BATTLE OF
BRITAIN
VOICES

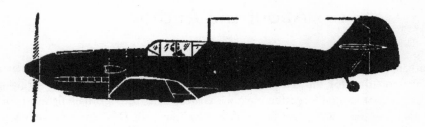

*To Zuzu & Quentin, my two-year-old twins, who
made writing this book a pleasure*

*My parents David and Eileen Reeve (thanks for the
loan of the books Dad, you will get them back)*

About the Author

Jonathan Reeve studied History at the University of Liverpool. He has been a history publisher for the last fifteen years and has been responsible for bringing back into print several forgotten memoirs written by Battle of Britain fighter pilots including the best-selling *Gun Button To Fire* by Tom Neil, DFC. Married with four children, he lives in Bath in a converted bomb-proof ARP centre built in 1943 as a response to Hitler's Baedeker Raids.

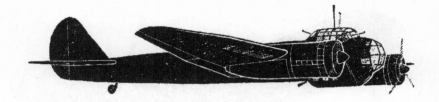

BATTLE OF BRITAIN VOICES

37 Fighter
Pilots Tell Their
Extraordinary
Stories

JONATHAN REEVE

AMBERLEY

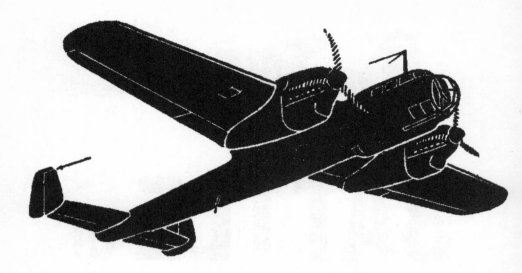

First published 2015

Amberley Publishing
The Hill, Stroud
Gloucestershire, GL5 4EP

www.amberley-books.com

British Library Cataloguing in Publication Data.
A catalogue record for this book is available from the British Library.

ISBN 978 1 4456 4264 2 (hardback)
ISBN 978 1 4456 4274 1 (ebook)

Typesetting and origination by Amberley Publishing
Internal illustrations in prelims and on part pages courtesy of Jonathan Reeve.
Printed in Great Britain

Contents

Introduction

What Was the Battle of Britain?

On 18 June 1940, Britain stood alone in the war against Nazi Germany. From September 1939 the Allied and neutral countries of Europe – Poland, Norway, Denmark, Belgium, the Netherlands and France – fell one by one to the Blitzkrieg tactics of Hitler's Germany, and by the end of May 1940 the British Expeditionary Force had just been forced out of France at Dunkirk. America had made its neutrality clear; Russia had agreed a non-aggression pact with Hitler. The only country remaining to fight on against Hitler's Germany was Britain. All that stood between Hitler's invasion plans was the English Channel and the pilots of RAF Fighter Command. Britain's position was precarious; should they fight on against such seemingly impossible odds? Should they capitulate? There were plenty of British politicians who thought the latter was the only option.

However, after Neville Chamberlain stepped down as Prime Minister, Winston Churchill, the politician who had argued most virulently against Hitler and his appeasement, garnered the most support and took over. His task was to both motivate a beleaguered (but not dispirited) population and organise the defence of the realm. The name 'the Battle of Britain' is derived from a speech Churchill delivered in the House of Commons on 18 June 1940, a month after he had become Prime Minister, and declared, 'The Battle of France is over. I expect that the Battle of Britain is about to begin.'

The Battle of Britain (which officially began 10 July 1940) was the epic air battle fought over Britain during that summer. It was initiated by the German Luftwaffe to gain air superiority (the ability to operate freely in an area of airspace without insupportable losses) over the RAF and enable a successful invasion of Britain. Hitler's objective was to 'eliminate the English home country as a base for the continuation of the war against Germany'. Head of Fighter Command Hugh Dowding's task therefore was to marshal his fragile resources (as in most European countries, Britain's rearmament had not kept pace with Germany's) of fighter aircraft and pilots carefully, using limited force to disrupt bombing attacks, but not so much that his Air Force would dwindle and become ineffective. The Luftwaffe on the other hand did as much as possible to tempt the RAF into the air so they could destroy it. Dowding fully understood the Luftwaffe's strategy – ULTRA decrypts

(German military communications intercepted and decoded at Bletchley Park) of Hermann Goering's (politician and commander-in-chief of the Luftwaffe) orders to his commanders confirmed that this would be a war of attrition. The Luftwaffe would fly over Britain hoping to bring the whole RAF up to battle as it was the only way to destroy the Air Force in the time they had. Operation Sealion (the code name Hitler gave to his plan to invade Britain) had to be started before the autumn weather made the crossing of the Channel by 125,000 troops too perilous. The RAF's victory caused Hitler to cancel his planned invasion.

Historians of the Battle of Britain generally divide the course of the Battle into four phases. The first phase was 10 July–12 August 1940, when the Luftwaffe launched concentrated and escalating daylight attacks on coastal convoys, ports and coastal airfields. The second covered 13 August–6 September 1940. This started with Goering's four-day offensive, code-named *Adlerangriff* (Operation Eagle Attack), to obliterate the RAF on the ground. Large-scale daylight raids targeted airfields, communication centres, radar stations and aircraft production factories. In addition, Luftwaffe fighters made 'free-chase' sweeps over southern England to tempt a Fighter Command response; fortunately the raids were identified as such by 11 Group commander Keith Park and ignored. This has generally been regarded as the decisive phase of the Battle of Britain. Fighter Command came close to breaking point but was able to cling on as an effective defensive force at the same time as it inflicted real damage on the Luftwaffe.

Phase three took place from 7 to 30 September 1940, when the Luftwaffe switched from attacking airfields to attacking London and other major British cities. This was a critical strategic blunder. During phase two the Luftwaffe had Fighter Command on the ropes. By concentrating raids on its airfields, the Luftwaffe was disrupting the very support systems that kept the fighters in the air. The tactics of trying to draw large numbers of Fighter Command's fighters into the air for the Luftwaffe to destroy had not worked, so the decision to change approach was understandable. Luftwaffe intelligence on the true state of Fighter Command was woefully inaccurate. Hitler thought redirected daylight raids would force Fighter Command to use all its reserves in defence of its urban populations, enabling the Luftwaffe to smash it once and for all. The Luftwaffe failed, and in a week of air battles from 7 to 15 September Fighter Command managed to turn the tide, shooting down almost 400 Luftwaffe aircraft while sustaining losses of only 120. This proved once and for all that the RAF was far from beaten and that the Luftwaffe had failed to achieve air superiority.

The fourth and final phase began at the end of September after Hitler had indefinitely postponed Germany's plans to invade Britain. The escorted daytime mass bombing raids almost ceased and the Luftwaffe concentrated on the night-time 'Blitz'. During the day, Fighter Command also had to contend with large-scale fighter sweeps and high-flying, bomb-equipped fighter formations coming in high over Britain. Radar could not differentiate between the two, forcing constant standing patrols.

In the end the raids on London and Britain's other major cities of winter 1940/41 became an alternative to invasion as a means of, in Hitler's words, 'eliminat[ing] the English home country as a base for the continuation of the war against Germany', that is by terrorising it into surrender. In this, as in the Battle of Britain, the Luftwaffe failed. With a quick victory over Britain eluding him, by early 1941 Hitler had turned his attention east to Russia. Britain had lived to fight another day.

RAF Fighter Command

RAF Fighter Command was the section of the RAF tasked with protecting Britain's airspace. At the beginning of July 1940 it consisted of seventy-one squadrons with around 700 Spitfires and Hurricanes, with a further 100 Spitfires and 240 Hurricanes in reserve, which were in turn organised into four Groups. Each Group defended a specific geographical area: 10 Group, Wales and the West Country; 11 Group, the south-east and London; 12 Group, the Midlands and East Anglia; 13 Group, the north, Scotland and Northern Ireland. Squadrons saw very different levels of air fighting during the Battle and pilots were rotated among the Groups to allow them to rest after weeks of sustained contact with the enemy. The pilots' accounts often show a sharp distinction between time as a fighter pilot in a quiet sector, with occasional contact with lone reconnaissance planes, and the hurried move to an 11 Group airfield and being pitched into intense combat, flying up to five sorties a day and experiencing a life-and-death struggle each time. In reality, at any one time there were under 400 fighter pilots flying out of London and the south-east of England (11 Group) to take on the brunt of the Luftwaffe raids.

The territory protected by each Group was split into sectors (see illustration 41). Each sector had its own sector station, with an ops room relaying information to pilots operating from its sector station and surrounding airfields. Uniquely, Britain's Fighter Command had established a high-tech early warning system to detect aircraft approaching the British Isles. This was built around radar, still in its infancy in 1940. Twenty-one radar stations along the coast relayed information on incoming formations of Luftwaffe aircraft up to about eighty miles out from the coast to the filter room at Fighter Command HQ. As the direction of the raid was established (cross-referenced with sightings by the small army of Observer Corps volunteers), they were plotted on a giant map table. This information was then relayed to the ops rooms of Group HQs and sector stations from where squadrons received the command to 'scramble' (take off) to intercept the incoming raid. This command-and-control system was little understood by the Luftwaffe, who therefore failed to disrupt it, apart from a couple of attempts to destroy radar masts and the occasional stray bomb severing landlines that carried the telephone links between radar stations, Fighter Command HQ and the Group HQs and sector stations.

From the pilots' perspective, this all meant that they had to be at a state of 'readiness', i.e. ready to jump into their fighters as soon as the telephone call was received. It is photographs of fighter pilots waiting around 'at readiness' that form the most enduring image of 'the Few'. What these pictures rarely communicate is how tense the pilots felt; fortunately, the memoirs in this book do.

Once fighters were airborne, the sector station controller, who was based in the ops room, would speak to the leader of the fighter formation via radio telephone and relay further details and instructions on approximately where (radar was an imperfect tool) the enemy aircraft or 'bandits' were located, their height and their number.

How did Fighter Command stand in comparison to the Luftwaffe at the beginning of the Battle? Against Dowding's advice, valuable fighter pilots and aircraft had been lost in the defence of France. Aircraft production was speeding up, but the supply of newly trained pilots would be difficult to maintain against heavy losses. Fighter Command had 1,200 pilots as of 1 July. The secret weekly document 'State of Aircraft in Operational Command' listed, as of Monday 5 July 1940, Spitfires, nineteen squadrons of sixteen aircraft each, totalling 304; Hurricanes, twenty-four squadrons of sixteen aircraft each, totalling 384. So 688 front-line fighters with a reserve (at air storage units and the squadrons themselves, often not fully serviceable) of a further 100-odd Spitfires and 240 Hurricanes. The Luftwaffe had 900 single-seater Me 109 fighters and 1,700 bombers. Although clearly outnumbered in terms of total aircraft (the RAF pilots had to try and shoot down massed raids of bombers escorted by fighters), the number of fighters remained roughly similar throughout the Battle. The British fighter pilots did have some advantages over their Luftwaffe counterparts, though. The German fighter pilots were fighting at the limit of their aircraft's range, giving only ten minutes' combat time over Britain; the British were flying over their home territory so could land, rearm and refuel and be back in combat within twenty minutes. Also, if an RAF pilot was shot down and either crash-landed or parachuted out they would land on home turf and could rejoin their squadron within hours and quickly return to combat, while the Luftwaffe aircrew would be lost to the fight as POWs.

A Fighter Command Squadron

Each Fighter Command squadron was led by a squadron leader. A full-strength Fighter Command squadron consisted of sixteen operational pilots, twenty aircraft and two reserves. The squadron would be expected to field at any one time twelve aircraft and pilots. The twelve aircraft were split into two 'flights', named 'A' and 'B', which are in turn commanded by flight lieutenants. Each flight was then split into two colour-coded 'sections' of three aircraft each, so 'A' flight would have a 'Red' and 'Yellow' section, 'B' flight would have a 'Blue' and 'Green' section. Each coloured section of three fighter aircraft were identified as 'Red 1', 'Red 2' and 'Red 3' and so on.

After squadron leaders and flight lieutenants, next in line of pilot seniority were the flying officers and pilot officers, the latter of which was the rank of a newly commissioned officer pilot. Then followed flight sergeants and sergeant pilots, who were non-commissioned officers or NCOs. Sergeant pilots were the poorer cousin of the commissioned officers (flight lieutenant, flying officer and pilot officer). They were paid less, lived in less salubrious accommodation on the airfield and had to make their own tea in the morning (a pilot officer and above had a batman). Tellingly, they were often the 'weavers' or rearguard at the back of the formation of a flight, whose job it was to cover the rest of the flight by keeping an eye out for attacks from behind. This of course also left them most exposed to such attacks by enemy planes, and meant they were unlikely to shoot down enemy aircraft compared to the officer at the front of the formation – for the initial part of any attack at least – who was usually the first to be within range of any enemy aircraft (a point made by Battle veteran Bob Stanford Tuck). They generally socialised separately from officers, airfields having both an officers' mess and a sergeants' mess. Messes, which are discussed in most of the following accounts, are where military personnel, confined to a military compound, would socialise. Sergeant pilots made up about a third of the pilots in the RAF in September 1939, though many were promoted to officer ranks during the Battle.

The Pilots of Fighter Command

The quality of first-hand accounts left by the Battle of Britain fighter pilots is astonishing. Many were written in the midst of the epic air battle; hastily jotted-down diaries, contemporary interviews with journalists or radio broadcasts and, most poignant of all, the short books that were written to while away the weeks stuck in hospital beds recovering from wounds received in battle. Some were written up in the cold light of day later in the war or just after, but they all share one feature – they were written before 'the Few' truly became etched in the minds of the British people. The fighter pilots' modesty shines through.

In all, 2,937 British and Allied airmen are listed on the Battle of Britain London Monument and now officially recognised as having taken part in the Battle. The qualification for this was having flown in at least one sortie – combat mission – with a squadron of RAF Fighter Command between 10 July 1940 and 31 October 1940. 544 of them would lose their lives during the battle, and another 795 would die before the end of the war. 595 Battle of Britain pilots were non-British. There were 145 Poles, 127 New Zealanders, 112 Canadians, 88 Czechoslovaks, 32 Australians, 28 Belgians, 25 South Africans, 13 French, 10 Irish, 9 Americans, 3 Rhodesians and one each from Barbados, Jamaica and Newfoundland.

This series of accounts uniquely gives full coverage of the wide background of the participants, including not only many British pilot accounts but also those given by fighter pilots from America, Australia, Canada, Czechoslovakia, France, New Zealand and Poland. These brave Allied airmen not only fought the Nazis in the skies over Britain, but in many cases had to fight their way across occupied Europe to get to Britain in the first place and then contend with British bureaucracy in order to be allowed to fight on in the RAF.

The pilots' accounts have been split broadly into four chronological parts, but within some extracts earlier or later combat sorties are sometimes covered too. The longer accounts have often been split into several parts and placed in their respective periods. Each pilot account is given a short introduction which explains a little of the background of the pilot, and where possible I have attempted to ascribe dates to the sorties described in the text. These are not intended to be comprehensive, and I let the pilots speak for themselves. Where an account was originally written anonymously, and there are quite a few, I have identified the pilot concerned.

I have attempted to offer the 'score' for each pilot during 1940; the figures for these come from Kenneth Wynn's excellent *Men of the Battle of Britain* (new edition out August 2015) and John Foreman's *RAF Fighter Command Victory Claims of World War Two: 1939–40*. Claims of combat victories by pilots and aircrew were exaggerated on both sides by the confusion of aerial dogfights. In the RAF it was the job of the squadron intelligence officer to interrogate pilots to assess whether a claim of an enemy 'kill' would be officially recorded as such. The Fighter Command rules were that the pilot had to observe the enemy aircraft explode in mid-air or crash into the ground/sea or see the pilot bale out. Anything less than this was recorded as 'probably destroyed' or just 'damaged'. There is no official list of RAF kills per pilot, although many of the aces have had their combat histories picked over by post-war historians.

The aim of this book is to provide a far broader range of fighter pilot accounts of the Battle, and in doing so use significant-sized accounts rather than the gobbets used in other books. I aim to give depth to our understanding of what it was like to be a pilot and to pin down the dates of the sorties described, which was rarely done in the original texts. This both allows the sorting of the accounts chronologically and gives some sense to how experiences of pilots changed during the evolving Battle. I try to note where the action took place, for instance whether in the white heat of the skies looked after by 11 Group, operating over London and the south-east of England, or in the relative calm of the north (13 Group). I have made a special effort to include accounts actually written up during 1940, not in the years after. These accounts can be trusted to give a more accurate account of the pilot's true feelings, unaffected by passing years, fading memory and rose-tinted glasses. I was also drawn to lesser-known memoirs by sergeant pilots, i.e. the non-officer rank of fighter pilot, usually drawn from what was politely known in the 1940s as 'the lower orders'. Finally, I aimed to bring back into print the many forgotten accounts which I have been delighted to discover during the writing of this book.

This book also includes a large number of illustrations, over 150, many rarely reproduced, as well as classic images. For both I have attempted to put names to faces where previously there were none or where earlier sources disagreed. I would welcome clarification for future editions if I have made an error.

The Aircraft of the Battle of Britain

The pilots' extracts often compare the relative strengths and weaknesses of their own fighter aircraft with the German equivalent, and a basic understanding of these fighters and the bombers they tried to destroy is therefore useful. What were a Hurricane pilot's chances if he was 'bounced' by an Me 110? Which German bomber was easiest to shoot down? Which RAF aircraft were viewed by their pilots as 'flying coffins'?

Battle of Britain expert Dr Alfred Price sums it up thus: 'In the Battle of Britain most fighter-*versus*-fighter combats took place in the height band between 13,000 and 20,000 feet, because that was where the German bombers flew. At that altitude the mark I and mark II Spitfires were roughly equal to the Me 109 in capability. In the fleeting air combats that were the norm, tactical initiative counted for far more than the relatively small performance differences that existed between the opposing fighter types.'

Britain had two single-seater fighter aircraft, the Hurricane and the Spitfire, to the Luftwaffe's single equivalent, the Messerschmitt Bf 109, which was known by pilots at the time simply as the 'Me 109'. The Luftwaffe also had a twin-engined 'heavy fighter', the Messerschmitt Bf 110 (Me 110). For the purposes of the Battle of Britain, it is only the Luftwaffe's bomber force that features below.

The Luftwaffe had four bombers: the Junkers Ju 87 (Stuka), Junkers Ju 88, Heinkel He 111 and Dornier Do 17. The bombers flew in formation for protection, as all of their air gunners were then able to focus their fire on any attacking fighter plane. The bombers usually would be accompanied by a fighter escort (Me 109s or Me 110s). The typical battles over the south-east would involve anything from twenty to two hundred Luftwaffe bombers escorted by ten to one hundred Luftwaffe fighters. The size of the RAF response, as you will read in the pilots' accounts, varied enormously but they were often outnumbered. A brief description of the aircraft follows.

Hurricane. Most numerous variant/mark in the Battle: Hurricane I. The most numerous RAF fighter in the Battle. Two-thirds of Fighter Command's squadrons were equipped with them. Battle of Britain ace Robert Stanford Tuck: 'I shot down 109s when flying Hurricanes, but only when I had the advantage of height. I'd stick my nose down and go for them. But a Hurricane couldn't match the 109 on the same level. I spoke to German pilots after the war and they said, "Hurricanes? We didn't worry about them. It was the Spitfires we worried about."' But these pilots must have been fighter pilots; the bomber aircrews certainly had plenty to fear from the Hurricane.

The Hurricane squadrons were generally vectored to attack the bomber formations, while the faster Spitfire was deployed to deal with the escorting German fighters. The Hurricane had a top speed of 320 mph and was armed with eight Browning .303 inch (or 7.7 mm) machine guns (300 rounds per gun), in two blocks of four on each wing. This battery of four could produce a higher concentration of fire than the guns on the Spitfire, which were spread along the leading edge of the wing. For both Hurricane and Spitfire the ammunition consisted of a mix of ball, armour-piercing, tracer and incendiary bullets, allowing fifteen seconds of continuous fire, harmonised to converge on the target at 200–250 yards.

Early in May 1940, in France, Mark 'Hilly' Brown (see chapter 2) had a chance to pit a captured Me 109 against a Hurricane in a mock dogfight to assess the relative merits of the two fighters. The 1 Squadron log noted, 'The Hurricane is infinitely manoeuvrable at all heights and at ground level is slightly faster. The Me 109, however, is unquestionably faster at operational heights and although appearing tricky to fly and not particularly fond of the ground, possesses many fine features to offset its disadvantages.' The Hurricane did indeed have a tighter turning circle than an Me 109, and although it was slower, its pilots shot down plenty of 109s. However, exactly how much of the machine's potential performance could be extracted was down to the skill of the individual pilot; physical fitness, strength, mental agility and endurance mattered.

Interestingly, statistical analysis by historians of combat records has shown that the Spitfire was twice as safe as the Hurricane in combat. This was due to its metal construction and it having fewer vulnerable areas, whereas the Hurricane was made vulnerable by the position of the fuel and glycol tanks. A small *critical* hit on a Hurricane (although its ruggedness meant it could take a lot of punishment in less critical areas) would put it out of action or, worse still, cause the cockpit to become engulfed by flames, severely burning or killing the pilot. In essence, if you were hit by enemy bullets or canon shells in a Hurricane you were half as likely to get home as if you had been flying a Spitfire. Almost 15,000 Hurricanes of various types would be produced.

Spitfire. Most numerous variant/mark in the Battle: Spitfire I, with the mark II coming into increasing use in the second half of the Battle. It had a top speed of 353 mph and was armed with eight Browning .303 inch machine guns. The first forensic examination of how the Spitfire compared in combat to the Me 109 was recorded by Alan Deere on 23 May 1940 in a dogfight where Deere and his fellow fighter pilot were outnumbered three to one. Deere concluded that the Me 109 could out-climb the Spitfire and always out-dived it but that the Spitfire could turn inside the Messerschmitt. The Spitfire took two and a half times as long to build as the Hurricane. By the end of the war, 22,000 Spitfires of various types would be produced.

A small number of Fighter Command squadrons were equipped with Defiant and Blenheim 'fighter' aircraft, although neither was a pure-breed fighter like the Spitfire or Hurricane. They played a brave yet relatively minor role in the Battle.

Defiant. Most numerous variant/mark in the Battle: mark I. Armament: four Browning .303 inch (or 7.7 mm) machine guns in a powered Boulton and Paul turret, no forward-firing machine guns. Crew of two, pilot and gunner. First deployed during Dunkirk in late May 1940; Luftwaffe pilots were initially taken by surprise by what appeared to be a Hurricane. The turret gunner could of course fire rearwards on the unsuspecting attackers. Defiant crews scored some amazing successes: Pilot Edward Thorn and gunner Frederick Barker shot down seven over Dunkirk and three more in August. However, the Luftwaffe pilots learned quickly and after two disastrous sorties on 19 July and 28 August, when two squadrons of Defiants were virtually wiped out, they were moved onto night fighter operations like the Blenheim. During the Battle itself, Defiants accounted for about eighteen kills.

Blenheim. Most numerous variant/mark in the Battle: mark IF. Twin-engined fighter version of the Blenheim light bomber. Top speed 260 mph. Armament: five forward-firing Browning .303 machine guns (500 rounds per gun) plus another in a turret. It carried a crew of two or sometimes three. Fighter Command equipped six squadrons with the aircraft in mid-1940 but soon discovered they were highly vulnerable to fighter attack and they were transferred to the embryonic night fighter role, where they had some success against Luftwaffe night raids during the Battle, amounting to about six confirmed kills (three by New Zealander Michael Herrick).

Messerschmitt Bf 109 (Me 109). Most numerous variant/mark in the Battle: Me 109E 'Emil'. The Luftwaffe's only single-engined fighter. It had a speed of 350 mph, twin MG FF 20 mm cannon with sixty rounds of explosive shells per gun (and a greater range than that of the Browning .303 machine guns) giving seven seconds of fire and twin MG 15 7.92 mm machine guns with 1,000 rounds per gun giving sixty seconds of fire. The rate of fire was a little slower than that of the Hurricane and Spitfire but the 109's weapons packed a more powerful punch; a single cannon round could destroy an aircraft if fired close enough and could slice through armour plate. The cannon was selected separately, with separate 'fire' buttons for each gun. One key advantage of the 109 is that it could operate more effectively than both the Spitfire and Hurricane at greater heights. By the end of the war almost 34,000 Me 109s of various types would be produced, more than any other fighter. Later in the Battle they were also armed with a single 550 lb bomb.

Messerschmitt Bf 110 (Me 110). Most numerous variant/mark in the Battle: Me 110C. The *zerstörer* ('destroyer') fighter was intended for both offensive and defensive capabilities. The capability of the 110 fell short of the Luftwaffe's expectations, although it did have a longer range than the Me 109. It was fast (349 mph) but insufficiently manoeuvrable to engage with Hurricanes and Spitfires in dogfights. There were two crew: a pilot, who fired the two fixed, forward-firing MG FF 20 mm cannon (180 rounds per gun) and four MG 17 7.9 mm machine guns (1,000 rounds per gun); and the radio operator/gunner, who fired the single defensive rear-facing MG 15 7.92 mm machine gun. It also fulfilled a role as a fighter bomber, notoriously under the Luftwaffe unit Erprobungsgruppe 210, which operated them as a 'fast' Stuka, with similar levels of accuracy and twice the bomb load. Later in the Battle, as with Me 109s, they were used as tip-and-run bombers, dropping their bomb load from a high altitude of 25,000 feet almost indiscriminately.

Junkers Ju 88 (Ju 88). Most numerous variant/mark in the Battle: Ju 88A. The Ju 88 was the most advanced German bomber in 1940 and considerably faster than the He 111 and Do 17. It was also designed to take the stresses of dive-bombing. The Ju 88 needed a crew of four: pilot, navigator/bomb aimer, flight engineer/ventral gunner and radio operator/rear gunner. From some angles it was very similar in appearance to the Do 17, but it was distinguished by its single tailplane to the Dornier's twin tailplane. Its top speed was 286 mph, and it could carry 2,200 lbs of bombs. Defensive armament: three to four separately mounted MG 15 7.92 mm machine guns. Unlike the Do 17 and He 111, the Ju 88, according to Battle veteran Tom Neil of 249 Squadron, 'could fly just as well on one engine as two'.

Junkers Ju 87 (Ju 87 or Stuka). Most numerous variant/mark in the Battle: Ju 87B. The 'Stuka' dive-bomber was the very epitome of the Blitzkrieg (lightning war). It was a brilliant light bomber when unopposed in the air and could achieve pinpoint accuracy. It had been designed to operate ahead of panzer columns effectively as long-range artillery. However, over Britain, where the Luftwaffe never achieved air superiority, the ponderously slow Stuka presented 'easy meat' for the advanced fighters of Fighter Command and the Stuka was unable to take much punishment before exploding or catching fire. They also caused their much faster fighter escorts, the Me 109s, huge problems as they had to crisscross the skies to stay in formation, which used considerably more fuel. The Stuka needed two crew: the pilot, who dropped the bombs and controlled two fixed, forward-facing MG 17 7.92 mm machine guns, and a rear gunner/navigator, who fired a flexibly mounted rear-facing MG 15 7.92 mm machine gun. With a top speed of 232 mph, the Stuka could carry 990 lbs of bombs.

Dornier Do 17 (Do 17). Most numerous variant/mark in the Battle: Do 17Z. Known as the 'flying pencil' due to its slim side profile. The Dornier was slower than the Ju 88 and lacked the bomb load of the He 111. As the least important of the three twin-engined Luftwaffe bombers, it was almost obsolete by the summer of 1940. Its top speed was 260 mph, and it could carry 2,205 lbs of bombs. The

Dornier was usually crewed by four: a pilot, two gunners (with two separately mounted MG 15 7.92 mm machine guns each) and a bomb aimer. Often confused by RAF pilots in combat reports with the much rarer 'export' version, the Do 215, which was near identical to the Do 17 but wasn't much used during the Battle. This confusion was probably caused by contemporary aircraft recognition manuals (put together by intelligence staff at the Air Ministry), which included both.

Heinkel He 111 (He 111). Most numerous variants/marks in the Battle: He 111P and He 111H. This was the most numerous and 'heaviest' bomber in the Luftwaffe fleet, and the He 111P could carry 3,300 lbs of bombs. The crew of four comprised pilot, navigator/bomb aimer/front gunner, radio operator/rear gunner and flight engineer/ventral gunner. Its top speed was 240 mph. Defensive armaments: three to six separately mounted MG 15 7.92 mm machine guns.

Heinkel He 113 (He 113). Although these never actually flew in the Battle, plenty were sighted and claimed as shot down by RAF pilots (including in the extracts that follow). This was because of their inclusion in Air Ministry aircraft recognition manuals at the time and the difficulty distinguishing between them and the Me 109 (which those sighted actually were). The aircraft was the creation of Josef Goebbels' propaganda ministry, possibly to fill the gap between Britain's twin team of single-engined fighters and Germany's lone Me 109. Twelve Heinkel 100s were built in competition with the Me 109, but they were never taken up by the Luftwaffe; instead a group were painted up with fictitious markings, designated as Heinkel 113s, photographed and announced to the international press.

The German Luftwaffe and the Battle of Britain

The Luftwaffe was split into self-contained 'air fleets' or *luftflottes*, each one maintaining its own fighter, bomber, reconnaissance and other, more specialist units. For the Battle of Britain the two primary air fleets tasked with attacking Britain were Luftflotte 2 and 3. For the period of the Battle of Britain a boundary was drawn down the centre of England, with Luftflotte 2 setting its sights on targets to the east of this line and Luftflotte 3 on targets to the west, although these boundaries were not strictly respected. Luftflotte 2 was led by Albert Kesselring and its bases were in Belgium, the Netherlands and northern France. Luftflotte 3, led by Hugo Sperrle, was based to the west of Luftflotte 2, in north-west France. Another, Luftflotte 5, was based in Norway and was barely used in the Battle. Britain was in range of its long-range fighters (Me 110s) and bombers, but out of range of the critically important single-seater Me 109 fighters. It did make one major attack in the north of England (supported only by the twin-engine Me 110), but suffered terrible losses of 20 per cent of its aircraft and did not return. The numbers of Luftwaffe aircraft and pilots quoted by historians as being available for attacking Britain tend to exclude Luftflotte 5.

Glossary & Fighter Pilot Slang

Like all organisations, the RAF developed – officially and unofficially – a plethora of jargon. Below are those that most commonly occur in pilots' accounts.

AA/ack-ack Anti-aircraft shells fired from the ground. The exploding shell could either land a direct hit on an aircraft or damage it or its occupants with its red-hot and razor-sharp pieces of metal – 'shrapnel'.

Ace A pilot that has shot down at least five enemy aircraft.

Angels Height in thousands of feet. 'Angels ten' means '10,000 feet'.

Astern Behind or towards the rear of an aircraft.

Bandits Enemy aircraft.

Blitzkrieg German for 'lightning war', a method of warfare typified by the Nazis in 1939 and 1940 as they stormed through Europe whereby an attacking force is spearheaded by a dense concentration of armoured and mechanised infantry formations, and heavily backed up by close air support.

Bogey Unidentified aircraft.

Buster Maximum cruising speed.

Call sign Each Fighter Command squadron had their own unique call sign so that information from ground controllers could secretly reach members of the correct squadron.

CO Commanding officer.

Combat Report Air Ministry 'Form F'. This personal combat report was filled in by the pilot or squadron intelligence officer (after interviewing the pilot) after every combat sortie. Generally it was a single page, nearly A4-sized, detailing the date and time, squadron and flight, number and type of enemy aircraft, location and height and any casualties (RAF and enemy), together with a short (or sometimes long) narrative describing the action. These reports were copied and sent to group HQ and used to assess every aspect of the Battle. Hundreds of these from 1940 survive and can be viewed online at the National Archives, Kew.

Control/Controller The control or controller was the ground-based officer who (together with a team of support staff) gathered up intelligence from radar stations and the Observer Corps reports on where and how high formations of enemy aircraft were in the skies approaching Britain and predict where they were heading. They relayed instructions via the R/T to the fighter pilots in the air, directing them to where the formations of enemy aircraft could be found and attacked.

DFC Distinguished Flying Cross, a medal for bravery.

E/A Enemy aircraft.

11 Group See 'Fighter Command'.

Fighter Command The RAF organisation commanded by Hugh Dowding that ran RAF's fighter squadrons. Its headquarters was at Bentley Priory, Stanmore, Middlesex. It was subdivided into four groups, each responsible for the aerial defence of a geographical region of Great Britain.

Fighter Command HQ, Bentley Priory Orders were dispatched from the ops room and filter room here to the four Group HQs (10, 11, 12 and 13). Bentley Priory would receive reports direct from radar stations and its network of Observer Corps, plot the path of Luftwaffe attacks and dispatch orders to the ops rooms at Group HQs and sector stations to pass on to pilots in the air.

Flight A military grouping of six aircraft. An RAF fighter squadron is usually split into two 'flights', A and B. Each flight is usually split into 'sections' of three aircraft each.

Huns/Jerry/Boche Contemporary slang for Germans.

Glycol Radiator fluid to cool aircraft engines.

Mae West Slang term for the pneumatic lifejackets worn by fighter pilots in the event of having to bale out over the Channel. Mae West was a big-busted film star of the 1930s. It was an appropriate name when you see what they do to a pilot's contours.

Pancake To land, refuel and rearm.

Readiness There were various levels of 'readiness'. Essentially it was how ready a pilot had to be to jump in his fighter and take off. 'Readiness' meant to be able to take off within three minutes, 'standby' meant sitting in the cockpit ready to start the engine and go, and 'available' meant able to take off within fifteen minutes.

R/T Radio telephone, used by pilots to communicate with their fellow pilots and ground staff.

Satellite airfield Hastily prepared forward air bases nearer the coast than principal airfield, saving fighters valuable minutes in reaching the enemy. Pilots were often dispatched there at first light and would return to their home airfield in the evening. Facilities were basic, with tents and a wooden hut or a caravan as a makeshift ready room.

Scramble Take off.

Section See 'flight'.

Sector stations Each Fighter Command group was split into several sectors, with the principal airfield as the sector station. From here, controllers in the operation room would direct the squadron by R/T based on orders from Group HQ.

Snappers Enemy fighters.

Sortie/patrol/mission Various names for a combat mission flown by at least a flight or section of a squadron to intercept enemy aircraft.

Squadron A military unit in an air force comprising a number of aircraft, its aircrew and support staff. In the RAF in 1940 a fighter squadron was made up of twelve to eighteen aircraft.

Squadron code/aircraft call sign (RAF) Each squadron was identifiable by its own two-letter code, which was applied to the aircraft fuselage next to the RAF roundel. Individual aircraft were then further identifiable through a single-letter 'call sign' ('G' for George and so on) painted on the opposite side of the roundel. Aircraft from A flight were given 'A–K', and B flight 'L–Z'.

Tally-ho Originated as a call in fox hunting for when a rider sees a fox. It was used by fighter pilots over their R/T to let their fellow pilots know that were going to attack.

Vector Steering course to intercept.

V formations or vics 'V'-shaped formation of three or more aircraft.

Chronology & Statistics

Rather than being used strictly as a reference tool, this subsection is designed to be read to give a concise overview of the course of the Battle of Britain through key events and statistics. Only particularly heavy raids by the Luftwaffe are included as there were simply too many to list individually. The period of the Battle, 10 July to 31 October 1940, is split into the generally accepted four phases of the Battle as used by most historians. I start with the key events in the lead-up to these four phases.

COUNTDOWN TO THE BATTLE OF BRITAIN, FIGHTER COMMAND & THE BATTLES OF NORWAY & FRANCE & DUNKIRK

2 September 1939 Hurricanes of 1 and 73 Squadrons arrive in France as fighter element of the Advanced Air Striking Force (AASF).

4 September–15 November 1939 Hurricanes of 85, 87, 607 and 615 Squadrons arrive in France as Air Component of the British Expeditionary Force (BEF).

24 April 1940 263 Squadron of antiquated Gladiator biplanes flies from aircraft carrier Glorious to their base in Norway. They last a few days before all their aircraft are destroyed and return to England by sea to re-equip.

April 1940 Air Ministry achieves record 45 per cent increase in aircraft production.

10 May Germany invades France and the Low Countries. Luftwaffe attacks seventy French, Belgian and Dutch airfields.

10 May Neville Chamberlain resigns as PM and Winston Churchill takes over.

10 May 501 Squadron fly out from England to join the AASF in accordance with the reinforcement plan, and is in combat with forty He 111s within an hour of arriving in France.

10–12 May Hurricanes of 3, 79 and 504 Squadrons arrive in France.

13 May A further thirty-two Hurricanes and pilots (equivalent to two squadrons) from a variety of British-based squadrons (including 32, 56, 145, 151, 213, 229, 242, 245, 253, 601) fly out to reinforce British air forces in France.

14 May Anthony Eden launches the Local Defence Volunteers (later renamed the Home Guard) on national radio. Within six days it has 250,000 recruits.

14 May Ministry of Aircraft Production created as separate ministry with the energetic, no-nonsense newspaper baron Lord Beaverbrook (Max Aitken) placed in charge. His own son, Max Aitken junior, is a Hurricane fighter pilot who fights in the Battle of France and at the beginning of the Battle of Britain with 601 Squadron (nicknamed 'Millionaires Mob' as many of the pilots are very wealthy) and shoots down four enemy aircraft in 1940.

15 May Hugh Dowding, Commander-in-Chief of Fighter Command, attends a meeting with the Chiefs of Staff, with Churchill as chair, where he lays out the case that if the flow of fighters to France is not halted Fighter Command will be too weak to defend Britain.

16 May Despite Dowding's insistence that it would reduce Fighter Command's ability to protect Britain from invasion, Churchill deploys eight 'half-squadrons' to France. Flights from 56, 145, 213, 229, 242, 245, 253 and 601 Hurricane squadrons fly over to further reinforce British air forces in France and are attached to existing squadrons based in France. Flights from 17, 32, 111 and 151 Hurricane squadrons fly over to operate temporarily from French airfields and return to Britain later the same day.

18 May IAN GLEED (see chapter 4), on his first day of action over France, shoots down two Me 110s.

19 May Luftwaffe attack airfields used by British Hurricane squadrons in France.

20 May Planning begins for the evacuation of the BEF, code-named Operation Dynamo.

21 May 263 Squadron return to Norway with Gladiator biplanes.

22 May Around 200 sorties a day being flown from Britain over northern France in addition to those flown by Hurricane squadrons based in France.

26 May BRIAN LANE (see chapter 7), flying from RAF Hornchurch, Essex (11 Group), shoots down a Ju 87 and an Me 109 over Dunkirk.

26 May 46 Squadron (Hurricanes) join 263 Squadron in Norway.

27 May British Cabinet approves Chiefs of Staff's view that the primary military objective now that Britain is faced with enemy bases along the European coast is 'to prevent the Germans achieving such air superiority as would enable them to invade the country'.

27 May–4 June Operation Dynamo, the evacuation from Dunkirk, begins. Fighter Command offers fighter support to evacuating BEF, flying 2,739 sorties and losing ninety-eight Hurricanes and Spitfires but accounting for 200 enemy aircraft and 300 airmen.

4 June Winston Churchill: 'We shall defend our island, whatever the cost may be. We shall fight on the beaches, we shall fight on the landing grounds, we shall fight in the fields and in the streets, we shall fight in the hills; we shall never surrender.'

5/6 June First small-scale bombing raid on Britain.

7 June 263 Squadron leave Norway on HMS Glorious having destroyed their aircraft to avoid them falling into enemy hands. 46 Squadron join them but manage to fly their Hurricanes on to the aircraft carrier. The two squadrons leave Norway having shot down about forty enemy aircraft and flown 300 sorties. The carrier is sunk and only two pilots survive.

7 June SVATOPLUK JANOUCH (see chapter 6) flies his last sortie over France, attacking German ground forces approaching Paris.

8 June Hurricanes of 17 and 242 Squadrons arrive in France, the last reinforcements committed to French soil.

9 June French air force nearing collapse in the face of losses it is unable to replace.

14 June Paris falls to German forces.

17 June France requests an end to hostilities with Germany.

18 June Final withdrawal of last Hurricane squadrons of the AASF. In May and June, operations based in France had cost 386 Hurricanes and 67 Spitfires aircraft destroyed. Fighter Command had lost a further 200 fighters on associated sorties from Britain. The Luftwaffe had lost around 1,300 aircraft.

18 June Churchill delivers possibly his most famous speech to the House of Commons: 'The Battle of France is over. I expect that the Battle of Britain is about to begin ... Let us therefore brace ourselves to our duties, and so bear ourselves that, if the British Empire and the Commonwealth last for a thousand years, men shall still say, "This was their finest hour."' Churchill's speeches were very effective in inspiring the nation to work at victory against the Nazis.

19 June Fighter Command has 548 fighters ready for immediate action, and 200 in reserve at one day's notice.

2 July Hitler orders armed forces to undertake exploratory planning for an invasion of Britain.

5 July Air Ministry asks Dowding to postpone his retirement once again (already delayed from June 1939 to 14 July 1940) until 31 October 1940.

7 July Hitler orders armed forces to complete investigations into the possibility of an invasion to end the war against Britain.

THE BATTLE OF BRITAIN PHASE 1, 10 JULY–12 AUGUST 1940: ATTACKS ON BRITISH CONVOYS & LUFTWAFFE FIGHTER SWEEPS

10 July The first 'official' day of the Battle of Britain and the first mass dogfight of over 100 aircraft.

10 July HENRY FERRISS (see chapter 11) shoots down an Me 109 over Folkstone.

14 July Hitler instructs armed forces to prepare for an invasion any time after 15 August 1940.

14 July ARTHUR DONAHUE (see chapter 16) arrives from the USA by ship and signs up for the RAF.

15 July Fighter Command has 700 or so Hurricanes and Spitfires. Just under half of these based in 11 Group, protecting London and the south-east. The 1,200 aircraft of Bomber and Coastal Command would be of little help in the battle for air supremacy, though some pilots from its ranks would be seconded into Fighter Command later in the summer.

16 July Hitler's order number 16 is issued, stating, 'Since England has still not given any sign of being prepared to reach an agreement, despite her militarily hopeless position, I have decided to prepare an operation to invade England and if this becomes necessary, to carry it through. The objective of this operation is to eliminate the English home country as a base for the continuation of the war against Germany … the English air force must have been beaten down to such an extent morally and in actual fact that it can no longer muster any power of attack worth mentioning against the German crossing.' Operation Seelöwe (Sealion) was on and its prerequisite, air superiority, stated plainly by Hitler. This operation was for a surprise invasion to take place somewhere on the south coast between Ramsgate and the Isle of Wight if others means of persuading Britain to end its war with Germany failed.

19 July Hitler issues peace offer to Britain in speech delivered in Reichstag.

19 July 141 Squadron (Defiants) decimated by Me 110s.

20 July 80 per cent of the entire Luftwaffe is in place for air offensive against Britain. This consists of Luftflottes 2, 3 and 5. Between them they have 1,576 bombers and dive-bombers, 1,089 single- and twin-engined fighters and 200 reconnaissance aircraft.

22 July Official British rejection of peace offer of 19 July.

25 July Heavy attacks on Channel convoy. Luftwaffe lose eighteen aircraft to Fighter Command's seven. Eleven ships (over half of convoy) damaged or sunk.

25 July British daylight convoys in Channel suspended due to intensity of Luftwaffe attacks.

30 July Goering instructed by Hitler to prepare the Luftwaffe for intensive operations with half a day's notice.

30 July Hitler tells Admiral Raeder, 'If the effect of the air attacks is such that the enemy air force, harbours and naval forces, etc., are heavily damaged, Operation Sealion will be carried out in 1940.'

10–31 July Fighter Command loses sixty-nine fighters while shooting down 155

Luftwaffe aircraft, in almost daily bomber raids on shipping in the Channel and along coastal ports of the south coast, including Portsmouth, Dover and Portland.

1 August Hitler's order number 17 is issued to the Luftwaffe, urging them 'to overpower the English air force with all the force at its command, in the shortest possible time. Invasion preparations to be complete by 15 September.'

c. 5 August Goering takes over direct command of the air war against Britain.

8 August Heaviest fighting in the air so far; 150-plus aircraft involved.

9 August Fighter Command has 715 fighter aircraft ready for immediate action. A further 317 were awaiting repairs/servicing and 424 more were in storage units ready for use the following day.

10 August Luftwaffe has 805 Me 109 fighters ready for immediate action (a further 206 awaiting repairs/servicing) in Luftflottes (Air Fleets) 2 and 3 (i.e. those assigned to the Battle of Britain and excluding Luftflottes 5's Me 109s based in Norway, from which Britain was out of range).

11 August 38 Luftwaffe aircraft shot down. Highest figure in a single day by Fighter Command so far.

12 August RAF Manston, Hawkinge and Lympne as well as radar stations attacked in preparation for Adlertag on 13th.

12 August Thirty-one Luftwaffe aircraft shot down. Fighter Command, flying 500 sorties, loses twenty-two fighters with eleven pilots killed.

12 August Fighter Command has 750 fighters and 1,396 pilots available.

12 August GORDON OLIVE (see chapter 18) takes off in the middle of a huge bombing raid on RAF Manston.

10 July–12 August Fighter Command loses 148 fighters while shooting down 286 Luftwaffe aircraft.

THE BATTLE OF BRITAIN PHASE 2, 13 AUGUST–6 SEPTEMBER 1940: THE MAJOR LUFTWAFFE OFFENSIVE AGAINST THE AIRFIELDS

13 August Signal from Goering (intercepted and deciphered by Bletchley Park): 'To all units of air fleets 2, 3 and 5. Operation Eagle. Within a short period you will wipe the British air force from the sky. Heil Hitler.'

13 August Adlertag (Eagle Day) was the first official day of the Luftwaffe military operation Adlerangriff (Operation Eagle Attack). Forty-five Luftwaffe aircraft shot down, thirty-nine more seriously damaged. Fighter Command loses thirteen fighters, only three pilots killed. Luftwaffe fly 1,500 sorties. Adlerangriff was Goering's big idea to break Fighter Command and secure air superiority as ordered by Hitler. Goering had requested input from his air fleet commanders at a conference held on 21 July, and on 2 August he issued his Adlerangriff directive. It was in essence a fortnight of attacks within a 50–150 km radius south of London, moving progressively inland to destroy Fighter Command on the ground and in the air, with a major emphasis on bombing Fighter Command airfields. Luftwaffe intelligence contributed to the plan but was woefully inaccurate, reporting that Fighter Command was down to 450–500 fighters when in reality the figure was 750. The over-reporting on both sides of enemy kills was far more critical on the German side to the formulation of strategy in the Battle. Adlerangriff also included attacking the radar masts, accurately identified as the 'eyes' of Fighter Command.

Luftwaffe intelligence underestimated the sophistication of Fighter Command's command-and-control system and the impact damaging or destroying it would have on the effectiveness of the British fighters.

15 August Goering goes for another killer blow, the Luftwaffe aircraft available numbering 1,790 bombers and fighters. This time the attack is on two fronts, Luftflotte 5 attacking the north of England while Luftflotte 2 and Luftflotte 3 attack the south. Luftflotte 5 attacked and lost 20 per cent of its aircraft.

15 August The Luftwaffe fly more sorties than on any other day in the Battle (over 2,000), losing not the 182 claimed by Fighter Command pilots but seventy-five. In Luftwaffe history, the day becomes known as 'Black Thursday'.

15 August US Ambassador orders embassy and its staff to flee Britain in anticipation of imminent invasion.

16 August Seven Hurricanes destroyed on ground by Ju 87 bombers at RAF Tangmere and eleven more at a maintenance unit, the largest loss of fighters on the ground in a single raid. Luftwaffe loses forty-five aircraft to RAF's twenty-one.

16 August James Nicolson earns the only Victoria Cross of the Battle of Britain for his efforts on his first sortie against the enemy.

18 August Known as 'The Hardest Day', when both the RAF and Luftwaffe lost more planes than on any other day in the conflict so far. Heaviest and most concentrated attack by Luftwaffe and hardest defence by Fighter Command pilots of RAF airfields (Biggin Hill and Kenley). Luftwaffe lose seventy-one aircraft to RAF's twenty-seven.

8–18 August 154 Fighter Command pilots killed or wounded (and unable to return to the Battle), less than fifty replaced by newly trained pilots.

15, 16 & 18 August Over 150 Luftwaffe aircraft lost over these three days and 172 officers dead or missing.

19 August Keith Park, commander of 11 Group, issues instruction no. 4 to all squadrons that they should concentrate on destroying enemy bombers, avoiding fighter-to-fighter combat as much as possible, and that 12 Group should be asked to provide patrols over Debden, North Weald and Hornchurch if all of 11 Group's squadrons are off the ground.

19 August Dowding issues new tactics to all squadrons in response to Luftwaffe assault on Fighter Command's airfields. Pilots are instructed to avoid contact with enemy aircraft over the Channel as the Luftwaffe was keeping groups of Me 109s in the skies here ready to escort back returning bombers and to pick off pursuing RAF aircraft. Pilots to engage Luftwaffe bombers first and to try and avoid dogfights with German fighters. Spitfires encouraged to engage fighters where essential, Hurricanes the bomber formations.

23 August Fighter Command has 672 Spitfires and Hurricanes operational with an additional 228 in storage units ready for dispatch to squadrons.

24 August ANTONI GLOWAKI and RONALD HAMLYN (see chapters 30 and 29) both shoot down five German aircraft each.

25 August RAF Bomber Command raid Berlin, a retaliatory attack for the Luftwaffe's – accidental – bombing of London.

26 August Heavy bombing of RAF Debden.

26 August Keith Park issues instruction no. 6, telling squadrons about to attack enemy formations to transmit their position and size of the raid over the R/T for the benefit of sector station controllers. He also sends secret memo to Fighter Command HQ highlighting heavy losses of rotated squadrons in London and the south-east from 12 and 13 Group, and in particular those sent from 12 Group, commanded by Leigh-Mallory, asserting Leigh-Mallory was sending him inexperienced squadrons.

28 August Defiant-equipped squadrons transferred to night fighter operations only.

29 August 700 Luftwaffe fighters flying 'fighter sweeps' across south-east England to tempt Fighter Command into battle. Dowding does not offer up fighters to repel raids.

30 August Heavy bombing of RAF Detling, Biggin Hill and Lympne.

30 August General Stapf reports to Hitler that Fighter Command must be down to only 200 fighters.

30 August Hitler lifts his ban on bombing London as it is proving impossible to avoid Luftwaffe bomber force accidentally hitting the capital.

31 August RAF's worst day for losses so far, forty aircraft destroyed, nine pilots killed and eighteen badly wounded.

31 August Heavy bombing of RAF Detling, Eastchurch, Croydon, Biggin Hill, Hornchurch and Debden.

31 August Dowding tells Churchill at dinner at Chequers that he considers it legitimate for Luftwaffe aircrew to machine-gun RAF pilots who have parachuted out of their aircraft over British territory and could return to Battle the next day. Churchill is horrified.

August 1940 Hitler's Chief of Operations, Alfred Jodl, states the Nazi regime's view on Operation Sealion: 'No matter what might happen, the operation dare not fail.' A botched invasion would be not just a military disaster but a political one too.

1 July–31 August Luftwaffe claim to have shot down almost 2,000 British aircraft; in fact it was only a quarter of that.

1 September Luftwaffe inflict serious damage to RAF Biggin Hill, Eastchurch and Detling.

1 September Fighter Command has 701 Spitfires and Hurricanes operational with an additional 256 in storage units ready for dispatch to squadrons.

3 September Luftwaffe inflict serious damage to RAF North Weald.

3 September RICHARD HILLARY (see chapter 33) is shot down and grievously burned.

4 September Goering decides to change tactics.

5 September Park issues instruction no. 10 to controllers, stating that bombers heading for aircraft factories must be intercepted well before they closed on their target.

6 September Fighter Command has 750 fighters and 1,381 pilots available (not all fully trained on Spitfires or Hurricanes).

6 September Goering inspects a fighter unit in France and attempts to fit into the narrow cockpit of an Me 109. He fails, to much quiet amusement.

6 September Reconnaissance flights photograph growing number of invasion barges at Belgian, French and Dutch ports.

6 September British order 'Invasion Alert No. 2', invasion likely in next three days.

13 August–6 September Luftwaffe have lost just under 700 aircraft, Fighter Command around 400.

13 August–6 September Luftwaffe flies over 13,500 sorties over Britain.

23 August–6 September The most intense period of Luftwaffe attacks on Fighter Command airfields. Ratio of Luftwaffe fighters to bombers changes markedly, with far more fighters sent over to escort bomber raids. Some newly rotated squadrons from north of 12 and 13 Group massacred as a result of this and their use of outdated 'fighter area' tactics.

THE BATTLE OF BRITAIN PHASE 3, 7–30 SEPTEMBER 1940: THE BOMBING OF LONDON

7 September, morning Air Ministry issues 'Invasion Alert Number 1', invasion imminent.

7 September BILL ROLLS (see chapter 37) collects a fellow pilot who has crash-landed in London from an East End pub; he never forgets the Londoners' gratitude and the silk scarf given to him by 'Emma' which later saves his life.

7 September Goering abandons free-chase and airfield attacks in favour of raids on London.

7 September First of nearly sixty consecutive days of bombing raids on London. Luftwaffe assault on London consists of almost 1,000 aircraft.

7 September Luftwaffe has suffered heavy losses in its fighter units, with only 533 Me 109s available ready for action in Luftflottes 2 and 3. This is caused by a combination of long supply lines for spare parts, rudimentary maintenance facilities in France and lower aircraft production of single-seated fighters in Germany than in Britain. Fighter Command are increasingly able to replace destroyed aircraft and repair battle-damaged fighters faster that the Luftwaffe.

7 September Church bells sounded in Britain (the signal for an invasion by German forces) by mistake; Home Guard mobilises and erects roadblocks.

7 September Park issues instruction no. 12 to controllers. He states that in recent weeks raids have not been intercepted due to controllers sending squadrons in too high, a problem compounded by pilots adding a further few thousand feet for good measure.

8 September Park starts sending up squadrons in pairs to achieve more concentrated force against large formations of bombers.

10 September Hitler postpones invasion decision until 14 September.

11 September One of the few days where Fighter Command losses exceeded those of the Luftwaffe. Fighter Command also vastly over-claimed, with eighty-seven enemy aircraft downed; in reality it was only about twenty.

13 September Buckingham Palace bombed, handing the British a major publicity coup. The queen says she can now look East Enders, bombed out of their homes, in the eye. They agree, and the monarchy's popularity soars.

13 September Having studied combat reports observing the effectiveness of head-on attacks, Keith Park sends dispatch to fighter squadrons that they should stay together in the face of enlarged Luftwaffe formations, stop following kills down to confirm crashes and stop wasting time on 'lame ducks' that were already finished, instead concentrating on attacking unmolested enemy aircraft.

14 September Hitler postpones final decision about invasion once more, until 17 September, to await the outcome of major attack planned for 15 September.

15 September The Luftwaffe pitches 1,120 aircraft (including over 500 Me 109s) against south-east England. Fighter Command has 802 Spitfires and Hurricanes immediately available. Largest bomber formations ever arrive over London but are broken up by more than 300 fighters of the RAF. A major British victory is claimed, with 183 enemy aircraft shot down to Fighter Command's losses of less than forty. Though the figures are inflated it is a resounding defeat for the Luftwaffe. Becomes known later as 'Battle of Britain Day' (still celebrated today) and as the day Britain won the Battle of Britain. Actual aircraft losses: sixty Luftwaffe to RAF's twenty-six.

15 September TOM NEIL and ERIC LOCK (see chapter 40), Hurricane and Spitfire pilots respectively and from different squadrons, meet in the air and share in the destruction of a Do 17.

16 September Goering announces that Fighter Command has just 177 aircraft left.

17 September Hitler decides to postpone the invasion of Britain indefinitely because, as the German naval war diary recorded, 'the enemy air force is still by no means defeated. On the contrary it shows increased activity.'

19 September Wind-down of the German invasion shipping begins.

19 September Fighter Command has 656 fighters ready for immediate action, 202 in reserve at one day's notice and 226 in preparation at the factories.

21 September Last day of favourable tides in the Channel.

21 September With Hitler's decision not known to the British, Dowding and Churchill discuss counter-invasion preparations over dinner. Churchill receives telegram from American President Roosevelt warning that invasion would be launched in the early hours of 22 September; the source was highly credible and had accurately predicted the earlier German invasions of Holland and Belgium.

27 September Heavy losses for Luftwaffe, with fifty-five aircraft shot down to RAF's twenty-eight.

30 September Last mass daylight bomber raid by Luftwaffe. Heavy losses for Luftwaffe, with forty-eight aircraft shot down to RAF's twenty.

THE BATTLE OF BRITAIN PHASE 4, 1–31 OCTOBER 1940: NIGHT BLITZ & DAYLIGHT FIGHTER-BOMBERS AT HIGH ALTITUDE

1 October Luftwaffe change tactics once more. Their principle bomber force is reserved for night raids on London. Throughout October, on average 150 bombers attack the capital each night. The real start of the London 'blitz'. During daylight, faster Ju 88 bombers and Me 109s carrying bombs raid Britain from high altitude.

8 October Josef Frantisek, Fighter Command's highest-scoring ace of the Battle with seventeen kills, is killed in action.

14 October London attacked at night by the heaviest bomber force yet. Coventry bombed by night too.

15 October London attacked at night by an even heavier bomber force (400 bombers).

27 October Churchill concludes that German invasion is postponed based on Enigma decryptions and aerial reconnaissance showing invasion barges leaving Channel ports.

31 October Official end of the Battle of Britain.

31 October The highest-scoring squadrons in the Battle of Britain are 303 (Polish) Squadron with 126 kills and 602 Squadron with 102 kills.

31 October Fighter Command has 729 fighters ready for immediate action, 370 in reserve at one day's notice and 110 in preparation at the factories, available in four days.

1 July–31 October Fighter Command pilots (of which there were officially 2,927) made 2,698 claims of 'kills' of enemy aircraft during the Battle. Of this figure, 806 claims were made by aces (there were 104 aces in the period). This shows how a significant proportion of total kills (around 30 per cent) were made by a small minority (around 3.5 per cent) of fighter pilots.

10 July–31 October Luftwaffe loses 1,733 aircraft to Fighter Command's 915.

10 July–31 October Total losses for both sides are Luftwaffe 2,698 airmen (killed and captured) and Fighter Command 544 (killed).

IMMEDIATE AFTERMATH

11 November PETER BLATCHFORD (see chapter 56) shoots down two Italian Air Force bombers on one of their rare incursions into British airspace. He later liberates bottles of Chianti from the wreck of one.

15 November Dowding forwards to the Air Ministry Keith Park's report on the air fighting in September and October.

25 November Dowding is retired as Commander-in-Chief of Fighter Command.

PART I
Prelude, the Battle of France, Spring 1940

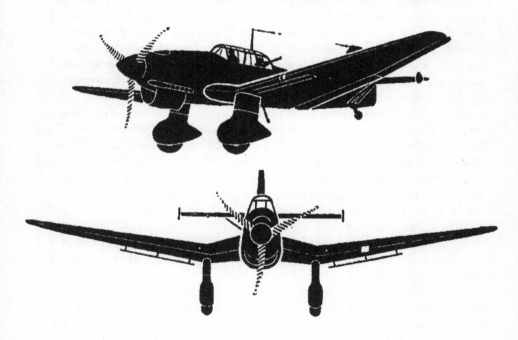

1 James 'Jimmy' Davies, Hurricane Pilot, Flight Lieutenant, American, 79 Squadron

Air Ministry & Ministry of Information-endorsed BBC radio broadcast by an anonymous RAF fighter pilot in June 1940. The pilot is Flight Lieutenant James 'Jimmy' Davies, who was an American pilot in 79 Squadron. While operating in France in May 1940, 79 Squadron flew from the airfields at Merville and Norrent-Fontes, both in the Nord-Pas-de-Calais region of the north-east.

As mentioned in the introduction, there was no such aircraft as the Heinkel 113; in reality the aircraft Davies encountered were Me 109s, which looked similar in the aircraft recognition manuals.

Within weeks of the broadcast Davies was dead. On 27 June he was shot down into the Channel by an Me 109. His body was never recovered. He had been due that afternoon to be presented with his DFC at Biggin Hill by King George VI himself. Good friend and fellow pilot in 79 Squadron Donald Stones recounts in his memoirs how the king was visibly moved when he was told why Davies wouldn't be making the award (see chapters 3 and 34, though extracts don't include this episode). Davies had shot down six enemy aircraft plus two shared kills.

I was born of Welsh parents in Bernardsville, near Morristown, New Jersey, in 1913. My father ran a big farm there. I went to school first at the Morristown High School, and when we left there for Connecticut, I went to the Gilbert School in Winstead, Connecticut. We lived for a long time in New Hertford, Connecticut, and I have many friends over there. I left the United States when I was about eighteen or nineteen years old. My parents, who had gone out to America two years before I was born, came back and settled down in Bridgend, South Wales. I went to Cardiff College to study wireless for a while, and after doing this and that for a year or two, I took a short service commission in the RAF. That was in 1936. I was posted to a fighter squadron immediately I had finished my training, and here I am, still a fighter pilot, and liking it more and more each day.

I got my first German in November 1939. It was the first enemy aircraft to be shot down in the Straits of Dover in this war. I was on patrol between Deal and Calais, leading a section of Hurricanes from my squadron when we spotted, at 12,000 feet, a Dornier 17 'flying pencil'. He was about 2,000 feet below us, and as we hadn't seen a German machine up to then, we went down carefully to make sure. We soon recognised him as an enemy, and as I turned to attack he tried to attack me. My Hurricane quickly outmanoeuvred him, I got on his tail, and gave him three sharp bursts of fire. Another member of the section got in three bursts too, as he dived towards the clouds. The last I saw of him was just above sea level. He had turned on his back, and a moment later crashed into the sea. When we got back to the mess we were handed a parcel. It contained a bottle of champagne – with the compliments of the station commander. You see it was our first fight – and we'd won. In those days, one German aircraft was something to celebrate.

We went over to France on 10 May, when Hitler invaded the Low Countries. We went up that same afternoon. That time we didn't see anything, but the next day we really started. We carried out three patrols east of Brussels, and on the third patrol we saw three Heinkel 111s. We shot down one, and badly damaged the other two. The day after that, we got two Heinkel 111s, one of which was credited to me. I shot mine down from 12,000 feet.

All the same, those skirmishes were child's play to what was to come later. On 14 May, after we had escorted a number of Blenheim bombers into enemy territory, we were on our way back when we saw three Dornier 17 'flying pencils'. It was a trap, for when we gave chase to the Dorniers, we suddenly found ourselves in the middle of between fifty and sixty Messerschmitt 109s and 110s. I was leading the flight that day and when I realised how hopelessly outnumbered we were, I gave orders to the boys to sort out their own targets and not to keep formation.

We broke up and began to set about the Messerschmitts. I got four Me 110s, and other members of the flight got four more. On the way back to our base, I saw two Heinkel 126s, one of which I shot down, and damaged the other with the rest of my ammunition. It was a good day. We routed an overwhelming number of enemy fighters, beat up two of their army reconnaissance planes, and we all got home safely. Our bag on that day was six. There were six of us, so we averaged one each.

There were several other days when we ran into heavy odds of enemy fighters. It is really amazing, looking back, that we should have had the success we had. But it certainly was a success each day. We never ran into the Germans without shooting some down. When we were patrolling Dunkirk, for instance, giving protection day after day to the BEF, we always got a few. I remember once, when we found ourselves in the thick of six squadrons of Me 109s and 110s, we saw an unusual type of enemy fighter. They were the new Heinkel 113s. Naturally we couldn't resist the appointment. We got one of each type, and three or four of what we call 'probables'. I was attacking an Me 110 when I suddenly realised that there were six Heinkel 113s on my tail. I made a very quick turn to get away from them, and then shot down the Heinkel 113 on the extreme left of that particular formation.

That was in the afternoon. We had an 'appetiser' before lunch, when we met twenty Heinkel 111 bombers. I got one. He went down in flames. And others of the squadron got their share.

The smoke from innumerable fires in Dunkirk and other French coast towns was terrific about that time. A fellow pilot described it as being like a gigantic piece of cotton wool lying right across the seashore, following the coast down the Channel as far as he could see, even from two or three miles up. There were times when we found that same smoke of great assistance in outwitting enemy fighters.

One of our squadron, for instance, used up all his ammunition in shooting down two Me 110s one day, and found himself being chased by two more. Without ammunition he could do nothing, so he dived into the smoke over Dunkirk. He emerged above the smoke a few miles away, and there the Messerschmitts were still waiting for him. They simply stuck above the smoke waiting for him to emerge, a victim for their guns. But he outwitted them by diving back into the smoke and was able to slip away home, only to be off again into battle the same evening.

We were stationed in France for eleven days. I remember that, when we went away, the roses were in bud; and when we came back they were in full bloom. In between we'd had eleven glorious days of action, but it was very hard work.

2 Mark 'Hilly' Brown Part 1, Hurricane Pilot, Pilot Officer, Canadian, 1 Squadron

First of three extracts from contemporary letters home, personal combat reports and part of a BBC radio broadcast covering his time during the Battle of France and Britain.

Born in 1911 in Manitoba, Canada, Brown joined the RAF in May 1936 and 1 Squadron in 1937. In early September 1939 1 Squadron was deployed to France as part of the RAF Advanced Air Striking Force (AASF). Brown soon showed his exceptional skill as a fighter pilot and became Canada's first ace of the war. In a ten-day period from 11–21 May 1940 he shot down twelve enemy aircraft. Brown was so busy shooting down Germans he only managed one letter to his parents, on the 13th ('We are getting a lot of action and liking it'), then nothing again until 27 May ('I have of course been very busy and have spent all my spare time sleeping or eating …')!

2 & 3 March 1940, France, letter home God, how I would like to get leave to go to Canada. I am not foolish enough to think that I would want to stay in one place and miss all the fun over here, but I do yearn to wander around and see how all my old friends and sisters and brother are getting along. I have had a marvellous experience over here, in studying people and types. When I think about how small I was when I left Canada, I believe that if the chances of getting back are only 10 in 100, it will have been worth it.

I will tell you about my latest excitement. On 2 March, I was leading two other chaps about the sky and we saw a Hun. I attacked, and had my prop shot away. I had to glide to a forced landing, but luckily I was high enough to get to an aerodrome. I landed safely (at Nancy). One of the chaps was killed – he was our first casualty. They got the Hun.

The next day, the survivor of the bout and I were up again. We saw a Heinkel 111. We made no mistake this time, and he came down with a bang. So now I have two 50 per cents, which makes a whole one. That is much better than the average have. Most of the boys haven't even seen one.

3 March 1940: Pilot's Combat & Gun Behaviour Report. Type of enemy aircraft: He 111; Position of enemy aircraft shot down: Forbach: No. of bursts: 4; Length of bursts: 2-3-7-3; From: F/O M. H. Brown; To: Officer Commanding, No. 1 Squadron. Sir, I have the honour to report that at 11.15 hours I took off with Sergeant Soper as No. 2 to patrol Nancy–Metz.

An enemy aircraft was reported in the vicinity twice, but we did not intercept.

At 1200 hours Sergeant Soper reported an enemy, so I told him to fly in the direction of it. It was about 10 miles SE of Etain, and flying north. I was at 24,000 feet but still below the enemy. Sergeant Soper was below it and behind.

I climbed on a parallel course and eventually attacked over Etain. The attack was not successful owing to the fact that the enemy turned and my attack was badly executed.

I then climbed east to cut the enemy off, and when again above him, 27,000 feet, I approached for a second attack. The enemy was then north of Metz, going east. He turned toward me, so I delivered a beam attack. I believe I silenced the upper rear gunner on this occasion. All the while during this attack, anti-aircraft bursts were going off indiscriminately.

The enemy then headed south-east and I was not in a position to attack again, until he was 20 miles SE of Metz.

My third attack was from directly astern and was quite a long burst, opening fire at 300 yards and closing to 50 yards. He was belching much smoke and bits flying off. My machine was covered in petrol and oil. I could see that both engines were out of action.

On my fourth attack I could see his undercarriage was down and both engines definitely out of action, but since he had turned north-east in the meantime and was gliding, I knew the pilot must be alive, so I gave it another burst. Sergeant Soper then began attacking again, and followed it to the ground. I kept at a height of about 8,000 feet to keep a lookout for enemy fighters.

Points: 1. The camouflage was very dark; 2. Rear gunfire was not experienced when attacking from directly behind; 3. I wasted very few rounds, but still the entire crew were not killed; 4. It is difficult for a Hurricane to reach the ceiling of a He 111, but with patience it can be nursed above, and is faster by at least 30 mph.

Around 30 April 1940 & 15 May 1940, France, part of BBC broadcast I was one of the lucky ones who got to France right at the beginning of the war – on 8 September 1939 – and I was there until the evacuation. By that time my squadron had knocked down well over a hundred of the enemy for the loss of four of our pilots killed, and three taken prisoner – which we thought wasn't bad. I put in nearly five hundred hours flying in France, and first I'll tell you about just two of these.

One of the most thrilling flights I made was, strange to say, not in one of our planes at all, but in a German one – an Me 109. It fell into our hands, complete, and I was the first British pilot to fly it, as I was told to fly it back to England. They gave me a nice, fat escort, and I felt I needed it. Not that I found the German fighter bad. It wasn't. It was a very good machine but it had no armour plating, and one squirt from one of our own fighters would have ended me if it had been mistaken for the enemy. I came home safely, in close formation with a Hudson and three Blenheims, with fighters above and behind, in case of trouble.

Another was 15 May (1940) and eight of us, in Hurricanes, were detailed to escort six bombers over to Maastricht, where there was a bridge that had to be destroyed. The bombers did their stuff as everybody knows. The first Air Force VC of the war was won that day by a leader who didn't come back. Our job was to keep the German fighters busy while the bombers did their work.

We didn't have much trouble on the way out, but when we got there we found plenty. There seemed to be millions of 109s in the sky and it was our job to keep their minds occupied. As the bombers went on to the bridge 10,000 feet below us, we waded into the 109s, and within a few minutes we had shot down four or five of them. My tail was badly damaged, and I set off for home with a limp. Just inside France, I met up with one of the squadron. He called me on the radio and told me to be very careful. He said, 'Half your tail's missing!' I can tell you, I was careful, and I got back all right.

3 Donald Stones Part 1, Hurricane Pilot, Pilot Officer, British, 79 Squadron

First of two extracts from his memoir, first published in 1990, this one covering ten days fighting in France from 10 to 20 May 1940 as part of the reinforcement of the Advanced Air Striking Force.

Donald 'Dimsie' Stones was born in Norwich in June 1921. He joined the RAF in May 1939 and 79 Squadron in March 1940 and was just eighteen years old.

Led by our CO, the squadron took off for France just before noon in bright sunshine and a cloudless sky, I in my trusty old fabric-winged Hurricane L1716. We crossed the Channel, calm as a lake with even a tinge of blue for a change to grace this beautiful day, in tight peacetime formation as if we were going to an air display. In minutes we were over the foreign-looking fields of France, so regular and formal after the jigsaw patterns of England and its 'rolling English roads made by the rolling English drunkard'. French roads all seemed straight from our bird's-eye view and were a navigational bonus. Soon we were touching down at Merville, a grass aerodrome which looked more like a flying club than an operational base, with few buildings and no runways, tarmac aprons or maintenance hangars. We were to be billeted in the village with local families and made use of the Hotel Sarafand as a mess. There was also no control tower or radio navigational aids. Refuelling was to be done by one bowser, and the first few of our newly arrived ground staff. While we awaited the arrival of the main body in other transport aircraft, we repaired to the Sarafand for a meal and heard on the French radio that Winston Churchill had been called to the palace to form a new government as Prime Minister. We gave three cheers, and one of the French villagers at the bar raised his glass and said '*Alors! La guèrre commence!*' The rest of the news was not so joyous. We gathered that the Germans had broken through the French near Sedan, bypassing the Maginot Line, and were hammering the Low Countries.

At once we were on patrol towards the fighting, but without our CO who was otherwise occupied with bowel trouble. We thought of Drake's famous words on hearing that the Armada was sighted whilst he was busy with bowls, not bowels. We patrolled from Lille to Roubaix and Mons-en-Chausée without seeing any German aircraft. Below us we could see British Army transport going eastwards to meet the enemy. We landed back at Merville, disappointed that we had had no action, but pleased to see that the Army was advancing. I was given the best bedroom in my billet by my French hosts. It was dominated by a vast *lit matrimonial*, brass-railed, with an ancient mattress which had taken generations of punishment.

We all met at the Hotel Sarafand that evening and I asked Bob Edwards what was wrong with our CO as he had still not appeared. 'Gut rot,' said Bob. 'You don't mean a "question of guts" do you?' I asked him in a whisper. 'Better not discuss it,' said Bob. 'We'll have to wait and see. We have no MO here as far as I know, so perhaps he's gone to some French quack.' This troubled me a lot and back in my billet I thought about it before I managed to get to sleep in the swaybacked mattress. The CO had been such a stern disciplinarian, on the ground and in the air, before we left Biggin and we knew he was a good pilot. What would happen to us if he did not recover quickly? The unthinkable question would not go away.

I had just got to sleep when my French hosts woke me with the news that another English pilot had arrived and would have to share my room. He came up the stairs dragging his opened parachute behind him like a bridal train. He was from another squadron, Auxiliary Air Force and, after apologising profusely for disturbing me, explained that he had been returning from patrol alone, having somehow lost contact with his squadron, and met three He III bombers over the middle of the garrison city of Lille. His instinct was to ignore them, discretion being the better part of valour, but had suddenly realised that thousands of British troops were in Lille and watching him, so *noblesse oblige* he had to turn round and attack them. He was promptly shot down by the rear gunners, baled out and hitch-hiked to Merville. We had to share the bed, head to toe.

The CO was still not to be seen next morning and it seemed that a cloak of silence had been instinctively drawn around the matter. I heard no one mention it at all after my brief exchange with Bob Edwards. Our NCO pilots were too well trained to ask questions. They rallied magnificently to the rudderless ship. There was no noticeable drop in morale but a general air of confusion was apparent.

Early next day we were on various patrols again to the east, now operating in flights of six Hurricanes, and I was in the air for eight hours. On one of these patrols I saw passing below me a German reconnaissance aircraft, Hs 126, recognised at once after all those hours of studying enemy aircraft silhouettes at Biggin. I shouted on the R/T and was told by the flight commander to stay in formation. On our return, this time to Norrent Fontes, we found that we were to operate from there as the advance to the Belgian frontier continued. A flight commander Bob Edwards was missing on one patrol but turned up later, having been shot down by something he didn't see and baled out. Excitement mounted as we patrolled towards Belgium and escorted Blenheims from England to bomb German positions. Still no contact with the Luftwaffe but on 14 May, with Lew Appleton leading Sergeant Cartwright and me, we patrolled from Louvain to Namur. Suddenly I saw below us three Junkers 88 bombers and yelled: 'Bandits! Bandits!' on the R/T. They were in a wide V formation and I heard Lew shout: 'Tally ho!' Harry Cartwright and I went after two of them and Lew disappeared, presumably after the other which had broken formation. We dived on our two. For the first time I felt the joy of firing my guns in hot blood and at a range of about 150 yards I saw my rounds flashing into the 88's port engine and his rear gunner firing tracer at me. The 88 started to turn to port and slowed down so suddenly that I overshot him and I shouted to Cartwright to finish him off. I now pulled out the emergency boost plug for the first time ever, which gave the Hurricane its maximum speed of just over 300 mph, and went after the leader of the 88s. The old fixed-pitch Hurricane was quite fast when really wound up and I gradually overhauled this 88, having still some extra speed from our initial dive, but it seemed ages before he filled my reflector sight. Adrenalin was now pumping into my bloodstream and I tried to remember to give only short bursts and make them tell. First his port engine and then switch to the starboard, silencing his rear gunner. His port engine was smoking and I thought I could see his airscrew windmilling. Again I overshot, and did a hard steep turn down above him and saw he was in a spin. I straightened out and saw him go into the west bank of a river, which I discovered later was the Maas. I felt nothing for him, only satisfaction and victory. As the adrenalin faded, I began to wonder where I was and belatedly reduced my engine power, alarmed by the high temperature. The only thing to do was fly west, and by sheer luck I eventually saw in the distance the unmistakeable bat-shaped Forêt de Nieppe, landmark for Merville, and Norrent Fontes.

Harry Cartwright had already landed and had finished off the other 88. Lew Appleton had not returned, and we never saw him again. My poor old L1716 had suffered hits from the 88's rear gunner in its port wing main spar and would have to await a new wing.

Bob Roberts, our other flight commander's aircraft had been damaged by ground fire near Maastricht and he was temporarily grounded, so by now we had the CO and both flight commanders out of action, which was to prove a great disadvantage, as the rest of us had very little experience in leading a section of three let alone a flight of six. At about this time we had a brief visit from the Duke of Gloucester and his entourage. He was in a joyful mood but rather vague, with a high colour. I asked our adjutant, 'Fiji' Mortimer, if he thought our visitor had a touch of the sun. 'Sunstroke?' he laughed. 'Sunstroke? Dimsie your name suits you. No, it wasn't the sun. He had been celebrating, though God knows what!'

Patrols continued and I now had my own section to lead in a spare aircraft. In the early evening of 18 May I had returned from an uneventful patrol and was having a cigarette with my ground crew when an unknown wing commander came up to me and said, 'Which is your aircraft?' 'That one, sir, but it is out of action for an hour or so for a minor repair.' 'Right, get into that new one. It has just been delivered by a ferry pilot. Stand by for take-off immediately you hear any bombing or see any smoke. Get your ground crew up on your wings to listen and watch, and go off to investigate if they hear or see anything. There are reports that the Germans are bombing air strips to the east of us.'

This unknown wing commander turned up again later with similar disastrous results.

I got into the cockpit, which had a distinct 'straight from the factory' smell. My two ground crew, the fitter and rigger, stood on the wing-root either side of my cockpit and gazed out towards the east. As I sat there I thought that everything was getting very strange. Of all the cock-ups we had already had, this felt likely to be the biggest of them all. If the Luftwaffe was bombing air strips to the east of us, why were we not sent to attack them as a whole squadron? Why me, sitting here alone in a new aircraft, which I had not had time to fly and test that it was combat worthy? Were the guns harmonised? The ferry pilot would not have known as he was not a combat pilot. What was in the gun belts? Was it all ball, all tracer, all armour piercing or what? And what exactly was I to investigate or do when I was eventually airborne? Take on the entire bomber force on my own, or come straight back to our base and tell our sickly CO? Would the squadron still be here when I got back? For once my excitement was tinged with depression that no one seemed to know what was going on in France. We had already heard rumours that our unreliable telephone system to some distant operations room near Arras was being sabotaged by fifth columnists. We knew that even when it was working, the orders were vague and often countermanded at the last minute. Perhaps one of my ground crew was right when I overheard him say cheerfully, 'It's all a buggers muddle' in a Yorkshire accent.

I had been sitting strapped in for some minutes when one of my ground crew told me I had no radio as the crystals had not arrived with the brand new aircraft. I was absorbing this information when my rigger shouted 'Over there, sir – smoke!' Off I went and climbed south east to about 2,000 feet, from which height I could see several pillars of black smoke, which soon materialised as six or seven Hurricanes burning on the ground at Vitry-en-Artois aerodrome. I wondered who had set fire to these and where the other Hurricanes were. Looking upwards, I saw some aircraft at about 5,000 feet – they must be the surviving Hurricanes from this disaster and I climbed up to join them, keeping my eyes on the fires below me. The next thing I knew was that, on closing with these 'Hurricanes', they had sprouted twin tails and one of them, although still at a distance, was firing at me with guns in his nose. Good God, they are Me 110s – twin-engined fighters! Frantically I unlocked my gun button and fired wildly at him with the luckiest burst of the war, and hit him, but there was no time to see how badly, as his friends now fell on me from all angles and I dived for the ground. I pulled out at about 100 feet and a 110 I hadn't seen following me down, suddenly appeared bang in front of my nose and only 50 yards ahead, having actually gone under me and overshot, climbing to avoid some buildings. He went into a left turn and I fired burst after burst into him as I turned with him. We went almost completely round the village, about 100 feet above the rooftops. I remember a church flashing by, and I could see my rounds hitting him in the port wing, engine and cockpit, when suddenly there was silence from my engine and only puffs of white smoke coming out of my exhaust stubs. Total loss of power. A small field ahead on the edge of the village. Straighten out and try to get in. Leave the wheels up as you have been taught. You're a sitting duck for the next of the 110s but you have no height for baling out. You're going too bloody fast, put it down, you're running out of field – rumble – crunch – the Hurricane going vertical on its nose – will it go over? – no, crash back on to its tail and blood running down my face where it hit the glass of the reflector sight. Get out and run like hell before the others shoot you up.

One flew over and he must have thought I was dead in the wreckage, but I foolishly gave him a few rounds from my Webley automatic, which he couldn't have noticed because he didn't come back. Suddenly everything was quiet as the adrenalin ebbed and the anti-climax, which I was to get to know after every battle, was upon me. I lit a cigarette, which wobbled like a piece of rubber.

I sat at the edge of the field and gazed at the wreckage of my brand new

Hurricane. Lit another cigarette and was pleased to see that this one didn't wobble quite so much. So this is what it's like to be shot down. But how had it happened? That rear gunner in the Me 110 must have hit me somewhere before he died. Because he certainly can't have lived through that blast of fire from my eight machine guns which I saw lashing into the 110's cockpit at such close range. And nor could the pilot. The gunner must have hit some vital part of my engine with his dying burst. As I calmed down I began to make plans for leaving the scene. Walk north-west I suppose. Or try to find the RAF airfield where I had seen all those Hurricanes burning on the ground. There must be someone there with whom I could get a lift back to base? How far away were the Germans? No telling, because if the Me 110s who attacked me were the ones who had strafed the Hurricanes on the ground, they were long-range aircraft, so the German armour might still be miles away. This cheered me up a bit and suddenly a French rustic appeared. '*Vous êtes abbatu*' was his understatement of 1940 so far. '*Mais aussi les Boches*', which cheered me. '*Combien?*' I asked '*Deux!*' he replied, '*Les sales Boches!*' and offered me a grubby flask from which I took a small swig. It was raw cognac and I gasped. '*Encore*' he commanded, but I was saved by the noisy arrival of a British Army motorcyclist, attracted by my broken Hurricane. He was a despatch rider and was wearing a tin hat, with a rifle slung across his shoulder. He seemed in no particular hurry, so together we examined the Hurricane to look for any damage which could have caused my engine to fail. We eventually found a small bullet hole in my oil tank. This had obviously done internal damage and had probably made a large exit hole, causing the loss of all my engine oil and seizure of the engine. We could not look underneath as the Hurricane was very firmly on the ground. The 110s rear gunner had managed to hit me with only one round before my fire lashed into him.

The despatch rider offered to take me to the nearest aerodrome and I accepted only too gladly. Before leaving my wreck, I smashed the reflector sight with the butt of my Webley in compliance with regulations, as it was supposed to be on the secret list in those days of naïveté, then bundled up my unused parachute and clambered on to the back of the motorcycle. Off we went to the nearest aerodrome only a few miles away, which turned out to be Vitry where I had seen the Hurricanes burning. All was confusion there. RAF lorries were hurriedly packing to leave and, followed by the loyal despatch rider carrying my parachute, I searched for someone in authority and eventually found a squadron leader of an Auxiliary Air Force squadron. 'I have just been shot down, sir.' I got no further. 'So what,' he snapped. 'We've got troubles of our own here. The German tanks are only 15 miles away and we are leaving.' I asked if I could have a lift, mentioning that my Hurricane was wrecked in a field a few miles away. 'Did you burn it?' 'No, sir.' 'Then get back on that motorbike and burn the bloody thing.' Turning to Wilkinson, as I now knew him, he said: 'Take this officer back to his aircraft and help him burn it.' Wilkinson started to tell him he had a despatch to deliver, but was told: 'That's an order – get cracking.' I threw my parachute into a lorry and back we went to the wreck.

I had always been told that aircraft would catch fire easily if you fired bullets into a half empty petrol tank containing enough petrol air mixture. Taking careful aim, Wilkinson, prone at a safe distance, fired a magazine into the wing tanks with no result. We were both thinking about those German tanks approaching and there was no time to waste. I waved Wilkinson back to the edge of the field and, opening one wing tank, dipped my handkerchief in the remaining fuel and sloshed it all over the cockpit and wing root. I lit my handkerchief, threw it at the wing and ran like hell. She went up with a great 'woof' and I fell flat on my face. We only waited about a minute to see that she was a ball of flame before heading back to Vitry. Everyone had left except for one lorry with some ground crew, who were having starting trouble. I said goodbye to that splendid man Wilkinson, who sped off on his duties. I hope to God he survived. I only knew his surname, and that he came from Leeds.

Now what? With the gallant Wilkinson gone, heading east in the very direction of the German armour 15 miles away to deliver his precious message, the decision must be made about whether to start walking north-west or wait to see if the remaining ground crew could get their bloody lorry working. The last thing I wanted to be was a prisoner of war. Fighting was all right, lots of excitement and not much time to get scared while the blood was up, but sitting in a prison camp for the rest of the war was a ghastly thought and worse than death for a person of my impatient temperament. I wondered about that strange squadron leader who had ordered me to go back and burn my wrecked Hurricane. Was he in such a panic to get away from the onrushing German tanks that he decided a wreck was worth more to the enemy than a pilot who would probably be captured? It struck me that we were going to need some better senior officers to save our campaign in France. And what about the half-dozen or so Hurricanes I had seen burning on the ground at Vitry, drawn up in parade ground order, not properly dispersed, just waiting there to be destroyed by those Me 110s with one long burst of cannon and machine-gun fire? Sheer bad organisation, followed by panic. I was learning fast, but all the lessons were cautionary rather than exemplary, which would have been more use to me in those early days, still a month short of my nineteenth birthday.

Mercifully the solitary ground crew got the lorry started and we set off. The roads were by now jammed with French and Belgian refugees fleeing westwards in the path of the German advance and a pitiful sight they were. Many were on foot, wrapped in Red Cross blankets, others in ancient farm carts drawn by exhausted horses, some on bicycles. Many of them were women, carrying infants or leading children old enough to walk. There were many wounded amongst them, lying in the carts in their bandages and slings, some looking more like corpses. This, they told us, as we crawled by them when there was room to pass, was because they had been strafed by German aircraft the day before to keep them moving and to maintain the level of panic. Some younger ones, more nimble, grabbed the sides of our lorry and travelled with us. Our crew had scrounged a few hard rations and water from some abandoned store before we left Vitry and now displayed the charity for which British other ranks have always been famed and shared these with our hangers-on. We stopped at about midnight near Béthune and rested in a barn for a while. We got a bit of sleep cosily tucked into piles of hay, and then went on to Norrent Fontes, arriving just after daybreak. We had covered only about forty-five miles as the crow flies, at not much more than walking pace.

I reported to my CO, who asked, 'Where the hell have you been all this time?' I explained and was ordered to get another aircraft and come to readiness straight away. I washed the caked blood off my face, grabbed some breakfast and off we went again on patrol. I saw another Hs 126 on reconnaissance ahead of the main German forces and put him down with some difficulty as my Hurricane was so much faster. Every time I attacked he would turn on a sixpence and dodge round a tree or building, and I would have to find him again. Eventually it crashed into a field but the pilot got out of the wreckage and ran for cover. The next day I got another Hs 126 more easily, as he was over open ground near Arras, with the German main force not far behind.

On 20 May the same wing commander who had sent me off to Vitry appeared again with more orders. We were to take our six remaining combat worthy Hurricanes and patrol over Arras to rendezvous with some Blenheims coming out from England to bomb the German armour now approaching Arras. If the Blenheims did not show up, we were to engage enemy aircraft in the area. If we did not find any of these, we were to attack the German tanks ourselves. We thought it rather strange that he did not offer to lead us himself, as we had a non-flying CO and both flight commanders out of action.

John Parker took Dorrien-Smith and a sergeant pilot as his section, and I had my usual No. 2, Harry Cartwright, and Sergeant Pearce with me. We set out for Arras praying for the Blenheims to be on time. As we patrolled the western outskirts of Arras we could see fires and smoke to the east. We waited for the Blenheims for about forty minutes but they did not arrive. Inexplicably there were no enemy aircraft either. The dreaded third option was now unavoidable. John Parker, as senior pilot officer, called me on the R/T. 'Ok Dimsie, I'll take one road – you take the other', and down went his section in line astern towards the forerunners of a tank column we could now see clearly. I looked at my road and saw about half a dozen tanks apparently stationary. Ordering my section into line astern, I saw a great flash followed by a black cloud of smoke erupt from the ground between us and the tanks. It was probably an oil storage tank going up, and I decided to attack the German tanks, using this smoke as cover. Down we went through the smoke and there were the tanks with their black crosses, drawn up on the side of the road. We let them have the full contents of our gun belts but all they had to do was to fire their secondary armament all together to be sure of scoring hits on us as we flew through it. We were lucky to have had this black smoke cover and received no more than a peppering from the surprised panzers. We three landed safely with only minor damage. Not so the other section however. John Parker and Dorrien-Smith were both shot down by the tanks. Dorrien-Smith was killed. John ran into the outskirts of Arras where he met some British troops whose CO had no idea that the tanks were only minutes away, and actually had men off-duty on twenty-four hours' leave! That unit, I believe it was a Welsh regiment, had had no warning and we heard later that they had fought to the death.

My section's aircraft were no longer combat worthy, though only slightly damaged. My own was peppered with light machine-gun fire behind the cockpit and the armour plate at my back had kept me from death. Sergeant Pearce had a cannon shell in his armoured glass windscreen, from the heavier armament of the tanks. The windscreen was a mess but the shell had not fully penetrated and Pearce was undamaged. Harry Cartwright had some light machine-gun holes in his wings, but was also unhurt. John Parker's sergeant pilot also returned in one piece, with some holes in his aircraft. I could not stop Harry and the other sergeants getting heated about this attack and joined the discussion myself, regardless of king's regulations concerning criticism of the senior officer who had sent us off. When we analysed it, we did not know what had happened to John Parker and Dorrien-Smith until John turned up a few hours later. We all felt that it had been a totally irresponsible order from that wing commander that we six Hurricanes, carrying only machine-guns, should attack columns of tanks with their thick armour plating, if there were no other targets. There was no chance of doing material damage to them, other than chopping off a few tank crew heads if they were slow to close their hatches when they saw us coming at them. Our costs were two Hurricanes destroyed, one pilot killed, one missing until John Parker turned up, and four Hurricanes damaged and not officially airworthy.

John turned up later that afternoon, having hitch-hiked somehow from Arras. We were all furious at this ludicrous waste of life and aircraft on a crazy attack. Dorrien-Smith was a nephew of Marshal of RAF Lord Trenchard, the architect and founder of the Royal Air Force. But the day's excitements were not yet over by any means. That evening we were ordered to return to England as we had no more aircraft fit for combat. Those which could make the short flight to England were patched up. The remainder which could not were to be destroyed by our ground crews, who would quickly go to evacuation ports after we had left. Our CO now made a brave recovery from his bowel trouble and took to the air in a Hurricane, unseating a sergeant pilot who had to return by sea with the ground crews.

The sergeant pilot told us later on his return to England that their evacuation troopship was bombed in its harbour but not critically damaged. Just before it pulled away, and as the last stretcher cases of the wounded were being carried up the gang planks, a very scruffy and elderly man arrived at the dockside on a motorcycle and wearing shabby civilian clothes. He claimed to be a British fighter pilot who had been shot down and escaped from advancing German tanks on a stolen German motorcycle. He showed some identification to a medical orderly who at once saluted him and, pulling a blanket off a corpse, said: 'Well this one's very dead, sir. If you don't mind taking his place, I'll tell the stretcher bearer to put you aboard.' The pilot got on the stretcher and pulled the blanket over his face. Legend has it that the pilot was Flight Lieutenant Sir Archibald Hope, baronet, who survived to fight again in England. He was already well known as the oldest flight lieutenant in the RAF.

The CO now led us into Northolt instead of Biggin Hill for some mysterious reason of his own. We saw him in conversation with the station commander of Northolt as we stood around our seven Hurricanes, the only ones which were fit to make the homeward flight. He walked towards us after his conversation with the station commander. We could hardly bear to look at him. He gave us a happy grin and said, 'Right. Now we can fly back to Biggin' and we followed him there. We walked into the mess in exactly the same clothes as we were wearing ten days earlier, and carried the same small hand luggage that we had crammed into our cockpits. Everything else had been left with the ground crews in France. The CO disappeared. 32 Squadron pilots, our friends and my old comrades in arms, gave us a huge welcome and bought us a drink, holding their noses in mock disgust and told us we needed a bath, which was true. They also pointed out that we were improperly dressed for a gentleman's mess. This was also true, as we had no ties and some of us were in flying boots. At the same time the 32 Squadron boys were longing to hear about France, but we were too tired and confused to tell them. The CO returned, looking spruced up and properly dressed, the only one of us who was. He announced that we could all have forty-eight hours' leave. There was a mad rush to cash cheques, arrange transport vouchers and go to our old rooms to see if we had left anything fit to wear that we had not sent to France. I found an even older uniform which was cleaner than the one I was wearing, and some old shoes and underclothes. Then I went down to the hall, where the CO asked me if I wanted a lift to Bromley railway station in his official car. I didn't but accepted the offer as the quickest way to get there on my way to London and Suffolk. At the station he said, 'Blast! I have no small change for my train fare. Have you by any chance got 1/9*d*?' I had, and gave it to him. 'Until we meet again then,' he said cheerily. I saluted and turned away to go to my train, and that was the last any of us ever saw of him.

On the train from London to Suffolk there was much to ponder concerning our ten days in France. I looked at the other passengers in the first class compartment to which my travel warrant entitled me. They were mostly civilian, businessmen I supposed, reading *The Times* and looking comfortable. If they could have read my mind, they would not have been at all comfortable, but they could not be blamed for that, as whatever news they were reading was not half the story of what we had just left behind us in France. If they had asked me, and I had been foolish enough to try and describe the shambles, they would not have believed me. They could quite rightly have reported me for 'spreading alarm and despondency'.

4 Ian 'Widge' Gleed Part 1, Hurricane Pilot, Flight Lieutenant, British, 87 Squadron

Contemporary memoir published in May 1942 as *Arise to Conquer*. Born in Finchley, London in July 1916, Gleed learned to fly privately before joining the RAF in 1936. He started the war with 266 Squadron on 9 September 1939 and was injured while testing a Spitfire which broke apart in mid-air. Fully recovered, Gleed joined 87 Squadron flying Hurricanes in France on 14 May 1940 at Lille/Seclin airfields while it formed part of the Air Component of the British Expeditionary Force (BEF). This is where this extract, the first of two, begins. He fought over France until 22 May when his squadron was withdrawn to RAF Debden, Essex (11 Group).

Gleed had met several writers including Somerset Maugham and Hector Bolitho (see chapter 8) before the war while indulging his passion for sailing and this is thought to have encouraged him to try his hand at writing. The memoir is part-fiction but closely based on his personal experiences. Pseudonyms are used throughout, for example Richard William Forbes or 'Shuvvel' for 87 Squadron's New Zealand CO Terance Lovell-Gregg (KIA 15 August 1940), and Gleed himself is referred to as 'Widge' Leeds.

Chapter 4, Combats Before Lunch: France, c. 14 May 1940–c. 28 May 1940 As the French express roared across the country side I thought what a strange world it was: a little while ago I had been in a damned uncomfortable troop-train; now I was in a very comfortable train, eating a delicious roast chicken and sipping champagne. Soon it was dark. I was surprised how slack the French were about black-out as nearly every village had many windows showing bright lights; the train itself was only blacked out with blinds which half the time were up, as passengers peered out.

After several halts, the train drew into the outskirts of Lille, and steamed very slowly into the station. As soon as I was on the platform I heard the crack of anti-aircraft, and the dull thud of bombs bursting in the distance; through the glass roof of the station I could see searchlights sweeping the sky. I thought, 'Well, this is a good welcome to the war.' I wandered along to the RTO's office and tried to get the aerodrome on the phone. After about half an hour I got through to the 87 Squadron mess. The adjutant said that the best thing to do was to stay the night in Lille and report in the morning; he suggested that I should stay at the Metropole, and he would send transport at ten in the morning.

The French didn't seem to take much notice of the air-raid, except that this time the black-out was a hundred per cent effective, for the simple reason that all the lights were turned off. The station was absolutely crammed with refugees; it was with the utmost difficulty that I managed to get out of the station, after parking my main luggage with the RTO.

I soon found the Metropole, a tall, rather smart hotel with a lot of glass and chromium plate in the foyer. The receptionist seemed to think that it was a hell of a joke when I asked for a room; there wasn't a room in the place. She told me that I would find some RAF officers in the bar. She was right. The so-called bar was a low room with crowds of tables, overflowing with uniforms and French girls. A table of slightly tight RAF blokes hailed me and stood me a drink. 'You're the new flight lieutenant for 87, are you? Well, ol' boy, you stick along with us; we're staying somewhere in this goddamned town tonight, and will take you out to the 'drome in the morning.'

'Damn it, ol' boy, I'm off after that one', so off went one of the blokes after a very ropy blonde. A few drinks and I was feeling muzzily pleased with life; all I wanted now was a damned nice bed. The party was gradually growing smaller, as one by one the boys disappeared with various women. I gathered that most of the blokes were from 504 Squadron, who that afternoon had shot down about fourteen Jerries, but had lost six of themselves, including the CO. Eventually there were only two of us left. The other bloke felt like me, so we pushed off in search of a pub that wasn't full. We found that we couldn't walk more than a few feet before we were accosted by women; the place was swarming with prostitutes. Neither of us was feeling at all inclined that way that night. At last we found quite a decent small hotel which gave us a double room and bath for fifty francs, cash before you sleep. As it was now in the early hours of the morning, this place seemed empty of the crowd of women.

The sun was streaming through the window when I woke. *Petit dejeuner* was brought up to our rooms. We ate it hurriedly, and went downstairs, where we found an RAF driver with a Citroen van. We bumped through Lille, then down a small road leading to the country. My companion left us at the first small village. We bumped on across the cobbles for about another half-mile, then turned into a drive lined with trees, round a bend, and stopped by what looked to me to be a cricket pavilion. Several types were lying about in deck chairs. A tough-looking pilot was adjusting a small petrol engine of a model plane. I soon discovered that he was 'Watty', one of 'A' flight boys – 'A' flight was to be my flight. I introduced myself rather nervously. They seemed pleased to see me. After many questions of what London looked like, I managed to hear something about my new squadron.

87 Squadron had come out to France right at the beginning of the war, in company with 85; they had been together at Debden for several years before the war. They were a happy bunch, and loved France. Terrific parties were had in Paris. The squadron had moved around to various 'dromes: Le Touquet, Senan, Lille, Seclen, Amiens. All these 'dromes became familiar to the pilot boys. Each place had its amusing memories: Le Touquet, where the inevitable 'Cock' overshot and fell into a reservoir; Senan, where 'Robbie' landed with his wheels up: 'Just forgot them, old boy.' France liked them and they liked France. Life was rosy and spring was coming.

They had lots of adventures but little action. Flight Lieutenant David Rhodes, 'B' flight's commander, shot down a Heinkel, the first one to be shot down in France, and received the Croix de Guerre avec Palme and the DFC.

The CO, 'Dusty' Miller and Beaver force-landed in Belgium five miles the wrong side of the frontier on the sands at La Panne. They were jumped upon by the Belgian army and whipped away to a castle in Brussels. They were soon called the mad English boys, because every afternoon they went for a run round the grounds. It was a medieval place, surrounded by a moat. Every day they made their run a bit later; gradually they worked it that they didn't get back until after dark. The British Consul and various friends visited them and made secret arrangements. One evening they ran very hard, slipped down the bank of the moat, swam it, ran like hares, hid in a wood for a couple of hours, then picked up the car driven by their Belgian friend, who hid them where they could slip across the French frontier undetected. Back to the squadron they came, dressed in the most fantastic clothes.

A new CO was posted to the squadron, Johnny Carswell, whom everyone grew to love and respect. The squadron swapped planes with a French squadron and had a grand dogfight. Our pilots had a hell of a job landing, as the throttles were the opposite way round to ours, and nearly everyone slammed the motor full on just as they were touching down. There were some terrific parties in the evening.

Sergeant 'Dinkie' Powell force-landed one evening 100 yards in Belgium. Dinkie ran like hell, and got pulled through the barbed wire by the French, just as the Belgian frontier guards caught him up. He managed to throw his parachute through first. He said afterwards that he daren't leave that behind as actually it belonged to Dickie Lylles, another pilot. That night most of 87 massed on the frontier, armed with ropes and a tractor. A plot had been hatched to pull the plane across the frontier. Unfortunately, our 'spies,' consisting of some of the boys in civvies, who sneaked across the frontier and hung about the plane, reported that it was guarded by three machine-guns, so they all went back to bed feeling very browned off. Such had been the life of my new squadron before the blitz.

'Wake up; you're at readiness in half an hour.' Hell! It was about three-thirty, and we were to be at readiness by four. I leapt out of my camp bed; a quick wash, then downstairs, where I met other sleepy pilots snatching a quick breakfast. A hoot from the outside told us that the Citroen van was waiting to take us to the dispersal points on the aerodrome. We bundled in. Cries of, 'Wait a moment! Where's Watty?' Watty arrived, running out of the mess half dressed; then off we went down a dirty, cobbly road. The van lurched from side to side as the flight sergeant who drove it cursed. The steering was as loose as hell we seemed to be in a permanent speed wobble.

At last, after a hectic three miles, we turned off the road. 'All out for "A" flight.' I scrambled out with Watty and Chris; the van bumped off down the road for 'B' flight.

It was my first day of readiness with 87. It was cool, as the sun had only just appeared over the horizon and was slowly climbing into the cloudless blue sky. We were to do a dawn patrol across the lines towards Brussels. 85 Squadron was to have two sections to meet us over Lille; they were operating from the 'drome south of us. We wandered to our planes. They had already been warmed up. We checked that our parachutes and helmets were handy, then there was nothing to do but wait. We sat by the phone; it might ring at any time, giving us patrol orders. Nothing happened. We idly turned the pages of well-thumbed books; several of them were the pornographic literature collected by the boys from the shops of Paris, Amiens and Lille. The sun grew warmer. I asked Watty and Chris how many planes they had shot down. Chris told me one, a Heinkel over Valenciennes about a week ago. Watty was like me, nothing.

Gradually, steadily, the time passed. Six o'clock was zero hour. At ten to, the engines were started; we clambered in. The plane I had got only arrived from England the day before, a brand-new one, with the latest variable-pitch Rotol airscrew. Already a black cat, my mascot, was painted on its side. We taxied out. On the other side of the aerodrome we saw 'B' flight turning into wind for the take-off. Soon we roared across the ground. Airborne, we swung southwards for the centre of the town. Where the hell were 85? After a few minutes, which seemed to me like hours, three Hurricanes climbed towards us. There seemed to be only nine of us, then. 85 were the leaders. Their section turned eastward; we followed, keeping well up. Looking either side, I saw Watty and Chris weaving (weaving means that the last planes of any formation fly on a twisting, snakelike course. By doing this the pilots can get a view behind them to their right and to their left alternately. This is the only way in which single-seater fighters, which are blind to the rear, can prevent enemy fighters from getting on their tails and shooting them down); farther across, 'B' flight wing men were doing the same thing. We droned onwards, climbing to 12,000 feet, then levelled out.

Beneath us the country was looking peaceful; except for patches of fog, the visibility was good. Looking back, Lille shone in the sun. There was nothing to show that there was a war on. Suddenly to our right appeared a black burst, then another; a score sprang into existence. Our formation started evasive action climbing, diving, twisting and turning. I looked down; there was nothing below that showed me that now we were over the enemy lines. The AA (ack-ack) was uncannily accurate: whenever we changed height the bursts seemed to follow us, always just a bit behind just as well for us! Soon we were past the guns, and once more everything looked peaceful.

We drone on. On the R/T a guttural voice starts talking. Blast these sets! Why can't they keep them tuned? I turn the volume down and move my tuning-arm. Hell! It's German. Wish the hell I could understand the language. It sounds hellishly close. I crane round, searching the sky behind. Nothing, not a cloud even, just steady blue. The weaving of our wing men becomes more vigorous.

In the distance I can see a haze of smoke, steeples and towers. Brussels… Christ! There they are, five specks coming towards us well below. I waggle my wings, 'Line astern, line astern. Go.' Messerschmitt 110s; nine of us against five of them. This looks easy. What the hell are the leading section doing? Still in vic formation, they sail on. 'Well, here goes, boys.' I bank over for a right-hand diving turn. Out of the corner of my eye I see 'B' flight's section, in line astern, wheeling towards us. The enemy are flying in rather a wide vic formation. I decide on the right-hand plane, 'Echelon port, echelon port. Go.' Watty and Chris swing up on my left. They still haven't seen us. We are diving steeply now, doing about 300 on the clock.

'Throttle back a bit; otherwise you'll overshoot them. Hell! They've broken. What the hell! They have turned to meet us. Steady, now; get your sights on before you fire. Rat tat tat, rat tat tat. Hell! You can hear their cannons firing. Blast it! I am going too fast: they are past me, on either side so close that I thought we would hit.'

As they pass, their rear gunners fire at me; their tracer goes over my head.

'A quick left-hand turn. Steady, or you'll black out.'

As I turn, the sky seems full of black crosses; another one overshoots me.

'Hell! They must have dived out of the sky.'

To my right a Hurricane goes down in flames; by it there's a white puff as a parachute opens.

'Keep turning tighter, tighter. God! They turn badly. I wonder if I'll get out of this alive? Another couple of turns; it's only a question of time before one of those rear gunners hits me.'

At last I can get my sights on a full deflection on the inside of the turn. I thumb the firing-button; a tearing noise as my guns fire.

'Got him.'

My bullets hit his petrol tanks, a stream of white vapour pours from his wing tanks, a whouf! almost in my face, his wings on fire. He turns on his back, trailing fire and smoke behind, plunges into a wood below.

'Keep turning.'

My lips crack, my cockpit smells of the oily compressed air that fires my guns.

Only three thousand feet up now. Three of the bastards at me seem to be the centre of their circle; their rear gunners banging away at me. Silly bastards! One of them overshoots me in front of me; only twenty-five yards' range. Brrrrrrrrr, brrrrrrrrrm. God! I can't miss. Brrrrrr; a blur of white and black.

My windscreen is covered with muck. I've hit his oil and glycol tank. I still turn tight as I can. A flash from below means that last one has just hit the deck; no parachutes.

'God! I wonder if I am going to get out of this. Not a sight of another Hurricane in the sky. Far above there seem to be a lot of planes; these damned Huns are bloody bad at turning.'

A few more turns and one of them is in my sights again. I thumb the gun-button. Nothing happens. I press again.

'Oh, Hell! I am out of ammo.'

A shiver runs down my spine. Still turning as steeply as I possibly can, I dive for the deck.

'Down, down. Thank God they've broken away from me.'

At about 100 feet I straighten up, pull the tit (this is the emergency control which, by driving the supercharger at its very maximum pace, gives the aeroplane considerable extra speed, but the strain on the engine is terrific so it must only be used in case of need, and then not for long, or the engine may blow up); a jerk as my supercharger goes up to twelve boosts.

'You bloody fool! You're going the wrong way: swing round and head for the sun.' The Jerries must be above me some way away. Oh God, don't let them see me. 'Streak along, dodging trees and houses. Thank God, another Hurricane's doing the same thing. I'll follow him home.'

Just as I am drawing up to formate on this Hurricane, he dips; I catch a fleeting glimpse of flying brick, and, seemingly quite slowly, a Hurricane's tail, with the red, white and blue stripes, flies up past my cockpit. I glance behind, and see a cloud of dust slowly rising.

'Hell! He must have had some bullets in him to hit that house. Wonder who it was? I seem to be the only survivor. Blast these fog patches! Keep going west. Untwist the emergency boost button (the tit), boost sinks back to normal. Now let's have a look at the map.'

My hands are shaking and my feet are drumming on the floor. I can't stop them. I'm sweating like a pig. Glancing at the cockpit clock, I see that it is exactly six-thirty; yet the sun seems hellishly hot.

'Oh, I can't make head or tail of these French maps. A town on the left, so sheer off southwards and have a look. It seems quite a big town; but I can't find it on the map. Now keep cool; go west wards for fifteen minutes, then turn north, and you'll hit the coast.'

At last, after what seemed hours, I saw the coast. Now it was only a case of guessing which way to turn to find an aerodrome. I turned westwards, as I was damned if I wanted to run into any more Huns just yet. Soon I came upon an airfield. For a second I had a nasty jolt, as the planes that I could see looked exactly like Jerry dive-bombers. Immediately I saw the French markings and felt at ease. I circled once, saw the direction of the wind, and came in to land. There were a few bomb-holes on the 'drome; several hangars looked the worse for wear, no roofs and bulging walls. I taxied up to some of the other machines. Several French airmen ran to meet me as I jumped out. God! How lovely it was to be on firm ground again.

Nobody appeared to speak English. I was shepherded to one of the huts by the hangars, where I was greeted in very broken English by a capitaine, who told me that I was at Berck, near Le Touquet. They shoved me in a car and rushed me off down a dusty road to a small chateau, where it appeared they had their officers' mess; there they rapidly produced for me a colossal breakfast of two eggs and multitudes of rashers of bacon. I did not feel at all hungry, only slightly sick. My hand was shaking so much that the coffee cup rattled against the saucer, which added to my embarrassment. A rather one-sided conversation went on. I managed to make them understand that I had shot down two Messerschmitts and that I thought my friends had been killed. They told me that they were the fleet air arm, and of late had done several raids on German-occupied Rotterdam.

I managed to borrow a map back at the aerodrome and to show the French crew how to crank the handles to start my Hurricane. She soon started, and off I went. By now the fog had cleared and the country looked green and clear beneath the cloudless sky. Soon the chimneys of Lille hove in sight and I was throttling back for the landing on the aerodrome, which I had left only three hours before. In that time I had seen death in flaming planes, heard the crack of the cannon-shells aimed to kill me, felt fear and exultation, despair and hope, helplessness and strength.

As I taxied in the crews ran to meet me, and, God! Can it be true? Watty and Chris were there too. 'How many, sir?' 'Two.' 'Damn good shooting, sir.' 'Hullo, Watty. How many did you get?' 'One.' 'Damned good show. What about Chris?' 'He got a probable; he was having too hot a time to see what happened to it. Whew! It was hot. They fought like hell, the swine. Where the hell have you been, Widge (Ian Gleed's nickname)? We thought you were finished. We were just saying, "Wonder who the new flight commander will be."'

'Well, old boy, it was like this. I hadn't the remotest idea where I was when I broke off the scrap. I started following another Hurricane; he hit a house, so I pushed off west; then what with fog and French maps I was properly foxed, so after a bit I turned north, hit the coast and landed at a French fleet air arm 'drome at Berck. They stuffed me with breakfast, and here I am. I thought that I was the only survivor.'

'That's what we thought, too. Poor 85 must have lost their boys. I saw two Hurricanes crash definitely. When I left the scrap after my ammo was finished I saw one "Hurribox" fighting five Jerries; I was scared stiff that they would come after me.'

By the time we had told each other what had happened, the sun was flaming down from a clear blue sky. We took off our tunics and lolled in the heat. The Citroen van rolled up with a pile of pilots to relieve us. We scrambled in, off to the mess for breakfast a second one as far as I was concerned. The trees looked very green and the world unusually happy; we all thought how good it was to be alive. In the mess we met the CO and some of the ground staff; they showered congratulations on us, and made us shoot them a line.

Breakfast tasted good. I managed to eat much more than my first one, which seemed years ago. As soon as we were finished we had a quick shave, then back to readiness.

Most of the squadron wore soft, dark-blue shirts, bought from the local village; the service type that I had on cut your neck when you craned round to see that nothing was on your tail. It was best to look behind at least four minutes out of every five: most people who had been shot down, and had got back to tell the tale, had said that they never saw what had hit them. I asked 'Chiefy', the flight sergeant, to get a village shirt for me, and in the meantime I took my collar off.

One of the things that had rather shaken me while I was in the mess was that the ginger-haired stores officer, who was mess secretary, had relieved me of 500 francs for the mess fund. He explained that everyone gave that, just in case they didn't come back. This was the real thing… war.

From the end of the aerodrome a red Very soared up; we sprinted to our planes – it was the emergency signal, meaning every plane off the ground. We slammed the throttles open; planes were taking off in every direction, the Rotol airscrew planes getting off first, scraping over the variable-pitch models, who in turn soared over the wooden prop versions.

I was petrified, heaving at the stick to get some height. Up in the sky ack-ack bursts showed where the Jerries were. There were about thirty bombers, with showers of fighters. I was fairly well in front of about fifty Hurricanes, climbing flat out. The Jerries saw us coming and swung round eastwards. 'Good show!' I thought. 'At least we've turned them back.' We were all gaining on them. Behind me I saw some of the 109s dive at the straggling 'Hurries'. A dogfight developed. We in front climbed upwards; the bombers, for some unknown, foolish reason, started breaking formation and dispersing in all directions. I had my eye on a Heinkel III which had separated itself and was some way away from the protecting Jerry fighters. I was soon up to him, aimed carefully and gave him a short burst; a stream of smoke from his port engine. I was closing rapidly now, sights on again; this time I gave him a long burst.

'Hell! Everything has gone black; his whole oil tank must have burst. Slam the hood open. All over the wings the oil glistens. Hell! I'm nearly ramming him.'

I shove the stick forward and just miss his tail. As I passed, a black object flashed past my cockpit; a puff of white as a parachute opened. The Heinkel fell away to my left, going down in a gentle, ever-increasing spiral. He hit the ground in the centre of a large wood and blew up with a terrific flash; chunks of wood and flaming debris drifted up towards me. I turned to see where the parachutist had got to; he had just landed in what appeared to be an empty field. In a matter of seconds the field was full of sprinting men, some soldiers and some civvies; the parachutist disappeared under a crowd of people.

As soon as I had landed, the crew were asking the usual question: they knew from the oil on my machine that I had got something. Robbie also got one of the Heinkels, and several of the other chaps had shot down 109s. So far Jackson, the Australian, and 'Joycey' weren't back. After an hour we phoned ops, and, as they had no news, reported them missing. Jackson we never heard of again; Joyce landed, with his wheels up, with half a leg blown off by cannon-fire. Some French soldiers looked after him and got him back to hospital at Amiens, where he had his leg amputated. Of course we didn't hear those details for some days, so to us they were just missing. One bullet hole was found in my machine; it had just missed the petrol tank.

No sooner was the oil cleaned off, and the machine rearmed and refuelled, than there was another panic take-off. This time I was first off the deck. I saw a mass of Jerries in close formation over Lille, which they were bombing heavily; the usual fighter escort was weaving above them.

'Blast them! They were dropping a packet. God! You are swines. There's nothing in the town itself except thousands and thousands of refugees. Come on, boys.' I glanced behind at the crowd of Hurricanes behind me. 'Hell! Wish I wasn't in front. Blast you bastards! You've dropped your dirt. We'll smash you before you get home.' I was gaining on them quickly. 'God! What marvellous formation flying.' The bombers sailed through the sky, their metal-work glinting. High above, the protecting fighters darted here and there. 'If they come down, there's going to be a hell of a party. Damn! don't shoot now, you fools!' Black anti-aircraft bursts appeared unpleasantly close to us; as usual, behind and below the bombers: the bursts were just about landing in the middle of the pursuing Hurricanes.

'On; not much farther. The return fire is going to be bloody hot. Now, don't be a fool: wait until some of the others catch up before you close.' I throttled back a bit and did a quick weave. High above, the escort fighters looked like skylarks; they seemed to show no signs of coming down to attack us. The left-hand back one will do me nicely. 'Waste your ammo; you won't hit me yet.' The whole formation was pouring tracer bullets at us.

'Here goes, full throttle again. Sights on. Close a bit. Steady. Now Brrrrrrmmmm. Got him! A huge flash; the starboard engine is blazing furiously. Go down, damn you! Brrrrrrrmmm.'

The Dornier sailed on, still in close formation, his whole wing burning; even in the sun the flames seemed bright. Then suddenly it toppled onto its side and just dropped from the sky. 'Look behind, look behind,' the warning voice inside me was screaming. I glanced behind. 'Hell! 109s. Let's get out of this, quick. Blast you!' A Hun was just about dead on my tail. Out of the corner of my eye I saw the massive formation splitting, with several bombers spiralling down. But two 109s seemed to have picked on me. Around me a gigantic dogfight was taking place; it was impossible to see which was friend or foe until you were close enough to see the aircraft markings. Round and round I went. Slowly but steadily I was turning inside the 109. Round and round until I felt sick and hardly knew which way up I was. Now and then I flashed by other planes, sometimes with black crosses and sometimes with roundels.

'You're a stubborn swine, a few more turns and you'll have had it.' Damn! It was as if the Hun had heard my thoughts. He turned on his back and dived vertically. I followed. Brrrrrrmmmm, Damn! That was a shaky shot. Christ! A large chunk of something flew off. A snaky white trail suddenly appeared by my cockpit. 'Someone on your tail; aileron turn, quick. Stick hard over to one side.' That's lost him. Thank God for that! Now for home.

I searched the sky. The bombers had beat it, closely followed by fleeing 109s. I roared low over several burning wrecks. I was soon at the 'drome, and landed quickly. What a morning! It was only midday, but I felt as if it was late evening. I had got five. How long can this go on? All my boys were back safely. Robbie had knocked a Dornier down and had about twenty bullet holes in his plane. The others had only inconclusive scraps with the 109s.

The intelligence blokes went into Lille to see if they could find anything worth having from any of the crashed. We piled into the Citroen and hurtled off for some lunch. Nearly everyone that we met had got something down that morning. A lot of shop was talked at lunch. We were all very cheerful. We had lost three pilots. Nobody talked about that. I managed to scribble a letter to Pam and home, saying that all was well and that my score was mounting.

Then back to readiness. As we drove along the road this time half the British Army seemed to be on it, straggling along in single file. We stopped and asked one of the blokes what the hell they were doing. They said they were retreating. Hell! we thought, that wasn't so funny. There were still a pile of refugees. Things didn't look so good. As we sat at dispersal the stream of army increased; quite a lot of them were hanging on to lorries and Bren gun carriers. They repeated the refugees' story that Jerry had a Panzer division five miles up the road. We dismissed these ideas as fifth-columnist rumours. A rumour was also going round that half the French generals had been given the sack, and that Gamelin was reported to be the head of the fifth column in France. Our men began to get uneasy. They jokingly asked how the hell they were going to get away if the Jerries appeared. They joked, but it was obvious that they were worried. Very few of them had rifles, the others had just nothing. Opps were getting worried too. They gave orders that the squadron was to get ready to move at half an hour's notice. So down came our tent and everything that could be piled high on lorries. Nobody seemed to know where the front line was, or what the hell was happening. Still the army went by. A large convoy of ambulances passed, full of wounded. The war seemed to be getting very close to us.

Chapter 5, The End of France: Last Two Days in France, c. 30 May 1940–c. 31 May 1940 That afternoon we sat and waited. Everything seemed very quiet. Along the road more and more army straggled, the sun beating pitilessly down on their sweating forms. We lay in our shirtsleeves, sunbathing and chatting quietly, watching the road and wondering what the hell was happening. Now and then a section or flight of planes took off, and returned having seen nothing.

Teatime came along. We were just arguing whose turn it was to go first, when one of the crews shouted that there was a plane in flames. There it was over Lille, very high. As we looked it came plummeting down, trailing a dirty black streak behind; at about 20,000 feet there was a puff of white as a parachute opened. A cloud of dust rose from the ground where the plane had hit; high above we could see the tiny white canopy bringing its pilot slowly down to safety. 'Theirs or ours?' Whoever it was, he was going to have a long ride down, and would eventually land fairly near us, as there was a gentle wind blowing our way.

I rushed off to tea with my section, Watty and Banks. Tea tasted good. The batmen had fantastic rumours that the Jerries had broken through south of us. They told us that the village behind the mess was practically deserted. Back to dispersal to relieve the others for tea. When we arrived there about forty minutes after we had left, the parachutist was still about 5,000 feet, and looked as if he would land slap in the middle of Lille. Opps had phoned us and said that it was one of ours, a 504 bloke who had been shot down by a 109.

We still sat around and waited. Things weren't so comfortable now, as most of our comforts were piled high on the lorries, waiting for the move to Heaven knows where. At about six the phone rang. The squadron was to move to Merville immediately. Hell and damnation! We hoped that our batmen had packed our kit ok. 'Well, here goes, boys. Cheerio, Chiefy; we'll see you at Merville.' It wasn't too big a move, as Merville was only 40 miles behind Lille. It took us a bare fifteen minutes to fly there.

We arrived over the aerodrome in company with another squadron. The ground seemed covered with aircraft already. Where we were meant to go nobody seemed to know. We taxied round the 'drome trying to find somewhere to put our planes. At last we found a corner not too far away from a cafe, we noted. Several of the boys knew Merville well, as they had been stationed there earlier in the war.

There we were, with no men to start us up, even. We got the starter handles out and arranged to start each other up. We had left one of our Hurriboxes back at Lillemark. It was Watty's old 'G', which had had its control wires and main longerons shot away that morning; the tail was just about falling off. We hoped to send a crew back to fix it up; we never saw G again.

We sat about and waited, not feeling at all happy with life. Several of the squadrons had already left for England. But we were told that we would be escorting the transport aircraft back later that evening. We didn't like the way that the inhabitants had walked out. Nobody in authority seemed to know exactly what was happening; there wasn't any actual panicking, but the panicky feeling was affecting everybody.

Nothing happened. We sat around feeling rather lonely and very hungry. Robbie and I suddenly had the bright idea of borrowing the 'Winco's' [wing commander's] car and driving into Merville to get some sandwiches for our lunch. It was now six o'clock, and we were all famished. The town was crowded with refugees, and we had a job squeezing our way into the bar. A charming girl about fifteen years old was behind the bar dealing with crowds of people; we barged our way in. Robbie produced a torn 100 franc note. *'Avez-vous quelque chose à manger, Mademoiselle?'* *'Oui, Monsieur, un moment.'*

She yelled through to the back room. A terrific woman arrived, and started spitting French at us. We eventually understood that she could let us have some omelette sandwiches and beer. We said, *'Très bon!'* In the meantime, while they were being made, we would have some beer. It tasted damn good as it slid down our rather parched throats. Soon a mass of extremely thick omelette sandwiches arrived, so we piled them and a few bottles of beer in the car, and hurtled off back to the 'drome. We arrived just as the Winco's plane landed. The boys were overjoyed to see us. The sandwiches were damned good and cheered us up quite a lot. The Winco was very browned off, as he had seen nothing. He leapt into his car and tore off, heading for Boulogne. We didn't envy him, as the roads were absolutely congested by the refugees. We sat and waited. Still nothing happened. Now and then a few planes took off, turning northwards for the shores of England. David Rhodes got a raspberry from some senior officer for asking if we could leave for England. Back came, 'Wait for orders.' So we sat and waited.

A shower of Army types arrived; they said that they had been ordered to defend the 'drome. We showed them where our ammunition was, and how to work our 'sheep dippers', the multiple machine guns. These were four Browning guns which had been salvaged from a crash. They were mounted on a universal joint. Our armourers had managed to shoot down three Jerries with them. The Army were very pleased to get our ammo, as they were down to ten rounds each. We gave them about three million rounds; I hope they pumped most of them into the Jerries.

At last Opps phoned. '87 will take off and escort an Ensign and two Dragons back to England. You will land at North Weald.' 'Come on boys, off we go!' We ran to each other's machines and started them up. B flight were to lead us home, Johnny, our CO, leading them. We took off, quickly followed by the transport plane. We left poor old J standing on its nose. I looked behind as we headed north. On the horizon there was a red glow; here and there fires burnt, with black columns of smoke rising up vertically in the still air. So we should see England again. My heart somehow felt hollow at the idea: we were leaving France to the Huns.

We all kept low, weaving fiercely. Soon the coastline loomed on the horizon. 'Hell! What's that?' A series of black dots in front of me. 'Oh God! We'll have to fight our way home, after all.' Cold fear gripped my heart. We soared on. 'Oh Christ! They're only balloons.' It was Calais balloon barrage. We sailed across the coast. The sun shone warmly on us; across the Channel we could see the white cliffs of Dover. It seemed to take years off us to cross that twenty miles of water. I had enginitis badly: the whole plane vibrated. I realised that I hadn't got a Mae West. At last we reached the shores of England. We crossed the coast between Dover and Ramsgate. To our right I could see Broadstairs, where Pamela would be. We sailed on, heading for London. The transport planes swung onto a different course: they were to land at Gatwick.

I was happy now. We were in England again. I looked down at the little Kentish hamlets, the green fields and woods. England looked very beautiful and fresh after France. We passed just outside the silver balloons of London, passed very nearly over my home in Finchley, then round to North Weald aerodrome. We landed in quick succession, taxied into the dispersal positions, waved and pushed into the pens by crowds of airmen. We leaped out. 87 was back in England.

It was very strange being back in an officers' mess. The blokes there plied us with beer, and were very disappointed because we were all so tired that we went to bed early.

5 Barry Sutton Part 1, Hurricane Pilot, Pilot Officer, British, 56 Squadron

First of two extracts from a Barry Sutton's memoir *The Way of a Pilot: A Personal Record*, published in 1942 (reissued by Amberley Publishing in 2010 as *Fighter Boy*). Born in January 1919, Fraser Barton Sutton, known to everyone as Barry, was twenty-one during the Battle and joined 56 Squadron in September 1939. He became engaged to Sylvia Vicki Sutton, a WAAF, while on seven days' leave at Christmas 1939, and they were married in February 1940. They didn't have a honeymoon until 1944. The first extract covers 16–23 May 1940 and comes direct from the diary he wrote in France on scraps of paper soon after part of 56 Squadron was sent there on 16 May 1940 to reinforce the British air forces. He was based at Vitry-en-Artois, near Douai.

Chapter 13: France, May 1940 In those early days of spring, the war, though already a terrible reality to thousands of our countrymen in France, was still to many of us in the Air Force a remote, almost intangible thing.

But with a suddenness which we did not bargain for, the bottom dropped out of our comparatively humdrum existence and we plunged between the hours of lunch and tea, on a certain day in May, into a new, exciting world.

Coffee in the Mess in Essex, and a bite from a sandwich and drink from a thermos flask at the decent hour of four-thirty in a Flanders field ... the fates had a sense of drama after all.

We climbed out of our machines, took one look at each other and burst out laughing. Over the fields came the sounds of a village clock striking four. Someone asked whether it would strike seventeen instead of five.

The events of that whirlwind, crazy day were a fitting prelude to what was to follow. During the short time I was in France, I kept a diary. It was the first time I had undertaken a self-imposed task of this kind, but I stuck to it assiduously. I wrote it on any odd piece of paper I could find, and though I subsequently arrived back in England with no hat, collar, or tie, one shoe and without even my aeroplane, I still was able to recover from various pockets of my tunic, my diary.

As a literary effort it is poor stuff, but as a basic record it will, I hope, be of interest in these pages. I present it without alteration or adornment.

The Diary, 16 May 1940 The 'Fuehrer' came in to lunch with the stationmaster (CO of the station, Group Captain 'Paddy' O'Neil), both looking pretty excited. I heard him tell Ian [Soden] to get his boys together in the anteroom immediately. We troop in and learn the astonishing good news. The squadron is to split, 'A' Flight to remain at North Weald and 'B' Flight to stand by to crack off to France in the afternoon. What excitement! Our immediate orders are to leave for Manston at two-thirty. Shall get our final posting from there.

Tried to get Sylvia on the phone but without success. I decided against a telegram; it would only scare her, however I might word it. The 'Fuehrer' told us that we shall only be away for a few days, anyway.

Tommy Rose, Peter [Down] and I pooled our luggage in Tommy's suitcase. This will go by transport machine with the troops who are to go in Dragon Rapides. Terrific activity down at flight. Apparently we are to revert to TR9Ds (old type radio sets) for the trip. Radio section in a worse flap than anyone. No wonder, with six radio sets to install and wire up in an hour and a half, for provisional zero hour is now three! My own machine 'N' for Nuts was U/S, so I am given 'C' for Charlie, my old machine in 'A' Flight. Poor old thing was already showing signs of getting a little deadbeat when I gave it up, and I hope it won't let me down now. I got Charlie started up and ran him on the chocks; everything seemed to be ok, except the radio. They haven't fitted anything yet, hope everything will be ready in time.

Group Captain Bowman (a Great War member of 56) and Paddy O'Neil shook hands with all of us on the tarmac and wished us godspeed.

We took off on time and circled the aerodrome in two flights of three, climbed away for the north and turned and flew over very low in our pansiest formation before setting course for Manston. The Thames Estuary is still a prohibited area, so we flew over London itself before finally turning south-east for the Kent Coast. It was a beautiful afternoon and almost every building seemed to stand out.

I looked for our flat in Woburn Place, but the district was obscured too much by factory smoke haze drifting from the East End for me to pick out individual streets, much less houses. Still, I couldn't help feeling a bit homesick.

Ten minutes later we landed at Manston. Four other flights of Hurricanes arrived from other squadrons after we landed. We joined up with 229, a new squadron in the charge of Freddy Rosier, an old friend of Ian's.

Rosier and his boys were at North Weald about two months ago. They came to collect our old Hurricanes when we changed to the new Tin Winged jobs.

The allocation of bases in France was simple – just 'first come first served', and take your pick. Ian [Soden] and Freddy decide on Vitry-en-Artois, near Douai.

Everyone taxied out. Except me. Charlie lost no time in getting temperamental. He just would not start. The others waited for me until their engines became too hot ticking over, and finally left without me. Ten minutes later having exhausted two battery starters, I gave a hand in swinging on the handles and I finally got started. No sign of the others, of course. So it was me for France alone with no course worked out. I looked at my maps and guessed 150°. This landed me to the east of Calais. The cliffs showed up well and were a good landmark. I now had to start map reading in earnest. This was difficult as I was passing over an industrial district, and railway lines – usually the best landmarks in times of trouble – were no more illuminating than a tangled wool skein.

A machine rushed up to identify me. I was just beginning to get excited when it turned out to be a Hurricane. As I turned the firing button back on to 'safe' again, I saw the pilot push back his roof. In spite of his oxygen mask, I recognised him. Extraordinary coincidence; it was Sergeant [Peter] Hillwood who joined 56 at about the same time as I, and who had been posted to another squadron which had gone to France before us!

I followed him and we both landed at Merville, which was his base. I discovered that he was with 79 Squadron, whose home station in peacetime was Biggin Hill. Met Jack, Tommy Rose's brother, who was at FTS with me. He said they had had a bit of action, and some of the chaps had got one or two confirmed victories.

I eventually landed at Vitry, only a few minutes after the others. They had been led by a Blenheim and must have taken it easily.

The aerodrome was a large field with very long grass. There were no obstructions except a crashed Blenheim in the middle.

We spent most of the evening looking for billets in Vitry which turned out to be more like a very large farmyard than a village. Cobbles everywhere, no kerbs, lots of straw and smell.

We ate pork chops in an estaminet, drank some terrible red wine, and after Ian and Freddy had given us our orders to report on the aerodrome at dawn, we yawned off in search of our billets conducted by a Frenchman who seemed to have been appointed as our guide by wing headquarters. Incidentally, they had pinched the only hotel as their mess.

Ian, Peter, Tommy, and myself ended up in a house with a huge sign outside announcing that it belonged to a painter. Sounded as though he might be Dutch. The name was 'Van' something or other. Anyhow, we found he had left, taking with him every stick of furniture except a bedstead and two mattresses. Ian and Peter slept on the mattress on the bed, Tommy and I on the floor. It was cold, so we decided not to take off our clothes.

17 May What a night it was! None of us, except Peter, slept a wink. Getting up, even at three, was no effort. We boarded transport at the estaminet and arrived at the aerodrome to find a few French soldiers already making coffee. A ramshackle wooden hut served as our flight office. No furniture except a phone, linking us with wing headquarters in Vitry and operations hut on the far side of the airfield.

At five, we took off on our first patrol. The sun was then well up, but it was still cold. East of Lille we ran into a barrage of AA fire. Shells were bursting all around us, but miraculously no one suffered a direct hit. Something burst directly underneath me and the blast lifted poor old Charlie as by an invisible hand. But Charlie appeared to be still undamaged. Frankly, I was a little frightened, but I told myself I would get used to that sort of thing.

We returned to Vitry, having seen no signs of enemy aircraft. Others had fared a little worse than I. [Clifford] Whitehead's machine showed evidence of a hit by splinters on the tailplane, while Ian had lost a port wingtip, but appeared quite unconcerned.

We were apparently in for a busy day. No time for breakfast, for at eight orders came through for another patrol. Ian took off with Tommy, Peter, and [Fred] Higginson. Whitehead and I were left behind to come to readiness with a section of 229.

Terrific excitement! All returned safely at about 9.20. They had sighted a formation of eight Heinkel 111s and immediately attacked from dead astern. Between them they brought five down. Tommy told us it was a 'piece of cake'. None of the Huns took evasive action and, strangely enough, there was no return fire from any of their rear gunners.

We lazed about in the sun until the alarm went again at 10.30. Freddy Rosier and some of his boys took off on patrol but returned at 11, having seen nothing.

At noon, Ian took off again, this time with Higginson and Whitehead.

Higginson and Whitehead landed first about forty minutes later with alarming news. They had been jumped on by a force of about fifty Me 109s and, wisely, Higginson and Whitehead had dived for cloud cover and got away. They had lost Ian. No-one dare say what had become of him. We could only hope that he was safe, having either baled out or force-landed.

Dramatically, when we all must have secretly given up hope, 'S' for Sugar – Ian's machine – appeared. The ground crews saw it first and raised a cheer.

Ian told us his story a few minutes later. He had seen the 109s a few seconds later than the other two, but judged that they had not seen him. He rushed in from astern, firing in the midst of them, and then half rolled and made for home. He told us that the 109s had followed him but somehow he had shaken them off.

Our next bit of excitement of the day came in the middle of the afternoon. A Dornier appeared over the airfield, flying high and out of the sun. This was the first enemy aircraft I had seen, either from the ground or from the air, and I was so engrossed in looking at it that I had to be thrown into the small trench at the back of our dispersal hut by a lusty charge in the back from an airman who showed more presence of mind than I did.

A second later there came the scream of a falling bomb and the teeth-rattling crunch of what must have been at least a 500-pounder bursting on the airfield, luckily on the far side.

Ian, Higginson, and someone from 229 were forming the 'Flap-Flight' at the time, and soon the first of the machines, Ian's, roared off. He must have had everything wide open, for he rushed off down-wind, just getting airborne a few yards from the hedge, but saving valuable time.

The Dornier had now overshot the airfield and turned as if to make a second run on the target. He also lost height and was at about 800 feet. Spellbound we watched him turn away suddenly as he apparently saw Ian climbing hard after him.

Then followed the most thrilling spectacle I have ever seen while standing on solid earth. Ian, by now well on his tail, started firing. We heard the noise of his Brownings above that of the engines of both machines and saw the tail of gun-smoke issuing in a black wisp in the Hurricane's slipstream. The Dornier dived and began hedgehopping in an effort to get away, but Ian followed him, firing all the time. We watched them disappear behind some trees.

The Dornier was apparently a decoy, for a second German bomber now appeared flying from the east, the opposite direction. He didn't wait long, either, for the other two Hurricanes were soon after him. Before he disappeared in the direction of Douai he dropped one bomb on the town. He must have hit something pretty important, for almost instantly a black column of smoke arose. The town was only about four miles away and we could soon see flames as well as smoke.

Ian landed about twenty minutes later. He told us that he had watched the Hun crash into a field; as there was plenty of room, he had himself landed beside the wreckage.

He said it was obvious that none of the crew could have got out alive, and he waited only to pick up a trophy from the wreckage, an ammunition pan. (As our first trophy of the present war, this was naturally much prized. It is now used as a paperweight on the CO's desk.)

The other two Hurricanes failed to make contact with the remaining Dornier, but unless a great deal of damage had been done in Douai, this particular German sortie can hardly have been a success.

No further activity of note during the day, but we did not leave the aerodrome until half an hour after dark. It is about 1015 when we arrive back in Vitry again. Everyone is naturally very tired and hungry. We had not had a square meal since last night.

The others went to the same billets as before, but Ian, Tommy, Peter, and myself decided to try elsewhere. Ian and Peter found a house, while Tommy and I tried a large house which had already been taken over by an Auxiliary squadron which had been operating from our aerodrome, but whom so far we had not met. This was because they had dispersed their machines on the opposite side of the field and seemed at the moment to be doing only a little flying.

When we arrived at the house, we found most of the inhabitants had already gone to bed. One of a small party remaining in the dining room, a flying officer, explained that quarters were cramped, and that except for the CO everyone was 'doubling-up' in bedrooms. He, as did the others with him, looked worn out. We had bacon and eggs and some wine with them, and learned that they had all had a very busy time, and that most of them were due for leave shortly.

We were shown the only sleeping accommodation in the building, a couple of forms with rugs, in the attic.

We made the best of a bad job and tried to make ourselves comfortable. There were no panes in the windows, and because of this and the few bedclothes, we decided once again not to take off our clothes. Tommy soon dropped off to sleep, in spite of the discomfort and the additional nuisance of a particularly nasty smell. The smell seemed to get worse and, although I was dog-tired, I could not sleep.

I eventually ended up by sleeping in a wicker chair in a room downstairs which was apparently used as an anteroom of sorts.

18 May I was called at 315 by the airman working in the kitchens with whom we had left instructions last night. Found that I had had a roommate. He was an Army officer who must have come in later than I had, and who must have been even more tired. When I left in search of Tommy, the Army man was fast asleep in his chair. He was apparently too tired to take off even his tin hat and Sam Browne. Wonder what his job was and how he arrived here.

Tommy seemed to have slept well. Said he only noticed the smell when it was time to get up. He had tracked it down to a bowl of what had perhaps been washing-up water many months before. Before we left for the airfield he told the sergeant in charge of the house servants, who was much obliged. Officers who had been quartered on the upper floors had complained about the smell for some weeks, but although he himself had led more than one search to track down the source of the stink, they had not been successful. So at least we had earned our board!

By the time we arrived at the airfield, the *poilus* were making coffee. They seemed a curious lot. None of them bothered to wear full uniform: one man was always in carpet slippers. Their whole energies seemed to be taken up in making coffee and playing a game called 'le couteau'. For this, a group of them ranged themselves in a circle at the centre of which was a matchstick stuck in the ground. Squatting on the ground, each man took his turn in throwing a clasp knife at the match. The first man to cleave the match won the kitty, to which all subscribed. The rules seemed simple enough and one would have thought there could have been little doubt as to what constituted a winning throw, but every time there was a claim on the kitty there was the father and mother of a row.

In charge of these troops, which could not have numbered more than a platoon, was an elderly major who seemed to me to be more engrossed with some perpetual trouble with his small Renault than looking after his men. Sole armament of the platoon appeared to be a small, incredibly ancient-looking whippet tank. If these few men with their poor equipment were our only defence against ground attack, God preserve us! One could only hope that they were not typical of the French Army as a whole. As it was, someone had said that the Germans were less than fifteen kilometres away.

Few of the Army lorries and cars which passed along the Douai road were even properly camouflaged. Some of the cars had been covered in what appeared to be a mixture of clay and gravel to produce a sort of khaki colour.

At about eight, orders came through for us to take off and fly to Brussels and maintain a patrol for half an hour between there and Ghent. Brussels was about thirty-five minutes away, but long before we reached there, Ian's section, of which I was a member, sighted an unescorted Dornier 17, flying below us and roughly on the same course as ourselves.

We peeled off and dived on him, all three of us firing.

He must have had either very good armour plating or else our shooting was bad, for he continued to keep his height and course for some seconds, though we swarmed all around him like wasps. I was flying in number three position, so followed the other two in our first dive. Higginson, who was number two, 'crowded' me off the target, so that after only a very short burst I had to pull out of the dive to avoid hitting Higginson. Turning to make a second attack, I found that I had overshot the Dornier and that he was coming for me, practically head on. I kept him slap in the middle of my sights and broke away at about eighty yards, having given him a good long burst.

Again there was no apparent effect, but as I again prepared to get round after the breakaway, something hit the underside of poor old Charlie with a terrific 'woomph'. I felt like a fullback diving at the other chap's legs but missing and crowning himself on the goalpost. The machine seemed ok so I followed Ian in for another attack astern.

We both got in a burst of about five seconds this time and watched the Dornier stick his nose down and hare for the ground. Ian had gone in a little too fast and had to pull away before he overshot, leaving me alone on the Dornier's tail. I followed him right down to a few hundred feet. One of us had obviously crippled the machine and put the rear gunner out of action, because there was no return fire. The Hun may have been feinting, so I gave him a very short burst, but almost as soon as I had put my finger on the button it was obvious that he was well and truly in trouble. Flames leapt out of his port engine. Somehow the pilot got the machine down the right way up and Ian and I circled round at only about fifty feet as the Dornier skidded across one field and through a hedge into another on its belly before finally pulling up in a cloud of dust. By the time we had climbed again and regained formation, the Dornier was blazing furiously.

We were greeted at Brussels with intermittent bursts of AA fire – red stuff which seemed to be coming up from the aerodrome, but the firing was inaccurate and did not trouble us much. No further incident during the patrol between Brussels and Ghent, or on the return journey. It was just as well, for on landing I discovered that I had only a few rounds left. Worse still, Charlie had been hit – a bad show. I cursed myself for coming in head-on to that Dornier. One of his cannon shells had hit the underside of my port mainplane, but luckily glanced off, leaving no damage apart from a small hole which could be patched up by fabric and dope; had it been a few more inches to the left I should have probably been blown to kingdom come for less than a finger's-length away from the hole was the outside end of Charlie's un-armoured wing petrol tank.

Round about lunchtime a few strangers – pilots from other squadrons – began to assemble at our dispersal point. They were going on leave and were waiting here to pick up a transport machine to take them back home. Among them was Flight Lieutenant Dickie Lee, who already had his gong up and whose name was then almost legendary in both the RAF and L'Armée de l'Air. His bag even then was well into double figures. Like the others, he looked very sunburnt and tired.

But two pilots arrived who were not strangers. One was Sergeant Hillwood again. He had his hand bound and his face was inflamed, and he told of baling out when his machine blew up. And the other was dear old 'Minney'.

Red tape was very properly swept aside out here, and we took both pilots under our wing again without any formal posting. Minney had been at Vitry for some time with 615 Squadron and had seen plenty of action. Naturally we were very happy to have him back.

20 May (written in Le Tréport Base Hospital). So much for good intentions! The diary here petered out but not the way I thought it would. I had a good excuse.

What exactly happened after midday on the 18th is still a bit of a mystery, and so is what became of the rest of the boys. All I can remember is taking off with the whole squadron to escort some bombers which were to be picked up east of Douai at about two o'clock.

I was in the last section of three aircraft led by Tommy Rose. The other machine was flown by [Tony] Dillon a young pilot officer in Rosier's squadron.

We had just taken off and had barely got our wheels up when things began to happen. Bullets began blasting and rattling all over the machine – one must have hit the glycol pipe in the cockpit, for steam began to shoot everywhere. The sheer unexpectedness of it must have knocked the wind right out of my sails, but somehow I did the only thing that could have saved me. Funny how the brain seems to rev up in these circumstances! Although we were at only about 300 feet, I whipped over in the beginning of a half-roll – better to go straight into the deck than stop any more of that stream of lead from behind. It was the most unlovely of manoeuvres, but it worked. Glycol was now everywhere. I felt that it had penetrated even through my tunic sleeves and shirt, for I could feel it warm on my flesh. The windscreen was fogged up too, so that by the time I had got level again I had to think about getting down somewhere. Vitry was still only about a mile away and I managed to scrape in the aerodrome. No signs of Tommy and Dillon (it was afterwards confirmed that they had both crashed, killed) or the rest of the squadron or of what had attacked us.

I taxied poor old Charlie back to the tarmac. This was his nemesis (When I eventually met my fitter back in England, he said that he had found upwards of three hundred holes in the bottom of the fuselage) if not mine! The radiator was almost completely shot away. A few more minutes in the air and the motor would have seized up. Everyone on the ground was in a hell of a flap. I climbed out of the cockpit and gave orders for another Hurricane, bearing strange letters and obviously belonging to another squadron which was dispersed near the flight office, to be started up. My foot felt a little numb and blood was beginning to ooze from the heel but somehow it only hurt when I tried to walk. I took my shoe off, but could see no signs of damage, so tried to put it on again. The injury, whatever it was, must have been in the heel, because in using my forefinger as a shoe-horn I felt some pain. They were already wheeling away the starter battery from the machine and the fitter was signalling to me with his thumbs up. Here was I fiddling about on the grass trying to get a shoe on when a battle was probably raging near by. I was too excited to bother about things like shoes, so I flung mine aside and climbed into the cockpit and taxied out in my stockinged foot. After all it wasn't hurting and I was not quite so ham-footed that I had to wear shoes to work the rudder bar.

The machine was a museum piece, one of the oldest Hurricanes I had seen. In my excitement and hurry to be off the ground I started the take-off run in coarse pitch, so that I had to pull the tit (emergency boost control giving extra power) to get off at all. Somehow we clambered into the air.

Looking round, I could see some activity several thousand feet above. I kept the tit pulled but found that for some reason the wheels would not come up. I tugged and heaved at the selector but with no effect. The machine was deadbeat all right and must have been abandoned because it was U/S. Even in fine pitch I could hardly get enough revs to out-climb a Tiger Moth. Still, if only I could have got the wheels up and decreased the drag, I could have coped. As it was, I stood no chance of getting anywhere, so I made two or three circuits, keeping a good look-out for anything which might try to 'jump' me again, and tried to get the wheels up with the emergency hand-pump. I tried holding the selector lever in with my right foot, but it was no good. The thing just would not engage. So there was nothing for it but to land again.

The fight must have been almost dead overhead now, though I still could see nothing of what was going on beyond the odd Me 109 and Hurricane wheeling and swarming round a thick white cloud which probably hid a formation of enemy bombers.

As I came in a second time, a Hurricane shot clean across me, careered across the aerodrome and finished up on its nose on the far side in a cloud of dust (I never found out who it was). Some poor devil trying to get back in a hurry. Looked as though he might have been badly shot up.

As soon as I landed the second time and stepped out on the wing before jumping on to the ground again, I noticed that the foot had decided to pack up. The bleeding was worse and I found it too painful to stand.

Someone drove me to Vitry in a car. We pulled up at a kind of barn which had been converted into a field dressing station. I got my foot dressed and waited on the steps outside watching the fight which was still raging overhead. The scene was fantastic. There seemed to be machines everywhere – there must have been a hundred. By far the greater part of these appeared to be He 111s, no longer in formation but split up and being chased in all directions by Hurricanes. The 109s were probably higher up but I never saw one from the ground.

I was told by the MO in charge of the field dressing station, which was the official designation of the barn, that he had another pilot in a back room. He had baled out a few miles from Vitry about half an hour before and had been brought there with bad burns. As soon as he came round from the anaesthetic he had been given when his wounds had been dressed, we would both be moved by ambulance to hospital.

Everywhere in Vitry there seemed to be terrific excitement. Oblivious of the danger of what might have fallen on their heads from the battle above, the natives ran like mad things up and down the streets. Men and women danced in the frenzy of impotent fury, weeping and shouting, always pointing to the sky.

Seeing me sitting on a step at the door of the barn, an old woman rushed from the opposite side of the street.

She embraced me, weeping profusely, and pointed over the roof-tops behind.

'L'àvion allemand est tombe, là-bas!' she shrieked.

I felt too excited to be embarrassed and together we rejoiced.

A second later a 111 screamed at only a few hundred feet above us, with a Hurricane close on its tail. Squirts of gun smoke issued from the fighter as they disappeared from view. Our boys were certainly giving the Hun a warm reception, for though the major part of the melee was hidden by low cloud, we could still hear the thunder of our Brownings and the unmistakeable whine of Merlins as the Hurricanes milled into the fray. So far we had not heard a single bomb drop, so that in spite of the Hun's preponderance in numbers, and his fighter escort, our base, which must have been their objective, was so far unscathed.

At last two orderlies carried out a form in RAF uniform on a stretcher and placed it in the waiting ambulance.

It was the signal for me to move too, so I climbed in. Half afraid at what I might see, I looked at the stretcher on the other side.

Underneath its black coating of tannic acid I recognised the face. It was Fred Rosier.

Although still befogged by his anaesthetic, he grinned and tried to speak. Instead, he was sick. I honestly thought he was going to die.

Our destination was Frevént, which normally, I suppose, may be reached from Vitry in a matter of two or three hours by road, but as soon as we struck the main road out of Vitry it became obvious that it would take us considerably longer. Everywhere the roads were choked with Army vehicles and the cars and carts of refugees who had already begun their trek westwards. News of the speed of the German advance seemed to have reached even the remotest villages.

If the tedium of that journey, which lasted seven hours, was a discomfort to me, it must have been a misery for Fred, who had come round completely soon after we set off and was now feeling pain. His hands were the worst burned part of him, and he held them above his head as he lay to keep the blood out of them. His face was now swollen out of recognition and his eyes were both closed. Even so, he managed to carry on a conversation and smoked cigarettes which I held for him.

Frevént turned out to be a large château which had been converted into a hospital. We were both borne on our stretchers up the wide marble staircases, and put to bed in a ward at the top of the building.

Soon after our arrival we were both taken to the operating theatre, Freddy to have fresh dressings and I to have whatever was in my foot removed.

Life was good when I came-to. While I was under the dope they had taken me out of my tunic and trousers, so that for the first time since I had been in France I found myself wearing pyjamas and lying between sheets. Freddy too seemed a little more cheerful. He must have got used to this business of anaesthetics by now.

In the morning we were off again. Two wounded Army officers joined us in the ambulance. One was a major who had been brought in only a few hours before with a scalp wound, and the other was a young second lieutenant who appeared to be still in his teens. He was very ill.

Again a nightmare journey. After an age we wound up at Le Tréport, a large military hospital under canvas, and here we are again all in the same tent and in adjacent beds. Mercifully we all managed to sleep most of the way. The only piece of excitement occurred soon after we set out. The driver pulled up dead, shooting all our luggage in a heap and the VAD who had been keeping an eye on us on top of it. My stretcher was one of the top tiers, commanding a restricted view through one of the small darkened windows, and through it I was able to see the cause of the trouble. It was an Me 110 doing steep turns around a small spinney less than 500 yards from the road. What he was doing I never found out, but the pilot must have been either blind or a man of pity, for he turned away after flying at only about 100 feet over the road and we never saw him again.

Life here at Le Tréport is not so bad. I managed to get up this morning for the first time. We found some crutches so that I could get about a bit. Fred was quite cheerful but I knew his hands were giving him hell.

An unhappy thing happened last night. A bomber boy, who was already in his tent before we arrived and who, I believe, had lost a leg when he crash-landed and one of his bombs went off, became very delirious.

Sister Gutteridge, a young Yorkshirewoman, who had been on duty here as a night sister for some weeks, called in the CO about midnight. When I awoke the following morning, the bed opposite was empty and I noticed that poor Sister Gutteridge had been crying. No need to ask any questions.

22 May Gutteridge and another sister came on duty late. They told us that as they had left their billets in the village, a Hun had beaten up the main street with machineguns. The two British girls had torn up their linen caps and bandaged a woman they had found lying on the street seriously wounded.

In the afternoon I managed to walk quite a way round the camp on my crutches. I found I was getting more used to them now.

All that day there was a lot of activity upstairs, mostly our bombers, some of which must have been based near by. An He 111 came and had a look at us in the afternoon. I was smoking my pipe in a deckchair just outside the entrance to the tent when I saw him circling round at only a few hundred feet. Like the 110 we saw on the road, he must have been a perfect little gentleman, for after a few circuits he flew off, not so much as dropping a pamphlet.

23 May Fresh news arrived of the incredibly rapid German advance. It seemed that we ourselves were in danger again. Transport began to arrive soon after breakfast, and by midday preparations had been completed for us all to evacuate. Orders came through for us to go to Dieppe, so it seemed certain that we were going back to UK.

The major, and the young second leiutenant, Fred, Sister Gutteridge, and myself travelled together in the same ambulance in a huge convoy. A few MOs, including the camp commandant, stayed behind with some troops to fire the tents and equipment, for there was no time to get any of it packed. We somehow managed to get all our personal belongings in the ambulances. This meant travelling in even greater discomfort than usual, but it was worth it.

The journey proved more miserable than ever. The others, I think, were shot with a little morphia to ease the physical discomfort caused through our joltings on the rough country roads, and this probably accounted for them all, including the second leiutenant, who looked very ill and had scarcely spoken at all before, being quite cheerful. The major, whose name was Linton, and I discovered we had the same Christian name. Nothing extraordinary in that, I suppose, but we would have talked of anything to take our minds off serious things. Freddie and I christened the second leiutenant 'The Colonel', and Sister Gutteridge insisted upon sticking to 'Sweetie-Pie', the name Freddie had given her as soon as we arrived at Le Tréport.

How long the journey took I don't know. In any case it couldn't have been measured in time. Everyone was nearly exhausted when we arrived at Dieppe, particularly 'The Colonel' and Freddie, who both seemed to be in great pain again. The major was asleep, still clutching a black rag doll which he had tied to a small chain round his neck. He never seemed to leave go of it. It must have been a very special mascot. (It was. He later told us that it belonged to his little girl, who had given it him before he sailed for France).

We waited on the dock-side for fully an hour and then unaccountably moved again to the railway station.

Here the current account of that dismal French episode ceased, the last few pages having been scribbled as we jolted along in the ambulance.

Up to the time we had arrived at Dieppe, our adventure had been exciting enough for me to forget most of my own discomforts, but under the shock of our greatest disappointment which was shortly to come, I lost what incentive or propensity I had had to describe for my own amusement what was going on. Life had ceased to be a passing show, in which I had seemed to be little more than a spectator. It was as though all the time I had been watching the drama from the wings but had by some awful mistake found myself precipitated on to the stage.

The edge of all our sufferings and discomforts (perhaps in my own case they could have scarcely been described as such) had been taken off to some extent by the golden prospect of 'Blighty', but now like a cruel mirage the prospect had faded, and we were jolted painfully back to the present.

Our horizon had narrowed to the miserable skyline of Dieppe looking south again instead of north, for fresh orders had come. We were not to sail, but were to travel back into the hinterland. Someone had made a mistake, a ghastly bungle, but who were four men on stretchers, lying on the uncharitable stones of the platform of a foreign railway station, to question the voice of authority? We were to know that it was all the workings of providence after all.

For this it undoubtedly was. The *Maid of Kent*, the hospital ship which was to take us home, was blown to eternity less than half an hour later as she lay in her berth while, all oblivious of the fact, we were trundling south again aboard a hospital train. Nor did we know of the other stroke of good luck which had befallen us. The train which had pulled out of Dieppe a few minutes before us and which we had somehow missed, was bombed and seven coaches, completely destroyed, and most of the casualties were in that part of the train reserved for stretcher cases.

We paid in some measure for our own good fortune. We were machine-gunned as we pulled out of Dieppe. Miraculously, there were no casualties. Yet the journey, even when we were free of attack, proved easily the worst experience we had had.

There were over six hundred aboard that train, which was normally equipped to carry half that number. There were few rations or dressings, and though we crawled southwards for nearly thirty hours, never exceeding 15 kilometres because of the air-raid warnings and the incessant danger of damage to the line, we never had a chance to get out at any of our frequent stops.

In the front part of the train were the more seriously wounded troops. We travelled in a long coach at the rear, together with fifty or sixty less serious cases.

There was nothing to read and little to occupy the time and lessen the tedium. I lay for hours on my stretcher, watching the countryside all too slowly unfolding itself.

Sometimes we passed through orchards and farmyards. What a delightfully inconsequential habit French railways seemed to have of wandering through the countryside! In England it is different. Rail travel is a much more serious business. There is always the embankment, or a skein of telephone wires, to shut you off and serve as a reminder that, whatever the beauty of the scene beyond, you are no more than something moving in a box. Although this journey was far from fun, in normal times it no doubt would have been.

After twelve hours, cooped up in close quarters with the suffering in the carriage, I managed to get up and hobble through to the next compartment. This was full of troops. I sat talking to them on the steps of the carriage – there was no door.

Poor fellows, they must have had a rough time and would be looking forward to some Blighty.

One of them summoned up courage to disillusion me.

'There'll be no Blighty for us. We are bad boys.' The others grinned, obviously embarrassed. We exchanged cigarettes and talked of other things.

I made friends also with the venerable guardsman of the train who sat alone in his van amid a pile of luggage. He spoke a little English and showed me photographs of his sons, who, as he had done last time, were serving France. Once we stopped for a few minutes at a small country station while we changed engines. The old fellow leapt down on to the track and made a bee-line for some cottages. He returned just as we were moving again, his arms full of vinegar bottles containing home-made wine.

Rough stuff though it may have been, it was refreshing. So far as I remember he called it 'Pinard'. I took some to Freddie to cheer him up, but he was sleeping. As he lay, 'Sweetie-Pie' was swabbing his eyelids, which had begun to discharge badly. I made her have the wine instead.

We were making for Brest. At our present rate of progress that meant two and a half days more of this purgatory. No time to take more food, nor even to get dressings for the wounded, which had already run dangerously short.

A young British Army captain, who was in charge of the train, first told me the bad news. Why we couldn't be taken off at a port nearer, nobody knew. The nurses were aware of the design, but it was going to be a hard job to explain to the patients, especially the very sick, that it was for their ultimate good that they should be imprisoned so much longer on this hell-train. One of the French orderlies had already told me that some had died on the journey; undoubtedly there would be many others who would not be able to withstand the strain of travelling.

Again fresh orders came, altering everything at the last moment. We had been waiting for some hours in a siding just outside Lisieux when the glad tidings came that we were to leave almost immediately for Cherbourg.

This time the train was in a different mood – our mood. Joyfully we rushed towards the coast. In less than four hours we arrived at Cherbourg. How different we found it from Dieppe! The town was quite unscathed by air raids and, on board ship at last, as we lay at anchor waiting for darkness before we finally set course for England, we looked landwards and marvelled. Could this bay, broad and serene and bathed in the soft evening sun, really be part of the France we had known?

It was a happy ending for all of our little party, except for the poor 'Colonel'. By the time we had arrived at Cherbourg, our journeyings had completely exhausted him and he was in no condition to go further. I learned in England some months later that 'The Colonel' had died in Cherbourg. It was then that I found that he was the son of General Sir Alan Brooke.

Freddie, Major Linton, and I were taken on our arrival at Southampton to a Hospital. Eleven days later I was discharged and given a month's sick leave.

6 Svatopluk Janouch Part 1, Hurricane Pilot, Pilot Officer, Czech, 310 Squadron

The first of two extracts of Janouch's experiences, this account is written by fellow Czechoslovakian and 310 Squadron fighter pilot Jaroslav Maly, who would shoot down one enemy aircraft during the Battle of Britain. It describes a patrol flown in the Battle of France by an anonymous Czech, 'Lieutenant J', in an anthology of first-hand accounts of Poland's fight against the Nazis first published in early 1941. Born in 1913 in Jincina in Czechoslovakia, he served in the Czech air force before it was disbanded by the occupying Nazis forces. Janouch then escaped to Poland and then France, where he joined the French air force and shot down three enemy aircraft while flying a French Morane 406 fighter.

This extract covers a near-suicidal mission on 7 June 1940, while flying for the French air force, when Janouch and two other pilots were sent to strafe advancing Nazi forces heading for Paris. Within days the French air force had ceased to operate as a fighting force and the Czech airmen decided to head for England. Injured by shrapnel from the ground fire he encountered in the attack on 7 June, using bicycles and a cattle truck Janouch reached the French coast on 19 June, where he caught a ship, the *Karanan*, to England. He was admitted to the RAF, joining 310 Squadron on 12 July 1940.

It was at the time when the German armoured units were advancing through northern France and breaking through all the fortified defence zones. By fierce blows they broke through the fortified area of the Weygand Line. After crossing the Seine and the Marne they advanced further to the south through open country.

When only small hope remained of their advance being stopped by the land defences an air striking force was thrown into the battle consisting of units equipped with light two-engined battle aircraft aided by; single-seater fighters: these aircraft were intended between them, by means of fighting operations, bombing and cannon fire, to stop the forward sweeping waves of steel and iron. Their intervention successfully slowed up the German advance. But there were few such units and as, in consequence of the character of their tasks, they suffered great losses and they were exhausted in a few days.

The attacks on the German armoured columns were indeed what our pilots called with a smile a hard nut to crack. Most of the armoured fighting vehicles of the Panzer units are so armed that they can shoot against aircraft without stopping in their onward drive; the others only take a few minutes to make ready for anti-aircraft fire. They can therefore begin to fire already before the attacking aircraft begin their raid. The aircraft almost always are flying close to the ground, and the tanks can thus set up a concentrated barrage of fire in which it makes no difference whether the aircraft manoeuvre to the right or to the left, as it is chiefly chance and the fortune of battle which determines which aircraft is hit.

This, therefore, was the reason for the great losses of the battle aircraft which were so quickly exhausted that soon fighters had to be used to help the battle aircraft, for the most part squadrons equipped with aircraft of the types Morane 406 and Bloch 151, which were armed with cannon.

Towards the evening of 7 June 1940, one of the sections of the Czechoslovak squadron in the 1/6 Fighter Wing received orders to set out on a task of this kind in an area 25 km south of Amiens.

The commander of the section was a young lieutenant, who explained to his comrades the nature of the task. One of his comrades was a French second lieutenant, the other was the Czechoslovak, Sergeant B. The commander of the section was a little surprised that his commanding officer shook hands with him as he left the station and told him emphatically to be careful, but he did not reflect on this, absorbed as he was in his task. It was only when he was flying back that he remembered this.

In a moment the noise of the engines is heard as they warm up, a cloud of dust arises from the dry ground of the airfield. The noise of the engines dies away in the distance and the section with its three members disappears in the blue sunlit sky. The commander of the section has spotted the area in which he is to operate already from some distance and has quickly noted a few landmarks among the burning villages and the clouds of dark smoke for the moments when he will not have time to look at the map; he has also noted the direction for the return flight: he must keep the sun on his right hand.

Before he concluded these reflections the familiar white lines became visible quite close to the section.

But surely they cannot be here!

But it is useless to wonder, for the lines of white smoke increase. But he must be quite certain. The section dived swiftly towards the ground. Before the eyes of the pilots could be seen in clouds of dust on the white country a column of cars hurrying onwards filled with soldiers in grey uniforms with the characteristic German helmets on their heads. So there they are after all! But this is not yet the region in which they have been ordered to operate; he must fly on further, and there may be more of them there. When they had flown on for a while and the fire had not ceased the commander of the section decided to attack the column beneath the section. The section only sprinkled the first column from the side without any obvious result; there was not much time in which to fire.

After flying over a few hills he suddenly saw right in front of him on the road coming directly towards their line of flight a new cloud of dust.

He climbed a little in order to have a better view, and after turning a little to the left he saw a column of vehicles about 400 metres long moving along the road before him. The crews of the armoured vehicles had no idea that the section was near them. The commander of the section began to attack the end of the column, and keeping his hand on the trigger he swept the whole column with fire for its entire length. There was not even any need to take special aim. The bursting of the shells from his cannon clearly showed where they had fallen. And they fell on the target with complete accuracy. They struck one vehicle after another, leaving behind them whirls of dark smoke and great tufts of flames. Some of the vehicles – whose drivers had probably been killed swerved off the road, falling into the ditches on either side and turning over. Some of the bodies hurled out of the vehicles were thrown far into the fields, where they lay spread in a macabre fan.

After he had flown past the column the commander of the section turned round. The two other aircraft of the section followed him at a short distance and continued the destructive work. He cast his eyes along the instruments on the dashboard and looked around for the other column. He caught sight of it at a halt under the trees a few hundred metres further on. The column had been made aware of the presence of aircraft by the firing, and welcomed them for their part with a terrible barrage of fire. In the air there were so many white lines and small black clouds that the commander of the section refrained from turning aside and flew straight on, crouching in his cockpit. But it was only an optical delusion, well known to all who have flown through barrages of this kind, when he thought that the fire was thicker to either side of him. The effect is as in a shower of rain when it appears to the eye that it is heavier a little further on while actually the rain is equally heavy everywhere.

He therefore swiftly set about attacking the middle of the column; its cars were empty, all the crews had run into the fields to hide from the attack or were tending the guns which kept up an uninterrupted fire.

He flew over the column without any visible result. When he looked round he saw a great fire on the ground. He shouted for joy because at least one of the vehicles was on fire. But all at once he froze in horror. The fire was far from the road and was a big one. And suddenly in the flames he caught sight of the dark outlines of an aircraft with the rapidly disappearing remainder of a gay tricolour on the ruins of the rudder.

One of the aircraft of his own section was shot down.

One of his comrades had fallen.

A bitter smell in his cockpit rapidly brought his thoughts back to his own position. The control levers were moving smoothly as usual, but the glass of the cockpit was smashed in a few places. In addition he saw in each wing a hole caused by cannon fire; the metal covering of the wings was pierced by holes 60 cm wide. His first reflection urged him to caution: 'You are deep in country occupied by the enemy and close to the ground,' he thought.

But then he saw another column on the horizon. Sudden rage seized him and he had only a single idea – to avenge his fallen comrade. The column was just driving into a small village.

All the better; they would have nowhere to escape to.

Again he attacked the whole column and again the shell explosions burst along the vehicles throughout the length of the column. A few soldiers hastily jumped out of the cars as the column stopped. There was little fire from the ground, there were few white lines, two vehicles in flames.

The commander of the section climbed further from the ground, and on his right wing a second aircraft appeared which, putting on speed, came up to the same level as himself and remained for a minute close by. He caught sight of the pilot's face. It was Sergeant B. His aircraft, too, had yawning holes in the wings.

Another column. It was going too fast, it was not possible to fly along it. He began to fire from a distance at the centre of the column. Soldiers jumped out of the vehicles as the column stopped and ran into the fields in small groups. A few groups of them pulled something behind them, a few were carrying something in their hands, and when he approached the centre of the column their guns set up a barrage of fire.

In front of the aircraft he saw a wall of white and fiery lines interweaved with small black clouds – shell bursts from small calibre cannon. He distinctly heard the noise of the explosion which suddenly seemed unreal and ridiculous; it sounded like a click of the tongue.

Every now and then dust poured into the cockpit. Dried grass and sand flew up into his face from the floor. He smelt something burning and felt a sudden heat. He instinctively crouched forward, but something immediately compelled him to look out of the cockpit. Sideways above him, only a few metres from the ground, he saw a terrible picture which lasted only a few fragments of a second. The other aircraft of his section had suddenly exploded in the air after a direct hit, had disintegrated and fell to the ground. And on the ground it rolled on for a few metres as if it were a rock of red flames enveloped in thick black smoke.

He was alone. Somewhere in his body he felt a dull pain, suddenly he felt faint. A sudden jerk of the joystick in his right hand woke him from his inactivity. The aircraft wavered, the rudder rose suddenly of its own accord and the joystick strongly resisted the pressure of his hand. He swiftly moved the steering apparatus to see if it was working – and the aircraft again came under control. It must have been a cannon shot in the tail. In the left wing there was a new hole. The cockpit was also riddled with holes.

Through the fields a herd of frightened cows was rushing.

Suddenly there again arose in his mind the picture that he had seen a few seconds ago – the death of his second comrade. And through this image he caught sight of a new column below him. He saw it too late. He was able only to attack the front of it. He aimed and pressed the trigger. No cannon fire was heard, only the barking of machine guns. The aircraft was no longer accurately obeying the movements of the joystick and the nose was slipping from side to side. He took aim again; he fired, and clouds of dust arose around his target. With his last effort he turned his guns on the first vehicles of the column. At this time he was already close to the ground. The vehicle contained some twelve officers. He saw their sallow faces and the braid on their shoulder straps. The vehicle suddenly stopped in flames. The driver pulled motionless bodies out of it.

New dust and a new smell of burning in the cockpit; new fire from the ground, fans of white lines and the black, ridiculously popping clouds around the aircraft.

He drove his aircraft right down to the ground; the fire was now above him and the white lines swept over him like the arches of a Gothic cathedral.

The sun on his right hand, he made for home.

He saw nothing but cows madly running about the fields and burning villages all round.

He saw nothing more except a final weak burst of fire as he flew over the lines. He felt peculiarly weary and through his head there passed the vague outlines of ideas forming the strange muddle; grief at the loss of his comrades, a feeling of joy but of a specially exuberant joy – at the successful fulfilment of his task, a keen sense of the horrors he had just gone through which now all at once seemed so far off and unreal, and amid all these ideas there suddenly burst forth a feeling of joy immediately suppressed again, of joy at being able to see those beautiful rich fields below him, the blue sky above him, the setting sun on the horizon. And at the fact that he was flying home to his comrades. At the fact that he would soon be jumping out of his plane and would be able to lie on the thick grass at the side of the airfield, close his eyes, stop thinking and rest for a while. And while he was thinking thus he felt a fierce pain in his left leg. And only now did he notice that his boot was full of blood. He tried to move his foot and it moved. So it could not be so bad.

On the roads below him waves of cars, refugees, cattle were sweeping onwards. A familiar sight in those days.

The knowledge that he was wounded caused him to ascertain more carefully the results of the enemy fire. It occurred to him that some part of the aeroplane might fall off, and he remembered that at one moment the aircraft had not been fully under control. When looking at the safety harness of his parachute he realised that the cord which served to open the parachute, in case of need, had been shot away. So this time he would not bale out. From habit and from his newly awakened caution he looked round and started. A little above him at a height of about 1,000 metres a large group of German fighter aircraft were calmly circling. It was a bad feeling to be immediately underneath them, alone, wounded, without munition, with a severely damaged aircraft, carefully crawling along and keeping close to the ground so as to keep above fields of a similar colour of that of the aircraft, so as to avoid the attention of the German fighters. He hopped over an avenue of trees constantly looking for places in front of him where he might land if the worst came to the worst. He turned his head round and looked for the enemy. In the meantime the enemy fighters had disappeared somewhere in the distance.

Weariness again overtook him; he could go no further; he would land in a field. But who would take him with them, for everyone ran away like this, especially if he could not reach the road. He must hold out until he reached home. He reached the Seine south of Rouen; soon he saw Paris before him and on its north eastern outskirts a green meadow with a mown strip of turf in the middle. That was home. When he landed they helped him out of his aircraft. No one could believe, not even he himself, that such a collection of holes could still fly.

Before he was taken to hospital he had yet to write his report:

Start: 17.40 hours.

Landing: 18.55 hours.

Crews: Commander of the section: Lieutenant J. No. 2: Second Lieutenant Paturle. No. 3: Sergeant Bendl.

In the region of operations eight attacks were carried out on columns. Two were almost completely destroyed, eighteen vehicles (one of them leading the column) were set on fire, many others damaged. Strong anti-aircraft defence.

Two of our own aircraft (Nos. 2 and 3 of the section) were shot down in flames. The crews did not bale out.

PART 2
Dunkirk & the Beginning of the Battle in July 1940

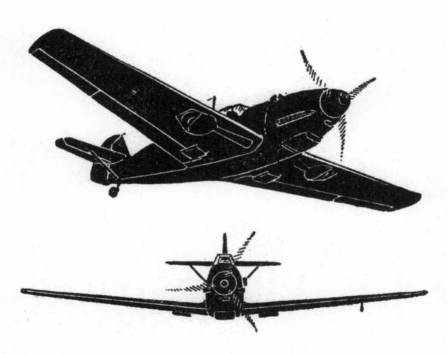

7 Brian Lane Part 1, Spitfire Pilot, Squadron Leader, British, 19 Squadron

Memoir written under the pseudonym 'Squadron Leader B. J. Ellan' and published in 1942 as *Spitfire!*. The author was in fact Squadron Leader Brian James Edward Lane of 19 Squadron. This, the first of four extracts, covers 11 May to 5 June 1940. The RAF airfields Lane flew from are indicated at the beginning of each original book chapter in the memoir. Fellow pilots are given pseudonyms also, some based on their actual nickname at the time.

Brian Lane, from Pinner in north-west London, was twenty-three when he fought in the Battle of Britain. He first joined 66 Squadron at RAF Duxford in 1937, and had a short stint at RAF Northolt with 213 before settling at 19 Squadron in September 1939. Lane married the famous racing driver Eileen Allison just before the Battle in June 1940.

The memoir is first-class and one I consider among the very best by Battle of Britain pilots. It covers Dunkirk and intense Battle of Britain action as well as quiet periods outside of the front line of 11 Group. It is a detailed account of the day-to-day activity focusing on the air-to-air combats and was written during the Battle itself and in 1941 in 'spare moments between flights and after the squadron has been released in the evening' before Lane was sent overseas to the Middle East in June 1941.

Chapter 2 First Blood: 11–25 May 1940 (based at RAF Coltishall, Norfolk in 12 Group, apart from 11–16 May 1940, based at RAF Horsham St Faith, also Norfolk and 12 Group)
On 11 May 1940, Wilf with a section of B flight was sent up after a reconnaissance machine over the East Coast. They intercepted him and saw It was a Ju 88 at about 20,000 feet. The section formed line astern and turned into the attack. The Hun saw them coming and put his nose down, going hell for leather towards a layer of cloud at about 5,000 feet. Wilf and Flight Sergeant S each managed to give him a squirt, and then he was into the cloud. A game of hide and seek followed, and Wilf told John, who was flying No. 3 in the formation, to go beneath the cloud layer in case the Hun should come out below.

As luck would have it, this was what actually happened, and John was able to deliver a good attack, closing to about fifty yards and giving the Hun all he had got. The Hun disappeared in the clouds again and the Spitfires returned to the aerodrome. John came in a few minutes later than the others, touched down and came to rest in the middle of the aerodrome with his engine stopped. We all went out to him to see what was up, and although he personally was all right he had a bullet hole in his oil tank and several more in the wings and nose. The German rear gunner had put in some good shooting and John had come back from thirty miles out to sea with no oil pressure at all. He had only just managed to make the aerodrome before his engine seized up.

This was the first action in which the squadron was engaged, or as Michael our adjutant put it in the squadron diary, 'The first shots to be fired in anger by the squadron in the World War of 1939.' A few days later came the news that the crew of the Ju 88 had been picked up in the North Sea. The rear gunner claimed to have shot down one Spitfire – he was nearly right!

Just about this time we heard that the squadron was to move to France at short notice, the first Spitfires to be sent overseas. This meant terrific activity for us all in order to be ready for the great day, but the great day never came. Thanks to somebody's foresight 'up top' we never went to France but moved south instead to relieve a squadron down there, and incidentally to take part in the Dunkirk evacuation. Although events were moving rapidly, King Leopold had not yet given in and I don't think any of us fully realised what was so soon to happen around that onetime peaceful gateway to the Continent.

It was at five o'clock in the evening of 25 May that the squadron took off and headed south into the gathering dusk. Nature herself might have been warning us with that grey sky that all was not well and that a stern task lay ahead of us.

As we circled our new station and glided down towards the ground past the innumerable balloons of London's barrage, each standing out blackly against the sombre grey of the sky, it was already getting dark. The sections landed and taxied in to their dispersal points and their pilots climbed out. As they stood silently about waiting for the others to come in, a curl of smoke rose here and there from a cigarette. Apart from the cracking noise of the cooling exhausts, and an occasional remark in quiet tones, the only sound was the distant drone of a tractor bringing the tanker out to refuel the silent aircraft. It was very peaceful that evening of early summer, though so few miles away on the other side of the Channel hell was going on.

Having seen the aircraft refueled and ready for the morrow, we walked up to the mess, the sergeants giving us a quiet 'Good night' as they left us to go to their own quarters. As we got nearer to the mess we could hear rounds of laughter and talking floating out across the lawns to disturb the silence. As we went in, our eyes blinking a protest against the sudden light, all was noise. Snatches of conversation hit our ears. 'I gave him a squirt and he broke up and went straight in–,' 'Bill should be back soon. I saw him put it down on the beach and get out, so he's ok–', '…went into the drink. A destroyer picked me up – lucky for me it was going the right way,' this from a pilot disguised as a seaman in a blue sweater, trousers and monkey jacket, which the Navy had given him when he was rescued.

I wandered, off to the bar to get a drink. A rather dishevelled officer stood there with a glass in his hand talking to the barman. He turned as I came in. 'Good Lord!' – 'Well, I'm damned!' It was Ian, who had been at FTS with me. I hadn't seen him for years. He had left the Air Force and gone back to America some time back, but here he was again, once more in uniform.

We had a lot to talk about and I found that he had just returned from France. He had been shot down out there but had managed to get back to his aerodrome – only to find that his squadron had left for England. After sundry adventures he managed to elude the Germans, get to the coast and find a boat to bring him over. But except for the clothes he stood up in and a French tin hat he had taken from a poilu who would never need it again, he had lost everything he possessed. He was very proud of the tin hat. 'Rather distinctive, what!' he said.

After supper the CO called us together in the writing room, and introduced the CO of one of the other squadrons on the station who gave us some tips on the sort of thing we might now expect to get. It was while we were thus engaged that an orderly interrupted the talk by calling Squadron Leader L to the phone. When he came back he told us, 'They wanted an aircraft to go over to Dunkirk and drop an important message. But the weather's too thick, never have found it in the dark; I told them so.'

The long shadow of Dunkirk had fallen across our path, and tomorrow would come the reality. It was now getting late, so we gradually drifted off to bed. We had to be up in the morning in time to take off on patrol at seven o'clock. I don't know about the others, but I slept like a log.

Chapter 3 Dunkirk – First Patrol: Morning, 26 May 1940 (based at RAF Hornchurch, Essex in 11 Group) Save for a layer of hazy cloud high up in the sky, through which the sun shone mistily, the next morning dawned bright and clear. We ate our breakfasts in silence, and not much of it at that. Eggs and bacon don't sit too well on an excited stomach.

Smoking, talking, fourteen pilots assembled on the tarmac wondering who would be the unlucky two who would have to stay behind. We had brought twelve aircraft with us, and two extra pilots had come down by road the previous night. The section leaders alone looked quite happy, for they knew they were definite starters. For fairness we drew names out of a hat and face after face lighted up as its owner's name was called. In my flight the unlucky one was Flight Sergeant U, and he stood looking at me with a hurt expression on his face, for all the world like a dog who has been told he can't come for a walk. I went over to try and console him, but he just shook his head sadly and said, 'Well I'm damned, sir!'

I couldn't help it, I burst out laughing, while the other pilots shot humorous remarks at him.

'Go on, Grumpy, you'll live to fight another day!'... 'Don't get too drunk while we're away!'

And that was why; from that time on, one flight sergeant was called Grumpy.

We, the lucky ones, got into our aircraft and started up, the fitters fussing round the cockpits polishing mirrors and windscreens which were already spotless. A pat on the shoulder – 'Good luck, sir. See 'em off good and proper!' – and they jumped down to guide their pilots out onto the aerodrome.

As we turned into wind and opened up, I noticed a lonely figure walking slowly back along the tarmac – it was Grumpy!

The CO was leading the squadron with a section of A flight, myself with a section on his right Wilf with one of B flight on his left and Eric, with a section, above and behind us all, the rearguard and lookout section.

We set course for Calais and climbed away south towards the thickening clouds over the French coast. Our instructions were to patrol Calais-Dunkirk at 17,000 feet. As we went higher and higher we kept running into straggling wisps of cloud, thin misty stuff which shone dazzlingly white in the light of the sun above. Below, the earth showed through as a dark mass, the Channel a slate grey ribbon with the reflected sun showing like a streak of silver paint down its middle.

We crossed the English coast at Dover. Ahead rose up a great black pall of smoke from Calais, drifting out in a long trail across the water. To the left another inky column showed the position of Dunkirk. There was something infinitely sad and terrible about that towering mass of smoke. I cannot describe just how I felt as I gazed fascinated on the dreadful scene, but I know that a surge of hatred for the Hun and all his filthy doings swept over me, and I felt that no mercy must be shown to a people who are a disgrace to humanity.

As these thoughts were racing through my mind, the CO turned and we flew up the coast towards Dunkirk. We were at 18,000 feet, just below the layer of high cloud; and turning at the other end of the patrol line we gradually lost height towards Calais. Suddenly from behind a bank of cloud, appeared twenty-one Ju 87 dive-bombers, heading out to sea over Calais and looking like some sort of strange bird, with their big spotted undercarriages and upswept wings. We turned in behind them and closed to the attack.

The Huns flew on unheeding, apparently suffering from the delusion that we were their own fighter escort, until the leading section of Spitfires opened fire. Panic then swept the enemy formation. They split up in all directions, hotly pursued by nine Spitfires, while Eric & Co kept watch behind us. I picked out one dive-bomber and got on his tail, staying there as he twisted and turned this way and that, trying to avoid the eight streaks of tracer from my guns. Finally he pulled up and stalled, rolled over, and then plunged headlong towards the sea out of control.

I felt happy! I had often wondered what it would be like really to shoot at an aircraft and bring it down. Now I knew, and it was definitely exhilarating! I turned to try and take stock of how the fight was progressing. Two other Stukas were spinning down, and several Spitfires were wheeling about over Calais looking for more targets. I soon found one for myself, a Stuka just starting his dive on to the town. I plunged after him firing at long range in the hope of putting him off. I saw him release his bomb, and then he was away as fast as he could go, heading east over the trees. I had turned and climbed up over the town again when Eric's voice came over the R/T: 'Fighters, fighters!' A pause, then, 'My God, there are hundreds of them!' This was an exaggeration, but there were about fifty, and I couldn't help smiling at his tone of voice.

There weren't many Stukas left now, but Eric turned and tried to hold off the German fighters, Me 109s, while we completed the rout. But before we could complete this job the 109s were down on us. A burst of tracer came over my left wing and I turned violently as a grey painted shape with black crosses on it flashed past. I saw the pink blur of the pilot's face turned towards me as he passed, and then another darker shape, only yards in front of my airscrew, flashed after him. It was a Spitfire after that 109.

To my left I saw Watty, hot on the tail of a Hun. As I watched, I saw another Me 109 get on Watty's tail. I switched on my transmitter and yelled a warning to him, at the same time turning to try and cut the second Hun off. Even as I did so I saw a flash on the Spitfire as a cannon shell hit it. The Spitfire went into a steep dive, smoke pouring from the engine. I circled and saw a white puff as a parachute blossomed out far below.

The noise of machine-gun fire behind me suddenly reminded me that I was still in the game, and I found that three Messerschmitts were honouring me with their undivided attention. An awful fear gripped the pit of my stomach. I knew I had very little ammunition left, probably only enough for one burst, and three to one wasn't so funny. I pulled round in a tight turn, the aircraft shuddering just above the stall. I knew I could out turn the 109s but I had very little petrol to play with now as well as being short of ammunition, and obviously it was time to go home!

The leading 109 was firing short burst every now and then, his tracer going behind me as he strove to get his sights far enough ahead of me. I remember I was cursing at the top of my voice. I was in a jam, I was frightened, and I was furious with those Huns for making me frightened. Something had to be done and done quickly. I tightened the turn still more. The aircraft flicked as she stalled. I rolled over on my back and out into a reverse turn, a trick I had learnt back at FTS. This manoeuvre temporarily got me away from the Huns and I dived hell for leather towards the sea, flattening out as near the water as I could and then opening the throttle wide.

I was beginning to breathe again when rat-tat-tat behind me and a tracer appeared over the cockpit, the bullets churning up a patch of foam in the water a hundred yards ahead. It was then that I remembered the automatic boost cut-out, a device giving maximum power from the engine for use in an emergency. I pushed the lever down and felt the surge of power from the Merlin in front of me as the aircraft accelerated. Twisting and turning, I managed to keep clear of the Hun bullets, very nearly hitting the water several times while doing so. One of the 109s had evidently climbed up to one side and now came diving at me from the beam. I turned towards him and gave him the last of my ammunition at point-blank range. I think he went straight in, for as I drew well away with my superior speed I could see only two Messerschmitts behind me.

At last I saw the white cliffs of Dover, never a more welcome sight than now, and feeling sick and rather limp I throttled back, climbed up to clear the cliffs and flew on to the aerodrome.

As I circled, putting everything out before coming in to land, I noticed three other Spitfires already on the ground refuelling. I had barely touched down when another appeared from the south, roared low over the aerodrome and came in. My crew came running out to meet me as I taxied in, caught the wing tips and guided me to the tanker.

With a sigh of relief I switched off and climbed stiffly out of the cockpit whilst and army of armourers fell on the aircraft and reloaded the guns at top speed. A crowd of airmen and pilots surrounded me, questions were shot at me right and left. Before I could collect my wits and answer, the intelligence officer pushed his way through, handed me the green combat report form, and guided me to the tailplane. 'Come on! The report first please. You can talk to the chaps afterwards.' Slowly I tried to sort out all the thoughts racing through my head and remember the sequence of events.

'How many did you get, first? I want the final score.'

'I got a Ju 87 and I'm pretty certain I got a 109 as well.'

'Good show,' he said, and made a note in his little book.

At last I had finished writing out my report and more pilots had returned. After a while no more came in and ten pilots trooped back to the mess, smoking and talking for all they were worth.

'I saw one of our kites spinning down. Nobody stepped out.'

'I saw Watty go down, but he got out.' Eventually we decided it was the CO we had seen spinning. Sergeant P had seen that the pilot who baled out was wearing black overalls. Watty had been in black overalls, the CO in white. Rather sadly we reached the mess, to flop down somewhat exhausted in an armchair, have a well-earned drink and count the score. Seven Ju 87s and three 109s certain, and one Me 109 probably destroyed. Not bad for the first show.

Our casualties were the CO and Watty missing, and Eric unserviceable with a crease across his forehead made by a bullet from one of those Me 109s and a flesh wound in his arm.

'I thought I was dead,' he said amidst roars of laughter. 'Then I saw some more tracer coming past me, so I came to the conclusion I must still be alive.'

A very near thing, but with an Me 109 to his credit he was more than quits.

Chapter 4 More Patrols: Afternoon, 26–27 May 1940 (based at RAF Hornchurch, Essex in 11 Group) In the meantime the NCOs and crews were working like niggers, patching bullet holes and checking everything over, to get the aircraft serviceable for the next patrol. I had only two bullet holes in the wings of my kite, and two strikes on the tail, where bullets had been deflected. Those Huns must have been darned bad shots! But some of the other aircraft were worse off than mine, one of the other sections having seventeen holes in the fuselage.

By lunchtime we had mustered seven aircraft, and soon after we managed to get nine serviceable. A quick lunch and we were down on the tarmac again. As acting CO I was leading the squadron this time, and nine Spitfires taxied out and took off, the thundering roar of the Merlins reverberating across the 'drome.

We circled and climbed away south east, the sun shining and glinting on our wings. It was a lovely afternoon. Several broken layers of cloud hung across the sky, the lowest being at about 9,000 feet. As we neared the French coast, I decided to patrol below this bottom layer, as it was obvious that any bombers knocking about would be flying below it in order to see their target; and at the same time it afforded us protection against a surprise attack from above.

We flew up and down that stretch of coast which was to become so familiar to us. Half an hour passed, and still nothing happened, though we scanned the ground below eagerly for bomb bursts and the sky above for enemy aircraft. Suddenly came a shout from the lookout man: 'Eight 109s right above!'

We had come out into a clear patch just north of Calais and the Huns had evidently emerged from the clouds now behind us. I looked round but could see nothing.

'Where are they? I can't see them!'

'Right above us. About a thousand feet. Look out, they've seen us, they're coming down!'

I pulled round in a steep turn to the right, the rest of the squadron spreading out in line astern behind me. By this time we were over a convenient patch of cloud, and as I circled I saw a Spitfire dive into the cloud with a 109 on its tail. It was G, who was leading his section. I turned to follow, but the Hun pulled up clear of the clouds and climbed away inland. I opened the throttle wide and climbed after him, keeping a good lookout behind in case anything was after me. The sky was clear of aircraft. Half a minute before there had been seventeen aircraft within that small clear patch. Now, in the miraculous manner which defeats the logic of the eye, there was only that Hun and myself.

I was overtaking fast, just below and behind him. He obviously had no idea I was there. Carefully I maneuvered my sights on to him and then slightly ahead, to get the deflection. Then I let him have it. It must have given him the shock of his life if he knew anything about it at all. His aircraft lurched, fell over almost on its back and went screaming vertically down. I half rolled and followed him, in case he was shamming, although I knew I had got him with that one carefully aimed burst. Down, down I went, watching for him to pull out, but he never did. I suddenly realised that I was perilously low myself, and doing a fair rate of knots as well. I had lost sight of my Hun, and realised he must have hit the ground by now; for he had been well below me and still in a vertical dive.

I pulled back on the stick and felt my head droop forward. At the same time everything went purple and then black in front of my eyes as I 'blacked out.' I came round again, climbed out to sea and made once more towards the clouds. Looking at my watch I noticed that only about three minutes had elapsed since the beginning of the fight. It had felt like a quarter of an hour at least.

I wondered how the rest of the chaps had got on. The English coast slipped by underneath me. Ahead the tower of Canterbury Cathedral shone in the sun and the estuary glinted beyond. I came to M aerodrome, circling to see if anybody had landed there to refuel. Yes there was a Spitfire just landing. I dived and flew low across the aerodrome, noting the letters on the fuselage as I flashed by. It was one of ours. A glance at my petrol gauge showed that my fuel was getting low, so I came in and taxied up to where the other Spitfire was parked. As I switched off, G walked over to me. He was swearing like a trooper.

'What's the matter with you?' I demanded.

'Did you see that little swine on my tail? Well, he got young B. I saw him spinning.'

'Blast him,' I said. 'Well, I got him, anyway, so we're quits. He climbed up after you went into that cloud, and I tailed him. He never knew what hit him and went straight in. Did you get anything yourself?'

'Yes, I got one of them after I came out of the cloud. A flamer.'

'Good show. That's two, anyway.'

Another Spitfire came in and taxied towards us. Out stepped young B. We looked at him as though he were a ghost.

'Didn't you go into a spin when that Hun had a crack at you?' asked G.

'Oh, yes, but I came out and everybody had disappeared, so I came back.'

G and I looked at each other. 'I wish you wouldn't give people such frights,' said G, 'I thought he'd got you.'

One by one more Spitfires came in. I got on the phone to our own station to see if anybody had turned up there. None had, which meant two were missing, Michael and Sergeant I.

But after the aircraft had been refuelled and we had been up to the mess for a cup of tea, we flew back to our own station and found that news had come through that Michael had parked down on the beach at Deal with a bullet in his knee. Sergeant I was still missing, though.

The following day was dull, with huge banks of grey cumulus cloud cutting off the sun. But in the afternoon it cleared, and the evening turned to perfect summer weather, without a cloud in the sky, as we took off after tea. The operations room had rung through to tell us that there would be 'hell over Dunkirk this evening' and it was with a tremendous feeling of excitement that we climbed up over the aerodrome and settled down on the now familiar course over the Thames for Dunkirk. Once past the estuary we could already see, miles away, the huge black column of smoke from the burning oil tanks, rearing up nightmare fashion into the quiet evening sky.

Soon we were out over the sea and in a few minutes came to Dunkirk, turning eastward to run up the coast to Nieuport past those rolling yellow sand dunes and beaches on which a chapter of Britain's history was beginning to be enacted.

The sea far below shone blue and gold under the westering sun. Above us was the deep blue dome of the heavens. Anxiously we scanned it, looking for the tell-tale glint of the sun on a pair of wings which would show us the enemy was above. Suddenly, just off the south mole of Dunkirk harbour below, appeared three white circles in the water near a tanker which was lying offshore. Bombs! Frantically I searched the sky to the right of us, trying to see the aircraft which had dropped them. It was the barrage put up by our anti-aircraft batteries which showed me his position. There was only one enemy aircraft.

Thinking it might be a decoy, I called up Wilf on the R/T and told him to stay on patrol while I took a section after the Hun. I turned away to give chase, but I think the Hun must have seen us, for he immediately turned inland, pursued by bursts of Ack-Ack. We crossed the coast diving slightly, as our quarry was below us. Gradually we overtook him, to find the enemy aircraft was a Hs 126. As we neared him he began to turn and twist this way and that, the sun catching the dark green camouflage and the black crosses on his wings. I came up with him rather fast over Ypres and gave him a short burst as he turned back underneath me. Although he had a far slower aircraft he used his manoeuvrability to escape our fire and fought us off magnificently, and after another burst I lost him as he dived away behind me. Feeling that we shouldn't really be playing with a Henschel miles inside Belgium when we were supposed to be guarding the Dunkirk beaches, I called up the section to rejoin formation. Frankie, my No. 2, was soon beside me making faces, as apparently he had found the Hun again, but Grumpy was not to be seen. The two of us dived down and tore back at twenty feet over the peaceful Belgium countryside. I tried to spot signs of either Germans or our own troops, but not a soul could be seen. Cattle browsing in the fields seemed to be the only living things in a deserted landscape. We passed over farms and villages all equally deserted, and then the dunes of the coast showed in front of us. As we flashed over the beaches and out to sea I saw hundreds of khaki-clad figures on the front and among the dunes waving to us as we went by. Under the huge black pall of smoke that hung over the town and drifted slowly out to sea it was almost like full night.

Out of reach of any German guns we climbed up again trying to find the rest of the squadron. I called Grumpy and heard him answer faintly. He was telling me his position, but I could not quite get what he said, though I did hear his triumphant voice repeating, 'I got him, I got him!'

Later on I had his story. When that Henschel had seen Frankie and me reform and turn back, he had thought himself safe, whereupon Grumpy, sitting unsuspected above him in the sun, had dived on him and sent him crashing into a field with his engine on fire.

But to go back a little, we still continued our patrol, having fetched up with two aircraft of B flight, but at last I called up the others and said we were going home, and we turned north-west towards our supper. As we came to the aerodrome in the dusk and sank down to mother earth the balloons of London seemed to be made of gold and silver. The weather was still beautiful and calm.

Soon after the rest of the squadron arrived. They had been lucky. Wilf, searching the sky for a target and wondering where I had got to, suddenly espied a Dornier just ahead and above him. He attacked and the Dornier burst into flames, plunging like a comet down into the blue water below. A few minutes later he saw two more, and a section between them sent down one of these on his last long dive to the sea. The ear-splitting 'blue note' of his over-revving engines must have sounded like music to the weary troops on the sands, ending abruptly as he hit the water far below in a huge cascade of white foam.

The other Dornier, the third, had suffered a similar fate at the hands of Sergeant J, and then, petrol getting low and no more Huns being in sight, they had followed us back.

I pounced on Grumpy after we landed. 'Why didn't you join up when I told you to?' I demanded.

'I must have had my R/T switched off, sir!' he said with a sly grin.

'You're a damned liar,' I said, unable to suppress a smile. 'You know perfectly well you heard me call up.' His grin just got a bit wider. I added: 'It was a good show, your getting him like that, but you obey orders in future.'

He was still grinning as we said 'Good night,' before parting to go up to our respective messes.

Chapter 5, 'First Wing Patrol': 28–30 May 1940 (based at RAF Hornchurch, Essex in 11 Group) Up to now we had encountered two big snags. In the first place we were operating at the limit of our operational range – we could only stay on patrol for a maximum time of one hour – and secondly we were almost always outnumbered.

The latter disadvantage was temporarily overcome on the following day, 28 May, when the three Spitfire squadrons on the station took off together and patrolled as a wing. The Huns were now beginning to escort their bombers more strongly, and the idea was that the leading squadron of the wing should take on the bombers whilst the other two tackled the fighter escort.

This was the first time we had tried operating as a wing, and on this first patrol we met with quite a fair measure of success. The weather was dull, with big masses of thundery-looking cloud covering the sky, the base varying from 5,000 to about 10,000 feet. We hadn't been on patrol long when the leading squadron dived away through a fantastic ravine in the mountainous black clouds and disappeared from view. Although we gave chase we weren't able to find them again, but we found something else instead.

As we emerged from the valley between the towering clouds into an open space I suddenly spied, just above and in front of us, about sixty Me 109s and a dozen Spitfires in a tremendous dogfight. Climbing as fast as I could, and keeping clear of the fight, I circled round the edge of this cloud arena until I had reached the height of the combatants. The squadron behind me then broke up and dived into the fight. As I went in I saw five more 109s come diving out of a tunnel high up in the black wall of cloud on my right, and then another five, and another. By this time I was well into the battle, and as a Hun crossed my nose I turned after him and closed in on his tail. Glancing in my mirror I saw coming round in a turn behind me another 109. 'I'll have to be quick getting the one in front,' I thought, 'before his pal gets on my tail.'

I got my sights on and pressed the firing button. My guns fired, but only very slowly and spasmodically. I swore as another glance in the mirror showed me Hun No. 2 just on my tail. Then I half rolled and let the aircraft plummet down in the ensuing dive until the clock showed 400 mph. Slowly, I eased back on the stick, feeling my eyelids and head grow heavy with the pressure that was pressing me down in my seat. But now I was out of the dive and soaring up and up, the black wall of cloud in front of me dropping out of sight below the nose of the aircraft as it reached the vertical. I tilted my head back to watch the clouds on the opposite side come slowly down to meet the nose as the aircraft came over on its back at the top of the loop. Then I eased the stick forward and to the right and rolled out right way up.

This had brought me out to one side of the dogfight, and at the same height, and I cruised around, trying to find the cause of the gun trouble. I looked at my air gauge, which showed the pressure in the compressed air bottle operating the guns, and it read 80 lbs. I swore again. No wonder the guns wouldn't fire properly. I wondered if I had been hit; a bullet might have struck a pipeline, causing a leak.

However, I turned into the fight again to have another squirt and see what happened. A 109 saw me coming and turned to meet me. Tracer appeared from his guns and passed just underneath my starboard wing. Not a bad shot, as I was a rather awkward target from his position. I turned hard to the left as we passed and slowly began to come round on his tail. He suddenly came out of his turn and gave me a fleeting shot, but as I pressed the button there, was a single 'crack' and a single bullet sped on its way.

'That's a fat lot of good,' I thought, seeing the Hun rolling away out of sight below me. I pressed the button again but nothing happened at all. There didn't seem much point in sticking around in the middle of so many Huns with guns that didn't work, so I dived down into the clouds and flattened out below them at 2,000 feet. Looking at my watch I saw that only five minutes had elapsed since we first sighted the Huns!

Suddenly coming towards me I saw three twin-engined aircraft. If these were Heinkels I was going to look an awful twerp. But as I got nearer I saw they were Ansons and heaved a sigh of relief. The worthy Coastal Command pilots, however, apparently did not recognise me so easily, for they turned in line astern into a tight circle. I rocked my wings and circled round them. They still appeared suspicious, but eventually straightened up and continued on their way whilst I steered for home.

As I climbed out of the cockpit my crew came up. 'Did you get anything, sir?'

'Not a ruddy thing,' I said in disgust. 'There's no air in the bottle, it must be leaking.' I added, 'I only fired about twenty rounds before the guns petered out.' Grimacing their disappointment the men started in to check the air system.

I was one of the first down but one by one the others came in until all had returned! Good show, no one missing! I wandered round talking to the others as they climbed out. Flight Sergeant S and Grumpy claimed one each, both flamers. Several of the others thought they had got one but they couldn't claim as they did not see what had happened to their opponent. As Wilf put it, 'There wasn't time to see anything. I just fired when something came into my sights and then turned like hell as something fired at me! What a party!'

It seemed amazing that everybody had come back from that fight. I had a word with Grumpy and S. Grumpy was grinning happily, but S only made a face.

'What's the matter?' I said.

'I got one in flames and the poor swine got stuck halfway out of the cockpit. Rotten sight.' And he turned away to light a cigarette.

Back in the mess we learned how the other squadrons had fared. Two pilots were missing but the next day one of them returned. He had parked down on the beach at Dunkirk and had got back on a destroyer. He reported that he had seen two 109s come down in flames and two more go straight into the sea. The leading squadron had sighted some Dorniers and given chase, when we had lost them in the clouds.

That evening the weather cleared and after dinner I was strolling in the garden in front of the mess when Wilf, standing on the lawn, called me over. 'What does that remind you of?' he asked, pointing above his head. I looked up and saw a cloud of gnats milling about in the evening air, looking for all the world like that dogfight in the morning.

We both laughed.

Next day the two other squadrons went to another station and were relieved by two more squadrons, both of which had at one time or another been on the same station with us. They both had grand COs in Squadron Leader M and Squadron Leader H. We were now the veteran squadron on the station, and after one or two wing patrols during the course of which nothing was seen, it was decided that we should lead the wing to try and change the luck. For two fruitless days it seemed as though we were still going to be unlucky, but on 1 June things really happened. *Chapter 6 Dawn Patrol: Dawn, 1 June 1940 (based at RAF Hornchurch, Essex in 11 Group)* On 1 June the wing was on the dawn patrol. Still full of sleep we rolled out of bed at 3.15 a.m. and staggered downstairs to the anteroom for tea and biscuits. Then down to the tarmac, to the rising and falling thunder of noise as fitters ran up the engines, to the sight of dim aircraft, shown up by the blue flames from the exhausts which stabbed the half light.

Still dazed with sleep I climbed into the cockpit, tested the oxygen supply and the R/T and then taxied out to the far end of the aerodrome and turned into wind, there to sit yawning whilst the other aircraft formed up around me. Thumbs up from each section leader and I waved my hand over my head, the signal to take off, and opened up.

A throbbing roar all around cut off the outside world as we sped across the aerodrome. The bumps from the undercart became less and less, until with a final bump we beat gravity and the green blur of grass slipped away beneath us. My right hand dropped to the undercart control, moved it back, and then felt for the pump. A few seconds later two faint thuds told me the wheels were up, and with a confirming glance at the cockpit indicator I reached behind me and pulled the hood shut. Changing hands on the stick, I closed the radiator and put the airscrew into coarse pitch, throttling back to cruising revs, and then glanced at the rev counter, boost and oil gauges to make sure that everything was ok.

As I turned left round the 'drome I glanced in the mirror to see the rest of the squadron formed up behind me. Three circuits and the other two squadrons were in position, Squadron Leader M, 'Tubby' to everybody, immediately behind us and Robin (Squadron Leader H) bringing up the rear with his squadron.

I straightened up and climbed away towards Dunkirk and the rising sun, circling as we left the English coast to pick up a fourth squadron of Spitfires from another aerodrome which had a rendezvous with us. Then out over the North Sea, forty-eight Spitfires looking for trouble!

When we reached the Belgian coast I turned left run up to Nieuport, past the packed beaches looking oddly like Blackpool or Margate on a bank holiday, past the hundreds of small craft lying offshore to ferry those heroic troops to the bigger vessels standing farther out. Every kind of craft was represented there, Thames barges, lighters, rowing boats, lifeboats, in fact anything that would float. Stretching back towards the cliffs of England was an unending stream of ships, some taking precious loads from the hell beneath us now to the comparative peace and safety of our island, others returning in the opposite direction, back to the inferno to save some more of that undefeatable little army.

From 5,000 feet we watched the drama being enacted below us. Above was a thin layer of cloud, not more than fifty feet thick, through which the sun was just visible. Suddenly in front of us appeared a twin-engined aircraft followed by eleven more, all heading towards Nieuport. I switched on the R/T: 'Twelve Me 110s straight ahead,' I said, then opened the throttle and gave chase.

The Messerschmitts evidently saw us coming, for they went into a circle and tried to get into the clouds. For once the odds were in our favour, and four to one at that. I was still out of firing range when, to my astonishment, one of the enemy aircraft staggered and then plummeted down, down with a strange pendulum motion as its tail came off. None of my section had fired, and since we were leading and out of range still, I could not imagine how on earth the Hun had been shot down.

By now we had closed with the enemy and turning right I got on the tail of a Messerschmitt and chased him down as he dived away, the rest of the squadrons fighting to get a target! It really was pathetic. By our standards of training those pilots should never have left FTS, yet here they were; trying to fight four times their number and with no idea of how to do it. War is war but I remember cursing the Hun for a cold-blooded devil in sending out pilots like these to fight us. Even as I cursed I realised what a queer thought this was. We ought to be thankful for cold meat like this!

I fired several bursts at the 110 I was after and saw his port motor splutter and stop. As he tried to turn away I pulled round inside him and gave him another squirt, this time hitting his starboard engine, which was immediately enveloped in smoke. By this time we were pretty low, and as I pulled up I saw him go down into the deck. Looking round I was in time to see the tail come off another 110, and down he went too.

Since every Hun in sight had a Spitfire on his tail I climbed up through the clouds to see if there were anything left up there. As I came out on top I saw two

Spitfires cruising about. As any Me 110s came up through the cloud they jumped on them, sending them down again. Unfortunately for those wretched Huns the cloud was too thin to hide in – there was no escape. I came down again, and as a Me 110 came towards me head on, I fired, then turned to come back after him. But another Spitfire was on his tail before I could get there. A few seconds later a dull flash appeared on the ground below, followed by a huge tongue of flame. And that was another Nazi less in the world.

After this there didn't seem to be any more Huns left, so I dived down almost to the water and came home, there to find most of the aircraft already on the ground. Two more came in as I was landing, and the squadron was complete. The second squadron came in by ones and twos, and then the third squadron in formation. The latter had apparently not seen much and had been unable to find anything to fire at.

The first pilot I saw as I climbed out of my aircraft was Sergeant J. He was grinning from ear to ear. 'How many did you get, sir?' he called.

'One,' I answered.

'Only one, sir! I got two.'

I grinned myself. 'If people like you weren't so damned greedy, I might be able to get a few more!'

A car pulled up by the aircraft and Cras, our intelligence officer, stepped out.

'Good morning, gentlemen. Any luck?'

A chorus answered him, whereupon he was heard to mutter a few remarks about the unearthly hour at which he was forced to rise, merely on account of bloodthirsty young devils whose idea of fun was a fight before breakfast.

Having received our reports Cras counted up the score. Seven 110s had been accounted for, and three 109s.

I hadn't seen any 109s and said so, whereupon it turned out that Wilf, with B flight, had had a little private dogfight with some 109s which had appeared out of nowhere. B flight had apparently made the best of it! As for the 110s, Sergeant J had got two, and so had G and Grumpy. B and I had each got one.

Back in the mess it was still too early for breakfast, so, we sat about in the anteroom swapping yarns. Tubby M, who had been responsible for shooting down the first 110, told us a really *stirring* tale. Literally, I mean, for Tubby volunteered the information that the miracle had been achieved by use of his *stirring* attack. By stirring it was discovered he meant stirring the stick round the cockpit once his sights were on, thereby getting a hosepipe effect from his guns. This, then, was the secret of how to shoot down a Hun when at 1,200 yards range! However, another of his pilots had got an Me 110 by means of more orthodox methods. Two more pilots were missing, apparently shot down by flak.

But any patrol that Tubby was on invariably turned out to be an amusing one, at any rate in retrospect when he got back to the mess. He was a great humourist, and now he improved the shining hour until breakfast by giving an exhibition of his actions and reactions on a previous patrol when he had found himself short of oxygen. He had us all rocking in our seats with laughter. It was the first time I ever remember being convulsed with mirth at such an hour of the morning!

Chapter 7 Dunkirk – the Last Patrols: Morning, 1–4 June 1940 (based at RAF Hornchurch, Essex in 11 Group) Breakfast over, we went down, again on to the tarmac.

The order of battle was as before. Again we circled as we left the coast to pick up the other squadron, then out over the glassy sea, down the long line of ships to Dunkirk.

The weather had not changed since dawn, and as the enemy bombers would have to come below the thin layer of cloud in order to drop their eggs, I decided to patrol just below the cloud base again.

As I turned off the harbour I glanced back over my shoulder at the mass of aircraft stretching away behind. It was an impressive sight, and I only hope it cheered up those poor devils five thousand feet below us on the shore.

Nieuport slowly appeared beneath my wings, and I turned to run back down the coast. I had just turned again at Dunkirk, and was heading back once more, when something moving on my left caught my eye. I looked round in time to see an aircraft diving down towards the shipping off the harbour. Coming hard round I dived after it, the rest of the squadron chasing after me. The aircraft flattened out over a destroyer for a moment and then turned, climbing towards the coast. As I followed there was a terrific flash below and a huge fountain of water was flung high into the air, to fall slowly back into the sea. As the disturbance subsided I saw that the destroyer had completely disappeared. So the aircraft in front of me was a Hun. A blind fury gripped me.

I was gaining on him as he strove to reach the safety of the clouds, but he was into them before I could get close enough to fire. I went up through the clouds in the hope of finding him, but he had disappeared. As I circled, waiting to see if he would appear again, some anti-aircraft fire inland attracted my attention and I caught sight of three Dorniers just above the clouds. Easing the stick forward I dropped down until I was almost in the clouds and then began to stalk the quarry. I don't think they saw me until I came round behind them and came up into position to attack. The Huns were flying in 'Vic' formation and I picked out the right-hand aircraft, closing in behind him. I fired a short burst from about 400 yards in the hope of killing the rear gunner, or at any rate frightening him.

As I closed in to shorter range, another Spitfire climbed out of the clouds to the left and turned in behind the left-hand Dornier. I grinned to myself, then concentrated on holding my aircraft steady in the slipstream from the Hun in front of me as the sights came on to his fuselage. My right thumb felt for the firing button on the stick and pressed it. A muffled 'B-r-r-r-p' came from the wings and I felt the aircraft check slightly as eight streams of tracer spanned the space between us.

The Spitfire bumped in the slipstream and my sights drifted off the target. I stopped firing to correct the aim and noticed tracer from the Dornier passing over my left wing. Then – 'Spang!' and I looked down to see a shining furrow along the top of the wing, where a bullet had bounced off the metal taking a sliver of paint with it.

I fired again, and as the Hun seemed to rush back to meet me broke away down to one side, muscles tense as involuntarily I tried to contract my body, half expecting to hear the sound of bullets hitting the aircraft. I made a good target for the German gunner before I got safely out of range. If he fired he missed me, and as I flattened out I saw the Dornier losing height very unsteadily and disappearing into the cloud. I dived down and searched frantically for him, as one more burst seemed to be all that was needed to put paid to his account. But I couldn't see a Dornier anywhere, so I made a few remarks about the parentage of the pilot and of Huns in general and turned out towards the sea.

Crossing the coast again a Heinkel passed just in front of me and I tagged on behind and gave him a couple of squirts as he climbed into the cloud. By this time my windscreen had become covered in oil, owing as I later found out to a leak in the airscrew, and it was impossible to see through the glass or use the sight. I was getting more and more annoyed, and when two more Heinkels in tight formation appeared above me I had to open the hood, pull down my goggles and peer round the edge of the windscreen in order to see what I was firing at.

A terrific blast of air hit my head as I looked out, nearly knocking my goggles off. Closing in below and to one side of the Huns I gave them the last of my ammunition, though without much hope of hitting them. But at least it had the effect of sending them up into the cloud, and as they melted like ghosts into the grey vapour above I turned and dived down to the water and headed out along the line of ships for England.

As we had run into the first lot of Huns only when it was almost time to go home, I was by now getting very short of petrol. Ten feet above the sea I raced along past the strange collection of vessels heading from hell to heaven. A mile ahead I recognised a cross-Channel steamer. I smiled to myself, remembering the long hours I had spent on her in happier days, crossing to the Continent. She would take a good two hours more to get home now, whereas I would be there in ten minutes.

Just as I came abreast of the ship the whole sea suddenly erupted immediately behind her, and only a few hundred yards away from me. I nearly jumped out of the cockpit, with fright! I had been rudely awakened from my dreaming by a Dornier sitting at about 2,000 feet, nearly over the top of me. As I looked, four little black objects left the belly of the bomber and came hurtling down towards the ship. I turned sharply and began to climb as hard as I could, feeling absolutely wild that the Hun had given me such a fright. He looked so insolent, sitting up there throttled right back and letting his eggs go in that deliberate fashion. Luckily for me it hadn't helped him to aim accurately, but I felt like ramming him. I was not, however, forced to dwell further on this suicidal measure, for the Hun then turned back towards the French coast and climbed away as hard as he could, pursued by bursts of AA fire from a cruiser a mile or so to the north east. Looking at the cruiser I watched the flickering stabs of flame from one of her 'Chicago Pianos.' Though it certainly looked a wicked and deadly performance enough, I couldn't see whether the Dornier was hit or not.

Once more I turned for home, on again up the line of ships, over the rusty wrecks on the Goodwin Sands, glistening like gold in the sun, and then the coast slipped by beneath me. I landed at M to refuel, then back over the peaceful English countryside to our own aerodrome.

A myriad silver dots ahead, the balloons of London, told me I was nearly home, and soon the aerodrome hove in sight. Usually I was never able to find it easily and spent the last few miles looking everywhere for a glimpse of some hangers, finally, just as I was beginning to think I had passed it, finding it as a rule hidden from view beneath the nose or a wing. But today I hit it straight off for once. As I sighted the hangars I put the nose down and dived across the aerodrome, to pull up in a climbing turn to the left round the circuit, throttling back as I did so. My left hand went up to the hood catch, pulling the hood open far enough for me to put my elbow against it and push it right back.

The airspeed dropped to 180 mph; I pulled down the under carriage selector, and the little white indicator pegs in the wings came slowly out until I could read 'Down' in red letters on both of them. A glance at the electric indicator in the cockpit told me that the wheels were locked down. Then I opened the radiator wide.

The speed had now dropped to 160 mph, and throttling back still more as I turned at the downwind side of the aerodrome I waited until the clock showed 120 and then pulled down the lever to lower the flaps. I felt the aircraft slow up, the nose dropping slightly at the same time. I pulled the control to put the airscrew into fine pitch, then – stick over to the left a little and back, and the aircraft was gliding into wind towards the aerodrome. I pulled the throttle back and felt it stop. Then I remembered the mixture control was still forward in the 'weak position' and was preventing the throttle from being closed. I pulled it back and then closed the throttle more as a belt of trees slid by underneath and the boundary fence came to meet me. A glance at the airspeed indicator – 95 mph, ok – and I closed the throttle completely, easing the stick back as I passed over the fence. Back a little more still as the aircraft flattened out – hold it! – then right back, and a second later some jolting and a slight bump from the tail. We were down.

Pulling the brake lever to and fro, I eased the brakes on and off to slow down without tipping up on the nose, and gradually came to a standstill. A glance behind as I put the flaps up showed me that nobody else was coming in, and I turned and taxied to the dispersal point and switched off. My fitter jumped up on the wing as I took my helmet off.

'Any luck, sir?'

I grimaced. 'Look at that ruddy windscreen!'

The fitter frowned and shook his head. 'Sorry, sir. It's the airscrew, I'm afraid. It's very bad on this kite.'

I climbed out, lit a cigarette and wandered over to where a group of pilots stood talking to Cras and making out their combat reports. As I approached, Cras turned and held out a green form.

But I shook my head. 'No luck, I am afraid. I pushed a Dornier into the clouds looking a bit shaky, but I couldn't find him again. He may have come down but I can't claim.'

'Bad luck.'

Everybody was talking and asking questions. Bit by bit I began to get an idea of what had happened to the others. G had got two, a Heinkel and a Dornier, both on fire, Leonard had got a 'probable' (a Heinkel), and so had Grumpy and Sergeant J. Sergeant P was missing.

'Not so good,' somebody remarked. 'That damned cloud was just ideal for them. It was a bit thicker than it was this morning.'

Still talking we wended our way up to the mess, to sit at our ease for the rest of the morning, drinking on the lawn. Robin had the best tale to tell. He had led his squadron after some Ju 88s up towards Ostend, and on the way back, having finished his ammunition, he had met a Hun going home. They passed each other at a respectful distance.

A few minutes later the same thing happened again, by which time Robin was getting a bit annoyed. When, a few miles out to sea, he saw another one, he couldn't stand it any longer and charged straight at the Hun as if to ram him. They were both very low over the water, and to his absolute amazement the wretched Boche dived straight into the sea.

'Pity I hadn't got just one bullet left,' he said. 'I could have claimed it then.'

Next day we did another patrol, but all was quiet over on the other side. The evacuation of Dunkirk appeared to be completed. When we landed at the aerodrome again we were overjoyed to find that Sergeant P had got back. A bullet in his oil-tank had forced him to come down in the sea, and he had been picked up by a French fishing boat, the *Jolie Mascot*. Her captain was trying to get back to Dunkirk from England but had got himself lost. P took over the duties of navigator and got his craft to the Belgian coast, where he took part in the rescue operations, finally coming back with some of the last of the BEF. A darned fine show.

Another early patrol on 3 June, and then the next day the last show we were to do before going back to our home station. At 4 a.m. we were taxiing out, and took off flight by flight. The clouds were at 200 feet and completely covered the sky, but we managed to rendezvous above them, and after circling for a while picked up the other two squadrons. We then set course to pick up the fourth squadron from R, and more by luck than anything else met them just as they came through the cloud. Then the wing set off on the familiar course.

The wind was south east and the smoke from Dunkirk stretched right to London, a black ninety-mile trail! Over on the other side there was no activity to be seen. A few derelict Thames barges, a sunken destroyer, an overturned lorry on the beach, such were the only reminders of the conflict now over. Only the pall of smoke, greater than ever now that our own demolition people had been around doing their particular job.

The whole scene rather reminded me of a theatre after the audience has gone. Nothing to remind one of the show but the litter left behind. Yes, the show was over now. The enemy was within twenty miles of our coasts, but another show would be put on, many shows perhaps, and Hitler would never speak the last line.

5 June 1940 On 5 June we took off from the aerodrome for the last time and headed away towards our home station. It was with some regret that we left. We had had a grand time there and everybody, from the station commander downwards, had been kindness itself. Nothing had been too much trouble if it had helped us at all.

Our stay had been very successful too. We had succeeded in destroying 28 German aircraft and probably destroying nine others. This for the loss of the CO (prisoner of war), two pilots killed, Watty and Sergeant I, and one wounded, Michael. Eric and John had been slightly wounded but were fit again. Not bad arithmetic at all.

It was Eric and John who were to be the next pilots in action, but more of that later. As we headed home our thoughts were dwelling on leave. Woody, our station commander, had promised us forty-eight hours when we got back, and I think we all felt very carefree and happy as we came over the aerodrome, went into our own special formation, and one by one peeled off to come screaming across the aerodrome. One by one we landed and taxied up to our dispersal point, to be met by a smiling Woody and Squadron Leader P, our new CO. Then to the mess for some drinks before lunch, with everybody shooting questions at us. We managed to answer most of them, I think, and cleared up the various tales, which had reached the aerodrome of our doings down at H.

A phone call to my wife to tell her to pack for forty-eight hours leave and then lunch. I was drinking, my coffee afterwards when I espied through the window a little grey Lancia come up the drive, a golden head showing behind the wheel. Good show – my lady hadn't wasted much time! A hurried farewell and I dashed up to my room to collect my bag and then we were away.

8 John Simpson Part 1, Hurricane Pilot, Flight Lieutenant, British, 43 Squadron

A series of letters from John Simpson to his friend Hector Bolitho, who was an RAF squadron intelligence officer. The first selection covers 43 Squadron's move south to RAF Tangmere to help cover the Dunkirk evacuation, flying from a temporary base in France and back to Tangmere for the first days of the Battle of Britain.

John Simpson joined 43 Squadron in 1936 and was stationed at RAF Tangmere, West Sussex (11 Group), one of the archetypical Battle of Britain bases in the heart of Sussex. Note that the dates in italics refer to the events described in the letters, not the date of the letters themselves. Bolitho published a 'memoir' built around these letters and first-hand accounts of his combat missions that Simpson had relayed to him in person (*Combat Report: The Story of a Fighter Pilot*, 1943).

Early May 1940 I am slowly losing all my friends in 43 and now I am the oldest member. Peter [Towsend] has been posted today to command a squadron in the south.

Caesar [Hull] is still in Norway, I suppose, with Batchy Atcherley. And now Peter has gone. I am pleased for him as he has done so well with us. I know he will be magnificent with a squadron of his own. I think he is getting a DFC. It will be the first DFC for our squadron. He is an extraordinary person. Do you remember how shy and self-contained he was? It has all gone now. He loves his gay parties and the squadron worship him. He is the hero of the squadron to the ground staff. What a lesson one can learn from a person like that, in watching the way he works with the men. He never needs to be angry or tiresome, or even particularly firm with them. It just comes from inside him and I suppose they know a gentleman when they meet one. I have noticed it a lot when I have been censoring the men's letters, how they all think the world of him. I shall miss him. I bet he'll do the best of all of us in this bloody war. George Lott, Eddie Edmonds and I are becoming very good friends. Eddie used to be in the Fleet Air Arm. He has a brother in the Service also. Eddie has many of Caesar's characteristics. He is always laughing. The chaps love him. He's a good pilot and the greatest fun in the world on a party. We share a room in the hotel and I think that we are Elsie's pets. After we have been flying late into the night and come back dog tired we get the next morning off until one o'clock.

Elsie and Dan Sutherland always wait up for us and give us a drink before we go to bed. And they have a great deal of work to do in the hotel. She usually wakes us up herself, fairly late next day, and *brings us our breakfast in bed*.

The war has taught me that these are really the great British people, who work hard and seem to have more to give people because of it. They are very fond of each other and completely unselfish. They are really marvellous to the whole squadron.

Did I tell you that they give us a bottle of champagne every time we shoot down a Hun?

We have at last got an adjutant, Stuart Cary. He has fitted into the squadron straight away. He is a charmer and already has the 43 spirit. We have had some pretty terrific parties with him. I think he will help George a great deal, which will allow him to fly more.

I am a lucky person, Hector. The squadron is really grand in spite of losing Caesar and Peter... and now Frank Carey. He is getting a commission so he has to leave us. We are such a happy family and have such a wonderful team spirit. I sometimes think that other squadrons are a bit jealous when they see us all having fun together. When we all go on a party we usually take the sergeant pilots with us. They are grand chaps who have all been in the squadron for a long time and they have a tremendous respect for it and the officers. I think they will get commissions in time. In many ways I think they have an advantage over us because, being sergeant pilots first, they see every side of the picture and this should make them good officers.

I fly with a wizard little chap as my number 2. He used to fly with Caesar in the old days, so I have something to live up to. His name is Tony Woods-Scawen. He's the biggest and smoothest flirt that I have yet come across. His room is surrounded with pictures of naked jobs much to the delight of Knockers [Harold] North, who is also in my flight and a bloody good type. He hails from New Zealand so you must meet him sometime. He has a tough time because he nearly goes mad if he is tickled. Naturally, when we are at dispersal and have nothing to do, we menace him the whole time and he gurgles and doubles up when we tickle him.

George and I are going into Thurso tonight to have a few drinks and some dinner. I think that the war in France is depressing him. It looks pretty bloody. I wonder whether it's the army's fault. I wish we had more squadrons there. Poor No. 1 Squadron must be having a pretty bloody time. I hear that dear old Laurie [Lorimer] is missing. I must say that it will leave a gap in my life if I never hear his Irish laugh again. Do you remember how he used to cook sausages in the kitchen and yell to you, 'Heigh! The bangers are coming up like nobes!

The other squadron, 605, is moving south tomorrow and we are told that we are getting a squadron from France. I cannot believe it. The squadrons can't be coming back yet unless, of course, they have had terrible casualties. I wish they would send us out there. I know that we'd do well. I hear that Dickie Lee has done wonders. You see how those boys, who were always looked upon as being the naughty ones, are doing so well. They needed a war to convince the old gentlemen in Whitehall. Do you remember that Dickie was almost given his bowler hat for low flying? That same low flying has apparently stood him in good stead.

I met some of the chaps from Walter Churchill's squadron [3 Squadron], and they were full of stories of Belgium. They all say Dickie did marvellously. In the first ten days of the German invasion of Belgium and Holland his squadron brought down between sixty and seventy Huns. Dickie was actually taken prisoner on the second day. On the first day he was wounded but he carried on. So like him. Next day he shot down two enemy aircraft and then he was caught by the German flak. He came down in a field and asked the way. The man told him to go to some tanks which were nearby and said that they were Belgians. Dickie was a bit of a sucker about this and, with a Belgian officer, he went towards the tanks, armed with a machine gun. The tanks turned out to be German so the machine gun was not much use. Dickie had an overcoat and the Huns did not realise that he was one of us. They popped him into a barn with some refugees.

Now comes the piece that is so like him. There was a high window in the barn. Dickie climbed up the wall to look out. Of course, he's a lucky blighter. There was a ladder beneath the window so he just climbed out and walked four miles, got a lift from some Belgians and he was back with the squadron to fight next day.

31 May 1940 A hurried note. We are to move back to dear old Tangmere today. To help in the evacuation from Dunkirk. I am taking off in about an hour. We have had little time to pack and we are all flapping a bit. The ground crews are delighted. They all love Tangmere and feel a bit resentful if anybody else is there. Crackers [Malcolm] Carswell, our other New Zealander who crashed into the sea a month or so ago, has turned up today from hospital. When he crashed he went to the bottom of the sea and got out of his aeroplane. It must have been a bit much. He escaped, however, and one of the ships in the convoy he was protecting picked him up. He always sings those Maori war songs when he is a bit tiddly. They mean nothing to us so we call him Crackers. He is always washing his hands. He has a thing about cleanliness of his hands. He is delighted that we are moving as he hasn't had a crack at the Hun yet.

I have just heard from the station intelligence officer that 605 Squadron were sent from here to cover the evacuation from Dunkirk. News has come through that they have lost nearly all their chaps on the first day, including their CO, George Perry. Such a charming person with a delightful wife.

I am ashamed to think I was the least bit sorry when I shot down my first Hun. There were so many good types in 605, and so many of them were my friends. Most of them are missing. It must be hell for the army in France.

1 June 1940 On the first day of our Dunkirk patrol, we took off from Tangmere while it was still almost dark. I shall never forget the mass of balloons all down the Thames, from London. We saw them in the distance, glittering in the morning light. They were so thick that they seemed to form a line, like silver battleships in the clouds, following the curves of the river.

We breakfasted at Manston and waited by our aircraft for the hour of our patrol. We were lying on the grass, reading the morning papers and I came upon the announcement that dear old George had got his DFC. There he was, lying next to me. And I realised, I don't know how – a sort of instinct – that he had read it himself and had not said a word.

I congratulated him and he said, 'Christ knows what I got it for.'

I could not have been more pleased about any decoration. George is an extraordinary person and he deserves it. Behind that slow, quiet manner, there is a lot of courage and a good brain. What was so nice was that when we returned from our patrol and he asked his batman to buy a DFC ribbon for his tunic, the twizzet bought a DFM ribbon by mistake. George wore it without even noticing until we told him.

On that first morning we made our way across the Channel to Dunkirk. 43 flew 'above and behind.' We crossed the water above clouds and saw nothing of the evacuation which was going on below. But the smoke from the oil tanks at Dunkirk had reached us at Tangmere and we knew what to expect. We had smelled it in Sussex as we flew through it. You can fly from Brighton to Dunkirk on the smoke trail… just follow it and find Dunkirk at the other end.

All the harbour at Dunkirk seemed to be on fire with the black smoke from the oil dumps. The destroyers moved out of the pall of smoke in a most uncanny way, deep in the water and heavily laden with troops. I was flying at about 1,000 feet above the beach and the sea. And there I could see the *Brighton Belle*, and the paddle steamers, and the sort of cheerful little boats you see calling at coastal towns on Sunday. Hundreds of boats! Fishing boats and motorboats, and Thames river craft and strings of dinghies, being towed by bigger boats. All packed with troops, and people standing in the water and awful bomb craters in the beach, and lines of men and groups of people sitting down. Waiting, I suppose. And I could see rifles – stacked in threes. And destroyers going back into the black smoke. And wrecked ships on the beach: wrecked ships of all sizes, sticking out of the water. And a destroyer cut in halves by a bomb. I saw it! A Junkers 87 came low over the water and seemed to fly into the destroyer and drop its bomb. That was pretty terrible. It was shot down after, thank God. I saw the destroyer crack in two. And I saw parachutes coming down from wrecked aircraft, landing in the water and on the beach and on the land.

The first day we were patrolling, there were nine of my squadron, flying in a sort of oval-shaped route over the coast at between 10,000 and 20,000 feet. We flew two miles out to sea and then two miles inland. And suddenly, I realised that there were more aircraft flying than had come with us across the Channel. That was a bit disturbing! A squadron of Messerschmitt 109s had joined us and they were sharing our patrol peacefully, waiting to take their chance in getting a straggler. It was a bit shaking. I signalled to my CO when I recognised them. We had only come on bombers when we were in the North. Before the CO had time to give the order to attack a lone Messerschmitt dived down on him. The battle was on then. We picked our opponents, while two squadrons of our fighters flew low to protect the shipping. After avoiding several on my tail, for what seemed to be ages, I got on to one and opened fire. We chased about and lost height rapidly, coming down to 5,000 feet above the land. When he was diving I got in a steady burst and he crumbled up as if he were made of cardboard. He crashed in flames on a golf course.

I climbed up again and found that more German fighters, Messerschmitt 110s, also strangers to us, had joined in. I got on to the tail of one of them, which was firing at a Hurricane piloted by Crackers. I got so close that when I fired, his tail just blew off in mid-air. Crackers was on fire too. But he baled out and he was brought home by a destroyer two days afterwards.

Then I dived to the sea and made for home. I thought it was all right, but I made a silly mistake. In the heat of it all, I flew towards Calais instead of Dover. When I realised this, I turned and thought I was alone for the journey across the Channel. But I looked back and saw that I was being followed by an enemy aircraft. We weren't more than three or four feet above the water. I zig-zagged to avoid his bullets. God was kind to me. We continued that mad, zig-zagging journey, so low over the smooth water, and he kept at me until I was eight miles or so from Dover. Then he turned and went home. It was our first combat with anything more than five aircraft... our first combat with any fighters. We got nine destroyed and six probable and we lost two.

7 June 1940 Abbeville, France It was a fine, clear summer day. Our squadron was ordered to patrol with nine aircraft on a line between Le Tréport, Abbeville and Amiens. We flew straight from our base on the English coast and made our landfall south of Le Tréport. Along the whole of our patrol line were smouldering villages, columns of black smoke and burning forests. Others had been there before us. As we turned to make for Rouen, where we were to land for lunch, a squadron of Messerschmitt 109 fighters attacked us from out of the sun. In a second we had broken our formation and each one of us engaged an enemy in a dogfight. There were more of them than of us and it was difficult to fire at one without being attacked by two others at the same time. I finished my ammunition, having fired at three of them. But the battle was too hot for me to follow and see if they crashed. I dived to the ground and made my way over the tree tops to Rouen which I found by following the Seine. When I landed I found that six pilots of my squadron had arrived before me. We were two short. Dickie Bain, the Station Commander, would not allow us to stay. The aerodrome had been bombed that morning and they were all preparing to move south. So we had to take off again for an aerodrome thirty miles away. I had only ten minutes petrol left when we landed in a cut wheat field. While the ten men in the field refuelled our aircraft with only one petrol tanker between them, we climbed on to an American car and were driven at a hellish speed to a village. It seemed to be very peaceful, except for the motor cycles which flashed through on their way to headquarters. There was a cart, with flowers and fruit and vegetables for sale. We were hot and thirsty. We talked of the combat, but not much of those who were missing. We just felt that they would turn up. We had a miserable lunch of cold sausage meat, brown bread, and quantities of watered down cider. We had no French money and we had to pay the angry madame with an English pound note.

We went back to the farm but the telephone wires had been cut. While the CO went back to the village to telegraph for orders, we stripped to the waist and lay in the sun, in the middle of the wheat field. We were seven, very white and clean, lying in the wheat. In one corner the Frenchmen were making a haystack and in the other corner some Cockney airmen were belting ammunition. We became thirsty again as we lay in the sun, but nothing could be done about it.

The Germans had advanced many miles while we were lying there. Our orders came. We were to patrol the same line, but two miles into enemy territory. We seemed to be very small... only seven... taking off. We flew in peace for ten minutes after arriving on our line and then the sky was filled with black puffs of smoke, like hundreds of liver spots. We dived and climbed and none of us was hit. When we turned at the eastern end of our patrol line the sky was fantastic. The black puffs of smoke from the anti-aircraft guns had woven weird patterns in the sky.

The guns stopped firing. We knew then that the German fighters were on their way. Coming towards us, in layers of twenty, were what seemed like a hundred of the enemy, looking like bees in the sky. Some were level with us. Some above. Some below. My CO climbed up with us to sixteen thousand feet and there, while we were being circled by all of those hungry fighters, he gave the order to break up and engage. Forty were bombers. They flew south: perhaps to bomb Rouen. I singled out a Messerschmitt 109 and had a very exciting combat with him. He was a good pilot and he hit me several times. We began to do aerobatics and while he was on his back, I got in a burst which set him on fire. He jumped out, but I did not see his parachute open. His machine was almost burned out before it hit the ground. There were scores of fighters about me, but I still had plenty of ammunition. I got on to the tail of another 109 and while I was firing at him two Messerschmitt 110s fired at me from either side. I continued to fire at the 109 which was badly winged. He suddenly stall turned sharply to the right, went into a spin and crashed straight into one of the other Messerschmitts which was firing at me.

I couldn't resist following them down. It was a wonderful sight. They stuck together in a sort of embrace of flames, until they were a few hundred feet above the ground. Then they parted and crashed, less than twenty yards apart.

I turned for home, flying as low as I could. Crossing the Channel seemed to take hours. I was wet through with sweat. I had been fighting at full throttle. The sea looked cool and it made me feel cooler. But I was afraid that I might be caught without ammunition and go into the sea. There were no boats to rescue me. Luck was with me for there was a mist above the sea. I flew in it for twenty minutes before I emerged into the sunlight again. I was lucky. The Germans had lost me. I could see nothing but the sea and the English coast.

My wireless had been disabled so I could not inquire of my friends. At last I flew over land and very soon I was circling the aerodrome. I landed to find that I was the first home. My CO followed, having bagged two himself. We sat in the sun on the aerodrome for a long time, waiting for our other pilots. We searched the sky for them for what seemed an hour. But no more arrived. So we went to the mess and we drank to ourselves and to them.

11 July 1940 I have just been to see George at Haslar Hospital. He is in terrible pain. They have operated to try and save his eye, but it has failed. Tonight they are taking his eye out. It will relieve the pain. His other eye will be ok.

Hector, I think I admire him as much as any human being I know. He began in the Service as an AC2. I think he's been in the RAF something like eighteen years. I remember you saying to me once something about the RAF being a school for character. The phrase was something like that. If ever a great character emerged from the RAF, it is George. God, I do admire his guts. I am sorry if I did not make it clear about Tony. George and I were having a lunchtime drink in the hall when Tony walked in, wearing an army shirt and a tin hat. Under his arm was his same old parachute. On the 7th [June], when we lost him, he had baled out over the German lines. He landed all right and hid in a ditch. After it was dark, he crept out and he walked twenty miles, still hanging on to his parachute. He found a British patrol with whom he was eventually evacuated.

But I wish you could have seen him walk into the mess, his face covered with smiles. He said to George, 'I am sorry I am late, sir.'

All George did was to call Macey and say, 'Bring us a drink.' George asked Tony why he had lugged his parachute all the way home with him and Tony said, 'Well, I know that this one works and I might have to use it again'. [He was shot down and saved by his parachute no less than six times. The seventh time he was shot down he was killed.]

The new boys are doing fine. Tom Morgan is first rate. He shot down his first Hun yesterday – a Heinkel. There's a lot of activity now that the blitz has really begun. Caesar is out of hospital and on leave in Guildford. Carey and I are going up to London to have a party with him tonight.

19 July 1940 It was a lovely evening and the wind was warm about us as we passed through the slipstream of our aircraft to our cockpits. We were to patrol the coast at 10,000 feet and we soon reached the patrol line at this height. I could see for miles. There was a thin layer of cloud one thousand feet above us and it shaded our eyes from the sun.

We were flying east when three enemy aircraft were seen flying west in the clouds overhead. I told my leader that I would climb above the clouds with my flight and investigate. As I did this, no less than twelve Messerschmitt 109 fighters emerged from the clouds. Still climbing, I made for the sun and turned and gave the order for my flight to break up and attack. In a moment our battle began. Our six Hurricanes were against the enemy's twelve.

The eighteen aircraft chased round and round in and out of the cloud. I chose my first opponent. He seemed to be dreaming and I quickly got on to his tail and gave him a short burst which damaged him. I flew in closer and gave him a second dose. It was enough. He dived, out of control, and I followed him down to 6,000 feet. There I circled for a minute or two and watched him dive vertically into the calm sea. There was only the telltale patch of oil on the water to mark where he had disappeared.

I opened my hood for a breath of fresh air and looked about the sky. There was no sign of either the enemy or of my own flight. I was alone, so I climbed back into the cloud which was thin and misty. Three Messerschmitts, flying in line astern, crossed in front of me, so close that I could see the black crosses on their wings and fuselages. I opened fire on number three of the formation. We went round and round, in decreasing circles, as I fired. I was lucky again. I had the pleasure of seeing my bullets hit him. Pieces of his wings flew off and black smoke came from just behind his cockpit. He dived and I fired one more burst at him, directly from astern. We were doing a phenomenal speed. Then my ammunition gave out just as the other two Messerschmitts attacked me. The cloud was too thin to be of help. It was merely misty and you could see the blue of the sky throughout. So I had to rely on my aeroplane. I twisted and turned and dived towards the coast. I was flying at about 16,000 feet, eight miles or so out to sea. But they were too accurate. I could hear the deafening thud of their bullets hitting the armour plate behind my back and I could see great hunks being torn off my wings. There was a strong smell of glycol in the cockpit, so I knew that the radiator had been hit. What little wisps of cloud there were, were far beyond my reach and my engine was chugging badly. It was terribly hot.

Then came a cold stinging pain in my left foot. One of the Jerry bullets had found its mark. But it really did not hurt much. I tried to dive faster to the sea and make my escape, low down, when the control column became useless in my hand. Black smoke poured into the cockpit and I could not see.

I knew that I must leave the aircraft.

Everything after this was perfectly calm. I was now at about 10,000 feet, but still some miles out to sea. I lifted my seat, undid my harness and opened the hood. The wind was my ally. It felt like a hand lifting me from the cockpit, by my hair. But it was actually a combination of the wind and the slipstream catching under my helmet and pulling me free of the aircraft. It was a pleasant sensation. I found myself in midair, beautifully cool and dropping without any feeling of speed. It seemed hours before I reminded myself to pull my ripcord and open my parachute. This part was quite easy. The noise of the wind stopped and there was a terrific jerk. It seemed that my body was being pulled in every place at the same time. Then I began to swing like a pendulum. Then I vomited, just as I looked down and saw the coast and the sea near Worthing.

I stopped swinging and settled down to look about me. Then I had a horrible fear. I felt terribly afraid of falling out of my harness into the sea. I put my hands up and held the straps above me. I was frightened of touching the quick release box on my tummy by mistake.

I became calm and I was able to enjoy the full view of the world below. The beach was some miles away, with soldiers. And there were the long lines of villas in Worthing. There was no sensation of speed. I knew I was descending only because the ripples on the water became bigger and the soldiers on the beach seemed to grow.

Then came a minute of anxiety. As I floated down one of the Messerschmitts appeared. The pilot circled around me and I was alarmed. He was near enough for me to see his face... as much as I could see with his helmet and goggles. I felt very much that he would shoot me. And I felt helpless. But he didn't shoot. He behaved very well. He flew so near the noise of his aircraft was terrific. He flew around me about one and a half times and then he suddenly opened a piece of his hood and waved to me. Then he dived towards the sea and made off across the Channel to France.

I'd like to know why he let me get away. He could have got me as simply as anything. But he didn't try.

When I recovered from my fear I found that the wind was still being friendly. It was carrying me in towards the beach. I took out my cigarettes and lit one with my lighter without any difficulty. Ages seemed to pass and I was quite happy. I had forgotten about my foot but I suppose that it had been bleeding all the time because I began to feel rather sleepy. I threw away my cigarette as I came nearer and nearer to the beach. I heard the 'All Clear' siren and as I passed over the beach and the houses on the sea front, I could see people coming out of their shelters – people looking up at me. I was then at about 1,000 feet.

The changing temperature of the air at a low level seemed to affect my speed and I began to sway a little. I could hear my parachute flapping like the sound of a sail in a small boat. The soldiers' faces became quite clear. I could see their rifles but they were not pointing at me. I must have looked English, even at a thousand feet. This was comforting.

I became anxious again, for the first time since the enemy pilot circled around me. I was afraid that my escapade was to end by my being killed against the wall of a seaside villa. It did not seem possible that I could reach the fields beyond. It was all very quick after that. I seemed to rush… and then I hit the roof, or the edge of the roof, of a house. I suppose my parachute crumpled then because the next thing I realised was that I was going through a garden fence backwards, and then, bang into a cucumber frame.

I lay still for a moment. Then I released my parachute. I don't know quite what happened. I was in pain. My collarbone was broken and I was pretty badly bruised from hitting the house and the fence. And my foot was still bleeding. But I remember that when I released my parachute and lay still, my brain was quite clear, and I whimpered because I was so grateful for being alive.

It was a little house and a little garden. The woman ran out and others came, because they had seen me coming down I suppose. The woman brought me tea and then a policeman came with a glass of whisky. He was in the street and he handed it over the garden wall. I drank the whisky and then the tea. There seemed to be about twenty people wanting to be kind to me. The woman who owned the garden brought me a blanket. My ankle and shoulder were bound up and an ambulance arrived…

I was in awful pain, but my mind was quite clear. I remember that as I was being lifted into the ambulance, there were some men who had seen the battle and they seemed to know that I had brought down a Hun. One of them said, 'we saw what you did, sir,' and then a woman pushed a little boy forward and said, 'Ernie, give the gentleman those cigarettes.' And the little boy came running up to me and said, 'Good luck, sir. When I grow up I'm going to be an airman too!'

9 Gordon Batt Part 1, Hurricane Pilot, Sergeant Officer, British, 238 Squadron

Leslie Gordon Batt, known to everyone as Gordon, was born in 1916 in Wolverhampton. This is the first of two extracts from his memoir, first published privately in 1994 as *Sgt Pilot 741474 RAFVR: A Flying Memoir* and then republished by the Battle of Britain Historical Society in 2001 as *Scramble! A Flying Memoir of One of the Few*. To aid with identification of his fellow pilots I have adjusted the spelling of a couple of names and inserted first names where Gordon had just listed a surname.

The first extract begins on 15 May 1940 when he joined an operational squadron through to his experiences of the first days of the Battle. The extracts are used courtesy of Pam Hurn, daughter of Gordon Batt, and many thanks also to her husband Mike.

Halfway through May 1940 with an above average assessment as a pilot, I was posted to 253 Squadron at Kenley. There were no operational training units at that stage, one went straight from training school to a squadron.

253 Squadron had one flight in France, and one at home, the actual aerodrome was quite small, as compared to Little Rissington, there were however some open bunkers for the aircraft. It was all a bit like a dream. The CO saw me, handed me over to the flight commander, he gave me the pilot's notes relating to a Hurricane,

he said read these, sit in the cockpit, and when you think you know all about it, I will check you out and you can have a flight.

For the uninitiated, the pilot's notes for an aircraft are similar to the driver's handbook for a motor car, the only difference is that with a car, if you don't remember a certain thing, you can pull into the side and have a quick recheck. There was no dual instruction, the Hurricane was a single seater fighter, also there are no parking places, you just keep going, or else.

After a couple of hours I had absorbed the basics, nice cosmetic cockpit, all controls nice and handy, very slightly different basic instruments on the blind flying panel. The Harvard was to USA layout, this was back to the UK type. So I was back home so to speak.

I reported back to the flight commander, who checked me out, and my log book records that on the 19 May 1940. I did some local flying from Kenley. The next day I had another trip, local flying and R/T practice. This R/T was not exercised to the same degree in training command, things change when one gets into the operational area. No problem with the aircraft, the extra power was super, and the Hurricane is a most docile, easy aircraft to fly.

I was only at Kenley for a week, and during this stage what was left of the 253 Squadron in France arrived back in dribs and drabs very bedraggled, extremely tired and a little demoralised. The real war had started, and reasonably read people will know how rapid was the retreat in France, the RAF ran out of airfields, and ground staff to back them up, so it was a simple question, save the aircraft, and get out now.

During this exodus of France, a Fairey Battle aircraft landed at Kenley, with a sergeant pilot at the controls. I was most interested, because the RAFVR pilots were to have flown these. I asked the sergeant, 'What are they like?' 'Absolutely bloody useless, the Me 110s and 109s slaughtered us. They are slow, carry a pitiful bomb load, under armed and not very manoeuvrable.'

They were taken out of service, and I never saw another one.

The next morning the CO sent for me. The squadron was being posted to Scotland to rest and reform, but as I was fresh I was being posted to Tangmere, to a squadron just forming. Just think, if that bod had not stamped on my hand in that seven a side rugby game, I could have been in France, fate, it seems, plays some funny tricks.

So I reported to Tangmere, found the 238 Squadron office and reported to the adjutant, Sergeant L.G. Batt, 741474. Sir. Tangmere was a grass airfield, with the traditional hangers and typical layout and design of the other buildings developed from the late 1920s onwards. The squadron was equipped with Spitfires.

None of the pilots from the CO downwards had any operational experience, so we set about training, but it was a bit like the blind leading the blind. After studying the pilot's notes for the Spitfire, and being cross examined by my flight commander as to where all the knobs, buttons and tits were located, landing speed etc. I was allowed a flight.

This first flight was on the 23 May 1940. It was only three days previous that I had done my second flight in a Hurricane at Kenley. That's not bad going by any standard. We carried out various training exercises, formation flying was high on the list, then there was firing into the sea, quite frankly, I was beginning to feel at home with a Spitfire really is a lovely aircraft. The love affair was short lived. The Dunkirk episode was in progress not very far to the east of us, and the powers that be decided that they wanted these precious Spitfires in that area, in the hands of operationally experienced pilots.

I flew my last practice flight in a Spitfire on 9 June, and on 13 June back onto a Hurricane, which the squadron had been re-equipped. There is one thing for certain, I did by now know how to read through the pilot's handbook notes. The Hurricane after the Spitfire was like a carthorse compared to a racehorse, still, it flew, and that was what our business was about.

By 19 June we were moved to Middle Wallop. Ok, you've never heard of the place, neither had I. It is to the north east of Nether Wallop, and to the south east of Over Wallop. Actually, about half way between Andover and Salisbury. At the same time as this move our original CO Squadron Leader Cyril Baines was posted and replaced by a Squadron Leader Harold Fenton, they were as different as chalk and cheese. The former seemed to be only training orientated, with no other experience, he talked to us more like a school master. The new bloke was more friendly, he talked to us more like fellow pilots, irrespective of rank.

We did more training through June, and I don't know exactly when we were made operational, but our first operational trip was on the 3 July. It is interesting to note at this point that my total flying hours were 275 hours. Now, this is far in excess of those less fortunate pilots who were trained during the war, and were thrown into the deep end without this length of training. The VR pre-war preparation held me in good stead.

My interpretation of the Battle of Britain was in four distinct phases, and was not confined to just September. Phase 1 Protecting shipping in the Channel who had the cheek to sail south a month after Dunkirk; Phase 2 Fighter and fighter bombers probing our defences; Phase 3 All out attacks with large bomber formations with fighter formation cover; Phase 4 Fighter and fighter bombers trying to lure us to fight out in the Channel. This last item was in an effort to destroy both aircraft and pilots, with no chance to force land or parachute to safety.

While we were at Tangmere there were two incidents which stick in my mind. 601 Squadron (City of London, university air squadron) were also at this airfield and had the hanger next to us, actually the officers had there greatcoats lined in hunting pink, my impression was, what a lot of pompous show offs. During the Battle of Britain I changed my mind about them, they were in the thick of things, and fought and fought, with great bravery.

As I mentioned they had the hanger next to us, and for convenience for setting the reflector sight to the guns, they had marks on our hanger door, that end was seldom opened. They jacked this particular Spitfire up into flying attitude, straight and level pointing at the sighting marks.

The erk (a fitter or rigger) working in the cockpit imagined he was a fighter pilot and pressed the firing button. Now if all the rules had been complied with, all would have been well, unfortunately this was not so, first the firing button was not in the safe position, and secondly the guns were armed.

Now, if my memory serves me correctly a Browning gun delivers 800 rounds a minute, one little press delivers quite a hail. Some went through our hanger door, some ricocheted off. There was pandemonium, the erks working in our hanger didn't have time to get flat on the deck, until it was too late, and a 601 erk who was standing in front of the Spitfire with his arm drooped over the covered gun port was a hospital case. I have an idea that our CO said! 'Please move your gun sighting arrangements'.

The other episode involved one of my mates, a Sergeant Eric Bann. He was instructed to carry out a petrol consumption test on a Spitfire, now, he had not been brought up with a technical back ground, and they did not explain to him precisely how he should conduct this test. He took off, noted the time, flew round just doing practice manoeuvres, and when the fuel looked very low he circled the airfield, and when it ran out completely and the engine stopped, he made a forced landing on the airfield, and had previously noted the time when the engine stopped.

He made a perfect landing with a dead prop and of course could not taxi back to the hangers. They had to go and tow him in. He thought he had done a good job until he was marched in front of the CO. He then explained that the way to do it, was to fly round until the fuel was low, but not dangerously so, then land, the ground crew top up, measure how much, then calculate from that. Now you will understand my remark, the blind leading the blind. However we did not break any Spitfires.

Referring back to the four phases of the Battle, phase one, when we were instructed to escort ship in the Channel, the first thing we did was to check what signal we had to indicate to them on arrival, so that they would know we were friendly aircraft. This was done by firing a Very cartridge of a certain combination of colours, depending on the time of day.

I soon learnt that one fired the correct colour on arrival, and kept very well away, well out of gun range. These brave mariners took no notice of any signals, if you came within range they opened fire. This included the Navy, at this stage I don't think they had any training in aircraft recognition.

Having been made operational we quickly settled down into a routine, the system was on a four day cycle. Day 1 Stand by, this meant that you must be on the base and available to fly within an hour; Day 2 Available to fly within 15 minutes. This meant you had to be at the flight hut or near enough; Day 3 Readiness immediately available to take off, with parachutes on the wing or in the cockpit, depending on the weather; Day 4 Stand down, this condition meant you could leave the base with permission from the flight commander. However he had to maintain a full flight of operational pilots. This day could also be used for training.

This routine, in practice, went by the board. At the height of the battle (third phase) in August and September even from 'stand down' you could find yourself 'available' and actually airborne within half an hour.

One day we were 'scrambled'. That was the jargon of the day for the order to take off. There would be a phone call from our local controller, like, 'Scramble, angels fifteen Portsmouth'. Once in the air the instructions could be altered to suit the changing circumstances. This particular day we finished up over the Channel where a small convoy was being attacked. The water thrown up from the bombs landing round these ships was enough to sink the damn things without a direct hit. As soon as we arrived the bombers quickly turned tail, but that did not stop the trigger happy clots in the ships firing at us.

Over one such convoy in the early days, the CO and Pilot Officer Charles Davis caught some Ju 87s dive-bombing a similar convoy. The CO got one and Davis three, some people are lucky, it must have been like duck shooting. The Ju 87s were withdrawn from this area, they were only effective when there was no opposition. Just my luck, I never ever saw one. This phase in the Channel lasted long enough for us to know we needed air sea rescue.

My first shooting encounter with the enemy was over Weymouth, a flight of us (six aircraft) were scrambled to engage a force of hostile aircraft. We made contact about 15,000 feet above Chesil beach, there were six Me 110s. The flight commander ordered us into line astern, ready to attack. As he started to attack the most rear aircraft in their formation, the others went into line astern. Now, as I was, to put it very crudely, 'arse end Charlie' of our formation, the leader of theirs was forming the circle behind me. So, I broke formation, did a very steep turn in utter panic, and managed a frontal attack on the leading aircraft. I could see my tracer bouncing off his starboard wing, we were on a collision course and he chickened out and pulled up above me at the last moment. Even now, when I think about it I break out into a sweat.

It is quite strange that I fired my first shots on the Chesil beach, and my first shots in anger were directly above. I must mention here that we had a mix of bullets in the gun harness, ordinary, armour piercing and incendiary, it was the latter which I could see bouncing.

Later I learned that a bullet had gone through my port wing between the engine and the oil tank. It was taken away for repair at a maintenance centre to be fixed. I flew it again about ten days later, and encountered a hail storm, it stripped all the paint off the repaired wing, obviously someone had missed out a process of undercoat, I felt very naked with one bright wing.

Our living arrangements at Middle Wallop were quite reasonable for wartime standards, we were in a brick built building of the sergeants' mess. However, because of the sudden influx of sergeant pilots, we were two or three to a room. This did give rise to a little mental pressure when one of your roommates failed to return from a mission. I just do not know how those people fighting on the ground with their mates being killed around them, could ever sleep again. At least our battlefield was clean in seconds. I suppose it's every man to his trade.

The sergeants' mess food was excellent, and equal in every way to that of the officer pilots. Obviously we did not enjoy the same degree of service and mess etiquette was most strongly imposed by the station warrant officer. We had a bar, the beer was at very near cost price, and we only paid a very reasonable amount for the extra services for the manpower employed. The station warrant officer was strict on all discipline, and was also feared by the junior officers, he would report them for not correctly returning a salute. We drank off the station when time permitted, so as to avoid his wrath if we committed a minor misdemeanour.

Mark you, from my experience, the behaviour in the sergeants' mess, was most likely to be of a higher order than that in the officers' mess, where the CO and the adjutant were in charge. The station CO had to rely upon the station warrant officer for the main discipline, there were more troops than officers, so SWO had to be most firm. I received this extra training early, because eventually, before being injected with blue blood, I was a warrant officer.

Mixed social life in the sergeants' mess was very limited, the married regulars who lived out, were invited to bring their wife, and mature children to a party once a month. The officers had their dining-in night, and the occasional mixed do.

At Middle Wallop at this time was 'Cats Eyes' Cunningham's night flying squadron. They originally flew Blenheims, but progressed to Beaufighters. They took over from us when darkness fell, they also took over our R/T frequency, mark you, they could only operate four aircraft at one time, because there were only four friendly signalling segments available.

During the day, each squadron in our wing of four, could be controlled with a segment each. This friendly signalling device, of fifteen seconds to each unit, with automatic R/T transmission, enabled the radio stations to monitor our positions, and distinguish friend from foe. This information, coupled with his radar information, gave the controller a fairly good idea of the situation. Setting this automatic friendly device in the cockpit, with a precise count down from the controller, to a pre-selected pilot, is not to be undertaken when the squadron is climbing in formation through cloud. Both jobs require undivided attention.

These combined systems were so precise, that with a really slick team on the ground, which of course included the WAAF operators moving the symbols on the ops table, the controller could tell you which way to look for the main force of attackers, but also warn you of higher and to the rear, together with approximate numbers.

Our radios were push button type, pre-set. There were five or six buttons. I think four of them were squadron frequencies and the forward one for MAYDAY calls only. Obviously this frequency was manned continuously, you gave your call sign, if you had time and said mayday three times, then offered up a prayer. There was no point in using this facility if you were over land, but more often than not we were over the sea, not very far out, but too far to swim.

It must be appreciated that at this time the air sea rescue service had not been developed, we took pot luck with whatever the coast guards could muster. We had a small dinghy in our parachute pack, and even if you were all in one piece when you dropped in 'the drink' (the sea) it was not easy to get into the thing, oh yes, and also a marker dye. All good and well to see when it was calm, otherwise it was the needle in the haystack trick.

One day about this time in July, one of our pilots was shot down, and baled out into the sea, someone registered the rough location. The CO obtained permission to look for him. In the same location was a German seaplane, looking for any of their pilots who had ditched, the CO ventured too close to it and it shot him down. Now he was so low there was nothing he could do except force land in the sea. I think he must have undid his safety harness before landing, because he was thrown out, he caught the top of the screen, and it made a mess of his face. Fortunately, a small Navy vessel saw him go in and picked him up, there was no news of the original casualty.

At this time we alternated between our base at Middle Wallop, and Warmwell. RAF Warmwell was a grass airfield just outside Weymouth. This was of course nearer the frontline line so to speak, in practice it gave us very little advantage, because all the enemy were coming in at between fifteen and twenty thousand feet. Still if some had tried to sneak in at low level we would have been there.

A typical day for us would be, report to the flight hut on the airfield half an hour before dawn. We would be allocated an aircraft, we had our own mostly, but servicing upset this sometimes. We would put our parachutes in the cockpit or on the wing, don our Mae Wests, then return to the Nissen hut, which was mainly full of beds, lay down and wait. If you had no feelings you could sleep!

The main trouble was the phone, this was manned by an erk, he was our communication link with the controller, and all and sundry on the station. So the damn thing would ring for things like, permission granted for someone to carry out a test flight, then maybe a time check, change of duties etc., until you got to the stage when you said sod the thing, I am going to sleep. Then it would ring again and the erk would shout, 'Squadron, scramble, angels fifteen Portsmouth.' He would also run outside and ring a bell, as a signal for the ground crews to start engines.

We would dash out to our aircraft, the engines would burst into life, and as we put on our parachutes the fitter would get out of the cockpit, then stand on the wing ready to help strap us in after we had donned our helmet which had been draped over the control column, wave chocks away, and move off.

Invariably we could take off straight away as the flight hut was located on the east side of the airfield. However, if the wind was strong from the east we had to taxi to the opposite side of the airfield before taking off. It was a glorious sight to see twelve aircraft taking off, although I must confess I always felt vulnerable until I had the wheels up and the cockpit hood closed.

The CO would waggle his wings, to get the two flight commanders to form up either side of him, at the same time climbing on a course for Portsmouth. The respective numbers two and three in each section would form up in line astern, then the final section (Yellow) would tag on behind, making a neat pack of twelve.

We would climb through cloud in this formation. The CO did the instrument flying, the two flight commanders holding V formation on him, and the rest of us in tight formation line astern, no problem when you get used to it. This was all done in silence. The controller would come through to the CO and pass on any further instructions.

As soon as we broke cloud Yellow section would break formation to do some gentle weaving about so as to ensure no one jumped us from the rear. Yellow section was the domain of sergeant pilots and it was known as the weaving section. As a matter of interest the other sections were, CO's Red, and the others Blue and Green.

At this time, through the controller one of us would set the auto friendly signal, and we were all set. We did not always make contact with the enemy, sometimes they would veer away and attack further east, or just push off. Some were just nuisance raids, but the tempo was being stepped up, and each time the ratio of the bombers was being increased, not to any great extent initially, a couple of dozen bombers with about a hundred mixed fighters was a nasty combination.

When we did make contact the CO would radio 'Tally ho', that was the time to turn the firing button to fire, then wait for the CO to put us into a position to attack. Now, being in the weaving section this made Yellow section most vulnerable. However, after the initial attack, we always tried to have a go at the bombers, there was all hell let loose, fighter aircraft all over the place. We were usually outnumbered by four to one, in a way this was not a bad thing, we had more targets than they did.

It was on one such encounter over Portland Bill, and we were operating out of Warmwell that day, we met a mixture as described, and I was having a squirt here, and a squirt there, and looking over my shoulder at the same time. With these fights I always kept in the thick of it, I never went looking for stray lame ducks to shoot down, that was the most dangerous area, the German aces picked their victims on the fringes.

Then I had a squirt and my guns made a funny noise, I was out of ammunition, to say I was panic stricken would be putting it mildly. I just turned upside down and went straight down with full throttle, when I felt safe I tried to come out of the dive, I pulled on the control column, and all that happened was that the aircraft went even steeper. Now it is written in the pilot's notes that under no circumstances are you to use the elevator trim to recover from a dive. Portland Bill was coming up fast, I can draw a picture of it to this day.

So I said sod the book, I am out of control, I wound the trim wheel back, pulled hard on the stick, there was a Christ-almighty bang and I was flying straight and level. The only thing was I could not see out, the seat was below the level of the cockpit, so I pulled on the lever that controls the height of the seat, let go when it was at the correct height, and promptly descended to the base of the cockpit again. The ratchet on the seat mechanism was not functioning. This made the aircraft very difficult to fly, I could not see forward. Anyway, I made my way back to Warmwell, did a circuit and landed with a little difficulty, with my head well back I could just see about thirty degrees to the line of flight, I taxied as near as I dare to the dispersal area, then shut off. With great relief I clambered out of that Hurricane.

Subsequently I heard that one of the erks had seen me come round and land, and of course he could not see me, my head was too low. He evidently said, 'Cor blimey there's one of the bloody things coming back on its own.'

The flight sergeant told me the seat ratchet was broken, the panel below the cockpit was stove in, and he did not know why I had not gone clean through the floor. After that my bursts of fire were very short and sharp in such encounters.

I notice from my log book that my first operational flight was on 3 July, and on 17 July I was involved in four operations, there are however three entries missing in this period.

10 René Mouchotte Part 1, Hurricane Pilot, Flying Officer, French, 615 Squadron

First of two extracts from *The Mouchotte Diaries 1940–1943*, first published in France in 1949 and translated into an English edition in 1956. René Mouchotte, born in Paris in 1914, was a pilot in the French Air Force and was stationed in French Algeria in North Africa when France capitulated on 17 June 1940. This extract covers 17 June to 3 July 1940 and details Mouchotte's epic escape together with fellow pilots Henry Lafont and Charles Guérin from Algeria via Gibraltar and on to England. All three Frenchmen would fight in the Battle of Britain. Mouchotte was a French patriot who decided at great risk to himself to defy the Vichy regime, who had ordered all those in the French forces to lay down their arms when France capitulated.

Chapter 1: Oran, June 1940 [17 June 1940, French Oran, North Africa] I have just heard the incredible news of the capitulation on the radio. The thing is so inconceivable that you boggle at it, shattered, imagining all manner of things – a nightmare, a mistake, enemy propaganda – to try and efface the horrible reality. The wretched radio completely shattered our over-strained nerves by sounding forth a ringing *Marseillaise*, the last call of a France that yesterday was free.

I cannot remember ever feeling anything so intense and sad. I wanted to run, to show everyone I still had the strength and energy to go on fighting. France must always be France. Her heart still beats in spite of those who want to kill her without letting her struggle. I was possessed by a huge disgust for the twenty years since 1918, when our politicians showed the world their squabbling and incapacity.

Today is the reckoning for them. Why did our elders fight if not for honour and peace? Yet from 1919 onwards steps were taken to see that the 'last-war soldiers' had no right to a voice in the councils of the nation. The embarrassing folk who had died a thousand deaths for four years to keep their native land free were thrust aside. How could they have foreseen such sabotage of their victory?

Four o'clock It isn't possible. Our spirit is coming back. France can't be beaten like this, even if she has been the victim of saboteurs and traitors. Thank God there are active men who still have faith and courage. Many will arise to revive the spirits who fail at the sight of shameful examples...

North Africa will break away from metropolitan France. Armed, she will stand firm. What will be the terms of the armistice they have announced? Who can we believe now? They seem to be using Marshal Pétain, that living legend, as a banner. He was appealed to when the situation was obviously desperate. Is what he is going to tell us to do what his French heart really implores him to say?

18 June France surrenders: her army, her navy, her air forces. General Noguès has just issued a rousing appeal to the troops in North Africa. A little hope. No other news. I haven't much faith. What will happen to England?

19 June I haven't been in action yet. Not because I haven't the skill; I have enough flying hours. Others with less have been fighting since September. Nor because I'm in love with being grounded; I've put in three applications to go, which resulted in my being posted – after five months of war – to the course of higher training for instructors. I've been an instructor. Impossible to get out of the toils. Yet I have got something out of it: *my pupils have taught me to fly.* Then Avord was bombed. Everything destroyed. We moved to a château. Night and day we hunted intangible parachutists.

Guérin and I received orders to go back to Algeria. At Marseille we learned that we were being posted to Algiers as instructors on twin-engined machines. The end of our hopes of going to the front on fighters. We were furious.

We decided to risk it. After all, there was a war on. The only fighter instruction unit in North Africa was at Oran, the fighter springboard. We had to pass out there to make our dream come true. Without tampering too much with our posting orders (we could use our colonel's name: Avord was no more), after many verbal assertions, the Marseille area commander sent us off to Oran. What a day that was! We were no longer instructors. But what sort of a welcome awaited us in Oran where we were not expected? For once the breakdown of the French staff was on our side. Not only did Oran accept us when we landed as fighter pilots in training but Algiers never claimed us.

Yet it was written that we should not fly.

20 June So North Africa is not putting up a fight. But why do so many planes from France crowd our aerodrome? There are a thousand today, jammed wing to wing. Some take off for the south, others land direct from France, some vainglorious, some damaged, to take shelter. Or have they had orders to go far away to Southern Tunisia to be put out of action?

Our squadron leader has just sent for us to appeal to our sense of discipline and resignation. How very wretched the man was! It was hard for him to find words to express what he didn't believe. We sensed an appeal in his eyes, like hope. Perhaps I am not the only one who is thinking of a different future than the one they are preparing for us.

I mean to go to England. Since my country has rejected me as a combatant I will fight for her in spite of her and without her.

I have just been to see Colonel de Fond-Lamotte. He is a tough last war veteran with thirty two wounds, twenty seven of which could have killed him. 'Steel-all-through' is his nickname, because of the platinum 'extras' skilful surgeons have fitted into his body to replace broken bones. He always volunteers for dangerous missions and still flies, despite his age.

I was sure he would see me and understand. I found him in front of a hangar.

'We must clear out, my boy, and I'm taking those with guts.'

'But where to, colonel?'

'Come and look at the map with me.'

I was unlucky; two majors came up to talk to him. The three of them went away, leaving me alone and disappointed.

Charles Guérin came to me, too, to confide that he wanted to go. I am glad he shares my feelings. Damn you, Charley, you and I were born to follow one another. We swore not to escape without each other.

A succession of news items from France, each more worrying than the last. And my poor dear little mother, always so uneasy about your son, what dreadful ordeals are you going through at such a time? Should I succeed if I tried to rejoin her? Won't France become a second Czechoslovakia, her young people mobilized to work in German camps and factories? What a dilemma.

My poor little mother, how I hate these savages. The thought that they might touch a hair of your head makes my blood boil. I have a calm, mild nature but I have not been myself for over a week. I dream only of fighting, of shooting down some of these Boche vermin. *I see red,* as they say; my life no longer matters to me. Only on the day when I kill my first Boche shall I be able to congratulate myself that I have followed my destiny.

I have made up my mind. I am going to England, or Malta, or Egypt; I don't know when, where or how, but I shall never contemplate remaining under the orders of Franco-Boche authority. Maybe in the future we shall know the truth about these painful days we live in. I want to be one of those who will chastise the men responsible for this war, for justice will inevitably be done. That same harsh justice will punish those who have now surrendered France while she could still fight, who abase themselves before the invader, and hand over, despite itself, the nation which was entrusted to them. The propaganda is filtering through even here; many are already turning their backs on England, their former ally, to blame her for the catastrophe. That is enough about that. It hurts too much. *I've got to get away.*

When I woke this morning I learned of a plane escaping with three men on board. Yesterday two succeeded in getting away. The commanding officer at Oran has decided to stop any further attempts. A Germano-Italian commission is arriving in a few days. The clauses of the armistice will have to be respected. The government has given strict orders that no unit of the naval and air fleets shall go to England. Fear of responsibility? Fear of reprisals? Confusion? Whatever the reason, nothing will excuse the draconian measures that are being taken to prevent Frenchmen avenging their country. I have been back to see Colonel de Fond-Lamotte. He is no longer in command of the station. Significant. Colonel Rougevin Baville has replaced him. He seems even more respectful towards orders received.

I met old 'Steel-all-through' in the corridor.

'Excuse me, colonel,'

He took a good look at me, then, without a word, turned his back on me and went into his office. It was enough. I understood. Poor man.

28 June One day after another. We do nothing. Flying is forbidden. I feel myself more and more a prisoner. The multitude of ultra-modern aircraft spread over the aerodrome looks more like theatrical scenery than the real thing. Charles and I wander about on our own looking for the slightest loophole. There was an unsuccessful attempt this morning: a Bloch 174 bomber, piloted by two youngsters, unluckily crashed while taking off. The imprudent ones were unhurt. It was the first time they had flown that type of aircraft. The commanding officer has gone crazy. He is having the petrol tanks drained, the magnetos removed and the planes locked wing to wing. The ones who escape now will be pretty crafty characters.

Chapter 2: The Flight of the Goéland, 29 June Things are happening fast. Charles and I have decided to go today or tomorrow, for the mechanics are busy draining the petrol from the tanks. We have considered several plans. It would be possible to get to Dakar either by stealing a car or by train. Poles are leaving there for England and it would not be difficult, with their complicity, to get Polish uniform. We settled on another scheme: to escape by plane to Gibraltar or Egypt. An inoffensive Goéland, perfectly camouflaged, bang in the middle of the landing ground, seems to be inviting us to escape.

Guérin knows several pilots who also want to get away. I am afraid that if there are too many of us we shall be risking failure. Our plan is beginning to get even more delicate because I have brought two new recruits to our little group. We have therefore decided, working together, to go in two Goélands, each carrying six men.

Every hour that passes brings new problems. Our objective is settled: Gibraltar. It is the nearest point (about 475 kilometres). We shall have to economize fuel, not being sure of finding full tanks, and we shall consider ourselves lucky if we have enough to reach the Rock (the range of our plane is about 1,200 kilometres).

Will there be an aerodrome to receive us? A transport plane can't land on a pocket handkerchief. But we have resolved to come down in the sea if necessary; that won't stop us. The awkward bit is undoubtedly our getting away from Oran.

The aerodrome looks as if it is under siege. Each plane is guarded by day by an armed sentry. Mechanics are busy draining petrol. Others are working on the batteries and even dismantling propellers. The landing ground and the camp have been invaded by armed men. Finally, they have taken care to barricade the armoury windows.

How slowly the hours of this 29 June 1940, are flying! 11 a.m. Shall we be gone tonight? I never cease mingling the thought of my mother with the act I am about to perform. I do not intend making the slightest modification of what I believe to be my duty but I cannot help thinking that my decision will cause many a tear to the mother I shall not see for months, perhaps for years. My other comrades will be demobilized; soon they will return to France. They will help their families to bear the sufferings of the occupation. What is my duty? To give moral and material help to those I love or attempt a dubious adventure to satisfy an idea of vengeance? Should I be of more use with them or in a fighter? I am not ignorant of my mother's poor health and weak heart. I close my eyes in despair. What would she advise me to do? Would she speak to me as a mother or as a Frenchwoman, if she were at my side? Once I am over there I shall not even be able to write to her… When she no longer has news of me, will she think I am a prisoner, or sick, or dead, perhaps? Poor mother, I'm trying to think how I can let you know. A good friend I knew at Istres, in whom I have great faith, has promised me that when he returns to France he will write to you.

I simply cannot understand our leaders' mentality. We see some dumbfounding things here: it is a question whether the men who command us today still deserve the name of French officers.

A meeting at one o'clock of those who have agreed to escape with Charles and me. My room looks like a headquarters. On the table I have spread a map. We count up and there are fourteen of us! We do not conceal from ourselves that our attempt is a pretty risky one. If we have the luck to get away we shall be the only ones who have done so. Yesterday's two unfortunates are in prison at this moment, waiting to be sentenced by court martial for stealing an aircraft and desertion. Shall we be luckier? Whatever happens we must try, cost what it may, and not let ourselves be influenced by the obstacles that are bound to stand in our way.

We have decided to take two Goélands and a little Simoun. Charley will pilot one Goéland and I the other. We are allotting five passengers to each. Later we will consider the possibility of flying together but it is settled that each crew shall form a unit independent of the other; thus, if one party is caught, the chances of the other will not be prejudiced.

Fayolle will pilot the Simoun, with Sturm. An admiral's son, he is also the grandson of the famous General Fayolle. In my plane I am taking two sous-lieutenants, an infantryman and a cavalryman, deserters some days old who escaped from France in the bunkers of a collier after dodging endless pursuits and stealing a car to reach a port. In his, Guérin will have comrades who are already in his own squadron, whom he has incited to escape with him.

When shall we go? Another meeting at five o'clock.

Each of us has an individual task to fulfil both on his own account and for the team: to see which way the wind is, to find out what the latest measures against escapes are, to be sure of the help of trustworthy friends. As pilot, I have to see to the plane, its position, its working condition, how much fuel it has. One point worries me: starting the engine. A transport plane doesn't start as quickly or as easily as a passenger plane; it is essential to warm up the engines for at least ten minutes before taking off. But there is no question of us doing that. We shall press on. I therefore had to find out as much as I could about starting the engines. Not much success; the mechanics I asked, fighter specialists, did not know the Goéland engine. Impossible to go near the one selected for me. How can I find out if it has petrol?

One of my friends confesses that he has been to see the British Consul in Oran this week. He came back completely discouraged. Far from approving, they painted a grim picture of the existence awaiting him if he succeeded in reaching England. The poor fellow therefore has no further desire to desert. He nevertheless thought it might be useful to let me know that England may not be in the least what we imagine and that it is very likely we may be sent back to France. As deserters our fate would be sealed. Unless they kept us in a prison camp, another charming prospect. It is probable that if we are accepted we shall be left penniless, that we shall not be employed as pilots but used as infantry, etc. On the other hand, he thought that by staying here he would soon be demobilized. I turned my back on him, not wanting to waste any more valuable time. What good could his suppositions do me? Haven't I decided to go? Besides, I feel I shall succeed. I must succeed.

I have just heard that our colonel is calling all the squadrons together at 4.30 to talk to them. I cannot help seeing a connection between this speech and yesterday's abortive escape. Is he going to threaten us and tell us of the latest measures against these untimely flights? A fine time for us…

I met Guérin looking dejected. His Goéland had been moved. They have towed it across the landing ground into a hangar and shut it in. So everything is going against us. How shall we manage to overcome these obstacles? It is lucky, though, that the police have not yet invaded the aerodrome, as an officer gave us to expect yesterday. I went with Charles to look at *my* Goéland. It is still slumbering peacefully there in the middle of the landing ground. As long as it has petrol… How can I find out?

I have decided to take Guérin with me. One of our comrades will give up his place to him. After all, it was we who took the initiative in the escape. It is only fair that he should be in on it. As for the little Simoun, Fayolle has contrived to approach it without being noticed and is radiant with joy. The plane has a full supply of petrol and oil; it asks for nothing better than to leave this unhospitable land.

I have just learned that the training unit is being disbanded in a few days' time. The pilots are being sent to the mountainous region in the south to form youth camps. The Hitler regime is beginning. I must get away, the sooner the better.

We have to go and hear the colonel's speech. Surely it will be about the last untimely departures of planes from Oran. We shall see. We are somewhat uneasy. Have they taken new measures to prevent any attempt at escape? Or are they, on the other hand, trying to appeal to our emotions? The sudden *contretemps* is holding up our preparations. Have our superiors got wind of our project? Why did they move the first Goéland from the landing ground? I am going to have a look at the other. It is still in the same place.

Four o'clock. I have been noting down on paper all the information, fugitive as it is, about the engines and how to start them, details obtained for me by an excellent mechanic whose silence has been assured. As for the state of the fuel, I shall try and get to the Goéland at nightfall. There is no question (on account of the speech) of leaving tonight. Tomorrow morning, which gives us more time to prepare.

The colonel, as we expected, began by talking discipline and good example. Without excessively bemoaning the ordeal of France, he tried to give us a glimpse of the France of tomorrow, built by the resigned youth of the nation, full of prudent courage: work, discipline! He made a savage attack on stupid 'quixotry', the lamentable and cowardly attempts to escape, the work of idle adventurers seeking to avoid the hard work before them. They will go before a court martial charged with stealing military material and with desertion... They will return to France only to be shot; their families and their descendants will suffer the shame of one of their kin being a traitor to his native land, etc.

Will all this discourage certain of our comrades? I suspect some of them of joining our group in an imitative spirit or to boast about having done so, being sure that the attempt will not come off. I admit that so far everything is against us and only boldness can help. The test is hard, our plan flimsy, our chances slender... Guérin met me as I was getting ready to go and examine the tanks of my Goéland. He had come from it and, according to him, had not been seen. He was radiant. It is full up with petrol and oil. Nothing to fear in that respect.

11 p.m. The time for action is near. Fifteen of us gathered in my very small room, talking in low voices by candle-light. We looked like real conspirators. We were divided into three teams: the Goéland team, six; the Simoun team, two. The rest are going to try and get away in an American bomber which is not far from our Goéland. The question before us was whether we should embark tonight or tomorrow morning. Nearly everyone chose tomorrow. I succeeded in convincing my team that it would be wiser to make the attempt tonight. Guérin agrees with me. We are getting ready.

I wrote a letter to a good friend who is staying behind. I charged him to look after my baggage and reminded him once more of his promise to reassure my mother. Poor mother...

We have the password, the position of all the sentries, the time of the rounds, etc. On the landing ground two cars with headlights are plying to and fro in front of the hangars. It will have to be done quickly. We have three revolvers; one never knows, and we are resolved on doing everything to succeed. The die is cast. We count up for the last time. We are off...

The darkness was far from complete. A very light sky. We went forward cautiously, in Indian file, avoiding stones. Five minutes later we entered a danger zone. No more trees, nothing to hide behind, sentries near. We had to cross the embankment of a railway which ran through the camp; this was the difficult bit. Having conferred in undertones, we decided to cross it as quickly and as quietly as possible. The first man went, then the second. My turn. What a racket! The stones clattered noisily; we must have been heard within a 200 metre radius. The moon was shining.

Damnation! A sentry's 'Who goes there?' burst forth less than 20 metres from us. We were flat on our stomachs, behind a bush. One of us, still on the slope, sent stones cascading. We held our breath... The sentry was a native; I gathered that from his accent. We remained there, motionless. The sentry kept equally still. He must have been more scared than we were. Would it be better to spring on him and disarm him, or try to hold him in parley? Five mortal minutes passed. Suddenly more pebbles fell. A metallic noise accompanied them. The sentry had drawn back the bolt of his rifle. We could not stay where we were; he was quite capable of opening fire on us. Just as I was getting to my feet, I heard 'Paris!', the password, spoken by Guérin as he advanced.

'Well, everything all right in this sector? Nothing to report? This is the security patrol. Fine, you're doing a good job.'

His voice may have trembled a little with the recent excitement. During this time, in twos and in step, we passed behind them and made for the hangars.

'Now go and keep a lookout at the other end; there's no sentry down there. Goodnight!'

The trick worked. Revolver still in hand, Guérin rejoined our little group, hidden in the shelter of a hangar. We were still nervous; there were officers on rounds everywhere tonight and the man might tell them his story.

The light vehicles came and went quietly on the landing ground. From time to time the headlights swept the vast field with its hundreds of sleeping planes. Then we heard the sound of the engines die away while from the opposite direction the sound of engines grew louder.

We had to cross this zone and get to our Goéland. We waited for another car to pass and then moved, praying that no sentry might spot us. We were walking exposed and no one could doubt our intentions. We went fast; despite our care the cement rang under our feet. At last there was earth and the first planes' shadows. We went on. The car behind us appeared again, advancing slowly... Should we find our plane easily in the dark? At last we had it before us. Incredibly happy, we climbed in and hastily drew the curtains over all the windows and locked the door. Each in a seat, we tried to get some sleep; unsuccessfully because we all felt too nervous.

Only a quarter of an hour after our arrival came the first alarm. The sound of footsteps. We all lay down flat and held our breath. The sounds came closer. This was it. Voices whispering breathlessly. Our hearts beat an extra pulse. The door was roughly and insistently shaken. Then there was calm again; the footsteps went away. I peeped out and saw three shadows disappearing, carrying suitcases... We were not the only ones intending to depart. Half an hour later and *we* should have found the door locked.

We settled down once more. I shut my eyes. Where should I be tomorrow at this time? Too late to draw back now. Anyway, I didn't want to draw back. Each minute that passed brought me nearer to my departure into exile, a departure considered and willed, the consequences of which I had taken into account. Tomorrow I should be on English soil or I should be dead.

The quarter hours passed slowly. We had fixed the time of departure at 4.30 and it was now 1.00. I wanted to sleep. I could still hear the car engines on the landing ground. From time to time one of them came into the midst of the planes; the headlights swept our machine, lingered an instant, then went to seek elsewhere. I could not stop myself mentally retracing the events, as rapid as they were tragic, which had thrown into confusion and annihilated thousands of lives in the space of a few days. What I was about to attempt this morning, how many other rational beings were not attempting or dreaming of attempting? If I had stayed behind, should I have been able to stand the incessant vexations, obeying each day the orders the Boche gave to humiliate us, witness to the shame and cowardice of a government continually flaunting its arrogance? Eventually seeing France being engulfed little by little beneath the Nazi dust, and watching all this while trying not to react? I could not have done it. The concentration camp awaited me. God, how I should have loved to go to sleep and not wake up till I was in Gibraltar! I felt absurdly apprehensive. I should soon have need of all my resources. Five lives and mine as well to transport far away. As in the dentist's waiting room, I longed for the door to open quickly and be done with it. I looked at my watch every two minutes. Once more the car left the hangars and came close. Once more we came out of our torpor to fling ourselves face down while one stayed by the door with his revolver and I knelt down between two seats to watch, lifting the corner of a curtain. This time the alarm looked more serious, for after sweeping us with its headlights the car drew up barely 30 metres away. Two shadowy figures got out and came towards us. I gave the alarm. All were stiller than stones. I could not stop my heart dancing a mad saraband; I felt its beating must be audible. The shadows were certainly heading for us. There was no doubt about it. We were caught.

Our plan had been discovered. Flight? Too late. Defend ourselves? Six against two, we should easily overcome them and then take off in the darkness... Now they were at the door. They knocked. As long as they didn't think of climbing on the wings; the emergency door beside me was not fastened. They shook the door, but it would not open.

'Open up in there!'

We held our breath. Suddenly the beam of an electric torch lit up the interior of the Goéland, through the uncurtained window of the entry. Catastrophe... Overlooking the scene, I saw the beam stop on Sorret's arm and wristwatch. This time the door was shaken roughly and – blessing! – we heard: 'Open up. It's Georges.' It was the friend who had given us the password. He had changed the sentries and had come to give us the latest tips. We could have embraced him in our joy. Delightful to stretch one's legs and jump down to the ground for a few moments. Five minutes later we got in again and shot the bolts of our prison. In an hour it would be nearly time to take off. We should need good visibility; fifty planes were drawn up in no particular order around us and it would be preferable not to run foul of them. In case of accident we had planned to make for the other end of the aerodrome, where one of our friends was in command of the guard.

Four o'clock. I got out my bit of paper and, with my fingers over the torch, let through just enough light to spell out what I should soon have to do. The car continued its tireless exercise; twice more it came dangerously near our machine... One of us managed to get to sleep and his regular snores created a sense of security in the cabin. Idiotic!

4.30. The day had not yet broken. A faint light was barely outlined down in the east. Impossible to go yet; it would be stupid to risk an accident by being over precipitate. We must, however, be off about five o'clock, the hour at which the patrols were relieved and the watch on the landing ground became extremely strict. We had no intention of finishing the war in prison. We would leave at 5.50, but we must be able to see to take off. Behind me they were protesting that the time had been fixed for 4.30, the sooner the better. We settled on 4.45, time to get the engines going, which would be perfect. I noticed that as the line of the horizon grew lighter the hangars, which had stood out clearly in the darkness, seemed to be becoming indistinct, so that the contours were barely visible. Mist. We really were in luck. What did it matter how we did it, the great thing was to get away. That was our sole immediate objective. Afterwards, we would see. I got into the pilot's seat. Guérin sat beside me. Off we go!

We thought for a moment. Two engines had to be started. If one were recalcitrant, we were lost. Ah, how gratefully I pay homage to Renault Motors! Petrol, switches, magneto... The starboard engine started. I opened the throttle in order to pull up the flaps, while Guérin braked the port wheel to swing the plane towards the take-off. During this time the port engine started. The terrible noise must have been ear-splitting in the darkness. We learned later that the aerodrome car rushed towards us. The navigation lights blinded us. Without a second's delay I opened the throttles and started the take-off, my two hands clasped round the stick. The engines had to be warmed up for a quarter of an hour before taking off. Too bad. We should see. Fifteen seconds had been enough to start them. Alas! Guérin had braked too much to the left. A bad direction. The speed increased. I saw the shapes of several bombers in front of us, a little to the left... we just scraped past. And the plane was still moving. How long it took! In the dark it is hard to judge. Even so, the engines did not seem to be pulling. What was the matter? The landing ground was enormous but I had the impression we were already at the other end. I pulled the stick back timidly; the plane lifted but fell heavily. Yet it had to be done. I helped it again; we took off. Coming down again, the port wing tip touched down. What now? This was a calamity. I strove desperately with rudder bar and stick, trying to relieve her. We were skirting the great salt lake of the Sebkra. She returned to the horizontal, but with great difficulty. Over my shoulder, Lafont caught the lever of the undercarriage and retracted it. That lightened the Goéland a little. I looked at the rate of climb indicator Hurrah! We were climbing. But what a take-off! I was sweating all over. I coarsened the pitch of my propellers. No change, or only a hundred revolutions less on the rev counter. The plane gained altitude painfully. We circled over the Sebkra in the hope of seeing Fayolle's little Simoun appear. If only they could manage it! Then we headed for the sea. I had great difficulty in gaining altitude; each time my rate of climb indicator showed plus one or plus two, my airspeed indicator immediately dropped to 120. I got it up to 130, 135, but to do so I had to put the rate of climb at zero or minus a half. What was not working? The engines were going well. I tested the propeller pitch control. They answered well, but each time without much change on the rev counter. Suddenly I understood. Our plane had been visited by the sentry. Instead of emptying the petrol tanks, they had simply *put the propellers out of order*. This criminal act nearly cost us our lives. Our Goéland, loaded with six passengers, had taken off at coarse pitch when at fine pitch it would already have been a near thing. It was as if one had expected an overloaded car to start in top gear. How had we done it? A miracle! The darkness was less thick. Behind us the day was breaking slowly. Many little efforts got the plane up to 800 metres. A heavy mist hid the ground details. But we preferred to fly over the sea, the anti-aircraft batteries on the coast being wicked and numerous. Were we not deserters now? Deserters! That would have made me want to laugh, if my nerves had not been so strained. I went on gaining height, still very painfully. The cruising speed of the Goéland was 220 kilometres an hour. We were doing 120. Slower than a tourist machine. Anyway, the great thing was to reach Gibraltar.

My right hand went instinctively to the propeller pitch control. I came to the conclusion that the propellers were nearly fully feathered, that is to say, in the position of propellers turning at engine speed but without producing a useful effort: the plane became a glider. I could not bless Providence enough. How did we escape being smashed at the take-off? How did the machine, overloaded as it was, contrive to stay in the air when I had torn her off the ground at such impossibly low speed? It really was a miracle. I tremble when I think of the frightful second when the wheels had left the ground and I felt the plane sink after the determined lift and then, despite my efforts, drag to port while I was tensely holding my stick and rudder bar to starboard. The darkness made the thing more dramatic. I distinctly remember having a vision of crashing. Luckily I had told little Lafont to stand behind us; his weight in the tail of the machine might have been fatal.

What a strange sensation that ascent into the night was! The sky was full of stars, in which we seemed to swim in unreality. My shirt was soaked, I was dazzled by the instrument panel light, with only my instruments to guide me: I acted more or less as an automaton, only my reflexes working for me. Then suddenly I roused out of my torpor. I saw the end of the immense salt lake of the Sebkra. Here was the sea. Our joy burst out at last and we all sang in chorus, howling as loud as we could, almost breaking our voices: 'Four o'clock in the morning, tomorrow already and the day is breaking!' If old Lyne Clevers had heard us singing one of her hits! Sorret told us that just as we left he had seen through the window the aerodrome car coming full speed at us, headlights fixed fiercely on the fleeing bird. They saw a lovely take-off... As long as they hadn't sent any planes in pursuit. At the speed at which we were going they would soon have caught up with us. I would rather have landed in Spanish Morocco than have gone back. I looked at Guérin out of the corner of my eyes, seated next to me; he had his eyes closed, exhausted. I sent him to go and sleep in a seat at the back. I looked at the map. Heavens, how slowly the coast was passing! We were about 30 kilometres out to sea.

I preferred to take the short cut and leave the coast of Spanish Morocco well to port. The altimeter rose painfully. A layer of transparent mist covered the sea and the shore. I dared not think of fog. It would surely vanish when the sun was up.

I had the impression of living in a dream, a wonderful dream. So destiny was on our side: all those obstacles overcome, that mad departure. We should soon be in Gibraltar. We should land without accident. I visualized our arrival in England, my battles as a fighter pilot. I foresaw my success everywhere, my return to a France delivered from the oppressor. Why not? Is not success a question of will-power... and a bit of luck? The take-off and the flight had proved that luck was with me; it would not abandon me. Nothing would stop me accomplishing what I had marked out for myself.

The sun was on the point of rising. To port we saw the great Tres Forcas peninsula.

Lafont wanted to take photographs. He asked Guérin to return to my side. Now the sun was rising. 'Smile please, gentlemen!' We turned round. Click! The snapshot was taken. After the crew the passengers, then Spanish Morocco. What a souvenir if the negatives were all right!

We had now been flying for over an hour. We flew horizontally, which gave me a speed of 130 kilometres, according to our airspeed indicator. Not much, but we were in no hurry. No one was expecting us! I was dreadfully hungry. We had climbed to 2,000 metres. I considered it useless to reach a higher ceiling. It had taken fifty laborious minutes to attain that altitude. Well, there we were, but alas I had other things to worry me. Far from vanishing, the mist had grown thick enough to hide the sea and the coasts of Africa beneath us altogether. I therefore kept faithfully to my course. Only the Balearic Isles, very far to the north, were visible. It was a problem to know whether this thick compact white cloud went down to ground level or whether, once we were down through it, we should have enough altitude to navigate. At present only the Balearics and a faint shadow of the Spanish coast served as landmarks. Never mind. We should see.

Another thing was rather alarming, too. My petrol gauges instead of showing less, showed more! There even came a moment when the needle on the dial passed the 'full' and went back to 'empty'. Gauges out of order. At any moment I expected to hear the fatal splutter of the engines, then the silent descent, down through that accursed cotton cloud... Then the open sea... I smiled, not seeing myself swimming dozens of kilometres. What a grand splash we should make for the entertainment of the Spaniards! ... 'The six French deserters, avid for heroic adventure, ended their epic wretchedly in a Spanish gaol.' But the engines were still going full blast.

My passengers were quiet enough. They did not guess the bizarre thoughts passing through my head. Perhaps they thought themselves on a regular Air France flight. I was thinking of my mother. If only she were aboard with me. I should be so much reassured then than by knowing she was in that hostile country. But I do not know that she would feel very reassured up here with me...

We could not be far from Gibraltar now. I never stopped looking at the map. The Balearics were unmistakably north-north-east of us; ahead was mist. The same to port. If it had been clear we should have had the famous Rock in sight long ago. In flying through the mist we must not crash on it. Ten more minutes went by and suddenly I thought I could pick out, just ahead, cloud of a different kind. It no longer had that uniform, cotton-ish consistency but revealed deeper crevasses of less regular and darker colour. It might be that the sea stopped here. It could be the North African point of the Straits of Gibraltar. I had to make up my mind: the invisible Rock inspired mistrust. I turned about fifty degrees to starboard and we were on our way down. The delicate moment had come. If only I had made no error in my navigation! The cloud drew close. We were at only 900 metres. I slowed down the engines a little. An instinctive and useless action, but it would not do to neglect anything. Six hundred metres... 500... 450... We were in the cloud now. The bank was not too thick. But oh, miracle! Gibraltar, the magnificent Rock, rose up there before us, five or six kilometres away. It was planted there, its summit hidden in the clouds. We should have shouted 'Alleluia'.

The end was attained. Emotion choked me. We wanted to throw ourselves into each other's arms. But the surprise had been too sudden; our reaction was numbed. We were flying at about 250 metres above the waves. We were going in. To port I saw a destroyer, across whose course we were cutting. I thought it wise to show our friendly feelings by putting down my undercarriage and waggling my wings a little. Then, for greater security, I swung away slightly and left the ship well to port. Only too clearly I recalled the anti-British propaganda which had broken out in the Germano-French press as soon as the Armistice was signed. That campaign is still going on, incidentally, so much so that some people envisage the possibility of war between France and Great Britain. My measures of caution, if taken in a somewhat ironic spirit, were none the less excusable. I accentuated the waggling of my wings to show my markings clearly, for the Rock was getting close. We were less than 100 metres above sea level. I raised the engine speed to the maximum, which gave me 150 kilometres an hour. I was looking greedily at the celebrated and menacing Rock, for I knew its reputation for formidable defences. We were very close now. We soon passed its huge spur. I had little time to examine it, which I regret. We flew parallel with the cast flanks of the Rock. Huge cemented walls, almost vertical, sank into the sea, probably to make access on this side more difficult. We flew along the vast fortress at less than 100 metres. Suddenly it broke, as if split by a sword, and gave place to a level shore. This part of the peninsula is flat and only a few metres above sea level. I knew the Spanish frontier was close. Once over the wall, the frontier of the two countries was the first thing I looked for. I soon spotted it. It took the form of a line of barbed wire. To avoid it I had to turn steeply, and my sick Goéland was very heavy. I had not the slightest desire to die from a Spanish bullet.

So far the English had given no indication that they were aggressive and I could disregard Spanish hostility. I turned timidly, but I felt a heavy, heavy machine. We were perhaps overloaded. However, the turn to port was made, steeply enough, and we passed just above the top of the wire. All was well, or at least so I thought, but Jimmy told me later that he had clearly heard machine-gun fire. Joy! Flying along the diabolical wire I saw a splendid race course with – stupefying! – a huge white 'T' indicating the direction of the wind and an immense white circle in the middle. Had they turned their race course into an aerodrome just for our benefit? What a good augury! We did not hide our delight. We continued the turn, hesitant and very timid, making a wide circle above the roads. I noticed I was losing more and more height and we scraped over the masts of a multitude of ships. My kite was not one of the most reassuring and I was not to be at my ease until shortly afterwards, when I had a good hot cup of tea in front of me. My wide turn had taken me well out and gave me time to regain 50 metres on the new direct course. If I fluffed the landing, should I have enough power to take off again? I approached the race course, and from where I was it looked terribly tiny. I concentrated hard. I put my flaps down rather soon; I prefer it that way. But it made me lose altitude too fast. A big burst from the engine; the plane was dragging; I was getting near the limit. I cut down the speed. In spite of my concentration on the landing, which went off very well, I noticed hundreds of English soldiers to right and left, running and waving wildly. But our eyes were also drawn to three or four French planes whose tricolour markings rejoiced our hearts. So others had preceded us? There were people here to expect us and greet us. Our nerves relaxed. Cries of joy filled the plane, all the louder because the engines were running quietly. Once we touched down I braked, lightly at first, then increasing the pressure. The plane stopped in the white circle in the middle of the landing ground. There is no doubt about it: the Goéland is a marvellous aircraft. M. Renault and his engineers are entitled to my eternal gratitude.

From habit, I turned to port. They were waving a little red flag there. As I taxied along I could not help being delighted by the exquisite sensation of being bounced by the slight shock of the wheels on the grass. Guérin pointed out a French airman on my right. I opened a panel. There were welcoming shouts of 'Cheerio!' coming towards us. I manoeuvred the plane into position and then, once the propellers had stopped, there was a rush to the door to see who would be first to set foot on the soil of Gibraltar. It made me forget to turn off the petrol, to turn off the switches, magnetos and main switch, to turn off the navigation lights, to close the circuits, to lock the controls; my flaps were left down. I rushed like my pals but, being the furthest forward, I was last out. A crowd of soldiers surrounded us. There were handshakes, great smacks on the back. What big, kind fellows they were! They fought to offer us the first cigarette. There must have been fifty of them at least. One came forward with a notebook to write down our names. Another collected cameras. A third asked for our guns. They could not help smiling at the sight of the positive arsenal we pulled out of our pockets: revolvers of all types, pistols of every calibre, and I had a retrospective thought of the lovely scrap there would have been if anyone had caught us in Oran. We had all been resolved to sell our lives dearly rather than let ourselves be stupidly ensnared into finishing the war in a cell or in front of a firing squad.

Chapter 3: Gibraltar, 3 July 1940 Here we are, aboard a small ship which might at first sight pass for some sturdy, inoffensive cargo steamer but which, to us who are in her, turns out to be almost as heavily armed as a naval patrol vessel. Crammed with mines, it has six machine guns, two guns, and its hold is stuffed with ammunition. This is comforting when one considers the value of the bait the convoy offers to the enemy's unholy desires. We are sailing in a convoy of twenty-one ships which ours, the *Président Houduce*, is escorting, together with an English destroyer.

What a feeling of well-being I have as I lean on the poop rail, fascinating by the water sliding along the hull! My heart is prey to uneasiness about the dark and uncertain future, but my body is relaxing lazily from an over powerful effort. I am remembering…

Once the formalities were over, our first need was breakfast. Kindly Tommies took us to the officers' mess, where we had a royal reception. We were so hungry that we postponed the indispensable wash. Our exhaustion and our plans were forgotten; we were nothing but poor creatures fascinated by the lavishly loaded table. Ah! We did not have to wait to satisfy our desires. Soft-boiled eggs, fried eggs, bacon, toast, jam, all in abundance. Never have I found these simple dishes so attractive.

One thing struck us, though it did not astonish us: the difference between the country we had just left and this one. In the former there was quietude akin to indifference, then the surprise of alarm, and lastly bewilderment, dejection and degrading submission. Here there were young men with open, smiling faces, sure of their strength, with confidence in their leaders, ardent, and able to find words of comfort for the friends who had sought them out.

The mess president was quite young. He spoke a little French; our flight had aroused his enthusiasm. A car came for us. Destination? The Admiralty.

Our drive through the town attracted the attention of swarms of people. News of the arrival of a French aircraft had travelled as fast as a lighted train of gunpowder. Arms waved. We had to salute, smile back. France, after all, was still France.

If the population was curious to see us, we were no less so to admire the town, seven-tenths of the population of which are Spanish, the rest English: soldiers, sailors and officials. Fortification walls everywhere, blocks of concrete crowned with iron teeth. On all sides a tangle of barbed wire, deep trenches crossed by frail foot bridges. Tank traps here. A concentration of anti-aircraft guns there. New discoveries every moment, but we never tired of admiring the rigid discipline of the troops, grimly devoted to their orders. It is this respect for law and order, this love of tradition, this confidence in her own strength that multiplies Great Britain's power tenfold. The Rock, in a way, is the symbol of English unity. Each man seems to be doing his duty, and more. A lorry full of soldiers came towards us; hands waved. '*Vive la France!*'

Three times we were stopped and each time a secret password cleared our way. A formidable studded door halted us for some minutes. This was the sanctuary of the Admiralty. Docks and courtyards flanked by severe buildings, a quay. The roads appeared. I had more time to admire them now than from my Goéland. Packed with naval units. There was an aircraft carrier. I learned it was the famous *Ark Royal*, supposed to have been sunk by the Boche!

We were in the corridors of the Admiralty. Vague uneasiness. What sort of reception would they give us? I remembered the words of the British Consul in Oran: concentration camp, return to France, etc... Who could prove we came in good faith? One thing tormented me: had the French Consul in Gibraltar enough influence to cause French pilots who landed here to be handed over to him? If so, I would escape to Portugal. One more escape, more or less...

All the corridors in the world are designed to keep wretched visitors waiting for long hours. This one kept up the tradition. No sound in the building. Officers in shorts and shirts passed, silent as shadows. The sun had come out. It must have waited for us to land, confound it! It was almost too warm. At last a door opened. We went in. To our stupefaction, two French officers rose as we entered. A captain and a commandant. The latter took the initiative in questioning us.

Hair cut short, rectangular head, eyes that seemed to shoot at us, so hard they were. On his feet, he seemed immense. A curt, harsh voice. He wasted no words. Hands behind his back, his rapid questions exacted rapid answers. Where do you come from? How many of you are there? Who took the initiative in escaping? The captain wrote swiftly. I looked at Charles. Like me, he had been seized by a terrible doubt: had we fallen out of the frying pan into the fire? Sweat damped my forehead. Stupor possessed us, making our answers awkward and often incoherent. Now he was taking our names, our papers; now he set about each of us individually. All the agony and despair of the last twenty-four hours were laid bare before this man, not a muscle of whose face showed his feelings. Not a word came from his mouth that might enable us to guess what fate awaited us. He let us talk, his eyes boring into us. Finally, when Jimmy, who was last, had ended his story, which, like the rest of us, he had tried to cut as short as possible, an amazing and unforeseeable miracle took place. The commandant's face lost its savage look, his eyes softened and a smile lighted up the severe prosecutor's face.

'Boys' he said 'what you have done is all the better for being difficult and dangerous. You were on the horns of a tragic dilemma. Your affections your families, the interests, perhaps, of a whole life, opposed themselves to your duty. You made the choice…'

His voice was rapid, abrupt, but the tone was fatherly. He himself had deserted a few days before. He was going to join General de Gaulle in England. *This was the first time we heard General de Gaulle mentioned.* We knew vaguely that he existed and what he had done, so we were eager to know what he was like. At every sentence he spoke, multitudes of questions were on our lips, and little by little, patiently, he slaked our thirst. Now we knew under what leader we were to be the first legionaries.

Suddenly there was a droning in the air. A plane… French, perhaps? Then we thought of our comrades in Oran, those in the little Simoun, de Joffre and Fayolle, whose absence was worrying us. Then there was silence again and once more our questions poured forth. Others had landed before us. Some young pilots with barely thirty flying hours had escaped in a Morane 230. Others, under the fire of the police, had dived into the water and boarded a Polish ship as it sailed. A sergeant major, revolver in hand, with a few men, had seized a military vehicle and, after endless wanderings in southern France, succeeded by a miracle of boldness in getting aboard a tiny collier. Two pilots, flying to Gibraltar in a grounded plane, had come down in the harbour, not having seen the racecourse. What emotion when they found themselves received by two French officers! Like us, they had thought they were in the snare. How many heroic acts there had been, performed by many who fell, but the survivors knew the joy of having fought to remain free and French.

One question burned on my lips.

'Can we hope to fly with our English comrades in the RAF?'

The reply was reassuring. We were expected in England, where everything was ready for our rapid training on English planes. Our delight turned into enthusiasm when, after a bustle in the corridor, we saw our two friends Fayolle and Sturm come in. We surrounded them and bombarded them with questions. The commandant had hard work to restore calm. Something rather amusing had happened to them. They had first intended to escape in a Glenn Martin, a difficult business, for it is a ticklish aircraft to handle, especially for people who know nothing about it. But the luck of the draw had decided it so, just as it had decided that two of our other comrades should take off in the Simoun at the same time as ourselves. The fact is that the latter two, whose names I have no desire to remember, although they had contrived, like us, the previous evening to reach their little plane and spend the night on board, experienced such fear of the act and its consequences when they heard us take off that at the very moment when they should have set off, when they had everything on their side, abandoned it like cowards and went wretchedly back to their quarters. I doubt whether they would have made very excellent fighters if they had reached Gibraltar. You can't be lukewarm in this business.

Our take-off had awakened little Fayolle. The time we took to get off the ground made him shiver in his shoes but his fears soon gave way to joy when he saw us succeed. After losing no end of time, he and Sturm managed to get to the aircraft, which was fortunately by a hangar a good distance from the middle. They took off without trouble and reached Gibraltar as if on a pleasure flight. To describe the emotion which gripped us is difficult. We met like brothers after years of separation.

11 Henry Ferriss, Hurricane Pilot, Flying Officer, British, 111 Squadron

Air Ministry & Ministry of Information endorsed BBC radio broadcast by an anonymous RAF fighter pilot in July 1940. The pilot is Flying Officer Henry Ferriss. The combat he describes took place on Wednesday 10 July 1940 when 111 Squadron were flying from RAF Croydon, South London (11 Group).

Born in Lee, London on 1 August 1917, Ferriss joined the RAF in 1937. He was posted to 111 Squadron in 1938. The 10 July was the first 'official' day of the Battle of Britain and the first mass dogfight of over 100 aircraft. Ferriss was a key player in the battle that day. Although the account below doesn't mention it (but fellow 111 Squadron pilot William Dymond in chapter 21 does), 111 Squadron employed what was then a unique tactic. They attacked the enemy bomber formation head-on, en masse. This proved highly effective in splitting up the enemy, forcing them to abandon their bombing run, but required a great deal of nerve and relied on the more experienced members of the squadron. This tactic was used less and less as the experienced members of the squadron were reduced during the Battle to be replaced by inexperienced and less battle-hardened pilots.

Ferriss was KIA less than a month after his broadcast. On 16 August he collided with a Do 17 after making the squadron's signature head-on attack. Neither pilot veared away and both aircraft were destroyed. He is buried in St Mary's churchyard, Chislehurst in Kent. He had shot down 11 enemy aircraft.

I suppose many people who watched the air battle from the shore saw a lot more than I did, although I was in it. As you can imagine, you don't see anything but your own particular part of the show when you are actually fighting.

Our squadron was ordered to fly to the spot where ships were being attacked.

In a few minutes we had reached the scene. We were at 8,000 feet, the clouds were about 2,000 to 3,000 feet above us, and below we saw very clearly a line of ships and a formation of bombers about to attack.

The bombers were between 100 to 200 feet below us. There were twenty-four Dorniers altogether and they apparently intended to attack in three ways. The first bunch of bombers had already dropped their bombs when we got there and the second formation was about to go in. The third wave never delivered an attack at all. It was a thrilling sight I must confess, as I looked down on the tiny ships below and saw two long lines of broken water where the first lot of bombs had fallen.

There were two distinct lines of disturbed water near the ships and just ahead were fountains of water leaping skywards from bombs newly dropped. In a second or two the sea down below spouted up to the height of about 50 feet or more in two lines alongside the convoy.

Our squadron leader gave the order to attack. Down we went. He led one flight against a formation of bombers and I led my flight over the starboard side. It was a simultaneous attack. We went screaming down and pumped lead into our targets. We shook them up quite a bit. Then I broke away and looked round for a prospective victim, and saw, some distance away, a Dornier lagging behind the first formation. I flew after it, accompanied by two other members of my flight, and the enemy went into a gentle dive turning towards the French coast. He was doing a steady 300 miles an hour in that gentle dive, but we overtook him and started firing at him. He was in obvious distress. When fifteen miles out from the English coast we turned back to rejoin the main battle.

I was just turning round when I saw an Me 109 come hurtling at me. He came from above and in front of me, so I made a quick turn and dived after him. I was then at about 5,000 feet and when I began to chase him down to the sea he was a good 800 yards in front. He was going very fast, and I had to do 400 miles an hour to catch him up, or rather to get him nicely within range. Then, before I could fire, he flattened out no more than 50 feet above the sea level, and went streaking for home. I followed him, and we still were doing a good 400 miles an hour when I pressed the gun button. First one short burst of less than one second's duration, then another, and then another, and finally a fifth short burst, all aimed very deliberately. Suddenly the Messerschmitt's port wing dropped down. The starboard wing went up, and then in a flash his nose went down and he was gone. He simply vanished into the sea.

I hadn't time to look round for him, because almost at the precise moment he disappeared from my gun sights I felt a sting in my leg. It was a sting from a splinter of my aircraft, which had been hit by enemy bullets. There were some Messerschmitt 109s right on my tail. Just as I had been firing at the enemy fighter which had now gone, three of his mates had been firing at me. I did a quick turn and made for home, but it wasn't quite so easy as all that. My attacker had put my port aileron out of action, so that I could hardly turn on the left side. The control column went rough on that side too, and then I realised that my engine was beginning to run not quite so smoothly.

There were no clouds to hide in except those up at 10,000 feet and they seemed miles away. Practically all my ammunition had gone, so it would have been suicide for me to try and make a fight of it. All I could hope for was to get back home. I watched my pursuers carefully. When they got near me I made a quick turn to the right and saw their tracer bullets go past my tail. I gained a bit on them and then they overtook me again, and once more I turned when I thought they had me within range. I did that at least twelve times. All the time I was climbing slightly and when I reached the coast I was at 2,000 feet. My course had been rather like a staircase. They had not hit my aircraft after that first surprise attack and finally, on the coast, they turned back.

I went on and landed at my home aerodrome, got a fresh Hurricane, and rejoined my squadron before going on another patrol.

12 Eric 'Boy' Marrs Part 1, Spitfire Pilot, Pilot Officer, British, 152 Squadron

First of four extracts from letters to his father sent 26 March 1940 – 2 December 1940. The first covers 26 March – 29 July 1940 when Marrs flew from RAF Acklington, Northumberland, (13 Group), up to 12 July 1940, thereafter from RAF Warmwell, Dorset (10 Group). The sortie mentioned in the 29 July letter is that flown on 25 July, and 'Jumbo' is Edward Deanesly.

Eric 'Boy' Marrs joined 152 Squadron on 17 March 1940 aged 18. He probably gained his nickname from his relative youth amongst the squadron's pilots. From the very start he kept his father up-to-date with regular letters detailing his progress as a fighter pilot. The dates below are those actually on the letters, but may contain details of sorties flown earlier. The vivid and personal account benefits from their immediacy to the actions, Eric wrote the letters the same day or within a few days of his patrols.

26 March 1940 I have flown at last. On Friday I went off in a Gladiator without any other dual instruction. It is a very easy machine to fly and handles something like the Hinds which I have just been flying. When I have done a certain number of hours on this type I shall go on to Spitfires, and then I shall have to do a number of hours on Spitfires before I become operational on them. I have done about four hours on Gladiators since I started and I like them very much. They are very nippy and maneuverable and are easy to land. Their top speed is supposed to be about 250 mph. Life is quite interesting on the whole, but it ought to liven up soon if the Germans are going to do anything at all.

2 April 1940 I have got on to Spitfires at last. I had my first trip on Sunday and it was rather hectic. They are very sensitive and delicate on the controls at low speeds and after the other aeroplanes I have been flying I found myself being very ham-handed with the controls. Apart from this, they are very nice machines. The view forwards and downwards is not too good but is otherwise excellent, though when coming into land the approach is made with the nose up, and that makes you very blind. A special curving approach is thus necessary, which only leaves you blind for the final hold off. The speed is not noticeable until you get near the ground. On the whole they are very gentlemanly aircraft and the only really bad habit is a tendency to tip up on its nose very easily, on the ground. This necessitates great care in using the brakes. There has been very little excitement here and we are all longing for the sight of a a Hun.

14 April 1940 I am getting on quite well with the Spitfire and have begun learning the methods of attack. These we practise in sections of three on one or three aircraft flying in a steady, straight line. It would be much more amusing if we had a bomber at our disposal on which to practise these attacks, while it did its best to evade us. The bombers, however, have more serious work to do.

21 April 1940 I am nearly up to operational standard on Spitfires having done about 10½ hours on them. Even when one is operational one gets plenty of training and practice flying, and as the Hun seems to be too preoccupied with Norway to do anything about Britain I expect to get in a good deal more practice before I have to fly in earnest.

15 May 1940 Our sector still remains deadly quiet, though we are all at an advanced state of preparedness and ready for anything. I am taking my part in day operations now and have been off on one chase. We were sent about 50 miles out to sea but saw nothing. When you start going out to sea like that, it makes you listen very carefully to your engine.

I have also started night flying. Spitfires are very nice at night as they are very stable machines and can be trimmed to fly hands and feet off. We also have to get up very early to be at readiness an hour before dawn; this works out that we get up at 3.30 about four mornings out of six, and if you have been night flying the night before it means that you get about 1½ to 2 hours' sleep some nights. It is surprising though with what little sleep one can do when the need arises. Besides, our work is not at the moment strenuous.

29 May 1940 I think our squadron will move soon; in fact I am nearly sure it will move soon. We will not be leaving this sector unguarded for another squadron will move in. The southern squadrons, however, cannot carry on indefinitely and our job will be to relieve one of them for a spell. We are supposed to be next on the list for either France or south of England, from where we will guard the evacuation of the BEF or escort bombers.

When the system really gets going there will be a continuous rotation of squadrons to and from the battle area.

9 June 1940 We were left out of the Dunkerque show and have been stuck up here all the time, and very quiet it has been, too. Still, we're bound to be given action some time and the war won't end yet awhile.

Leave has been resumed in the Air Force now for periods of four days. I am due for mine on July 13–16 inclusive. Just time to get down and spend a day in town and a day at Heronden and nip back again.

7 July 1940 I was very interested to hear that Hawkhurst had been bombed and machine-gunned and I'm very glad that worse casualties were not sustained. You mention that no British fighters were around, but they were probably all above the cloud. In these cloudy conditions it is almost impossible to catch these lone raiders. They nip out and in again and don't give one any time to get near them. We are having the same difficulty up here in catching them. One dropped four bombs on Newcastle the other day. There were 15 fighters up at the time but he got away. He could have flown back to Germany in cloud if he had wanted to for that day the cloud went from about 6,000 feet, to 20,000 feet, in several layers which merged into each other in places.

We have been having some work to do these nights, but up to now only two have been shot down in our sector. One by anti-aircraft fire and the other by the other squadron. On Friday night we had a proper go at them. There was however, a general over-excitement of the ground defences, and searchlights and guns were not up to much. Most of our own fighters were fired on and some had a bad time. The guns did, however, get their one enemy aircraft that night. They also received a large and powerful raspberry for firing on us. I was not actually on duty that night, but was aerodrome control pilot and was out on the flare-path all the time. The next three nights they did not visit us again. On the fourth night my flight was on again and I went up this time. The guns and searchlights were, however, too shy this time and they never even picked up a friendly aeroplane, much less an enemy one. We searched and patrolled and did what we could, but unless the searchlights illuminate aircraft for us we are not much use. The next day we had a big conference with searchlight officers from all the sectors round and cleared up many points and questions. That night the other squadron was on. The searchlights were a 100 per cent better and they fixed on a Hun which was promptly shot down. We now feel that with good cooperation between searchlights and fighters we can do fairly well. That happened last night. Tonight we are on again, but it is the other flight's turn.

23 July 1940 There has been quite a lot of enemy activity down here just lately, chiefly against shipping. Our squadron unfortunately has been off duty during most of it. We have, however, had one small engagement, when one section shot down a Ju 88. I myself have not yet been in anything.

29 July 1940 Our squadron had another little engagement some days ago. They came up against some Ju 87s escorted by Me 109s and with a Do 17 as a decoy. I say they because I was unfortunately at breakfast during this show and missed it. They shot down the Do 17, a Ju 87 and the two Me 109s confirmed, with one or two others rather doubtful. We had one pilot, Jumbo, shot down, but he got out all right with a leg wound and was picked up from the sea shortly afterwards. Since then things have been very quiet indeed round here. The Germans seem to be concentrating chiefly round Dover and Folkestone at the moment. Probably because that is the narrowest part of the Channel. The raiders that we have to deal with come, I think, from the Channel Island aerodrome at Jersey. We often fly more than halfway across and can see France quite clearly. The other day one section chased an enemy machine right over to France before they gave up.

13 David Crook Part 1, Spitfire Pilot, Pilot Officer, British, 609 Squadron

Memoir published in 1942 as *Spitfire Pilot*, and based on his contemporaneous diary of 1940. Born in Huddersfield in 1914, David Crook joined 609 Squadron in August 1938. He was called-up to full-time service on 25 August 1939 and completed his training to join 609 Squadron in May 1940. This is the first of three extracts which covers the end of June to 28 July 1940 when he was based at RAF Northolt, West London in 11 Group to 6 July 1940, then RAF Middle Wallop, Hampshire in 10 Group.

Like most wartime books real names were not used for security reasons but I have been able to work out the real names behind most of the pseudonyms: Andy, Andrew Mamedoff (American); B, Paul Baillon; Buck, James Buchanan; CO, Horace Darley; Franck, Frank Howell; Sergeant F, Alan Feary; G, Henry Goodwin; Geoff, Geoffrey Gaunt; Gordon, Gordon Mitchell; Jarvis, Adolf Jarvis Blayney; John, John

Dundas; Johnny, John Curchin (Australian); Mac, James McArthur; Michael, Michael Appleby; Mick, Rogers Miller; Noel, Noel Agazarian (a great friend of Richard Hillary); Novi, Tadeusz Nowierski (Polish); Ogle, Alfred Ogilvie; Osti, Piotra Ostaszewski-Ostoja (Polish); Peter, Peter Drummond-Hay; Pip, Philip Barran; Red, Eugene Tobin (American) see chapter 39; Shorty, Vernon Keough (American); Sidney, Sydney Hill; Stephen, Stephen Beaumont. I didn't manage to work out who 'Bishop' or 'Squadron Leader R' were.

My knee was now improving rapidly, and on 16 June Dorothy and I left Peebles. We returned home and spent a few days in the Lakes, and on 29 June we departed for London. I said goodbye to Dorothy at Marylebone and went out to Northolt, to start the most exciting and eventful time of my life.

A great change had come over the squadron since I had left them only seven weeks before. We had a new CO and there were several new pilots to replace the Dunkirk losses.

The old easy-going outlook on life had vanished, and everybody now seemed to realize that war was not the fairly pleasant affair that it had always seemed hitherto. Altogether the general mood now appeared to be one of rather grim determination.

My first two days at Northolt were spent mainly in practice flying, and I soon felt quite at home in the Spitfire again.

On the Monday evening, 1 July, I came down into the anteroom, just after dinner, and found Pip gathering everybody together, as an order had just come through that twelve of us were to do a reconnaissance of some aerodromes in northern France the following morning, in order to see what machines the enemy was assembling there. If our patrols reported a good concentration at any aerodrome then bombers would be dispatched immediately to beat the place up.

I don't think anybody was particularly enthusiastic about the idea, but anyway it had to be done, so we got out maps and discussed the route: down to Hawkinge (Folkestone) at dawn to refuel and get breakfast, then straight over to Boulogne, along the coast to the mouth of the Somme, and then turn in to Abbeville to inspect the aerodrome there. After this we should turn south west again to Rouen, inspect the aerodrome, and turn north towards the coast, crossing it at Dieppe and having a look at that aerodrome also. We reckoned that we should get to Abbeville easily, but that we might expect a lot of trouble any time after that.

And so to bed to get what sleep we could. I gathered afterwards that nobody slept well, and I certainly didn't. I had never seen the enemy before, and I kept wondering what it would be like to go into action for the first time.

We got up about 3.30 a.m. It was a lovely morning and we got into cars and went down to the point where our machines were already being run up. I checked up everything in the cockpit particularly carefully, and a few minutes later we took off and headed south east, down through Kent to Folkestone. It was the first time I had flown with the whole squadron, and it was certainly a rather inspiring sight to see eleven other Spitfires all thundering on together.

We landed at Hawkinge, and the ground crews immediately started to refuel the aircraft. We stood around and smoked cigarettes incessantly and made some rather forced conversation, and suffered from that unpleasant empty feeling in the tummy that one always experiences at such moments.

Altogether a very good specimen of squadron 'wind up'!

So many recollections come back to me at such moments. I thought of a summer's evening two years before, when Glen had been at camp here and I had come down to see him. How different it had all seemed then.

I thought of those grand July weekends that we had spent at Brenley, only a few miles away, and most of all I thought of those occasions when we had sailed from Folkestone *en route* for Boulogne and Switzerland. I had a feeling that I wasn't going to enjoy this cross Channel trip quite as much as those previous ones!

The machines were now refuelled and we climbed in, started the engines, and taxied out to take off. A few moments later we were in the air. We made one circuit of Folkestone, and then headed straight out for the French coast. But an anticlimax was in store for us. As we approached France we could see a ground mist covering the countryside, and the ground itself was invisible. This was no good, so we turned about and landed at Hawkinge with our task still unexecuted.

We spent an unpleasant day at Hawkinge, and although somebody went over to have a look at the weather at lunchtime, it was still too misty.

During the afternoon instructions came through that one machine was to go over at 6 p.m., and if the weather was suitable, we would take off at 7 p.m.. Our scout returned at about 6.45 p.m. with the news that the weather was now ok. The time had arrived. I really didn't care very much any longer; after waiting all day I was so fed up that it was a relief to get going and try to get it done this time at any rate.

We took off again, and, having circled Folkestone, we steered out towards Boulogne. The CO was flying below with two other machines in order to do the actual 'spotting', while the other nine machines flew above and behind to guard him and look out for enemy fighters.

In a matter of four or five minutes I saw Boulogne ahead and we turned right and flew down the coast to the mouth of the Somme, where we turned inland towards Abbeville and started to dive at very high speed. As we approached the aerodrome, an accurate burst of AA fire appeared just in front of us, and I swerved to the right and climbed slightly. We soon passed out of range of the battery, and, the CO having inspected Abbeville, turned right for Rouen. From now onwards we could expect enemy fighters, and we scanned the sky anxiously, looking above and behind us almost the whole time. But none appeared, and soon I could see the Seine ahead, winding down to the coast in great S bends.

Only a few weeks before, the bitterest fighting of the war had taken place in the countryside below us and along the banks of the Seine. But it all looked very peaceful that evening, and travelling at the height and great speed that we were going, I could see no signs of the great struggle that had just finished.

We flew over Rouen aerodrome and then turned north for Dieppe and the coast. We were on the last lap now. The coast loomed up ahead and a moment later I gave a sigh of relief as we left French soil behind us. But our troubles were not quite over, for after we were a mile or so from the coast, another accurate burst of AA fire came up from a flak ship anchored off Dieppe. This burst came up just ahead of us and rocked several machines violently, though no damage was done.

Shortly afterwards we crossed the English coast at Dungeness, and turned up towards Folkestone. Gosh, it was good to be back!

When we landed we found that the cook had gone, so had to cook ourselves some eggs and bacon. But we just didn't care a hang about anything, and sat and ate our meal and felt jolly glad to have got the job over at last!

Our stay at Northolt was now almost up because on Thursday morning, 4 July, the enemy bombed Portland, and so orders came through later in the morning that 609 were to move to the south west as reinforcements.

The squadron accordingly moved down on the Thursday afternoon, but I stayed behind, as it was my day off, and I had to have another medical board about my knee to see that it was now ok. So I spent the night at Hampstead with Dorothy and turned up at Kingsway the following morning.

I was prodded and pushed and altogether thoroughly 'vetted' and pronounced A1, though the doctor was a bit annoyed to find that I had already been flying, as the last medical board at Peebles had passed me as unfit for flying till my knee was examined again. However, he soon calmed down.

So I went out to Northolt again, and flew down that evening.

We were the only squadron in that sector at the time, and so we had to get up at 3.30 *a.m.* and went to bed again at about 11.30 p.m. – altogether a pretty long day.

We had a number of alarms and went out over the sea as hard as we could, hoping to see some enemy, but I think most of these scares were quite without foundation, and after a day or so I came to the conclusion that I might spend months at this game and never see any action. How little I knew!

A few days later we moved to a new aerodrome near Salisbury. This is a very good strategic base for the defence both of Southampton and Portland, and it was to be our home for some time to come.

We continued, however, to use the advanced base and we flew down at dawn every day and returned home at dusk.

I was sharing a room with Peter, and we rose as usual on the Tuesday morning, 9 July, and had early breakfast at 4.30 a.m., and then flew down to our advanced base in bad weather.

At about 9 a.m. a report came through that a German machine was attacking ships off the coast, so Peter and I took off to investigate. The clouds were so low that they were actually covering the hills between us and the sea, but we found a gap just where the road runs through a little valley. We roared through this gap just above the road (we heard later that two cyclists were so alarmed by these two Spitfires racing through just above their heads, that they threw themselves into the ditch), and then found ourselves over the coast. But it was a false alarm, and so, rather disappointed, we turned back to the aerodrome.

We sat in the tent again and listened to the rain dripping steadily outside, and Peter and I fixed to go up to London together on the following day in his car, as we both had the day off, and he was going up to see his wife.

At about 6.30 p.m. we were ordered to patrol Weymouth, and so Peter, Michael, and I took off, Peter leading.

We circled round for about three-quarters of an hour, and saw nothing at all. Peter was getting very fed up with this apparently unnecessary flying, and we circled round the aerodrome and asked permission to land. We were told, however, to continue our patrol and turned out again over Weymouth at about 7,000 feet. A moment later, looking out towards the left, I saw an aircraft dive into a layer of cloud about two miles away and then reappear. I immediately called up Peter on the R/T, and he swung us into line astern, and turned left towards the enemy.

A moment later I saw one or two more Huns appear, and recognized them as Junkers 87 dive-bombers. I immediately turned on my reflector sights, put my gun button on to 'fire' and settled down to enjoy a little slaughter of a few Ju 87s, as they are rather helpless machines.

I was flying last on the line, and we were now travelling at high speed and rapidly approaching the enemy, when I happened to look round behind. To my intense surprise and dismay, I saw at least nine Messerschmitt 110s about 2,000 feet above us. They were just starting to dive on us when I saw them, and as they were diving they were overtaking us rapidly.

This completely altered the situation. We were now hopelessly outnumbered, and in a very dangerous position, and altogether I began to see that if we were not jolly quick we should all be dead in a few seconds.

I immediately called up Peter and Michael and shouted desperately, 'Look out behind, Messerschmitts behind' – all the time looking over my shoulder at the leading enemy fighter, who was now almost in range.

But though I kept shouting, both Peter and Michael continued straight on at the bombers ahead, and they were now almost in range and about to open fire.

I have never felt so desperate or so helpless in my life, as when, in spite of my warnings, these two flew steadily on, apparently quite oblivious of the fact that they were going to be struck down from the rear in a few seconds.

At that moment the leading Messerschmitt opened fire at me and I saw his shells and tracer bullets going past just above my head. They were jolly close too. I immediately did a very violent turn to the left and dived through a layer of cloud just below.

I emerged from the cloud going at very high speed – probably over 400 mph, and saw a Ju 87 just ahead of me. I opened fire (my first real shot of the war), and he seemed to fly right through my tracer bullets, but when I turned round to follow him, he had disappeared.

I then climbed up into the cloud again to try to rejoin the others. I saw an Me 110 some distance above me, and I pulled up into a steep climb and fired at him but without result. He turned away immediately, and I lost him.

At that moment I saw dimly a machine moving in the cloud on my left and flying parallel to me. I stalked him through the cloud, and when he emerged into a patch of clear sky I saw that it was a Ju 87.

I was in an ideal position to attack and opened fire and put the remainder of my ammunition – about 2,000 rounds – into him at very close range. Even in the heat of the moment I well remember my amazement at the shattering effect of my fire. Pieces flew off his fuselage and cockpit covering, a stream of smoke appeared from the engine, and a moment later a great sheet of flame licked out from the engine cowling and he dived down vertically. The flames enveloped the whole machine and he went straight down, apparently quite slowly, for about five thousand feet, till he was just a shapeless burning mass of wreckage.

Absolutely fascinated by the sight, I followed him down, and saw him hit the sea with a great burst of white foam. He disappeared immediately, and apart from a green patch in the water there was no sign that anything had happened. The crew made no attempt to get out, and they were obviously killed by my first burst of fire.

I had often wondered what would be my feelings when killing somebody like this, and especially when seeing them go down in flames. I was rather surprised to reflect afterwards that my only feeling had been one of considerable elation – and a sort of bewildered surprise because it had all been so easy.

I turned back for the coast, and started to call up Peter and Michael on the R/T. But there was no response, and as far as Peter was concerned, I was already calling to the void.

A moment later I saw another Spitfire flying home on a very erratic course, obviously keeping a very good look behind. I joined up with it, and recognized Michael, and together we bolted for the English coast like a couple of startled rabbits.

I made a perfectly bloody landing on the aerodrome and overshot so badly that I nearly turned the Spitfire on her nose in my efforts to pull up before hitting the hedge. I got out to talk to Michael and found to my surprise that my hand was quite shaky and even my voice was unsteady, due I suppose, to a fairly even mixture of fright, intense excitement, and a sort of reckless exhilaration because I had just been in action for the first time and shot somebody down, and the full significance of that rather startling fact was beginning to dawn on me now that I had time to think.

Michael had left his R/T in the 'transmit' position instead of 'receive' and so had not heard my warning shouts at the beginning of the action.

Fortunately for him, however, he turned it over just in time, and heard me say 'Messerschmitt'. He whipped round and found himself being attacked by three Me 110s. He had very great difficulty in escaping, got into a spin, recovered and then spun the other way, and came home having fired almost all his rounds at various Me 110s and Ju 87s, though without being able to see any results.

He saw a great flurry of machines in the sky about a mile away, which must have been Peter's last effort against an overwhelming number of Messerschmitts. Knowing Peter, I bet he put up a hell of a fight before they got him down.

As soon as our machines were refuelled and re-armed, six of us flew out over the sea to look for him. But there was no sign of him at all, and his body was never recovered.

I think there is no doubt that he also had left his R/T on 'transmit' and so did not hear my warnings, or else perhaps he was thinking that there were only a very few enemy, as we had been told, and therefore the possibility of attack from the rear simply did not occur to him. There had been so many false alarms that he was rather in the frame of mind – 'Nothing can ever happen at Weymouth.'

We took off just before dusk to return to base. Gordon could not come as his machine had been slightly damaged earlier in the day, and I left him standing outside the tent, looking rather disconsolate because he had not been able to take part in the action with Michael and me. It was the last time I ever saw him.

We got back and I went up to my room in the mess. Everything was just the same as Peter and I had left it only eighteen hours before; his towel was still in the window where he had thrown it during our hurried dressing. But he was dead now. I simply could not get used to such sudden and unexpected death, and there flashed across my mind the arrangements we had made to go up to London together the following day. It all seemed so ironical, so tragic, so futile. I felt that I could not sleep in that room again, and so I took my things and went into Gordon's bed next door and slept there.

But I could not get out of my head the thought of Peter, with whom we had been talking and laughing that day, now lying in the cockpit of his wrecked Spitfire at the bottom of the English Channel.

I felt much better next morning, had a late breakfast, and made out my combat report, and then went into lunch with the others.

In the middle of lunch Pip was called to the telephone, and a few minutes later I went out into the hall and found him standing there looking very worried and unhappy. Peter's wife had just been ringing up, wondering why he had not telephoned her about his trip to London that afternoon. The telegram had not yet reached her, and so Pip had to tell her the news. It all seemed so awful; I was seeing for the first time at very close quarters all the distress and unhappiness that casualties cause. I walked out of the mess and drove to the station, very thankful to be doing something that took my mind on to other subjects. And I never saw Pip again, either.

I met Dorothy in London and we had a pleasant dinner together. She was delighted about my first Hun, though naturally very worried and depressed about the other events. I also rang up home and told the family with considerable pride that I had at last been in action and managed to bag a Hun.

We went out to Hampstead for the night to the flat where D was staying, and early next morning I went down to Waterloo to catch the train back. I arrived at the aerodrome at lunch time and was walking up the steps of the mess when I met a squadron leader who was working in operations room. He told me that there had been another fight early that morning and both Pip and Gordon had been killed. The whole squadron was now in the air and apparently a lot of fighting was going on all along the south coast.

I could get no details of what had happened, and I sat alone in the mess all afternoon, feeling more miserable and more stunned than I have ever felt before.

Everybody arrived back after dark, dog-tired and utterly depressed. I shall never forget seeing them all come into the mess – people who, normally, appeared not to have a care in the world just flopped into chairs and sat there and said not a word.

I rang up Dorothy and told her the news, and I think that she was as shocked as I was. She had only met Pip on a few occasions, but knew Gordon very well indeed.

What happened in the morning was this: a ship was being bombed by a large enemy formation south of Portland, and five Spitfires led by Pip took off to go to the spot.

They saw the enemy while they were still some distance away, in the usual German formation with bombers below and fighters guarding them above. The Spitfires were outnumbered by ridiculous odds, but Pip, who had never hesitated for one second at rugger or anything else in his life, did not hesitate now in this last and greatest moment of all. He detached two machines to try and hold off the enemy fighters (of which there were at least twenty), while he led the other two Spitfires against the enemy bombers below which were attacking the ship.

It was hopeless from the very start. The Messerschmitts dived down on top of our small formation and everybody was separated immediately. Gordon was last seen diving down into the attack and after that nobody saw him again.

After a brief but very sharp fight, during which two enemy dive-bombers were almost definitely destroyed, the enemy formation departed, and Jarvis saw a Spitfire flying back towards the coast, going very slowly and with smoke pouring from it.

This was Pip. A moment later he jumped out, opened his parachute, and dropped into the water. Jarvis circled round him, but Pip gave no sign of recognition, and shortly after, when a boat picked him up, he died as soon as they got him on board. He had been hit twice in the right leg and was also burnt, but it was probably the shock and being for so long in the water that killed him. I think that if he had dropped on land and been attended to quickly he would have lived, because he was incredibly strong and tough.

An immediate search for Gordon was made both by aeroplanes and also naval launches from Portland, but he was not found.

It is difficult to describe my feelings during the next few days. We had lost three pilots in thirty-six hours, all of them in fights in which we had been hopelessly outnumbered, and I felt that there was now really nothing left to care about, because obviously, from the law of probability, one could not expect to survive many more encounters of a similar nature.

When one thinks of the losses sustained in war, particularly by the Army, to lose three people in two days seems very trifling. But in a squadron there are so few pilots, and it really seems more like a rather large family than anything else, and therefore three deaths at once seems very heavy indeed.

Again compared with the experiences of squadrons during the fighting in France, such losses are small, because some squadrons in France were wiped out almost to a man in a few days. But they were taking part in heavy and continuous fighting where one expects losses and also they were destroying very much greater numbers of Germans than they themselves were losing, so they could feel, to put it bluntly, that they were getting value for money, which is a very big factor in maintaining spirits and morale.

But our losses had been sustained in two small encounters, and we had hardly anything to count against it in the way of enemy shot down.

So, quite apart from the death of one's friends, we all felt very depressed, because obviously things weren't going well.

Gordon's death in particular made a deep impression on me, because I knew him much better than I knew Pip. We were at school together, and he, Michael, and I had spent the whole war together, and were so accustomed to being in each other's company that I could not then (and still cannot now) get used to the idea that we should not see Gordon again or spend any more of our gay evenings together or rag him about the moustache of which he was so proud.

He was a delightful person, a very amusing and charming companion, and one of the most generous people I ever knew, both as regards material matters and, more important still, in his outlook and views.

He was also a brilliant athlete, a Cambridge Hockey Blue and Scots International. It always used to delight me to watch Gordon playing any game, whether hockey, tennis, or squash, because he played with such a natural ease and grace – the unmistakable sign of a first class athlete.

He could not have wished to die in more gallant circumstances.

But if Gordon's death was a greater shock to me personally, Pip's death was a terrible blow to the squadron.

He was more than a mere member of the squadron; you might almost say that he was the foundation stone upon which it was first formed and built. He was one of the first people to join the squadron when it was started, and he was, I think, easily the outstanding personality of us all. I don't think anybody could mention 609 without immediately thinking of Pip, and his death in the face of such overwhelming odds was characteristic of his brave and resolute spirit.

I admired the CO very much in these difficult days. He flew as much as everybody else, never batted an eyelid, and remained as imperturbable and serene as ever.

It was a very fine example of what can be done by one man's courage and determination, and very shortly matters began to improve, as other fighter squadrons were sent to the south west to reinforce us.

The lesson about going out in such small numbers had also been learnt, and from now onwards we generally flew as a complete squadron, which is a very much more formidable and powerful adversary than three aircraft only.

Two days later, three of us, Stephen, Jarvis, and myself, took off in cloudy weather to intercept a lone enemy aircraft which was on a reconnaissance flight.

We flew for some minutes on a given course and were then told by operations room, 'Look out for him now on your left.' A moment later both Jarvis and I saw him up in the clouds on our left, just as 'operations' had forecast. Stephen, who was leading, did not see him, and so after a few seconds, I broke away from formation and went hard after the Dornier, with Jarvis just behind me.

We opened right up to full throttle, and overhauled the Dornier very rapidly. He didn't see us coming till I was about 400 yards away, and then he turned and ran for the nearest cloud with black smoke coming from both engines as an indication that he also was 'flat out'.

The rear gunner opened fire at me and I could see his tracers flicking past like little red sparks, but he was very inaccurate, and a moment later I opened fire and am certain that I killed him immediately as there was no more return fire and I saw my bursts going right into the fuselage. Jarvis said later he was certain that I had shot him down, as he also saw my fire going right into the Dornier.

However, the cloud loomed up ahead and a second later the Dornier vanished. I turned left hoping to intercept him on the other side of the cloud, but did not see him again. Jarvis had three short bursts at him in gaps in the cloud, but unfortunately lost him also, and so a rather badly damaged Dornier got away safely. Had the cloud been only half a mile farther away, I think we should have got him easily.

A few days later, news came through that Gordon's body had been washed up near Newport on the Isle of Wight. The station ambulance went down and collected the body, and on Thursday 25 July, exactly a fortnight after his death, I travelled up in the ambulance to Letchworth to his funeral.

His death had been an overwhelming tragedy for his parents, for he was an only son. I think they felt that after his loss there was really very little left to live for. But they were marvellously brave about it and very kind to me and touchingly grateful for the letter I had written to them, giving all the known details of Gordon's death, and the approximate time it occurred, etc.

The service was short and simple, and he was buried in a lovely little country church near Letchworth. Mr Bisseker, our old headmaster and a very old friend of the Mitchells, came over from Cambridge to conduct the service.

I went up to London after the funeral and spent the night at Hampstead with Dorothy and returned to the squadron the next day.

All through July and early August we used to get regularly the unpopular task of escorting convoys up and down the Channel.

The Germans at that time were concentrating mainly on attacking shipping rather than land objectives, and some very fierce fights used to occur when they bombed the ships.

We all disliked this work; the weather was brilliant and the Huns invariably used to attack out of the sun, and sometimes took the escorting fighters completely by surprise.

Also we were always outnumbered, sometimes by ridiculous odds, and a lot of pilots were lost. Some of these were drowned, without doubt, when their machine was hit and they descended in the water ten or fifteen miles from land, and were not found despite all the searching that took place afterwards.

Two days after Gordon's funeral, on 27 July, a convoy was lying in Weymouth Bay when a German formation approached, and we went out to intercept it. A very confused action followed, in which most of us never saw or engaged the enemy, but we lost one pilot, Buck, who was almost certainly shot down by Me 109s.

Johnny and I could never quite understand what happened to him, because he was leading us in Green section and we were turning all round behind him, guarding his tail while we patrolled. We both turned away to have a good look behind, and when we turned again he had vanished quite suddenly, and we never saw him again, though we stayed together for the rest of the patrol. Neither of us saw any Huns near us, though there were a lot of Me 109s some distance above, and we came to the conclusion that he must have seen a Ju 87 in the broken clouds just below us and dived down immediately to attack it and then been shot down. But we both felt rather unhappy about it, although there was certainly nothing that we could have done to prevent it, and he was definitely not shot down while he was with us.

Johnny and I went out to search for him afterwards and saw something in the water, so we directed a patrol boat to it as it looked like a parachute, but actually it was a stray barrage balloon. As a matter of fact, no trace of Buck was ever found.

We stayed out there for nearly an hour, circling round very low on the water, till the boat arrived to confirm that it was a barrage balloon, and I was quite thankful to get back again afterwards, as we were forty or fifty miles out to sea, very near the French coast, and at the mercy of any Me 109s that happened to see us. But fortunately none of them appeared.

I think Buck's death also was very largely due to inexperience and faulty tactics. We had not yet learnt that it did not pay to go out to sea to meet the enemy, but to let them come to us. Also we did not realize the importance that height meant.

Afterwards we used to get as high as possible before going into action. This is the whole secret of success in air fighting.

But Buck's death was another in the series of unnecessary losses, against which we had very little to show in the way of success, and I think that we all felt depressed and discouraged. He was a jolly good chap and a sound pilot.

However, we learnt our lesson from these deaths, though it seems so grim that in a war experience is almost always gained at the expense of other men's lives. But the end of July came, and with it the end of our bad luck.

August was to produce many successes and at least one brilliant victory.

14 Barry Sutton Part 2, Hurricane Pilot, Pilot Officer, British, 56 Squadron

The second extract from Sutton's 1942 memoir covers a sortie flown on 25 July 1940 where he makes his first full official 'kill'. He was shot down on 28 August 1940 over the Thames Estuary and seriously burned, spending a year in hospital. His tally for 1940 was four enemy aircraft and one shared kill.

Sutton fought in the air over Burma in 1942, where he shot down a further four enemy aircraft, and wrote a second volume of memoirs, *Jungle Pilot*. He survived the war despite being shot down three times. Each time his wife received the dreaded 'missing in action' letter from the Air Ministry. Together with his wife he had two daughters, one of whom, Julia Gregson, became a writer and wrote among other books a historical novel, *Jasmine Nights*, partly inspired by her father's experiences of being seriously burned. Forty years after the war he wrote a long poem about his Battle of Britain experiences, *Summer of the Firebird, Soliloquy of a Fighter Pilot Shot Down During the Battle of Britain*. He died in 1988.

Chapter 17: First Blood, 25 July 1940 Clear skies, brilliant sunshine were the devilish beguilements of the heavens during those midsummer days.

Day after day, week after week, the fierce turmoil raged high up in that blue dome, while the very elements stood aside and watched.

A break in the weather, if only for a day, could alone have given us respite from the full ardours of a battle in which we were so sadly outnumbered in men and machines.

Even clouding of the sun would have helped. Climbing into a brilliance which the enemy wisely exploited as a tactical advantage, was a hazardous and often nerve-racking business, for it meant that escorting German fighters were able to see us long before we saw them.

If the weather was not wholly on our side, however, the fates were. We believed it, and we were proved right and rejoiced when we knew that we in our few had the full measure of an enemy who, with the recklessness of desperation, daily threw more and more machines into the fray in an attempt to crush all resistance by sheer weight of numbers.

The failure of this policy and the way it came about is now history.

To those of us, however, who found ourselves embroiled in that struggle, dates, places, and events, which of course are the very stuff and substance of history, are as lifeless as monuments. The imprint of emotional experience, the thrills and sickening fears of a moment, these are the pictures, vivid, indelible, and above all, vital, which remain uppermost in the mind.

To make fabric out of these shreds, to give these isolated impressions any place within the cohesive whole of a story, is an almost impossible task, for the events of those hectic days still seem disjointed as in a dream.

Through the starboard side of my window I could see France, while the mainplanes easily spanned at our height of 30,000 feet the Straits of Dover. Strung out in search formation, we had been combing a patrol line between the Estuary and Dover, when the CO's voice crackled over the R/T. At last we had seen something. Flashes from the guns of a couple of destroyers out in the Channel had held our attention for some minutes, but what the target was had not become apparent until now. Swarming above the ships and some 12,000 feet below us were aircraft in two layers. Three Hurricanes on my right heeled over until I could see the light blue of their bellies before they plunged down in to the attack. They were 'A' Flight machines, and were carrying out the CO's orders to attack that upper layer, which must be fighters. A second later, Gracey, Page and myself followed, diving almost vertically towards the ships, which had now ceased fire. We had been spotted by our quarry. That lower layer, which, as we thought, consisted of Junkers 87 dive-bombers, had already begun to disperse. Two in front of me turned steeply and headed for home. Their fighter escort was of no use to them now.

I overshot the first too quickly to observe the effect of my short burst, but I was able to fasten on to the tail of the second. Twisting and turning, he was now only a few feet above the water. I pressed the firing button as he tried a sudden steep turn to the right which brought him right across my gun-sights. The worst shot in the world could not have missed.

The Junkers tightened its turn but skidded violently towards the water as its nose dropped. In less than a second it was all over. It had hit the water with the full momentum of its three tons travelling at 200 miles per hour, but it plunged in like a stone and made little splash. As I watched, something wound up in my stomach. It was my first Hun but there was no immediate feeling of elation.

For a moment I was conscious of a sickly, nauseating wave of sympathy for the wretched men I had sent to their doom.

It was a sensation which, thank God, I never had again.

As I broke away, a second 87 flashed over my head. He was already being dealt with by another Hurricane which was snapping at his heels like an angry terrier.

The Hun stuck his nose down until he was only a few feet above the top of the waves, and turned in the direction of the French coast.

The evening sun picked out the cliffs east of Calais ahead of us, so that they shone pale gold above the cobalt water of the Channel. Against this background the end of the fugitive, which came a moment later, presented its brief, fantastic scene.

The Hurricane continued firing until flames peeped out of the Hun's fuselage and almost instantly lengthened until they flapped and bellowed in his slipstream, making a huge red banner.

The fighter broke away – there was no need to use more ammunition, the flames would do the rest. As he turned, the 87 became enveloped in one huge sheet of flame, hung for an instant on the horizon, and then plunged into the sea.

By this time all the dive-bombers had disappeared. Climbing back into the sun, I saw that 'A' Flight were still dealing with the few 109s that were the remnants of the forty-odd machines which had formed the escort for the 87s. 'A' Flight had done their job well, for they had had the task of driving off the 109s unaided. As we had gone into the attack the CO had detached 'B' Flight to deal with the dive-bombers, so that we had only six machines to deal with each enemy force. We were outnumbered, but we had the powerful element of surprise in our favour in that first attack out of the sun, which had at once split up the Huns.

As in so many air battles, it is impossible to describe exactly what took place. Our tactics had broken up any organised manoeuvre which the Huns might have employed, and the result was a number of separate combats in which our boys had to deal with sometimes as many as three Huns at a time. We had to weave in and out taking a shot at anything in range. This freelancing is sometimes more of a nuisance to one's comrades than it is to the enemy, but it is the best way of keeping the greatest number of them busy defending themselves. This is obviously the most important consideration in cases where we were so outnumbered.

I turned at about 1,500 feet and looked down-sun again. I could see only one 109 and he was going flat out for home. Things so often happen like that. One minute the air seems as full of hostile aircraft as it does of gnats on a summer evening, and the next, everything disappears. As most fighter pilots did sooner or later, I learnt to distrust the first evidence of my own eyes on these occasions. I was destined to be 'jumped on' a few weeks later in just the same way as I had been in France, before I fully learnt this lesson.

I was in the very act of turning once again to make sure there were no aircraft about when a red stream, rather like the issue from a Roman candle firework, shot past me on my port side.

Had we not been well out of range of Dover, I would have sworn it was pom-pom fire, but I knew that was impossible and that what I had seen was cannon-fire. I kicked on the rudder hard to skid out to the right, and yanked my Hurricane so hard that it seemed my stomach was being wrenched out. I came round again just in time to catch a glimpse of the 109 which must have fired at me. He had not bothered to follow me but had kept straight on for the French coast, leaving a wraith of black exhaust smoke behind. That meant he was somewhere at full throttle, and as he was already a full mile on his way and I was climbing and turning at about 160 mph, I had not a hope of catching him.

He must have been the last of the stragglers, because I continued climbing and circling for about five minutes and saw nothing more.

Heading home at last, I became aware of a strange emotion I had never known before.

I have since been in tighter corners, been much more conscious of danger and perhaps become more casual with the experience, but that feeling of supreme elation, almost lightheadedness, has never left me immediately after a battle.

I slid back the roof of the cockpit, put my seat in its proper notch, and took a deep breath of the fresh air. Looking over the side, I thought the fields of Kent had never looked more green. Crossing over the Estuary, I looked towards the west – surely the setting sun had never smiled so genially through the smoking skyline of London.

I began to sing.

15 George Stoney, Hurricane Pilot, Flight Lieutenant, British, 501 Squadron

Air Ministry- and Ministry of Information-endorsed BBC radio broadcast by an anonymous RAF fighter pilot on 3 August 1940. The pilot is George Stoney and the combat took place on Monday 29 July 1940 with 501 Squadron flying from RAF Gravesend, Kent (11 Group). The Spitfire squadron mentioned was 41 Squadron, and didn't fare as well as the Hurricanes of Stoney's squadron against the eighty-strong Me 109 escort. 41 Squadron shot down three Me 109s and a Ju 87 but one pilot was shot down and killed and four others crash-landed, although the pilots were unhurt.

Stoney was shot down and killed within weeks of the broadcast on 18 August 1940 by Manptmann Foezoe of JG51. 18 August later became known as 'the Hardest Day' as both the RAF and Luftwaffe lost more planes than on any other day in the conflict so far. Stoney had flown on his own at a formation of fifty Dornier bombers, disrupting the entire force before being 'bounced' by Me 110s. He is buried at St Helen's Churchyard in Lunt, Sefton. He was twenty-nine and had shot down two enemy aircraft.

On Monday we were up bright and early and waited by our Hurricanes enjoying the fine summer morning and wondering whether we'd be sent up before breakfast or not. Suddenly we received the alarm, enemy bombers were over the Channel. We raced to our aircraft and just as the engines were starting up the air raid siren was sounded. I wondered as we took off how I was going to behave if I saw the enemy. I was excited of course, it's a strange experience to find myself going out on my first action against the enemy. Would I be frightened? Would I want to bolt? I genuinely wondered.

Then, when we were at 8,000 feet we made a turn and saw the German aircraft. There were thirty or forty Junkers 87s, in threes, about to dive down and bomb four ships in Dover harbour. As we raced to intercept them I watched the first lot begin their dive. They dropped their bombs at about 2,000 feet and I saw them disappear in the water. The ten bombs at one time and the water all around the ships was heaved up into huge fountains. As we raced along at 300 miles an hour I could see the bombers waiting their turn to go in and attack. Not all of them got a chance. Somewhere above were the escorting Messerschmitts, they were being looked after by a squadron of Spitfires so we had the bombers pretty well to ourselves. It was only a matter of seconds before we were diving down to our targets. First I saw a Junkers 87 being chased by six Hurricanes, and I felt like cheering when the bomber went down in flames. Immediately afterwards another Junkers flew right across my bows, I hared after it for all I was worth. I got him in my gun sights and let him have it. I was overtaking him fast and when I stopped firing he was covering my entire windscreen, only 50 yards away. I stopped firing because he blew up.

Then blow me I saw three Ju 87s tearing off for home. They were only 50 feet above the surface of the water going away from our shores as fast as they could. I dived down and attacked them in turn, chasing them about a dozen miles out to sea. I gave the first one a good burst and I know I hit him, but I was attacked from behind and had to break off. We were in the air for exactly 36 minutes, though I suppose the fight itself didn't last more than 5 minutes. When we got back we had breakfast.

When I first saw the Germans I felt a kind of fascination. And I was surprised that I was able to see so much of the battle. After dealing with my first Junkers 87 I was able to notice other members of the squadron shooting down other German bombers. There is no doubt that we shook them up an awful lot. As I said, some of them didn't even get the chance to drop their bombs.

One of the things that stands out in my mind was a sailing boat with a big red sail steadily passing down the coast. Aircraft were blazing away at one another in the sky above, occasionally one would crash into the sea and disappear. That little boat with the red sail appeared to take no notice at all – a cheerful sight. Our squadron, by the way, came out of the combat untouched except for one bullet-hole through the wing of one of our aircraft. One bullet-hole for four bombers destroyed and six others damaged.

I've been a pilot with English and Irish airlines, and I've put in more than 5,000 hours flying time and I don't think I've ever had a more enjoyable few minutes in the air. This morning I saw the first enemy machine since this fracas, after one burst he was off home. My father and brother who live in Victoria at the moment will probably be glad to hear that I'm hale and hearty.

16 Arthur 'Art' Donahue Part 1, Spitfire Pilot, Pilot Officer, American, 64 Squadron

The first of three extracts from Art Donahue's 1941 memoir, *Yankee in a Spitfire*, covering June and July 1940 and including his convoluted route to England and entrance into the RAF. 'Art' Donahue, from Minnesota, was twenty-seven when he joined 64 Squadron on 3 August 1940 at RAF Kenley. He was among a very small band of Americans who ignored their country's neutral status to join the fight against Nazism in the Battle of Britain. He had held a pilot's licence since he was nineteen. He aimed his memoir at an American market, probably to encourage engagement with the European struggle, and his memoir is particularly good in that it assumes little knowledge on the part of the reader, explaining every feature of being a fighter pilot for the laymen.

For wartime security reasons other members of the squadron were referred to by first or nickname only. I have identified some of Donahue's fellow pilots and what became of them. 'Peter' is Peter Kennard-Davis, KIA 10 August 1940; Ernest 'Gilly' Gilbert, one shared kill in 1940, survived the war; Jack Mann, four kills in the Battle of Britain and survived the war; James 'Orange' O'Meara, seven kills in 1940 and survived the war; 'squadron leader'/'CO' is Aeneas MacDonnelly, squadron leader and CO of 64 Squadron, eleven kills in the Battle, survived the war.

Chapter 1 A Farm Boy Goes Abroad: 1 June–15 July 1940 I'm afraid that if this story is to be judged by the standards of the thousands of air stories that have been available to the American public in magazines the last few years, it will be classed as a failure. It is not very bloodcurdling, with fewer people taking part in the entire story than meet death in the first three pages of most air stories.

The hero is not tall and muscular and steely-eyed, with grim, wind-bitten, hawklike features; and his accomplishments in the story are few. Worse yet, he's anything but fearless; he scares as easily as you do, perhaps more easily, and in the whole story he never does anything particularly heroic. Worst of all is his identity, because actually he's only me.

But this story is true, and I hope that some of you may consider its shortcomings compensated for by the fact that the characters in this story really exist – or existed; that the occurrences in this story, though less spectacular, really occurred; and that the characters who meet death in it really did meet death, in the savage and desperate struggle that is being fought for the safety of the world, including you.

The most that can be said for myself is that I tried and tried hard, and fought hard, as I hope to be still trying and fighting when you read this; and I have probably accomplished as much against the enemy as the average of those who were in action at the same times as I. And I did have the privilege of being numbered among the few score pilots who met the first German mass onslaughts in the air blitzkrieg against England. Of these facts I shall always be proud, even if I fail to add more to them.

And in this tale of an ordinary American from a mid-west farm coming to a warring country, joining its fighting forces, mingling with its fighting men, and finally fighting and falling and fighting again, I hope that I can tell you enough of 'what it's like' to keep your interest. If I fail it will be my fault as a writer, for I'm sure that what I've seen and experienced will interest average Americans if I describe it right. I'm an ordinary American myself, and it has been tremendously interesting to me!

I was born and raised on a farm at St Charles, Minnesota, and at the age of eighteen I went into commercial flying. During the years of the depression this wasn't always too lucrative, and at various times I worked as garage mechanic, construction worker, and truck driver, in addition to working on my father's farm quite often. Always, however, I tried to work at some place where I could also keep my hand in flying part of the time – barnstorming, instructing, and the like, and working as aircraft mechanic. For the most part of the year and a half before I went to war I was engaged as an instructor at the International Flying School at Laredo, Texas.

As I remember, when I started flying there were about a hundred and twenty licensed pilots in Minnesota; and if you had lined us all up at that time and ranked us according to our possibilities of ever flying in a war, I'd have been in about the one hundred nineteenth place. The only one less likely than myself would have been my good friend Shorty Deponti of Minneapolis. Shorty would never fly in a war for two very good reasons: first, there wasn't enough money in it; and second, there wasn't enough money in it. My flying instructor, Max Conrad of Winona, would be more easily moved because he'd get higher pay out of allowances for his five daughters. I didn't have any of the qualifications of a soldier. I was neither big nor very strong; I was quite mild-tempered and absolutely afraid to fight, and I was more cautious in my flying than the average pilot then. Yet I believe I am the only one of them all to have gone to war. Tom Hennessy, whom I'd have ranked in those days as the most likely prospect, is now married and settled down sensibly on an airline.

When the war started I should have liked to volunteer at once for England. I felt that this was America's war as much as England's and France's, because America was part of the world, which Hitler and his minions were so plainly out to conquer. Consideration for my folks, whom I didn't want to saddle with a lot of worries, held me back. As the next best thing, I applied for a commission in the United States Army Air Corps Reserve, so that I could learn something about military flying anyway. This looked easy on paper, but I found myself frustrated for months by delays that were mostly hard to understand.

I paid a visit home in mid-June of 1940, and was cultivating corn on my dad's farm at the time of the collapse of France and the evacuation of Dunkirk. I had heard that American pilots were being hired for noncombatant jobs with the Royal Air Force, so when I left home I went to Canada to investigate. I was promptly hired, and about ten days later I boarded a boat for England.

It was a big passenger liner and should have been gayly painted and lighted, with flags flying and decks lined with tourists as it sailed – at least that's the way they were in all the pictures I'd seen. But instead it was painted in dull drab colors and there were only a handful of passengers. Nevertheless it was my first ocean trip, and I was plenty thrilled. Orders were posted about that we must keep our portholes closed at night and not show any lights on deck; and I realized that whether I fought or not I was in part of the war now.

I boarded the ship in late afternoon, and after I was settled and had had my supper I went out on deck. We were sailing down the St Lawrence River and it was nearly dark. Not a light showed on the ship. At the stern I saw some men on a platform above the main deck swinging what looked like the boom of a big crane out so it hung over the water, and I wondered what they intended to lift with a crane out there. Then my eyes became accustomed to the darkness and I saw that it wasn't a crane at all, but a big cannon being prepared for use – more evidence of war! Remember, I was just an ordinary American, to whom war and battles and actual shooting at human targets were unreal things that only occurred in newspapers or movies or books. This was real, and it wasn't in a newspaper or movie or book, and I just stood there a while gawping at it!

I enjoyed every moment of the trip across. I had a whole cabin to myself, and the excellence of the service and food gave me a feeling of luxury. Here on the smooth Atlantic life was so peaceful and relaxed that it was difficult to remember, except when I looked at the grim cannon at the stern of the ship, that within a few days I should be among a people fighting for existence, with their backs to the wall.

The prettiest sight of the trip was furnished by a number of icebergs one afternoon – something I didn't expect to see in July. The sun was shining brightly, making them appear crystal-white and gleaming. We were nearly always within sight of half a dozen, for several hours, and we sailed quite close to some. One which passed close had apparently shifted its position in the water, and a wide ring of blue marking its old water line was visible. It contrasted beautifully with the white of the rest of the iceberg, cutting across it diagonally. The blue band, I suppose, was clear pure ice, while the rest of the berg was ice and snow, very white. It was about a mile away and was at least one hundred fifty feet high. It was one of the most beautiful and striking pieces of scenery nature ever produced.

We arrived in an English port on a dreary, foggy Sunday morning after a final twenty-four hours of constant zigzagging by our ship to upset the aim of any lurking enemy submarines. The ship stood in midstream for hours while we passengers leaned on the deck railings and dodged the sea gulls that flapped overhead, squawking and bombing indiscriminately.

We left the ship in late afternoon and an RAF officer took me in tow and escorted me from the dock to a green and tan camouflaged automobile which was parked near by. Instead of a license plate on the front of the car there was a plate with three big letters: 'RAF.'

My baggage having been loaded on, we set out for the railway station, and I got my first look at an English city. I had never realized that English cities were so different from American cities, with their winding irregular streets and their closely packed stone houses and business buildings of wholly different architecture from ours. Traffic is left-hand in England, and it seemed impossible for so many cars to be driving on the wrong side of the street with no accidents! I expected we'd crack up every minute. We didn't, though, and at the railway station the officer got me a ticket for London.

I found that my train didn't leave until midnight, so I set out to find a restaurant and eat supper. On the ship each passenger had received a gas mask in a little cardboard carrying case, and I now carried mine. However, after walking about a block I realized that it looked out of place. No one else carried any, and people were staring at mine. I went back to the station and put it away in my suitcase!

Then I sallied forth again and found a restaurant; but I still didn't get any supper. I understood but little of the menu on the wall and nothing of the prices, which were in English money of course, with its set of signs absolutely foreign to any American. Furthermore I realized that I didn't have any idea of how you ordered a meal here, and I just didn't have the nerve to try to bluff it. Retreating to the station once more, I got some chocolate bars from an automatic vendor.

After a time an English girl came in whom I had met on the boat, and I found that she was waiting for the same train. At my suggestion we went out together for supper, and by that time it was dark.

And I *mean* dark. Not a street light showed, not a window or doorway gave a crack of light. It was my first experience in a black-out, of course. The few cars and busses on the street crawled along at five miles an hour, with nothing but dim little parking lights to see by. Many of the people walking had lighted cigarettes, and it helped them to keep from running into each other. That was once I wished that I was a smoker.

There was a sense of freedom about it, though, for we could walk in the middle of the street, as many did, because the cars moved so slowly we didn't have to worry about being run down. We just stepped out of their way! There were a few very dim stop and go lights, and here and there dim blue lights marking the entrances to air-raid shelters. These and the little lights of cars, the glowing cigarette tips, and an occasional dimmed flashlight were the only breaks in the darkness. Posts, stairways, building corners, and similar objects were all painted white so that people wouldn't walk into them.

That was a cloudy night. On clear nights it isn't so bad and the traffic moves faster, particularly if there is moonlight too. Houses and buildings, of course, have their windows and doorways curtained so that the lights can be used inside; and until I got used to it I always had a sensation of bewilderment when I stepped out of a brightly lighted restaurant or other building, absently expecting to be in a brightly lighted street, and then found nothing outside but total darkness.

The passenger car in which we rode to London was divided into little carriage like compartments, each having room for four passengers riding forward and four facing backward. The lights in our compartment were very dim and shielded so they only lit up a little section of the middle of it, and even then we had to have curtains drawn all around. We rode 'First Class.' 'Third Class' coaches are less comfortable, but are cheaper; there isn't any second class. I marveled at the speed the train made through the blacked-out country. The locomotive used only the faintest headlights or none at all, and the engineers must have had cats' eyes to do it.

I'm still glad it was a beautiful fresh morning when we walked out of the station at the end of the journey, for my first glimpse of the world's greatest city.

I'll always try to keep my first impression of London, for it will never be like that again. The streets, houses, buildings, trees, and parks were all at their best in the bright sunlight. Far over head the silvery barrage balloons hung silent and motionless, like sentinels. The raids hadn't begun then, nor the devastation. But everyone knew they were coming; and London impressed me so much with its greatness and beauty as it stood that morning awaiting its trial, prepared and unafraid.

It's hard to give a specific reason why I became a combat pilot. Of course I'd always wanted to be one; and once I was in England the significance of the struggle seemed to carry me away. This was mid-July. France had fallen, and the invasion of England seemed imminent. Its success would open the whole world to a barbarian conquest. I had a growing admiration for the British people and a sincere desire to help them all I could. I couldn't help feeling that it would be fighting for my own country, too.

I felt drawn into the struggle like a moth to a candle. That's a pretty good comparison, too, for it developed that I was to get burned once and be drawn right back into it again!

Knowing that one of England's greatest problems was inferiority in numbers in the air, I felt it a duty as a follower of the civilized way of life to throw my lot in if they would take me. To fight side by side with these people against the enemies of civilization would be the greatest of all privileges. I had never done any military flying, but was confident of my ability to adapt myself.

Inquiries revealed that the way was wide open. I could be a fighter (pursuit) pilot if I wished, by first taking an advanced training course. Also I could probably get where the fighting was heaviest if I wished, because pilots as a rule were given preference in this regard. I shouldn't need to tell my folks I was fighting, because they wouldn't expect me to tell much about my work on account of censorship. The whole set-up had too much appeal for my resistance.

I knew I should be scared to death many times and should regret my decision often, for as I said before, I am not overendowed with courage; but I also knew that I'd never forgive myself if I rejected this opportunity. So in a fateful moment on the day after my arrival I held my pen poised while making one last reflection on what I was doing, and then signed on the dotted line. I thereby surrendered my independence for the duration of the war and became a proud member of the Royal Air Force. I also presumed that I was surrendering my citizenship, for I understood that the law was so interpreted at that time.

I was given a commission as pilot officer, which corresponds to the rank of second lieutenant in the Army; and was allowed two days' leave to buy a uniform. I was impressed with the swiftness and lack of red tape with which I was accepted. I had simply shown them that I had the goods and they had said in effect: 'All right. We'll buy. Sign here, and you can start delivering.' It was a refreshing contrast to my experiences in my own country.

My uniform was soon made up, and on the evening of the fourth day after arrival in England I walked down the streets of London a full-fledged officer of His Majesty's Royal Air Force. That is, I walked a little way. I was with an American boy working in London whom I'd met the day before, and who was going to show me about. We walked about a block and then met a couple of airmen in uniform ('airmen' is the term for all non-commissioned ranks in the RAF). They of course saluted me as an officer; and I of course was obliged to return their salute. Then the terrible realization dawned on me – not having been inducted into the RAF in the normal way, I hadn't learned how to salute!

It was do or die, though, and I 'did' – in a terribly blundering fashion, it seemed to me; and I fancied them to be staring back at me, wondering what was wrong. There were plenty of soldiers and airmen on the streets, and by the time I'd walked a few more blocks and been saluted half a dozen times I had lost all interest in the sights.

I said to my companion: 'This can't go on. Let's find a cafe or restaurant where we can stay inside until after dark.'

He suggested a little place on Kingsway, where we could get American Coca-Cola, and I sighed thankfully as we entered this haven. There was a girl sitting at the table next to us, in the uniform of the Women's Auxiliary Air Force. This is the women's branch of the RAF. Its members work side by side with RAF men at RAF stations, doing work that they are capable of, and their status is exactly the same. They are usually called 'Waffs' from the initials of their organization, WAAF. I appealed to her, and she instructed me in the proper way of saluting. I suppose that was one of the few times in history when a member of the ranks instructed an officer on how to salute!

Fortified with this instruction and a little practice I felt safe in sallying forth again, and we went for a long walk about the interesting parts of the town, looking at some of the sights I had often read about – Buckingham Palace, St James's Palace, the buildings of Parliament, the great clock 'Big Ben,' the home of Scotland Yard, Trafalgar Square, and many other places that were a big thrill to me. Even bigger were the thrills I got walking past Buckingham and St James's palaces when the guards there presented arms to me, and I began to realize what a weight of tradition I had taken on when I put on the king's uniform for my first time that evening.

One didn't have to walk far through London then to realize there was going to be no thought of declaring it an 'open city,' or of abandoning it except building by building and street by street if the barbarian Hun came; and I began to realize that the type of resistance that the Nazis would face here was very different from what confronted them in France.

London was a fortress. Anti-tank barriers and traps were located all about. Sandbag and concrete barricades and breastworks were erected everywhere, protected every building. Gun emplacements marred the beauty of the parks.

The Prime Minister had said, 'We shall not falter.'

I got a feeling, realizing the implication of all these preparations, that history would prove him right.

Chapter 2 Apprenticeship in War! 16 July–4 August 1940 (based RAF Kenley, London in 11 Group) Next day I journeyed by train to the advanced training school to which I had been assigned. Traveling this time by day, I found the English landscape surprisingly like that of southern Wisconsin – rolling country, very green, with lots of small pastures and a great deal of woodland. The one big difference was that there were no red barns. Many of the barns in England, like other buildings, are of stone, and the rest all seem to be painted white or gray.

My school was one of many such that are known as 'Operational Training Units.' At these places newly trained pilots are given their final brushing up and actual experience in flying the latest fighter planes under the guidance of experienced fighter pilots who teach them the newest tactics. In addition, experienced pilots who have been doing other kinds of flying and want to become fighter pilots, as well as pilots from other air forces, receive the same training in order to learn British fighting tactics and the behavior of fighting planes. There were many Polish pilots and a few Belgians at this place undergoing training.

It was my first visit to a wartime airdrome, and I found it an impressive contrast to airports I was familiar with. In the United States everything possible is done to make an airport conspicuous and easy to locate – bright markings on hangars, buildings, etc., conspicuous runways, big arrows pointing toward the airport on the tops of buildings nearby, and so on, for the convenience of visiting pilots.

The visiting pilots who come here are not welcome, and everything is done to hide the airdrome from them. Hangars, shops, offices, and even driveways and roads are camouflaged, as well as vehicles themselves. All are painted in crazy wavy combinations of dull greens, grays, browns, and black, so designed that at great altitudes the airdrome merges in with the countryside and can scarcely be seen.

Most impressive of all to me was the grim dull coloring of the airplanes themselves. They were painted dull green and brown in the wavy pattern, except the undersides, which were gray. Concession is made even in the national markings, which for British planes consist of a red bull's-eye surrounded by concentric white and blue rings. On the top side of the wings this is altered by omitting the white ring, because that is too conspicuous from above, so there is just a larger red bull's-eye and a wider blue ring around it. The Spitfire fighting planes have a peculiarly shaped wing, very wide and tapered in such a way that it resembles the wings of some moths. The round red and blue marking near each tip enhances this resemblance so much that the planes themselves look like giant moths from above.

The entire airdrome bristled with sandbags, trenches, dugouts, and machine-gun and anti-aircraft emplacements.

A building known as the 'officers' mess' is provided for officers at airdromes and other military stations in England. This usually contains a dining room, bar, billiard room, and a large comfortable lounge. Here the officers spend most of their leisure time, and the officers' mess is a large part of their life. The building may or may not contain quarters for the officers as well. At this station it did not, and we roomed in other buildings. Each officer has the services of a 'batman,' or valet, who takes care of his room, makes his bed, presses his uniform, polishes his buttons, wakens him in the morning, and in general makes himself useful. This was all quite strange to me, and I went to bed pondering on the many strange things I must get used to in fighting the Huns.

Next morning I was assigned to a 'flight' of several pilots who arrived for training at the same time I did, and I reported to my flight commander's office. While waiting to see him I read a notice on the wall advising students to take their training here seriously. I still remember the closing words: '… for in all probability this is the last training you will receive before being committed to combat with the enemy.'

It gave me a little thrill. I was getting close to realities.

An instructor took me up in an American-built military plane, a North American, which is a type widely used for advanced training here, and I did a couple of landings for him. He seemed satisfied and assigned me to a single-seat advanced trainer of English make and gave me some practice work to do in it.

I had never flown anything that cruised faster than one hundred ten miles per hour before I left the States. This machine cruised at one hundred eighty; and I thought it more wonderful than anything I'd ever imagined. I practiced in it for a few days and then was told I might go on to flying Spitfires.

This was the very height of my hopes. Of all England's superb fighting planes, the Supermarine Spitfires are generally considered masters of them all and the world's deadliest fighters. The pilots assigned to fly them consider themselves the luckiest of pilots. They are single-seat low-wing monoplanes. The engines are twelve-cylinder Rolls Royce of about ten hundred fifty horsepower with an 'emergency boost' giving them nearly fourteen hundred horsepower for actual combat. Each has eight machine guns, mounted in the wings. All the guns point forward and are fired by a single button on the top of the pilot's control stick. The Spitfires, together with the Hawker 'Hurricanes' which are contemporary fighters also carrying eight guns, are often called 'flying machine-gun nests.' The cruising speed of a Spitfire is nearly three hundred miles per hour and the top speed nearly four hundred.

To myself, who had been instructing for the last year and a half in trainers of forty horsepower that cruised at sixty miles per hour, this was such a change that there just didn't seem to be any connection with my former flying. The first time I took a Spitfire up, I felt more like a passenger than a pilot. However, I began to get used to the speed after a few hours. I practiced acrobatics mainly at first, to get familiar with the behavior of the airplanes. In doing this I got my initiation to a new factor, which limits a pilot's ability to maneuver at high speeds. This factor is known as the 'black-out' – no connection with the black-out of cities at night.

If you swing a pail of water over your head the water will stay in the pail even when it is upside down, because centrifugal force pushes it against the bottom of the pail. Similarly, if an airplane is turned or looped quickly the centrifugal force tends to push the blood in the pilot's body downward, toward the bottom of the plane and away from his head. In ordinary airplanes this doesn't matter because his heart keeps pumping the blood right back up to his head. But modern fighting (pursuit) planes are so fast that it is quite easy in a turn or loop for the centrifugal force to drain the blood from the pilot's head. When this happens his brain stops working. At three hundred miles per hour only a few degrees of change in direction per second is enough to cause a pilot to 'black out.' A pilot's physical strength in resisting black-out is what determines the rate at which he can turn at high speeds, but it is impossible for any pilot to turn very quickly at three hundred miles an hour or more.

Strangely, when one starts to black out in a turn or loop his eyes fail before his brain. My first experience in blacking out occurred the first time I tried to loop in a Spitfire. I was cruising along at about two hundred eighty and drew the control stick back about an inch, rather abruptly, to start my loop. Instantly the airplane surged upward in response, so hard that I was jammed down in the seat, feeling terribly heavy, feeling my cheeks sag downward and my mouth sag open from the centrifugal force on my lower jaw, and a misty, yellow-ish gray curtain closed off my vision! I eased the stick forward again to stop the change in direction and my sight came back instantly. I saw that I had raised the nose of the plane only a few degrees.

This loss of vision is the warning a pilot receives. If he continues to turn or loop that hard he will lose consciousness in a few seconds. In looping I found that I had to ease the nose up ever so slowly at first until the speed had dropped to around two hundred, after which I could pull the plane around quite fast without blacking out.

It's an uncanny thing. In combat you may be circling to get your guns to bear on the enemy. He is circling, too, but you have almost caught up with him. He is just outside of your gunsights; and if you could only pull your plane around a few extra degrees, all at once, you would have him in your sights and be able to open fire. But you can't do that. You can turn just so fast and that is all, for if you turn any faster your vision fades and you can't see either him or your sights!

A pilot can increase his resistance to 'black-out' by practice in doing lots of tight turns at high speed. He learns to contract the muscles of his abdomen and take deep breaths and hold them while he's turning, because that leaves less room for the blood to drain to down in his body. In this way physical strength often enters modern air fighting. The pilot who can resist black-out best is the one who can maneuver fastest at speeds much above 200.

Leaning forward also helps, because then one's head isn't as high above his heart, and so his heart can pump the blood up to his head easier. I have some very vivid recollections of moments in combat when trying to throw an enemy 'off my tail' (in other words from directly behind me which is the best position to shoot from) when I was leaning forward as far as my straps would permit, taking big gasps of air and holding them, and tensing my body muscles in the desperation one feels when his life is at stake, trying to fight off that damnable misty curtain from my eyes while fairly hauling my plane around in the most sickening turns. It invariably worked, too, and when I 'came up for air' after a few seconds and looked around I usually found that my enemy had lost his advantage and it was my turn to take the offensive.

There was an English boy named Peter, a big dark-haired husky fellow, who started this training course the same time I did. We took to each other as soon as we met, and became very close pals. He had been in the Navy at sixteen, and at twenty he was bronzed and hardened and looked and acted several years older. We practiced nearly all our flying together and with a squadron leader who was also taking the course.

We did a lot of 'dog fighting' practice. We would take off together, Peter and I, and climb to ten or fifteen thousand feet. Then we would separate and fly in opposite directions a few seconds, so that we could turn around and fly back toward each other. Then when we'd meet we'd engage in vicious mock combats – turning, twisting, rolling, climbing, and diving to get into firing position on each other. When one of us succeeded in getting the other in his gun sights he pressed with his thumb on the guard over the firing button on his machine, sending salvo after salvo of imaginary bullets after his pal. This guard over the firing button was just a temporary affair, to keep the pilot from accidentally pressing the button itself when he didn't want to use the guns; and across it were painted in red letters the words 'GUNS LOADED.'

I became well acquainted with some of the Poles who were training here. They were a fine bunch of fellows. Most of them had fought the Hun over Poland and again in France. Now they were being prepared to fight with the Royal Air Force. They were cheerful, happy-go-lucky fellows – except when the subject of Nazis was brought up. Then you saw evidence of the terrible hatred for the dogs who had ravaged their homeland and their people.

On one occasion one of the English boys, joking, chided one of the Polish boys, saying that he was supposed to love his enemies. It didn't anger the other because he knew it was a jest; but he replied with a pitiful attempt to smile and keep his voice light, 'Would you love your enemies when they kill your mother, and put your sister in a brothel for soldiers?'

I hope I never find myself in as perilous a position as that of a Nazi pilot being attacked by one of our Poles.

Days passed, and we began to develop a polish in our handling of the Spitfires. I had been at the training base about ten days when the papers carried the news that the State Department of the United States had announced that Americans fighting for Britain would not lose their citizenship. My friends congratulated me, and I felt pretty good. But I also felt proud that I hadn't waited to learn that before I volunteered.

In the lounge at the officers' mess I was often the center of conversations about the United States and the war. I was continually asked if I thought the United States would join or at least give more help, and when. I answered their questions as well as I could, giving the American people's side as I had seen it but not necessarily taking that side. A mean of all such conversations would have run something like this:

'When's your country going to give us some help, America,' ('America' is about the only nickname I have in England outside of the usual 'Art.')

'I don't know,' I reply. 'They've sent me, haven't they?'

'Yes, but we're never sure whether that was helping us or Germany. Seriously, though, what do they think about it – don't they realize this is a world menace we're fighting?'

'Yes,' I admit, 'most of them seem to realize it now. They seem pretty well agreed that if Hitler wins here it will only be a matter of time before their turn will come. But they'd rather have it that way, it seems, than to take any chances of having their boys fight on foreign soil.'

'What? You mean they'd rather wait and fight in their own country?'

'I guess so,' I admit again.

'Do they know what that means?'

'They should.'

'Sounds as if they don't like their women and children,' says one.

'Or their homes and cities,' from another.

'Besides,' I add, 'they say, "What did we get out of helping England in the last war?"'

'They got rid of their menace, didn't they? Where do they think they'd be if the Kaiser controlled England and France and Canada?'

'They forget that they ever had a menace then, and all they remember is that it cost them money.'

'Do they think England got rich on it?'

'If you ask me, they don't think, very deeply.'

I wasn't standing up for my countrymen in these conversations because I didn't sympathize with their attitude. I'd fight the battles which were America's as well as England's in the air, but I wouldn't fight America's battles in the officers' mess.

I had just come out of the officers' mess from dinner one noon when the local air-raid sirens sounded. It was the first air-raid warning I had ever heard.

It was a cloudy day, there being a high dark overcast that covered the sky. Lower down there were a lot of scattered thick clouds; and looking between these I could see, very high up, a long curving trail of smoke across the sky. I asked some of the boys who were watching what it was, and one of them said, 'It must have been a Jerry made that. See, there's some Spitfires going up after him.'

I could see several Spitfires above the clouds, and as I knew that my flight commander was up on a training flight with some of the boys I wondered if theirs were the Spitfires I could see. I had never seen a German airplane, and I strained my eyes trying to see this one, but couldn't.

Suddenly above the sound of the several engines roaring up there we heard a distant *r-r-rat-a-tat-tat!* The engines kept on droning as the machines scurried about, and now the Spitfires were so high we couldn't see them either. They all seemed to be working north of the airdrome.

All activity at the airdrome had of course stopped when the air-raid warning sounded, but no one was in shelter. Everyone was outside trying to see the show. Now little black puffs of smoke began appearing here and there far up in the sky north of us, and a few seconds later we heard a succession of little noises like a feather duster being shaken outside a window – anti-air-craft shells exploding, I realized – the first time I had ever seen an attempt to take a human life. Then came a succession of heavy distant 'booms' – bombs exploding, the others said.

Now the planes seemed to be getting closer overhead again. Another and longer *r-r-rat-a-tat-tat!* reached our ears and every one grew tense and breathless watching the sky. A long minute elapsed, and then:

'There he *is!*' The voice of one of the overwrought boys who called out almost ended in a scream; and then we saw it too. First there was just an indistinct swirling in the bottom mists of one of the clouds, and then it came clear. It was an enormous strange-looking twin-engined airplane, and it was in a tailspin, nose down and gyrating round and round as it fell. It was the first time I had ever seen a big airplane in a tailspin, and I was spellbound.

'It's a Jerry, all right!' said an awed voice.

A tiny figure parted from it, fell a way, and then the white canopy of a parachute blossomed above it. Then another and another came clear, and their parachutes blossomed out.

The great machine kept spinning down and down, seeming slow and majestic even in this, its death dive. As it got lower and lower I tried to realize that it wouldn't be recovering from the spin at the regulation 1,500 feet minimum altitude, as exhibition or student planes that I watched always did. It wasn't going to pay any attention to the nearing ground. It was going to spin in! Almost unbelieving, I watched it make its last great corkscrewing revolution, just sweeping over the tree tops of a nearby grove and disappearing behind them.

A moment later there was a heavy crash, and then everyone was running in the direction of the grove and the victorious Spitfires were diving and zooming and rolling over the spot and some of them went to circling around the descending parachutes with their unhappy occupants, like Indians doing a dance around trussed-up captives. The Polish boys who were watching with us were very angry because none of the Spitfire pilots shot the Nazis in their parachutes – Nazi pilots had machine-gunned many Polish pilots in their parachutes in the Polish campaign!

We soon learned the whole story. The machine was a Junkers 88 bomber that had come to raid a nearby village. When the Spitfires took chase the pilot tried to get away, jettisoning his bombs in open country, but one of the Spitfires caught him anyway. It was the plane piloted by our flight commander; with his second burst of machine-gun fire he had dislodged one engine from the bomber so that it fell completely out of the airplane! The German pilot was then unable to control his unbalanced airplane and it went into the fatal tailspin. One other member of the crew baled out in addition to the three we saw, but he wasn't as fortunate. They found his body in a wood. The rip-cord by which he could have opened his parachute was severed by a bullet.

Every day we wondered when the promised German invasion would start. This was the last of July and Hitler had promised to take over London by 15 August. Peter and I hoped the invasion wouldn't start until we finished our training. The mass air raids had not yet begun on England, but there was a great deal of air fighting over the English Channel.

We had made our requests to be posted to a squadron near the Channel – the same squadron for both of us if possible. Those were the squadrons getting the action now, and if the invasion were launched it seemed likely that the Channel would be the hottest place then, too. We were spoiling for all the action we could get.

Peter and I reported as usual in our flight commander's office on the morning of the day before our training was scheduled to end.

'What shall we do this morning, sir?' I asked, meaning what flying should we do.

He looked at us a little oddly and then said: 'Nothing. You boys have been a little ahead of your schedule, and you've covered everything I can give you. The rest you'll have to learn – other ways!'

We knew what he meant by that. Our next instruction would be from our enemies!

'You boys can take the day off,' he added.

We saluted and went out. When we were outside, we turned to each other and shook hands, grinning. Peter said, 'Congratulations, war pilot!' We had arrived.

That afternoon we were informed, to our delight, that we had been posted to one of the squadrons close to the English Channel. We asked how close it was to the Channel and were told, 'From your advance base you can see the French coast on a clear day!'

We were given railway warrants and told to leave the next afternoon. I spent most of the rest of the day studying pictures of German fighting and bombing planes.

Next morning we packed. In the afternoon a large lorry left the airport for the railway station carrying a precious cargo. More than a score of newly trained fighter pilots rode in it, all bound for various squadrons. Over half were Poles and Belgians, eager for vengeance; and most of them were to exact their vengeance from the Nazis soon.

We all took a train to London, where we separated on various lines for our destinations. There was plenty of handshaking and goodbyes.

'Take care of yourself, and watch your tail, Pal!'

'Thanks, old man, same to you! Hope you get a hundred of them!'

Many well-wishes such as these, and then Peter and I were alone waiting for the train that would take us on a branch line to our squadron's home base, an airdrome near London.

Sitting and walking about in the gathering darkness, waiting for our train, we got to talking about America.

It was Peter's ambition to go to America after the war, and to stay there if he could find a job with a future in it. I told him I thought it would be swell if we could go back to the States together after this was over, that I was sure he could find a job and get ahead. He said: 'Let's plan on that. If we both come through this war in one piece I'll go back with you.'

I thought of what a swell pal he'd be to have over in America, and was glad of the plan.

We arrived at our airdrome late in the evening, and were fixed up with rooms in the officers' mess and told to report to our squadron leader in the morning. We met some of our new mates, who hadn't gone to bed yet. Conversation was all about the news they had just received from one of the oldest members of the squadron. He had been missing since a battle over the Channel some time back, and had been counted as dead. Now they had received word that he was alive, a prisoner of war in a German hospital. They were jubilant over the news.

An elderly, thin-featured, dark-haired man in the uniform of a pilot officer introduced himself to us.

'My name's F,' he said, speaking slowly and with a solemn mién that was contradicted by a twinkle in his eye, 'but everyone calls me "Number One." You see, I am Number One stooge of your squadron. You know stooges are people who don't fly, don't you? There are three of us officer stooges in the squadron. We're really very nice people, too. I hardly count myself. I'm just the intelligence officer, sort of a father-confessor to whom you are supposed to tell all the blows you've struck at your fellow men, the Huns, each time after you come back from shooting holes in them. You'll meet the other stooges in the morning. "Number Two" is the squadron's chief mechanic, and "Number Three" is the adjutant.'

We liked the man at once, and from the twinkle in his eye and the dry humor with which he spoke about himself and the rest we suspected that our squadron must be a good-natured bunch.

We were right. From commanding officer right down to the lowest ranks, they were all a cheerful, easy-natured, hard-working, happy-go-lucky group, an ideal bunch to work with or fight with or have fun with.

And as time went on I was to learn that the same was true of nearly all the boys and men in the RAF – good-natured, fun-loving, informal chaps, laughing in the face of tragedy because it did no good to cry, and fighting because their country is forced to, not because it's their trade or because they want to. No professional soldiers, most of these: they are your brother who was working in a drugstore to earn money to go to college and study to be a lawyer, until his country had to rise to call a halt to world gangsterism; and young Joe who was doing well in the insurance office downtown; your neighbor's boy who had just graduated from high school and had his head full of changing ideas, all involving a secure future; the Smith boy who had just gotten married and settled down on his father's farm – his father is running the farm again now, after having planned to retire; and young Ray King, the spoiled, spendthrift, ne'er-do-well son of the local banker, who everyone had prophesied would come to no good, chastised and sobered now by his consecration to a high cause.

Certainly no 'international bankers,' these lads, in whose plans war had had no part – nor in the plans of their parents either. Their parents, too, are ordinary people, who had approved their government's course in giving beaten Germany a chance to rise again so that her people could live happily and normally, until an insane, hate-crazed spellbinder had wrested control of the nation and turned it into a great war machine and started it on a march of world conquest and murder.

Then and only then, completely educated on both sides of the question by a free press, and by a free radio from which they could listen daily to thousands of words of Nazi propaganda in the English language, these ordinary people had risen and demanded that their government call a halt and make a stand now, because they could see that there was no other way out. And so these boys had abandoned all their cherished plans and gone into training to learn how to kill, and were now making the best of their new task of defending the existence of their people and of civilization.

Next morning, 4 August, we reported to our squadron leader, whose rank in the RAF corresponds to that of major in the Army. What follows will make him blush if he reads it, but I must describe him a little.

He is one of the most impressive personalities I have known. He is slender, with fine wavy hair and mustache, and piercing blue eyes. I seldom remember the colour of a person's eyes, but I couldn't forget his. He is very witty in his speech, has a personal magnetism that lends an almost feminine beauty to one's impression of him, and he fairly radiates strength of character and will power. We liked him at once and felt great confidence in him.

He outlined to us the work that his squadron was doing and the tactics they used; and gave us advice from his experiences with the Huns. This was all done in matter-of-fact tones that initiated us to the detached, impersonal, and unemotional attitude that fighter pilots quickly develop toward the taking – and losing – of human life.

He told us apologetically that it appeared to be a quiet time just now. There had been no fighting over the Channel for a week. We knew from the papers that, a week before, his squadron had played the main part in the biggest battle yet fought over the Channel.

'We gave them a good licking that time,' he said, 'and apparently they've been staying home licking their wounds ever since. We haven't seen a one all week, but perhaps it's the lull before a storm.'

He explained that the squadron spent most of its time at this airdrome, its home base, and the pilots all lived here. But part of the time was also spent in shifts with other squadrons at the advance base, an airdrome close to the Channel, from which the enemy planes could be intercepted more quickly when they came across.

He told us the type of German fighting plane encountered most frequently was the single-seat Messerschmitt 109 fighter, and he gave us some pointers on fighting them. There was another type fighter, the Heinkel 113, which was supposed to out perform the Messerschmitt, but none had been seen in this area yet.

Then there was the twin-engined Messerschmitt 110 to watch out for. It could be used either as a fighter or as a light bomber, but was considered easy meat by our fighters. The only danger lay in a surprise attack by one of them, because this type carried very heavy armament including two cannons, and if one of them got a good shot at you it would be bad. They weren't to be feared otherwise, though. 'You can shoot them down very easily,' he said.

There were three types of large bombers used by the Germans: the Dornier, the Heinkel III (made by the same company but otherwise unrelated to the little Heinkel 113 fighter), and the Junkers 88. All these were twin-engined. And of course there was the Junkers 87 dive-bomber, more familiarly known as the 'Stuka.' This was the type which terrorized the armies in France with mass attacks, dropping screaming bombs on them. This type was particularly easy meat for fighters and easiest of all to shoot down. It was an awkward-looking, slow, single-engined machine.

Our squadron leader said that up to this time the only raids had been on ship convoys in the Channel. 'But we have every reason to expect,' he added, 'that they will be sending bigger raids over to bomb our coastal cities and perhaps even London itself, as soon as they get their bases organized in France.'

How truly he spoke!

That afternoon we were taken on a short patrol to familiarize us with our new territory, because the next morning the squadron was scheduled to fly to its advance base at about eight o'clock. There we would put in a shift of several hours 'at readiness' – staying close to our machines ready to take off at a moment's notice.

I might explain here that most patrolling by fighter squadrons is done under the direction of a controller on the ground who gives the squadron orders by radio. Each plane has a radio receiver and transmitter, and the pilot keeps his receiver turned on all the time. He has headphones in his helmet and a microphone in the oxygen mask that fits over his nose and mouth.

Part 3
The Height of the Battle, August & September 1940

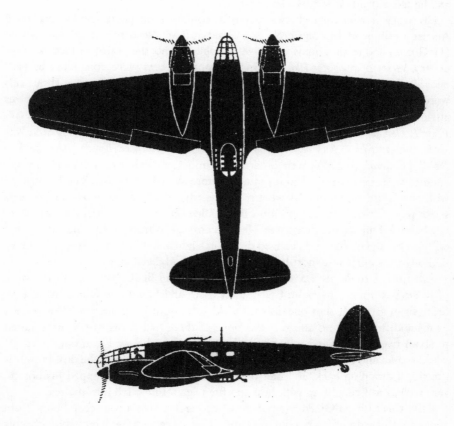

17 Archibald Nigel Weir, Hurricane Pilot, Pilot Officer, British, 145 Squadron

Archibald Nigel Charles Weir, Nigel to his family and fellow pilots, was born in June 1919 in Hythe, Kent. He followed his father into the RAF via the Oxford University Air Squadron but a slight eye defect threatened to end his flying ambitions. However, Nigel applied his formidable intellect to the problem, and uncovered a treatment using exercise alone that rectified his eye defect sufficiently to pass the RAF medical. Or perhaps, like Tony Woods-Scawen of 43 Squadron, he just memorised the eye-test cards. He was made an officer in the Volunteer Reserve in June 1939, joined 145 Squadron in May 1940, and flew during Dunkirk and throughout the Battle. As near as dammit an ace by September 1940, he was killed in action on 7 November 1940, shot down in the sea off Ventnor on the Isle of Wight by an Me 109. He was aged twenty-one. Nigel's body was never recovered, and he left a brother and two sisters.

His story is told through two personal combat reports he hand-wrote on 8 August 1940 when 145 Squadron was based at RAF Westhampnett, West Sussex (11 Group) and in six poems which were published posthumously in a book of his poetry, *Verses of a Fighter Pilot*, in 1941. Combat reports were completed by each pilot after they had encountered enemy aircraft on an operational sortie. Thousands were filled in by pilots in the Battle and many are preserved in the National Archives at Kew, London. They can now be searched and viewed online for a small fee.

Form F, Combat Report, 8 August 1940. Time attack delivered: 09.00; Enemy casualties: 1 Me 109 and 1 Ju 87 both destroyed unconfirmed; Place attack delivered: 5 miles SSW of Needles; General report: We were ordered to reinforce A flight over a convoy, as many bandits were approaching. About a minute before we arrived we saw A flight engaged with the fighter cover and as we arrived the first of numerous waves of bombers swept past. Green section went after them. Blue section followed and I was rather left behind. During the dive three Me 109s crossed in front of me and one peeled off onto the tail of Blue 3. I changed direction slightly, fired and followed him down. Although my burst was short he began to smoke and dived straight into the sea.

After this I could see no aircraft for a minute, and finally saw the second wave of Ju 87s passing on my right. I went after them and found one Hurricane already firing from astern. It shot one down. I picked the right hand aircraft (there were 9 or 10) and fired with no affect, but as none of them had returned my fire I closed to about twenty yards and gave him a short burst from below. He at once gave out white smoke and broke away from his squadron. I followed him as he dived towards the ships, dropping back, as I had throttled back sharply. He dropped his bombs, very wide, and I caught up with him and fired again till he fell into the sea.

After this I joined Green 2 in pursuit of a straggler, fired a two second burst from about 250 yards, and then ran out of ammunition. Green 2 subsequently brought this one down. I returned to base to rearm at about 09.30 hours.

Form F, Combat Report, 8 August 1940. Time attack delivered: 12.45; Enemy casualties:

1 Me 109 confirmed; Place attack delivered: 30 miles south of the Isle of Wight; General report: We had climbed after twenty-six He 111 and Me 110 but as they were far above us and heading home we were unable to catch them. We returned to shore above Dungeness and were then told that the convoy south of the Isle of Wight was being attacked. The squadron streamed back west, Blue section being at the rear, since it had been in front before. We headed well south of the convoy, hoping to cut off the bombers' retreat, for we could not hope to reach the convoy in time.

About 15–20 miles south of the convoy we found two squadrons of Me 110, about 5 miles apart, flying round in defensive circles low down (at about 2,000 feet). There were only three of us and we circled round at 12,000 feet for a long time wondering how best to attack and asking for help. We were split up, watching for other possible attackers, and just keeping note of where each member of the section was. After about ten minutes I had decided on the manner of attack I would adopt, and was about to dive when an Me 109 flew across in front of me – a decoy, I think. I pulled round to get on his tail, and we flew round in circles till I was just gaining a position from which I could fire. At this point he dived steeply – almost vertically. I went after him, but could not get closer than 500 yards, so I opened fire straight down onto his tail, and when I was sure he was hit, I pulled out and continued towards the 110s, where he had tried to lead me. My flight commander, Blue 1, saw him dive straight into the sea, as he was not engaged himself. He and Blue 3 attacked later.

At about 500 yards I opened fire on one of the 110s of the approaching side of the ring, allowing 6–8 lengths' deflection, and after a short burst began to pull out. One came up to meet me, but as I was doing over 500 mph I could not pull my sights on to him. I fired a burst behind him to put him off, and then flashed over the rear gunners quite low but quite safe, with a relative speed of about 700 mph.

After this I made off towards the convoy, in case it should be attacked again. There were no E/A there, but one had crashed and sunk leaving a patch of vivid blue green smoke to mark the spot. One could see it for miles.

I then returned to base and landed.

Perfect Workmen
Aero-engine, I trust you;
you manufacture motion
with a uniform precision that is constant.
In this unflagging gang of co-ordinated workmen
No-one is jealous,
nobody moves out of turn—
They concentrate keenly, and quicken the pace together
when ordered:
they obey. Towards their hardest foremen they bear no malice.
They labour uncomplaining,
and finally fail
together, when their nourished energy is all quite spent.
Hours of work irregular you share contented—
You have never grumbled,
fixed parts and moving; I place

well-earned confidence in you.
August 1938

Rearmament
I have heard the sullen howl of madness
rising, falling, from afar;
I see the desperate hate of nations
boiling up; it reeks of war.

I have dreamed of joy, unmeasured gladness,
planned my joys—for I am young;
England was weak, and dreams were broken;
England meet the day—be strong!
September 1938

Evening Flight
The blue bound fires of evening
sink quietly in the West;
the soft twilight is deepening
and teal return to rest.

But we sit by the salting
to meet their flight with lead,
and here they do no halting
but the halting of the dead.
Solway, January 1939

War
When the bloom is off the garden,
and I'm fighting in the sky,
when the lawns and flower beds harden,
and when weak birds starve and die,
the death-roll will grow longer,
eyes will be moist and red;
and the more I kill, the longer
shall I miss friends who are dead.
September 1939

To Elizabeth
Is th' enchanting light that plays
all in gold across your face
that same light whose myriad rays
are found in every place?

Yes, ah yes, the light that's nearest,
ever thrilling in my sight,

may have just left you, my dearest,
at the speed of light.

Now whenever I see flowers
in the light, or clouds, or dew,
or sunlight flashing after showers
I shall think of you.
(Undated) 1940

To Elizabeth
To each potential nobility is given,
the gift of heaven,
awaiting but the breath of inspiration
found in the chance encounter, or in the fleeting hour;
and here there is a power
beyond imagination:
'twas you held forth to me the lamp of beauty.
But now there is a war, there is a death,
and the great call of duty
took away those eyes, that hair,
those hands adorable, your hands,
and all that gentle loveliness—
Elizabeth!
This the vision everywhere,
here and in far distant lands,
will ever shine before me,
happily, my darling, happily.
In the field or in the wood,
and even mid the smoke and blood
'twill stay delightful none the less—
And should the thread of life be snapped within me,
that wondrous dream shall yet be carried with me
in its entirety
into eternity.
(Undated) 1940

18 Gordon Olive, Spitfire Pilot, Flight Lieutenant, Australian, 65 Squadron

Memoir written in the 1960s and '70s and published posthumously in 2001 as *The Devil at 6 O'Clock*, edited by aviation historian Dennis Newton. Olive was born in Bardon, Queensland on 3 July 1916 and was twenty-four at the start of the Battle.

He joined the Royal Australian Air Force in 1936 and sailed to Britain in 1937 to join the RAF as a pilot officer. He completed his training in May 1937 and joined 65 Squadron.

The extract below follows Olive's most active period during the Battle, 2–14 August 1940, when he was fighting continuously in 11 Group in the south-east of England (from RAF Hornchurch, Essex and RAF Manston, Kent) clocking up four kills. By the end of 1940 he had shot down at least six, making him an ace. Olive flew with such luminaries as Paddy Finucane (one of the top-scoring aces of the Battle) and Jeffrey Quill (Supermarine's top Spitfire test pilot and attached to 65 Squadron). Olive mentions bumping into 'Hilly' Brown (see chapter 23) in London while both were on leave, after he was shot down in flames on 15 August, however Olive's memory of the dates is incorrect here.

He survived the war and returned to Australia with his wife, London-born Helen Thomas, whom he had married in July 1940. Tragically widowed in 1946, Olive married fellow Australian Beryl North in 1948. A talented artist, Olive painted many scenes from his Battle of Britain experiences after the war. These paintings are unique, as they depict aerial combat scenes impossible to capture by photography (see colour section). His family still retain a photographic record of all his works and thirty can be seen in colour in the new edition of his memoir, retitled as *Spitfire Ace* (Amberley, 2015). He died in 1987.

Chapter 10 Fatigue & Fire: 2–7 August 1940 We soon took to Sawyer. He was a big man in every way and unusually good-looking. I had seen him a couple of years before when attending a camp concert at Cranwell where he took part in the evening's entertainment. He had been the outstanding performer and was a very able artist. He probably would have made a star in the theatrical world had he chosen it instead of the Air Force, especially with his physique and his good looks.

He also had a delightfully generous and happy nature and it was a rare bonus for a unit to have such a type as its leader. We knew we were lucky to have him.

He took it in turns to fly with 'A' Flight or 'B' Flight. When he flew with 'A' Flight I led the Squadron, when with 'B' Flight, Sam led. However, as most of the work at this stage was escort of convoys by flights, there was little opportunity to employ the whole unit.

It was his turn to fly with 'A' Flight one afternoon about four weeks after Cookie's death and on this occasion he was going to lead if we took to the air. The weather clamped down as a warm front came in from the Atlantic. Flying conditions became progressively worse and the forecast was that it would deteriorate into heavy rain – with little possibility of a clearance until morning. For the first time that summer the weather had broken and reverted to the average foul English day. For the first time since I had arrived in England I welcomed that murk and drizzle – it meant an early night and some sleep.

We were 'released' early, about three o'clock in the afternoon, and Sawyer invited me to join him in his little sports car and we took off for an hour or so at the local pub.

Over a few beers we talked of many things, but mostly about the other pilots. Sam Saunders, MacPherson, Smart, Franklin, Phillips all came in for a mention. We philosophised about life and the shortness thereof in our trade. In particular he was interested in the joint attitudes of Sam and I, neither of whom believed in claiming kills.

Sam and I both felt that it was the urge to confirm a kill which led so many boys to follow a stricken plane down and in the process make the perfect target of themselves for the ever outnumbering enemy. If we were going to survive, let alone win, we had to abandon all forms of claims and never give them a thought. This of course was hard when others subscribed to the opposite philosophy and some impressive scores were already being tallied up. Franklin, Sam's most experienced sergeant pilot, claimed no less than twelve kills at this stage, and Sam and I knew that if we had accepted the same standards of certainty for kills, we could both match him. In Sam's case he would be two or three ahead. Nevertheless, the prospects of survival were too grim to alter our attitudes and we would be very lucky indeed to come through the onslaught which was steadily mounting. No deviations were to be encouraged and in a matter such as this, examples were all important.

Sawyer was very unhappy that neither Sam nor I had a gong. Already most flight commanders were wearing at least a DFC and many already had bars or other recognition added. He knew of Cookie's unpopularity with the station commander and felt that but for that fact, Cookie would almost certainly have had a DSO and Sam and I something too. We both already had some sixty to seventy operational trips up including forty odd over Dunkirk. Being on the forward aerodrome was no help either – out of sight was out of mind where decorations were concerned and the station commander never ventured to Southend, far less to Manston.

As we parted company for an early night he announced that the first thing he would do the following morning would be to recommend both Sam and I for a DFC.

I made for my cot in the caravan by the Spitfires with a pleasant feeling in my middle. It was not just beer – Sawyer was one in a million and it was pleasant music to hear some appreciation for all the blood, sweat and tears. Anyway I was really dog-tired.

As the German attacks on the convoys had become routine, we had reverted to a flying to exhaustion routine. This was similar to the situation at Dunkirk when we were flying turn and turn about on the patrol lines behind beaches. Now, however, we flew cover over the convoys being relieved every hour or so. When there was a fight the tempo would step up. Thus once again tiredness had become the all-consuming sensation of life and we were lucky indeed from this point on to get four hours sleep during a night.

The German High Command must have been aware of the exhausting effect this would have on us, so they began a programme of bombing our airfields at night in order to ruin what little sleep we were able to snatch.

Every night one of our more experienced pilots who could fly a Spitfire at night had to sleep fully dressed in a caravan near the Spitfires. In the case of our squadron this was Sam, MacPherson, Phillips, Tubby Franklin or myself. When the night 'sleep disturbers' came over we were called to make some sort of effort to intercept them.

Sailor Malan had the record so far. Searchlights had picked up two in the one trip and Malan had destroyed them both. Thus whoever was detailed for this job consoled himself with the hope that if he were lucky, he could match Sailor's feat – it was largely up to the searchlights.

It came around to my turn every fourth night, and I was sleeping in the caravan on this night which followed the session with Sawyer. Suddenly I awoke to hear a Spitfire start up. After a few seconds the engine roared to full throttle for takeoff.

Strange, I thought, as I rang the controller to find out what was happening.

'Oh, it's all right,' said a voice at the other end, 'Squadron Leader Sawyer said you hadn't had a decent night's sleep for weeks and that if there was a scramble he would take your turn.'

The roar of the Spitfire's engine suddenly stopped in an abrupt explosion and I looked out of the caravan window to see a fierce fire blazing about a mile from the end of the runway.

It was a very dark, murky, moonless night after the day of rain and there were no stars. It was easy to see what had happened. Sawyer had never flown a Spitfire on a truly dark night. He had been dazzled by the exhaust flames lost his orientation and crashed. It had almost happened to me over a year ago and had happened to the three pilots killed on the night of the London blackout test just a year ago. It was not his lucky night.

I jumped in the flight truck and drove to the scene of the crash. The ambulance and fire men were in the process of extracting Sawyer's body from the blazing inferno which was all that remained of the Spitfire. After being violently sick I returned to the flight caravan and reported to the controller.

'Oh, it wasn't a raider after all', he said, 'so you can go back to bed'.

To bed, yes, but not to sleep after that. Poor Sawyer, trying to do me a kindness and let me sleep a little longer had paid for it with his own life. He had a beautiful wife and two little children – oh, the tragedy of war! It seemed that it was always the Sawyers and the Cooks who were killed. Eventually sheer exhaustion put me into a fitful sleep and I awoke at 6.30 – three hours after first light. It seemed impossible – the weather was clearing and a strip of blue sky was visible to the west.

I had some breakfast, almost unheard of these days, but I was still feeling sick from the sight of the crash the night before, and ate little.

Eventually we were brought to readiness at 11.00 a.m. and as Sam was away for a forty-eight-hour leave pass, I was acting as squadron commander. The sun was shining and once more it was glorious summer.

At 11.30 we were alerted to take off and patrol Manston at 20,000 feet after the patrol we would land at Manston and stay at readiness for the remainder of the day.

I led the squadron off. In those days the twelve Spitfires took off simultaneously in two groups of six, forming up in the air in four sections of three, each flying behind and below the one in front. In this way we could fly through thousands of feet of cloud and still keep together.

At five hundred feet as the last two sections steadied down in line astern, I wheeled the squadron around in a turn at full climb and turned on oxygen supply, as we were going to 20,000 feet.

Immediately there was a sharp explosion and the oxygen regulator dial blew up. I could see a fierce flame burning behind the instrument panel on the petrol tank. Sparks and dense smoke filled the cockpit and I realised with horror I was in trouble.

My first thought was 'perhaps this killed Sawyer' – I had to think of a way out. The Spitfire would obviously blow up in a few seconds – as soon as the oxygen fire heated the petrol tank to flash point.

If I rolled the Spitfire over and fell out I would be blown back through propellers of the following section leaders. If I turned they were so well drilled they would follow me. My radio was dead – wrecked in the explosion – so I could not tell them what was had happened.

I could see MacPherson on one side and Nicky on the other, and I realised that they would act on hand signals as we had done months of formation aerobatics by hand signals, so I decided on giving them the break-away signal – that at least would give me a chance to get clear of the squadron and those churning twelve foot propellers.

It worked – they peeled off and I pulled up into a vertical climb. Five hundred feet was too low for a parachute to open, so I had to get extra height, if possible.

The Spitfire rocketed vertically. I unfastened the straps of the harness and tore off my flying helmet. Many pilots had broken their necks trying to abandon an aeroplane with the helmet still attached. It worked like a hangman's rope. As the Spitfire stalled on the top of its climb, I kicked the left rudder hard and put it into a stall turn. This blew the flames over to one side of the cockpit as I pulled the canopy back, and jumping up on the seat, pushed out into the cool, sweet, fresh air.

I could see the Spitfire rapidly separate from me, then the tank blew up with a huge orange flash.

I lost interest in it at that point and pulled the parachute ripcord and waited for the jerk. Nothing happened. I looked down and saw the parachute all caught up around my legs, not streaming out as it should. With some horror I tried to free it and found that the little pilot chute, an umbrella-like device with springs to flick it open had fouled my flying boots and was not doing its job, pulling the silk out. I grabbed it and tore it free, then threw it clear.

After what seemed an age I felt a most violent jerk and for a few seconds could see nothing but stars. These cleared and I realised I was now supported by the parachute.

As my vision improved, I took stock of the situation. A violent crump told me the Spitfire had hit the ground and the main petrol tank had exploded. I could see it clearly, not far below – it had crashed next to some high tension cables which carried 330,000 volts across the countryside. I was dropping, as far as I could calculate, precisely on those cables, too!

The experts claimed a parachute could be guided by partially collapsing one side and side slipping. This, I told myself, I must do. The important thing was to avoid collapsing the canopy too close to the ground, and I was getting awfully close.

I looked up to take stock of the effect of pulling on one of the main straps, when I received my next nasty fright. The parachute looked like two half moons! Two complete panels forming a diameter across the canopy were just not there – a couple of fragile seams kept the whole from completely disintegrating.

Now I remembered – I had not had that parachute aired and packed since before Dunkirk. It had been sitting in my cockpit for almost four months, in water and damp and was in no shape to be used.

Miserably, I abandoned the idea of a sideslip. It would fall to pieces if I sneezed.

With a cold clammy feeling I watched the high tension wires come up. I missed them by inches.

Before I hit, I heard a loud 'thunk thunk' report then braced myself for a heavy arrival. The parachutes we used were supposed to break our fall to the equivalent of jumping off a fourteen foot wall. The thump I made as I hit was equivalent to considerably more, but I was lucky – I landed on a beautifully heaped up row of potatoes – my feet, hands, face and bottom making quite an interesting pattern in the loam.

I got my wind back to find myself surrounded by Land Army girls.

'Ee luv,' said one chubby lass, 'be you one of us or one of them?'

I was wearing my RAAF uniform which was dark blue and they were justifiably uncertain.

So was the Home Guard who ran up and, rightly or wrongly, was going to finish me off with a shotgun full of swan drop. That was the 'thunk thunk' I'd heard on my way past the high tension cables! Fortunately, a bit of the Australian vulgar tongue was readily identified as friendly. That problem resolved, we were soon all very matey.

The tubby one rolled up the parachute. 'It's a luvly bit of stuff,' she said. 'See 'ere Gert' to one of her mates, 'make luvly knickers, wouldn't it?'

Gert replied, 'It's not much good, luv, it's all ripped to ruddy ribbons. Better take it back and trade it in for a new one.'

All the drama had been acted out in the circuit area of the aerodrome and a sudden crescendo of ringing bells announced the imminent arrival of the station fire engine. In its wake was the ambulance.

I put the parachute into the ambulance and we set off but did not get very far. We ran into a ditch which was invisible as the grass had been scythed flat with the rest of the field. The ambulance rolled over. Fortunately, nobody was hurt.

Next, I mounted the fire engine and with bells ringing madly in my ear, we charged at full throttle down the country lane to the Spitfire. It was still burning furiously and we still had some stubble which had to be doused.

This done, we turned back for the aerodrome. Apparently, our fire engine drivers seldom had a run outside the aerodrome, but when they did, they liked to open the engine up. Their philosophy was a simple one – fire engines must proceed at top speed! We thundered down a straight stretch of road, the wind in our faces making the tears run from our eyes, whilst our ears were pounded by the bell which rose to a crescendo as the speed mounted.

The driver did not know the road. Around the corner was a bridge in the centre of a hairpin bend. At our speed there was no chance of making the turn. As we crashed down the embankment, I hurled myself into the air once more and landed for the second time with an even greater crump on the far bank of the creek. The bank was rock hard.

Looking back, the fire engine was upside down, slowly disappearing in a great doughnut of foam. The driver called his crew together and established that all were safe. No one was in the foam or under the engine.

I set off along the road to walk the mile or so back to the aerodrome. A local farmer passed me in his old bull-nose Morris, stopped, and as I caught up to him, offered me a lift.

'Not bloody likely,' I replied, 'I'm going to walk!'

He did not seem to understand that I'd had enough. I just wanted to walk back under what was left of my own steam.

Between us the camp doctor and I took stock of my condition. Eyebrows, eyelashes, moustache and hair mostly missing. Skin burnt but not badly. One damaged foot (it turned out I broke a bone in the right one) and a considerable assortment of severe bruises. In his opinion I would be little use for 48 hours so I'd better get to bed.

I explained that I had a wife up in London whom I hadn't seen since we were married nearly a month earlier, so I was given a pass for forty-eight hours.

One of the new boys flew me up to Hornchurch in the Maggie, where I caught a train to London.

Before I left I heard that Wigg had taken two boys up at Manston to investigate a raid above the overcast. They broke through the clouds immediately under a German fighter formation which promptly shot the three of them down. Warrant Officer Phillips and one of the new sergeants were killed; Wigg escaped once more by parachute.

It was a bad day for 'A' Flight, five Spitfires down, all destroyed by fire, the squadron commander and two others killed, Wigg and myself out of action – that just about eliminated 'A' Flight for a couple of days. It was a day I am unlikely to forget.

When I arrived in London I immediately rang Helen. She was working in St Thomas' Hospital as a social worker and was not expecting a visit from me.

We met at Leicester Square and regardless of my burns and bruises, made for a restaurant called the Queen's Brasserie, known to all fighter pilots in Fighter Command as 'the Queen's Brassiere'. It was a delightful spot with a distinctly Austrian atmosphere. It was popular with the boys because it reminded them of their skiing holidays. Skiing was a generally popular sport with the RAF and Austria had been cheap and unspoiled. Thus most of them found their way there in the balmy days of peace – 'the Queen's' because of its decor and its associations was thus our peacetime rendezvous and this had continued on into the war.

We walked straight into Hilly Brown, a Canadian flight lieutenant who was stationed at Tangmere – Hilly's face was the colour of beetroot and about twice its normal size. His ginger moustache and most of his ginger hair was gone and his hands were bandaged up. I knew him well from other get togethers in the relaxed days of peace. He was a great friend of Bob Tuck and Caesar Hull, the South African.

We joined forces and compared notes. Hilly, too, was on forty-eight hours leave – had been shot down and his Hurricane had caught fire. He had been burned on his way out, but it was not sufficiently incapacitating to keep him in bed either.

Others joined in the noisy reunion and we had quite a party. No doubt the civilian patrons of the restaurant thought the rowdy red faced fighter pilots who got so drunk and sang songs out of tune were a raucous nuisance and behaved like that every evening – getting off with the prettiest of the girls, too. Well, such was life. They had no idea what it was like working each day from Manston, nor that it was our first night off for a drink for over a month and we would not have had that if we had not both been burnt that morning.

For all the noise and enjoyment we turned in early. It was the last time I saw Hilly, later he was killed on Malta.

Two days later I was back on the job. Sam Saunders was acting squadron commander again but we were told a new CO would be posted to take Sawyer's place. While I had been away one of 'B' Flight's officers had been killed and my boys were desperately tired from lack of sleep.

Except for the party on the first night, I had slept most of the forty eight hours, so I was feeling much refreshed, if still bruised and stiff. I arrived back at Hornchurch by midday, had a meal in the mess, then flew a new Spitfire back to Southend.

Within half an hour I was climbing up to the east with Nicholas on one side and MacKenzie on the other – we were ordered to investigate some plots which had appeared near Dover, estimated at 20–30,000 feet.

We climbed in perfectly still air towards France at 20,000 feet and the view as always was superb. Below was the Channel no bigger it seemed than a large river. In fact the Thames Estuary seemed wider, as we flew down I looked at Nicholas and he waved back. Then as usual I glanced at my other companion. He seemed to be looking down at the floor of his cockpit. I waited for him to look up, but he did not move.

Gradually his left wing dropped and he slipped away from the formation. I turned towards him and called him on the radio.

'Red three – you ok? Over?' No sound. I called again – by this his was down and with full climbing power he was gathering speed rapidly.

I called him more urgently. 'Red three – what the hell's the matter. Wake up Red three! Red three! Wake up!'

He continued to roll to the left and dive. The speed was mounting to the high 400s. In a few seconds I would have to break off or hit the speed of sound, which could break up the Spitfire. Obviously MacKenzie had gone to sleep. They were all so tired it was amazing how they kept awake.

I called control. 'Red three's gone to sleep – I can't wake him. If you can't wake him in a few seconds, his wings will come off and he'll be killed.'

I listened as the more powerful radio of control called.

'Red three. Wake up! Red three wake up! Wake up – do you hear me? Wake up.'

The tone got more urgent, but it was no use. The Spitfire was now diving vertically and slowly spiralling to the left. There was nothing more I could do. I lost sight of him in the haze over the Channel.

Nicholas and I continued on the patrol to 30,000 feet, but apart from a very remote vapour trail over France there was nothing to be seen.

Half an hour later we returned and landed. No response from MacKenzie. He had gone to sleep and that was it. It could happen to any of us – we were a depressed flight that afternoon. Only Nicky and I were left of the officers and Nicky was in pretty bad shape. He was becoming even more nervy as he became more weary – he desperately needed a rest. Wigg was still away for a couple more days recovering from the effects of being shot down in flames two days before.

MacPherson who had been one of my best friends over the years had risen to rank of warrant officer. He was easily the best of my bunch, so I had to appoint him as my deputy to lead the other section of three in the flight. The only problem was that we were now down to five pilots in total – no rests and no time off unless one of us was hurt.

The following day at about three in the afternoon, the five of us returned from an escort job in the Straits of Dover – already I was feeling exhausted again, and we had seven more hours to go before we could be released. We landed at Southend and taxied in to our dispersal point. As I climbed down from my Spitfire, I saw MacPherson's machine still out on the aerodrome where it had finished its run.

I leapt in my little truck and drove out to see what was the trouble. MacPherson usually taxied in without delay and a Spitfire could not be left with the engine ticking over like other aeroplanes, because its radiator was offset and not cooled by the slipstream from the propeller. As a result, it would boil in five minutes and that involved a major engine overhaul.

I reached the Spitfire and climbed up on the wing. MacPherson was out cold – fast asleep. He had gone off between landing the Spitfire and coming to rest at the completion of the landing run. I woke him up and he looked around stupidly, shook his head, opened his throttle, finished his taxiing and switched off.

In the caravan we discussed it. MacKenzie, we knew, had gone to sleep in the air. Now MacPherson had missed doing so by moments. Yet with five pilots to fly six aeroplanes, none of us could get any rest. It was some problem and the fatigue made us feel so damned miserable all the time – yet the real fighting, we knew, was still to come.

That night three new pilot officers showed up, two for 'A' Flight and one for 'B' Flight. We welcomed them wearily and Sam shot a few questions at the senior boy – or rather the one among them who seemed to be an old timer. He was at least thirty or so and had a very mature look about him. The others seemed to be children.

The new boy smiled self-consciously as Sam paused for him to reply and said.

'Sorry, Sir, I do not understand very well.'

'We are Poles,' said one of the younger members of the trio with fair curly hair. In fact, he looked too young to be in long pants, far less in an Air Force officer's uniform.

'We do not spik the English too good – pliss to talk very slow and I think I understand.'

'Hell,' I thought, 'it's come to this – we have no pilots left, only bloody foreigners who can't talk to us.'

I suddenly felt too tired to cope but Sam took up the interview.

'You are Polish,' very slowly – 'Good, I'm very glad you have come – we need you very badly. Can you fly Spitfires?'

'Oh yes,' said the curly-headed boy with a grin which lit up his whole face. 'Very good aeroplane – I fly for two hour – Szulkowski he fly for one hour, Gruszka fly for one hour, too.'

So. Their names were Szulkowski and Gruszka. It turned out the boy's name was Drobinski. One hour – two hours on Spitfires – what the hell – and unable to communicate with us!

I won the boy and the short, stocky, fair-haired Gruszka. I explained to my pair very carefully to get to bed and get plenty of sleep, because it might be the last they would get, and to see me at midday the next day when I returned from the morning visit to Manston. Then I would see if I thought they could fly Spitfires.

When we got down to business next afternoon, I was pleasantly surprised to find that they knew all the controls of the Spitfire and that they knew the various procedures for takeoff and landing perfectly. They could even locate every tap, switch and tit with their eyes shut. Further, I learned that they had four hundred hours flying to their credit, albeit in somewhat less advanced planes. Also, they'd had many hours in combat and could fly formation and do aerobatics.

I sent Gruszka off and he started by doing a circuit and a landing, the latter a perfect job. I waved him off and he disappeared for half an hour, returned and landed. Drobinski then did the same. Then, with one on each side, I took them off in formation. They obviously knew their business. I gradually stepped up the manoeuvres until we were doing aerobatics. Both of them sat either side as if riveted to my main planes.

We landed and I had a new respect for these boys. They were really good. The phone rang in the caravan. It was Sam.

'How are your Poles?'

'First class. Yours?'

'Same. Most capable.'

That was all we said but I knew we both felt a little more hopeful about the immediate future.

Chapter 11 Ordeal At Manston: 8–12 August 1940 MacPherson returned from a convoy engagement with an assortment of bullet holes in his Spitfire, and when it came to the point where he lowered his undercarriage for landing, the wheels would not come down. Mac went through all the emergency and panic procedures, but still no wheels, so with much reluctance he landed in the centre of the aerodrome on his Spitfire's belly. This grieved him considerably, because he had flown the same aeroplane for some eighteen months and had formed quite an affection for it.

So now he had to go and collect another Spitfire as a replacement. This was an inconvenience because we were again short of pilots as well as aeroplanes. Nicky was off on necessary leave to give him a bit of rest, and we had lost one of our new sergeants. A couple of hours later MacPherson was back and he was very unhappy. His trouble was, he told me, that his new aeroplane was virtually unmanageable – it would only fly with its wings about ten degrees down to the left unless an effort was made to force it to fly level. In air force parlance, it was 'left wing low'.

I took the Spitfire up for a test flight. Mac was quite right. It was useless.

Whilst the aeroplane could be flown, this defect was a great curse to the pilot because it flew along like a ship with a list to one side and the only way to correct it was by continual pressure on the control column against the tendency to lean. This could be tolerated for a few minutes at a time, but if the machine was in the air for an hour or more, the effect was like holding a small weight at arm's length for that period. You hardly noticed it for the first five minutes, but at the end of ten the weight felt like a hundred pounds. In half an hour the weight was quite insupportable, an hour meant cramps and general muscular agony – two hours was pure hell.

Another result of this defect was that as soon as the wing dipped, even a degree or so, the aeroplane sideslipped quite significantly. With a five degree list the slip was far too serious for continuous formation flying, as the aeroplane tended to slip in and ram the leading aeroplane. If on the other hand the list was to the other direction, the aeroplane tended to float away from the formation.

To fly such an aeroplane in formation was an unexpected form of physical hell – especially for a trip of two hours or so.

'Why did you accept it, Mac?' I asked him.

'Remember that bloke Quill who was the Spitfire test pilot at Southampton? Well, he was up at Hornchurch for some reason or other and when I rejected it the engineer officer appealed to Quill who stated that he had flown it two days ago and it was quite ok.'

Thus overruled, Mac had been obliged to fly it down to Southend. As it was only flyable in an emergency I gave instructions for it to be put at the end of the line until I had a chance to sort it out. It seemed odd to me that Jeff Quill could pass a machine so badly rigged. I was moodily contemplating this latest annoyance when who should walk into my caravan but Mr Quill, all fitted out in a flight lieutenant's uniform.

'I was just thinking about you,' I said, 'what brings you down here to this forsaken outpost?'

'The Air Ministry has agreed that a few of us test pilots can fly with operational squadrons to see what goes on under battle conditions. Bad luck old boy, I've been attached to your flight.'

'By the way,' as an afterthought, 'have you got an aeroplane I could fly?'

'I certainly have – there's one over there at the end of the line – you might recognise it,' I said.

'Isn't that the one Warrant Officer MacPherson was bitching about this afternoon? That's a good aeroplane.'

'Fine,' I said, 'it's yours. I suggest you collect your bits and pieces and put them in the cockpit – taxi it up here near mine and you can fly number two next to me for a few trips until you feel you have the score.'

It was late in the day and we were let off the readiness list to relax at 'available' so Jeff and I talked for some time about the finer points of the fighter pilot's trade and in particular what to do when the dogfights set in.

At 4.30 the following morning we were ordered into the air to patrol Manston at 25,000 feet. Jeff took off with me and with Wigg on the other side, we climbed to our altitude in a cloudless sky. We spread out to about ten spans and every now and then I glanced at Quill to see how he was going. For the most part his Spitfire remained on an even keel though now and again I noticed it sliding in towards me.

We were ordered around the sky on various courses, but after two hours of scanning the horizon and the sun, we landed at Manston. Jeff was some time before he climbed out of his Spitfire and I was just beginning to think that I must have been imagining its imperfections when he slowly struggled out of the cockpit and eased himself gingerly on the ground.

He was not smiling when he announced, 'I'll condemn that bloody aeroplane if it's the last thing I do – where's a phone – I want to ring up the Works.'

He disappeared wearily inside the crew room for a phone to ring the Spitfire factory at Southampton. I don't know what he said, but we never had a Spitfire from the works which flew other than perfectly level in flight from that day on.

For the most part Spitfires were superbly well put together and could be flown 'hands off' at most speeds. Occasionally one would need a small adjustment to make it fly level. This was usually achieved by attaching a piece of cord along the top or bottom of the aileron trailing edge. Rarely, the trouble was a warped aileron, when considerably more rectification was necessary. Usually this was done, but in the case of this particular Spitfire, it was necessary to send it back to the works.

The exchange was arranged and in a few hours Jeff had a new aeroplane or rather MacPherson had it, as Mac had the prior claim to the machine.

It was easy enough to understand. Quill normally tested the Spitfires as they came off the assembly line for only a few minutes, he was very experienced and could tell almost immediately if there was any serious fault in the assembly. During these tests he seldom flew them for more than a minute or two in a straight line and a tendency to drop a wing slightly on one side or another was common in most makes of aeroplanes, but it was not viewed as a serious fault especially in the heavier aeroplanes where trimming controls were available in the cockpit to correct the tendency in flight. There was no such control on the Spitfire. Having spent most of two hours wrestling with this imperfection, Jeff was physically a very tired man, and it was quite unnecessary to mention it again.

Two days later Jeff and I landed at Manston. Paddy Finucane and another pilot were with us. As there were only four planes to refuel, we took a chance and landed together. The intention was to refuel quickly and then continue escorting a convoy a few miles out in the Channel.

The tanker had just started to refuel the second of our Spitfires when we heard an unusual snarling growl from an unfamiliar aero engine. We looked up to see six Me 109s coming in over the hedge with rows of tracer squirting out of their guns.

We scattered at tremendous speed, most heading for the nearest dugout shelter, about a hundred yards away. Our yellow life jackets (Mae Wests) were obviously noticed by the attackers, as two of them turned off from shooting at the parked aeroplanes to try to hit us on our run to the shelter.

We hit the back of the shelter mound as a barrage of cannon shells and bullets zapped into the other side of the low earth mound over the trench. The 109s snarled past only a few feet above me and hauled up into a steep climb. Another and another screeched past and I judged from the absence of missiles slamming into the mound of earth that I might have time to make the entrance and safety.

Above, the 109s stall turned and came down on the opposite side. They were after me, but I whipped around to the other side in time to get down the funkhole. I was second in.

As I made it, a shower of cannon shells and slugs spat filling the shelter with the stench of exploding cordite.

There was silence for a couple of minutes during which Paddy Finucane hurled himself down the entrance. He only just made the tunnel as another broadside hit the opening – Quill arrived shortly after Finucane, and we were all safe.

The roar of Mercedes engines faded and we emerged into the sunlight. Two of our four Spitfires were burning furiously – the other two were unharmed.

Jeff was furious. If there was one thing which made his blood boil, it was to see Spitfires being destroyed on the ground by Me 109s. He was even more livid on account of the undignified scramble necessary to avoid being massacred by the ground strafers in their efforts to kill the pilots.

We had learned a lesson – never refuel without a top cover. The 109s had come in fast at wave height from Calais. They were so low that the radar had not had a chance to pick them up and warn us.

We continued our convoy patrols but, for some reason we could not understand, there was a lull in these attacks for a couple of days. In between escorts, we were alerted regularly and sent scrambling into the air only to return as the alleged raid disappeared, and according to control dispersed. After five or six such false alarms, we became sceptical about the reliability of the radar. The controller insisted that they were unusually large concentrations of aeroplanes according to the radar screens, thus we were anticipating a dramatic increase in enemy effort, but each alarm was a fizzer.

The days were hot and we were irritable at being endlessly disturbed as we tried to snatch a few winks of badly needed sleep on the dusty floor of the crew room. Each hour and each day made us feel worse. Already Jeff Quill was looking like one of the old timers. He too was tired and sported a two day's growth of black beard which somehow made him look like a pirate from a bygone age.

Things changed dramatically late in the morning on Monday, 12 August.

According to Adolf Hitler's favourite English-speaking radio personality, Lord Haw Haw, Britain would lie in ruins by 15 August, in just three days time. It was a hot, still, humid morning – the light breeze blowing in from the west had dropped and clouds had begun to build up over the Straits of Dover. Nature, it seemed, was holding its breath.

We knew that Hitler had smashed all air resistance in Poland in two days. The same pattern had been repeated in Holland and Belgium, again in a couple of days. France, one of the most powerful nations in the world, had collapsed after three days of air onslaught and the complete and unconditional surrender had been achieved in under six weeks, about the time it took the infantry to walk across the territory. Now, according to 'the voice', whose prophesies had proved so right each time, it was our turn!

As it was, our fighter defences were desperately thin. More than half of the force was necessarily dispersed north to protect the major fleet installations in Scotland and Scapa Flow, as well as the vital Rolls Royce factories, the bomber bases and the industrial heart of England, which could not be left unguarded. They were all at least two hundred odd miles to the north and beyond effective range of help.

What was left, some two hundred and fifty pilots and fighter planes, were dispersed around the south of England from Cornwall to Kent and Essex, a distance of some 250 miles. Opposite us, across the powder blue waters of the English Channel, Hitler had ten times that number of planes poised to strike, or so our intelligence experts had told us – so too did Lord Haw Haw. Directly across that strip of water, which we could see through the crew room door from Manston, was the hazy outline of the white cliffs of Calais, barely twenty-five miles away. There, although we could not see them, were some six squadrons of Me 109s on the airstrips near the town.

All we could do was wait.

The squadron's pilots looked a motley bunch as they sought relief from the deadly weight of fatigue. The fighting strength of the squadron was twelve, we had virtually no reserves so most of us had been on continuous duty since the Dunkirk fighting twelve weeks earlier. The hours of duty were from first light to last light, a spread of twenty hours, with an average of four hours sleep each night. This was exhausting even in good times, but when the stresses of continuous operational flying and battle were superimposed, the effect was overwhelming. Sleep – just eight hours of peaceful sleep – represented the most precious commodity in life.

There was MacPherson, the tall spare warrant officer pilot who would not accept a commission because the medical examination involved would risk detection of his secret. One of his eyes was virtually useless. He had tricked his way into aircrew four years earlier and knew he could not do it a second time. He was a superb pilot and incredibly courageous. He never claimed a kill although his score was already in double figures.

Remarkably handsome, Paddy Finucane was a veteran already. He was only eighteen and looked younger because he did not yet shave. His beard had not begun to grow and I suspected he was even younger than he claimed. Yet such was the superb vitality of the boy that he always appeared bright eyed and full of fun.

His boon companion was Dave Glaser, another eighteen-year-old who was as tall and blond as Paddy was short and dark. He too did not shave, nor did he have any fear. He and Paddy produced the only real sign of life when the squadron was on the ground, when they horsed around tirelessly like a couple of playful pups. It was a classical David and Jonathan friendship and under the most impossible conditions they seemed determined to get the most out of what little life they could anticipate.

'Sam' Saunders was, at twenty-three years old, in temporary command of the squadron. Tall, thin and blond, he was rude to everyone except one or two of us who were spared his barbs. I was one who was excluded, as was Jeff Quill. Sam had to be shyest man I have ever met and without exception the bravest of a very brave lot. He led us most of the time, except on odd occasions when his duties as *de facto* squadron commander demanded his attendance elsewhere. Then I led the team. In our eyes Sam had already earned two VCs, but it seemed that fighter pilots did not qualify for this rare honour as the number of witnesses and other conditions required by the charter could never be met. He would earn half a dozen more in our eyes before the crisis was over.

Tom Smart was a plump easy going Englishman of twenty summers. He had the joviality of a fat man and was as friendly and outgoing as Sam was introspective and reserved. They were great friends – no doubt their personalities complemented each other in some way.

'Butch' Franklin was a tough, prematurely balding warrant officer who claimed twenty odd kills already. He alone of the squadron kept a jealous tally of his victories which he collected with a savage and ferocious satisfaction. His father had been killed in the First World War.

Drobinski, one of the Poles, was another youngster, with blond curly hair and a pinched look due to enduring fantastic hardships in escaping overland from Poland, then from France. He had the appearance of a prematurely old man who had suffered greatly. We called him Ghandi-ski, but he, too, was a most intrepid boy. He was later to receive the Polish 'VC', which was richly deserved.

Szulkowski was another Pole, a much older man who had great difficulties with the language, but none at all with a Spitfire, In his thirties, he had over 3,000 hours flying to his credit, more than three times the flying Sam or I had, more even than Jeff Quill. He was in Quill's class as a pilot, probably one of the best in the world. He had been a squadron commander in Poland, now he was a humble pilot officer in the RAF, but there never was a better one, nor a more cheerful one.

Oh! How we wished we had an extra thousand Spitfires just to back up our meagre waiting twelve. According to Jeff Quill, he had been loaned to the RAF partly to help replace the appalling losses of skilled pilots and partly because of the failure of the main Spitfire shadow factory to supply a thousand or more fighters to date. This was due, he said, to communist subversion and obstruction in the works. This latter achievement of the comrades was part of their contract under the Hitler-Stalin Pact of non-aggression and mutual friendship and assistance signed on the outbreak of hostilities against Poland a year earlier. It was the joint Socialists contribution to the struggle against British capitalist imperialism led by Winston Churchill, the arch warmonger!

What we could have done with another 1,000 Spitfires! We had a bare two hundred and fifty out of the seven hundred odd fighters available, but the Spitfire was unquestionably the best.

It was eleven o'clock. Saunders, Quill and I were discussing the villainy of the industrial sabotage at the Spitfire works. A sudden clatter of boots running on floor boards jerked us out of our chairs and off towards the aeroplanes a few yards away outside the crew room door.

'Scramble!'

We were all half-asleep and wearily dragged ourselves to our planes. There was no ginger in our stride, though from so much practice we were all taxiing briskly across the aerodrome for a take off into the west within a couple of minutes of the call.

'Scramble base angels ten' shouted the voice, as we jumped into our Spitfires. I took my flying helmet off the control column where I always left it attached to its wires and tubes and pulled it on. An airman had jumped up on the wing and handed me the straps of my parachute over my shoulder and I clicked them into the main coupling box; next the webbing belts of the safety harness were secured. I turned on the petrol cocks, switched on and pressed the starter button.

A cloud of bluish smoke appeared and the Rolls Royce engine growled into life with customary staccato belches and coughs – I opened the throttle enough to roll away and out on to the field. There was now a light wind blowing from the west, so we taxied across the aerodrome to the opposite side and as we did so Sam called control to check that radio contact was normal.

'Control – Petal Squadron taxiing. Scramble one minute.'

The twelve Spitfires turned into wind and formed up as we had done a hundred times in the last month. We paused a moment for Sam to call the usual take off command over the radio. We would take off all together as four sections of three, Sam leading the first six, I following with the second six. Sam's six aeroplanes were ahead and to my left.

We had not begun to roll when there was a violent 'crump' and to my amazement I saw two hangars near the hut we had just vacated erupt into the air in two vast geysers of black smoke and earth. Two more crumps in quick succession sent two more buildings skyward. I could not believe my eyes. We had never been bombed before and I had never seen a large bomb explode except on films.

Two vast fountains of dark grey earth suddenly erupted thirty feet away to my right eclipsing the first explosions and a fraction of a second later the shock wave hit the Spitfire like a huge invisible hammer. It seemed to move two yards to the left.

Sam called over the radio in his usual calm voice.

'Let's get out of here'.

He need not have said a word. Already each Spitfire was at full throttle. I glanced up as we started to roll, scarcely daring to look and saw a huge massed formation of some two hundred bombers about five hundred feet above us, the black crosses of Prussia were quite unnecessary to tell us they were hostile, their bomb bays were open and the bombs were right there in front of us and above, falling down exactly above us.

At first it seemed they would all land in front of us, but as we gathered speed they drifted back in their path. I watched fascinated as stick after stick raced along and speared in about twenty yards to my left, chasing Sam's flight as they gathered speed. They seemed to explode in a solid line rushing right up to the Spitfires and bursting amongst them. For a moment they were completely lost in the smoke, then the Spitfires were out in front again. One was hit and trailed back behind me, its propeller stopped.

I looked in the rear vision mirror to see what was happening to Jeff Quill and his two boys. They were inches in front of a huge cascading wall of black smoke and dust which reared up like some huge tidal wave about to catch up, crash down and engulf us all.

I knew just one of those bombs in front of us now would kill us all, yet for some curious reason I felt no fear, only a tremendous interest in getting into the air as quickly as possible to avoid that pursuing tidal wave of disaster.

The time dragged but the Spitfire leapt into the air at last. At full throttle plus override, I forced it up to hang on its propeller as I clawed for enough height to escape the bomb blasts if they came.

A pair of Me 109s streaked past, going at twice our speed. Fortunately, we must have been obscured from their approach by the bomb blasts as they had obviously not made a pass at us. They could not have missed.

I looked back and was amazed to see both my wing men, MacPherson and Drobinski in position and Jeff Quill, imperturbable as ever, moving into his station under my tail. Ahead of me Sam continued to climb with four of his five followers in immaculate formation. I moved in behind and below his rear section.

We could still see the bombers too far ahead to be in range of our guns and they wheeled around and turned east. It was an impressive sight. The clouds had massed up now and were almost a complete cover over the Channel so once the bombers reached them we had no chance of seeing them again.

Two Me 109s broke through the cloud in front of Sam. They had no idea they were just in front of eleven Spitfires and paid the price. Both blew up as Sam got one and Paddy Finucane the other.

For the next half hour control wheeled us around, but it was all over. We returned to Manston and flew around for a while. The entire surface of the aerodrome was covered in white chalk dust. Six hundred large bomb craters were visible, over two hundred of them in two distinct straight lines marking our recent take off run. From start to finish the bomb lines were over a mile and a half long. Just one of those bombs, had it dropped in front of us, could have destroyed our entire team.

We returned to Southend as it was impossible to land at Manston. Later that day we heard Lord Haw Haw's version of what happened from Germany. He boasted that over three hundred bombers had struck Manston in the most massive attack in history and that twelve Spitfires caught taking off had all been destroyed on the ground!

We had already heard that the Spitfire pilot who had failed to take off was safe. A bomb blast had stopped his propeller, but done no other damage. He would return when it was possible to use the aerodrome again.

Well – it was on – the massive attacks on the aerodromes which we had been warned of. The mystery of our few days respite was solved too. The Germans, with their Teutonic thoroughness, had been practising forming up large formations to give a hitting force of three to four hundred aeroplanes, roughly half fighters – half bombers. As there would be ten or more of their aerodromes involved in each raid, the organisation and timing could not be taken for granted. They had been practising the art of marrying up three large formations of the size they had been employing against our convoys with such success.

Such a massive onslaught on our aerodromes could reduce us to ruins in a few days like Poland, France, Holland and Belgium.

This new turn in events woke us up from our weary exhaustion. If we thought the prospects of survival against a hundred or so of the enemy were slim, our prospects against forces four times as large were much less. That attack on 12 August marked the beginning of the main assaults of the Battle of Britain.

It was a notable day in my life too, for from that day on I believed in miracles. *Chapter 12 Death in August: 13–14 August 1940* By the following morning it was clear to everyone that this was a new phase in the fighting. 54 Squadron had been bombed at Manston that morning in almost identical circumstances to our own. This time they made it with a few more yards to spare than we did, as they were alert to the dangers.

To my dismay I found we were to go down there again at midday to relieve 54 Squadron. It seemed impossible that anyone could operate off Manston after the mess made by the carpet bombing of the previous day and again on this morning.

When we arrived I discovered how the miracle had been achieved. An army gentleman in a new device called a bulldozer had succeeded in filling in enough bomb holes to give us a clear strip a hundred yards wide to land and get off on. It was flagged out like a runway and we were back in business.

It seemed to me the height of absurdity that we should risk Spitfires for another attack by the German bombers. We were only twenty-two miles away from their nearest aerodromes and our hopes of surviving by another miracle were nil in my opinion. It took the bombers less than five minutes to cross the Channel at that point. But it seemed the politicians had decided that Manston would be held and operated regardless of danger and inconvenience to the pilots.

Right or wrong we were on Manston at 12.00. The place was a greater mess than I had imagined. All the dozen or so huts had been destroyed except for two. Two Me 110 fighter bombers had been caught by the explosions of their own bombs. They had crashed and rolled themselves up in front of the crew room in an unrecognisable tangle of metal and wire. Four bodies were still trapped in them – dead – but it had so far defied the resources of the ambulance and rescue teams to extricate them.

Sergeant Franklin came in sporting a pair of very smart German flying boots. He had managed to get them off one of the corpses! They were much dressier than ours.

A belly-landed Me 109 was a few yards away. It was in quite good shape and we spent some time studying it. It was almost the same size as a Spitfire but the petrol tank was behind the pilot instead of being in front of him, as in the Spitfires and Hurricanes. This was a big advantage from the pilot's point of view.

An aeroplane was a structure full of petrol, oil, inflammable engine coolant and explosive bullets or bombs. Once a bullet holed the petrol tank the fumes of petrol and oil in the fuselage became highly explosive. A single tracer bullet was more than enough to explode the lot.

Once the petrol tank was set on fire a vast sheet of brilliant orange flame trailed back from the tank, rapidly melting and consuming what was left of the frail aluminium structure. No human could survive the heat of the burning petrol. The few who made it through the flames were always terribly burned.

The Germans on the other hand had a reasonable chance to get out without too much personal incineration unless they were hit by bullets, when their end would be somewhat slower than that of their opposite numbers in the Spitfires and Hurricanes.

One disadvantage of the Me 109 was that the pilot sat immediately over the wing and this gave him a much greater blind area below him than was the case with both the Spitfires and the Hurricanes, however, this was a minor disadvantage and merely meant that he would miss seeing some of us, especially if we were underneath him. That was worth remembering!

Already the ground crews at Manston had got themselves organised. A slit trench was dug to the side of each Spitfire's parking area, the starter batteries were plugged in and as soon as the engines started, the crews slapped shut the plug covers (where the battery plug was inserted) and dived into their foxholes.

Now we knew the real heat was on, we took off every time a sizeable plot was picked up by the radar, even at extreme range. There was no more taxiing out into wind and forming up. We just opened up as soon as the engine was firing evenly and took off straight ahead. This cut down our take off time by about three minutes and although we did not know it at the time, this was enough of a margin to prevent the Germans catching us on the ground again.

The aerodrome now looked like a white desert with thousands of bomb holes everywhere. A bulldozer growled and creaked away in the bright sunlight as we sat around at readiness, more or less holding our breath waiting for the phone to ring.

The crew room table had to be man handled down from the roof. It was a big table and it took some manipulating to get it back inside the hut and through the narrow doorway. It was the mystery of the week how it had been heaved out through the door in the first place, although once out it was not hard to figure how it had got up on the roof.

Wigg had a theory that during the bomb raid even the table legs had turned to jelly and that was how it had been blown out of the room in the first place.

The laugh of the week had been provided by the duty pilot. His hut was drunkenly perched on the side of the biggest bomb crater of the bombing, which was some thirty feet or more across and about fifteen feet deep. A huge pile of chalk was heaped on its roof like some crazy mass of snow. It seemed the duty pilot had taken cover under the table during the bomb raid and somewhat predictably everything shook and rocked like a violent earthquake. When the noise had stopped and all was quiet, he gingerly emerged head first from under the table like some prehistoric tortoise and as he did so the electric clock, which had broken loose from the wall and was swinging back and forth, finally broke its wire. It fell on his head, knocking him out cold. Nine stitches and a week in hospital after surviving some thousands of bombs – one, the largest, only inches from his own head at the time.

I think the remaining duty pilot felt his mate was the lucky one. He had no great hopes of surviving many more such bomb raids – and there were bound to be more.

About three o'clock, pounding boots from the direction of the phone sent us all headlong to our Spitfires. Mine was already ticking over as the orderly shouted, 'Base 10,000 feet'.

We took off in some sort of loose order, but squadron formation on takeoff was now out of the question as the chalk dust blinded everyone. This time we took off in threes and formed up in the air.

The sky was clear this time and the attackers would not be able to elude us by making for the clouds.

At 7,000 feet, we could see a great cloud of aeroplanes. They were well above our level. There were several hundred bombers in a mass with little packets of fighters everywhere. Sam turned away and we climbed at full throttle. They did not seem to take any notice of us as we continued to climb and eventually we were about 5,000 feet above the top bombers and to their south.

We headed in towards them, still climbing, and I felt my stomach curl up into a hard knot. There were twelve of us and about four hundred of them. Slowly they came down below us at about two o'clock ahead. We were almost over the top of them when Sam called 'Number one attack go'.

We nosed down one behind the other, the speed mounting rapidly. Perhaps they did not see Sam as he started his dive, but before he got within range of the nearest bomber, most of the two hundred and fifty odd bombers were firing tracer at him or at us. He and his wingman, Tom Smart, were virtually obscured by the crazy maze of tracer.

As we flew down along parallel paths, the tracer grew as thick as rain and it had a curious negative effect on us – even the old trails somehow seemed lethal. It seemed quite impossible to traverse that barrage with any hope of survival.

All of a sudden large bombers were everywhere in front – big ones – with endless streaks of tracer coming from them at point blank range. Then – we were in the clear blue sky again and the attack was over.

I had fired as I went past one of the bombers in such a way that I should have hit him and another which was in line with him, but the whole attack had been futile as far as I was concerned.

I pulled over to the side and found myself flying along with six or seven groups of

Me 109s. They seemed to be more interested in the bombers than in me, so I lined a group of four up and fired at the leader. If my deflection was out, some of the slugs should have found their mark on his followers.

They wheeled off wildly towards the main formation and I made a pass at a group of three. I don't think they even noticed me and I ran out of ammunition as I pulled around behind them. There was not much future in sticking around without bullets, so I made a tight turn and, satisfying myself I was not being stalked, opted out of the fight.

I was more than a little pleased to be alive still and as I made for the aerodrome, I called control to see if it was still possible to land there. It was so I made for it without too much haste because I wanted to be sure that the bombers were not going to clobber it as I landed just for a change.

I wondered how many of our boys would be alive after that suicidal attack of Sams. It would not have surprised me if only half of them made it, or so I decided before I landed. Half an hour later we were all back or all accounted for. Wigg and one of Sam's boys were walking back from some remote Kentish village, but we were all in one piece as a squadron. It seemed incredible.

The refuelling over, we discussed the raid at some length. Sam had made a pass at the leader, or the one he thought was the leader, but this had left the rest of us to dive through the main body of the tightly massed bomber formation, where the risk of collision seemed overwhelming. Somehow, we had missed and at the same time we had been unsuccessful as far as we could see in hitting any of the enemy machines. Sergeant Franklin claimed two Me 109s, but that was routine with him.

Apparently the target of the raid had been Eastchurch and the raid had made quite a mess of that aerodrome; but before the attackers returned to their bases, other Hurricane and Spitfire squadrons in the group had destroyed about a score of their machines.

There was another raid that evening, but it was a hundred miles or more to the west near Tangmere and although we went over to give a hand, the bombers were back in France by the time we arrived.

The first two days of the big blitz were over. The much advertised 'Eagle Day' was about to be launched. 'The practices had been run, now it was to be for keeps'. So said the German radio in their English broadcasts and Lord Haw Haw laconically claimed that the squadron of twelve aeroplanes taking off from Manston on the 12th had all been destroyed by the invincible Luftwaffe. Well, that was us, and we were still all alive and kicking, even if we were not landing too many kicks at this juncture.

We were dreary with the fatigue from insufficient sleep next day when we landed at Manston at midday to do our turn at readiness. There had been some attacks in the morning, but by the time we had been mobilised from available and despatched to the area, the scraps were over.

I sat on the floor in the chalk dust, too tired to read and too tense to go to sleep. Our aerodrome was due for another blitz. As soon as the telephone bell rang, we would have to reach our Spitfires in even time and make no mistakes starting off or we would be in for real trouble.

At three o'clock the controller rang. A warning had come through that the German crews were getting into their bombers in France and that another 'carpet raid' was under way. The French resistance were getting warning messages through on their radios so we checked to see that all was set and waited.

A quarter of an hour later the controller warned that the radar was registering a build up about sixty miles to our south-east, but not to go yet as it might be a feint – aimed to get us into the air long enough to have to land and refuel – the main attack would then hit as we were refuelling.

A few minutes later and it was clear that it was on. We took off and climbed out over the Channel, then turned back to the west, climbing over England. At 20,000 feet we turned east again and after about five minutes we could see them – somewhere between four hundred and five hundred aircraft. Two hundred to two hundred and fifty of them were bombers, which made quite a spectacle. As we rapidly drew nearer on a head-on approach, the much smaller fighters could be seen rather like wasps escorting a large flock of pigeons. The bombers were rock steady except for the odd ones out on the flanks where formation flying was most difficult. The fighters, on the other hand, gave an impression of movement as some, if not all, were weaving around using their superior speed to turn continually in their search for us.

There were several large cumulus clouds towering up to thirty thousand feet and the formation leader would have to avoid these or they would wreck his fine formation. We had decided that I would try to cover Sam's attack this time to cut down the risk of hostile fighters attacking him as he attacked the leader.

We closed rapidly, within a couple of minutes or so, and Sam was on his way down. Two Me 109s had seen him and were after him, so I gave chase and opened fire on the leader. He must have seen me or the bullets registered on his machine, for he hauled up in a full powered climbing turn with me and four other Spitfires on his tail. Several groups of Me 109s came in from both flanks and we were forced to break up and take avoiding action.

Thus I found myself surrounded by about forty odd fighters with no visible friendly support. They were above, at the same level and below me, whilst a mile below again the great armada of bombers ground on its course up the estuary.

The fighters all seemed to have their eye on me. No matter which way I looked they were all turning in my direction. The most immediate threat came from the leader of twelve 109s, who had tightened up his turn so that he was almost able to get a head on attack on me. As he was almost straight ahead of me, at this instant, I straightened out abruptly and flew straight at him, the eight guns snarling. I was out of range at first, but in four or five seconds he was only a couple of hundred yards away, closing fast.

He lost his nerve or I hit him, because he suddenly nosed down under my attack. All his squadron followed him. They were all firing their guns but they had no chance of hitting me as they followed their leader. Why they did not break up and attack me separately I'll never know.

That reduced the odds so I then fastened on the next nearest and he opted out together with a friend who was trailing him.

There were still half a dozen other groups still above me and I had no chance of out climbing them while they could all get down on to my tail. At this stage I could see no chance of surviving the odds, so I suddenly dived on one of the few below me and as I passed him, kept on going.

The bombers had vanished from below and I made the safety of one of the large clouds before my pursuers could open fire effectively. The cloud was rough and threatened to pull the wings off the Spitfire at the high speed I dived into it, but I had no chance of surviving a thirty-to-one fight with most of them above me, so the cloud was my only hope. A dozen seconds later I broke out of the cloud only to see more clouds banked up in front. I could see no sign of my pursuers, so I weaved around the clear spaces on the off chance that I might find something to expend the remainder of my ammunition on, but everything had vanished. I called control and they told me to return to Manston.

One of our Poles and one of 'B' Flight's new boys were not accounted for. Later that evening we heard that they had been killed. The odds were too severe for all of us to escape unscathed.

The following day the events were almost identical. This time, however, the skies were clear except for a few thin strata patches over the Channel and one or two at higher levels around the twenty thousand feet – no big cumulus to play hide and seek in or to use as escape hatches!

Once again we had plenty of warning and were above twenty thousand feet when we saw them coming. The only difference was size – this time there were almost twice as many bombers. The fighter strength was harder to estimate as they were hard, if not impossible to see at first.

Sam called up, 'Red leader you go in as high cover and try to occupy the fighters – I'll have another go at the leader'.

'Ok,' I replied, and climbed for height over their topmost fighters.

As the raid came towards us in its massive grandeur, the fighters became visible. I seemed to be well above the highest of the escort. Realising that for the first time I was up sun, and therefore probably not visible to them, I cautiously closed in. Six 109s were flying along quietly just below me so I slipped down and in behind the rear most one. It was a perfect shot, and as I pushed the button the 109 dissolved in a huge puff of black smoke.

'Bullseye!'

I pulled up in case the flight tried to attack me, but to my surprise the leader just put his nose down and dived for France, firing all his guns. His four remaining stooges dived and fired also. They disappeared from sight.

As if by magic, four more, flying almost in line abreast, appeared from nowhere in a perfect position for a repeat performance. I did the same thing again. To my amazement my target exploded again, but before I had time to pull up, the other three dived abruptly, wheeling back to France.

There was another group a few hundred yards to the right. I went across and opened fire on the nearest and down he went, back to France, closely followed by his mates. He did not oblige by exploding.

A single Messerschmitt below was too tempting to ignore, so I dived on him. He saw me coming and dived. I was close on his tail, so I sprayed him for about five thousand feet. We went through two layers of cloud and by this were down to 10,000 feet. I pulled out as the speed was very close to the speed of sound and the Spitfire was believed to disintegrate if this speed were attained. The 109 continued on its dive to the cloud layer over the sea. It showed no sign of pulling out or slowing down as it entered the cloud.

I allowed the speed to drop as I circled at 4,000 feet, then descended through the cloud. It was a thin layer and directly below was a large patch of white on the dark water which could have been left by my quarry. There was no other sign of aeroplanes, so I climbed up to see if I could find the large raid again.

Above the top layer the air was absolutely empty of all aeroplanes. I called control and was given a course to steer; a minute later and I saw a dot on the horizon. I was flying straight at it and it was not moving. Either it was going the same way as I, or it was coming towards me.

A few seconds later and it was clearly a single-engined fighter – either a Spitfire or a Me 109. Which? It answered the question for me and dozens of tracer streaks flashed towards me. As we did not fire tracer I instantly knew he was not one of ours, but before I could make a move to put my sights on him, he flashed by overhead, tracer still pouring out of his guns. He was travelling at his full speed, I should think, and running slightly downhill at about 400 mph. My own speed would have been around 350 mph, so our combined closing speed would be about 750 mph or twelve miles a minute. As neither the Spitfire nor the Me 109 could be seen five miles distant from head on, this meant that he had come from a position beyond my range of vision to point blank in thirty seconds. He probably opened fire a mile away when he still could not be sure of my identity about five seconds before he passed me. I turned as rapidly as I could through 180 degrees, but as this took about a minute at the speed I was going at, he was out of sight by the time I was going in his direction.

It was a good lesson on the speed at which things happened out of sight to point blank in thirty seconds, with five seconds to identify friend or foe, then out of sight again in the same time. It meant that at any time a clear blue sky could produce an enemy who could destroy you in half a minute – much less if he came from the sun.

I was ordered to return to Southend as Manston had been savaged again.

When I told my ground crew that two of my victims had blown up and another had crashed into the sea in all probability, they were almost delirious with excitement. They took my success as part of their own – and very rightly so! These two youngsters, both in their early twenties, were fanatical in the care they lavished on my aeroplane. In addition to being on duty whenever I was (which was about eighteen hours a day), they worked through the night as well, and usually slept on the ground under the plane's wing during the day, once they had the machine checked over and serviced to their satisfaction. They were the most loyal and devoted boys with whom I have ever had anything to do. The proof of their work was in the performance of the machine they serviced.

However, while I basked in their elation, I could not help thinking that it might so easily be my turn to be blown up next. I had destroyed other aeroplanes and the men in them but it was kill, or be killed. These formations had to be destroyed or we ourselves would suffer the same fate.

Our duties as interceptors of the enemies' fighter screens took us up to greater and greater altitudes. A week or so before the battle began, the de Havilland people who made the variable pitch propellers on our Spitfires, had turned up with a supply of little boxes which they attached to an oil tube on the back of the Rolls Royce engine. This was a constant speed unit and it weighed about a pound or so. The effect it had on the Spitfire was truly magical.

Prior to its attachment, a Spitfire was staggering at 24,000 feet and was only just flyable at 25,000 feet and it took some twenty minutes to make that altitude. Now it shot up at twice the speed and reached 25,000 feet in less than ten minutes. It continued to climb beautifully to 38,000 feet, when for some reason the spark plugs started to give trouble and the engine ran roughly. New type plugs were provided and the Spitfire was able to make 40,000 feet comfortably and still climb, if necessary.

However other problems immediately plagued us. Intense cold in what was essentially an unheated and unpressurised cockpit froze hands and feet in minutes. If we put sufficient clothes on to combat the cold it was impossible to move around and keep a reasonable look out.

Worse still, after reaching 30,000 feet, the perspex and windscreen frosted up badly due to the condensation of the water vapour in the breath and it was only possible to see at all by continuously scraping off the frost as it formed.

Even though we scraped away furiously, the little patch of clear Perspex quickly re-frosted and the combination of ice crystals and frozen leather scratched the canopy badly making it even more difficult to see. As it was, we could only see through the hole in the frost for a few seconds before it fogged over again and we could only get an all round view by progressively scraping the frost off in patches all round the canopy from left to right a peephole at a time!

What we could see of the other planes in our own formation revealed that we were leaving vast streamers of vapour behind us as if we were some kind of rocket. If the opposition were not similarly cursed with frost, they would have no difficulty in locating us and closing in for a kill. We would not even know they were there and we would not even get the warnings of seeing the tracer go past.

Sometimes we would spot other vapour trails and we would set off after them. However, it was most difficult to keep them in sight and as we approached they would usually dive for the lower altitudes and that would be the last we saw of them.

It was a curious game of blind man's bluff – we could see, but only just and then only for a few seconds at a time.

I was going through this routine at 35,000 feet one afternoon when I suddenly felt a delightful sensation of relief from all the tensions of the combat area surge over me. It was a lovely afternoon for a little snooze. I was weary and at last I was at peace with the world and not the slightest bit afraid. To hell with the Kraut, and frost, and the ice crystals, and the damn cold.

The engine noise changed and I could not care less – the rush of air grew to a shrill scream, but I loved it – I was so happy and relaxed. Then I realised – I must have run out of oxygen! My brain faintly registered I was passing out. The oxygen must have given up or perhaps the pipe to my mask had become disconnected. Faint fear began to register and I blanked out visually as I felt around for the pipe. I found it and managed to push it clumsily over my nose – I took a couple of deep breaths and began to come back to reality. I could see again. The nose was down – the speed well up over the 400 mph, altitude 15,000 feet and the engine screaming – I had dived some four miles in the process.

I pulled the throttle back and eased out of the dive. There was plenty of time and no danger at all, but I was very lucky that I realised I was passing out and found that oxygen tube, or it might have been the North Sea for me.

The oxygen attachments were crude and far from efficient. Mine had become caught up around the back of my neck where it passed so as to prevent undue clutter in front of the pilot. As I turned my head from side to side to keep a lookout, the tube had come off the little pipe attachment on the gas mask and thus in a few seconds at 35,000 feet, I was due to pass into unconsciousness.

Others had similar experiences. Alan Deere of 54 Squadron actually passed out, coming to in a shallow dive at very high speed at about 5,000 feet, where there was enough oxygen to revive him naturally. He was lucky that his aeroplane was not by then in an unmanageable dive which no doubt happened to many others in those days who were not so lucky.

19 Arthur 'Art' Donahue Part 2, Spitfire Pilot, Pilot Officer, American, 64 Squadron

Art's second extract from his 1941 memoir, covering 5–13 August when he was flying from RAF Kenley in London, the centre of the Battle.

Chapter 3 Tally-Ho! AM, 5 August 1940 Our last instructions by our squadron leader before we left for our advance base next morning were in regard to staying in formation, any time the squadron was looking for the enemy.

'It's essential that the squadron stick together as a compact unit as long as possible, until the enemy is actually being engaged. So whenever we're on patrol, and especially when the scent is good and warm, stay in formation. Fly wide enough apart from your leader so that you won't be in danger of colliding with him, but don't lag behind if you can help it. If you see a Hun don't go after him until I give you the ok. And if we sight a bunch of them, stay in formation until I call out the "Tally-Ho!" Then you can break formation and pick your targets. And then,' he added, patting us both on the back, 'Heaven help your targets!'

We got our airplanes ready and put on our flying equipment. As it was warm, we didn't wear any flying suits over our uniforms, but we put on pneumatic life jackets that were issued to us. These are called 'Mae Wests' – quite appropriately, too, as you would agree if you could see what they do to a pilot's contour.

We took off in sections of three and assumed squadron formation over the airdrome. An RAF fighter squadron consists of twelve planes normally, and we flew in sections of three, the leader in front with his section.

It was a tremendous thrill for me to be aloft with a fighter squadron for the first time. We circled the airdrome majestically and then swept out eastward toward our advance base on the sea coast. I was enjoying this, even though it was only supposed to be a little cross-country jaunt.

I heard the whine of a radio transmitter in my headphones, and then our squadron leader's voice.

'Hello, Control! Hello, Control! Tiger Leader calling. Are you receiving me? Are you receiving me? Over.' ('Tiger' was the call name of our squadron.)

There was another transmitter whir, more distant, and a cheery voice sang out, 'Hallo-o, Tiger Leader, Tiger Leader! Control answering you. Control answering. Receiving you loud and clear, loud and clear. Are you receiving me, please? Are you receiving me? Control over to Tiger Leader.'

Another whir and our leader's voice answering again. 'Hello, Control. Hello, Control. Tiger Leader answering. Yes, receiving you loud and clear also. Loud and clear. All Tiger aircraft are now airborne. We are now airborne. Tiger Leader over to Control, listening out.'

Control called once more to acknowledge this message, and then there was radio silence as we roared onward. We had to cover about seventy miles, which would take about fifteen minutes. It was a clear morning, and I idly wondered if we should be able to see the French coast that day. If so I should be seeing France for the first time. Also it would be my first view of enemy country, for that was German-occupied France.

Perhaps seven or eight minutes had elapsed when Control called us again. There was the transmitter's whine and a voice calling Tiger Leader and asking if he was receiving him. Then Tiger Leader's answer that he was 'receiving you loud and clear.'

Then the voice from Control again, this time slower, and with careful enunciation: 'All Tiger aircraft, patrol Dover at ten thousand feet; patrol Dover at ten thousand feet.'

Our leader immediately opened his throttle and put his plane in a steep climb, at the same time altering his course in the direction of Dover. We of course did likewise to stay in formation with him.

I wondered what it meant. Had something been seen there, or were they expecting an attack? It still didn't seem possible that I actually might see an enemy. Planes with black crosses and swastikas still didn't seem to exist in reality to me, in spite of the one I had seen that spun in at our training base. Somehow that one, a great broken thing lying on the hillside after it crashed, didn't seem real to me in memory. It still didn't seem possible that I should actually see airplanes with black crosses in the air, whose pilots would be trying to kill me, and I them.

In less time than it takes to tell, our altimeters were registering ten thousand feet and we were racing level. The coast was visible now, not far ahead, with the waters of the English Channel beyond. I guessed that we were nearly over Dover.

Another command came through from Control. 'Climb to fifteen thousand feet.' And then the message that electrified me:

'There are bandits [enemies] approaching from the north!'

My pulses pounded, and my thoughts raced. This was *it!*

In quick response to this information, our leader sang out a command: 'All Tiger aircraft, full throttle! Full throttle!'

That meant to use the emergency throttle that gave extra power to our engines.

I was flying in our leader's section, on his left. As he gave the command 'Full throttle,' his plane started to draw ahead, away from me. I pushed in my emergency throttle lever in response to the command, the first time I had ever used it, and my engine fairly screamed with new power. I felt my plane speeding up like a high-spirited horse that has been spurred.

Our leader now led us upward in a steeper climb than I had ever dreamed an airplane could perform. Trembling with excitement, trying to realize that this was actually happening and I wasn't dreaming, I pulled the guard off my firing button. For the first time in my life I was preparing to kill! The button was painted red, and it looked strangely grim now that it was uncovered. I turned its safety ring, which surrounded it, from the position which read 'SAFE' to the position which read 'FIRE.'

Then I switched on the electric gunsight. This projects an orange light in the image of a machine-gun sight upon a glass in the middle of the windshield. It's more accurate than mechanical sights.

We were going forward and upward at terrific speed, and reached fifteen thousand feet shortly. A new command came over our radio receivers: 'Steer one-three-zero and climb to twenty thousand feet.'

We obeyed, every pilot now watching above and below and on all sides, the sections of the squadron closing in more tightly and the rear-guard pilots wheeling in swift vertical banks one way, then the other, to watch against any surprise.

Our course led us out over the middle of the Channel, and the coast of France was plainly visible – answering one of my hopes. I was getting my first view of France, and enemy France at that.

I was using oxygen now, controlled by a little valve on my instrument panel that released it into a hose connected with the mask that covered my nose and mouth. Oxygen is necessary at high altitude to keep your mind working keenly and to keep you from getting tired and weak. Pilots who don't use it at high altitude tire out quickly, and their minds become sluggish. Also they are apt to faint without warning.

More orders followed. New courses to steer. New altitudes at which to fly.

'Circle your present position.'

'Watch to the left.'

'Believe the enemy is now heading south and passing behind you.'

Such orders as these interspersed the radio silences and kept us busy and on our toes while we hunted about for perhaps half an hour. I was in a sweat trying to look in every direction and still keep my place in formation. Our leader led us about like a group of charging cavalry.

As time went by, my hopes of seeing an enemy flagged.

We were at about twenty thousand feet altitude and a few miles north of Calais on the French coast, and doing a sweeping left turn. Looking in the rear vision mirror above my windshield I saw what looked like a little blazing torch falling in the sky behind me. For the instant I didn't realize that the first shots of battle had been fired, and I had to put my attention again on our leader's plane, to keep my place in formation with him.

I was flying on his left, and that meant I had to look to the right to see him; and out of the corner of my eye I noticed far below and beyond him the distant shape of another airplane heading for France. I hated to call out, in case it didn't mean anything, but it didn't seem reasonable that a British plane would be out here alone, heading in that direction. Also it seemed to be colored blue-gray on top, and I was quite sure no British planes were colored like that. It was too far away for me to make out its markings or even its design. Hesitating to call out, I looked at our squadron leader, to see if he had noticed it.

I saw that he hadn't, for he was looking the other way, to our left, where several distant black dots were visible in the air at about our level. And as I watched him I heard his transmitter whine and his voice sing out the Royal Air Force battle cry: 'Ta-al-ly-ho-o!'

As he sang it he swung his airplane over viciously into a wild vertical turn and laid out for the black dots on the left, which had now grown into airplanes; still little and distant but headed toward us. There weren't very many of them, and the entire squadron was breaking formation and wheeling toward them like a bunch of wild Indians.

I remembered the one I had seen heading the other way and our squadron leader's words that we might pick our own targets after the 'Tally-ho' is given; and a second later I was peeling away from the squadron and down in pursuit of the lone machine which I had decided should be my target.

I went down in a screaming dive, pushing everything forward – throttle, emergency throttle, propeller control and all. The other had a good start, but I had the advantage of several thousand feet more altitude, and was gaining speed by diving. The wind shrieked against my windshield and the Rolls Royce engine bellowed, while the air-speed indicator needle moved steadily around its dial and on up past the four hundred miles an hour mark.

The Spitfire grew rigid in its course as if it were following a groove. The controls became terribly stiff, and I couldn't move the stick a quarter of an inch in any direction. It was hard to level out from the dive when I got down near the other's altitude. I had to pull out very gently to keep from blacking out too much. The misty curtain kept closing down in front of my eyes as I pulled the nose of my plane up, and I leaned forward and tensed my muscles to resist it. I was still a way behind the other when I got down to his level, but I was gaining on him fast, because of the extra speed I had from my dive.

I was holding my thumb over the firing button now and keeping my eyes glued to the little silhouette ahead, except for an occasional glance at the rear vision mirror to see that I wasn't being chased too. I imagine my heart was doing about fifteen hundred rpm, from the pounding I felt.

The other machine grew steadily larger in the circle of my gunsight as I drew closer. I could tell its distance by the amount of space it covered in the sight: six hundred yards, five hundred, four hundred – my speed was dying down a little, and I wasn't gaining quite as fast. He apparently was going wide open too.

Now I was only three hundred yards behind – close enough to open fire, but something made me hesitate. From directly behind, where I was now, it was hard to identify its type. Suppose it was a British machine after all?

To make sure I eased my machine upward just a little so I could look down on the other and see the upper side of it. The old feeling that airplanes with black crosses and swastikas on their wings and sides couldn't exist in reality still had hold of me; but it was banished forever by what I now saw.

For I could see that the other machine's wings were not curved, with nicely rounded tips, like a Spitfire's; and it was not camouflaged green and tan; and there were no red and blue circles near the tips. Instead, the wings were narrow, stiff-looking, with blunt, square-cut tips. They were pale blue-gray in color, and near each tip, very vivid, was painted a simple black 'plus' sign!

I knew from pictures that it must be a Messerschmitt 109, and I dropped back into firing position behind it. My sights centered on it, and I squeezed the firing button with my thumb. *B-r-r-rup-pup-u-pup!* The sound came to me muffled by my heavy helmet; but it was a venomous sound, and I could feel the Spitfire shudder and slow from the recoil as the eight Browning guns snarled and barked their terrific fast staccato. I held the button in for about a full one-second burst – about one hundred and sixty bullets.

Then my plane bounced sideways as it encountered the turbulent slipstream of the other, and I lost sight of him for a second. He must have gone into a diving turn just then, for when I spotted him again a few seconds later he was far below. Mentally cursing my carelessness or dumbness, I rolled over and went down after him again; and while I was overtaking him I reflected that for the first time I had tried to take the life of another man. It didn't bother my conscience.

I caught up with him just over Cape Gris Nez on the French coast, and that was how I entered France for the first time! As I drew close he abandoned flight and turned to face me like a cornered animal; but I was too close behind him now, and I simply followed him in the turn, cutting it shorter than he could and crowding in on him.

I knew I was outmaneuvering him, and felt I had him now. He was almost in the circle of my gunsights. This time I'd keep him there!

Powp!

It sounded exactly as if some one had blown up a big paper sack and burst it behind my ears; and it shook the plane and was followed by a noise like hail on a tin roof.

I realized that I had been hit somewhere behind me in my machine by a second Hun, and guessed that it was an exploding cannon shell that made the noise. Most German fighters are equipped with cannon as well as machine guns.

I put all the strength I could muster on my controls to whip my machine into a turn in the opposite direction, then saw that I'd wasted the effort. My new attacker had already flashed by below and ahead, and I now saw him wheeling to come back, his black crosses vivid on top of his wings as he appeared spread-eagled in a vertical turn. The square-cut wing tips of his Messerschmitt looked crude but grim.

He must have dived on me and fired a shot as he went down past. I reflected a little grimly that a new 'first' had occurred for me – for the first time another man had tried to take my life!

It's hard to recall details of the ensuing combat, but I know it was pretty wild. I made lots of blunders. It was terribly hard for me in my inexperience to try to get an advantage on one of my enemies, so I could open fire, without the other popping up immediately in firing position behind me. The three of us scrambled about in a terrible melee, climbing, diving, rolling, and pirouetting in screaming vertical turns to get at each other. A combat such as this is well called a 'dog fight.' One moment I would be maneuvering for my life to get away from one who was almost on my tail, and in the next moment I would have one of them in the same kind of spot and would be trying just as desperately to hold him long enough to get a shot.

And sometimes when I got separated from both of them a moment I would see bright flashes and puffs of white or black smoke in the air near me – shells from

German anti-aircraft guns. The batteries on the coast below had joined the fight and were shooting at me whenever they got a chance to do so without hitting their own machines.

This went on for several minutes, before I finally managed to get one of them all by himself away from the other for a few seconds. I was in a beautiful firing position right on his tail.

Then I got a heart-breaking shock: my gunsight wasn't working! The precious image in orange light wasn't to be seen on the glass in front of me. Feverishly I fumbled and found the switch for it. Yes, it was on. I tried the rheostat which controls the intensity of the light for day or night use. It was on full bright.

It was hard to do this and keep behind the other's tail. He was dodging wildly, expecting my bullets every second, I suppose. I jiggled the rheostat and turned it back and forth, and hit the reflector sight base with my hand and shook it. Still no result. It took precious seconds to do this checking, and the loss of time was very nearly fatal.

A set of four long vibrating snaky white fingers reached across my right wing from behind and stretched far ahead. They were about an inch thick and made of white smoke and pulsated with bright molten-looking objects streaking through them. I knew they were tracers – the trails of smoke left by bullets to mark their course. Chemicals coated on the bullets do it. They show the pilot where his bullets are going. In this case they showed me too, and I knew I was being fired at by the other German pilot from behind. I panicked and rolled into a turn so violent that my machine shuddered terribly and slipped over into a tailspin – at more than two hundred miles an hour! It must have made me look like an amateur, but it shook off my attacker.

I felt that I was in a pretty bad spot without a gun-sight, but decided to bluff them a little bit rather than to turn tail right away and let them know something was wrong.

The melee continued. I was terribly hot and tired and sweaty, and was conscious of that more than of being scared. I wished I could rest. The bright sun beat down hotly through the transparent hatch over my cockpit. My clothes were heavy and I was hampered by my parachute straps and seat harness straps as I twisted about in the cockpit trying to see above, below, behind, and to the sides to keep track of my playmates.

During those next few minutes I think I must have blacked out at least twenty times in turns. I remember starting to spin at least once from turning too violently. I wanted to flee but couldn't get my directions straight because I was maneuvering so fast. My compass couldn't help me unless I'd give it a chance to settle down. It was spinning like a top.

Finally I noticed across the water, in the distance, a ribbon of white lining the horizon, and I remembered reading years ago in my geography book about the 'white cliffs of Dover.' Just then that looked like the promised land.

One of my enemies was heading the other way. I made a pass at the second and he headed in the opposite direction from Dover, too, and I turned out across the sea and homeward. It was an ignominious way to end a fight which had begun with such promise, but I thought it was the wisest. My enemies took after me, but when they drew close I turned around as if to go after them and they turned back. They were apparently willing to call it a draw, and I didn't feel quite so badly after that.

When I went to land at our advance base I found that the trimming controls for my tail were out of order. The wheels actuating them spun loosely, so I knew the cables must be broken.

On landing I taxied to one end of the field, where I saw the rest of my squadron's planes, already down. I was flagged into place, and mechanics and armorers swarmed over my Spitfire. Some jerked off the removable metal covers above and below the machine guns in the wings while others ran up with belts of ammunition and began to refill the guns. A gasoline truck roared up and stopped in front of the plane, and they began refilling the tanks. In a few minutes my machine would be completely checked, refueled, and refilled with ammunition.

My squadron mates crowded around to hear my story. All but one of them were down now, and they had already heard one another's stories. I told them mine as well as I could remember, and had to admit regretfully that I had come away without bringing down either of my enemies.

We examined my plane, and it was easy to see that it had been struck by an exploding cannon shell, as I had thought. The shell had blown a fairly large hole in one side of the fuselage just behind the cockpit, in the lower part of the red, white, and blue insignia. It would have been a bull's-eye if it had been a foot higher.

The control cables which ran close by where the shell had hit, were in bad shape. In addition to the trimming control cables being broken, the main elevator and rudder cables were also nearly severed by the blast. A battery connection was broken by the explosion, and that explained the failure of my electric gunsight. The bottom of the plane was littered with bits of light shrapnel from the shell and there were a myriad small holes in the other side of the fuselage from the shell hole, where pieces of shrapnel had gone out. The shrapnel must have made the noise 'like hail on a tin roof' that I had heard after the explosion. My machine truly carried an 'after the battle' appearance. It would have to have a new fuselage installed.

I heard the story of the rest of the squadron. They had charged into the formation of Messerschmitts that they were heading for when I left them, and had shot down two for sure. There were also two other 'probables' which they had seen going down but which they couldn't claim definitely because they weren't seen to hit the sea. One of the boys had damaged still another – had seen pieces fly off it when he fired.

In addition a Henschel 126 German reconnaissance machine had come steaming along right into the center of the melee, a terrible mistake for its pilot to make, for these machines only have two or three machine guns and can't travel much over two hundred miles an hour, so that they are cold meat for fighters. He must have been going on some business of his own and blundered into the middle of the show somehow, before he realized it. Two of our boys spotted this machine and went to work on it, but they were nearly out of ammunition by that time and they emptied all the bullets they had left into it without bringing it down. It just kept sailing right on, but they thought they killed the rear gunner at least because he quit shooting back at them. It was credited to the squadron as being 'damaged.'

This is one of three categories into which RAF successes are divided. The other two are 'probably destroyed' and 'confirmed victories' (definitely destroyed). Only the number of confirmed victories is given out in the report of enemy aircraft destroyed.

The score for the squadron that morning was two confirmed, two probables, and two damaged.

None of our planes that were back was even hit except mine; but one had not returned yet and the out look grew bad. Two of the boys remembered seeing what looked like a Spitfire going down in flames in the distance behind the squadron at the start of the battle. This boy who was missing was one of the 'rear guard' pilots, protecting the rear of the squadron. I also remembered the glimpse I had in my mirror at that time, of something that looked like a torch falling in the distance behind us. When no trace could be found of him and it was learned that no other British planes were missing, we knew he must have been the pilot [Sergeant Lewis Isaac]. There were a lot of Messerschmitts about that morning, and it was pretty evident what had happened.

He must have seen some Messerschmitts coming up to attack the squadron from behind, had turned back and engaged them, and thus, fighting alone to protect his mates, he had gone out in a blaze of glory. Our squadron leader paid him a simple but meaningful tribute that we wished he could have heard.

'I noticed,' he said, 'that we *weren't* attacked from the rear.'

I sought out Peter, and we lay on the grass near our machines and basked in the warm sunshine. There were a lot of scratches on my flying boots from shrapnel, and we found a little piece imbedded in one of them.

I felt strangely tired and lazy, not realizing that this was my initiation to a strange feeling of exhaustion with which I was to get better acquainted in the following days. I didn't want to sleep, but I didn't to move, or talk, or fly, or anything else either, just relax. It's a feeling that's always pervaded me after a fight or a nerve-racking patrol. As nearly as I can describe it, it is a sensation of being drained completely, in every part of your body, though I don't know what of. But you seem to want to just surrender to relaxation, sitting or lying inert and absorbing whatever it is back into your system. I've heard many other pilots say they get the same feeling.

Peter asked, 'Will you do me a favor, chum?'

'Sure. What is it?'

'Let me have your notebook for a minute and I'll tell you.'

I gave him the little memorandum book which I always carry, opening it to a blank page. He wrote a girl's name and telephone number in it.

'If anything happens to me,' he said, 'will you telephone this number and tell her the story? And then –' He paused, and indicated the silver identification wristlet which he wore on his left wrist. It had a little nameplate, and also little charms of some sort strung on it. 'If it's possible,' he finished, 'I'd like to have you see that she gets this.'

'Ok,' I said lightly, 'and let's hope that I never have to do that for you.'

Looking at the notebook, I tried to realize that I had bought it only three months before, in a drugstore in Manitowoc, Wisconsin.

I still have that notebook, Peter, and the page you wrote on that day is still in it; though, of course, I don't need it any more because I've telephoned the number and told *her* the story, long since.

Chapter 4 Victory – & Its Price: PM 5 – AM 10 August 1940 It was hard to realize that this had all actually happened and wasn't a dream. This was 5 August, scarcely six weeks from the time I had been at home in Minnesota, cultivating corn! That corn wouldn't be big enough to cut yet!

In England the letters 'U-S' have a different meaning than they do in America. Here they mean 'unserviceable.'

My machine was U-S now, because the fuselage was ruined, so I couldn't fly back to our home airdrome with the rest of the squadron when our shift was over at noon. However, the squadron had a little two-seat training plane for the use of the pilots, and after the boys flew home one of them came back in this machine and picked me up, and I had a nice ride home.

In the afternoon I visited 'Number One,' our intelligence officer, in his office and made out my first combat report. After I finished I spent some time in his office, studying models of various types of German bombers which showed their gun positions and the arcs of fire of the guns.

Next morning when we were collected in our pilots' hut, Number One visited us and passed around some mimeographed papers to us, saying, 'Here's the latest intelligence dope for you boys to look over when you have time.'

I found that one set of papers was full of information about the enemy's activity during the past two or three days and nights, what units of their air force were operating and where, changes in the status or position of enemy *staffels* (squadrons) and *gruppes* (wings), and developments in design and armament of enemy aircraft.

Another set gave summaries of recent activities of the three divisions of the RAF: Bomber Command, Coastal Command, and Fighter Command. A third set proved most interesting to me. This gave accounts of activities of the front-line fighter squadrons during the past two days.

Each squadron that was called up on patrol during this period was listed, and its activities detailed. In the case of engagements the name of each pilot who made contact with the enemy was given, together with a summary from his combat report; and if he was credited with destroying, probably destroying, or damaging any of the enemy this was also given. Our own casualties were listed, with names, and details where known.

These summaries are published every two or three days and given to the pilots of all the squadrons to read, so that each of us is able to know just what our losses and successes are. I have never seen them omit any losses by my squadron or other squadrons whose activities I knew of, nor have they exaggerated our successes; and they never fail to check with the information concerning RAF successes and losses that is given in public communiqués.

You can see that we pilots are in a position to know if the information in RAF communiques is true, and any fighter pilot will tell you that it is. It was quite interesting and edifying for us to read the papers Tuesday, the day after our combat, containing the German report of our encounter, taken from a German High Command communiqué that was relayed from New York. This stated that we lost eight machines in the fight and all the German planes 'returned safely'!

Tuesday and Wednesday were quiet. Apparently the Boche aviators were staying home and 'licking their wounds' again.

We had plenty of leisure; and Peter and I visited the 'operations' room from which our orders came by radio while we were on the chase. It was an intriguing and interesting place. In the middle of a large room was a table several feet wide and long, on which was an enormous map of southern England, the English Channel, and northern France. Little wooden blocks were placed on it to represent planes and their positions, as well as ship convoys. As reports came in of new positions for planes or ships, girls standing around the table moved the blocks to the new positions. Enemy planes and ships were 'plotted' on this board in the same way as our own.

There was a gallery around the room, in which the control officers sat so that they could see the complete picture of the positions of their own and enemy planes and ships. All the time we were looking for the Nazis that morning our moves and those of the enemy were plotted about on this map. Our controller was able to see our relative positions on it at a glance; and on the basis of what he saw in that room he ordered us about in the air far out over the Channel until we found the enemy!

Daily he played a deadly game of chess on that map, using the pilots as chessmen, with unseen controllers on the other side of the Channel who directed the movements of our enemies.

Wednesday morning some of our squadron cooperated in giving the ground defences at our home airdrome some practice. The station commander had arranged to have a mock attack on the airdrome by combined air and ground forces. We were to furnish six airplanes to play the part of defending fighters, while a Hurricane squadron which was also based here was to furnish six airplanes to play the part of 'enemy' bombers. The six Hurricanes were to fly over as if they were bombing the airdrome, and our six Spitfires would attack and pretend to shoot them down.

There was only one flaw in the station commander's plans: he forgot to take into consideration the friendly but intense rivalry between the pilots of Hurricane and Spitfire airplanes. Pilots of these two types of fighters argue by the hour on which is the better, and the pilots of either type never pass up an opportunity to demonstrate the superiority of their type over the other.

Everything went according to plan when the mock attack began. The six Hurricanes which were to take the part of the bombers had left earlier in the morning and gone to another airdrome from which to start on their 'raid.' Our six Spitfires went up and began patrolling the airdrome, waiting for the bombers. I wasn't included in the six pilots used, so I watched the show from the ground, standing in front of our pilots' hut. Soon the Hurricanes appeared, flying in good bomber formation, right over the airdrome. The Spitfires went in to 'attack' – and that was where the plans went wrong.

Now bombers, when attacked, endeavor to stay close together in formation so that the gunners of all of them can fire on each enemy that gets close, all at the same time. These six Hurricane pilots probably intended to stay in formation originally, until the Spitfires attacked and the full import dawned on them: six Spitfires were going to get on their tails and pretend to shoot them down.

Never!!

As the Spitfires closed in, the formation of Hurricanes literally exploded, in all directions, in the most unorthodox manner for bombers as their pilots broke

1. Gordon Olive (see chapter 18) took up painting later in life and his little-known and, indeed, unique paintings of his Battle of Britain experiences convey combat scenes impossible to capture in photographs. 13 August 1940: 'We nosed down one behind the other, the speed mounting rapidly. Perhaps they did not see Sam as he started his dive, but before he got within range of the nearest bomber, most of the two hundred and fifty-odd bombers were firing tracer at him or at us. He and his wingman, Tom Smart, were virtually obscured by the crazy maze of tracer.'

Left: 2. A famous shot of a formation of KG55 Heinkel He 111s bombers heading for England, summer 1940. The He 111 was the most numerous bomber in the Luftwaffe fleet, delivering 2,200 lbs of bombs. *Right:* 3. The waist gunner position on a He 111, 1940. Such defensive machine-gunners took a considerable toll on British fighter pilots, a bullet in the right spot disabling many a Hurricane in particular.

Above: 4. A photograph of Hurricane pilots from 249 Squadron taken at the height of the Battle of Britain at RAF North Weald (11 Group), 21 September 1940. Left to right: Percy Burton (KIA six days later ramming an Me 110 which he destroyed), Robert 'Butch' Barton (4 kills, survived the war), Albert Gerald Lewis (15 kills in 1940, survived), James 'Ozzie' Crossey (survived), Tom Neil (13 kills, only pilot still alive today from this photo, see chapter 40), John Beazley (2 kills, 2 shared kills, survived), John Grandy (survived), George Barclay (an ace in 1940, KIA 1942) and Keith Lofts (6 kills, survived). *Left:* 5. René Mouchotte (on the right), French, 615 Squadron (see chapters 10 and 52) with fellow pilot *c.*1940.

6. A Hurricane dogfighting with two Me 109s, while a critically damaged Dornier 17 plummits to earth in the background, 1940s period illustration. David Crook, 609 Squadron on dogfighting: 'A very tiring business owing to the high speeds and heavy strains involved, and after about ten minutes we had generally had enough.'

Above left: 7. Richard Hillary (see chapters 33 and 50), Hurricane pilot with 603 Squadron, author of the bestselling fighter pilot memoir *The Last Enemy*. Portrait by Eric Kennington, an official war artist. *Above right:* 8. Albert Gerald Lewis (South African), 85 and 249 Squadrons, Battle of Britain Hurricane ace. He shot down 5 Me 109s on 19 May 1940 and 6 E/A on 27 September 1940! *Below:* 9. Rupert Smythe of 32 Squadron sitting in his Hurricane P3522 (each fighter had its own unique military aircraft serial number admisistered by the Air Ministry), August 1940 at the advanced landing base of RAF Biggin Hill, Kent. Note the tape covering the gun ports on the leading edges of both wings is still in place indicating that the machine guns have not yet been fired. Tom Gleave, 253 Squadron: 'It was good to be in a Hurricane, especially in a jam; the Me 109s couldn't cope with them when it came to turning; they could dive and climb quicker than us but were not nearly so manoeuvrable.'

Top: 10. A *schwarm* (similar to a *flight* of Spitfires of Hurricanes) of Me 109s. Here they are flying low over the White Cliffs of Dover, summer 1940. *Above left:* 11. An Me 109 in flight, 1940. *above riight:* 12. Me 109s in France, summer 1940. The Luftwaffe's only single-engined fighter, by the end of the war almost 34,000 Me 109s of various types would be produced, more than any other fighter. Most British pilots referred to it as the 'Me 109' rather than its official designation, Bf 109 (same for the 'Me 110').

Above: 13. Another stunning visualisation of a Luftwaffe aerial armada and Me 110s in defensive circles by Gordon Olive (see chapter 18). 25 August 1940: 'Sam led in with an attack on the leader of the uppermost wing of fighters and followed on towards the formation on the outer flank. He appeared to be lining five or six aeroplanes up in his sights simultaneously. His attack must have panicked the fighter leader for all four elements of the fighter escort began flying around in defensive circles. They went into it so simultaneously that it must have been a radio command. I remained five thousand feet above the formations. I was puzzling over the best way to attack these defensive circles when a flash of inspiration showed me a better way. While they wheeled around in their merry-go-rounds, the fighters were rapidly losing their bombers who were flying on up the Estuary unescorted.' *Right:* 14. Arming up an Me 110 fighter, summer 1940.

15. Me 110 over the White Cliffs of Dover, summer 1940. The 'A2' unit code on the fuselage denotes an aircraft of Luftwaffe unit ZG2. The naming of Luftwaffe units equivalent to RAF 'squadrons' was very complicated. Arthur Donahue, 64 Squadron (see chapters 16, 19 and 53) on the Me 110: 'Considered easy meat by our fighters. The only danger lay in a surprise attack by one of them, because this type carried very heavy armament including two cannons, and if one of them got a good shot at you it would be bad.'

16. A *section* of three Spitfires emerge out of the blinding sun in a surprise attack on Me 110s, 1940s period illustration. The shoe was more often on the other foot as David Crook (see chapters 13, 24 and 45), 609 Squadron describes: 'On 8 August, soon after dawn, we were ordered to patrol a convoy off the Needles. It was a very clear day with a brilliant sun – just the sort of day that the Germans love, because they come out at a very big height and dive down to attack out of the sun. By doing this cleverly, they used to render themselves almost invisible until the attack was delivered. We hated these clear days and always prayed for some high cloud to cover the sun.'

17. Gun camera film still showing machine-gun and tracer fire (the curling white streak) from the Spitfire of 74 Squadron's Irishman Wilfred 'Paddy' Treacy hitting a Me 110 during a dogfight near Dunkirk late May 1940. Treacy was shot down twice during the evacuation and escaped twice, the latter time via Spain. He shot down several enemy aircraft in spring 1940 but was KIA in 1941.

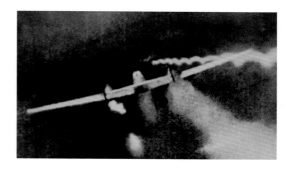

18. A formation of Ju 87 'Stuka' dive-bombers in flight, summer 1940. The epitome of the German Blitzkrieg, the rather fragile and lumbering aircraft held no fear for RAF pilots who shot them down with relative ease. George Stoney, 501 Squadron, 29 July 1940: 'I got him in my gun sights and let him have it. I was overtaking him fast and when I stopped firing he was covering my entire windscreen, only 50 yards away. I stopped firing because he blew up.'

19. A convoy in the English Channel under attack from Ju 87 dive-bombers. 1940s period illustration.

20. Escorting Me 109s make a head-on pass to disrupt the Spitfires attacking their bombers, Gordon Olive painting (see chapter 18).

21. A 1941 cutaway drawing of a Spitfire mark 1. American Art Donahue (see chapters 16, 19 and 53) on being told he was assigned to fly Spitfires: 'This was the very height of my hopes. Of all England's superb fighting planes, the Supermarine Spitfires are generally considered masters of them all and the world's deadliest fighters. The pilots assigned to fly them consider themselves the luckiest of pilots. The engines are twelve-cylinder Rolls-Royce of about ten hundred fifty horsepower with an "emergency boost" giving them nearly fourteen hundred horsepower for actual combat. Each has eight machine guns, mounted in the wings. All the guns point forward and are fired by a single button on the top of the pilot's control stick.'

22. Richard Jones (64 and 19 Squadrons) sitting in his Spitfire in 1940. He joined 64 Squadron at the beginning of the Battle in July 1940 and flew throughout the Battle. One of the more light-hearted entries in his log book read, '28 October, shot down and crash-landed at Hawkhurst, Kent. Killed three sheep. What a bloody mess!!!'. Such light heartedness hid the real story; 'arse-end Charlie' to a patrol at 20,000 feet, he had been picked off by Me 109s coming out of the sun, his starboard wing disintegrated, his engine died and he lost 10,000 feet in an uncontrollable spin. When he finally recovered some element of control he realised his hood was jammed shut. His precious Spitfire was recovered with only minor repairs needed.

Right: 23. A Spitfire pilot return from a sortie. This is Colin MacFie of 616 Squadron at RAF Fowlmere, Cambridgeshire, September 1940. Born in Cheltenham, he made 1 kill in the Battle, crashed in France in 1942 and was made a POW. *Left:* 24. A Spitfire in flight, 1940.

Left: 25. Portrait by official war artist, Eric Kennington of John W. C. Simpson, Hurricane Pilot, 85 Squadron (see chapters 8 and 48). *Right:* 26. Pilots scramble to their Spitfires early 1940. In reality a squadron's aircraft were dispersed rather than being 'parked' in a neat row. This was to avoid presenting the Luftwaffe with an easy target for its bombers.

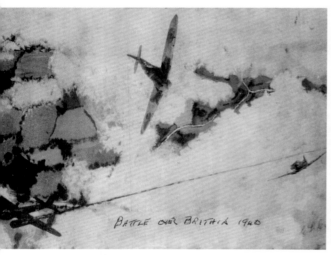

BATTLE OVER BRITAIN 1940

Above right: 27. A sergeant pilot (he has three angled stripes on the sleeve of his left arm) in the cockpit of a Spitfire. The gun firing button is at the top of the control column just to the left of his right hand and the pilot would operate it with his thumb. *Right:* 28. Spitfire with a black/white under wing surface scheme. This was used on many British fighters early in the Battle. 1940s period illustration. *Above:* 29. *Battle Over Britain 1940* painting by 605 Squadron Hurricane pilot Christopher 'Bunny' Currant. Currant shot down 10 enemy aircraft in 1940 and later starred as 'Hunter Leader', alongside David Niven and Leslie Howard, in the aerial sequences of the film *First of the Few*, a huge success in 1942.

30. 610 Squadron Spitfires from RAF Gravesend patrol over Kent in July 1940.

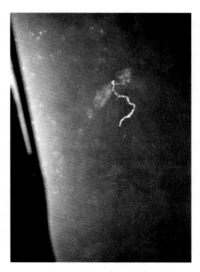

Right: 31. Photograph from the window of a German aircraft of a doomed British aircraft, summer 1940. *Left:* 32. This is the terrifying vision a He 111 crew would have when attacked head-on by the Spitfire. 1940s period illustration. Brian Lane of 19 Squadron (see chapters 7, 43 and 55) describes attacking Luftwaffe bombers in such a manner on 11 September: 'It must have been rather frightening to see the Spitfires rushing to meet them apparently in a head-on collision, forty-eight guns of the leading flight spanning the space between with white pencils of tracer. I held on to the last minute and then ducked to one side as a huge dark green monster flashed past. I caught an impression of the whirling airscrews, a black cross outlined in white, a gun in the rear cockpit swinging after me, a pink blur of the gunner's face showing behind it. Then they were gone.'

Above: 33. Cockpit of the Heinkel 111 bomber, pilot is on the left, the bomb aimer/front gunner is lying down looking out for RAF fighters, 1940. *Below:* 34. Gun camera still taken from the Spitfire of Adolf 'Sailor' Malan, 74 Squadron, at around 5.20 p.m. 21 May 1940 over Dunkirk. Unbelievably it was only counted as 'probably destroyed', since Malan didn't actually see the Heinkel crash (he was too busy shooting down a Ju 88). Though if it had struggled home it would have suited the South African ace who favoured damaging aircraft and sending them back to base with dead crew as a warning to others. His 'ten rules of air fighting' would become unofficial textbook tactics for fighter pilots and found their way onto squadron notice boards throughout Fighter Command. *Left:* 35. Heinkel 111s in formation on a raid, summer 1940.

36. A Dornier 17 bomber, summer 1940.

Right: 37. Two individual rear-facing guns at the back of the cockpit of a Dornier 17, summer 1940. David Crook, 609 Squadron: 'It is an odd thing when you are being fired at by a rear gunner that the stream of bullets seems to leave the machine very slowly and in a great outward curve. You chuckle to yourself, "Ha, the fool's missing me by miles!" Then, suddenly, the bullets accelerate madly and curl in towards you again and flick just past your head. You thereupon bend your head a little lower, mutter "My God," or some other suitable expression and try to kill the rear gunner before he makes any more nuisance of himself.' *Left:* 38. A Heinkel 111 bomber crew 'suit up' with parachutes before embarking on a daylight raid over Britain, summer 1940.

Above: 39. A formation of Ju 88 bombers in flight on a raid, summer 1940. The fastest and most rugged of the Luftwaffe bomber fleet, they proved the most difficult for RAF fighter pilots to shoot down. *Below:* 40. A Ju 88 flying in formation, summer 1940. *Opposite:* 41. 1940 RAF Fighter Command map showing HQs, group boundaries, sectors boundaries, sector stations and airfields.

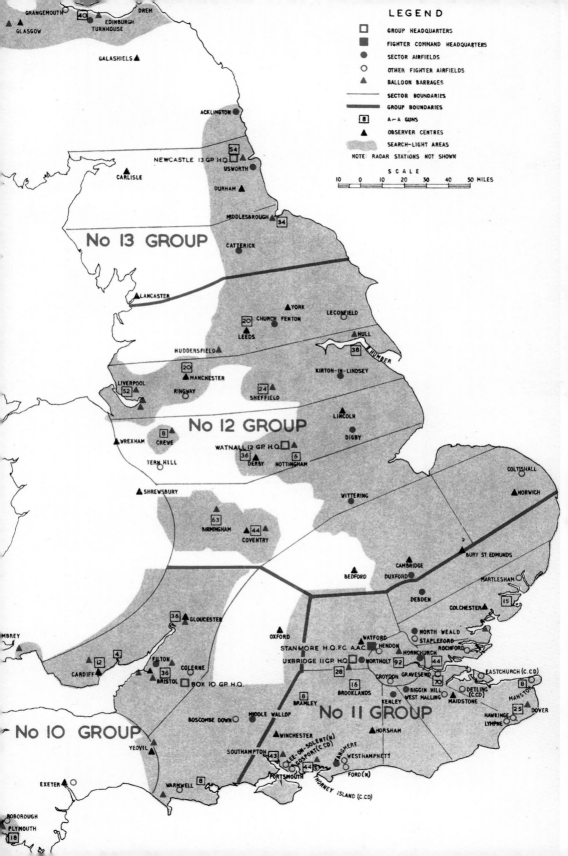

Left: 42. Front cover of the first edition (1941) of Arthur Donahue's Battle of Britain memoir, *Tally-Ho!* (see chapters 16, 19 and 53). *Centre:* 43. Front cover of the first edition (1942) of Esther Wright's memoir, *Pilot's Wife's Tale.* Her husband was Battle of Britain fighter pilot David Hunt of 257 Squadron (see chapter 27). The book was adapted into a radio play broadcast during the war. *Right:* 44. WAAFs about to send a barrage balloon up into the sky above London. These balloons were deployed to deter low-level bombing raids (inherently more accurate) by the Luftwaffe. *Below:* 45. Hurricane shooting down a Dornier 17, 1940 period illustration. 242 Squadron's Douglas Bader's combat report of 15 September echoes a similar attack: 'Opened fire at 100 yards in steep dive and saw a large flash behind starboard motor of Dornier as wing caught fire: must have hit petrol pipe or tank; overshot and pulled up steeply.'

away to do combat with their rivals, our Spitfire pilots. It was absolutely earnest combat in everything except that they didn't use their guns, and for the next few moments the air above the airdrome was full of milling, wheeling, twisting, diving, zooming, rolling, and gyrating Spitfires and Hurricanes, as the rival pilots strove their mightiest and cleverest to prove the superiority of their respective machines.

It seemed impossible that they could avoid collisions. The din of Rolls Royce engines racing at full throttle nearly made our ears ring. Number One, who was standing beside us watching the show, remarked in his slow, sage manner, 'I'm awfully glad that all our boys are crazy. No sane pilot could possibly fly in that melee up there for a minute without colliding with some one!' I agreed with him.

After a few minutes the boys had all had enough, for dogfighting even in fun is a terrific strain, and the machines of both types came stringing back in, one by one, and landing. Little was proved by it all, because it was such a melee that no one knew whom he was fighting – in fact at times Spitfire pilots had found themselves engaging other Spitfires, and Hurricane pilots other Hurricanes! It merely started another endless chain of arguments in the mess.

It was very illustrative of the high spirit of all the boys. Our squadron leader, remarking about the spirit in his squadron, had said the day before: 'It's like holding in a team of wild horses when I keep them in formation when there are Huns near. I'm almost afraid to give the "Tally-ho" because I know I'll be alone about two seconds later! They just peel off like banana skins when they get the word to go after the Huns!'

Thursday of that week, 8 August, was the beginning of the German mass air raids on this country – the date commonly referred to as the start of the great battle over Britain. Of course we didn't know it that morning.

We had to fly to our advance base at dawn, and it was an unforgettably beautiful flight for me. It was just getting light when we took off, and the countryside was dim below us. Wicked blue flames flared back from the exhausts of all the engines as I looked at the planes in formation about me.

We seemed to hover motionless except for the slight upward or downward drift of one machine or another in relation to the rest, which seemed to lend a sort of pulsating life to the whole formation; and the dark carpet of the earth below steadily slid backward beneath us. The sun, just rising and very red and big and beautiful, made weird lights over the tops of our camouflaged wings. We were like a herd of giant beasts in some strange new kind of world. It reminded me of a motion picture named *Dawn Patrol* which I had seen in some other life in another world far away.

We landed at our advance base, and saw our airplanes refueled and ready to take off. It was a chilly morning, and most of us turned in under blankets on cots provided for us and hoped that the Huns slept late and wouldn't bother us until we had completed our night's sleep. We had gotten up at about 3 a.m.

It seemed like it would be another quiet day. Nothing happened until about 11 a.m. Then the telephone rang, and the call was for our squadron leader. When he finished speaking he turned to us with a little smile and said: 'Operations just called to tell us to be on our toes. There's a lot of activity on the other side, and they have a "fifty plus" raid plotted, coming across farther down the coast. It may turn and head our way though.'

A 'fifty plus' raid meant a group of fifty or more enemy airplanes!

In a few minutes the telephone rang again. The telephone orderly listened a moment and then turned to us and said, 'Squadron into your aircraft, and patrol base at ten thousand feet!'

Instantly we were on our feet and racing pellmell out to our airplanes. An airman helped me on with my parachute. I climbed into the cockpit of my machine and, trembling with excitement, adjusted my straps and put on my helmet. Down the line of planes starters whined, and first one engine then another coughed to life. I pressed my own starter button and my engine joined the chorus. There was no 'warming up,' no taxiing across the field to take off into the wind. Upwind, downwind, or crosswind, we took off straight ahead. Better a difficult take-off than to give a deadly enemy a minute's extra advantage!

We roared off like a stampeding herd of buffalo, climbing steeply and wide open. Two thousand feet, four thousand – there were thick fluffy clouds at five thousand, and we flashed up through their misty chasms, caverns, hills and valleys; and then they were dropping away below us and forming a snowy carpet for us to look down on. The sun shone brilliantly above. New orders came over the radio from our controller, much as on the previous chase. Sometimes we were over coastal cities, sometimes over the Channel, circling here, patrolling there, watching for the elusive enemy. I recalled the scene in the operations room and wondered if the girls plotting our positions were any less nonchalant now when there was a real chase on.

Nearly an hour passed without our seeing anything. One flight (six of our twelve planes) was ordered to land, and I guessed that the trail was getting cold. Peter and I were in the flight remaining on patrol.

We were about eight thousand feet up, the six of us patrolling over the Channel, and for a couple of minutes we had received no new orders. The sun was very hot, and I wished I hadn't worn my tunic.

Our only warning was the sudden whine of a transmitter and a voice shouting 'BANDITS ASTERN!!'

It was blood-chilling. Our squadron leader was quick on the trigger and led us in a violent turn, just in time. A myriad gray Messerschmitts were swarming down out of the sun, diving from above and behind and shooting as they came.

'Tal-l-ly—ho-o!'

Our leader's voice was steady and strong and reassuring and in that moment filled with all his personal magnetism and strength of character. It was reassuring in its calm call to battle, and caught up shattered nerves and self-control in each of us. He led us together down into the middle of the swarm of Huns, whose speed had carried them far down ahead of us and who were now wheeling back towards us as they came up out of their dives.

There seemed to be about thirty; it was probably a *gruppe* of twenty-seven, and they simply absorbed the six of us. We picked targets and went after them and were soon completely lost from each other. One Messerschmitt was coming up in a climbing turn ahead of me, and allowing for its speed I aimed a burst of fire just ahead of its nose. I had no time to see if I hit it.

My guns gave me a feeling of power. They sounded terribly capable and completed the steadying effect of our leader's voice on my nerves.

Another Messerschmitt coming head-on spat his four white tracers at me but they arched over my head. We seemed to be milling about like a swarm of great gnats in this giant eerie amphitheater above the clouds. Sets of long white tracers criss crossed the air and hung all about, like Christmas decorations! They stay visible for several seconds after they're fired.

Something about the shape of the Messerschmitts reminded me of rats sailing about on their little narrow, stiff-looking, square-tipped wings. I think it's because of the shape of their noses, and the way their radiators are carried tucked up under their noses like the fore-feet of a rat when he's running close to the floor.

One came at me from the side, his guns blazing out their tracers and his cannon firing through a hole in the center of his propeller, puffing blue smoke for all the world like a John Deere tractor! It wasn't a pretty sight. Two of the tracers erupted from guns on either side of its nose, at the top, and two from the wings. It looked like a hideous rat-shaped fountain spurting jets of water from its nostrils and mouth corners!

We meleed about for several minutes, the fight quickly spreading out over wide territory. I got short shots at several of our playmates, just firing whenever I saw something with black crosses in front of me and not having time to see the result.

Then one got on my tail and gave me a burst just as I saw him, and I laid over into a vertical turn; and as he did likewise, following me, I hauled my Spitfire around as tight as I could. We were going fast and I had to lean forward and hold my breath and fight to keep from blacking out, and I turned this way for several seconds. Then I eased my turn so that I could straighten up and look out of my cockpit, and I spotted the other in front of me. I had turned so much shorter than he could that I was almost around and on his tail now. He apparently became aware of it at the same time, for he abandoned his turn and took to flight; but he was a little late now.

He went into a dive, twisting about wildly to upset my aim as I opened fire. I pressed my firing button three or four times for bursts of about a second each, and then he quit twisting. I was able to hold the sight dead on him while I held the firing button in for a good three-second burst, and let it go at that.

I didn't think he needed any more, for I knew of only one reason for him to stop twisting. He disappeared into the clouds below, diving straight down, and although he might have gotten home he certainly wasn't headed right then.

Two more were following me down closely, and in pulling out of my dive I plunged momentarily through the clouds and then up out of them, turning to meet these two. The powder smoke from my guns smelled strong, and I felt good. This was battle royal!

But my newest opponents failed me. As I zoomed up out of the clouds I saw them just disappearing into the clouds and heading homeward. Another diving out of nowhere took a snap shot at me as he went by and down into the clouds, also heading for home.

Recovering from the shock that gave me, I looked around and found no more planes of either nationality in view. I appeared to be in sole possession of this part of the battlefield. This was well out over the Channel and I knew I must be nearly out of ammunition, so I headed for shore and our advance base.

All but one of our planes were already down safely when I taxied into line on the ground. Peter was 'still adrift,' I learned, and it gave me a little shock. There was still plenty of time for him to show up, though.

We compared notes. Others of the squadron had sent two Messerschmitts down in flames. I couldn't claim mine as a confirmed victory unless someone saw it hit the sea, because it wasn't in flames. We can claim a victory if the enemy is seen in flames or if the pilot jumps out in his parachute; but otherwise it must be seen by some one to hit the sea or ground. Mine went down quite a way out over the Channel (if it went down) and there wasn't much likelihood of its being seen.

We began to worry about Peter when he didn't show up after a reasonable time. One of our boys remembered seeing a parachute floating down during the fight, but didn't know whether or not it was a German. Our squadron leader got on the telephone to try to get news of him. Our shift at the advance base was over now and another squadron had arrived to relieve us. Our squadron leader sent us home and remained himself to try to locate Peter.

We were late for dinner when we got home, and it was warmed over and I suppose that was partly why I couldn't eat. But the main reason was Peter. The chances of good news were growing smaller each minute; but it finally came! Peter had been picked up, wounded but alive, and was already in a hospital. Later we got more details. He had several bullet wounds but none of them was serious in itself, and his only danger was shock and loss of blood. He was 'in wonderful spirits, cursing the Huns and spoiling for another go at them!' They thought that if he pulled through the first night he would be out of danger.

The world seemed brighter after that. I thought a lot of this big tough good-natured pal of mine.

It developed that our fight was only one of a series of battles all along the Channel. The mass raids had started, and the aerial 'Battle for Britain' was on!

The next day, Friday, we were scheduled to take the readiness shift at our advance base for the afternoon, from 1 p.m. until dark. In the morning we were just a reserve squadron. There was some activity in the morning but we weren't called out, and it quieted down about noon; looked as if it would be a quiet afternoon for us.

Our squadron leader decided not to go with us and had one of the flight commanders take over the squadron for the afternoon. He couldn't fly with us always, as the commanding officer of a squadron has lots of office work to do, and he wanted to get caught up with his that day. He reassured us though: 'I'll keep in close touch with Operations and have a machine ready, and if anything big starts turning up I'll be blazing down there at "four pounds boost and twenty-six hundred rpm" to join you!'

There was some activity about mid afternoon, and we were sent up on two patrols; but our squadron failed to make contact with the enemy. However, toward the end of the second patrol two of our boys were detached and sent to intercept two Messerschmitt 109s that were attacking the balloon barrage at Dover. They found the 109s and had a short, sharp dog fight among the balloons and low clouds and bursting anti-aircraft shells over the city. The Messerschmitts ran for it and got away in the clouds, but the boys thought they had damaged both of them.

Mann got a cannon shell in the wing of the Spitfire he was flying and was very worried about it because it was our squadron leader's regular machine. By that time the CO, as we usually called him, had arrived, carrying out his promise to come down if anything started to happen, and he forgave Mann for it, good-naturedly.

Then while we were getting refueled the main battle of the afternoon was fought near us over the Channel, between other British squadrons and a large mass of Huns. We all stood on top of a bomb shelter trying to watch it. We could hear the roaring of engines and machine guns, but it was too high and far away for us to see anything of it.

By the time we were refueled and ready to go it was over, and there was nothing more for us to do until about eight o'clock in the evening, when we were given permission to take off and return to our home base.

The first thing I did when we got home was to telephone the hospital for news of Peter. It was encouraging. He was still holding his own and doing fine, and they thought he was practically out of danger. I wrote him a letter, cussing him out for lying around in bed when we had lots of work to do. The CO told me I could have the following Tuesday off to go and visit him. His hospital was quite a distance away.

We weren't scheduled to do readiness the next day, although we were supposed to be available on the airdrome in case something big came up and the squadrons that were on duty needed help. I got up rather late and learned from the station commander, who had already been in touch with the hospital, that Peter was still holding his own.

Breakfast tasted good. I took stock of the events of the week in relation to myself, and decided it hadn't been bad. I certainly wasn't sorry I had come here. Although I was still pretty scared while on patrol I felt that, given a little more time to get used to it, I'd be all right. I'd been through two good engagements and felt quite sure that I'd already accomplished a little for the flag I was fighting under. Moreover I'd learned a lot and thought I'd be able to accomplish a lot more in time to come.

I was in our squadron office about mid-morning when an orderly brought in a telegram for the adjutant. The adjutant looked at it and then handed it to me, and as I read it my mouth went dry and part of my world went crumbling.

It was from the hospital. Peter had had a relapse that morning and passed away. *Chapter 5 Defeat: PM, 10–13 August 1940* I kept trying to tell myself, in the dazed moments that followed, that this was good for me, that it would give me the hardening that I needed; and some how that seemed to help me keep control of my pounding heart and wild emotions. When I was alone I murmured aloud: 'I'll make it up for you, pal. I'll get the ones you won't be getting now. Wait and see if I don't!'

Gradually the waves of feeling grew less intense, and I felt cleaned and chastened, and toughened a little too, perhaps; and by keeping my mind away from the tragedy of it I managed to eat my meals and act normally.

The next day was Sunday, but I didn't get to go to mass. There were some other blood sacrifices being made, to the ambitions of a hate-crazed, power-maddened little man who wanted to take the place of God.

We had the morning shift at the advance base again, from dawn until one o'clock, and there was quite a lot going on. We did one patrol without managing to intercept the enemy, and on that patrol my oxygen apparatus broke down. It would take a while to repair it, so the CO told me I might fly without oxygen if I wished, and if we got ordered above fifteen thousand feet I should break away and come back down.

We had hardly been refueled before we were off again, and as the mechanics hadn't had time to fix my oxygen apparatus yet I went along anyway without oxygen, as the CO suggested. We patrolled around a while at ten thousand feet, then were ordered to fifteen thousand, and after a few minutes twenty thousand. Control said there were a large number of bandits which had gone inland and were coming back out, climbing; and our squadron was to try to intercept them on their way out.

I broke away from the squadron after they got above fifteen thousand feet, but I hated to go back and land with so much going on. I thought that if a fight started it would probably work down lower, and I might get in on the last of it if I stayed around. By listening to the orders the squadron was given over the R/T (radio telephone) I could keep track of where the squadron was and where the enemy must be expected.

I went back down to ten thousand feet, as I didn't feel too comfortable at fifteen thousand without oxygen; and then cruised around listening to the R/T messages and watching for Huns on my own. Suddenly I heard the distant voice of one of the boys in the squadron calling over the R/T, 'Many bandits approaching from the starboard!'

There was a moment's radio silence and then another voice: 'Look out ! There's more of them behind and above!'

Then our leader's voice, 'All right! Tally-ho!'

Then there was absolute radio silence and I knew that the battle must be on. I watched all around and above me, but couldn't see any airplanes and couldn't tell where this was occurring, though I knew it must be close by. I wished I could find some enemies at my altitude somewhere.

All at once I saw some puffs from anti-aircraft shells a few miles away and not very high. I reasoned that where there were anti-aircraft shells exploding there must be enemy aircraft, and I headed in that direction, toward Dover. As I got near I saw what it was all about. Enemy airplanes must be attacking the balloon barrage, for one of the balloons was burning beautifully. Great scarlet flames and clouds of pitch-black smoke were rolling upward from it. A furious barrage of anti-aircraft fire was going up on the opposite side of Dover over the harbour, and I headed wide open for it.

The fire ceased just before I got there, and I swung out over the harbour looking in all directions but couldn't see any enemy. Then I saw the smoke puffs of more anti-aircraft going up on the other side of town again and I wheeled and made a bee-line toward them. When I got there the shells were bursting all around me and some of them close enough to be uncomfortable, but still I could see no Hun. I got away from there, and the firing ceased.

As I neared the airdrome I saw a Spitfire coming straight down in a vertical dive, from very high. It looked as if it was hit, and my heart sank and I prayed that it wasn't another of our squadron's boys. Then I sighed with relief as it began pulling out of the dive at about five thousand feet and headed for the airdrome.

I was at about seven thousand feet now and losing altitude toward the airdrome and relaxing a little. There were some nice fluffy clouds below me and I would be dropping through them in a minute. A dot on my rear vision mirror attracted my attention, and looking back I saw what appeared to be another Spitfire quite a distance behind and above me but overtaking me rapidly. I guessed that both of these Spitfires were boys of the squadron returning from the fight.

I watched it idly as it got closer behind me. The pilot was doing something which is considered bad taste in following directly behind me. This is bad for a fighter pilot to do because the pilot of the plane being overtaken may not notice him until he is close behind, with the result that he gets an awful scare when he does see him, thinking it's an enemy on his tail. So normally, fighter pilots never approach a friendly plane from directly behind, but always from well to one side.

This Spitfire pilot kept on overtaking me from directly behind, and it irked me a little, like seeing someone go through a 'Stop' sign in front of you. Then when he kept getting closer I began to wonder if perhaps the pilot mistook me for a Messerschmitt or something. Airplanes aren't too easy to recognize in profile, and he was certainly acting like he was going to attack me. He was only five or six hundred yards behind me and gaining fast, so I decided to give him a better chance to see my identity before he got close enough for accurate shooting.

I tipped my plane over in a vertical turn so that he could see the shape of my wings, and the next instant I realized that it wasn't that pilot, but myself, who had made a mistake in identity. He knew I was a Spitfire all right, and that's why he was attacking – his 'Spitfire' wasn't a Spitfire at all, but a Messerschmitt 109, and his tracers were reaching out across the space between us! It was too far for accurate shooting though, and I got out of his way and he continued his dive and disappeared into the clouds.

It taught me a lesson, and since then I have never allowed another airplane to get anywhere near behind me until I have scrutinized it and made positive identification.

I didn't think any of his bullets had hit my machine until I went to check my air speed, then I found that my air speed indicator wasn't working. On landing I found that a bullet had gone through my wing, cutting the air speed indicator pressure tube, and causing the instrument to fail.

I had reason to be disappointed because I wasn't able to be with the squadron that time. They had a terrific show, having found far more enemies than they could take care of.

They had first intercepted a bunch of 109s (Messerschmitts) and had got all split up fighting them and chasing them. Our CO had shot down one and then chased another most of the way across the Channel, but ran out of ammunition before he got it down. It was losing height when he left it, though, with white clouds of steam and glycol (radiator fluid) streaming behind, and the pilot had jettisoned the hood of his cockpit preparatory to baling out.

'Orange' [James O'Meara] had got a 109 and then chased a formation of forty 110s (the twin-engined type of Messerschmitt fighter and light bomber) most of the way across the Channel. On catching them he 'sort of nibbled at one at the rear of the formation,' as he termed it, exhausting all the ammunition he had left and getting some small pieces to fly off it; but it stayed in formation and he assumed that it probably got home – 'though not in very good condition,' he added.

Others had also had good results, and the final outcome, after checking with reports of machines that crashed in the vicinity, was four confirmed for the squadron.

The only casualty was Bud. He was ruefully inspecting his rather battle-scarred

Spitfire. A good proportion of one side of his tail was shot away by cannon fire, one wing damaged, and one tire flat! A 109 had surprised him from behind as he was returning from the fight, and had scored a couple of pretty good hits. When Bud heard and felt the explosion of a cannon shell on his machine he had rolled over quickly and dived straight down and got away, not knowing how badly he was crippled.

We had one more patrol, which proved uneventful, and then our shift was over and we returned to our home airdrome. Our CO went to visit Peter's parents that afternoon, so before he left I told him the request Peter had made me about his wristlet and he said he would have it taken care of. The funeral was to be Tuesday morning, and I planned to attend.

Monday, 12 August, was a pretty busy day.

We had one patrol in the latter part of the afternoon without making any interception; and while we were on the ground getting refueled Operations telephoned and said there was a '450 plus' raid forming up over the French coast. I guess we were all feeling a little subdued when we got scrambled again a few minutes later. We knew that if we intercepted it we'd be fortunate if there was more than one other squadron at the most with us in the fight.

However, we were up only a short time when we intercepted a comparatively small formation of enemy fighters, perhaps twenty or thirty. The 'Tally-ho' went up and we got all split up. I saw a formation of three that were flying by themselves a short distance away from the rest, and they started going in a circle as I went in to attack, just following each other round and round.

Their wings were different and more graceful-looking than those of Messerschmitts, and I recognized the machines as the new Heinkel 113 fighters. They were good looking airplanes, and I remember that they were painted all white. We meleed about a little, and I ended up by getting chased down into the clouds below us, and I lost track of them for the moment.

I was cruising along in a rift between the clouds when I saw above me and to the south east more airplanes than I had ever seen at one time in my life. It was the '450 plus' raid coming across. It takes those big mass formations a long time to get organized. They have to circle around over one spot for a long time while the various groups of planes get into their places in the formation.

This raid was now organized and was halfway across the Channel.

I wasn't very high, perhaps seven thousand feet, and above me and to the south east at very high altitude the sky seemed to be filled with fighters. I could see their wings flashing high above, almost everywhere I looked. Farther south east, not far off the French coast yet, the bombers were coming. I mistook them at first for an enormous black cloud.

I decided I had better get back to the advance base to rejoin the others, who would be collecting there after the fight we'd just had.

I had gone just a little way in the direction of our advance base, cruising along among the clouds, when right across in front of me flashed a Heinkel 113 again, just skimming the tops of the clouds. I opened up throttle and emergency throttle and turned after it. I didn't think the pilot had seen me, because he was higher than I. I guessed that it was one of the three I had just engaged, and looked back carefully but couldn't see the other two. Then I was getting close enough to open fire, and didn't look back for a moment.

Powp!! Powp!!

The familiar sound of exploding cannon shells wracked my eardrums and my plane shook. Shrapnel banged and rattled and white tracers streamed by. For all my care, I had been surprised from behind by a second Hun!

I tried desperately to make a quick turn to evade him, but for some reason I didn't seem able to turn, and my plane was just going up in a gentle climb, straight ahead. The firing lasted only a second, but I expected it would start again. I was above the clouds just a little now, and I must get down into them for concealment!

I pushed ahead on the stick – that's how you make an airplane dive – but this time the stick just flopped limply all the way forward to the instrument panel, with no result. Elevator cables gone, I realized. Then I saw why I couldn't turn. My feet were pumping wildly back and forth on the rudder pedals and they were entirely loose too, and produced no response – rudder cables gone too!

This was bad. I could smell powder smoke, hot and strong, but it didn't make me feel tough this time. It was from the cannon shells and incendiary bullets that had hit my machine. Smoke from an incendiary bullet was curling up beside me. It was lodged in the frame of the machine and smoldering there.

My heart pounded and my mouth tasted salty, and I wondered if this was the end of the line. This was *very* bad.

I could still pull back on the stick and get response, but that didn't help because it made me go up and I wanted to go down, to get back to the safety of the clouds. If I could just get rolled over, I thought, my controls would work opposite and I should then be able to dive. The aileron controls on my wings seemed all right, and perhaps I could get rolled over. My attacker was off to one side of me, out of firing position, but I knew he would be back on my tail again in a moment. He had just overshot me and swung off to the side and would come back as soon as he could get behind me again. There might be a chance to get rolled over first, I thought, then down into the safety of the clouds below, and maybe I could land some how.

First I jerked open the hatch over my cockpit, so that I could get away in a hurry if things didn't work out.

I had just done that when I was suddenly receiving a salvo from a third plane behind me – no doubt the other Heinkel. The din and confusion were awful inside the cockpit. I remember seeing some of the instrument panel breaking up, and holes dotting the gas tank in front of me.

Smoke trails of tracer bullets appeared right inside the cockpit. Bullets were going by between my legs, and I remember seeing the bright flash of an incendiary bullet going past my leg and into the gas tank.

I remember being surprised that I wasn't scared any more. I suppose I was too dazed. There was a finality about the salvo, and it lasted at least two or three seconds. Then there was a kind of silence.

I wondered if one of them was going to open up on me again.

A light glowed in the bottom of the fuselage, somewhere up in front. Then a little red tongue of flame licked out inquiringly from under the gas tank in front of my feet and curled up the side of it and became a hot little bonfire in one corner of the cockpit. I remembered my parachute, and jerked the locking pin that secured my seat straps, and started to climb out just as the whole cockpit became a furnace.

There was a fraction of a second of searing heat just as I was getting my head and shoulders out, then I was jerked and dragged the rest of the way out with terrible roughness and flung down the side of the fuselage and away all in a fraction of a second by the force of the two hundred-mile-an-hour wind that caught me. Then I was falling and reaching for my ripcord and pulling it. A moment of suspense, and then a heavy pull that stopped my fall and there I hung, quite safe if not sound.

I was surprised at how nice and substantial the parachute felt. Everything was calm and quiet, and it was hard to realize that I was only a few seconds out of a battle.

Looking myself over I found that I was even less to look at than usual. I was aching all over, but it appeared to be mostly from bruises that I received from being dragged out of the cockpit so quickly. One of my trouser legs was torn and burned completely off, and my bare leg, which couldn't be called attractive at best, was anything but pretty now. It was bruised and skinned in a dozen places, and there was a sizable burned area around my ankle where the skin hung loosely.

But I could find no bullet wounds. Bruises and burns only – my right hand and the right side of my face were burned too. But it felt so good to be alive after what my prospects were a few moments before that I didn't mind the aches and pains.

I sighed and said aloud, feeling that the occasion demanded some recognition, 'Well, Art, this is what you asked for. How do you like it?'

But I was still in for one of the worst scares of my young life.

It was perhaps a minute or more after I baled out. I was down under the clouds now. The sound of an airplane gliding came to me and I wondered what its nationality was. I couldn't look up, because of the way my parachute harness held me, and I couldn't see it. I knew that in the Polish campaign some Nazi pilots often machine-gunned Polish pilots who were coming down in parachutes, and I had a little moment of anxiety. Then my anxiety was changed to panic.

A staccato burst of shots sounded, and my parachute canopy quivered with each shot! It lasted for perhaps a second. I could think of nothing but that a Hun was firing at me and hitting my parachute canopy. I knew that if I pulled the shroud lines on one side it would partly collapse the canopy and I would fall faster, so I just went hand over hand up the shroud lines on one side until the canopy was two-thirds collapsed – I wasn't taking any halfway measures!

That changed my position so I was looking up and could see the canopy, and I was surprised that there didn't seem to be any bullet holes in it. Then another volley sounded and the canopy quivered in the same way, and still no bullet holes appeared in it.

Then I looked downward and discovered where the shots came from. Smoke was drifting away from an anti-aircraft battery on the ground beneath me! They must have been firing at an airplane somewhere overhead, and the concussions made my canopy quiver. I can laugh at it now, but it was really one of the worst moments of panic I've ever had.

I landed in a little oat field near a group of soldiers, who held their rifles ready as they approached, until I stood up and they could see the remnants of my RAF uniform. They started to escort me to their quarters; when I was halfway there my left knee began to give out, and they carried me the rest of the way. That was the last I walked for three weeks.

They gave me first aid in their quarters, and the boy who worked on me gave me a shock. 'You'll get about a six weeks lay-up out of this, sir,' he speculated.

'Don't be silly!' I said. 'This won't keep me laid up more than two or three days, will it?'

'Well, you've got a couple pretty nasty burns there on your leg and your hand. The one on your face isn't so bad, but the other two ought to take a month to heal. Then you'll get a spot of 'sick leave' of course – yes, I'd make it all of six weeks before you're all fit again.'

This was something, I realized. I had expected they'd bandage up my hand and leg and give me forty-eight hours off and tell me to be careful for a day or two – that is, if they were worth bandaging at all!

Several Tommies were in the room watching the proceedings and talking and joking with me. One of them left and came back after a couple minutes with a flask of whisky.

'You want to appreciate this, sir,' he counseled. 'It isn't every day that a Scotsman will give you good Scotch whisky!'

After a time an ambulance came. I climbed off the cot I was lying on, onto a stretcher that they laid beside it, and they put me aboard. I was taken to a nearby village where they parked me a while, and then put me into another ambulance that drove for a long time before we got to a little hospital where I was unloaded and put to bed.

The head doctor, an Army captain, looked me over and said that he would have to cut away the skin from the burned areas; and so a cot on wheels was brought in by my bed and I climbed onto it and was taken into the operating room. A nurse pricked a needle into my arm, and then the lights faded. When I awoke I was back in my bed again.

The official British Air Ministry Communique issued early on the morning of 13 August 1940, stated:

> It is now established that sixty-one enemy aircraft were destroyed in yesterday's air fight over our coasts. Thirteen of our fighters were lost, but the pilot of one of them was saved.

20 Peter Stevenson, Spitfire Pilot, Pilot Officer, British, 74 Squadron

A personal combat report of sortie flown on 11 August 1940 to intercept enemy aircraft over Dover. Stevenson's squadron was flying from RAF Hornchurch at the time. He was incredibly lucky to be found and rescued from the Channel after baling out. The RAF, unlike the Luftwaffe, had very rudimentary air-sea rescue capabilities in 1940.

Stevenson, son of a decorated First World War pilot, joined the RAF in 1938 and 74 Squadron in February 1940. By the end of September he had shot down six Me 109s and nearly ended the illustrious career of the Luftwaffe's top ace, Werner Molders of JG51. In the dogfight between the two fighter pilots on 28 July, Molders was injured but escaped to crash-land in France. Stevenson was KIA over France in 1943, his body never recovered.

I climbed up to him [an Me 109]. He must have thought I was an Me 109 but when he suddenly dived away I followed him and gave a two-seconds deflection burst. The E/A lurched slightly and went into a vertical dive. I kept my height at 15,000 feet and watched. I saw the E/A dive straight into the sea fifteen miles south east of Dover and disappear in a big splash of water. I then climbed to 23,000 feet up sun and saw a formation of twelve Me 109s 2,000 feet beneath me, proceeding north of Dover. It was my intention to attach myself to the back of this formation from out of the sun, and spray the whole formation. As I was diving on them, a really large volume of cannon and machine-gun fire came from behind. There were about twelve Me 109s diving at me from the sun and at least half of them must have been firing deflection shots at me. There was a popping noise and my control column became useless.

I found myself doing a vertical dive, getting faster and faster. I pulled the hood back. I got my head out of the cockpit and the slipstream tore the rest of me clean out of the machine. My trouser leg and both shoes were torn off. I saw my machine crash into the sea a mile off Deal. It took me twenty minutes to come down. I had been drifted eleven miles out to sea. One string of my parachute did not come undone, and I was dragged along by my left leg at 10 mph with my head underneath the water. After three minutes I was almost unconscious, when the string came undone. I got my breath back and started swimming. There was a heavy sea running. After one and a half hours an MTB [motor torpedo boat] came to look for me. I fired my revolver at it. It went out of sight, but came back. I changed magazines and fired all my shots over it. It heard my shots and I kicked up a foam in the water, and it saw me. It then picked me up and took me to Dover.

21 William Dymond, Hurricane Pilot, Sergeant Pilot, British, 111 Squadron

Air Ministry- and Ministry of Information-endorsed BBC radio broadcast by an RAF fighter pilot in August 1940. The anonymous pilot is William Dymond of 111 Squadron as the facts fit the introduction given to a transcript of the broadcast published in 1941 where they mention that the pilot joined the RAF in 1935, had joined 111 Squadron in 1936 and that the pilot had already shot down six enemy aircraft. The first day described is 13 August 1940, when 111 Squadron were flying from RAF Croydon, South London (11 Group). 13 August was *Adlertag* (Eagle Day), the first day of the Luftwaffe military operation *Adlerangriff* (Operation Eagle Attack) to destroy the RAF and achieve air superiority. This was the prerequisite for Hitler's planned invasion of Britain, which was codenamed Operation Sealion.

His two kills of He 111s over Dunkirk were on 31 May 1940, and the Dornier 17 shot down over France was on the 18 May. Dymond was KIA less than a month after his broadcast on 2 September. He was shot down, probably by an Me 109, over the Thames Estuary and went down with his aircraft. Dymond's body was never recovered. He had shot down ten enemy aircraft.

Our squadron had a very enjoyable time last Wednesday before breakfast. We had a lovely party somewhere off the Isle of Sheppey in the Thames Estuary. It was a beautiful morning, and twelve of us were flying very high over Beachy Head. We were told to patrol below clouds over Dover and then we had orders to intercept enemy aircraft between us and the North Foreland. So we went down to about 3,000 feet just below clouds. We turned north and came over the Thames estuary. It was very misty so we went up again above the clouds to about 6,000 feet. The sun was coming up from the east – and so were the enemy. We saw two formations of bombers – two lots of twelve aircraft, one behind the other, with about two miles between them. They were 1,500 feet lower than we were, so we had an immediate advantage. Our squadron leader gave his orders quickly, and clearly, over the radio telephone. He would lead his flight of six Hurricanes round the back of the first formation, and the other flight of six, which included myself, was to deliver a head-on attack.

As soon as the leader of my flight went down towards the first formation, the enemy darted down for the clouds. I should have explained, by the way, that the squadron was in four sections of three each in line astern. The CO led the first two sections, and I was leading the last section of three. It is one of the duties of the last section to give warning of approach of enemy fighters.

Anyway, when the Dorniers went into cloud, I led my section down after them, and when we emerged at the bottom of the clouds I found we were ahead of them. So I swung completely round and led a head-on attack on the second formation of Dorniers which had now appeared. I'm sure they got an awful shock. They didn't expect an attack from the front like that. You could see that they didn't like it.

My section came up from below and slightly to one side of the bombers and we blazed away for all we were worth. It was impossible to miss them. We simply sprayed them with bullets, and then we broke away to the left. One of them was badly hit and he broke away. I pounced on him right away, fired from dead astern, and after another pilot had fired at him I believe he went down to crash into the sea.

In a battle you don't often have time to see what happens to every enemy aircraft you shoot at. But you usually have a chance to look round and see what is happening near you. I looked around after my head-on attack and saw a grand sight. My flight leader was leading his section up at the bombers head-on. I could see their machine gun bullets spurting from their wings, and I could see the Germans losing their formation under this terrific fire.

After that we began to look for odd enemy bombers which were now wheeling about in the sky and trying to form up together. I went up above the clouds again with another pilot and we saw three Dorniers, looking very sorry for themselves, heading for home. We took one each, and the one I fired at shed a lot of pieces from his wings and fuselage. I saw the other pilot – another sergeant, as a matter of fact – later when he landed. I asked him how he got on, and he said: 'Fine! I got him nicely. First the rear gunner baled out and then I saw the Jerry plane go into the sea.'

We had quite a good breakfast that morning, for including what we got the squadron's bag contained four certainties and a number of others probably destroyed or damaged.

I think my best day – by which I mean the day I enjoyed most – was one over Dunkirk during the evacuation of the BEF. Our squadron was patrolling Dunkirk at more than 10,000 feet – I doubt if our troops could see us at that height – when we saw a formation of about twenty Heinkel 111s. High above them were a lot of Messerschmitt 109s acting as a fighter escort. We were told to attack the fighters, but before we could reach them they sheered off, and left the bombers to us. We went down on them like a shot.

I got two of the easiest enemies of my life that afternoon. I dived on one Heinkel and gave him an incredibly short burst of fire. My thumb was still on the gun button when both his engines immediately caught fire. He put his nose down, and to my surprise, I must confess, he went straight down into the sea with a tremendous splash. He just went straight in from 10,000 feet.

I climbed up a bit and looked round. Then I saw another Heinkel going east, having attacked shipping in Dunkirk harbour. I started chasing him, climbing after him all the time. When I got fairly near I just crept up to him – we were doing just over 200 mph – that is what I call 'creeping' in a Hurricane. Anyway, I crept after him for a few minutes and I'm sure he didn't see me until I opened fire from close in. I just let him have it – a long burst of five seconds. The rear gunner opened fire at me almost at the same moment that I started firing. He was silenced immediately, yet he managed to put half a dozen bullets into my aircraft. The Heinkel began to emit black smoke and dived vertically towards the sea. I watched him crash.

There was another day in France when we ran into ten Messerschmitts and only one of them got away. That was a good scrap. If I remember rightly, it was our first morning in France, too.

One afternoon, in France, when on patrol, we saw anti-aircraft shells bursting high above us. I spotted a German aircraft and reported it to the leader of the squadron. He as good as said, 'Well, go and get it then, if you can see it'. I went up to 15,000 feet and found it was a Dornier 17. I attacked from behind and below and in a few moments the machine caught fire and a second or two later, began a dive which ended on the ground. Then I rejoined the rest of the squadron to continue the patrol. I was just lucky to be the one who happened to see the enemy.

I have about 850 flying hours altogether on my log book, half of them on Hurricanes. As a matter of fact, I have been with the squadron longer than any other pilot. A few have joined since the war, but most of the pilots came in two or three years ago. There isn't one of them who hasn't got a Hun. It's a grand squadron to be in, I can assure you.

22 James 'Nick' Nicolson, Hurricane Pilot, Flight Lieutenant, British, 249 Squadron

Personal combat report of James 'Nick' Nicolson, 249 Squadron. This combat, for which he was awarded the only Victoria Cross of the Battle of Britain, took place on Friday 16 August 1940 with 249 Squadron flying from RAF Boscombe Down, Wiltshire (10 Group).

Born in Hampstead, London, in 1917, Nicolson joined the RAF in 1936 and 249 Squadron on 15 May 1940. This sortie was Nick's first operational engagement with the enemy; 249 Squadron had only moved south the previous day from the quiet zone of RAF Church Fenton, in North Yorkshire (13 Group).

Later in the year Nicolson made a BBC radio broadcast retelling the events of that day, and omitted that he had been shot in the buttocks while descending to earth in his parachute by a trigger-happy member of the LDV (Local Defence Volunteers), or Home Guard, who mistook him for a German paratrooper. Candidates for this series of broadcasts were meant to be telling 'good' news stories, so unsavoury facts were often left out. Seriously burned in the incident, he did not return to operational flying until September the following year. He served in India and Burma, and was awarded the DFC while flying the twin-engined Mosquito. He was KIA on 2 May 1945 while flying as an observer on a bombing mission in a B-24 Liberator. The aircraft's engine failed and it ditched in the Bay of Bengal. His body was never recovered.

Form F, Combat Report, 16 August 1940. Time attack delivered: 13.45 approx; Enemy casualties: Inconclusive 1 Me 110 prob.; Place attack delivered: Near Romsey; Height of enemy: 17,000 ft; General report: F/Lt Nicolson now in Southampton and South Hants Hospital reports: I was leading Red section in a squadron formation – saw 3 E/A some distance to left – informed Blue 1 who was leading squadron, who ordered me to investigate. 12 Spitfires however, engaged this formation before I got into range. I turned to rejoin squadron climbing from 15,000 ft to 17,500 ft. Heard Tally-ho from Yellow leader and immediately after was struck in cockpit by four successive cannon shells (?) damaging hood, firing reserve tank and damaging my leg and thigh.

I immediately pulled my feet up on to seat and at the same time I put nose down and dived steep turning right. Saw Me 110 diving at same angle and converging – opened fire at approx 200 yds and fired till I could bear heat no more.

I then abandoned aircraft with difficulty and after dropping some 5,000 ft pulled cord – I was shot in buttocks by an LDV just before landing.

Reflector sight was on but cannot swear whether firing button was on 'safe' or 'fire'.

Eye witnesses on ground state that Me 110 zig-zagged and dived steeply after Hurricane opened fire.

This report forwarded on F/Lt Nicolson's behalf. Signed John Grandy [249 Squadron Leader].

23 Mark 'Hilly' Brown Part 2, Hurricane Pilot, Pilot Officer, Canadian, 1 Squadron

Back in England after fighting in France, Hilly sees more action in the south-east while based at RAF Tangmere, Manston and North Weald airfields during August and early September 1940. After being shot down into the sea, he was lucky to have been picked up. Many pilots who baled out over the Channel died of exposure or drowned.

4 August 1940, letter home Well, here we are back at Northolt again. That week at Tangmere was grand. I got around to see some old friends. Most of them had gone, but a few remained.

My DFC came through on 31 July. I don't know when I will be getting to see the king to have it presented. We have been doing a lot of work lately, but haven't seen much. I have a feeling that something is going to come my way soon. I am getting fed up, never getting a shot at anything.

14 August 1940, letter home The chaps here are getting a minor taste of what we had to put up with in France. I have not been lucky enough to run into any of the large formations, so my score has not been going up very fast. I got one confirmed on 11 August.

Form F, Combat Report 11 August 1940. Time attack delivered 10.50; Enemy casualties 1 Me 110; Place attack delivered 20 miles S of St Catherine's Point; General report: I was Acorn leader Red section. At a point approx. halfway between St Catherine's Point and Cherbourg an enemy aircraft was sighted slightly below me at about 18,000 feet, it was identified as an Me 110. I followed the enemy aircraft in a slight dive with 8 lbs boost, gradually overtaking it with an IAS of 300 mph.

I opened fire at 250 yards and no return fire was observed and I gave three bursts of 2 seconds each. After the first burst bits were seen to fly off the E/A and the port engine was obscured by smoke, he turned sharply in a banking skid to port and I gave two more bursts and had my aircraft and windscreen covered with oil. The range was now less than 50 yards, so I had to break away to avoid impact.

Throughout the engagement there was no return fire and the E/A used no evasive tactics, maintaining a very shallow dive.

Pilot Officer Harold Mann who was directly behind me during the engagement saw the E/A diving vertically with smoke and flames pouring out. He saw the port engine explode with a burst of flame.

It was noticed that the impact of the De Wilde ammunition was visible.

Casualty confirmed by Pilot Officer Mann.

15 August 1940 (account from later BBC broadcast by Brown) We went out to intercept some bombers which were supposed to be on their way to attack one of our convoys, instead of that, some 109s came down and intercepted us. I collected a hole in the gravity tank, and my Hurricane caught fire, and it took me twenty minutes to come down. I landed in the sea about five miles out – but near enough to a trawler to be picked up safely. I was burned about the face and eyebrows. But I was flying again at the end of a fortnight.

26 August 1940, letter home I have been having a convalescent holiday. Had a spot of trouble on 15 August and had to bale out. I landed in the sea, but was picked up almost immediately by a trawler. I suffered facial burns but they have healed very well, and I am almost serviceable again. I expect to be flying in a day or two … The next time you send me anything, you might include some Spanish peanuts. I was just thinking yesterday how I would like to have a chew at some.

Form F, Combat Report 31 August 1940. Time attack delivered 05.25; Enemy casualties nil; Place attack delivered 10 miles south of Beachy Head; General report: I was leader of Red section No. 1 Squadron. We took off at 05.12 hours to patrol base below cloud. At 05.20 I received order to vector 120 and was proceeding just below cloud 10 miles south of Beachy Head at about 800 feet. I saw a Dornier 17 travelling due north crossing our bows about 1 mile away at 900 feet. I ordered section into line astern and approached from rear, in and out of cloud. I attacked from directly astern. E/A opened fire from upper rear turret at a range of 400 yards. I closed and opened fire at 300 yards one burst of 485 rounds when E/A disappeared into cloud. I climbed above cloud and instructed Red 2 and 3 to scour under clouds north of coastline, whilst I did likewise above. Nothing further was seen of E/A so I returned to base. Red section landed at 06.10 hours. My A/C was not hit.

Form F, Combat Report 6 September 1940. Time attack delivered 09.05; Enemy casualties one Ju 88 damaged; Place attack delivered between Kenley & Tunbridge Wells; General report: I was Red 1 and leading No. 1 Squadron. We were told to patrol Kenley at 20,000 feet with 303 Squadron Polish, but however, we did not make contact. Just past patrol line going east at 18,000 feet (there were visible vortices in several parts of the sky) a formation of fighters was seen above and on the right. Just then a very large formation of E/A at 20,000 feet stepped up vertically and backwards – were seen going west. It consisted of Ju 88s and Me 110s. We had not been informed of the presence of this enemy formation. I put the squadron in line astern and turned left in an attempt to gain a position to attack the bombers. A favourable position was not gained I saw a Ju 88 crossing under me and attacked him. I gave him one burst of 5 seconds as I closed in until I had to break away to avoid collision. I silenced the rear gunner and his starboard engine was streaming a white trail. After breaking away I could not see him any longer. The E/A was last seen going SE towards Tunbridge Wells.

7 September 1940, letter home I went up to Buckingham Palace last Tuesday, to be presented with my DFC. I was allowed two tickets to my investiture, but used only one, and am sending the other to you.

The VCs and DSOs were decorated first, and as each of us got to the top of the queue, we stepped forward, turned toward His Majesty, bowed and took one step forward. The king pinned the medal on, said a few words and shook hands.

An investiture is usually held in the throne room, or in the open, but not this one. There were quite a number to be decorated, and I suppose they didn't want to have it outside on account of the chances of an air raid.

Roderick 'Babe' Learoyd was there to receive his Victoria Cross. I was on a navigators course with him a couple of years ago. I have been working very hard lately, but hope we shall get a bit of rest soon. Most of the boys could do with it.

24 David Crook Part 2, Spitfire Pilot, Pilot Officer, British, 609 Squadron

Second extract from Crook's 1942 memoir based on his diaries, covering 7–25 August, when he was flying from RAF Middle Wallop, Hampshire (10 Group).

There were several changes in the squadron when I got back. We had a new flight commander in B flight, Mac, who had been a test pilot at Farnborough for two years. Before that he had done a lot of civil flying, including some long-distance flights with Campbell Black, and, as a matter of fact, Mac still holds the London-Baghdad record. There were also several other new pilots, including two Poles and three Americans, and altogether the flying personnel of the squadron were now a very young, vigorous, and dashing crowd. I think that this influx of new blood played a big part in bringing to an end our run of bad luck, because from now onwards we started on an almost unbroken series of successes and victories.

But in less than a year 609 had altered completely its personnel and character. We had a new CO, and of the fifteen original members of the squadron, only four were now left.

Four others had been posted away as instructors and seven had been killed at Dunkirk or later. Only Michael, John, and myself were left, and we were joined a few days later by Geoff, who had just finished his course at Cranwell. It was grand to have him back, and so for the next six weeks we flew together and went out on most evenings to the 'Mucky Duck' for a little beer, and altogether enjoyed life, in spite of the intense air activity that prevailed.

The first week of August 1940 was very quiet indeed, and apart from a few enemy machines that flew over at a great height for reconnaissance and photography, nothing stirred at all. We used to go up after these machines and chase after them over most of south western England, but they always flew so high and so fast that we were never able to make any interceptions, or even to see one. It is not till you go hunting after single machines like this that you realize the vastness of the sky, and how easy it is, even on a clear day, to miss one aircraft or even a whole squadron, in the enormous spaces above.

We had a private and somewhat jocular theory that this unnatural peace was due to Goering having given the whole German Air Force a week's leave to get them fit for 'things to come'.

Certainly it was the lull before the storm.

The intelligence reports that we got told of the efforts the Germans were making to establish themselves at all the captured aerodromes in northern France, Holland, and Belgium, and obviously preparations were being made on the very greatest scale in order to launch a very heavy air offensive against this country.

I don't know whether many people yet realize fully the great strategical advantages gained by Germany through her occupation of the Low Countries and France.

Hitherto, the Germans had been forced to fly big distances in order to reach this country, whereas we possessed advanced bases in France from which it was only a short flight into the heart of the enemy industrial areas. But we never used these advantages when they were in our grasp, and for the first eight months of the war, there was no bombing of land targets by either side.

When the big German attack was launched in the west, the tables were turned immediately. We lost our advanced bases, and the enemy gained theirs. Nor was this the end of the misfortunes that fell upon us as a result of the disasters in France. A very big proportion of the German Air Force is composed of Messerschmitt 109s and Junkers 87 dive-bombers, both of which are essentially short range machines, and could not possibly operate against England from German bases. But their weight could now be thrown into the struggle, and so, instead of meeting Heinkel and Dornier bombers over this country, and being able to inflict wholesale slaughter on them, we had to face very large numbers of escorting Messerschmitts, which had to be tackled first. This made the work of our fighter squadrons very much more difficult and dangerous, and certainly saved the Germans from the murderous losses which they would have suffered had they sent over unescorted bombers.

Anyway, as it turned out, even their escorting fighters did not manage to save the bombers, and large numbers were shot down.

And so we enjoyed our few days of peace, and did quite a lot of practice flying and attacks, and waited for the storm to break.

At this time we were still working under an arrangement whereby we lived at our base and spent every third day down at the advanced base. We took it in turns with two other squadrons.

On 8 August, soon after dawn, we were ordered to patrol a convoy off the Needles. It was a very clear day with a brilliant sun – just the sort of day that the Germans love, because they come out at a very big height and dive down to attack out of the sun. By doing this cleverly, they used to render themselves almost invisible until the attack was delivered. We hated these clear days and always prayed for some high cloud to cover the sun.

This convoy was a big one and escorted by several destroyers and balloons towed from barges in order to stop low dive-bombing.

I remember thinking at the time that there was obviously going to be a lot of trouble that day, because this convoy was far too large a prize for the Hun to miss. How right I was!

However, nothing happened on our first patrol and after about an hour we returned to base.

About 11.30 a.m. six of us were ordered off again, but one turned back almost immediately with oxygen trouble, so there were only five left.

We steered out towards the convoy, which was now about twelve miles south of Bournemouth, There was a small layer of cloud, and while dodging in and out of this, Mac and I got separated from the other three, and a moment later we also lost each other.

While looking around to try and find them, I glanced out towards the convoy, and saw three of the balloons falling in flames. Obviously an attack was starting, and I climbed above the cloud layer and went towards the convoy at full throttle, climbing all the time towards the sun, so that I could deliver my attack with the sun behind me.

I was now about five miles from the convoy, and could see a big number of enemy fighters circling above, looking exactly like a swarm of flies buzzing round a pot of jam. Below them the dive-bombers were diving down on the ships and great fountains of white foam were springing up where their bombs struck the water. I could see that one or two ships had already been hit and were on fire.

I was now at 16,000 feet above the whole battle and turned round to look for a victim. At that moment, a Hurricane squadron appeared on the scene, and attacked right into the middle of the enemy fighters, which were split up immediately, and a whole series of individual combats started covering a very big area of the sky.

I saw several machines diving down with smoke and flames pouring from them, and then I spotted an Me 109 flying about 4,000 feet below me. I immediately turned and dived down on him – he was a sitting target, but before I got to him a Hurricane appeared and shot him down in flames.

I was annoyed! I looked round, but the attack was finished, and the enemy were streaming back towards the French coast, where it was very unwise to follow them.

Three ships in the convoy were blazing away fiercely and destroyers were taking off the crews. All the balloons had been shot down. I turned back for the English coast and landed at base, to find everybody back safely. The CO, Michael, and John had each destroyed an Me 110, while Mac had shot down two Junkers 87 dive-bombers. He would have got an Me 110 also and got his sights on it, but nothing happened when he pressed his trigger. His ammunition was finished. So a very lucky Me 110 lived to fight another day.

Mac was very pleased about this fight, and certainly a bag of two for one's first action is very good. But it made him rather over-confident, and for the next few days he regarded the German Air Force rather as an organization which provided him with a little target practice and general harmless amusement. He soon learnt better!

That evening, when we again patrolled the convoy, he led Michael and me almost over Cherbourg in search of enemy fighters and frightened us considerably! Finally I called him up on the R/T, and politely pointed out that we were now fifty miles out to sea and that the French coast was looming up ahead. So he turned back with great reluctance!

On 11 August there occurred our first really big action of the war. We were again down at advanced base, and about 11.30 a.m. we were ordered to patrol over Weymouth Bay. Several other squadrons soon joined us, and altogether it looked as though it was going to be a big show.

Shortly afterwards we saw a big enemy fighter formation out to sea, and went out to attack it, climbing the whole time, as they were flying at about 24,000 feet. Some Hurricanes were already attacking the Messerschmitts, and the latter had formed their usual defensive circle, going round and round on each other's tails. This makes an attack rather difficult, as if you attack one Hun, there is always another one behind you. We were now about a thousand feet above the Mes at 25,000 feet, and the CO turned round and the whole of 609 went down to attack.

We came down right on top of the enemy formation, going at terrific speed, and as we approached them we split up slightly, each pilot selecting his own target.

I saw an Me 110 ahead of me going across in front. I fired at him but did not allow enough deflection and my bullets passed behind him. I then closed in on him from behind and fired a good burst at practically point-blank range. Some black smoke poured from his port engine and he turned up to the right and stalled. I could not see what happened after this as I narrowly missed hitting his port wing. It flashed past so close that instinctively I ducked my head.

There were many more enemy fighters above me and a terrific fight was going on. I couldn't see another target in a good position for me to attack, and it was rather an unhealthy spot in which to linger so I turned and dived back to the coast and landed to refuel and rearm.

Everybody came streaming back in ones and twos, and to my surprise nobody was missing. It seemed too good to be true that we should all be safe after such a fierce scrap. We had shot down about five Me 110s and several more (like mine) were probably destroyed, but it is almost impossible to stay and see definite results in the middle of such a mix-up. All that you can do is to fire a good burst at some enemy and then, hit or miss, get away quickly.

Some bombers had got through to Weymouth and Portland, and there was a great column of smoke rising from a blazing oil tank, but no very serious damage had been done. The Germans, in spite of their great numerical superiority, had suffered considerable losses.

Mac came back feeling rather shaken. He had not shot anything down, but had been attacked by two Mes and in his efforts to get away, his Spitfire got into a spin and he came down about 5,000 feet before he could recover.

From now onwards he was a very wise and successful flight commander, and never went out looking for unnecessary trouble!

The following day, 12 August, a very heavy attack was made on Portsmouth and the dockyard. At midday I was due for twenty-four hours' leave and I was having a bath and shave in my room at about 11 a.m. when somebody rushed up and said that we had been called to readiness. I hastily wiped the soap off my face and we all jumped into cars and went down to our aircraft.

A moment later the order came through to take off and patrol Portsmouth and the Isle of Wight. Just as we were taxiing out, I switched on my R/T and found it was dead. The rest of the squadron took off, and I sat on the ground for nearly five minutes till the loose connection was found and put right. I then took off and headed for the Isle of Wight, but could see no sign of the squadron, and, as a matter of fact, I did not see them again for the whole of the action.

After a few minutes I saw a big AA barrage going up over Portsmouth, so I turned slightly in that direction. The dockyard at Portsmouth had been hit and I could see one or two big fires going.

A powerful force of German aircraft was circling over the east end of the Isle of Wight, and I went out towards them, climbing all the time. As I got nearer, I was staggered by the number of Huns in the sky. I think we had always imagined that raids might be carried out by three or four squadrons at the most – some forty or fifty aircraft.

And here, circling and sweeping all over the sky, were at least 200 Huns! 'My God,' I muttered to myself, 'what a party.' I was not the only person to be impressed. Several other people (not only in 609) who were also in this fight told me afterwards that their main impression had been one of blank astonishment at the numbers of aircraft involved. As somebody remarked – 'There was the whole German Air Force, bar Goering.' Later in the summer we got used to seeing these enormous formations, but this first occasion certainly made us think a bit.

I climbed out towards the Huns and saw three formations of Messerschmitts circling round, one above the other, between about 20,000 and 28,000 feet. Each layer had formed into the usual German defensive circle, going round and round on each other's tails. I decided to attack the middle layer, which was composed of Me 110s, as I did not like the idea of continuing to climb up more or less directly underneath the top layer.

I got into position about 2,000 feet above the Me 110s and then dived straight down into the middle of the circle. As I was going down I selected a target and blazed away madly at him, missing him at first owing to lack of deflection, and then, as far as I could see, getting in a few seconds' effective fire at very close range.

But I could not observe any results as I flashed right through the enemy formation at terrific speed, narrowly missing a collision with one fighter and continuing my dive for some distance before I could pull out. I think I was doing well over 500 mph and the strain of pulling out was considerable.

I looked round to see what was going on, and at that moment an Me 110, enveloped in a sheet of flame, fell past within 200 yards of me. I don't know if this was my victim or not, but I definitely think it was, as I had seen no other British fighters in the vicinity when I attacked. There were a lot of Huns all round and above me, and I decided it might be a good idea if I moved on elsewhere, particularly as I had very little ammunition left.

So I turned on my back and dived away to the English coast, and shortly afterwards landed safely at the aerodrome.

Once again everybody got back safely, and we had destroyed six or seven Huns and several more probables, including mine.

My dive through the Hun circle had been so fast and the pull out so violent (probably in the heat of the moment I pulled out far more quickly than I realized), that as a result both wings of my Spitfire were damaged and she had to go back to the factory for repairs. So I reckon I must have been going fairly fast.

Most of the squadron got rather split up at the beginning of the fight and adopted the same tactics as I did, ie diving through the Hun circles and trying to pick off a target as they went down.

It was a boiling summer's day and we all got back absolutely soaked in sweat, even though we were flying in shirt sleeves.

Teeny, having fired off all his ammunition, landed at a nearby aerodrome to refuel and rearm, and while the airmen were doing this he decided that he had earned a good drink. So he borrowed a bicycle and started off for the mess. While on his way he saw another Spitfire land and the second pilot also leapt on to a bicycle and pedalled hard towards the mess.

This was John, and the two met on the steps of the mess and without saying a word they went straight in and drank a pint of iced Pimms apiece, after which they felt much better and swapped experiences.

That afternoon, about 4 o'clock, Mac, Noel, and I had changed our clothes and made out our combat reports, so we started at last on our journey up to town, about five hours later than we had intended.

The car wasn't going very well, and near Staines it packed up for about half an hour while we cursed like hell and Mac fiddled with the petrol pump. I was rather worried as I had arranged to meet Dorothy in the Trocadero at 6.30 and knew I should be late and that therefore she would be having a very unpleasant time wondering if anything had happened. I could not ring up, however, as the delay was so great, so I just had to hope for the best. Finally I got a lift from a couple of Canadian officers, and Mac and Noel promised to follow in the car as soon as it would work. So I arrived at the Troc about an hour and a half late and found D there with Michael, who had left the aerodrome early in the morning, as he had the whole day off.

Poor D. She was very worried about my non-arrival, and Michael could give her no news except that he thought another big fight was starting just as he left. She must have had many bad moments through the summer, but she always says that this was easily the worst. Anyway, we all had several Pimms apiece and felt much better, and shortly afterwards Mac and Noel arrived, having at last coaxed the car into activity.

We had a hilarious dinner together, and parted in very good form about 11.30 p.m. It seemed so funny to be dining peacefully in Piccadilly only a few hours after being in such a desperate fight.

The following morning I met Michael in Piccadilly and we drove back together.

At midday the squadron flew down to advanced base. The date was 13 August – a very lucky thirteenth for us, as it happened.

At about 4 p.m. we were ordered to patrol Weymouth at 15,000 feet. We took off, thirteen machines in all, with the CO leading, and climbed up over Weymouth. After a few minutes I began to hear a German voice talking on the R/T, faintly at first and then growing in volume. By a curious chance this German raid had a wavelength almost identical with our own and the voice we heard was that of the German commander talking to his formation as they approached us across the Channel. About a quarter of an hour later we saw a large German formation approaching below us. There were a number of Junkers 87 dive-bombers escorted by Me 109s above, and also some Me 110s about two miles behind, some sixty machines in all.

A Hurricane squadron attacked the Me 110s as soon as they crossed the coast and they never got through to where we were.

Meanwhile the bombers with their fighter escort still circling above them, passed beneath us. We were up at almost 20,000 feet in the sun and I don't think they ever saw us till the very last moment. The CO gave a terrific 'Tally ho' and led us round in a big semi-circle so that we were now behind them, and we prepared to attack.

Mac, Novi (one of the Poles), and I were flying slightly behind and above the rest of the squadron, guarding their tails, and at this moment I saw about five Me 109s pass just underneath us.

I immediately broke away from the formation, dived on to the last Me 109, and gave him a terrific burst of fire at very close range. He burst into flames and spun down for many thousands of feet into the clouds below, leaving behind him a long trail of black smoke.

I followed him down for some way and could not pull out of my dive in time to avoid going below the clouds myself. I found that I was about five miles north of Weymouth, and then I saw a great column of smoke rising from the ground a short distance away. I knew perfectly well what it was and went over to have a look. My Me 109 lay in a field, a tangled heap of wreckage burning fiercely, but with the black crosses on the wings still visible. I found out later that the pilot was still in the machine. He had made no attempt to get out while the aircraft was diving and he had obviously been killed by my first burst of fire. He crashed just outside a small village, and I could see everybody streaming out of their houses and rushing to the spot.

I climbed up through the clouds again to rejoin the fight, but there was nothing to be seen, and so I returned to the aerodrome, where all the ground crews were in a great state of excitement, as they could hear a terrific fight going on above the clouds but saw nothing except several German machines falling in flames.

All the machines were now coming in to land and everybody's eyes were fixed on the wings.

Yes – they were all covered with black streaks from the smoke of the guns – everybody had fired.

There was the usual anxious counting – only ten back – where are the others – they should be back by now – I hope to God everybody's ok – good enough, here they come! Thank God, everybody's ok!

We all stood round in small groups talking excitedly, and exchanging experiences. It is very amusing to observe the exhilaration and excitement which everybody betrays after a successful action like this!

It soon became obvious that this had been our best effort yet.

Thirteen enemy machines had been destroyed in about four minutes' glorious fighting. Six more were probably destroyed or damaged, while our only damage sustained was one bullet through somebody's wing. I think this was the record bag for one squadron in one fight during the whole of the Battle of Britain.

Just after I broke away to attack my Messerschmitt, the whole squadron had dived right into the centre of the German formation and the massacre started. One pilot looked round in the middle of the action and in one small patch of sky he saw five German dive-bombers going down in flames, still more or less in formation.

We all heard the German commander saying desperately, time after time, 'Achtung, achtung, Spit und Hurri' – meaning presumably, 'Look out, look out, Spitfires and Hurricanes.'

Novi got two Me 109s in his first fight and came back more pleased with himself and more excited than I have ever seen anybody before.

And so ended this very successful day, the thirteenth day of the month, and thirteen of our pilots went into action, and thirteen of the enemy were shot down. I shall never again distrust, the number 13.

One member of the squadron remarked afterwards that he rather missed the 'glorious twelfth' this year – 'but the glorious thirteenth was the best day's shooting I ever had'. (From *The Times*, 14 August 1940: 'In the Southampton area alone fighter patrols destroyed twenty-two of the enemy. Of these, nine were Ju 87 dive-bombers, five were Me 110s, and the remaining eight were Messerschmitt 109 fighters. All the nine Junkers were brought down in the space of a few minutes by a single Spitfire squadron, as well as four of the Me 109s. This same squadron had brought down seven enemy aircraft the previous day. Many others attacked were severely damaged. Not one of the squadron's pilots or Spitfires was lost during the two days' fighting.')

I think that 13 August marked a very definite turning-point in the squadron's history. Hitherto we had not had many successes, but had suffered rather heavy losses, and this state of affairs always shakes confidence. But now, for the first time, the glorious realization dawned on us that by using clever and careful tactics we could inflict heavy losses on the enemy and get away almost scot-free ourselves. Whenever in the future the squadron went into action, I think the only question in everybody's mind was not 'Shall we get any Huns to-day?' but rather, 'How many shall we get today?' There was never any doubt about it. This success was also a very well-deserved tonic for all the airmen in the squadron who did not get all the excitement that we did. They were a grand crowd in 609, mostly the original Auxiliaries who were at Yeadon before the war, and they used to toil nobly in order to keep all our Spitfires serviceable. Frequently in those hectic days they would work all through the night in order to have a machine ready for dawn. Their loyalty to the squadron and their keenness and energy knew no bounds, and as a result we always had the very comforting feeling that our Spitfires were maintained as perfectly as was humanly possible. I don't think my engine ever missed a beat throughout the whole summer, and this means a terrific lot to you when you are continually going into action and any mechanical failure will have the most unpleasant consequences.

All the men are extremely interested in the fortunes of the squadron and particularly the pilot of the machine which they look after. When you return after an action they always crowd round asking for details, and if you can tell them 'One Messerschmitt down' then there is great rejoicing. Altogether, from this time onwards, 609 was an exceedingly good squadron and probably second to none in the whole RAF.

The following day was very cloudy, and soon after lunch the air-raid warning sounded, and we all dashed out of the mess and went down to the point where our Spitfires were.

There were no orders for us to take off, though three of our machines were already in the air and circling round the aerodrome.

So we sat in our aircraft and waited. A few minutes later we heard the unmistakable 'ooma-ooma' of a German bomber above the clouds. I immediately signalled to my ground crew to stand by, as I did not intend to sit on the ground and be bombed. I kept my finger on the engine starter button and waited expectantly.

Almost immediately the enemy bomber, a Junkers 88, broke out of the cloud to the north of the aerodrome, turned slightly to get on his course and then dived at very high speed towards the hangars. At about 1,500 feet he let go four bombs – we could see them very distinctly as they plunged down, and a second later there was an earth-shaking 'whoom' and four great clouds of dust arose. All this happened in a matter of seconds only, but by this time everybody had got their engines started and we all roared helter-skelter across the aerodrome. Why there were no collisions I don't know, but we got safely into the air and turned round to chase the enemy.

But this was unnecessary. Sergeant F had already been in the air, and attacked the enemy just as he was climbing up after releasing his bombs. F fired all his ammunition at close range and the Junkers crashed in flames about five miles away, all the crew being killed. I flew over to the crash and have never seen any aeroplane more thoroughly wrecked; it was an awful mess.

I certainly admire that German pilot for his coolness and determination, because he made his attack despite the Spitfires that were closing in on him. It was a very daring piece of work, even though he only lived about thirty seconds afterwards to enjoy his triumph.

For the rest of the afternoon we had a very exciting and busy time, as various Huns were coming over in the clouds to bomb us. I was able to engage two of them; in each case I spotted them just as they were breaking from cloud and got a good burst at each before they disappeared again.

They were both certainly damaged, but nothing more. The main thing was that it stopped them bombing the aerodrome, but during the afternoon one other German managed to drop his bombs and get back into cloud again before any of us could intercept him.

We destroyed two definitely, but unfortunately when everybody landed later that evening, G was missing, and he never turned up. We could not understand this, as all the fights had taken place quite near home and they had been so scrappy and disjointed that it seemed almost impossible for anybody (except Huns) to be killed.

However, the mystery was solved about ten days later, when his body was washed ashore on the Isle of Wight. Obviously he had chased some bomber out to sea and been shot down.

It was a great pity; for his younger brother, also in the RAF, had been killed only six weeks before.

Incidentally, in one of the Heinkels shot down three very senior officers of the German Air Force were found dead. They had probably come over to see how the operations against England were progressing.

I hope they were suitably impressed!

The following day, 15 August, we had another raid in the late afternoon, this time by a fairly big formation of Junkers 88s and Me 110s.

We got off the ground only a few minutes before they arrived at the aerodrome, and were unable to intercept them, or even to see them until they were practically over the aerodrome, as they dived out of the sun, dropped their bombs, and then streamed back towards the coast as hard as they could go. But we were attacking them the whole time and shot down at least five. Oddly enough, less damage was done to the aerodrome by this large raid than on the previous day, when only single machines came over.

Most of these German bomber formations rely on one very good bomb-aimer in the leading machine. When he gets his sights on, the whole formation release their bombs and if the aim is accurate, the effect is generally rather devastating, but on this occasion the bomb-aimer misjudged by about two seconds and the whole salvo of bombs fell just beyond the aerodrome.

This occasion was the now famous one when I shot down one of our own machines – a Blenheim.

There was a Blenheim fighter squadron stationed with us; they are not fast enough for day fighting but are used a lot for night work. Incidentally, they are twin engined machines and very similar in appearance to the Junkers 88.

One of these Blenheims happened to be doing some practice flying near the aerodrome when the attack started, and in a fit of rather misguided valour he fastened himself on to the German formation as it ran for the coast and started attacking the rear machines.

We were rapidly overhauling the German formation, and when I was in range I opened fire at the nearest machine, which happened to be the Blenheim.

Quite naturally, it never occurred to me that it could be anything else but a Ju 88. I hit both engines and the fuselage, and he fell away to the right with one engine smoking furiously. I saw him gliding down and noticed a gun turret on the fuselage which rather shook me, as I knew the Ju 88 did not have this.

Fortunately the pilot had been saved by the armour plating behind him, and he managed to make a crash landing on the aerodrome and was quite ok, though the Blenheim was full of bullet holes and looked rather like a kitchen sieve. The rear gunner was not quite so lucky, for he got a bullet through his bottom which doubtless caused him considerable discomfort and annoyance, but was not serious.

Nothing was said about this mistake, as it certainly was not my fault, and equally the Blenheim pilot could scarcely be blamed for his desire to engage the enemy, even though it was rather unwise, since his machine was so similar to the Germans.

The Blenheims had sometimes got in our way before, and we had often remarked jokingly, 'If one of those blasted Blenheims gets in our way again we'll jolly well put a bullet through his bottom.' And now it had come to pass, and everybody was very amused (except possibly the rear gunner).

The whole story became very well known and I was ragged about it for a long time afterwards.

Our other Polish pilot, Osti, distinguished himself in this action. He chased an Me 110 which in its efforts to shake him off dived to ground level and dodged all over the countryside at over 300 mph, even turning round a church steeple. But Osti stuck to him and refused to be shaken off, and finally the German, as a last desperate resort, flew right through the Southampton balloon barrage.

Osti went through after him, caught him up over the Solent, and shot him down in the Isle of Wight.

These two Poles, Novi and Osti, were grand chaps and we were all very fond of them. They had fought in Poland during that desperate month of September 1939, when in spite of inferior equipment and being hopelessly outnumbered, they nevertheless resisted to the bitter end, and then escaped through Rumania to France, where they joined l'Armee de l'Air, and again fought till the French collapse, though they were shabbily treated by the French, who gave them only very obsolete machines to fly.

They told us some astounding stories about conditions in France during the disasters in May and June.

They were stationed near Tours, and on the aerodrome were a number of very good new American Curtis fighters. The Poles, who had been given Moranes which were old and hardly fit to fly, begged to be allowed to fly the Curtis's.

But the French refused, saying they wanted the Curtis's themselves.

Everyday the Germans used to fly serenely over Tours, bomb the city at leisure and fly back again, while nobody raised a finger to stop them, and the French pilots sat in the bar and drank their vermouth, with a lot of brand new fighters standing on the aerodrome outside. Incredible but true.

After the French collapse Novi and Osti and several thousand more of their indomitable countrymen escaped once more from a ravaged country and came over to England. It is easy to imagine their pleasure at finding themselves in a really good squadron, efficiently run, and with first class equipment. They could now fly the finest fighters in the world, and meet their persecutors on equal terms.

They certainly made the most of their opportunities, and their delight when they shot down a 'bloddy German' was marvellous to see.

They were both very quiet, possessed beautiful manners, were very good pilots, and intensely keen to learn our ways and methods. Their hatred of the Germans was quieter and more deadly than I have ever seen before.

They had undergone so much suffering and hardship, and had lost almost everything in life that mattered to them – homes, families, money – that I think the only thing that concerned them now was to get their revenge and kill as many Germans as possible.

They were certainly two of the bravest people I ever knew, and yet they were not exceptional in this respect when compared with other Poles in the RAF.

All the squadrons that had Polish pilots posted to them formed an equally high opinion of them, and the feats of the Polish Squadron, who in five days' fighting over London destroyed at least forty-four German machines, as well as probably destroying and damaging many more, must rank as one of the best shows of the whole summer.

Such indomitable courage and determination cannot go unrewarded, and when this war is won we must see that Poland is again restored to her former liberty and freedom, which her sons fought so valiantly to maintain.

After this raid life became much quieter for a short period, and while we had a number of alarms and went up on patrol quite a lot, we did not come into contact with the enemy for some little time to come.

In the middle of our 'busy time', when every day seemed to bring a bigger and heavier raid to deal with, we used to long for bad weather to come and give us some relief. Now when matters became quieter and we had no fighting, we all got very bored after a few days and longed to shoot down some more Huns. Human nature is never satisfied for long.

I was still managing to get up to London once or twice a week to meet Dorothy. We used to have some enjoyable dinners, sometimes with Michael and Geoff when they were up in town also.

Serious bombing had not yet commenced in London, and life was still proceeding much as usual, so after dinner we used to go to a flick or a show and then back to Hampstead for the night. I always had to leave in fairly good time in the morning in order to catch the train from Waterloo.

On 23 August I managed to get my twenty-four hours' leave as usual, and met Dorothy to celebrate the first anniversary of our wedding. We had a good dinner at Hatchetts, listened to an excellent band, and altogether enjoyed our little celebration.

What an eventful year it had been! But in spite of all the worries and anxieties of the present, I think we both felt much happier and more confident than we had done a year previously, when we were married under the shadow of impending war and the whole future seemed so black and full of doubt.

It was still equally uncertain now, but we were getting more accustomed to the idea of never thinking about the future (one never dared to hope for a future in those days), and we had made the necessary mental adjustments to be able to face the worries and doubts.

In this year there had been so much personal happiness, and such good times, so many outstanding people met, and so many new friends made.

There had been the finest flying I have ever had, and the most exciting and wildly exhilarating moments of my life, such as the fight over Weymouth and that first engagement with the enemy when I dived on to the Junkers 87 and sent it crashing down in flames into the sea.

And on the other hand, there had been so much monotony and anxiety, both inevitable in war, and in the latter part of the year there occurred the tragic deaths of so many gallant friends, among them being some of the finest people I ever knew.

But on the whole it had been easily the happiest and the most vivid year of my life. I certainly could not feel now (as I used to feel occasionally before the war) that I should lead an uneventful life and grow into an old man without possessing any really exciting and stirring memories to gladden my old age!

The following day, 24 August, I returned to the squadron. The weather was brilliantly clear again, to our intense disgust, and we anticipated a lot more trouble.

Mac was very amusing on the subject of the weather, and always used to scan the sky anxiously, looking for clouds. When we saw any rolling up, he would express great satisfaction and announce that it might keep the 'Grim Reaper' at bay for another few days. Mac and his 'Grim Reaper' became a stock joke, and if anybody had a very narrow escape, we always used to congratulate them on keeping the 'Grim Reaper' at bay.

Certainly it was typical of our English weather that in a normal summer it is quite impossible to get fine weather for one's holidays, and yet in war time, when every fine day simply plays into the hands of the German bombers, we had week after week of cloudless blue skies.

24th August proved to be no exception to the general rule, and about 4 p.m. we took off with orders to patrol Portsmouth at 10,000 feet. A number of other squadrons were also operating, each at different heights, and on this occasion we were the luckless ones sent low down to deal with any possible dive-bombers.

We hated this – it's a much more comforting and reassuring feeling to be on top of everything than right underneath. Superior height, as I said before, is the whole secret of success in air fighting.

However, 'orders is orders' and so we patrolled Portsmouth. Very soon a terrific AA barrage sprang up ahead of us, looking exactly like a large number of dirty cotton wool puffs in the sky. It was a most impressive barrage; besides all the guns at Portsmouth, all the warships in the harbour and dockyard were firing hard.

A moment later, through the barrage and well above us, we saw a large German formation wheeling above Portsmouth. We were too low to be able to do anything about it, but they were being engaged by the higher squadrons.

They were now releasing their bombs, and I cannot imagine a more flagrant case of indiscriminate bombing. The whole salvo fell right into the middle of Portsmouth, and I could see great spurts of flame and smoke springing up all over the place.

We spent a very unpleasant few minutes right underneath the German formation, praying hard that their fighters would not come down on us.

However, the danger passed and a very disgruntled squadron returned home, having seen so many Huns and yet not having fired a single round.

Also, one of our Americans, Andy, was attacked by an Me 110 which, in his inexperience, he never saw following him, and the Hun put a lot of bullets into Andy's machine. Fortunately Andy was not hit and managed to bring a battered Spitfire safely home. He was very lucky to get away with it.

These three Americans – 'Andy', 'Shorty', and 'Red', had come over to join the French Air Force. They reached France in May just at the beginning of the German attack, and when things started to crack up they hitch-hiked down to Saint-Jean-de-Luz and got away in the last ship, without being able to get accepted by the French. In London they got a pretty cool reception at the American Embassy, who obviously weren't going to assist them to break the neutrality laws. They even tried to send them back to the States.

But fortunately Red had got an introduction to some MP and went along to the House to see him. After that everything went smoothly; twenty-four hours later they were in the RAF, and after a short training they came to us. They had been civil pilots in America and had done a lot of flying. But civil flying is one thing and military flying, particularly in war, is quite another, and they were very raw and inexperienced when they came to us. However, they were keen, and soon improved.

They were typical Americans, amusing, always ready with some devastating wisecrack (frequently at the expense of authority), and altogether excellent company. Our three Yanks became quite an outstanding feature of the squadron.

Andy was dark, tough, and certainly rather good-looking with his black hair and flashing eyes.

Red was very tall and lanky, and possessed the most casual manner and general outlook on life that I ever saw. I don't believe he ever batted an eyelid about anything, except possibly the increasing difficulty of getting his favourite 'rye high'. After a fight he never showed the slightest trace of excitement, and I remember that after one afternoon's fairly concentrated bombing of the aerodrome, during which a number of people were killed, he turned up grinning as usual but with his clothes in an awful mess and covered in white chalk because he had to throw himself several times into a chalk pit as the Huns dropped out of the clouds. He made only the grinning comment, 'Aw hell, I had a million laffs!'

Shorty was the smallest man I ever saw, barring circus freaks, but he possessed a very stout size in hearts. When he arrived in the squadron we couldn't believe that he would ever reach the rudder bar in a Spit; apparently the medical board thought the same and refused to have him at first, as he was much shorter than the RAF minimum requirements. However, Shorty insisted on having a trial, and he produced two cushions which he had brought all the way from the States via France, specially for this purpose. One went under his parachute and raised him up, the other he wedged in the small of his back, and thus he managed to fly a Spitfire satisfactorily, though in the machine all you could see of him was the top of his head and a couple of eyes peering over the edge of the cockpit.

One day the Duke of Kent came down to see us. The Americans were very intrigued about the forthcoming visit; being good Republicans they are always much impressed by royalty. Shorty said, 'Say, what do we call this guy – dook?' We hastily assured him that 'sir' would be sufficient. Anyway, the 'dook' arrived, shook hands with each of us, and spoke to us, and had a particularly long chat with Shorty, who amongst other jobs in a very varied career, had been a professional parachute jumper. Shorty was immensely gratified.

Unfortunately, after about six weeks with us, and just as they were becoming really good, they were posted away to form the Eagle Squadron. We were very sorry to lose them, because they were grand fellows.

They are all dead now. Shorty was last seen spinning into the sea near Flamborough Head during a chase after a Heinkel. Red crashed behind Boulogne, fighting like hell against a crowd of Me 109s, while Andy hit a hill in bad weather and was killed. As Red once remarked with the usual grin, pointing to the wings on his tunic, 'I reckon these are a one way ticket, pal.'

I think it was a very fine gesture on their part to come over here and help us to fight our battles, and they came at a time when trained pilots were worth a great deal in Fighter Command. They are in the first half-dozen of that small but honourable band of Americans who have already been killed in this war, while serving in the RAF.

About this time we received a visit from Lord Trenchard. He seemed remarkably young for a man who commanded the RAF in the last war, and he chatted to us for a long time in a very paternal and charming manner, congratulated us on our successes, and said that the only way to win this war was to give the Hun such hell as he had never had before and would never want again. We all felt that this was remarkably good advice, to be followed whenever possible.

On 25 August we took off in the afternoon and patrolled Swanage as a large German raid was approaching the coast.

Shortly afterwards we sighted a very big German formation coming over the coast below us, and the CO swung us into line astern and manoeuvred into a good position for the attack. Then, down we went. I happened to be almost last on the line, and I shall never forget seeing the long line of Spitfires ahead, sweeping down and curling round at terrific speed to strike right into the middle of the German formation. It was superb!

The great weight and fierceness of this onslaught split up the Huns immediately and they scattered all over the place, with Spitfires chasing them right and left. I saw an Me 110 below me and dived down on him going very fast indeed. Unfortunately I was going too fast and in the heat of the moment I forgot to throttle back, with the result that I came up behind him at terrific speed and overshot him badly. I had a good burst of fire at practically point blank range as he flashed by and then I had to turn away very violently or I should have collided with him.

His rear-gunner took advantage of my mistake and fired a short burst at me, and put several bullets through my wing, very close to the fuselage and only a few inches from my leg.

When I turned round to look for the Hun he had disappeared. Though there was a lot of fighting in progress and machines were turning and diving all over the sky, I had dived down below them all and couldn't do much about it.

A moment later most of the Germans turned out to sea again and chased home.

I went as hard as I could for Weymouth, thinking that I might pick up something there. I got to Weymouth, but the fighting was almost finished there too, although some battle must still have been going on up at a very big height, because one Me 109 dived vertically down into the sea just off the Chesil Bank and another one with its engine stopped and a Spitfire watching it carefully, glided down and made a forced landing in a field near the coast. I saw the pilot get out quite unhurt, set fire to his machine, and then walk away calmly across the field.

I returned to base absolutely furious with myself for having missed that Me 110. He was right in front of me, and if only I had not gone at him so wildly I should have had him easily.

Anyway, it taught me to be a little more cool in the future. One lives and one learns – if lucky.

I found that everybody had got back safely and we had destroyed six or seven Huns. Various other squadrons had got some victims also, and in all thirty Huns were definitely destroyed on this raid. Bombs had been dropped only at Warmwell, where nobody was hurt, slight damage only was caused, and a few craters made in the aerodrome, which were immediately filled in.

Not a very good return for the loss of thirty machines and crews.

This was Geoff's first action, and he shot down an Me 110 together with Noel. Officially they were credited with one half each.

Osti had an amazing escape in this fight. An Me 110 got on to his tail and put one cannon shell into his engine, where it blew out most of the induction system, while another shell hit the armour plating behind his head, and the explosion almost stunned him.

He managed to get back home with a big hole in his wing as well, but had to land very fast as his flaps were damaged and he ran through the hedge. His machine was a complete 'write off', but he was quite ok, apart from a headache.

Nothing else of interest occurred in the last few days of August, and at the end of the month we were able to add up our score.

This was forty-seven enemy aircraft definitely destroyed, as well as a number of others probably destroyed or damaged, and our only loss was one pilot killed.

This result is astonishing when compared with that of the previous month, July, when in a very few engagements only we lost four pilots and shot down about five Huns – almost equal numbers.

We had now learnt our lessons, though the price of this experience had been the death of several members of the squadron.

We realized now the vital importance of getting above the enemy before going into action; we knew that cool thinking and the element of surprise can more than compensate for inferior numbers, and can sometimes produce astonishing results; we knew from experience that if you attack out of the sun the enemy will hardly ever see you till the last moment; and vice versa, how essential it is to maintain the most intense vigilance always in order to prevent being surprised oneself.

We also realized the importance of constantly dodging and twisting during a fight, because if you steer a straight and steady course for more than about five seconds a Messerschmitt will probably be sitting just behind you and firing as hard as he can.

But after all this, a very great deal of the credit for our changed fortunes was due to the CO. He came to command the squadron at the beginning of July when, owing to lack of experience, we were not a particularly efficient fighting unit. He was with us all through the bad times when we lost more than we shot down, and when the morale of the squadron might have suffered. But he flew as much as anybody else, led us skilfully, and throughout remained so imperturbable, so confident, and so cheerful that he held us all together by his example.

And so the end of August found us with a very satisfactory and solid background of success and victory, and we now faced the future with an ample confidence that whatever the Germans might do, we could do it far better.

25 Ian 'Widge' Gleed Part 2, Hurricane Pilot, Flight Lieutenant, British, 87 Squadron

The final extract from Gleed's 1942 memoir covers 13–25 August. The RAF airfields Gleed flew from after this are indicated at the beginning of each original book chapter from the memoir.

Concern from his publisher at his 'bachelor' status (Gleed was gay) led the fighter pilot to create a fictional girlfriend, 'Pam'. Gleed kept his homosexuality a secret as same-sex relationships were illegal in 1940s Britain and were a court-martial offence in the services. His family probably didn't know about his sexuality and it wasn't until the 1990s that fellow pilot Christopher Gotch revealed his wartime affair with Gleed in a BBC interview.

Gleed dedicated his book to the RAF's ground staff. He had started a second book just before he was KIA on 16 April 1943, shot down over the Tunisian coast. He had amassed sixteen kills by this time, eleven during 1940. He is buried in the military cemetery at Enfidaville in Tunisia.

Chapter 7 A Hundred & Twenty Plus: 13–14 August 1940 (RAF Exeter, Devon in 10 Group) 'Hell, it's hot! Let's send to the mess for something to drink. What would I give for a litre of freezing lager? Where's the van, orderly? Get a driver to take you to the mess and collect some grapefruit squash; a couple of bottles for me.' 'I'll have a couple of bottles of ginger beer,' said Watty. 'Hey, Dennis! What do you want to drink? Grapefruit? Ok. Bring about a dozen bottles: Robbie will want some when he wakes up.' He was sleeping gently on his camp bed in the sun.

'Hullo! what's up? B flight are starting up. 'Rubber' bind Opps and ask what is happening.' Three of them roar off the deck. 'Johnny is flying with them, isn't he? He's got a pile of guts; I'll swear if ever I get to Winco I would never go near a plane again.' said Dennis. 'He certainly has got a packet of guts.'

'Well, Rubber what are they after?' 'A single plot, sir; off Selsey Bill, sir; coming this way.''Anything else on the board?''Not a thing, sir, according to Opps. You know what that means. I expect a shower of bombs will drop on us at any minute.'

We sit about; nothing happens. 'Hullo Opps, how are our boys getting on?' 'They are very close together now, and should have seen it. Hold on, something has just come through on the R/T. It's a tally-ho. We'll give you a ring if anything more comes through.' 'Hell, boys, B flight have seen another one; they are getting all the luck.'

'Hold this a second, Widge; I want to give it full winds and see what happens.' I hold one of Watty's models while he winds it with his drill. 'Hey, steady, Watty; if this damned elastic breaks I'll just about be murdered.' Watty finishes winding, takes the model and launches it gently into wind; it rockets up in a steep climbing turn and starts drifting slowly down wind. 'Hell! somebody start running after it.' One of the airmen starts plodding in pursuit. Watty, as he is at readiness, can't chase it. At last, about half a mile away, the model comes to rest. 'Two minutes, not bad,' says Watty. 'Hullo! here come the boys only two of them; I wonder where the other is? Good show! they have fired their guns. Wonder what they got?' 'Hullo, B flight! A flight here. Give us a ring as soon as you get the dope.'

Robbie wakes up. 'B flight have had a crack at something, a single recco plane, I think. Two of them have just landed now.'

'There's the phone. Ok I'll take it, Hullo, Derek! What? An 88 confirmed. Good show! What? Oh, hell! no. I suppose the rescue boats are out. Can we do a search or anything? Hell! that's tough. Rough sea, is it? Christ! I hope he gets picked up.' 'What is it, Widge?' 'Dusty Miller is down somewhere in the sea they knocked down an 88, but the 88 hit Dusty in the glycol tank. Johnny saw him going down with white smoke coming from him. The rescue boats have gone out after him and they are sending an air search up. B flight seem to be having all the luck – and bad luck.'

'Dusty has had showers of near escapes. I expect he'll come smiling out of "the drink". Do you remember when his glasshouse (another name for the perspex, transparent hood over the pilot's cockpit) got shot off, he never turned a hair? One thing, it is a damned nice day for a bathe.'

'It's just about time that we found a few Jerries to shoot at. This is really lovely weather for a blitz.' 'Not enough cloud for me, old boy; I like just enough cloud to do a steep turn in if I have to,' answered Robbie. 'Well, here's to some shooting, drunk in grapefruit squash.'

The bell rings: 'Two aircraft patrol Plymouth.' 'Off you go, Robbie; that's your turn.' Robbie and Vines, one of our new pilots, got off in one and a half minutes dead; not bad. Watty flies his model again, this time not so successfully: It takes off, climbs steeply, turns and crashes to the deck with a splintering crash. Watty doesn't turn a hair. 'Oh, I'll soon fix that up.'

We lounge about. Robbie and Vines return after forty-five minutes; they had seen nothing. Robbie swears at Opps; they say it never came anywhere near the coast. He returns to his bed. 'It's about time somebody bought something else to read to this damned hut. Who's going shopping tomorrow?' 'We'll be able to in the morning.' – 'Well, boys, for God's sake let's each buy a Penguin.' 'Watty what about getting me a model Hurry?' – 'I can never find your goddamned shop. It's our turn to have tea first; give Opps a bind, somebody, and see if we can go. Whose turn is it? Yellow or

Red?' 'Red's, I think.' – 'Right! Well, we'll go first. Opps say we can go now. Get our planes started if there's a blitz, Robbie; we'll be out like a flash.'

'Pile in, boys. We'll go across the 'drome and call on B flight on the way.' The Ford bumps across the 'drome; Derek walks up to meet us. 'Hullo! old boy. I am damned sorry about Dusty. Have you heard anything yet?' – 'Not a thing, old boy; it's nice and warm, but the sea looked quite rough. The worst of it is that none of us actually saw him hit the drink. We saw the 88 go in – it went straight in; no survivors. We must push off to tea. See you for a drink this evening.'

The mess is nearly deserted, as we are the first in for tea. We sit down, and the batman brings us toast and sandwiches. We munch them, idly turning over the pages of the latest magazines that litter the mess. All is quiet. We must rush back to dispersal to relieve Yellow section for tea. Evening falls; the blue sky gradually turns yellow, a red glow on the horizon shows the last tip of the setting sun. We put our jackets on. Watty produces his model; it flies high and smoothly, climbing and gliding in steady circles; it lands only a few yards from where it was launched. The evening is very beautiful. There is no news of Dusty.

At last the release comes through. 'Come on, boys; I'm pushing straight off to the town. Who wants a lift?' We pound down the road. We meet the B flight boys and 'Shuvvel', our CO, and wander along to the pub by the cathedral and have a bit of a party. Then to bed. The B flight boys go back to the 'drome and we to the Rougers. The night is very still.

Next morning (14 August 1940, RAF Exeter, Devon in 10 Group): 'Buck up, Widge; we'll be late.' – 'Hell! the damned alarm clock hasn't worked again.' I leap out of bed, wash and shave quickly, scramble into my clothes and start down the lift, still tying my tie. We have only got half an hour before we have to be at readiness: for reasons unknown, we have to be at readiness instead of thirty minutes this morning. We grab a quick breakfast and arrive at dispersal just in time. Opps tell us they are expecting a flap ('a flap' means a fuss, flurry, or commotion, and so, by extension, any emergency likely to produce a fuss, flurry, or commotion). Both squadrons are at readiness. 'B flight want you, sir I think it's the CO.'

'Morning, Widge CO here. Sorry you've missed your morning's shopping. I'll lead the squadron from B flight. Keep your flight about a thousand feet above us if there's a blitz, and protect our tails. We'll fix the bombers, and you fix the fighters.'

'Ok, sir. What's the form? How the devil do Opps know there's going to be a blitz?'

'Heaven only knows, old boy somehow they think there will be one.'

'Ok, sir. If they come we'll try to give them hell. I bet you a pint we knock down more than you.'

'Ok, Widge; that's a bet.'

We sit about. Nothing happens not even a single plot appears. Lunch time comes and a terrific bind starts as to who should go to lunch. Opps, In their usual way, seem to imagine that we shouldn't have any lunch. At last Shuvvel gives them a spot of his mind, and they agree that we can go one section at a time. We are told that we will be the fifth section to go, Yellow section the seventh. We shall get lunch at two-thirty if we're lucky. We sit around with rumbling tummies; breakfast seems years ago. At last Opps phone that Red section can go to lunch now. 'Don't be more than twenty minutes; Yellow section can go as soon as you get back.' Off we dash. The lunch is damned good; we swallow scalding coffee and burn our tongues. Dash to the Ford and charge out to dispersal. It is now two-forty-five, and Robbie and his boys are very hungry. The last two sections of 213 Squadron must be starved.

We sit and wait. Yellow section takes exactly twenty-five minutes for lunch. The other squadrons are very pleased to hear they can now go to lunch.

Once more the sun shines from a clear blue sky. There are a very few scattered cumulus clouds at about 2,000 feet. 'Well, Robbie, just enough cloud to disappear into, perhaps.' Everything seems hellishly quiet. Opps phone up, 'Sorry, chaps, but you'll still have to stay at readiness; I'm afraid you'll have to have some tea at dispersal. I'll ring the mess and ask them to get some ready. Send some transport for it. I should get it across because I don't think they have got many thermos flasks.' – 'Ok Opps. Thanks for the tip.' – 'Well, boys, they are still expecting this blitz. Orderly, go to the mess and pick up some tea for us. Pinch as many sandwiches as you can.' All is quiet once more.

The telephone rings:

'Hullo! It's for you, Widge.'

'Hullo, Opps! Yes. How many? Phew! Hell's bells! Ok?' – 'Super readiness (this means that the pilots sit waiting in the cockpits of their planes so that they can be airborne usually within 15 seconds) boys; there are a hundred and twenty plus. ('120 plus' means some number larger than 120 of German aircraft) Jesus Christ! let's go.' The boys run to their planes and clamber into the cockpits.

'Flight, tell my crew to be ready to start up and see that everything is set for a damned quick take off; I'll stay by the phone.'

I lift the receiver. 'Hullo, Opps; A flight now at super readiness. How are the plots?'

'They're coming now; I expect you'll be off shortly.'

I replace the receiver with mixed feelings. The sun seems very warm. I look out of the window. My plane is only about fifty yards away. The grass looks very green now. Oh God, let us be lucky! I sit on the bed. The hut is empty. All the men are out by the planes. The black telephone looks like some evil genius. Why doesn't it ring? Please, God, don't let me get wounded. Hell, let's have some music. I give the gramophone a few cranks, pick up the first record from the pile, 'Little Sir Echo.' The noise rather startles me; the tune conjures up a tea dance in Margate on my last leave. It's a damn good ballroom there, and damned good cream cakes.

Brrrrrrrrg.

'Hullo!'

'Start up.'

'START UP!' I scream.

Over the wire comes: 'Patrol Portland. You are to fix the escort fighters.' I slam the receiver down and run like hell.

'Start the bloody thing, you fools!'

A's prop is still only turning slowly over; it kicks into life just as I reach it. B flight are already taxiing out.

'Quick, help me with my parachute.'

I swing up into the cockpit. Good show! all the boys are started. I strap my helmet on, taxi a few yards, then open up full for the take off, just behind B flight's last man. I glance behind; all the boys are screaming off the deck. I throttle back for a second. Oh, good show, boys! Dickie and Dennis are in position, tucked in close to me already. Shuvvel has done a complete circuit to give me a chance to get into position. I swing in behind B flight, who are in close formation, climbing hard. 'Crocodile calling Suncup leader. Are you receiving? Over.' Clearly comes Shuvvel's voice, 'Hullo, Crocodile! Suncup leader answering. Receiving you loud and clear. Over.' – 'Hullo, Suncup leader! Patrol Portland. Over.' – 'Ok, Crocodile. Listen out.' I glance at the altimeter. 5,000 feet. Hell! a long way to go yet. We clamber upwards. I turn on the oxygen. Dennis grins at me through his perspex roof. Dickie the other side makes rude gestures with his hands. I give them both a thumbs up. Behind and slightly above, Yellow section is flying in perfect formation. We are going much too fast to weave. At 15,000 I give Dickie the two fingers sign, that means, 'Open to search formation.' Dennis and Dickie swing out to about two spans; Robbie's boys follow suit. Below me B flight have opened out. The long finger of Portland Bill stretches out into the sea in front of us. 'Blast! the sun is from the sea, that means they'll come out of the sun.' Far below us I catch a glimpse of another squadron, 213 I suppose. At last we reach 25,000; it has taken us fifteen minutes not bad. Shuvvel has throttled back. I pull the throttle back to O boost. Dennis and Dickie weave; Robbie weaves his section behind me. I peer seawards. 'Blast the sun! Can't see a thing.'

Faintly on the R/T comes: 'Crocodile calling Suncup leader. Bandits are just south of Portland now, heading north. Heights are from fifteen to twenty-five. Over to you, over.' – 'Suncup leader answering. Your message received and understood.' We head seawards. I open my glasshouse. I'm sweating like a pig. I strain my eyes looking seawards. I wonder what Pam is doing at this moment.

'Hell! there they are.' I speak on the R/T. 'Hullo, Suncup leader. Tally-ho! Bandits just to our right. Line astern, line astern, go.' I slam my glasshouse shut. 'Christ! it's worse than a Hendon air pageant.' A horde of dots are filling the sky; below us bombers flying in close formation, Ju 88s and 87s. Above them, towering tier above tier, are fighters, 110s and 109s. The mass comes closer. 'Now steady; don't go in too soon, work round into the sun.' The bombers pass about 10,000 feet below us. I start a dive, craning my neck to see behind. A circle of 110s are just in front of us; they turn in a big circle. Suddenly the white of the crosses on their wings jumps into shape. I kick on the rudder; my sights are just in front of one. 'Get the right deflection.' Now I press the firing button, a terrific burst of orange flame; it seems to light the whole sky. Everything goes grey as I bank into a turn. 'Ease off a bit, you fool, or you'll spin.' I push the stick forward, white puffs flash past my cockpit. 'Blast you, rear-gunners!' I climb steeply, turning hard. Just above me there is another circle of 110s; their bellies are a pale blue, looking very clean.

'Look out! look out!' Oh God! a Hurricane just in front of me is shooting at a 110; another 110 is on its tail. Hell! it's too far for me to reach. The 110 goes vertically downwards, followed by the Hurricane. 'Hell, you bastards!' A stream of tracer from behind just misses my right wing. I turn hard to the left; two splashes appear in the calm sea; already it is dotted with oily patches. For a second I get my sights on another 110. He turns and gives me an easy full deflection shot. I thumb the trigger; a puff of white smoke comes from his engine. Almost lazily he turns onto his back and starts an inverted, over-the-vertical, dive. I steep turn. Down, down he goes – a white splash. At the same time two other splashes and a cloud of smoke go up from the beach. Four planes have hit the deck within a second.

'Keep turning,' a voice inside me warns; and sure enough a second later I spot three 110s behind and just below. 'You fools! you'll never turn inside me; turn and turn.' About twenty planes are around me: black crosses seem to fill the sky. About half a mile away I can see the greenish camouflage of another Hurricane.

'Hell! where have the boys got to? Blast these rear-gunners! Oh God, my arm is getting tired.' (The actual physical strain on the arm muscles of pushing the stick hard over and holding it there in the violent manoeuvres of air combats is very considerable, for at these extreme speeds it may sometimes require all your strength to move the controls.) For a fleeting second I am on the tail of another. I give him a burst, then turn frantically as a stream of tracer goes over my head. 'Damn! we're getting out to sea.' Below me the bombers are now heading sea wards, no longer in their tight formation, but in ones and twos. 'Hell! this is too hot.' I over-bank, stick right in the bottom right-hand corner. 'Down, down.' The altimeter whirls round; 400 mph shows on the clock. I go flashing by 110s. Now I am below them I straighten out and head for the finger of Portland. The voice inside me again: 'Turn turn.' Rat-tat-tat, rat-tat-tat. 'Christ! 109's cannon; you silly bastard!' One is past me – overshot. Sights on, I thumb my firing button. Brrrrrrmmmmmm. A long burst from about fifty yards, a splash of oil hits my windscreen. Rat-tat-tat. 'Yank back on the stick.'

Nearly dead behind me is another 109, with two others just behind it. 'Oh God, get me out of this.' Once more I aileron. Down, down, down. The sea rushes up to meet me. I pull out and scream towards the pebbly beach about a mile away. The 109s are far above me, heading for the south. I pull up into a turning climb. The sea now seems littered with odd bits of aircraft and splodges of oil. On the cliff-tops smoke rises lazily from several wrecks. I weave gently, and throttle back. My engine has been flat out for about fifteen minutes. I glance at the instruments; the temperatures are high, but not in the danger mark. The sky seems empty. I climb to 5,000 feet. Nothing. Faintly on the R/T comes, 'All aircraft return to base and land.' Thank God for that! I open the lid. The country looks very lovely beneath me. I dive. Oh God, I wonder if the boys are ok. I dive down low. People are standing in the streets of a tiny village; they wave to me from under the eaves of thatched Devon cottages. I wave back; I am happy, my clothes feel dripping with sweat, but I am happy. I roar along, low flying towards the 'drome; my wings look free of bullet holes. 'Good old A! you have knocked down seven Jerries now definitely, and probably two more.' The red earth round the 'drome looks very warm and friendly. I roar round low over the dispersal points. Already most of the planes are in. I turn in and do a bouncy landing, taxi quickly into the dispersal hut.

The men leap on my wing-tips as I swing round. 'How many, sir?' – 'Three, two confirmed, and I think I got another, though I didn't see him hit. Is everyone back?' – 'Mr Knight and Sergeant Horsham aren't back yet, sir; some of B flight boys are still up, too.' – 'Ok, thanks.' I drop my parachute on my tail and sprint to the hut. 'How did you get on, Widge?' Robbie greets me. 'I saw you get one of them; it was a lovely flammer.' – 'How many did you get, Robbie?' – 'One certain; I couldn't see what happened to the rest of the sods; I am claiming three damaged.' – 'What about you, Dickie?' – 'I got a 110 at the same time as you, Widge then I had a hell of a time and couldn't get my sights on anything else.' – 'Hullo, Opps, Red leader here. Have you any plots of any of our planes? Who is missing from B flight? – The CO and Doran? Oh hell! I hope they're ok. I am very sorry to say that I saw one of our Hurries go down in flames. I am claiming two 110s confirmed and a probable 109. Let me know as soon as you hear anything of the other boys.'

'Hullo, Exchange. Get me B flight, please. Hullo, Derek! How did you get on? A 110? Good show, old boy! God, wasn't it hell? What's happened to Shuvvel?"

'I saw one of my boys go in – it must be Dennis or Horsham: they are both missing at the moment, I've never seen so many planes in the sky before; I saw a Hurry crash-land near Weymouth; the pilot should be ok. Mitch got two – an 87 and a 109; Bea got a 110 confirmed and a probable. God knows where Shuvvel is. He led us into a shower of 110s; that was the last I saw of him. There were some 87s just underneath us; he may have cracked at them. Opps is ringing up Warmwell to see if any of them have landed there. Ok, Widge I'll let you know. Hold on a second Ken (our intelligence officer) wants to talk to you.' – 'Hullo, Widge. Ken here. How many have you got? Two confirmed and a probable? Good show! How goes our score? Eight confirmed so far and two probables? Four of our planes haven't turned up; when they do I expect they will have got something. I'll be over with the combat reports for you to fill in as soon as I have got these boys to finish theirs.' – 'Ok, Ken; see you shortly.'

'Ken is coming over for all the dope. No news of Shuvvel. One of our planes has done a belly-landing near Weymouth: Derek thinks the pilot will be ok. Phone Opps and say we're refuelled, somebody ask them if they've any dope on our missing planes.

'Hullo Opps, A flight here. We are at readiness again, four planes only: we'll fly in two sections of two if anything happens.'

'Hold on A flight. Is the flight commander there?'

'Here, Widge; something for you.'

'Hullo, Opps! Leeds here. Oh no, hell! How did it happen? Crashed in flames? Horsham all right? Where? Bridgport hospital, shrapnel from a cannon shell in his bottom? Ok; thanks a lot. Let me know as soon as you hear anything else about any of the others.'

'Shuvvel is dead. Crashed at Warmwell trying to land. He must have been wounded. Horsham has crashed in a field near Bridgport; he's in Bridgport hospital with shrapnel in his bottom, and bruises. He is claiming a 110 confirmed and another a probable.'

Robbie breaks the silence: 'Well, Widge the plane you saw going in must have been Dennis' – 'I suppose it was, Robbie. He definitely got a 110; I'll claim it for him.'

A scream of brakes outside – Ken, our intelligence officer, walks in.

'Tea, blokes; B flight have pinched their share.'

'Shuvvel is dead, Ken.'

'I know, Widge: Opps phoned and told us. Here are the combat reports. Fill the damned things in for me. There's the phone hold on a second.'

'Hullo! Yes. Doran. He's ok? Where? Portland police station? Ok, we'll send a car for him. Oh, good show! Cheerio.'

'Frank Doran has baled out and landed in the middle of Portland; he got two 87s confirmed and a 109. He's sitting in the police station.'

'Ken, phone up transport and send something for him; get on to the adjutant; he can go with it, and visit Horsham on the way there.'

'Now let's fill in these damned forms. What's our squadron score for today now, Ken?'

'Thirteen confirmed and three probables and a shower of damaged.'

'How did 213 get on?'

'Damned well. They were below you and ran into the bombers, mostly 87s with a few 88s. They claim fifteen confirmed, and have two missing. Rouge, one of their Belgians, is missing; they think he started chasing the bombers halfway across the Channel and got shot down a long way out. They don't know what has happened to their other bloke. I suppose, Widge, that you will be taking over the squadron now.'

'I suppose I will, Ken.'

We sat round, helping each other with our combat reports. The evening gradually drew on, the sunset behind the hills; It was very peaceful. We cracked jokes and laughed a bit. At last the night was upon us, and just as darkness fell we were released.

Come on, boys; I'm off to the mess for dinner I feel starved again.' We rush up the lane in the Ford and hurtle into the mess. The bar is full of B flight boys and the other squadron.

'Have a drink, Widge,' Johnny yells across the bar.

'Thanks, sir; mine's a beer.'

'I'm sorry you weren't with us today; you would have loved it.'

'Ah Widge, you must remember my exalted rank; I mustn't favour 87 [Squadron]. I've been with the 213 boys, and managed to get a couple of 87s.'

'Oh, damned good show, sir! I'm hellishly upset about Shuvvel.'

'I know, Widge; it's rotten luck. Come up to my office in the morning and see about things.'

'Right, I will sir.' – 'Hullo, Frank! What the hell have you been up to?'

'Well, old boy, I managed to get a couple of 110s and a 109; then I ran out of ammo. I was surrounded by 109s. One of them eventually hit me; the engine went up in flames, so I thought it was time to get out. I baled out at twelve thousand over the sea, and got blown overland by the wind. I landed slap in the middle of Weymouth High Street, and damned nearly got run over by a bus. The police were damned good to me, and plied me with tea and whisky.'

Derek said, 'Good show, Frank! Where's the adjutant got to?' – 'He's pushed off home. He called on Horsham, who is really not too bad: evidently he has got a couple of lovely black eyes and bits of cannon shell in one leg. The adjutant says his plane's in a hell of a mess, and that he's damned lucky to be alive at all.'

'Derek, you old devil, what are you drinking?'

'Whisky, please, old boy. It was tough today. Have you heard the wireless? We knocked down a hundred and four today that beats all records. We lost twenty-eight. Bloody good!'

'I suppose we must congratulate you and call you sir now, Widge.'

'Don't be too previous, Frank. I hope so, but I don't know.'

'I hope so, too.'

'Thanks a lot, old boy. Let's have some more beer.'

At last, after a good dinner, we pushed off to the Rougers, had a few more drinks there and got to bed. I lay between the clean sheets and thought how narrow the line between life and death was. Next door is Shuvvel's room; it seems hard to believe that we will never see his cheery smile again. And Dennis – the grand, tough, happy Dennis. 'You were such a promising fighter pilot, Dennis.'

Will I be given the squadron? God, let me be! With such grand boys I can make a great show of it. Robbie can be OC A flight. I think everyone will be very happy if that is so. Perhaps that is what Johnny wants to see me about in the morning. Shuvvel and Dennis, may you be happy wherever you are.

Then I started thinking about the fight that day. Why the hell did those Huns turn back? Who gave the order to turn? Was an order given, or was it sheer funk? The way the bombers were broken it looked as if funk was the more likely answer. But why? Surely they had expected to lose planes, or were they so full of propaganda that they thought Germany already ruled the skies over Britain? There were strange stories going around about captured pilots arrogantly asking for the nearest German army headquarters, and being really bewildered when they were told to shut up. Who can say? If they had pressed home their attack England would have been a sorry sight. Perhaps it was true that only one out of twenty German pilots knew how to navigate; that these navigators led the formations; that when they were shot down the rest turned tail and fled. I didn't know. My last thoughts were, 'They most certainly had a lesson today; I wonder when they'll come again.'

Chapter 8 Shuvvel's Funeral: 15–24 August 1940 (RAF Exeter, Devon in 10 Group) Next day I woke up early. It was a grand morning. I lay in bed and thought. What would this day bring me? Perhaps the command of a fighter squadron.

'Come on, Widge; get up, you lazy dog.' Dickie burst in and threatened to chuck a wet sponge at me.

'Don't be so damned hearty, Dickie. We've got packets of time; don't tell me that Robbie is out of bed yet.'

'Yes, he is: he's in the bath singing.'

'Oh, hell! Keep me away from the bathroom, then.'

I leap out of my bed. 'Dickie, you swine, must you rip the bedclothes off? Anyway, at this time of the morning I'm never respectable. For God's sake leave me in peace while I shave, or I'll slit my throat. Go and get Robbie out of the bath, and tell him if he sings when we're driving up I'll do ninety all the way; that'll fix him.'

I washed quickly and jumped into my clothes. 'Come on, boys; the bus leaves in two minutes.' We crowd into the lift. 'Morning, Widge' says Robbie as he ties his tie. There is a general fight to push the right button. After a rapid ascent to the top floor and then descent to the basement, we eventually arrive at ground level. Each buys a paper from the hall porter, and we crowd out to the Ford.

'Wait a moment, boys; you'll have to push, as the damned battery is flat.' Curses from Dickie, Robbie and Chris, a series of terrific jerks and she starts; the boys pile in.

'Hey, wait a second, Widge.' Watty leaps down the steps, putting his jacket on as he runs. 'Come on, Watty; you damned nearly missed the bus.' At last we are off, sweeping along the main street, getting up to sixty before we are in the derestricted area. We scream round the last corner doing just on ninety; the usual prayers go up from the back. We turn up the narrow lane, nearly exterminate a couple of cyclists and at last swing into the iron gates of the 'drome. A screaming of tyres as we stop just by the door where the notice says, 'Cars must not park here', and dash in to breakfast. 'What's Jane doing today? Has she any clothes on?' We peer over Dickie's shoulder; he always buys the *Daily Mirror*. Bacon and eggs arrive. We eat quickly and in silence. Our papers' headlines all proclaim the big blitz yesterday. I suppose we all are quietly thinking of Shuvvel and Dennis, who aren't with us to look at Jane and laugh with us. We don't mention that at all.

'Robbie, look after things for me: I shall be a bit late getting to readiness, as I must go and see Johnny. If anything happens, get my engine started, and I'll be out like a flash. Take the car out and send it back at once with a driver. See you anon, boys.'

I get up and walk along to the offices, clamber up the stairs and walk into Shuvvel's office. Sutton, the adjutant, is already there. 'Congratulations on yesterday, sir. I'm hellishly sorry about the CO and Knight. I've sent off the casualty signals. The station adjutant has just phoned me and said Johnny wants to see you.' – 'Ok, adj, I'll go along and see him now.'

I knock at Johnny's door. 'Come in.' – 'Good morning, sir.' – 'Good morning, Widge I'm very sorry you have lost Shuvvel I've talked to group, and they agree to give you the squadron. I think that you can cope, Widge; but you must realise that if you don't, you'll go back to flight lieutenant.'

'Thank you very much, sir; I'll do my very best.'

'Good show, Widge! If you want any help, just come along and see me. I'm afraid that you won't find it quite such good fun as being a flight commander: there's a hell of a lot of bumf (paper) work to do. Get your adjutant to do most of the work, and just spend about a couple of hours a day in the office yourself: it shouldn't cut down your flying at all. Don't put your stripes up until it comes through from group.'

'Ok, sir; thank you very much for the chance. I shall make Robbie flight commander in my place.' – 'Ok, Widge; I thought you would. Send it up to group on the pro forma for acting rank. I'll still come and fly with you when I can.'

'That's grand, sir; we love having you. Whenever you come with us you bring us luck: we always seem to find some Jerries then.'

'See you anon, Widge.'

'Good luck.'

'Thanks, sir.'

Back to the office. 'Well, adj, I'm the new CO.' – 'Damn good, sir; I'm very pleased. You deserve it. I'm afraid the first thing that we have got to do is to fix up Shuvvel's burial. As far as I can make out, he has no relatives in England: his next of kin is his mother, who is in New Zealand. You had better write to her; and to Knight's parents. I've got the addresses and the file with the other letters written to the parents of our other casualties.'

I write two letters, saying briefly what had happened and how much we missed our comrades – a most unpleasant job. Sutton was ringing up the undertakers about a coffin for Shuvvel.

'Well, adj, I think I'll push out and be at readiness.'

'Could you see a charge first, sir? It's waiting in the orderly room now.'

'Oh, hell! I suppose so. What is it about?'

'The Service police have run in one of our squadron HQ boys for being absent without leave.'

'Ok, adj; get the sergeant discipline to bring him in.'

The adjutant kicks the wall – the signal for the orderly corporal to come in: no bells had been put in yet.

'Bring in the charge now, sir? Very good.'

'Prisoner, attention. Quick march. Right turn. Left turn. Halt. AC Wales, sir.'

'No. 5467834 AC1 Wales?'

'Yes, sir.'

'You are charged with while on active service being absent without leave from 0800 until apprehended by Corporal Rodson of the Service Police at 1600 hours on the 16.8.40. Corporal Rodson, what have you to say in evidence?'

'Sir, at 1600 hours on the 16.8.40. I was patrolling High Street when I saw this airman coming out of a cinema. I said to him 'Airman, let me see your pass.' He said, 'I have no pass; I was fed up, so I have had a day off.' I took his name and escorted him back to the guardroom.'

'Thank you, Corporal. Well, Wales, what have you got to say?'

'I am sorry, sir; I haven't been out of camp since I have been here, sir, and I wanted to do some shopping.'

'Did you ask for a pass?'

'No, sir.'

'Why not?'

'I don't know, sir.'

'Well, Wales, as you well know, there is a war on; you let yourself down and you let your squadron down by being absent without permission. May I have the man's conduct sheet, sergeant? Thank you. I see from your record sheet that you have only been in the service three months, and that up to now you have got a clean sheet. Have you anything to say in your defence?'

'No, sir.'

'You are confined to camp for seven days. Remember when you want to go out again to get a pass.'

'Very good, sir.'

'Carry on, sergeant.'

'Prisoner, right turn. Quick march. Right turn. Left turn. Halt.'

The door shuts. I have done my first job as CO.

'Well, adj, was that ok? Why are some men such damned fools?'

'That was very good, sir. I hope you won't have too many to do. I'll get the discipline sergeant to see that the men get passes when they ask.'

'Well, adj, I'm off to dispersal point. Oh, by the way, get some pro formas out to promote Robbie to acting flight lieutenant. I'll sign them at lunchtime.'

'Ok, sir; I'll fix that and Shuvvel's funeral.'

I roar out and call at B flight on the way. 'Derek, you old bastard, I'm the new CO.'

'Damned good show, Widge! that's a grand show! Hey, boys, you've got to say 'sir' to the Widge now – that's right, isn't it, sir?'

'Only in working hours, boys – or, at least, when other people are listening. Well, as you can guess, I shall lead the squadron from A flight. Johnny, when he flies, will lead us with you boys. See you at lunch.'

I bump across the 'drome to A flight. 'Congratulations, Robbie; you're the new flight commander. Johnny has made me CO.'

'That's grand, Widge; thanks a lot for giving me the flight. I suppose that you will still fly with us?'

'I shall, Robbie; so you will still be Yellow leader. Your first job will be to get squadron leader's markings on mighty Figaro.' (I called 'A', my aircraft, Figaro, because I had had the little cat Figaro, of Disney's film, painted on the side panel, in the act of smashing a swastika)

'Ok, Widge; I'll get it done right away.'

'What's the form at the moment?'

'Nothing, old boy – not a plot has appeared today.'

'Where the hell is my Mae West? Thank you, Rubber.'

All was quiet for the next few days except for occasional single recco planes that we never caught.

The next morning at the office the adjutant said, 'The funeral is at two-thirty tomorrow. I have asked Warmwell to get a wreath for us.'

'Thanks, adj; Derek, Dickie and I will fly over to Warmwell. For God's sake phone Warmwell and make dead sure that they have the wreath ready.'

'Right, sir.'

'I'll be in Opps if you want me, then out at A flight.'

I walked along to the Opps room; it was still very crude; a huge map spread on a wooden table nearly filled the room. The controller sat on a raised dais; round the table about half a dozen WAAFs sat with headphones on. They received plots from the Observer Corps and from group. On the table they had little notices showing what each raid consisted of and its height, These they pushed across the board. Other plotters pushed coloured plaques which represented fighters. The controller tried to get the fighters to intercept the enemy plots.

'Morning, Widge – sorry, I mean sir.'

'Good morning, old boy; any activity this morning?'

'Only the usual early morning recco plane; it came alone at 25,000 feet today. 213 chased it, but were miles underneath it. It did a grand tour of Plymouth. What can we do for you?'

'Find us some Jerries in a small quantity.'

'We'll do our best about that.'

'Actually I want permission for three of us to go to Warmwell this afternoon for Shuvvel's funeral. We'll fly there. It's at two-thirty.'

'I'll fix it with group to have your Red section released till four. I don't think that there is any special flap on today. They now think that the invasion is put off for a couple of weeks. Heaven knows where they get the dope from. Anyway, they don't seem very right at the moment.'

The afternoon soon came. Permission came through from group for us to go to Warmwell. We took off in close formation, but opened up to search formation, just in case. It only took fifteen minutes. England was looking her best in the hot August sun. The world seemed too beautiful for a funeral. As soon as we had landed we taxied to the watch office and dispersed our aircraft near the hangar. 'Hell! when did they do that?' The hangar was minus its roof and the tin sides were bulging outwards.

We walked towards the headquarters office, past several burnt-out and flattened wooden huts. 'I suppose they must have dropped these the other day.' We walked into the station adjutant's office.

'Oh, you've come for Squadron Leader Forbes' funeral? You might take these things; they were found in his pockets.'

He handed me a small white bag. I checked the contents: some letters, slightly burnt; a wallet with several pounds in; a bunch of keys and a car key on a rubber holder which was half burnt.

'Ok. You had better go along to the guardroom; the body is there. The escort and you will go on a lorry to Warmwell Parish Church, where he is to be buried. You are the only mourners, as I understand his home is in New Zealand.'

'Yes, that's right. Thanks for doing all the arrangements. We'll push straight back as soon as it is over. Cheerio.'

We walked along the road to the guardroom. There a huge open lorry had a coffin on it draped with the Union Jack. Standing near was the firing squad, with arms reversed.

The sergeant in charge came up to me.

'Good afternoon, sir. Do you know what you have to do?'

'No, I'm afraid I don't.'

'Well, sir, we all go in two lorries behind the coffin. When we arrive at the church the pall-bearers – that's four of the men – lift the coffin off the lorry, and you follow them into the graveyard. You take up your positions on the other side of the grave to the firing squad; I give the orders to fire and to sound the Last Post. When the coffin is lowered you salute, then step forward and throw some earth on it. Before you leave the graveside you salute the head of the grave.'

'Ok. Derek, Dickie. I think we've got the right idea. Have you got the wreaths?'

'Yes, sir – one from 87 Squadron and one from the station at Exeter, and another from Warmwell. It would be best, sir, if you carried one each and put it by the head of the grave.'

'Right. Well, let's start.'

We clamber into the lorries and move off at funeral speed. It seems impossible to believe that the Union Jack covers the remains of the cheerful Shuvvel. We crawl along the road. For God's sake, why the hell can't we get a move on? What the hell is the use of prolonging the agony? We pass through a narrow lane lined with oak trees. Oh, Shuvvel why were you so reckless? We come to a halt. I jump down. We are by a high stone wall; behind it is the small village church, a warm grey in the sun. The pall-bearers lift the coffin onto their shoulders, the Union Jack nearly slips off. We follow behind the coffin, up through the wooden lych-gate, up a stone path round to the graveyard. The rows of grave stones look very neat in the thick, uncut grass. It looked all right until you saw that hole, surrounded by newly dug earth; it is in the shadow of tall trees that surround the church.

'You would love your graveyard if you could see it, Shuvvel; it is very peaceful.

Perhaps you can see it: I wonder if you are smiling at us now.' The padre was in the graveyard in his flowing robes. The coffin was laid by the grave; we took up our positions opposite to the firing party; the padre stood at the head of the grave and said the burial service: 'Earth to earth, dust to dust,' etc., etc. My thoughts were elsewhere – with Shuvvel at a party in Leeds. I was suddenly startled into reality by the firing squad: they fired rather a ragged volley. A few leaves dropped down from the overhanging branches of the trees. The coffin was lowered slowly into the hole; the flag had been removed. The brass plate and fittings glinted in the sun: 'Richard William Forbes. Royal New Zealand Air Force.' I stooped down, picked up a handful of earth and threw it on top of the coffin. 'Shuvvel, I'm sure we shall meet. Happy hunting.' Derek and Dickie threw earth in the hole. It looked very deep – most unpleasant if someone fell in on top of the coffin! The Last Post rang through the air. The service was over. I walked round to the head of the grave and saluted. 'Au revoir, Shuvvel; you leave behind happy memories.' We walked out of the shade of the trees into the brilliant sunshine. Back to Warmwell – faster this time – and back to Exeter by plane.

One day Watty and I were sent after a recco plane reported approaching Plymouth at 15,000 feet. We just reached the outskirts of the town when, inland of us, a series of black bursts appeared.

'Hell! what on earth are they shooting at? Tally-ho, tally-ho! One bandit, over Plymouth.'

'There he is. Here goes. This is where I carry out a quarter attack. Wonder what the hell it is?' I swing round to cut him off. Watty is just by me, throttle hard forward. 'What a piece of cake! One Dornier and two of us. Hey! he's going damned fast. Instead of closing, we seem to be getting farther away. Blast you! not so fast. He has gone into a steep dive. Damn! it will be an astern attack, after all. Damn and blast! we aren't gaining. We're across the coast now, going flat out.' I switch on the reflector sight. 'He's much too far away – about a thousand yards. Blast!' I shove the throttle. 'Damn! it's hard against the stop already. Oh, hell's bells! not so far away are clouds: if he reaches those I'll never get him. We're down to ten thousand now, so here goes with the tit.' A jerk and my speed increases. Just behind, Watty is going flat out, black smoke pouring from his exhausts. I peer through the reflector sight. 'We're gaining slowly. About 800 yards now still much too far. The clouds are only a few miles in front now. Hell to this! Damn! the engine's getting a bit warm.' All my temperature instruments show high readings. 'Oh damn! he has reached the first clouds.' In a flash I am enveloped in white wisps of cloud. I shove the stick forward and dive out of the bottom. I peer forward – nothing is in front. 'Hell's bells! he's got away!'

I swing round for the coast. Watty appears out of the cloud just to my right. I waggle my wings, release the tit, and throttle back. Watty closes formation; he shakes his fist at the clouds and makes the thumbs-down sign.

'Hullo! Crocodile! Suncup leader here. I regret to say that bandit has got away seawards. We have given up the chase.'

'Hullo! Suncup leader. Return to base and land.'

'Ok, Crocodile.'

We swing eastwards. We must be a hell of a long way out: there is no sign of the coast. Minutes pass that seem like hours. I fish the map out of the map-case. Damn, the coastline goes in nearer Exeter. I swing farther round to the north. At last on the horizon looms up the shape of cliffs. We swing much more eastwards. Now I know where I am. Below stretches the harbour of Brixham. I dive lower. Yes, there it is the little cafe that I used to have cream teas at when I was in hospital at Torquay. How peaceful it looks! We carry on along the coast, and at last the estuary comes into sight and the town of Exeter glinting in the sun. We land and taxi in. Jump out.

'Watty, what a hell of a bind! (Used as a noun in this way the word means a bore, a fag, a troublesome incident. Derivation: to bind, to discuss or argue with: hence to bore: hence 'a bind', meaning a bore.) Christ! I thought we had him cold. I was going to do a quarter attack on him when he just opened his throttles and left us standing. I was balls out with the tit pulled. We were just gaining on him when he made the clouds. What the hell was he?'

'A Dornier 215. 1 think he must have had special engines in. That's the one time that I wish I had a Spitfire. What a life! I should think that they'll blitz Plymouth soon; they seem to spend their time sending recco planes there.'

Intelligence were very interested and impressed by our story. We were very annoyed to know that the Jerries had got something that would go as fast as our Hurricanes, even though it must have been a special recco plane.

Days passed slowly. There was a general invasion flap; it was expected within twenty-four hours, so we were perpetually at readiness. Awful flaps were going about defence of the station: terrifically long and complicated orders on what to do if the invasion came. Ken was a great help; being a barrister in civil life, he managed to deal with the secret code words and general bumf well. We formed a brain trust, consisting of Robbie, Derek, Ken, the adjutant, and me. With that we managed to keep most things under control. On the station huts were springing up like mushrooms. We all said that Jerry would wait until they were all finished, then blitz it like hell.

Chapter 9 A Hundred & Fifty Plus: 25 August 1940 (RAF Exeter, Devon in 10 Group)
'Morning Ken. Is it true that Opps are expecting the invasion today?'

'I don't know, sir; I'll nip along and find out.'

There had been terrific rumours floating around the camp. For the last few days we had been at perpetual readiness. One of the enemy rumours was that there had been an invasion, but it had been wrecked by the Navy; German bodies were reported to be washed up in thousands on the coast of Kent. I didn't believe it much, because Pam would have said something about it in one of her letters.

Damn the phone! 'Hullo! Yes, Ken, it is today? Where? Ok. Well, I'm retiring to readiness. I suppose we'll have to have a staggered lunch. Look after things, adj; give me a ring if anything interesting comes in. I'll slip up at lunchtime to sign any bumf. I'm just going along to Johnny's office, then out to dispersal.' – 'Good luck, sir.' – 'Thanks.'

I knock. 'Come in. Good morning, Widge. Heard the news? Today is meant to be the great day.'

'Yes, I heard from Opps, sir. I wonder where on earth they are meant to be coming. Do you think they'll try it, sir?'

'No, Widge, but I think there will be another big blitz today, so I'm coming to fly with you.'

'That's grand, sir. Will you take your old place and lead the squadron with B flight? I'll look after your tails with A flight.'

'Ok, Widge. Tell the B flight boys I'll be out in half an hour.'

'Ok, sir; that will be about eleven.'

I bump across the 'drome, stop at B flight and tell Derek what is happening. Then bump across to A flight.

'Is A serviceable?'

'Yes, sir, it's all ok. Are you flying today?'

'I sincerely hope so. The invasion is meant to be starting today.'

'It's a grand day for it, anyway, sir.'

It was: a cloudless blue sky. The boys were lying out on their beds in their shirt sleeves. 'Good morning, sir. Sleep well?' That was a crack from Robbie because I had overslept that morning.

'Good morning, Robbie. Very well, thank you. Have you heard the gen? Today is invasion day, and they are expecting a hell of a blitz. Johnny is going to lead us from B flight. We are going to fix the escort fighters. Dickie and Dinkie Powell, you will be Red section with me. Who have you got, Robbie?'

'I'll take Watty and Vines.'

'Ok. I bet you nothing happens at all, but still, here we are. Watty have you got any models ready to fly? You make them and I'll break them.'

'I've built you a special one, sir; it's a super acrobatic model.'

Watty produces a beautifully made little model powered with many strands of elastic.

'Thank you very much, Watty; do you think I'm getting fat or something?'

'No, sir, but I don't want you to break my big planes.'

'Ok, Watty; I trust that you will maintain this for me, anyway. Come on, Dinkie; you hold it and I'll wind.'

We wind the elastic up with a drill; steady the elevators.

'Ok. Well, here goes. Christ, what a climb!'

The model whips into the air, soars up to about 100 feet, rolls on its back, loops, then climbs in a tight circle. The elastic unwinds and the prop, starts free-wheeling; It settles into a steady glide and touches down and lands on its wheels. A minute and a half. 'Damn good, Watty.' I have a couple of hundred yards' walk to collect it.

We sit about. I lie on a bed and write letters, one to Pam, another to my mother, and yet another to the Upper Thames Sailing Club asking them about keeping my boat *Spindrift* there. The sun is very hot. Opps phone and tell me that A flight's job is to stop the escort fighters interfering with B flight and 213 Squadron, who have been ordered to deal with the bombers. All is quiet. The usual arguments ensue on who should go to lunch first. Robbie and I toss up, and he loses. So once more Red section goes first, with lots of moans from Watty and Vines (the new pilot), who swear that I must have a double-sided coin (unfortunately not true).

'Come on, Dickie; we haven't got all day. I suppose Vines will be all right.' – 'Oh, I think so, sir; he has done a lot of patrols now, but hasn't seen any Jerries.' – 'How much time has he done on Hurries?' – 'About fifty hours now.' – 'Well, that should be plenty. If he survives his first blitz I think he'll be a good pilot. He's very steady.'

We swallow our lunch and rocket out to dispersal. 'Hold on a second. I must just rush upstairs and see if there is any bumf to sign. Shan't be a second. Hullo, adj! Everything under control?'

'Please sign these two files, sir; then everything is under control.'

'Are you ready for the invasion, adj? Have you got your revolver? – Good show! Well, keep the Hun out of the office while you burn the files.'

'Ok, sir. I'll have a large beer for you when you are released.'

'Ok, adj; that's a date. I must rush off now. Keep everything under control, and ring me if anything interesting comes in.'

'Right; off we go.'

'Have you fixed it that we get lots of tea, Dickie?'

'Yes, Widge, it is all fixed.'

'Good!'

Back to readiness to have a siesta on our beds. All is quiet. Everything seems very peaceful. The afternoon drifts slowly by. My thoughts are far away sailing on blue seas with Pamela.

'I wonder if it will be a blitz like last time, Robbie?'

'I hope not, old boy; it was too hot for comfort.'

'I should like about twenty Junker 87s to appear with no escort.'

'That would just about suit me too.'

'Actually, Robbie, what do you think the best way of attacking those really big formations is?'

'I don't know, Widge. The only thing that I am certain of is that the 109s are miles above the 110s, ready to pounce on anything that attacks them, and the 110s in their turn pounce on anything that makes a dart at the bombers. In fact, the whole thing is damned unpleasant. We can't possibly get above those 109s – they're floating about at thirty thousand. The only thing to do is to try to get them mixed up, then nibble at the edges. Don't let's think about it, Widge; I'm going to sleep. Wake me when the tea comes, before you have ganneted it all.'

'Happy dreams, Robbie.'

We lie about. The birds fly. Watty brings out his new model, gives it many winds; it soars upwards, catches a thermal up-current and nearly disappears from sight. It lands after a flight of eight minutes right the other side of the 'drome. Watty sends a van to fetch it. He is very pleased.

'Come on, Watty; hold my little devil.' We wind it up; it soars up, does two loops, a roll off the top, then a steady glide.

'It's wizard, Watty. Blast! it's going to crash on the haystack.'

It does. We get the ladder to fetch it down. I am halfway up the ladder. Brrrrring … Hell! I jump off and run for the hut. The orderly is already at the phone.

'What is it?'

'Super readiness, boys.'

The boys drop their books and run to their planes.

'Flight, see that my men have everything ready for me in the cockpit. My parachute is out there. I'll stay by the phone.'

'Hullo, Opps. Squadron Leader Leeds here. How many are there this time? 150 plus… Whew! Hell's bells! Try to get us off in plenty of time.'

'You'll be off soon.'

I peer out of the window. The boys are already in the cockpits. 'Hullo, Opps! A flight now at super readiness. Thanks a lot.'

I sit on the bed, idly turning over the pages of one of Watty's model aeroplane magazines. My mouth is dry. God! why must there be wars? I wonder if all the boys feel as frightened as I do. They at least don't know that a hundred and fifty plus is on the way. Suppose the two squadrons from Warmwell go up with 213 Squadron and ourselves it will be at the most forty-eight planes, probably thirty-six. How the hell can we stop them? I wonder what the Jerries feel like, flying in their huge formations. I untwist the cock on my Mae West and give it a couple of puffs; it's working all right, anyway. Brrrrring. Oh God, here it is! Patrol Portland. 'START UP!' I scream. 'You are to fix escort fighters.' Phone down, I run like hell, bound towards A. The engine starts. Good boys! Dixon, the fitter, is out of the cockpit like a flash and holds my parachute ready for me to slip in, I clamber up the wing and drop in the cockpit. He puts the straps on my shoulders; I fix the safety-pin.

'Good hunting, sir.'

'Thanks.'

He jumps off the wing. I open the throttle and start taxiing. B flight boys are roaring off the ground – three, four, five. I have picked my helmet off my reflector sight and have buckled my chinstrap just as B flight's sixth plane is off. Throttle open and we are off. A quick glance behind shows the others taking off in quick succession. I throttle back a bit to give Dickie and Dinkie a chance to get into position. Johnny, the station commander, is leading us on a straight course for Portland. Hold hard, Johnny: we'll never catch you at this rate. In my mirror I can see Robbie's boys just catching us up; we are climbing hard.

'Crocodile calling Suncup leader. Are you receiving me?' – 'Suncup leader answering. Loud and clear.' – 'Crocodile receiving Suncup loud and clear.' – 'Listen out.' 'Crocodile calling Bearskin leader. Are you receiving?' – Faintly I hear, 'Receiving you loud and clear.'

I glance back at the 'drome. Twelve dots are climbing behind us. Lucky devils, 213 Squadron: they are after the bombers again. It's a glorious day. The sun beats down on us. The sea looks most inviting. Hope I don't have a bathe just yet. At last we are slowly catching B flight up. I glance at the instrument panel. Everything looks normal: radiator temperature on the high side, nothing to worry about, as it's a hell of a hot day. It seems hard to realise that over the sea masses of Jerry aircraft are flying, aiming to drop their bombs on the peaceful-looking countryside that lies beneath. Up, up. My two wing men are crouching forward in their cockpits, their hoods open. I slide mine open: it's too damned stuffy with it shut. My mouth feels hellishly dry; there is a strong sinking feeling in my breast. Thank God a doctor isn't listening to my heart. It's absolutely banging away. Turn on the oxygen a bit more. We are now at 20,000. It is cooler now, so I slam the hood shut. It's a hell of a long way to fall. Once more the sun shines from the sea; its reflection off the surface makes it nearly impossible to look in that direction. Yet that direction is where the Hun is coming from. At last, 25,000 feet. We all throttle back and close up. I climb to 26,000, level out. On the R/T rather faintly comes, 'Bandits now south west of Portland Bill. We are in perfect position to intercept them.'

Below us, like a model, lies Portland harbour. A sunken ship standing in shallow waters, half submerged, looks like a microscopic model. Back with the hood. I strain my eyes peering at the blue sky. Nothing yet. Far below us another squadron is weaving; just below me B flight is weaving violently. Dickie and Dinkie criss-cross behind my tail. I peer forwards, heading out to sea.

'Tally-ho.' 'Christ! there they are.' A weaving, darting mass of dots gradually drifts towards us, looking like a cloud of midges on a summer evening. 'Hell! was I born to die today?'

'Line astern, line astern, go.'

Dickie and Dinkie swing under my tail. The Jerries seem miles above us; lines of smaller dots show where the 109s are ready to pounce. Beneath them, about our height, circles of 110s turn, chasing each others' tails, moving as a mass slowly towards us. Far below, the bombers are in tight formation. Somehow they look like tin soldiers. 'Steady; don't attack too soon.' Johnny and B flight have dived, heading for the bombers; they have swung into line astern and now swing into echelon. The 110s continue circling. They seem to make no attempt to dive.

'Here goes.'

I dive at the nearest circle of 110s.

'Christ! look out.'

A glance behind shows 109s literally falling out of the sky, on top of us. Messerschmitts. I bank into a steep turn. Now we are in a defensive circle, the 109s overshoot us and climb steeply. Now's our chance. I straighten out and go for the closest 110. 'You silly bastard!' He turns away from me. I turn the firing button on to fire; at exactly 250 yards I give him a quick burst. White puffs are flashing past the cockpit. Another burst. Got him! A terrific burst of fire from his starboard engine, a black dot and a puff of white as the pilot's parachute opens. I bank into a steep left-hand turn and watch for a split second the burning 110 going vertically downwards. The parachutist is surrounded by planes, darting here and there. 'Thank God! got one of them. Now for another.' Below me another circle of nine 110s are firing at a solitary Hurricane which is turning inside them. I shove the nose down, sights on the last one, thumb the firing button. 'Oh, what a lovely deflection shot! Got him!' White smoke pours from one engine, more white vapour from his wings; his wings glint as he rolls on his back. Another burst. Hell, look out! A large chunk of something flashes by my wings; as I glance behind I see tracer flash by my tail.

A 109 is just about on my tail; the stick comes back in my tummy, and everything goes away. Now an aileron turn downward, down. 'Hell! that was a near one.' I miss a 110 by inches down; at 400 mph on the clock. The controls are solid. Nothing seems to be behind me. I wind gently on the trimming wheel, straighten out and start a steep climb. What seems miles above me the Jerries still whirl. I can't see any friendly planes at all. 'Hell! where am I? About ten miles off the coast. Hurrah! they're going home.' I turn for the shore, weaving fiercely. 'Hell! over to the west the bombers are haring back in twos and threes.' Two Hurricanes appear to be chasing them. I can catch them easily. 'Here goes. There's one. Looks like an 88. That will do me nicely.' The escort fighters still seem a long way above me. I am gaining fast about 400 yards now. 'Hell! ... the Hurricanes have black crosses on them – 109s; coming straight for me, head-on attack. Right, you bastards! I'll give you hell before you get me.' Sights on, I thumb the button. A stream of tracer tears over my head. 'Blast!

missed him. Now come on, number two.' He heads straight for me. I yank back on the stick, kick on rudder and turn down on to the 109. 'That shook you up, didn't it?' Sights on. Brmmmmm, brrrrrrrmmmmm. A streak of black comes from his engine, a stream of tracer flashes past my nose. 'God, I must get out of this.' Another aileron turn; 'Down, down, down. Pull out now, or you'll be in the drink.' The coast is nearly out of sight. 'Oh God, don't let them get me.' I screw round in the cockpit. Nothing is in sight. I scream along just above the water. I glance at the rev counter. I'm so deaf that I'm not at all sure that the motor is going. It looks all right. I hurtle past many patches of oil. At last the cliffs loom up. I turn westwards. Several patches of fluorescence show where pilots are in the water. Motorboats are chugging towards them. The sea is dead calm, glassy.

'I'm still alive.'

I skim past a tyre, many patches of oil. 'Poor devil! wonder what that was off?' I wonder if all the boys are ok. These damned Jerries don't press very hard. I bet they are feeling sore. Sidmouth looks lovely as I roar low over the coast.

'Whew! I could do with a bathe.'

People in the water look up and wave. I wave back and give them a thumbs up. 'Good old A! here we are at last.' I roar low over our dispersal hut. All of B flight appear to be down. Round the circuit and swiftly into land.

I bump across the 'drome into the dispersal position; then men run out to meet me.

'How many, sir?' I put two fingers up. 'And I damaged another.'

'How many of the boys are back?' – 'All but one now, sir. Sergeant Vines is still up. All of B flight are down. Every pilot seems to have got at least one.'

'That's grand. Have a good look for bullet-holes. I don't think there are any, but you never know.'

'Did you pull the tit, sir?'

'No, not this time.'

'Hullo, Ken! how are we doing?'

'Very well, sir. B flight have got six confirmed and three probables. What did you get?'

'Two 110s confirmed and a 109 damaged.'

'Damn good show, sir!'

'Hullo, Watty! How did you get on?'

'I didn't, sir. Nine 109s seemed to think that I was their pet Hurricane; they fought me for about twenty minutes till I thought my arm would fall off. I only managed to get one burst in. I definitely hit one of the bastards, though I'm damned if I know what happened to him. Anyway, eight of the bastards still chased me. Honestly, old boy, I thought they'd get me. There was a hell of a bang once; the crew have managed to find five bullet-holes in the tail plane. How did you get on, Widge?'

'Very fine to start with. I suppose you saw my flamer? It most certainly lit the sky up. Did you see the pilot bale out? God! I bet he was petrified. Planes were whistling by him. If I had baled out I should have done a delayed drop. Who the hell was surrounded by 110s just after we had attacked?'

'That was me, Widge.' Dickie said. 'I suppose it was you who butted in. Many thanks. I saw you hit somebody's glycol tank. God knows what happened to it. I got one of them – went in with a hell of a splash, then the 109s descended. I had a hell of a fight with them. They most certainly wasted a lot of ammo. For about five minutes solid tracer appeared to be just missing the windscreen. I smacked one of them in flames; after doing about a hundred steep turns, the other bastards went away.'

Robbie said, 'I've got one bullet through the wing tip that hasn't done any damage at all. I say, Widge, where do you think Vines is? Did anybody see him after we had attacked? I think he turned to meet those first 109s. I didn't see him after that. I fired my guns at heaven knows how many Jerries, but only saw one go for a burton; his wings fell off about 5,000 feet beneath me. It gave me a hell of a shock. Did you see that one that crashed on the beach? There was a hell of an explosion when it hit. It must have been a bomber. Every time I looked down there was another patch of oil. Thank God they turned back when they did, otherwise I think we should have all been swimming about the drink. My arm just about dropped off.'

'I hope Vines is ok. I'll phone Opps and see if they have got any dope on the crashes. Hullo, Opps. CO 87 here. Have you any dope on our crashes? We are still minus Sergeant Vines. Ok; give me a ring as soon as you hear anything. Opps don't now a thing. There has been a hell of a blitz all along the coast. They made a dash at London, but turned back. Already there are well over a hundred combats in Fighter Command.'

'Telephone for you, sir.' – 'Hullo, Billie. It's 213. How did you get on? Hey, I said it first. Come on, Billie, what's the dope? Ten confirmed and seven probables. Damned good! Who's missing? Two Belgians? I'm damned sorry; I hope they'll be all right. We got nine confirmed and four probables. One missing Sergeant Vines. Mostly fighters. No, you didn't get eighty-seven dive-bombers again? You lucky devils! We had the damned escort fighters to fix. See you in the bar.'

'They *are* lucky devils – they had the dive-bombers again. They have lost their two Belgians. Do you remember after the last show, when Matters asked one of them how many he attacked, he answered, "Me, I attack no one. I defence myself."'

He had shot down three. Now he was missing.

We sat around. The evening was incredibly still, the hills behind the 'drome turned purple, the sun sank. The day blitz seemed like some fantastic dream. The corn in the fields looked a glorious yellow. It was very wonderful just being alive. Watty got his models out and we chased them across the 'drome. It got cooler. We retired to our hut and put our uniforms on.

'Opps, any news of anyone? No. Hell! Well, what about getting us released?' – 'Ok. Just hang on and we'll bind group.'

'Damn good show on your boys' part today. We are all very proud of you.'

'Hullo! Group send their heartiest congrats to 87, and say you are released till 0530. Hold on a second, Widge. Who's doing the early morning readiness?'

'I regret to say A flight.'

'Ok. See you shortly. You like lager, don't you?'

'Thanks awfully; yes, please, Opps.'

We pushed off to the bar. There was the usual terrific crowd and jumbled conversation. Once more the colours of the different bottles and the healthy tan of the pilots' faces seemed to be more vivid than usual. My heart seemed free. Things gradually became happily bleary as we drank each other's health. At last the party was over. We staggered out to the car; the air smelt delicious. A bumpy ride across the 'drome and we fell into the dispersal hut, rather unsteadily clambered into bed, after carefully folding our clothes, ready to put on over our pyjamas in the morning. 'Last in bed puts the light out.' There was a hell of a scurry to put our pyjamas on. Dickie was last, as usual. So he had to blow the hurricane lamp out. Mighty curses as he bashed his legs on his camp bed as he clambered in. All was silent. Robbie was quietly puffing at a cigarette. 'Well, boys, I'm afraid that Vines has had it. I'll have to write to his people tomorrow. Thanks for a grand performance today. Happy dreams.' – 'Good night, Widge, sir. Happy dreams to you.'

The hut was silent now, except for muffled conversation from the men's section behind a thin wooden partition. I turned on my side and shut my eyes. Once again death had been very near to me. 'Pray God that they don't come tomorrow; that would be too much. I must buy a sleeping bag.' Before I slept, pictures of my sailing boat floated before my eyes. I saw Pam laughing as I got a wave over me as we launched her. I fell asleep.

26 Gordon Batt Part 2, Hurricane Pilot, Sergeant Officer, British, 238 Squadron

Gordon's second extract essentially covers 13 August to early September. During this time 238 Squadron operated from RAF Middle Wallop and its satellite airfield RAF Chilbolton, and had a rest period in Cornwall at RAF St Eval. 'Leo the Lion' mentioned toward the end of the extract is Sergeant Leslie Pidd, who was shot down and killed on 15 September. This is a rare view of the Battle from a sergeant pilot's point of view. It is notable that almost all the fellow pilots he mentions are also sergeants, showing just how little officers and sergeants mixed. Gordon survived the war and died in 2004.

13 August 1940 It was on another enemy intrusion that we had rather a shock. We were the first squadron to be scrambled to deal with one of these comparatively small attacks. As we climbed up towards Portsmouth, the number of enemy aircraft increased from the original of twenty to thirty to seventy to eighty, then a hundred plus, other squadrons were being despatched to help.

By the time we were in sight of the enemy, the number had grown to a four hundred-plus raid. Obviously we could not see all this number, all we could see was the vanguard of fighters, a mixed bag of Me 109s and 110s at various heights. The bombers were still only halfway across the channel.

The controller said, 'Split into two flights and attack.' We were into a mass of fighter aircraft. We were attacked first by Me 109s from above, that cut me off from the rest of the flight, then I saw a gaggle of Me 110s below and started to turn and dive to attack.

Then it felt as if a steam roller had hit me. The aircraft bucked and jumped out of my control, I can't even remember if there was a bang, I think there must have been. I went through the cockpit drill to evacuate, there was no smell of fire, but when I tried to look round and about I could not see. I realised that my eyes were shut. It's the instinctive action you take in emergency, so I prised my eyelids open, they were gummed shut with oil.

There was no one on my tail, but I was streaming engine coolant, and there in front of me was a mass of oil hanging onto the windscreen in a cone towards me, and the end was being flipped out of the cockpit in the slip stream. I was going down near vertical, and it was getting blasted cold with the hood open, so I levelled off, turned north, we had been out to sea a little, and shut the hood. That gallon of oil immediately landed in my lap, being no longer supported by the various wind pressures.

I glided north and eventually broke cloud at about two thousand feet, thank God I was over land. Selsey Bill in fact, it's a bit that sticks out to the east of the Isle of Wight. There was not a field bigger than a postage stamp, so I elected to land in a field near to a farmhouse, so that if I did get into difficulties the farmer would come to my aid.

Actually I landed with wheels up in a field of barley, made a nasty groove in the farmer's crop. Landing a Hurricane with wheels up is an experience on its own. The big air scoop underneath digs in and rocks you forward, then releases as other forces take over, then there are repeat performances. I thought I was going to knock my brains out on the reflector sight, every time my head was shaken forward. Eventually it came to a stop, I rapidly released my safety straps and parachute harness, heaved myself out of the cockpit and ran along the wing, fell apex aver base off the end into the dusty barley and dry earth, and retired to a safe distance.

The oil that had dropped into my lap when I closed the cockpit hood made the perfect absorbent for the dust and dirt of the barley field. The Home Guard men who came charging across the field with rifles held above their heads (so that they could run), frightened me a little, I thought they may have difficulty recognising my uniform as now it was a mixture of blue and brown. To be safe, as they got near, I put my hands up.

I cannot remember much of the next half hour or so, what I do know is that they were quite nice, and delivered me to Tangmere, which was the nearest RAF base. I was indeed a sorry sight, so after being checked by the guard, I made my way to the control tower, got them to phone Warmwell to report the reason for my absence from duty. They said, sit tight we will get you picked up and taken back to Middle Wallop. So having previous knowledge of the place I made my way to the sergeants' mess, there was no one about, it really did astound me. I thought, here is me, been fighting (well I would have been given another thirty seconds), shot down, collected and brought here, and these blighters are still in bed, don't they know there's a war on?

I cleaned myself up as best I could with the aid of much toilet paper, scrounged myself breakfast, and made my way back to the control tower to wait for my transport. On the way the station warrant officer saw me, 'Sergeant, where is your hat.' I do not remember exactly what I said, but it was not polite, and I doubt if any other sergeant pilot has seen a station warrant officer with his mouth open and speechless. I made haste to the control tower, and kept a very low profile. In due course I did tell my own CO of the incident, just to cover myself; it raised a smile.

Eventually I was collected by one of our spare pilots, and taken back to Middle

Wallop. I did not fly again that day. The strange thing is that on the day I was shot down there is no entry in my log book, the reason is that as soon as an aircraft has crashed, the '700', (that's the aircraft maintenance document) is confiscated. So my friendly erk had no reference. I only learnt of this when one of these Battle of Britain buffs, wrote and asked me the number of the aircraft I was flying when I was shot down, and quoted the date.

The one thing that really upset me was that only the day before, my rigger had fitted a rear view mirror for me that I had purchased from Halfords on my last leave. Eventually they were fitted as standard, saves you breaking your neck looking at things directly behind. It was great fun in the weaving section, to report fighters above, then watch them come diving to our rear, switch to the mirror, throttle back in the meantime, then at the correct time do a steep turn, then watch them dive by to an empty piece of sky and lose the height advantage.

During this phase, the Germans thought up another diversionary scheme, they just could not understand why, when they attacked there were always fighters there to meet them, in small numbers maybe, but there. This was of course our radar stations, and the super degree of detection this gave us. There is no doubt whatsoever in my mind, this was the one thing that saved us.

There is a lot of bull written about our gallant fighter pilots, a fat lot of good we would have been without radar. We would have been thrashing around the sky virtually blind. I really do not know who was responsible for the design and development of it, plus the implementation. Whoever it was, GOD BLESS THEM.

To return to my original theme, diversionary intrusions, these were intended to get fighters in the air, then follow up with bomber/fighter formations while our defending fighters were on the ground, refuelling and rearming. Now I laugh every time I recall this event, it must have been one of the daftest things the Germans ever cooked up, and must have been a first sign of their frustration. A flight of us were scrambled (that is six aircraft) to deal with about twenty intruders. When we arrived at the scene there were these fifteen to twenty Me 110s flying round in a circle, nose to tail. I could not believe my eyes. They were not going anywhere, there was not any top cover so we set about them. I climbed a couple of thousand feet above them, and did a vertical attack, pulled into the centre of the circle and with full throttle climbed up and repeated the operation. It was at this point that a funny thing occurred. One of our pilots took his mask off, put his finger in his mouth, and made a noise like a red indian attacking a waggon train.

Then one of our pilots came up from below and knocked one of the formation circle out. Quite dangerous I thought, but effective. That broke the circle, and there was a right shambles. The Me 110s fled in complete disarray, we, unfortunately were not fast enough to take advantage. In my vertical attacks I know I must have been putting holes in several aircraft, but not one of the damn things blew up.

I never saw another defensive circle, the instigator was most likely the first on the list for the Russian front. It was Pilot Officer Aubrey Covington who shot down the Me 110 and broke the circle. He did not stop to think how vulnerable he was in the process, and it is obvious that the Germans had not thought through the whole process of this defensive circle, otherwise they would not have embarked on such a hair brain project.

During this period it is with regret that I have to mention that we lost some damn nice blokes. The first thing that shocked me was the loss of our Australian flight commander the other Aussie flight commander. They were over here on that lend system that operated in those days. They obviously volunteered to stay and fight. Then Sergeant Henry Marsh. He was a regular who had worked his way through the ranks at his trade, and was one of the nucleus of 238 Squadron. I was not on the mission when he went missing.

Here it is appropriate to mention that 238 Squadron was formed with a squadron leader, two flight lieutenants, two flying officers and I think two pilot officers and one sergeant pilot. Plus, of course, all the ground staff. The remainder of the pilots were straight from training, and mainly from the VR (Volunteer Reserve). Now it is this VR content that was so important to the first, and second phase of the Battle. Plus the fact that through the second phase, we had Poles, Czechs, Free French, and one New Zealander, and of course, the complete mixture of the UK – Welsh, Scots, Irish (both sorts), and I think there were some other English pilots beside myself.

We lost pilots, and of course aircraft, in a devastating way. Yes, I do wonder why I was spared, it is just fate. After the loss of Henry Marsh, I took over Yellow section. I must confess however, I made no more friends on the squadron. You do get to a point where you do not wish to be hurt anymore. I just did my job, to the best of my ability, had jovial off duty parties, but no friends, no more than that. I do not even know the names of many of the people I flew with, and were killed, I just blotted that out of my mind. I just concentrated hard on doing my job, and staying alive.

Leading the weaving section was a job and a half. I think the CO appreciated my efforts. I certainly took it very seriously. One day I did miss some Me 109s until the last seconds, it was too late to say 'Bandits six o'clock', I just shouted 'Look out', the damn things went past me with virtually feet to spare. As I came out of my steep turn, the rest of the squadron had vanished into thin air. We reformed a few thousand feet lower, but when we landed the CO said to me, 'Don't ever do that again, you frightened the life out of me'. That's gratitude for you, at least I saved them from being shot at.

Some days, which were few in 1940, we did have low cloud cover. Then the bombers would raid on their own, they would stay in this low cloud most of the time, then pop out, take a quick look, then back in, very crafty. On one such day, with luck on their side they bombed Middle Wallop. They made quite a mess of one hanger, I do not know why I was on the ground that day, but when the air raid siren went, my first reaction was to get into the air. I was at the flight hut, so I grabbed my parachute and ran to a Hurricane, unfortunately the station CO arrived at the same time so I had to stand aside. There were no shelters at the dispersal site so I ran to the main buildings, and dived into a shelter as the bombs started falling. The ground shook, we were only about a hundred yards from where they landed. I came to the conclusion that the safest place in an air raid was in the air.

This same pattern of activities continued, we either operated out of Middle Wallop, or Warmwell, until the 14 August. That morning when what was left of us reported to the flight hut at dawn, I think there were five of us, with three aircraft serviceable. We were withdrawn from active duties, and moved to St Eval in Cornwall to reform. This turned out to be another traumatic episode in my life.

We arrived, found our billets, dumped our kit. By this time it was getting near dusk, I was ordered to lay a flare path as there was no one else who was capable. This was the old fashioned stuff, goose necked flares, but fortunately, with a 'chance light' (flood light). I had located this, and instructed the erks to pace out and place the flares while I went to the control tower to obtain the colour of the day, this I have explained previously (identification).

There was no one in the control tower, the officer of the day was down the shelter because there was an air raid on, three Gladiators had taken off to try and protect the base. At my insistence he ventured out, opened the safe, and gave me the information I wanted.

As I ran back across the airfield to the unlit chance light (as were the flares), the place was bombed, they were of the screaming variety, not very large but quite frightening. I went flat on the grass and as the eighth one landed the seventh one showered me with earth. I felt all over myself, there was no blood, so I made my way to the chance light. In the meantime the raiders had departed, they had however also dropped incendiary bombs, they were in the bomb storage area, and amongst the aircraft. I went into a shelter and ordered all personnel out to help. They were a little reluctant until I started to unbuckle my 38.

Outside again on the aircraft park, there was an erk standing on the wing of a Harvard stamping an incendiary bomb through the wing. I shouted to him to get off, as I knew where the petrol tanks were. Anyway the damn thing went straight through onto the ground as I shouted and he kicked it away.

The next morning I made a verbal report regarding this erk, praising his devotion to duty, whilst others hid in the shelter. There is no doubt he was brave and thoughtful in what he did, I doubt if he knew that there was a petrol tank so close.

The Gladiators landed safely, and this sergeant pilot who was frightened out of his wits the night before, ate a hearty breakfast. I have no idea where I slept that night, I was just exhausted. It was strange to see the hanger next morning, it was one of those cheap structures, a lightweight job with asbestos tiles on the roof, they had all been blown off, but the roof trusses were all still intact.

During the day replacement aircraft were delivered, and also replacement pilots arrived. I was allocated a great big Humber Snipe estate wagon, and we were billeted out at a nearby beach bungalow. I had a contingent of five sergeant pilots, Eric Bann was with us, having flown direct from Warmwell. There were only sleeping arrangements in the bungalow, unfortunately the beach was all barbed wire and metal stakes so we just had to dream of what might have been.

We were not at St Eval long, my log book indicates that we were there only two or three weeks. You will appreciate that my log book was not one of my major priorities, in fact it was rather a wasteful time consumer. Obviously with these new arrivals, we had to practice. Some were very green, others were green, a few more experienced than our few months. There were various operational patrols, but the activity was on a small scale as compared to the Portsmouth and Southampton area.

They were hit and run efforts mainly, I would think just sea training sorties, mainly by Ju 88s. Some of our patrols made contact, I didn't. The nearest I came was when I was on the circuit, about to land and I saw flashes over Falmouth about fifteen miles away. It was dusk of course, so I informed the controller, he said get over there and I will tell them you are on your way. I think I arrived before the message got through, the clots started shooting at me. I screamed at the controller, and got out of range as soon as I could, one thousand to one it was the Navy again. Those tracer shells were very close, and I do not know what mixture they used, all I do know is that it was a most unpleasant experience.

It was here that we were getting to know our Poles and Czechs, they were most experienced pilots, Sergeant Pilots Marian Domagala (Polish), Josef Jeka (Polish) and Jiri Kucera (Czechoslovakian), the former was an instructor at the Polish central flying school. He flew with me in Yellow section many times, and that is most likely the reason that I am able to write this now, his ability was way above the norm.

The only reason that I led Yellow section was that I could speak English, not because I was the most proficient pilot. Domagala and Kucera, the Czech, were older than myself by at least six or seven years. They were just damn good, sound pilots that years of experience of weather and all the other things that multi-flying hours give. I must include Jeka the young Pole. Six feet tall, blonde, damn good looking, excellent pilot but not in the high category that I place the previous two, his main difficulty was fending off advances of the females. Unfortunately he was shot down and killed later.

We returned to Middle Wallop early September and I think it was about now that WAAFs started to arrive in great numbers. At this point may I congratulate the recruiting staff, in general, at enticing such intelligent good looking young females into the Service. Mark you, it gave some pilots sleepless nights. It was quite easy to drop back into the old routine, but by now the formations were increasing in size. The bomber formations were about fifty to sixty in one oblong block, flying in close formation, they were covered by Me 110s, then above them were the Me 109s.

Also at this time, to counter these large formations, we increased our gang. If necessary we could muster two squadrons of Hurricanes, and two squadrons of Spitfires or scale it down to one and one, dependent upon the scale of the raid. Our CO was the senior Hurricane commander, so we led. He would manoeuvre into position, having been given the height and of course the location of the main force by the controller, we would get ourselves about two thousand feet above the bombers, directly in front of them. The CO would give the order to attack, we would dive quite steeply on to the bombers, it was possible to squirt along a whole line. The snag was that as we started to dive, the Me 110s would dive at us and try and cut us off, to my knowledge they never stopped us, but of course there was another squadron behind us. The Spitfires would come down to protect, and the Me 109s would come after them.

It only took seconds to dive into the attack, I can assure you it was like an age. From this near vertical attack it was virtually impossible to miss such a close formation, I must have put hundreds of holes into the damn things, it was of course impossible to know what you had achieved, except coming off the end of the formation in one piece. The shambles that was at the end of this first squirt was unbelievable, there were fighter aircraft all over the place. It was near impossible to hold the section together under these circumstances, it was usually every man for himself, sometimes it was possible to have another crack at the bombers, it depended mainly on what devastation we had caused on the first attack. There is one thing for certain, the Hurricanes stayed in the fight, we were the slowest aircraft in the pack, you just had to stay and fight.

In all these encounters, I think I have mentioned this previously, we were always outnumbered four or five to one, we had plenty of targets, although it was not wise to dwell on the target in case someone got on your tail. There are two incidents which stick in my mind. In one of these episodes with aircraft all over the place, I saw an Me 109 going straight down at a hell of a speed, then suddenly the wings came off, and they appeared to go upwards. Now that is of course impossible, it was just the acceleration of the main body which obviously caused this optical illusion. I thought to myself, if the poor sod has not jumped out he will have a nice neat burial in the floor of the Channel. That went through my mind in a flash, and looked down my back smartly.

The other one was when we caught some bombers returning home after a raid on Bristol. They had outsmarted our radar this time, they had dropped their bombs, and were still in a block formation heading south without top cover. We were closing in to do our head-on attack, a Spitfire appeared like a bolt out of the blue, diving onto the bombers. He must have misjudged things very badly, he hit about the third aircraft in the centre of the formation, there was a flash, a ball of black smoke and one solitary open parachute emerged with no one on the end, that was all. The bombers were knocked about no end.

It was in one of these free for alls that I saw an Me 109 on the tail of a Hurricane. I gave him a burst as I pulled through him in my sights, then let him fly through the reverse. I saw the pilot look up at me, by now I was right on his tail and we were climbing. He rolled over onto his back, so I followed suit expecting him to roll out or do a half loop, he did not appear, so I rolled the right way up again and there he was, still inverted, still climbing. That was very crafty. I must explain that the Me 109s were petrol injected, they could fly just as well inverted as the right way up without losing power, whilst our aircraft had no power when inverted. I was really mad, I had the sod cold and failed. The only consolation I had was that I must have put holes in him to make him look up after the first couple of squirts.

It was about this time we were moved out of Middle Wallop to a place called Chilbolton, having been bombed at the former. This was about five fields knocked into one, we were all billeted out in the village, and Nissen huts formed our HQ. This was a completely different way of life, Sergeants Domagala, Kucera and myself were billeted with a Mr and Mrs Payne at the top of Station Road, only a stones throw from the perimeter of the airfield. They had a daughter who was engaged to I think, a bloke in the Army, and Tony the son who was in his teens. Mr Payne was a signal man on the local railway.

We had three single beds in the attic, the toilet arrangements were a little Heath Robinson, but being young and active we just made the best of things. The food was plain and well cooked, Mrs P had our rations to work on, plus a supplement from the quite extensive garden. We were very quickly under her control, and part of her brood, well what do you say to a lady who stood all of five foot two, yes, five foot two. This is also where Domagala learnt to say, at my insistence 'Please pass the salt' instead of reaching across in front of me. He reminded me of this at a recent reunion (1987). His English was limited and we had fun improving it.

This was of course a major jolt for the family we were living with, but indeed for the whole village, the main beneficiary must have been the landlord of the local pub. They all welcomed us without reservation, in spite of the noise we created with our aircraft, and of course we did have birthday parties! Actually, the pilots normally drank very little, the main reason being that if you are on duty until about 10 p.m. and have to be on parade at dawn, there is only time for a quick couple of shandies before closing time.

We were of course still involved with patrols and the group formations against the bigger raids, if you have been in one you have seen the lot, it was terrifying, but time blots out the nasty things of war, and one remembers some of the funnies, even though death was just around the corner. Pilot Officer Brian Considine was shot down, his aircraft was spinning, and he was unable to recover, part of his tail plane must have been damaged. He baled out on the inside of the spin, if you go the other way the tail plane could hit you. He said 'I fell clear, and was doing somersaults, and every time I looked up the aircraft was just above me. I knew I was about fifteen thousand feet when I jumped, so there was no hurry, and the aircraft was still just above me. Then I went into cloud, and thought the bloody thing can't see me now, so I pulled the rip cord. The jolt of the parachute opening caused my flying boots to come off, and it wasn't half bloody cold floating down to earth.'

August was a rough month, it was all go, there is no doubt that we were stretched to our very limits, nearly every day we were on readiness. It was about this time that the CO put me up for a commission. I was interviewed by the group captain at Middle Wallop who pushed it forward. When the answer came back that they had commissioned the present quota from training schools, sir was very mad. He sent for me, said how sorry he was, and the only thing he could do under the circumstances was to offer me a weeks leave. Now, fate had played another part in my survival. This was the real blitz week, including 15 September. Actually I phoned in and asked if they wanted me back, but the answer was in the negative. When I did return there were four or five new faces in the Nissen hut, makes you feel quite queer. There were others missing, plus my aircraft with my bat flying through a moon on it, lost without trace, along with little Leo the Lion as he was known, I do not even know his surname. War is cruel, but when you're in it you have to maintain your sanity, and blot things out of your mind.

Towards the end of August and through September we were sometimes called to the London area. The controller would get us onto the western outskirts, and give us a running commentary on what was going on. We could hear him directing squadrons onto formations, while we patrolled up and down the outskirts. Then he would say 'Red leader, vector so and so', the CO would comply, then the controller would come in again, 'Twenty five bandits angels twenty, heading straight for you, they are all yours'. It really was slick control.

We could see them coming, with the ack ack just underneath them, in black bursts, the CO would shout 'Tally ho', the ack ack would cease, and in we went. Sometimes we would go over to the London area, and patrol up and down and not get involved, although we could see ack ack and condensation trails of the Spits and 109s over London. The boys of Eleven Group were obviously holding the situation and we were held in reserve.

We did of course still have the activity over the Portsmouth and Southampton area, and we had our wing of four squadrons well organised by now. One day the CO's radio went on the blink, so he asked Blue leader to take over, that failed, so did Green leader, as a last resort he asked me. We changed places, it was absolutely wonderful, all those aircraft behind me. The controller gave me the usual instructions, thank God I did it right and we attacked. I have often thought what the other three squadron leaders would have thought if they had known they were being led by a sergeant pilot. They never knew.

27 Esther Terry Wright, wife of David Walter Hunt, Hurricane Pilot, Pilot Officer, British, 257 Squadron

Extract from a memoir written by the wife of a Battle of Britain pilot, Esther Hunt (née Wright), published in 1942 as *Pilot's Wife's Tale: The Diary of a Camp Follower*. It was also adapted and broadcast as a radio play staring Hugh Burden and Wendy Hiller in 1943. Pseudonyms are used throughout the book, including for the author herself, 'Mrs Lachasse', her husband, 'David Walter Lachasse', and fellow RAF pilots and aerodromes. The memoir extract covers mid-August to 5 September 1940 and the various RAF bases 257 Squadron was based at during this time are noted at the beginning of each chapter. Esther's husband's real name was David Hunt. Hunt was born in Chapel Ash, Wolverhampton in 1919, joined the RAF in August 1939 and joined 257 Squadron on 20 May 1940 when it was newly forming at RAF Hendon, North London (11 Group).

Wright describes two kills made by her husband, a Ju 88 and an Me 110. In the official record the Ju 88 was in fact a Ju 87 awarded as 'probably destroyed' on 18 August 1940 and the Me 110 was awarded as 'damaged' on 31 August 1940. Quite who is right is open to interpretation; some squadron intelligence officers (whose job it was to report to group HQ the results of combat sorties) were very strict, others lax in enforcing the definition of scoring an enemy 'kill'.

David Hunt was shot down at about 10.30 a.m. on Tuesday 3 September 1940 by an Me 110 over Chelmsford. In the same action, 257 were joined by Hurricanes from 1, 17, 46, 249 and 310 squadrons, and Spitfires from 19 Squadron. 19 Squadron had to withdraw after their newly equipped cannon-firing Spitfires suffered stoppages. Hunt was badly burned and treated by Archibald McIndoe at the Queen Victoria Hospital at East Grinstead in Sussex and became a member of the Guinea Pig Club.

With the help of Esther and David's son, Charles Hunt (who has been kind enough to give permission for this extract), I have been able to work out the real names of most of the people mentioned by pseudonyms. 'T' is Gerald Maffett, who baled out too late and was killed on 31 August 1940; 'B' is Camille Robespierre

Bonseigneur (Canadian), shot down and killed in the same sortie in which Hunt was shot down on 3 September 1940. 'F' is Charles Frizell (Canadian) and 'NR' is Herman Taylor.

The reputation of 'Squadron Leader D' is contentious. From formation of the squadron in May 1940 to 21 July 1940, 257's squadron leader had been David Bayne. From 22 July 1940 it was Hill Harkness. 'Squadron Leader D' is Hill Harkness. After Hunt was shot down, 257 Squadron took a bit of a hammering, losing further experienced pilots. Fighter aces Peter Brothers and Bob Stanford Tuck were brought in on 9 September. After flying a couple of sorties with Squadron Leader Harkness, Brothers and Tuck came to the conclusion that he was actively avoiding combat. After a couple of stiff drinks, Brothers and Tuck rang Keith Park (11 Group Commander) and explained their concerns. Harkness was posted away to a flight training school on 12 September and Tuck was made squadron leader.

'S' is 257 Squadron's intelligence officer, Geoffrey Myers. Myers would go on to release his contemporaneous letters to his family to author John Willis, who published them as part of his book *Churchill's Few: The Battle of Britain Remembered* in 1985. In the letters Myers detailed how 257 Squadron had fared in the Battle and the shortcomings of the squadron leader, which exacerbated their poor luck. However, Hill Harkness was not named but referred to as 'Squadron Leader Sharp' (there is no such person who fought in the Battle). This was probably because the author was unsure whether Harkness was still alive, and/or unwilling to condemn a man for perhaps just not being up to the job to which he had been appointed. It was in an interview with historian Patrick Bishop (in about 2001 for his book *Fighter Boys*) that Peter Brothers was able to finally release this information.

Chapter 9 (c. 15 August 1940, RAF Debden, Essex, 11 Group) We had breakfast next morning in the farmhouse across the road from the aerodrome: bacon and eggs and plenty of tea, and farm things went on outside the window of the low and antique room; and when David had gone to work, I started out to find a home for us. The farm was short-handed, and they would not take me while the harvest was coming in. I left the old room and the lovely furniture and prints with a sad heart, for I had already decided to live here where David could be with me, and I started out along the hot white road. By the afternoon I had knocked at the door of every house in the little village. Some people had tried to cheer me by saying that they had no running water anyway, or that their little cottage bedrooms inter-communicated; all of them said that I should find nothing unless I went back to the town four miles away. I knew I should never see David if I lived there, and so I went on, and soon I was trailing up a hard white cart track, and there were men bringing in the bleached harvest, and a showplace at the end of it all, with terrifying tester beds, and drunken floors and candlesticks. I could have a distempered bedroom and breakfast for three-and-a-half guineas a week. Out of my weekly guinea and David's fourteen-and-six a day. It was miles too far for him to tramp after a day's work, and too frightening for me if I should have to visit him instead and come back at night; but there was nothing else at all, and I took a bed provisionally and went on. The young woman at the showhouse had had rather a lot to say about a brother of hers: who would be in soon, who was surely arriving at this moment, whom I should certainly see if I came back at night. I met him later on, down in the village. Some hours had passed and

I was still tramping on because I was wound up. There was nowhere else to try, but there was nowhere to sit down, and so I went on walking. And then the car pulled up, and I was taken in. I made my moan, and I learned then that I was with the showplace brother, and that he was slightly drunk; and that he had a wife somewhere who had gone off with a fellow with more money.

Now, whether it was thinking of the wife, or whether it was just the drink taken, he seemed to take my plight to heart; and when we had called at one or two out of the way houses where he had friends who would but could not take me in, we drove back to the farm we had left in the morning and settled like polite visitors in the sitting room. And, after all, they let me stay; and there we lived, David and I together, in a friendly room with candles.

The alarm would go off at dawn, and we would creep down in the magic, early light, he going out quietly into the soft morning, I back to the bed that had cooled in our absence. I spent all the days alone, reading in the grass down by the pond where the cows were, or going aimlessly round the wonderful, scorched country on an ancient bicycle without brakes, keeping to myself and eating in the airmen's cafe, beans on toast and watery coffee, rather than make work at the farm. And David would come home most nights, bending down in the very low doorway of our room, a candle in his hand, worn out and waiting for his boots to be taken off; and soon the alarm would go off again.

This was a real aerodrome, where things happened. There were priority signals the farm knew about, and there were times in the dugout, where we carried our tea one afternoon in a hurry: and the son, being a Home Guard while the emergency lasted, and then coming in for tea. And one grey and ominous Sunday, when a great deal had been happening, David came home to say that he had shot down a Junkers 88. Geoffrey wrote from his bomber station:

> It was grand seeing David th'other day. Fine show getting the Junkers – what sort was it? Will you tell him I'm very sorry; but briefing for the night's raids was going on when he shot this place up, and the GC, being unable to hear himself speak, sent somebody out to take the Hurricane's number, which I fear he did; but I doubt it will lead to anything.

And David had promised him only a married man's shoot up! We thought perhaps the Junkers might cancel it out, and certainly we heard no more of the affair.

Chapter 10 David threw down his Mae West and his anti-gas things and his flying-boots on the bedroom floor. It looked like leave. I would not ask. Soon he said that he was released until further notice. He went to sleep. Early in the morning I heard unintelligible voices over the Tannoy across the road. I watched David sleeping after dawn with great satisfaction. When we had had breakfast, he went over the road to see if anything was going on. He did not come back, and later in the morning I borrowed a bicycle and rode up the hill through the aerodrome, and found that his plane had gone. There was a car at the farm gates when I got back, and a pale-faced man with protruding eyes got out and asked if I was Mrs Lachasse. I supposed that David had been shot down and I should hear about it. He had not. He had merely wandered in at half-past ten, when he should have been on readiness all night; and everyone was against him. (The adjutant did not mention that the whole squadron had made the same mistake, that everyone was missing. It was just David spoiling the war.) We both had plenty to say, the Adjutant turning on me for my husband, I leaning on the bicycle defending him, feeling a fool, secretly glad that he had had a sleep at last in spite of everyone. The adjutant prepared to leave, then stopped to say that David had gone away for a few days. No, I should not be able to follow him. No, I might not ring him up; no one liked that. All this had to it the cruel effect of an unjust school imposition; and it was just as unanswerable. I gave the adjutant a few of David's things to take with him, and when he had gone I packed the rest of our cases and had them put in the cellar. I should take nothing with me but a toothbrush and some pants. I was going to mother. There were no buses running to the town at all. I sent off some wires, and hung about waiting for something to happen. A bull terrier bitch at the wooden café took one look at me, laid back its ears and calculatedly bit my thigh. And so the alarmed owner produced a car and drove me into the town, took me to a doctor, and put me down at the station. And so I caught my train in town.

Chapter 11 (The Move to RAF Martlesham Heath, Suffolk, 11 Group) We lived quietly together, mother and I, while David toiled through his outlandish life, from 330 every morning until 1130 at night. There were terrible telephone conversations to and fro, when neither of us heard a word; or I would gather only that he was out of socks; and buying those and sending them off would make something to do.

There were sirens at night, we putting on coats and talking low on the stairs, getting down to the hotel cellars as a matter of course. And there were actually bombs on London.

There was a little Polish girl with dead white hair, whom I mistook for a little old lady, coming upon her one night at the foot of the stairs, standing by herself saying: 'Afraid, afraid.' We took her in hand. There was a terse little father, spitting out that we were all like rats underground, and taking a party upstairs for bridge at four in the morning.

And then there was a message from the admirable S, the intelligence officer whose wife was in France with their baby. S said it would be quite in order for me to come over and join David. It seemed a bold undertaking, with the area banned and things beginning to happen at last. Mother saw me off next morning, with a hurriedly-bought collection of washing-things and talcum powder and chocolate to see me through the adventure we both thought it was. And after all, I just walked off the station into the banned area, and by evening I had found and taken a room in a little box of a house facing the aerodrome.

It was a sandy place, with tall firs everywhere. Through the trees I could see some of the squadron's planes, and ground staff working on them. I had spoken to David and arranged to meet him in the little café on the hill when his evening work was over; and so when the café closed and still he did not come I sat in the owner's sitting room and read her magazines. She obviously thought it odd, but I had come to see David. She told me an amusing story of how she had heard bells one night, and had hurried with her dog to the shelter and sat trembling in her gas mask, watching the little dog suffocate. And, after all, it had been a gun signal, and so they both lived.

I told her how the Germans had dared to single out our brother Geoffrey and the flare path he was laying for a bombing attack, and how he had had to throw himself in a bed of nettles to save himself. This animosity towards him had shaken us all, Geoffrey no more than the rest of us. We were indignant.

David was very late. He told me afterwards how he had set out at dusk to get back for me, and got lost in the dark and missed the aerodrome; and how surprised they had all been ever to see him again. But now we walked down the hill with not much to say. He had already written about the squadron leader forbidding him to leave the camp once they were back at N. I had wished things on him in advance, but we took it that this depressing rule did not apply yet: there would be no official ruling, we supposed, with everyone working from dawn to near midnight so that mass desertion was unlikely; and so we went by our own rules. It was a delightful and terrifying life. David would spend his last energy in coming over to the house, washing perfunctorily in cold water, and falling into bed. We had no alarm clock. I would get into bed too, and with David already asleep, prop myself upright against the wooden rails of the bed and watch the dark, and the searchlights away over the aerodrome. There was his breathing, an occasional plane engine roaring, when the plane itself might soar like a ghost across the window. There might be a bomb or two away in the distance. Time barely moved; certainly it was not to be measured. I had a supply of matches and cigarettes, and David's watch. Somehow it would be half-past three. I would rouse him, which is an overstatement, and dress him where he lay, and put him out into the night that was still secret and full of stars. Some mornings a lorry would grind to a stop, and I would go to the windows and mutter to the shadow of a driver that David was nearly ready; but usually he went on foot, the cigarette that we had lighted to awaken him to his responsibilities hanging at arm's length, bright in the blue darkness, and he lurching in his sleep. Always there was about that time something of the tense excitement of a child's Christmas. I would lie in bed, feeling the cold now, and by and by the engines would begin.

Chapter 12 (26 August 1940, RAF Martlesham Heath) David's birthday party was the first we had given together. He was visibly anxious for it to be a success, and his collar had come off its back stud. I sat on the table looking on, while he ordered drinks and was such a good host to his guests that he forgot all the time to include me in the rounds; so that most of the time some of us were sharing tankards.

There was an undercurrent of illegality to this party: it was like a midnight feast. There was a priority warning on outside that did not apply to us since the squadron was released: whistles sharply blown, and men running to and fro in the dark, outside the ladies' room window. Most of the lights in the little room were out of commission after a raid before our time. There were bird prints on the walls and the few lights shining fanshaped on the cracked ceiling. We were all very quiet: even the barman put down the brown tankards without a sound. We sat and watched the candles burning down on David's cake, until they set the paper frill on fire; and even then not many people helped. We talked about pubs. Between the ten of us we had been to a good few; and David told how in his home town people would take out licences, turn about, and drink their beer home-brewed, in each other's houses. Good, desultory talk it was, and the beer was good too. Even now I knew only three of the party by name. David would say: 'This is my wife,' and there we would be. A long, long time after, at a party in another mess, he came to me with pride bearing an officer with him, and said: 'This is Flying Officer Russell. My wife.' I was pleased that he had remembered at last. But he had made a mistake, and it was not Flying Officer Russell, but a complete stranger. And no one told me that my youthful neighbour was that same Squadron Leader D who had tried to wreck our married life by keeping David in like a child; and so we had plenty to say, and I was charmed, and it was only when we were driving home that David told me where I had expended my own charm. I was treated with uncommon respect. I was the one woman in the room, and most of the squadron had never seen the ladies' room before. They lived austerely now. Most wonderful of all, there was no shop talked, that I can remember. Here was T who had drunk a quart of beer in eight-and-a-half seconds: an interestingly ugly fellow with an Irishman's charm of manner. Would he please repeat his performance for me? He looked bashful; but in the end, out of kindness, he agreed. He looked into the tankard with disgust while he waited for the signal to begin. We watched him. He drank his quart in eleven seconds and went to the bathroom next door. No one thought to shut the door, and when T came back he apologised to me. I was not used to such politeness. Someone had poured a little beer into the tankard, and told T he had not finished.

T was killed five days later. He baled out too late, and came down on the bank of a river.

The party soon broke up. There was work again at dawn, and everyone was falling silent. We wrapped up the remains of the cake in brown paper and took it home in a car we picked up outside. There were a few bomb craters in the drive. Everything was very quiet. David had borrowed an alarm clock, so that I too should be able to sleep tonight.

There were eight pilots at the party, and S, the intelligence officer; and a Canadian pilot came over three nights after it for cake, a little drunk, sitting very straight and serious on the edge of a chair in my room. After three weeks, not one was left in commission. David and I made a list. It was too complete to be shocking. It was perfect in its completeness.

Chapter 13 (Return to RAF Debden, Essex, 11 Group) Quite a lot happened that week. There was the day we moved back to our old station. I saw David and the others fly away late in the morning, and I packed my things in a hurry and followed after him on earth. I always had a great fear of being left behind, like a child. That day there were air battles over the very train. We were a cheerful party, mostly of officers going on leave from the sea. A woman who had been bombed a lot said: 'They're coming for the train,' and it seemed feasible and added to the excitement as we crowded to the windows, watching. In a train you are very much exposed. A fighter and a German bomber were chasing each other in and out of a cloud. You saw them alternately, like the figures in a weather house. There was a bright and beautiful formation of German bombers, and neat explosions below them in the hot sky. We ducked for a Spitfire. The bombed woman said: 'It's racing the train!' Some of us laughed. It was all very cheerful and unreal.

As we got nearer London, the train slowed down. People on the little stations were looking up, in tin hats. We kept getting up and sitting down again. We were still excited. There was a warning on when we got to town. Mother was to have met me between trains, but she had been in the Croydon raids, and I knew she would be below ground somewhere. I rang her hotel, and heard that she had gone away that day. I could not understand that, but I had to catch my train. As it was drawing out, the all clear sounded. I imagined mother coming up from below in a hurry. It is a terrible thing that you cannot chase two people at once, with an air raid on. It is like a nightmare where you cannot round up your family. I had to get to David, and so I lost mother.

Chapter 14 I felt that I had achieved something that night when I got back to S. I had braved the hazards alone, while David went over comfortably by plane.

There were no buses going out to the aerodrome until about ten o'clock, and so when I had left a message for David in the mess, I went to a little pub for a drink. A woman was playing a fearful medley on a ringing piano: there were two chords for the bass, and they served for every tune. I wished David had been there to hear it. I rang up two or three times, to see if he had arrived. Mostly telephone stewards have very strong imaginations: they will tell you in all sincerity and sorrow that your husband has just this minute gone over to nights, when he is sitting eating lobster not ten yards away; or that there is no one of that name on the station (and then you wonder who you are). Once they told me that David had been posted to a station on the coast, and had gone (without saying a word to me) where I should not be allowed to follow. He came home for tea with S an hour later, and found me shaken by his desertion. And so if there was any reason for it, I would ring fairly often, and by and by they would give in and bring him to the telephone. In defence of stewards: I once heard this conversation, when the lines were crossed, on the morning after a dance.

'Is Pilot Officer Smith there, or Flying Officer Jones?'

It was a young woman, and her voice was rather common.

(Tramping of feet on the parquet.)

'I'm sorry, madam. They're not here.'

'*Oh, dear.*'

Heavy silence.

'Will you leave a message, madam?'

'Well, I don't know what to do. Well, *will* you tell them that Gloria ...!'

'*What* name, madam?'

'Just Gloria. Will you tell them that I *definitely* rang up?'

Not that the steward cared.

It was getting late now, and dark with it, and airmen were gathering at the bus stop just out of the town. I tried ringing again, to tell David where I should be. And now at last an officer told me that the squadron had not come over after all, but was still at M, where I had left it in the morning. He advised me to go back there. I was surprised at that, because wives do not matter at all, and I did not see why he should bother about me. It was much too late now to start back, and there was nothing for it but to finish the journey out to N, where I had taken a bed for the night. The bus had come in now, and I got on to it. It was David's time for coming home, and he would not find me at the gate; and this was terrible, with so much happening so quickly that every moment was precious. I called in at the farm where we lived before, to wait for the taxi to take me up the hill. They were sitting in the lamplight in the big, old room. They told me how they had had raids, and there were refugee children billeted on them. The café where the bull terrier bit me had been bombed and abandoned. Mrs H said: 'When you didn't come back, I said to Jack: "I know why that is. Mr Lachasse has had an accident.'" I thought it a poor thing to say with such assurance. On the way up the taxi driver showed me the things which were no longer there; but in the dark I saw no difference.

Next morning I was in my first air raid. I was having breakfast in bed when all the doors went bang-bang, bang-bang together, in excellent rhythm. I shot downstairs in David's pyjamas, and we all sat in the hall with the dog. I had to get to the guard room gates by ten, when David had promised me transport to take me back to him. I hurried through my dressing between sirens; and then, every time I got to the front door they would go sounding again. I played a crazy game of cards with the red-haired children. The boy cheated. I wanted to get to the aerodrome, or the transport would go. Mrs C had gone up to the attic to see what was going on. She took binoculars, and came down to say there was black smoke over the village.

The all clear went again. It had happened so many times now that it was funny. I said goodbye again. Mrs C said the troops would never let me through. I took my bag and ran down the lane. There were troops everywhere and chuntering lorries in the fields and all the way down the road. I dared not ask for a lift and so admit that I was there. The heel came off my shoe as I ran. It was fearfully hot on the white roads.

In the village all the telegraph wires were down. People were at their doors just looking at their furniture out on the grass. A car went by, full of Salvation Army women with white faces and untidy hair, looking squalid. A cottage close to the farm was burning nicely, and there were hoses untidy on the road, and knots of people talking in low voices. I knew some of them, but we were all too busy with our own affairs to speak or to notice one another. I asked the sentry on the gates if there was any transport. He thought there was. He began to grumble to me about there being a raid when he was on duty. He sent me to the guard room. A sergeant I knew by sight rang up for me, and said that all transport was stopped. He told me David had just been in to refuel. He grinned all over his face and said that he had shot down another plane, a Me 110. It was an amazing thing that he had been over to this very place this morning, and was probably still here! The sergeant went to try and find him; but he had only called in to refuel, and had gone off again. It was a very busy day. I waited about for a bus. Some nice bright planes were flying in the sun. One of them was David's, looping for me over the wrong house.

The farmer came out of his gate, and I shouted to him about David's Messerschmitt. He was very pleased. He showed me the ashes of an incendiary bomb in the grass by the gate. It did not look very dangerous. There had been another in his flax field, and a third in the wonderful field of clover he had shown me when we lived here. His little grandson had put out an incendiary in someone's washbasin. He told me he had lost a whole barn with a car in it; but he did not know whose car it had been, and so he was quite unconcerned. Mrs H came out, looking very neat for such a morning, and I told her about the Messerschmitt. An old farmhand joined us, and while we were talking the siren went again, and we all went down to the shelter. I was not getting back to David very quickly. Mrs H had a bowl of greengages, still warm, from a bombed tree. We had those, and hung about the shelter. I could not do much about getting on because there was only one telephone left whole in the village, and every time I tried to get to it the siren would go again. It was very hot and ominous, and the cowman's cottage was still burning and crackling, with everything he possessed except his savings. I kept taking shelter with my little bag of clothes in the dugout that was lined with blocks of straw. Some airmen came over from the camp. They had had enough. Once the daughter-in-law, who did not like me, came into the shelter backwards. She said: 'We shall be having Mrs Lachasse back soon!' I said: 'You have.' There was always one person missing, and no one could settle at all.

One time I came up – and mother was suddenly there. She had followed me from town the evening before, without knowing at all where I was, and she had only happened to call at the right place. We were delighted to see each other; and mother had a taxi with her. I told her we were going straight away to M, and we got into the car and drove back to the town. She had seen the smoking village, and so she was glad to find me safe. We talked all the way in the taxi. Mother had spent the morning in a hotel shelter in S, and had good bits to tell of a bold general making a dash upstairs for his bacon and eggs. I sent David a wire about his Messerschmitt, and said that we were on our way back.

It was fearfully hot on the train. I had left my clothes at the farm again, as we should be back in a few days, and I was wearing my thick shoes in place of the broken ones, and a flannel dress that was much too hot. We would not take the risk of going through town today; and the cross-country journey was very long. We kept slowing down for sirens, and backing into stations we had been glad to leave. We passed through some lovely hot, white country, with ripe corn in plenty, and rounded fields; but you could not use it at that time. We drank railway tea and went on and on; and at last we came to H; and now there was nothing left but to get a bus and find David. I went to the telephone and left mother to follow me.

When I got back she was still behind the barrier. There was a young, officious policeman, and he would not let her through. Such a thing had never occurred to us. She was explaining things to the policeman. I told him she was coming to live with me as long as I was here, which meant that it was no mere visit. He was pleased to contradict me, and to refuse to let her in. He said I could go to the police station if I liked, and they would say no as well. Mother would just have to go back to the next town, miles and miles away. It was dreadful to think of her being sent away when she had been so good and made no fuss about this mad journey; and of course we should never see her at all.

It was hotter than ever in the town, and people kept misdirecting me. The police shook their heads. I might try the county station if I *liked*. I went along and talked to a young man in a lounge suit. He was kind enough, but he explained that the chief was strict and very difficult. What was David's rank? He was only a PO, I said, but a good PO who had shot down a Messerschmitt that morning. I forget now if I said that on purpose, but the young man went straight to the telephone, and he was soon back to say that the news had pleased the chief, and that he and his car would be over right away; and so they were: a crusty old man in a lounge suit and a magnificent car. We drove down to the station, I saying all the right things in case he should change his mind and spoil everything. When we got to the station he was going to send me on for mother, but I was glad when he changed his mind and came too. He had stopped at the bookstall to buy a paper. The little policeman came over and asked me what I had achieved, pleased in advance at my failure. He was very young. I said: 'I've brought the chief of police.'

And the silly little policeman falls back and salutes!

Mother was waiting patiently on a bench, doing a crossword puzzle. I introduced them. I felt a very clever daughter. As we went through the barrier I put out the tip of my tongue at the policeman. No one else was let off the station; but, muttering of penalties, the old man drove us to our bus – because David had shot down a German.

Chapter 15 We found mother some digs close to mine, with a humble old woman. It was soon done, and I felt I was practised in these things. The old woman gave her a latchkey, and told her, as one might tell a schoolgirl, that she could go out and come in whenever she liked. Mother was tickled. There were two embossed cardboard texts on the bedroom wall. I said it would cost about ten shillings a week.

In the evenings I would wait for David at the gate. Once it was dark, it was better than my room with its black-hooded light like an old-fashioned train. The owners of the house would be out there too, talking quietly. Tonight I had mother with me. We looked at the immense sky, and the cage the searchlights made, closing us in almost. We agreed about their beauty. The sirens had sounded now, but the night was very, very quiet, and we talked low. The man with the lamp was stopping cars, that ground on slowly afterwards with their lights dimmed. Two bombs fell somewhere near. The husband always stayed to watch these things, but the woman had gone below with her children, and mother went after her. I was a bit excited. I left a note on the door for David and went down to the shelter, in a hurry in the end.

It was awful in that home-made dugout. There were the landlady and her two little girls, and a younger mother with a very new baby, all in bed, and mother and myself, down in the soil-smelling little place. There was one fading bicycle lamp which the woman kept turning off to save the battery. We talked quietly because of the children. One of them was awake with earache. They all slept down in this earth hole every night. Mother was taking it all in her stride, prescribing for the earache, being a mother even in this hole. The landlady kept on looking at the clock, and turning her enormous eyes on me and saying that David *was* late. People like to make you uneasy. I talked as if I had hot news from the aerodrome, and said that he was released and would be here in a minute; and I wished he would come.

After a time the door opened inwards, and someone else was coming in. It would make too many people altogether! But it was David. We went up into the clean night. Mother had had real raids, and did not want to come; but David said that everything was all right, so we all went back to my room. We had agreed that we would not tell him about our adventures and our complicated day; but somehow we soon began to slip in little bits here and there, and to boast about how we got mother in through the barrier. We told things turn about; and all at once David began to talk too, about how he had found himself flying all alone after twenty Messerschmitts; and how he had shot down one of them and come away. We listened to him quietly. And then he told how T was killed, who drank a quart of beer in eight-and-a-half seconds.

Chapter 16 I was down at my place at the gate, and mother was reading in my room, and a lorry drew up outside; what seemed like a crowd of men came out, lurching, it seemed in the darkness. It was David, and the Canadian C come for his share of the birthday cake. They had been celebrating the return of one of the squadron. But not T.

David lay on the bed with a pleasant smile. C sat scowling on the edge of his chair; and while mother talked to him with great charm, I cursed them both under my breath. By and by David mentioned that we had twenty-four hours' leave. As if it did not matter! As if it were not the first leave we had seen in a month! I was terrified already that we should waste our time next day; and sure enough, at five o'clock we were still in the digs. True we had found Geoffrey by telephone, and arranged to meet him at night in Bury St Edmunds in the unlikely event of any of us arriving there at all. Geoffrey had a car, so he had chosen this outlandish spot. There was a train that would start us on our complicated journey; but David will never use trains. He always says we shall get there without, and I never believe him, and we always do. Sometimes I have wished that we might not succeed, to prove to him that he is wrong.

And so, when we had had tea with mother, we started off in the cabin of a lorry. Every few yards the driver would pull up for airmen, until the back of the lorry was packed. It was like a snowball. We liked it. After that we walked, and took a bus and walked again; until I knew we were both mad, David the more so because he still had faith. And here was a car going to Bury St Edmunds. Now why? We climbed in. There was nothing left now but for Geoffrey to fail us.

We looked in all the public rooms of the hotel, and we knew soon that we had hoped too much. We started dinner alone, and in came Geoffrey, with oil on his hands from the inevitable recalcitrant car; and we were glad. He had been over Germany times without number since we had seen him in July, and here we all were drinking together, laughing in quiet lounges because there was no bar for a woman in the place. There was good talk in plenty. Geoffrey told how he had been second pilot over Germany the night before. How he had had nothing for his mind to work on, and had watched the shells come until he had no spit left for his chewing gum. We all laughed. We did not like it at all. They smoked cigars. They are six feet tall, the pair of them, and cigars dwarf them both, and I tell them so. Now Geoffrey invites David to tell about shooting down planes. David is so modest about it, choosing the humblest of parts, that we all three rock again.

By and by we went over to the Angel. Geoffrey had found some Army people who would drive him down to town for his leave, so that we should not have him for the journey that lay in the back of our minds all the evening, nor be able to bear him back for mother as we had hoped. Geoffrey was staying the night here, and as there was no train for us before midnight, we went to a gloomy lounge upstairs, and read about our old schools in the usual books, and they played the piano vaguely until the manageress came and asked them to shut it, and stood over them until they did. We drank our beer slowly. David was flying early next day, and so I poured a pint that was standing rather long, privately into a flower vase.

We could have had a car to take us home for £3, or four days' pay. We refused Geoffrey's generous offer of his own car. He had finished with it for good; and I told David, who did not know, of the behaviour of Geoffrey's cars at night on lonely roads where you are far from aid; and so we went on waiting. After a long time, we went out into the silent night. Geoffrey produced his fearful little car; and now the whole town rang. There were half the cogs missing from the differential, and when the other half did not engage he just opened the door and pushed with one foot on the ground until they did. The noise was alarming, and of course we got lost in the sleeping town that had been.

Geoffrey told us then that he would abandon the car as soon as he had dropped us at the station; but it lived for long enough after that to let him down several times, and was not finished when it burst into flames between a plane and a petrol bowser; because over a year after, we met some airmen from Geoffrey's squadron. They did not remember him by name, but when we mentioned the car they all talked at once, and agreed that it was still standing.

We went into the station waiting room, off the ghostly platform. It was very dark and mysterious inside, and there were shapes of swaddled soldiers sleeping on the floor. We talked in low voices, and by and by the train came in, and Geoffrey saw us off. We pictured him and his car making the night loud, and soon we went to sleep.

There was one last taxi going our way. We should be home by two now. Searchlights were out. We sat silent all the way. We pushed a note from Geoffrey through mother's window, and she called goodnight as we went home to bed for an hour and a half. We were glad to find we could have so much sleep as that.

Chapter 17 (3 September 1940) Perhaps if he had known, S would have come to the telephone, as I had always imagined someone kindly and discreet would do. As it was, when I rang at midday to see if David was feeling unsettled too, it was an airman who said: "'E's one of the ones o've come down.'

That is how it happens.

I tried saying that I was Mrs Lachasse, hoping for something better, because for all it was a busy morning, that seemed a bad way of breaking news; and so by degrees I found that David was in hospital in a place that sounded like the Highlands of Scotland. If I would ring again in an hour and a half they might be able to tell me more.

I was in the police station ringing up. I tried to get a car, but no one would help. I told them at the garages that I had a husband who had been shot down, but that made no difference. I managed to find a willing driver at last, and I said I would ring again, then I went and told mother; and we packed our things.

The little landlady peered up at me with a nervous grin and said: 'I'm sorry about your trouble.' I hope I was not short with her, but I did not feel that it was her affair at all.

I waited until the hour and a half had passed exactly, and this time they sent F to the telephone. He had been at the party. He was someone I knew. He told me David had come down by parachute and was burnt. They had taken him to hospital and he had been on the table for examination, and that was all they knew. I said to F: 'He's not going to die or anything?' F said: 'Nothing like that.'

To leave the subject, I asked F who else had been shot down. He said nothing, and I cursed myself for being gauche.

Much later on, an Army colonel who had seen it described B's end as graphically as anyone could have wished.

Chapter 18 After quite a long time I decided that David might be alive, and might even go on living, for all the journey to him was so long. Nothing was very real on that long drive: it was like the morning after a sleepless night, when your senses are doubly alert and yet register very little. I had two packets of cigarettes in the car. Mother sat in front with the driver. Once we stopped and she bought fresh sandwiches, and while we waited for her, I told the driver what our journey was for. He listened to me, and then he told me how he had had to abandon the car that morning to a dive-bombing attack in a main street; and here they both were safe after all.

It was a white-hot day. All the way, the streets were curiously empty. Mother said she had only counted two or three people since we started; and there was no traffic at all. After a time we noticed sirens, and that explained it.

I imagined a proper hospital like a town one, built of red brick; and I wondered if the matron would be kind, and if we should be able to find beds for the night. We knew from the map that we were going to no safe area; and I pictured tin hats and bombs, and public shelters at night: all things I knew not at all. And Lawrie had written a worried letter to mother when she decided to come to us at M, just because of the aerodrome there. It was better in the last war, when we all lived in one house together.

When we were getting near the hospital I asked mother if she would mind my going in alone. If there was any drama about, I would see it through better by myself.

Mother had already decided that for herself. I left her in the car, and when she had what news there was, she drove away to find beds for us.

They put me in the master's office and left me alone. There was a letter on the desk addressed to me, and so I read it: 'Dear Madam, I am writing to confirm my telephone conversation of this afternoon's date, stating that your husband, Pilot Officer D. W. Lachasse, is very ill in the above hospital. You may visit at any time you wish to come.'

On paper, the message was sinister. It did not cheer me at all. It took David from me, just like that, and made him a part of the hospital, and so a part of a government scheme, as the Air Force had never done. I had plenty of time to think things in that hot little office.

After a very long time, the master came in. I had expected something dignified; and here was a little bald north country man with protruding eyes, and a grocer's confidential manner. I told him that I had seen the letter, and I waited. He said that David was very badly burnt, but 'nothing that won't get better,' he said. He seemed to be sizing me up. He told me how they had watched him come down by parachute that morning, and how the air had been so still that it had taken him twenty minutes to come. And how they had him on the table a quarter of an hour after he landed. I asked tentatively if I might see him. The telephone bell rang before the little man could answer. Because I was listening acutely, I heard his voice change, as he said very quietly: 'Leave it to me.' He would turn round now and tell me that after all I had come too late. I wished it might have been someone else, and not this funny little man, and I was thinking how I would ask in a hurry if I might see one of the doctors, before he could get the words out and have it all over when, down the telephone, he began describing the morning's excitements: 'It was *hell on earth*!' he boasted.

He rang off at last, and now we went in the strong sun across the courtyard and round a pile of new sandbags into a cool corridor that they darkened. The master told me that we should be here for seven weeks. Then, it seemed an unbearably long time. And yet the implication that we should leave at all was cheering.

We found a doctor in the corridor inside, standing as I knew by David's door. The master left us – so that I might be prepared, I knew. The doctor was immensely tall. He wore a navy flannel suit with a loud white stripe, and a bad tie. When he talked, he blinked down at me. He told me, as the master had done, that I should find David purple. I made lighter of that than I felt; and said that I had seen such things, because years before I had had a burnt brother in a lint mask. He said that his eyebrows were gone; and in the same mood of unreal brightness that had prompted my question to F on the telephone, I made some fatuous remark about how proud he had been of those eyebrows. But successful conversation was surely not expected of me, and after all this, I was let into the room.

David was lying on the bed. The newness of his accident was a sensation in the room. He himself was something brand new and very real. I saw him just for a moment, his face and his arms purple with fresh dye, and very swollen. I thought he had no eyes; and I thought they had not told me that, but had left me to find out quietly for myself; and, curiously, how wise they were. Behind all this was David. I saw then, as I cannot see now, how we should manage his blindness. (The Irish colonel spat out later on, at his lunch-table, that without his eyes he would have been better dead.) The master was in the doorway, and I looked for his permission, and kissed David, and said the things I had ready to say. His lips were very red against the purple.

He told me how the hood had jammed and trapped him; and how after a long time he had remembered me, and got it open. NR said afterwards that it could not have been more than six seconds.

A nurse brought the wings and buttons and the buckle off his tunic. I made out a receipt for them and signed it; and she said it was all right and took it away. A wire came to say that I was on my way. There was a baby crying all the time. The sunlight was white and harsh outside the window. The baby cried and cried. After a time I got up and closed the window, and made the room my home.

Chapter 19 Mother came over in the evening and brought me more cigarettes. She had found a hotel for us both; but they had given me a room here for tonight, next to David's. Mother came and sat with me while I ate my supper, on a wooden form. I belonged to this life.

The doctors were in with David for hours. They were giving him injections of plasma. I had asked to be allowed to stay 'just for interest'; and when they turned me out, I thought that most wives must say just that. They promised to let me see someone else's husband being prepared, knowing that I should never ask. I waited a very long time with mother. Once we wandered out and found NR, the visiting surgeon, washing purple off his hands in the passage. He said we should know in thirty-six hours if David was going to live. It seemed a ridiculous thing that a person who could think and talk now should do otherwise; but there was always shock.

By and by mother went away. They gave me a rough hospital towel and I went to wash for bed. I had to go through a ward with two men in it: a good-looking boy with his leg strung up on a pulley, and a middle-aged man. I hung about talking to them, and they told me about their accidents. The boy had been in the Army; and then he had been under a lorry. The older man had been shot in the hip by a fellow Home Guard. He told me how he had been able to watch the artery beating in the hole, and how they had brought his trouser pocket and its contents, money and all, out of his leg. They were good men, both of them. They made me feel more ordinary, and they made light of David without pretending that there was nothing to fear.

After a long time they let me in to say goodnight to him. They had fitted up a drip for the plasma at the end of the bed. I told him I should be next door, just through the wall. There was a VAD on duty, in a white overall. I asked if I might look in if I was awake in the night. She said no.

I went to my room and sat on the unmade bed, and after a time someone noticed me and brought me sheets; and so I went to bed on a hard, hard mattress that nowhere let me in. There were bars on the window, a folding cage. I put out the light, but left the door ajar. There were small noises all the time. Sometimes I heard them go in to David. I wanted to go too. I was not sure that all was well. But I did not go.

Chapter 20 Things arrived in the room all the time. There was the radiant-heat apparatus, broken and standing on end like a pulpit, and the tall stand with the flask of plasma, and the thin rubber pipes joined to David so that he must not move his feet; and all the empty plasma bottles on the window sill, and the new bottles of dried crystals. He was running through a prodigious amount of bottles. There was the cage at the foot of the bed, and the chart at the head. The room was full, and efficient like a good machine, and soon all these things were familiar. I learnt to give him drinks from a feeding cup, without much spilling. We wrote on scraps of paper intake and output. The two never tallied at all. Output was not my affair for long enough, and there were battles and there were many furtive journeys to and fro before I was officially allowed in the little room next to the kitchen. But that came in time.

They made him purple all the time anew. There was a cloth behind his head with dried blood on it, and purple dotted on all the linen and on the floor and the walls and the chair. I never hoped that one day we should have him clean and tidy. There was a lean man who came to take blood counts, quiet at the foot of the bed. He said: 'I'm going to give you a *little* prick.' Every time he said that I made comments; but he was a kind person, and patted my shoulder when I did not know myself in need of comfort.

The second day was the hottest of the year. They had brought more blankets and put them over David. Surreptitiously I lifted them up from time to time and let in what air there was. David wanted fruit salts. Mother was there, quiet and unobtrusive in a corner. She went out in the hot sun and brought them up the hill for him; we gave them to a nurse to mix and never saw them again.

All the time there were kind people calling, and kind people sending messages, and offering beds. There was a bald man from the ARP post telling how they had adopted David and would keep him supplied with fruit; and there were many, many plums. I thanked all the people and was very bewildered.

NR came and told me that he was satisfied with David's progress so far, but they would not know until next day if he were going to live. I asked him what time that would be and he looked amused, and said that it was neither here nor there; but he would say about midday. I took that as the time.

S rang up, a sane and friendly voice, and asked for details, so that he could make his report on the day's operations. I went like an echo to and fro along the corridor, from the telephone to the bed and back again. Dry facts they were that we gave: the time, the place, and his position in the formation; though I remember that S rang again to ask what colour the flashes from the cannon had been, and that would be picturesque. It was only long afterwards that the full tale was told:

On the morning of 3 September 1940, at 1045, a squadron scramble came through on the ops phone. I had been allotted an old fabric-wing Hurricane of early war vintage, and had trouble in starting up. I took off five minutes afterwards, and shortly rejoined the squadron, which was circling D at 30,000 feet. We then sighted a large formation of German planes to port, heading for London, which we proceeded to intercept. Then a dazzling array of multi-coloured light appeared on the starboard side of the cockpit, accompanied by explosive concussions. Immediately flame came through the instrument panel, filling the cockpit and burning my hands, legs and face. The reserve fuel tank had exploded, and I had neither gloves nor goggles which I had pushed over my forehead in order to get a better view. I then tried to open the hood but found it had jammed. Using both hands on the one side, I managed at last to pull the hood open, undid my Sutton harness, grabbed my helmet off and plunged out of the starboard side of the plane. I pulled my ripcord immediately, and assured myself at a glance that the parachute had opened. I then began to feel a bit anxious about being shot up on the way down. However nothing happened, so I started to survey the damage. My hands were all bloody, like I was feeling, and they were covered with projecting tissue; that was the skin; and all that was left of my sleeve was a charred ribbon of rank. I was suspended in an ill-fitting parachute, and the air seemed so quiet after the roar of the plane that had terminated with the bang. All I could hear now was the fluttering of the canopy, which reminded me of a yacht, and the fading drone and crackle of the battle going on above. I was worrying about the landing I should make, as I was swinging about like a mad pendulum in currents and gusts. When I was about 1,000 feet from the ground the sounds of shouting, dogs barking and a train whistle in the distance came floating up to me. After a 20 minutes' drop the ground suddenly began to come towards me quickly. Someone called: 'There he goes.' There was a scrape, a swing and then a light bump. I had landed. I lay as I was for a time, then sat up, and leant my arm downwards so that the ridiculous ribbon fell off my wrist, attached by a single thread. Then people started to arrive. Someone shouted: 'Keep back.' I gave my name and asked them to ring the aerodrome to say what had happened. Someone offered me brandy, and I said: 'All I want is a nice drink of cool clear water,' which soon arrived and of which I drank a little. I was trying to explain to them how to undo my parachute harness. Someone else held up the parachute canopy to shade me from the sun, and someone said: 'Don't move him. He may have bullet wounds.' The ambulance came and I parted with a reminder to them to ring my wife: the telephone number I did not know. And on to the table where I mentioned that it was the first operation that I was glad to have, and I breathed in the ether heartily and went out.

And now, would S find David's lucky scarf for him? He had never flown without it without some small thing happening; and a fortnight ago he had left it behind in a plane. S would do his best.

In the afternoon, the crying began again. I put cotton wool in David's ears, and there it stayed for days.

Chapter 21 The second night, they put me to sleep in the female end of the ward, and there were bars on the window again. It seemed curious, and even sinister that I should twice be given the rooms for difficult patients; and I wondered idly if they expected trouble from me, and if so why. A nurse with buck teeth brought me Ovaltine and a biscuit. All night there were noises of people going to and fro.

I woke at four o'clock, and lay for a long time trying not to get up. Everything was very quiet. After a time I dressed and went out to the corridor. A nurse looked at me curiously. I asked her how David was, and if I might go in to him. She went away to ask the night sister. I had an idea that something was wrong, or why had I woken so suddenly? The nurse came back with a message: my husband had been restless, and now they had given him an injection and he was not conscious. The night sister had said that I was not to worry too much. Until that moment I had not. The nurse advised me to go back to bed; and she went away. They were just taking down the screens from the corridor windows, letting in the colourless light. David's door was ajar. The light was burning, and the room was oppressively silent. I asked someone if there was a nurse in with him. They said there was an orderly. That was sinister. I did not know then that orderlies relieved the nurses; and there was something weird about there being a man with him, and their not letting me in. What had he done that he needed a man? I went up and down the corridor very quietly, afraid of being seen and sent away; afraid of being a nuisance, that worst of all things. I went out into the fresh morning. There was no sun yet, but there were smears of pink on the sky. I had no cigarettes. A wide-eyed, weary man in an office by the gates gave me one and watched me with surprise. A robin in a tree with clear orange berries sang loudly. I took in a lot of things.

I went back to the corridor, but no one came or noticed me. I would not look into David's room because there was surely something I was not to see, and if I did they would send me right away. My head was light with the earliness and the cigarette. By and by the smallest orderly came out of the room. With someone there, my head spun. I told Tich in a complaining voice that I was going to faint! I do not know how to faint, and I can only suppose that I was trying to do the right thing, as women do who are sick before the boat starts because a boat is a place to be sick in. I blamed the cigarette and felt all right again. The little bow-legged soldier came along.

'He'll pull through,' he said.

I asked if they had sent for the doctor. Tich said no, he was not up yet.

At six o'clock they let me in. I was firmly convinced then, and had been since I went out in the garden, that David was worse and was going to die. I read significant things into the chart on the wall. The fact that they let me in at six o'clock, like the fact that they had kept me out at four, showed that things were going badly. They took down the blackout and let in the raw light. They brought me a breakfast of brawn with bristles in, and I ate it all. David was awake, saying nothing at all. I could not even hold his hand. The VAD with the white coat came in and bent over him. She said: 'They'll have to cut those eyelids if he's not careful.' Then she said: 'He's going to be an awful mess!'

'Do you mean his mouth?' I said loudly.

'No,' she said: 'All over.'

And after this she expressed surprise at his being awake. Later on I suggested to the two doctors that they might hold tact classes for nurses. They assured me that I was wrong, that what the anonymous nurse had meant was something entirely different. They thought I was worried for myself! They went on with their conversation, and I cursed myself and decided to be a better patient's wife in future.

I sat all morning with David. Before midday, NR came to me in the corridor, and told me that he was out of danger and going under his own steam after all. I thanked him for saving a good husband. He asked how long we had been married, and I told him nine weeks. He looked amused. But they still did not know about his eyes. Until he opened them, they could not know if he would see. Someone muttered deferentially that they had not appeared to be injured; but NR would not commit himself. And all the time, David was lying there with the comfortable knowledge that he had seen all the way down and after he had landed; but we had not asked him, and so he did not tell us so.

Chapter 22 There was a telegram one day from Air Ministry, that had followed me from place to place, so that I read it out with interest at David's bedside:

Immediate from Air Ministry P110 4/9 regret to inform you that your husband Pilot Officer David Walter Lachasse has been admitted to the hospital L with injuries and placed on the seriously ill list as a result of air operations of 3rd Sept 1940 letter follows stop any further information received will be communicated to you immediately stop suggest you telephone hospital before intended visit Under Secretary of State Air Ministry.

Reading the letter that followed some days later, I was filled with pity for those immobile women, perhaps with little children, to whom such notifications applied.

Madam, I am directed to confirm the telegram in which you were notified that your husband Pilot Officer David Walter Lachasse was admitted to hospital L on the 3rd September suffering from burns received during air operations. Any change in your husband's condition or location notified to this department will be communicated to you as quick as possible.

Sitting at David's side where I belonged, I wondered if it could be that I had less than my share of endurance; or why should this letter seem such a terrible thing?

Chapter 23 Later on that second day David opened his eyes and saw. His parents arrived in the afternoon, and I knew even before they came into the room that I had not told them enough over the telephone; but I had had my reports from the surgeon and had repeated them word for word, and on the whole I felt my conscience clear.

The days were curiously the same. I learnt to be tired as I had never been in my life, with the hard, hard floors, and my thick shoes, and the hundreds of things to do. There was a stage when lying down was exquisite pain, when I moved inch by inch into a bath or a bed, relaxing very, very slowly. I was staying now with the anaesthetist and his wife, over the road to be near at hand. There was a real bath, and breakfast in bed, and good talk.

28 Eric 'Boy' Marrs Part 2, Spitfire Pilot, Pilot Officer, British, 152 Squadron

Second set of letters from Eric to his father, covering 16–25 August, and one official personal combat report for 16 August 1940, detailing his first 'kill'. The air battle described in his letter of 22 August was fought on 18 August. In his letter of 27 August he describes the attack on RAF Warmwell of Sunday 25 August 1940 when Tim Wildblood (three kills and one shared kill) and Richard Hogg were both shot down and killed. Marrs claimed a Me 110 destroyed that day.

17 August 1940 Well I have been in the thick of things since I came back from leave. I had quite a good journey down here and arrived on time. I found that we had had two casualties and that was the reason for my recall. One was a flight commander and the other was the chap who only got married about a month ago – to a Red Cross at Sidcup. I came on duty at 4.30 the same afternoon and have been on ever since. We get no released or avilable periods now and we are at readiness all the time. This is an emergency measure, but is somewhat tiring.

We had no shows that evening. Next morning we had to get up at 4.30, but had nothing to do till about 7 a.m. Three of us were then sent after some enemy aircraft floating round the countryside. One of them eventually popped out of a cloud not far from us. I managed to get within 500 or 600 yards, too far to fire, but he popped into another thick cloud. I went round the other side but lost him. There was a lot of cloud that morning. The machine was a Dornier Do 17. The day then passed quite quietly though we flew quite a lot, until about 5.15 p.m.

As many aircraft as possible were ordered into the air. Nine of us took off and climbed up to 15,000 feet over Portland. Soon we were told over the radio 'Many enemy aircraft approaching Portland from south.' About two minutes later I had my first sight of them. A cloud of black specks milling round and round, about halfway across the Channel and about the same height as us. We climbed up another 2,000 or 3,000 feet up sun of them and about five miles south of Portland; and there they were. There must have been more than 100 of them – Ju 87s escorted by Me 110s. The 87s were in vees of three, in tight formation. They were more or less surrounded by 110s. Behind, and to the right of and above these 87s, was another formation of 110s.

I must say that at the sight of all these aircraft my heart sank. How could nine Spitfires stop all these? However, we were ordered into line astern and down we came out of the sun – straight in behind the bombers. That dive cheered me up no end. I was going too fast to get a good shot in (I shall know better next time), but sprayed an 87. Then down and to the left and up into the sun again. I looked for stragglers. There were German aircraft everywhere, though from after that first dive I never saw another Spitfire in the fight. I found a 110 fairly separated. I had a short dogfight and managed to get several short bursts in but noticed no effects. Then away again. It isn't healthy to stay on one aeroplane for any length of time. I looked for more stragglers and could find nothing that looked pleasant, so I just charged back into the main group of bombers. I was nearly head on to them, and opening fire at a fairly long range I plastered a vee of three 87s but did not manage to put the coup-de-grâce to any of them. I nipped under them at the last minute and went on down in a dive. I then met up with another 110. I couldn't help it, there were so many of them. We circled round each other for a bit in tightening circles, each trying to get on the other's tail, but my attention was soon drawn by another 110. Down underneath him I went, and pulled up giving him a long burst into the belly. Nothing seemed to happen. I was then occupied by yet another 110. I milled around with him for a bit, but when I wanted to get in a shot I found I had run out of ammunition. I rolled on my back and pulled out of the mêlée and went home. I had unfortunately shot down nothing, but as I came home I saw a Hurricane. Reinforcements had come up and were having their turn with the enemy.

We had one pilot wounded in that show and lost no one. Our score was five confirmed and one unconfirmed.

Twenty minutes after that show three of us were up again, but it was all over. Nothing more happened that day, but amongst all the news of other fights in the 9 o'clock news bulletin we heard 'An attack on Portland completely failed.'

Next morning we were up at 4.30 again. Nothing happened till lunchtime. We were sent up to 20,000 feet east of the Isle of Wight. When we arrived, enemy fighters materialised all around us. I was fully occupied with dodging and never had a chance to get my sights on anything. I was too busy trying to keep their sights off me. I finally went into a spin through doing too light a turn at low speed. I came out and there was nothing in sight. I climbed up again towards the sun, and looked around. I saw about six aeroplanes bearing down on me from my left. I thought they were Spitfires and did nothing. When they were too close to be comfortable, they turned out to be Me 109s. I did such a steep turn that I went into another spin. When I came out I had a good look round and then made for land. I must have been about 20 miles out to sea. I looked for trouble or friendly fighters and finally found five other Spitfires of another squadron. I stuck with them until I was short of petrol but saw nothing and finally had to return owing to shortage of petrol. I returned feeling rather a fool, not having fired my guns, but found that same had happened to most of the others. One chap, however, had managed to find three Me 109s by themselves and had shot down two of them.

That evening we had another patrol. We saw nothing. Not long before we were ordered to land, I suddenly saw two Heinkel 111s stooging along below us. I called up the leader on the R/T and dived straight after them as they were going into a layer of thickish mist. I managed to keep sight of the rear one, and when it came out the other side I was able to shoot it up. I left it with smoke coming from both engines, and my own machine covered with oil from it. I don't think it could have got home and I'm pretty sure it didn't.

My R/T message was not understood and so nobody else saw them. I am counting that as my first. I returned home much cheered.

Today nothing has happened at all as no doubt you heard on the news. Tomorrow? Who knows? Probably raids on a scale we have never dreamed of. At any rate we have had a day's rest and are feeling fine.

Form F, Combat Report, 16 August 1940. Time attack delivered: 16.15; Enemy casualties: 1 (category 2) He 111; Place attack delivered: 10 miles S of Southampton; General report: I was Blue 2. When on patrol over Southampton, I saw 2 He 111s about 800 feet below proceeding in a southerly direction. I called Red 1 and dived to attack in order not to lose them in mist. I did stern and quarter attack on rear E/A opening fire at 300 yards. Oil poured from the E/A covering my windscreen, spinner, and leading edges. The last seen of the E/A was that the propellers appeared to be rotating slowly, with smoke coming from both engines. I broke off the action as I thought the oil may have been from my machine, and as this was only 10 miles from the Isle of Wight it is considered he failed to get home. Rounds fired: 2296.

22 August 1940 We have only had one show since I last wrote and that was the day after I wrote. It was the day the Germans lost about 150 aircraft. There was a large scale raid on Southampton and Gosport consisting of Ju 87s escorted by Me 109s. We arrived on the scene just as the 87s had finished dropping bombs. There were other squadrons already there and we have since learnt that one of them took on the fighter escort. We were therefore lucky, and when we arrived we found about thirty Ju 87s making for France. We met them just off the east end of the Isle of Wight. We dived after them and they went down to about 100 feet above the water. Then followed a running chase out to sea. The evasive action they took was to throttle back and do steep turns to right and left so that we would not be able to follow them and would overshoot. There were, however, so many of them that if one was shaken off the tail of one there was always another to sit on. I fired at about six and shot down one. It caught fire in the port wing petrol tank and then went into the sea about 300 yards further on.

When I had finished my ammunition I turned away and found an Me 109 sitting on my tail. As I turned it fired a burst in front of me. I could see the tracer and I seemed to fly straight through it. I was not hit, however, and ran for home as it was senseless staying without ammunition. I was not followed and two other chaps shot down that 109 soon after.

The squadron's score was 11 that day: 10 Ju 87s and the Me 109. We lost no pilots or aeroplanes and were mentioned in the news that night, when it said that 'Eleven Spitfires shot down their own number of enemy aircraft without loss.'

There were celebrations that night. Since then there have been no shows and we are all enjoying a welcome rest.

Yesterday our section found a Ju 88 and shot it down and that now makes our squadron total of enemy aircraft confirmed to 33.

27 August 1940 Excitements have begun again. We had about five days of very acceptable quietness, during which we merely chased odd lone raiders. We managed to get several of these and another chap and I came across a Dornier 17 which we shot down. I get a half for that. Chasing these lone raiders is good fun and quite amusing for it means that, for once, the odds are in your favour.

On Saturday [24 August 1940] the big raids began again. There was one over Portsmouth which our squadron did not get into. We had to patrol an aerodrome which Control thought was going to be attacked. On Sunday [25 August], however, we had our share. A big raid came over with our aerodrome as its objective. There were dozens of escort fighters and as usual we got mixed up with these without managing to attack the bombers at all. Other squadrons which arrived were a bit too late to prevent the bombing and so the bombers were more or less unhindered in their work. Considering this, they did surprisingly little damage. They demolished the hospital – luckily there was no one in it – they ruined a hanger and damaged a second – luckily there was only one aeroplane lost through this; they dropped one or two bombs on the aerodrome. They also dropped a number of delayed action bombs around the place, some of which have not yet gone off. One is near the WAAF's quarters, which they can therefore not use, one is in an empty hanger, and there are one or two others around and about the aerodrome. One of those on the aerodrome went off just as I was falling to sleep last night. It shook me considerably.

Well, as for the air battle. To begin with, the squadron was spilt up in two flights. Our flight went into line astern to attack a formation of Ju 88s, but on the way in I, who was the last of the string, became tangled up with some Hurricanes which I thought were Me 109s. The bombers had disappeared by the time I had disentangled myself, and I could not find anything to shoot at. Then I saw a lone twin engined machine about five miles out to sea and about 5,000 feet below me, making for France. I dived after it and found it was an Me 110. When it saw that I was overtaking it, it whipped round and came head on at me. I held on as long as I could, but he seemed to be going to ram me, so I pushed the stick forward hard and just went under his wing.

I went round in a steep turn and found he was doing the same in the opposite direction. I opened up my turn in order to give him a wider berth and then when I had passed him steepened it up again to come round on his tail. This I was able to do, and with a longish burst I put his port motor on fire. I then found myself overshooting. I throttled right back but could not pull up in time and drew out to his right. I overshot him by about 300 yards, and I watched him over my shoulder. I saw him turning in behind me to get his sight on me, and, leaving it as late as possible so that he would not be able to follow me round, I went into a steep climbing turn to the left, going into it as quickly and violently as possible. His tracer passed under me. I continued my steep turn and came round behind him again. I took good care to stay where I was this time. With another long burst I put his starboard engine on fire and pieces flew off. I then left him. None too soon either, for I caught a glimpse of an Me 109 diving down out of the sun on to what would have been my tail. I was now about 20 miles out to sea and I made for home at top speed. About halfway back to land I passed six more Me 110s going back to France. I did not stop to argue as I was still about 10 miles out to sea. Arriving back over land I hung around for about a quarter of an hour looking for something to finish my ammunition on. I then landed. When I landed I found that I had a bullet through my oil tank and had lost nearly all my oil. I reckon I was lucky to get back from 20 miles out to sea.

We lost two people that day and only had three confirmed and one unconfirmed. We were rather depressed that night. We have now lost six people since we have been here and the squadron score stands at 40 confirmed and 15 unconfirmed. I don't suppose we ought to complain really, but it is always a blow when people don't return.

29 Ronald Hamlyn, Spitfire Pilot, Sergeant Pilot, British, 610 Squadron

Personal combat reports of Ronald Hamlyn covering three sorties flown on 24 August 1940 when 610 Squadron was flying from RAF Biggin Hill, south-east London (11 Group). Shooting down five in a day was very rare but you wouldn't have thought it from the rather perfunctory reports he wrote up. Perhaps a bit like 'Hilly' Brown (see chapter 2) and his missing letters at the height of the Battle of France, 'Ronnie' was probably just far too exhausted from the relentless round of patrols to dwell on his phenomenal success. A bit like buses, the next two chapters include accounts of two other pilots shooting down five in a day, one a little later on the same day as Ronald Hamlyn!

Hamlyn made a BBC radio broadcast shortly after, retelling the events of that day and omitting the fact that his number 3 (Claude Merrick) had been shot down. As mentioned before, these broadcasts are generally accurate, but did omit events considered a threat to morale. Hamlyn joined 610 Squadron in June 1940 aged twenty-three and was the first RAF pilot to shoot down five enemy aircraft in one day. He survived the war with a tally of twelve kills, ten of which he shot down during the Battle of Britain, and almost all were Me 109 fighters. He died in 1991.

Form F, Combat Report, 24 August 1940. Time attack delivered: 08.25 approx; Enemy casualties: Two destroyed 1 Ju 88 1 Me 109; Place attack delivered: 10 miles south east of Ramsgate; Height of enemy: 12–15,000 ft; Range at which fire was opened in each attack delivered, together with estimated length of bursts: Ju 88 250 yds 2 sec burst, Me 109 150 yds 2 sec burst; Total No. of rounds fired: 500; General report: I was Yellow 2. I saw three waves of bombers approaching the S Coast. I attacked one of the these waves in which there were about 15–18 Junkers 88 at about 300–350 yds. I received a large amount of cross fire but I didn't open fire until 250 yds. I gave a two second burst and saw one Ju 88 dive away from the rest and I watched it crash into the sea. I did not break away but throttled back an Me 109 overshot me and pulled up right in front at about 150 yds. I opened fire and saw it starting to smoke. I followed it down and saw it also hit the sea.

Method of attack: Ju 88 – astern and above attack aiming at port engine; Me 109 – astern aiming at centre of fuselage.

Form F, Combat Report, 24 August 1940. Time attack delivered: 11.35 approx; Enemy casualties: One Me 109 destroyed; Place attack delivered: Dover to France; Height of enemy: 18,000 ft; Range at which fire was opened in each attack delivered, together with estimated length of bursts: 250–150 yds six burst of three secs; Total No. of rounds fired: All; General report: I was Yellow 2. I was attacked while in formation over Dover. After a short dog fight I got on to the Me 109's tail and he at once flew for France. I followed and while I was chasing him I saw another dog fight between two Spitfires and one Me 109. The Me 109 went down smoking badly but carried on flying eventually going into the sea off Cape Grez-Nez. By this time I had got into range of the Me 109 I was chasing but did not open fire until I had crossed over the coast into France, after about three more bursts I saw it go out of control with smoke pouring out and watched it crash in a field. I did not experience any AA fire while over France. The Me 109 that I saw crash into the sea was the one destroyed by F/O [Peter] Lamb – Yellow leader.

Method of attack: Astern and underneath aiming at centre of fuselage.

Form F, Combat Report, 24 August 1940. Time attack delivered: 15.55 approx; Enemy casualties: Two Me 109s destroyed; Place attack delivered: Halfway between Southend and Hornchurch approx; Height of enemy: 15,000 ft; Range at which fire was opened in each attack delivered, together with estimated length of bursts: Two burst of three secs, Three bursts of three secs; Total No. of rounds fired: All; General report: I was Yellow leader, on taking off we started to fly towards Gravesend but on reaching 5,000 feet we saw AA fire over NE London, so we changed course. At about 12,000 feet I first sighted about 20 Junkers 88 heading in a westerly direction. I lead my section towards them but I saw a bunch of Me 109s just above me so I pulled up and attacked one, after two bursts some smoke started pouring out and he fell away out of control. I was just about to break away when I saw tracer bullets passing me. I at once turned sharply and saw my number three being attacked by a Me 109. So I attacked it and it started to pull up, I gave another burst and it started smoking after another burst it caught fire and went down with pieces falling off it. The last I saw of the Spitfire my No. 3 was that he was still diving and he looked out of control.

Method of attack: (i) Me 109 – quarter attack on E/A starboard side followed by astern attack aiming at centre of fuselage. (ii) Me 109 –astern from underneath aiming at centre of fuselage.

30 Antoni Glowacki, Hurricane Pilot, Sergeant Pilot, Polish, 501 Squadron

An account by an anonymous Polish RAF fighter pilot written for an Air Ministry & Ministry of Information booklet on the contribution of Allied air forces of the occupied countries to the war effort and published in 1944. The pilot was Sergeant Pilot Antoni Glowacki of 501 Squadron, as he was the only Polish pilot to record five kills in one day, on 24 August 1940 when his squadron was flying from RAF Gravesend, Kent (11 Group). He shot down three Me 109s and two Ju 88s, achieved over three sorties over Ramsgate and Gravesend. Also on that day several Defiants were shot down by Me 109s in the vicinity of the 501 Squadron patrols.

A flying instructor in the Polish Air Force, Glowacki took an active part in the desperate army defence against the German invasion but when this collapsed fled to Romania with thousands of other Polish airmen and soldiers. He made his way to France then on to England, arriving in January 1940. He joined 501 Squadron on 5 August and ended the war with at least eight confirmed kills. Glowacki emigrated to New Zealand, where he joined the New Zealand Air Force. He died in 1980.

At 6.40 we were already up in the air. We were directed by R/T to the south coast of England, and warned of a strong enemy formation making for one of the towns on the coast. We were heading for this direction and were going all out. Suddenly I noticed a lot of aircraft slightly above us. I immediately warned the squadron commander.

We changed course, went into the sun and then into the attack. It turned out that they were all Me 109s, without any bombers. Dogfights ensued immediately; we came up against odds of 1 to 6 and 1 to 7, but no one thought of that. I got hold of one Me and started to twist and turn with him. I then noticed that another Jerry was coming in on my tail. I made a violent turn and fell into a spin. I pulled out and then I saw an Me about 200 yards in front. I got on his tail and opened fire without using any deflection at all. Eight machine-guns did their work. Bits flew from the Jerry, and soon he went down to the ground in smoke. I followed him down and saw how he exploded about six miles north of·Dover. Soon after I saw several others falling down to earth. My squadron was at work! However, it did not last long. Jerry made back for home, and a few minutes later we too received instructions to return. We came back singly, but we all got back.

Sometime about 12.30 we were called up a second time. This time we saw a large bomber formation approaching with an escort of fighters. We met Jerry just over the coast, but on seeing us he made a sharp turn and dived down to attack some town beneath us. The CO led us in to head him off, and we almost succeeded. I got on the tail of a Ju 88 and pumped in round after round. Both his engines started to burn; he came down lower, turned out over the sea, and just as he crossed the coast, exploded. I circled over the burning remains, and just then I caught sight of a Defiant in a fight with an Me 109. Quite unseen by the Me, I came in under his belly and pumped in the rest of the ammunition, but it was just a bit too late, as the Defiant was already on fire and was dropping down to the water like a stone. A moment later my Me burst into a black smoke and crashed close by his victim. A few minutes later and there was no trace on the water of either machine.

I took a course for base and after 15 minutes landed, tired and perspiring, but happy that I had started to repay my debt to the Boche for September 1939. My CO and the whole squadron were overjoyed. Good lads – they shook my hands and congratulated me.

We were not given long for a rest. At 2.30 we were in the air again. Our squadron was in the second line of defence. We met Jerry well over land, but we were lower down. The CO made a turn and we started to climb, parallel to the column of Jerries. They, meantime, were throwing out their bombs on the towns lying on the road to London. Some 25 miles outside London we were above Jerry, and we went in to attack. Just as our first aircraft opened fire, about 30 Me 109s attacked us. The last two sections got to grips with the fighters, while the rest took on the bombers.

I was attacked by three Me 109s. I took evading action, closed down the throttle, and when the first Jerry shot past me, gave him all I could. Instantaneously he broke into flames, lost both his wings, and like a rocket went down to ground but the other Mes had already opened fire on me. I did a half roll, pulled back the stick, and at once lost sight of Jerry, but this manoeuvre lost me some 4–5,000 feet. I started to climb on full throttle so as to reach the nearest group of bombers, which were flying calmly along without any protection, and so far had not been attacked at all. After two or three minutes I was in a good position. At a convenient moment I opened fire and directed it on the nearest Ju 88. The rest of the Jerries fired at me with tracer bullets. This made a fine sight, as the smoke remained in the air and formed a fan-shaped pattern. My ammunition gave out after a few seconds, so I did a left climbing turn and dived down, as two machines had appeared quite near me. After losing several thousand feet I looked at my Ju 88. There he was, in flames, spinning down to the ground.

31 Tom Gleave, Hurricane Pilot, Squadron Leader, British, 253 Squadron

Extract from Tom Gleave's wartime memoir, *I Had a Row with a German*. This was first published in 1941 under the pseudonym 'RAF Casualty'. The title came from the author's response to his wife's question upon first seeing him in hospital after being shot down, covered in bandages.

Born in Liverpool in 1908, Gleave joined the RAF in 1930. On 2 June 1940, after having worked in various senior roles in the RAF, he was appointed squadron leader of 253 Squadron, then based at RAF Kirton in Lindsey, Lincolnshire (12 Group). The squadron moved south into the 'hot' zone on 29 August to RAF Kenley, London (11 Group). The extract below covers 30 August 1940, when he shot down five Me 109s (official records note one as 'confirmed' and four as 'probable'), through 31 August when he damaged a Ju 88 before being shot down himself and grievously burned, to his first days in hospital. Post-war all five Me 109s were confirmed, as was the Ju 88.

Gleave was one of the first patients treated by Dr Archibald McIndoe's groundbreaking reconstructive cosmetic surgery at Queen Victoria Hospital, East Grinstead, becoming the first and only 'Chief Guinea Pig'. Fellow burns victim Richard Hillary (see chapter 50) met him in hospital. He would remain a prominent member of the 'Guinea Pig Club' for the rest of his life, featuring in many of the books about McIndoe's work. He returned to non-flying duties and remained in the RAF until 1953. After that he spent the next thirty years working in the Historical Section of the Cabinet Office. Gleave worked as technical and tactical adviser to the 1969 film *The Battle of Britain* and died in 1993.

As with other wartime memoirs, the censor did not allow the real names of his fellow pilots to be used, so from the author's own originally marked-up edition are their real names: Jenks, David Jenks; Star, Squadron Leader Harold M. Starr; Percy, John Greenwood; Dopey, Colin Francis; Bruno, George Brown; Henry, Pilot Officer Henley, squadron intelligence officer; Bill, William 'Bill' Cambridge; the Colonel, Jefferson Wedgwood; Dicky, John Dickinson. Pilot Officer Colin Francis was just nineteen when he was killed on his first encounter with the Luftwaffe. His body lay undiscovered until 1981 when his Hurricane was identified and excavated at Wrotham in Kent, his remains still strapped in the cockpit.

The extract is used by courtesy of Angela Lodge, daughter of Tom Gleave, who stills works to support the Guinea Pig Club.

Next morning, August 30th, I was up early, determined not to miss anything. Star had asked me the previous night to take turns leading the squadron so that he could keep up with the paperwork. This suited me from the ground upwards and I felt buoyed up with new hopes. I had breakfast and wandered down to dispersal point. The squadron was all set for anything with Star in command.

About 10am, or it may have been later, they were ordered off. I stood by with the emergency section, but we were not required. The squadron returned after about forty-five minutes, and we ran out to meet them, eager for results. Percy had shot down a Heinkel 111 near a neighbouring aerodrome: he got it at 2,000 feet! Must have been a Nazi fanatic. There were several more claims and Henry, the squadron intelligence officer, started to sift the evidence. Jenks was missing, and we heard soon afterwards that he had tried to bale out but something had gone wrong: his blood-stained parachute arrived later and it was obvious that no attempt had been made to pull the ripcord; he must have hit something getting out. Jenks was one of our best pilots and his death was a bitter blow for the squadron.

I stood by for Star until shortly before lunch. His engine had been hit by an armour-piercing bullet and he spent some of the time checking up on the damage. One or two other aircraft had also been damaged and he was anxious to know the total effect on the state of serviceability.

Stand-off for lunch was arranged and I pushed off; but not for long. The squadron was suddenly ordered off and I rushed back to take over the emergency section. I had been unlucky so far; this was the second squadron show I had missed.

Bruno, Dopey, and I made up the emergency section and we climbed into our aircraft ready for take-off. We had only a few minutes to wait: I saw my fitter turn his head towards the tarmac and then jump up on to my port plane, stick his head into the cockpit and repeat the orders he had heard coming over the loudspeaker. We were to 'Patrol base at 2,000 feet.'

I took off, closely followed by Bruno on my right and Dopey on my left. At 1,700 feet operations asked my height. I passed it back and received orders to climb to 20,000 feet as fast as I could; they gave me a vector south-eastwards. It was a perfect summer's day, the sky was cloudless, and as we approached 15,000 feet the sun became dazzling, almost painful to the eyes. Somewhere below us the rest of the squadron was mixed up in a scrap with Hun bombers attempting to attack our aerodromes, and I concluded that we were to keep some of their escort above them occupied.

To the north lay the sprawling mass of London and her suburbs, and the Thames could be seen winding its way through the maze of red, white, and black buildings on the waterfront towards the estuary. Stretching from the south bank of the river towards the east and south, as far as the eye could see, lay the hazy outline of the Kentish coast; beneath were the rolling downs of wood and grassland, the heart of the county. I estimated our position to be three or four miles west of Maidstone, at a height of 17,000 feet, our course still south-easterly, when I heard operations warning us of Hun aircraft in the vicinity. I intensified my search and rocked my aircraft to bring Bruno and Dopey further in; they were searching the flanks and keeping an eye on the area behind.

I had just steadied up and checked course when ahead and about 500 feet above us I saw BLACK CROSSES. There, shown up clearly by the sun, were rows and rows of Me 109s flying in 'grid' formation, each row flying line astern slightly stepped up. They were travelling south-south-east, and I reckoned there were forty or fifty of them, perhaps more. There was no time to climb as we were already within range, and I knew they could outclimb us if they wanted to. We had the advantage of the sun, however, being to starboard of them, and we drove straight into their flank to cut them up.

It was a sight worth all the months of waiting and disappointment.

All these particular Hun fighters were coloured silver against which the Black Cross stood out plainly, fitting emblem of what they represented. The nose, under-cowling, wing-tips, and tailplane tips were yellow, so was the under surface of the fuselage, hence the nickname of 'yellow bellies' by which they were known.

I had already turned the button to 'fire' and adjusted the reflector sight for '109s' – now for some real practice. Taking a bead on the nearest aircraft – I was flying at about 20° to his line of flight and slightly below at about 175 yards distance – I pressed the button and saw the lines of incendiaries pouring out of the wings of my aircraft. The smell of cordite filled the cockpit and I felt the nose dip under the recoil; I held her steady. The Hun aircraft flew straight for a bit, then gently turned on its back. My shot appeared to be going straight into the engine cowling and cockpit, but as the Hun turned over I saw what appeared to be tracers spiralling the fuselage and coming aft. I learnt months later from a fellow patient in hospital that this was shattered perspex, the transparent material of which the cockpit cover was made; I must have been dumb not to realise that! The Hun turned slightly on his back and then dived beneath out of sight, going straight down; I had fired for about four seconds.

A shower of tracers whistled over my head and an orange-coloured streak, about an inch thick with a head the size of a tangerine, shrieked past the right side of my cockpit cover. I glanced in the mirror and saw a Hun about 200 yards aft; I dipped, turning slightly to the right, then pulled up again in a sharp left-hand turn. I could see nothing of Bruno or Dopey. As I came up another Hun crossed my sights, he must have been about 120 yards off and flying steady. I gave him a burst and turned with him. A column of black smoke poured from what appeared to be the leading edge of his starboard wing, about a yard out from the wing-root; I thought my shot had gone slap into the fuselage. He turned across my path and his nose dropped into a dive, leaving a long column of smoke in his wake. I lost sight of him, having pulled up to avoid hitting him.

It was at this point that I nearly collided with another Hun. He flew past me only a few yards out and had obviously not seen me. He flew slightly across my sights, and at about 60 to 70 yards I gave him the works. It was too good to be true, few chances like this come one's way. I gave him a five-second burst in all; after three seconds of fire he pulled the nose up, appeared to lose speed rapidly and then fell out of the sky, stalling into a dive; I gave him a bit more for luck. The cockpit seemed empty as he pulled up, but I saw no body come hurtling out.

I seemed now to be in the centre of the mass of Huns; they were all over the place but still trying to keep some semblance of formation. Tracers passed overhead and underneath, curving down ahead. I looked for another target, and as I turned to fly out towards the sun a Hun passed just to the right of me and slightly above. I raised the nose and turned, giving him all I had; I saw him roll on to his back, fly for a second inverted, then go straight down full out. My shot appeared to have gone into the lower half of the fuselage and belly, and I think I got the pilot as the armour plating does not protrude downwards as it does upwards in relation to the pilot's seat.

I was now out of ammunition and my mirror told me that three Huns, in line astern, were fastened on my tail. There was no sign of Bruno or Dopey, so I stuck the nose down, skidding and turning until I was diving all out. Glancing over my shoulder as I dived, I saw six Ju 87s in two lots of threes just to the east of me. They were going south in a great hurry and I bitterly regretted having to leave them alone. I pulled out gently at the bottom of the dive, turning to search above and behind, but I was not being followed. It was good to be in a Hurricane, especially in a jam; the Me 109s couldn't cope with them when it came to turning; they could dive and climb quicker than us but were not nearly so manoeuvrable.

I could still find no trace of Bruno and Dopey, so I returned to the aerodrome, landed, and taxied in. The squadron was already down, and Henry was busy collating reports; they had had a good scrap and there were several claims, certainties and probables. I checked up on pilots and aircraft and found that Bruno and Dopey had not returned; I began to get worried, more so as time passed. News came through later that Bruno had force-landed and hurt his shoulder, but was otherwise ok. I felt relieved; we could not afford to lose pilots, much less those of his experience. Dopey, however, was still missing. Days later, when in hospital, I heard he had been found; he had crashed and received fatal injuries. What toll he took of the enemy will never be known; the amount of lead flying about in that scrap could hardly have been for my sole benefit, and I know Bruno was out of the scrap right at the start. I like to think that Dopey got one, perhaps more; he was the youngest in the squadron and a likeable chap.

Henry met me on the tarmac and asked for details. I gave him a brief account of the scrap and told him that I thought I had accounted for four Me 109s. He stated that unless I had seen them break up, catch fire, or crash, they could not be counted as destroyed. I could not state that, although I somehow felt that those Huns would not need rations any more. The station intelligence officer gave me two probables and two possibles; he gave nothing away, and rightly so. That is why, when I read the official account of the Battle of Britain, I know in my own mind that those figures are the utter minimum; one could add another 1,000 Huns probably destroyed and still be within bounds. I can't imagine the German Luftwaffe having that faith.

I had late lunch and then stood by for Star. During the afternoon the other squadron was sent off and we were told to be on our toes. The Huns were coming in from the south, and shortly afterwards Ack-Ack fire could be seen to the east of us. Then an air battle developed, and away up in the blue the glistening shapes of friend and foe could be seen twisting and turning to the accompaniment of machine-gun and cannon fire. Tracer streaks and vapour trails wove fantastic patterns against the blue sky, and the shrieks and whines of diving aircraft added sound to a scene hitherto undreamt of, even by writers of 'air ace' fiction. It was a grand sight, tragic no doubt, but nevertheless a scene more spectacular and stirring than any film studio could produce.

We saw the scrap fade out and the other squadron return, refuel and rearm ready for further business. All was quiet until, just as we were arranging for tea, an order came through for us to stand by. We had two sections ready. I had three aircraft in one and Bill had four in the other, and we climbed into our aircraft to await the signal to be off. The other squadron was already on its way to attack another raid coming north and we were hoping to be sent up to deal with any Hun escort or following raids. Instructions came through to take off more quickly than we had dared to hope: 'Patrol base at 1,500 feet.' We were off and climbing fast in a few seconds, and I could see Bill way out on my right coming up like a shell; the rest were strung out behind racing for position. I turned left for a wide circuit, easing up a bit, and my No. 2 and No. 3 closed in. Then I heard operations calling again: 'Climb to 15,000 feet as fast as you can go,' came the controller's voice, shortly followed by instructions to proceed on a certain vector. Bill had heard it too, and I saw him, through the mirror, closing in astern and stepping up. I set course for the south, and when we had reached a point a few miles south-east of Tunbridge Wells, at a height of about 14,000 feet, Bill informed me that he had seen something to the east of us. He had already turned his section, and I opened up the throttle to regain position. The aircraft we were chasing proved to be Hurricanes on another scent, and Bill turned, rocking his wings as a signal. He was now slightly above and ahead of my section, and I manoeuvred to get the lead again.

We were flying south with the sun on our right, climbing once more, and keeping an eye on the sun side as the Hun had the advantage in that respect most of the day when coming in, an advantage which they never failed to use. At 17,000 feet I had drawn almost level with Bill's section when I heard the rat-tat of machine-gun fire, punctuated by the chug-chug of cannons, and tracer streaks and cannon-shell tracks appeared over his section as several Me 109s came hurtling down on their tails. There were about seven in one batch, followed by six more; the odds were two to one, which was more than even: some people reckoned three to one was evens by this time. I turned, and we waded into them. The fight became a wheeling mixture of Me 109s and Hurricanes; each one seemed to be firing at the chap in front of him. Two aircraft, one a few feet above the other, were both firing at something in front; a horrible sight for a Life Insurance Company to see. I was about to pick out a possible victim for burial when I saw a Me 109 fastened onto the tail of a Hurricane, blowing bits of fabric and wood off the fuselage with machine-gun and cannon fire. My blood boiled; no darned Hun would get away with that. I opened the throttle wide and raced after him, opening fire at something like 180 to 200 yards, all three of us, with the Me 109 in the middle, being in line astern and turning slightly. I gained on the Hun rapidly; he had obviously slowed down to keep on the Hurricane's tail and appeared not to notice me. I kept the button pressed the whole time, determined to get him before he finished off the Hurricane. My firing sight packed up as I closed in, but as I was now only about 70 yards astern of the Hun I was able to use the tracks of the incendiaries as a sighting. My shot appeared to be going home, yet he still maintained formation although I could not see if he was firing or not, due to the firework display from my own guns. Then gradually he rolled to the right on to his back and flew inverted for a while. I kept on firing. I was almost on top of him now, and saw patches of black material coming away from the starboard wing near the wing-root and from the fuselage. A piece of long wire or metal dropped off as the Hun turned, still inverted, and then gradually dropped away into a dive, turning slowly. I wanted to follow him down and see him crash, but a glance in the mirror made me change my mind. There were three Huns on my tail, the nearest only about 100 yards astern. Why he never opened fire I do not know. I can only assume that he was afraid of hitting his compatriot in front of me. I had now only a few rounds left in the guns, less than ten apiece, and once again I relied on the good offices of the Hurricane to get me out of a jam. I flicked over to the left and pulled the stick back hard, diving, turning, and skidding down to 10,000 feet, but by then the Hun had disappeared. What speed I reached in that dive I do not know, the needle had passed maximum figure long before I levelled out, but it certainly added even further to my confidence in the strength of the Hurricane. I eased the nose up, climbing like a rocket with all that stored-up speed; it was one of the finest thrills I have ever experienced in my years of flying.

I turned south again in the hope of picking up some of the squadron, but when I reached the scene – it was on the coast near Dungeness – everyone had vanished. It has always been a thing of wonder to me how an area full of whirling aircraft can suddenly become completely vacant; I could not have been away more than a minute and not a trace of anything remained. I returned to the aerodrome, wondering how many were safe, where that battered Hurricane had gone down, and who was flying it: had he got away with it? I somehow felt he could not have made his base after that beating-up. I was wrong! I landed, taxied in, and there on the tarmac was the very machine. I had been unable to read the squadron letter in the scrap, but the damage was identical. How the pilot ever managed to fly home I do not know. Flaps, undercarriage, elevators, and rudder, which now consisted of a few tubes and thin air, still worked; they must have done. No recommendation for British aircraft construction could ever surpass that amazing example of sheer aeronautical guts.

Clustered around the battered but unbent aircraft were people from all parts of the station. I joined the spectators and asked who had been flying it; it was 'the Colonel'. I saw him talking to Bill in the middle of an inquisitive crowd of pilots. He was giving vent to his feelings and his opinion of the Huns in general, particularly the one who had written his name on the poor old Hurricane. The Colonel had a very good command of the English language, both written and unwritten – though muttered in secret places – but no oration, however eloquent, could have matched this piece of verbal cannon-fire. Roars of laughter assured him of full agreement all round, and he seemed better for the outburst.

I gave Henry a verbal account of the scrap and heard a few minutes later that my Me 109 was confirmed, although I never knew whether it crashed on land or in the sea. I had the satisfaction, however, of knowing that at least one Hun had been added to the squadron's collection. This stood at something like 12 confirmed and 12 probables from the Dunkirk show, and now, the first day with the Huns in the blitz, I estimated that we had shot down 14 altogether. When the final figures arrived from operations, we were given something like 7 confirmed and 5 or 6 probables, a very gratifying day. Star was very bucked, and I was feeling like someone in another world: I had kept my vow.

One incident, however, spoilt my sense of accomplishment. News came through that Dicky, one of our sergeants who, unknown to me, had been missing, had been riddled by a Hun whilst coming down by parachute. It may be permissible in war to shoot someone descending by parachute from a wrecked or burning aircraft, though he is using the direct and indisputable counterpart of a lifeboat, but only those devoid of all sense of fair fight and chivalry could do it. Paratroops are different; they drop under special conditions and are 'offensive troops' in no less a degree than a landing party by boat. I felt bitter about Dicky and so did Star, but little did he know that next day he was to meet the same fate.

We were off that evening, and spent most of the time in the billiard room comparing notes. One thing always stands out clearly in my mind when I recall those times. Contrary to what one would suppose, there is no sense of strain or tension in a scrap, nor for some time afterwards. It is when one settles down to lounge, smoke, and perhaps enjoy a can of beer that fatigue becomes apparent: a feeling of pleasant drowsiness from which one has no wish to be disturbed. This was how I felt at any rate, and I found a great deal of will power necessary to rouse myself somewhere about ten o'clock and push off to bed.

Next morning, August 31st, I was down at dispersal point before breakfast. It was another grand day, full of expectations: would the Hun oblige?

All was quiet, and I wandered back towards the mess. On the way I stopped and chatted to an anti-aircraft machine-gunner. He had a battery of Lewis guns ingeniously mounted on a home-made stand. He had had the same instrument in France and, thanks to its prolific output of hot lead and the accuracy of the gunner, several Huns had come to a sticky end. The gunner had a fine sense of humour, unimpaired by his experiences in the evacuation from France.

After breakfast I spent some time in the portable squadron office whilst Star stood by. There was some activity during the morning and the squadron was eventually sent off. We, that is the emergency section, stood by, but were not required. The squadron returned in due course, several aircraft being damaged. They had had a scrap and shot up a Hun formation; the results were now being sifted. Star was missing, and I feared the worst: Jerry always paid particular attention to leaders of formations. I wandered over to the station aircraft repair section to check up on the number of aircraft I could raise to fill up depleted sections. The station CO arrived shortly afterwards and informed me that Star had baled out but the Hun had shot him dead on the way down. I could hardly believe that this could be the end of Star. That a fellow of his ability and charm, a fellow who had the right idea about everything and only wished to do his job in complete accord with all, regardless of rank, should die like this was too much.

I went back to the dispersal point and broke the news to the squadron. Nothing can describe their feelings; they were expressed by all, crews and pilots alike, in no uncertain terms. Tempers were raised to white heat; nothing that they had heard or read could ever have brought home to them more forcibly the ruthless type we were fighting against. Their determination to smash the Hun now knew no bounds. Although they had missed the first mass raids of the blitz, their subsequent efforts bear testimony to the fact that this act profited the Hun nothing.

With the help of Bill I arranged for two sections to stand by, the remainder of the squadron to push off to the mess for an early lunch. The Colonel had taken over Bruno's flight, and it was his turn to stand off: we remained on duty.

Relief had been arranged for lunch, and I had just started off for the mess when the order came through for all our available aircraft to take off. A large raid was coming in from the south, and the lull of the past two hours or so changed to frenzied activity.

I grabbed my helmet and parachute and ran to the aircraft which I was to use in place of 'X,' which I had lent to another pilot during a previous raid when it had been damaged. The crew had already started up – they never needed asking – and I jumped in.

We received orders to join up with another squadron at 2,000 feet over the aerodrome, and in a few seconds were climbing up as hard as we could go. The sections formed up as we climbed, and I turned slightly at 1,000 feet to make a wide circuit and to look out for the other squadron, which, a few seconds later, I saw coming south, flying in an inverted 'J' formation; one flight was in 'vic' with the other in line astern behind the left-hand man of the leading flight. We followed suit, but joining up on the right, thus making a total formation in the shape of an inverted 'U'.

After a few minutes we turned north, and I glanced up to see what we were chasing. Right above us were rows of Hun bombers – Ju 88s in line astern – and my aircraft were directly below one line of them and closing distance rapidly. We were soon within about 1,000 feet of them, well within cannon range and approaching machine-gun range, but the formation was still going ahead. I did some rapid thinking; if we maintained our position we would, in a few seconds, be sitting shots for both front and rear Hun gunners. I therefore decided to attack before they had a chance to open fire, and certainly before we came within danger of collision. I rocked my wings and then eased the nose up, taking a bead on No. 5 of the line of Huns and giving him a raking burst. I turned on to my side as I finished firing, kicked hard on bottom rudder to fake a stalled turn, and dived down, straightening out as I gathered speed. I repeated the process on No. 3 and, glancing over my shoulder as I skidded sideways over the top, saw clouds of greyish-white smoke issuing from his port engine. I could not see the effect of my fire on No. 5, he was too far behind. I was about to pull up to attack No. 1, who incidentally was now losing height preparatory to a dive-bomb attack, when I heard a metallic click above the roar of my engine. It seemed to come from the starboard wing and I glanced in that direction, but a sudden burst of heat struck my face, and I looked down into the cockpit. A long spout of flame was issuing from the hollow starboard wing-root, curling up along the port side of the cockpit and then across towards my right shoulder. I had seen neither tracers nor cannon tracks near my aircraft; the fire could not have been caused by structural or other failure, and I therefore presumed I had picked up a stray incendiary. I had some crazy notion that if I rocked the aircraft and skidded, losing speed, the fire might go out. Not a bit of it; the flames increased until the cockpit was like the centre of a blow-lamp nozzle. There was nothing left to do but bale out: a forced landing was out of the question as I was still 7,000 to 8,000 feet up. I reached down to pull the radio telephone phone lead out of its socket, but the heat was too great. The skin was already rising off my right wrist and hand, and my left hand was starting to blister, the glove being already partially burnt off. My shoes and slacks must have been burning all this time, but I cannot remember any great pain.

Shock is nature's anaesthetic; a blessing I now know to the full; something that hides the pain and blanks the mind, leaving a memory of something unpleasant yet a feeling that one has defeated that which was once a terrifying thought. I think that is why I still yearn to fly again, am still willing to take the chance and risk, without which life would be a monotonous existence, unworthy to be called 'living'.

I undid my harness and tried to raise myself, but found I had not the strength. I was comforted by the thought that I had my gun ready loaded if things came to the worst. I decided to pull off my helmet, open the cockpit cover and roll on my back so that I could drop out. My helmet came off after a determined tug: I opened the cockpit cover and that was the last effort I had to make. There was a blinding flash, I seemed to be travelling through yards of flame; then I found myself turning over and over in the air, but with no sense of falling. Gradually I ceased to travel forwards and fell downwards, still turning head over heels. My hand instinctively passed over the harness release and on to the ripcord handle. I pulled hard and felt the cord being drawn through the strongly woven fabric tubing; then came a gentle jerk as I was pulled into the vertical position, swinging comfortably, secure in my harness. An interminable space of time seemed to have elapsed whilst I was endeavouring to escape from that inferno, but actually it was less than a minute.

Everything was quiet, deathly still, an amazing contrast to the sound of flight. I remember thinking how grand the scene below me looked; fields of green grass, fields of stubble patched here and there with clumps of trees and hedgerows. Country lanes wound their way from farm to highway where the metallic surface seemed to shimmer in the heat. I had always longed to make a 'brolley jump', as a parachute descent is called in the service, but now I could raise no enthusiasm as I floated down. Only the earth below had any interest for me; I was feeling distinctly browned off.

As I approached the earth I seemed to gather speed; the swinging appeared to be accentuated, and the sight of a barbed-wire fence below gave my fuzzled mind a start. I was then about 50 feet up, and as I went through the last swinging motion the fence disappeared from view, the ground came up in an unfriendly way, and I closed my eyes. I felt my left hip and head strike the ground simultaneously and then all was still.

I sat up and looked around, and was surprised that I had not received any injury from my impact with the ground. Then I remembered the days of instruction in 'how to use a parachute'; how one should relax when striking the ground and on no account try to take weight on the feet. I never intended to take any weight on my feet, I was too disinterested. With an effort I stood up and surveyed the damage. My shoes still looked like shoes and I found I could walk; why, I don't know, as my ankle and each side of my right foot were burnt and my left foot was scorched and had several small burns. My slacks had disappeared except for portions that had been covered by the parachute harness. The skin on my right leg, from the top or the thigh to just above the ankle, had lifted and draped my leg like outsize plus-fours. My left leg was in a similar condition except that the left thigh was only scorched, thanks to the flames having been directed to my right side. Above each ankle I had a bracelet of unburnt skin: my socks, which were always wrinkled, had refused to burn properly and must have just smouldered. That my slacks should have burnt so easily is not surprising; oil mist percolates one's clothing, and I probably had enough on my person to lubricate a battleship. My service gloves were almost burnt off, and the skin from my wrists and hands hung down like paper bags. The underside of my right arm and elbow were burnt and so was my face and neck. I could see all right, although it felt like looking through slits in a mass of swollen skin, and I came to the conclusion that the services of a doctor were necessary.

There seemed to be nobody about, so I decided to walk to the end of the field where I could see a gate. I remember calling out in the hope that someone would come along as I made my way across the grass. I reached the gate, managed to open it, and found myself in a country lane. Lower down, on the opposite side of the lane, was a cowshed, and I walked towards it. A man came out; he had apparently heard me calling, and when he saw me he stopped and stared. I guessed I must be looking a little strange, and promptly blurted out, 'RAF pilot. I want a doctor.'

32 Alan Deere, Spitfire Pilot, Squadron Leader, New Zealander, 54 Squadron

Extracts from an Air Ministry- and Ministry of Information-endorsed BBC radio broadcast by an anonymous RAF fighter pilot in February 1941 and the Operations Record Book (ORB) of 54 Squadron.

The incident took place at noon on Saturday 31 August, when RAF Hornchurch was bombed by a large formation of bombers from 15,000 feet. The anonymous pilot is Alan Deere (New Zealand) and the short account below is of how his Spitfire (and those of Eric Edsall and Jack Davis) was blown up as the squadron desperately tried to get off the ground and escape the bombing. Richard Hillary, also based at Hornchurch at the time (see chapter 33), witnessed their dramatic escape.

Deere joined the RAF in 1937 and 54 Squadron in 1938. By the end of 1940 the rugged-looking twenty-three-year-old New Zealander had become a legend. He had been shot down seven times (including three balings out) and amassed fourteen kills, and remains one of the best-known pilots from the Battle of Britain. He survived the war and wrote his wartime memoirs, which were published as *Nine Lives* in 1959. In this book Deere comments on the broadcast below, explaining that he experienced a 'little bother' with the radio producer about the script, which had virtually been written by the Air Ministry press officer, but was persuaded to play along because he was paid! However, the broadcast is so similar to the fuller account given in his book that we can assume the Air Ministry stuck to the facts pretty closely. With Deere, you couldn't really invent better stories anyway. He remained in the RAF until 1967, leading his fellow Battle of Britain pilots in the main funeral cortège for Winston Churchill and acting as a consultant for the 1969

Left: 46. *THE PILOTS.* One of 87 Squadron's two Belgian pilots, Francois de Spirlet, standing on the engine cowling of his Hurricane, 1940. De Spirlet was in the Belgian air force at the outbreak of war. His squadron was moved to France after the German attack of 10 May 1940, then onwards to England on the SS *Apapa* out from Port Vendres on France's Mediterranean coast on 24 June 1940 and sailed via Gibraltar to Liverpool, where they arrived on 7 July 1940. He joined Ian Gleed's squadron (see chapters 4 and 25) on 12 August. *Right:* 47. Two ace Polish pilots of 501 Squadron, August 1940. Left is Antoni Glowacki (see chapter 30), who shot down five in a single day on 24 August. He died in 1980. Right is Stefan Witorzenc; he also survived the war and died in 1994.

Top right: 48. David Crook (see chapters 13, 24 and 45) and Geoffrey Gaunt, September 1940 at RAF Middle Wallop. Soon after this photograph was taken on 15 September, the high point of the Battle, Gaunt was shot down and killed during an attack on German bombers.

Bottom right: 49. 501 Squadron Hurricane pilot Sergeant Pilot James 'Ginger' Lacey (right) explains to his flight commander Christopher 'Bunny' Currant (left) how he shot down his second enemy aircraft. Lacey was one of the RAF's top-scoring aces of the Second World War, and number two highest-scoring in the Battle of Britain (18 confirmed kills). Currant shot down ten enemy aircraft in 1940 and later starred as 'Hunter Leader', alongside David Niven and Leslie Howard, in the aerial sequences of the film *First of the Few*, a huge success in 1942.

Above: 50. 32 Squadron Hurricane pilots relaxing in between sorties, July 1940 at RAF Hawkinge, Folkstone, Kent. Left to right: Rupert Smythe (Irish, an ace, survived the war), Keith Gillman (1 kill, KIA 25 August 1940, a photographic portrait was taken of him and printed around the world in July and August 1940 as the 'face' of the RAF fighting the Nazis), John Proctor (with his hands round his ankles; a sergeant pilot with 501 Squadron in the Battle of France, he shot down 7, joined 32 Squadron as a pilot officer in July 1940 and added 3 more during the Battle of Britain), Pete Brothers (10 kills in 1940), Peter Gardner (7 kills during 1940, survived war), Douglas Grice (leaning on his front, an ace, survived war) and Alan Eckford (later 253 Squadron and an ace by the end of 1940). *Left:* 51. John Dewar, Hurricane pilot, leader of 87 Squadron from December 1939 (Ian Gleed's commanding officer; see chapters 4 and 25). He became an ace during the Battle of France. In the Battle of Britain he destroyed three more but was KIA 12 September 1940. Drawing by William Rothenstein, June 1940, official war artist.

Above: 52. 310 Squadron, the first Czech fighter squadron, formed in July 1940. Left to right: Stanislav Zimprich (1 kill and 4 probables during the Battle, KIA 1942), Viktor Bergmann (2 kills and survived the war), Emil Fechtner (4 kills, died in an accident with fellow pilot Jaroslev Maly on 29 October 1940), Vilem Goth (2 kills, KIA October 1940) and John Boulton, a British flight lieutenant. *Right:* 53. Ian Gleed (see chapters 4 and 25) in his Hurricane 1940; note on the door of the aircraft his personal mascot Figaro (a cartoon cat that first appeared in Walt Disney's animated film *Pinocchio*). Gleed saved the original doors decorated with his Figaro emblem from two of his Hurricanes, P2798 and Z3779. A fragment of the Spitfire in which he died (AB502), with Figaro on, was recovered from the crash site by a childhood friend. All three were kept by Gleed's family until they donated them to the RAF Museum, Hendon. *Bottom right:* 54. Members of 43 Squadron, April 1940 at RAF Wick in the north of Scotland (see Simpson chapter 8). Left to right: James Buck (baled out off Selsey Bill and drowned 19 July 1940), Tony Woods-Scawen (shot down and saved by the same parachute six times; when asked why he carried his parachute 20 miles across France he'd said, 'Well, I know this one works'), Caesar Hull, W. C. Wilkinson (KIA 7 June 1940), Geoffrey Garton (later 73 Squadron, 2 kills in 1940).

Above left: 55. Arthur Clowes alongside his 1 Squadron Hurricane (P3395 JX-B), October 1940 at RAF Wittering. A caption for the picture published 16 November 1940 stated that each kill by this pilot was recorded by a black band on his wasp emblem. He served in France through the Battle of Britain and survived the war. *Above right:* 57. Robert Stanford Tuck in the cockpit of his 257 Squadron Hurricane, autumn 1940 with his then 23 kills marked as Swastikas. He was posted to command 257 at the height of the Battle on 11 September 1940 after the squadron had suffered major losses, including David Hunt (see chapter 27). One of the greatest aces of the RAF, by 1942 when he was shot down and captured in occupied France he had shot down 29 enemy aircraft. *Bottom left:* 58. Thomas Grier, 601 Squadron fighter pilot, 1940. Nine kills in the Battle and shared in the destruction of 5 others, he was killed in action in 1941. *Middle left:* 59. 54 Squadron just after the fighting over Dunkirk, June 1940. Back row, left to right: John Norwell (3 kills and 4 shared kills in 1940), Desmond McMullen (12 kills in 1940), Colin Gray (New Zealand), Phillip Tew (1 kill and 1 shared kill in 1940). Front row, left to right: John Allen (an ace, KIA 27 July 1940 and buried in Margate Cemetery), Alan Deere (New Zealand, shot down 14 enemy aircraft in 1940, see chapter 32), James Leathart, 54's squadron leader (an ace by the end of 1940), Basil Way (an ace, KIA 25 July 1940) and Dorian Gribble (8 kills in 1940, KIA June 1941).

Right: 56. The damaged wing of the Hurricane (V6799) flown by Pilot Officer Kenneth Mackenzie, 501 Squadron. On 7 October 1940, Mackenzie deliberately knocked the tail off a Me 109 in order to drive it into the sea after using up all his ammunition: 'At the time we were flying within 80 or 100 feet of the sea and I could just see the French coast. Then the idea occurred to me that I might knock his tail off with my wing. I flew on his port side just above him and came up until the end of my wing was just over his tail plane. Then I gave a huge amount of right aileron which brought my starboard wing slap down on his port tailplane. At once I saw the tip of my wing fly off up into the air while his tail plane collapsed and he simply dived straight into the sea and never reappeared.' The Me 109 Mackenzie collided with, flown by Erich Meyer of JG51, was miraculously discovered and most of the wreck recovered from the sea in 1976, minus its tailplane.

Above left: 60. Arthur Donahue (American), Spitfire pilot with 64 Squadron, see chapters 16, 19 and 53. *Above middle:* 61. John Simpson, 43 Squadron (see chapters 8 and 48). *Above right:* 62. Mark 'Hilly' Brown. See chapters 2, 23 and 57. *Below left:* 63. Dickie Lee. First flew with 85 Squadron and made their first kill of a He 111 on 21 November 1939. Barry Sutton (chapters 5 and 14) met him in France: 'he looked very sunburnt and tired'. He flew with 56 Squadron with John Simpson (see chapters 8 and 48) during Dunkirk and returned to 85 Squadron later in the summer. He was last seen in pursuit of the enemy on 18 August, and his body was never found. *Below middle:* 64. Christopher 'Mickey' Mount (2 kills in 1940), Spitfire pilot with 602 Squadron, portrait by Cuthbert Orde, 1940. *Below right:* 65. Keith Gillman (1 kill, KIA 25 August 1940), Hurricane pilot of B flight of 32 Squadron. This photographic portrait was printed around the world in July and August 1940 as the 'face' of the RAF fighting the Nazis.

66. Pilots of 242 Squadron at RAF Coltishall in Norfolk, September 1940. Left to right: George Eric Ball (5 kills during 1940), Douglas Bader (squadron leader of 242, best-known pilot of the Battle, double amputee with 10 kills in the Battle, see chapter 38) and William 'Willie' McKnight (Canadian, 18 kills in 1940, KIA January 1941). When Bader took command of the squadron he designed the squadron emblem, a caricature of Hitler being kicked in the bottom by a flying boot labelled '242', painted by ground crew artist Tom Elgey.

67. Some of the inaugural members of the Guinea Pig Club, including the 'Maestro', pioneering plastic surgeon Archibald McIndoe (far right), who reconstructed many terribly burned fighter pilots. Left to right: Tom Gleave (see chapter 31), Geoffrey Page (56 Squadron, 1 and 2 shared kills before was shot down by return fire from a Do 17, and after two years in hospital he returned to duty and shot down 2 more), Russell Davies, Peter Weeks, John Hughes, Michael Coote (600 Squadron). The photograph was taken by the club's first secretary, Bill Towers-Perkins (238 Squadron).

Above: 68. Donald Finley, squadron leader of 41 Squadron, in front of his Spitfire Mk 11 at RAF Hornchurch December 1940. Finley, an Olympic hurdler before the war, was shot down twice and knocked down three enemy aircraft by the end of 1940.

Right: 69. 19 and 616 Squadron Spitfire pilots, 1940 RAF Coltishall, Norfolk. On the wing, left to right: Brian Lane (see chapters 7, 43 and 55), Flash the Alsatian dog next to his owner George 'Grumpy' Unwin (died aged 93 in 2006, 14 kills in 1940), Rangy the dog, and Francis Brinsden (New Zealand, 1 and 2 shared kills in 1940). Standing, left to right: Bernard Jennings (an ace by the end of 1940), Colin MacFie (wearing a scarf and holding a pipe; 1 kill in the Battle, crashed in France in 1942 was made a POW), in the dark polo-neck jumper, Howard Burton (KIA 1943) and Philip Leckrone (American, killed 1941).

Bottom: 70. A trophy from 609 Squadron's hundredth kill, Ju 88 of 1/KG51 (9K+BH), shot down on 21 October 1940 (crashed near Milford on Sea, killing the crew) by Frank Howell (left, survived war) and Sydney Hill (right, KIA 1941).

71. *THE OTHER FEW*. Defiants of 264 Squadron, summer 1940. L7026 V-PS (nearest camera) was shot down on 28 August 1940 by Me 109s, the crew (pilot Peter Kenner and air gunner Charles Johnson) were both killed. N1535 A-PS was shot down by a Ju 88 on 24 August. Again the crew, pilot Squadron Leader Philip Hunter and gunner Frederick King, both perished and their bodies were never found. They had shot down 9 enemy aircraft, including five 109s.

72. Pilot and gunner crews of 264 Squadron (Defiants) at readiness outside their dispersal tent at RAF Kirton-in-Lindsey, Lincolnshire (12 Group), early August 1940. Many of these brave men would be dead by the end of the month. The slow and unwieldy Defiant was soon discovered by the Luftwaffe fighters to be easy prey. 141 Squadron had been virtually wiped out on 19 July 1940 when bounced by 109s. 264 Squadron suffered the same fate within days of moving from Kirton to the centre of the Battle at RAF Hornchurch on 22 August. On 29 August the remnants returned, and the Defiant was redeployed as a night fighter.

Above left: 73. Blenheim IFs over south-east England, 1940. The fighter version of the Blenheim light bomber played a brave but small role in the Battle of Britain. Its most successful pilot was New Zealander Michael Herrick, 25 Squadron, who shot down three enemy aircraft during the Battle.

Above right: 74. Roderick Chisholm, Blenheim pilot with 604 Squadron, a night fighter squadron during the Battle of Britain. The embryonic night fighter squadrons were experimenting and perfecting their technique during the Battle, and began to come into their own as the night-time Blitz of late 1940 took over from the daylights raids of summer 1940 and radar technology developed further to enable accurate interceptions of enemy aircraft at night. Drawing by William Rothenstein, June 1941, official war artist.

Right: 75. John Laughlin, Blenheim pilot with 235 Squadron. He shot down an He 115 over the North Sea on 3 August 1940. Drawing by William Rothenstein, January 1941, official war artist.

Above: 76. *THE FORGOTTEN FEW.* 73 Squadron pilots in France, spring 1940. Furthest left is Lionel Pilkington; an ace by the end of the Battle of France, he was posted to an OTU as an instructor on his return to Britain. On 20 September 1940, during his time at the OTU, he was flying a fully armed Spitfire and shot down a Ju 88 over north Wales. Despite this he is not recognised as having taken part in the Battle! He was KIA in 1941. Left to right after him: Harold 'Ginger' Paul (at least 4 kills over France, did not take part in Battle of Britain), Newel 'Fanny' Orton and Edgar 'Cobber' Kain.

Left: 77. Richard 'Dickie' Martin in full kit standing on the wing of his Hurricane, spring 1940. He shot down several enemy aircraft in the Battle of France but served as an instructor during the Battle of Britain.

Bottom left: 78. 1 Squadron Hurricane pilots, France 1940. Left, Patrick 'Bull' Halahan, who achieved several kills in the Battle of France but served as an instructor at an operational training unit (OTU) during the Battle of Britain. Right, Peter 'Johnnie' Walker, who claimed 8 kills in the Battle of France and survived the war. He didn't fly during the Battle of Britain. Several veterans of the Battle of France scored Battle of Britain kills while attached to OTUs.

Above: 79. Basil 'Tich' Pyne (KIA 14 May 1940) in his 73 Squadron Hurricane, France, spring 1940. Armourers load the .303 machine guns with ammunition. *Right:* 80. Robert Lorimer, left, and Leslie Clisby (Australian), right. Clisby was an ace by 11 May 1940, when he shot down three German fighters before the rudder of his Hurricane was damaged by enemy gunfire. He then found a Heinkel 111 bomber, took a shot at it, forcing it to crash-land. Clisby landed nearby and chased the German crewmen across the field, firing his revolver and capturing one in a rugby tackle. He forced the others to surrender at gunpoint. He then proceeded to march them over to French authorities before rejoining his squadron. Both Clisby and Lorimer were shot down and killed on 15 May in the same action when their flight went in to attack a force of over thirty Me 110s. The aggressive Clisby had notched up an impressive score of 16 kills. *Bottom:* 81. 73 Squadron ace pilots in France, May 1940. New Zealander Edgar 'Cobber' Kain, right, and Newel 'Fanny' Orton, left. Kain became a household name in Britain at the time for his success in downing German aircraft, with 17 confirmed victories. Neither would fight in the Battle of Britain. Kain was killed in a flying accident on 7 June, and Orton was so severely injured on 15 May that he didn't return to active duty until July 1941.

Top: 82. *AT READINESS.* South African Brian van Mentz of 222 Squadron, 27 August 1940 at RAF Kirton-in-Lindsey, Lincolnshire (12 Group). A veteran of the Battle of France, Mentz was an ace by the end of 1940 but was killed on the ground by a stray Luftwaffe bomb that struck a Norfolk village pub on a Saturday night in early 1941. Shortly before the bomb struck, Bob Stanford Tuck had left the Ferry Inn at Horning having failed to persuade Mentz to accompany him to Norwich.

Second: 83. Pilots of 610 Squadron (Spitfires) rest between sorties at RAF Hawkinge, Kent, 29 July 1940. The squadron was based at RAF Biggin Hill but had moved forward towards the coast for the day. Lying on grass: on the far left is Edward Smith (on his stomach and resting on his elbows), who shot down four during the Battle. He married his wife, a WAAF, in 1940 and died in September 2013 aged 98. Leaning on his left elbow is Claude Parsons, who recorded his Battle of Britain experiences in a chapter in the wartime book *Ten Fighter Boys* (3 kills in the Battle, KIA 1941). Douglas Corfe is the dark-haired sergeant pilot. He shot down 1 enemy aircraft in the Battle and was shot down twice himself, being KIA over Malta in 1942. Constantine Pegge is flat on his back; he made 6 kills in the Battle and survived the war. Group on the left standing is difficult to identify but could include Horatio Chandler, John Ellis, Norman Ramsey, William Warner, Ronald Hamlyn (see chapter 29) and Norman Ramsay (1 kill in 1940, survived the war, died 2002).

Third: 84. Three fighter pilots of 111 Squadron beside their dispersal 'hut', a caravan, at RAF Wick in early 1940.

Bottom: 85. 501 Squadron (Hurricanes) pilots early August 1940 at RAF Hawkinge. Standing, left to right: Stefan Witorzenc (Polish, 4½ kills in the Battle, survived the war), George Stoney (see chapter 15, KIA 18 August 1940, 2 kills in the Battle) and Antoni Glowacki. Sitting, left to right: Robert Dafforn (at 6 foot 6 possibly the tallest pilot of the Battle, shot down 6 and shared two more during the Battle of France and Britain, killed 1943), Paul Farnes (6 kills and 1 shared kill in 1940, still alive today), Kenneth Lee (4 kills in 1940, survived the war), John Gibson (New Zealander, 8 kills and 1 shared kill in 1940, survived the war) and Hugh Adams (1 kill in the Battle, KIA 6 September 1940).

Above: 86. German Luftwaffe Me 110 pilots relax in France in the hot summer weather of 1940. The Luftwaffe were mostly operating from hastily requisitioned airfields in occupied territory, with rudimentary maintenance facilities and long supply lines to Germany. *Right:* 87. Glendon Booth of 85 Squadron napping between sorties, August 1940. He was shot down in his Hurricane on 1 September by Me 109s and baled out but was burned and landed heavily with his parachute on fire. He died of his injuries five months later. *Below left:* 87b. An unnamed fighter pilot grabs a moment to sleep while waiting for the call to 'scramble', summer 1940. *Below right:* 88. Parachute placed on the Spitfire wingtip ready for the pilot to strap it on as soon as the 'scramble' call was yelled.

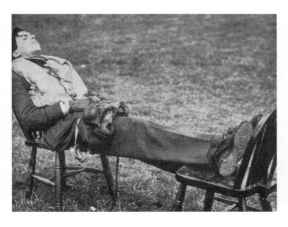

Left: 89. Pilots 'scramble' to their Spitfires.

Above: 90. Pilots 'scramble' to their Hurricanes, 1940.

91. Two 501 Squadron Hurricanes take off mid-August 1940 from RAF Hawkinge. Both aircraft would be shot down within days and destroyed by the same assailant on 18 August.

92. David Crook (see chapters 13, 24 and 45) in his Spitfire about to take off from RAF Middle Wallop for one of the London aerial battles, September 1940.

93. Me 109s preparing to take off, summer 1940.

Left: 94. A Hurricane coming in to refuel and rearm on 15 September 1940. *Above:* 95. Luftwaffe pilot helped out of his Me 109, 1940. *Below:* 96. The crew of a Heinkel 111 examining the damage to their aircraft inflicted while on a raid over England. They made it back to France and this photograph was found on a German prisoner who was later shot down over England.

Above left: 97. AERIAL COMBAT. An Me 109 shoots up one of the Dover barrage balloons in August 1940. The balloons were deployed to deter German bombers from low-level bombing, more accurate than bombing at 15,000 feet.

Above right: 98. British gun-camera images of German aircraft being shot down. John Simpson (see chapters 8 and 48): 'I singled out a Messerschmitt 109 and had a very exciting combat with him. He was a good pilot and he hit me several times. We began to do aerobatics and while he was on his back, I got in a burst which set him on fire. He jumped out, but I did not see his parachute open. His machine was almost burned out before it hit the ground.'

Left: 99. Gun-camera still taken from the Spitfire of John Bisdee (609 Squadron) at 4.30 p.m. on 26 September 1940. He is firing on a He 111 of KG55 which had just successfully bombed the Spitfire factory at Woolston, Southampton. Bisdee was awarded a 'probably destroyed' on a He 111 that day.

Bottom left: 100. A Spitfire shoots great lumps off a Heinkel 111; remarkable film taken from an automatic gun camera fitted to the fighter, 1940.

Clockwise: 101. Gun-camera film from David Crook's Spitfire (see chapters 13, 24 and 45) of him shooting down the first of two Me 109s on 30 September 1940. 'The Messerschmidt was now just ahead of me. I came up behind him, and gave him a terrific burst of fire at very close range. The effect of a Spitfire's eight guns has to be seen to be believed. Hundreds of bullets poured into him and he rocked violently, then turned over on his back, burst into flames and dived straight down into the sea a few miles off Swanage. The pilot made no attempt to get out and was obviously dead. I watched him hit the water in a great cloud of white foam, and then turned round to see what was going on.' 102. A Dornier Do 17 of KG76 shot down on 18 August 1940. It crashed near Oxted, Surrey. 103. Rear cockpit gunner of a Dornier 17, summer 1940. 104. Aerial combat, summer 1940. View from the rear gunner position of an Me 110. The rear canopy is hinged upwards to allow the gunner improved visibility. A Spitfire has been hit and is diving earthwards trailing smoke. It was rare for 110s to get the better of Spitfires. 105. A Do 17 with its starboard engine and wing on fire as recorded by the gun camera of an RAF fighter as it dives down to finish it off *c.* 15 June 1940.

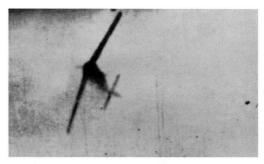

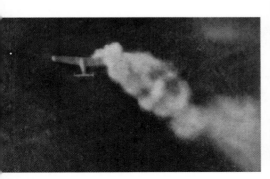

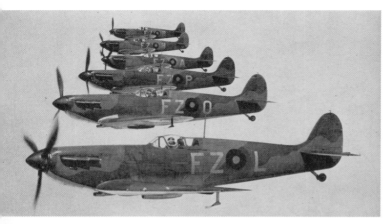

Top: 106. 56 Squadron fly for the benefit of the Air Ministry PR machine, summer 1939. This shot became the standard photo for formation flying. Flying the Spitfire closest to the camera is Robert Stanford Tuck. Fourth Spitfire in, flying Spitfire FZ-A, is Gordon Olive (see chapter 18). 56 Squadron identification letters/squadron code were changed from FZ to YT after the outbreak of war.

Middle: 107. Hurricanes of Ian Gleed's 87 Squadron (see chapters 4 and 25) in formation, 1940.

Bottom: 108. Vapour trails in the skies above London on 6 September 1940, marking the dogfights of the Battle of Britain.

Top: 109. Hurricanes of Ian Gleed's 87 Squadron (see chapters 4 and 25) swoop down on Me 110s. Pencil sketch by a Flight Lieutenant Richard Frost reproduced in Gleed's 1942 memoir, *Arise to Conquer. Middle:* 110. Hurricanes of Ian Gleed's 87 Squadron, bottom right, prepare to attack a raid of Heinkel 111s with Me 110s in a defensive circle above them. Pencil-sketch by Flight Lieutenant Richard Frost. *Bottom:* 111. Hurricanes of 85 Squadron in October 1940 in the standard RAF 'vic' formation, dubbed *idiotenreihen* (rows of idiots) by Luftwaffe fighter pilots in 1940 who had learned by experience in aerial combat over Spain, Poland and France to fly in looser, smaller pairs or *rotte* (a leader and a wingman). Tight formation flying took a great deal of effort and concentration, which could be better spent keeping a watchful eye for the enemy.

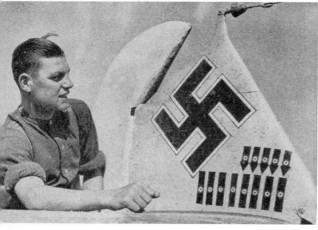

Above: 112. *THE VANQUISHED.* The Me 109 of Luftwaffe ace Franz von Werra. You can just make out the unit insignia on the panel below the windscreen (a geometric design of black and white triangles); it is of II/JG3. He was shot down at Marden in Kent on 5 September 1940 by either the Spitfire of Pat Hughes (234 Squadron) or Gerald Stapleton (603 Squadron, see Hillary chapter 33). The intense scrutiny of this 'kill' was because von Werra would go on to make a series of extraordinary escape attempts from British and Canadian captivity, succeeding eventually to become the only Luftwaffe pilot to escape back to Germany. Gordon Olive (see chapter 18) came across a belly-landed Me 109: 'It was in quite good shape and we spent some time studying it. It was almost the same size as a Spitfire but the petrol tank was behind the pilot instead of being in front of him, as in the Spitfires and Hurricanes. This was a big advantage from the pilot's point of view.' *Left:* 113. The tailplane of von Werra's crashed 109. The bars indicate the number aerial 'kills' achieved, the arrowheads the number of aircraft destroyed on the ground by 'strafing'. *Bottom left:* 114. Me 109 pilot Werner Voigt, of JG3, shot down at noon on 8 October 1940. He crash-landed in the Channel off Abbotts Cliff near Dover.

115. A KG54 Ju 88 (B3+DC) that crash-landed on Portland Head following a major raid on 11 August 1940, shot down by the Hurricane of James Strickland of 213 Squadron (an ace by the end of the Battle, killed 1941). Photograph taken two days later when RAF technicians were dismantling the Ju 88's engines. Chesil Beach is in the background. Note the underwing dive-breaks; these were deployed just before bombs were released in a dive-bombing run.

Above: 116. 18 August 1940, the day the Stuka dive-bomber met its match. Seventeen were shot down, all from the same Luftwaffe unit, StG77. This victim from StG77 (ST+UN) was shot down by Basil Whall of 602 Squadron and made a forced landing on a golf course near Littlehampton. Whall shot down two Stukas that day but his own Spitfire was damaged by return fire and he ditched his aircraft. His total for 1940 was 9 and he shared in 3 other 'kills (this includes 3 shot down while based in Norway in May 1940). He was shot down and killed by return fire from a Ju 88 on 7 October. *Right:* 117. The remains of an Me 110 shot down by the Hurricane of John Flinders, 32 Squadron, 18 August 1940. In his combat report: 'At 3,000 feet he levelled out and I found that I was gradually closing in. I was at about 600 yards. A running fight then ensued, [the 110] doing barrel rolls and half rolls in an attempt to get rid of me. We were now down to 200 feet and as I knew that I had very little ammunition left I refrained from firing until I had a certain target.' Flinders emptied his remaining ammunition into the twin-engine fighter flown by Rudolf Mai and navigator/ gunner Josef Gebauer. It burst into flames and crashed on Rough Common at Harbledown in Kent. *Bottom right:* 118. One of the Ju 87 dive-bombers that devastated RAF Tangmere on 16 August 1940. This Stuka (T6+HL) of Luftwaffe unit StG2 (3 Staffel) was shot down by Hurricanes of 43 Squadron. The pilot survived but his crewman fell out of the aircraft with no parachute.

119. The first Luftwaffe bomber to fall on *British* soil in the war. This bullet-ridden Heinkel 111 was shot down by Archibald McKellar of 602 Squadron on 28 October 1939. McKeller would go on to shoot down 21 enemy aircraft by the time of his death on 1 November 1940, making him one of the top-scoring aces of the Battle. Not to be confused with the first enemy aircraft to fall on *English* soil (or in English *waters*), another He 111, shot down by Caesar Hull and Peter Townsend of 85 Squadron on 3 February 1940. Townsend visited the surviving crew: 'Karl Missy, the rear gunner, had tried to kill me; he was prevented when the bullets from my guns sawed through his leg… despite the harm I had done him, he clasped my hand.'

Top: 120. A bullet-ridden Dornier 17 of KG3 (5K+LM), brought down in flames at Sandwich Flats, Kent, 31 August 1940 after attacking RAF Hornchurch (see Hillary chapter 33). *Bottom left:* 121. Captured pilot, Oberfeldwebel Lange, and crewman of the crashed Dornier 17 shot down at Sandwich Flats. *Bottom right:* 122. A bullet-ridden He 111 of KG55 (G1+FR) shot down at High Salvington near Worthing on 16 August 1940. Before it crash-landed, two crewmen were mortally wounded. Such images (distributed by the Air Ministry in large numbers) were a welcome antidote for a nation facing the horrors of the Blitz.

Left: 123. A crewman from a Dornier 17 of KG3 fished out of the sea by the Margate lifeboat on 28 August 1940. His three fellow crewmen were also rescued from the ditched plane, probably shot down by Antony Eyre of 615 Squadron (Hurricanes). *Right:* 124. Even though severely damaged by cannon shells, Hurricanes could bring their pilot home safe as seen in this photograph from around 16 November 1940. Plenty of photographs were issued to the press by the Air Ministry of crashed Luftwaffe aircraft but none of downed RAF aircraft unless there was a positive spin to be had, in this case the sturdiness of the Hurricane!

125. A badly shot-up Hurricane showing how much damage it could take and still land safely. The pilot of Hurricane DZ-G (DZ on the fuselage is the squadron code for 151 Squadron), P3065 (the unique aircraft registration number) was Henry Beggs. He crash-landed at Shorncliffe, near Folkstone in Kent after being shot down by an Me 109 and walked away injured on 15 August 1940.

126. Wreckage of a StG1 Dornier 17 (A5+EA) shot down on 25 July 1940 by the efforts of 152 Squadron Spitfire pilots Ralph Wolton and Frederick Holmes (see 29 July letter of Eric Marrs, a fellow pilot in 152 Squadron, chapters 12, 28, 42 and 54).

127. *SUPPORT STAFF*. Men of the Observer Corps on the lookout for enemy aircraft.

128. A pilot reports to the squadron intelligence officer his tally of 'kills'.

129. The operations room in the basement of Fighter Command HQ at Bentley Priory, Stanmore. It was at 11 Group HQ's similar ops room that on 15 September 1940 Winston Churchill joined Keith Park, C-in-C of 11 Group, and witnessed the decisive day of the Battle of Britain. Churchill later recorded his thoughts of the day: 'The odds were great, our margins small; the stakes infinite.'

Above: 130. Britain's air minister, Archibald Sinclair (left), visiting the all-Czech 310 Squadron. Sinclair, along with Air Chief Marshall Cyril Newall, was key in growing the RAF in 1937–40 and putting it on a sure footing for the onslaught of the Battle of Britain.

Right: 131. Keith Park, 11 Group Commander, in front of his personal Hurricane, which he used to visit airfields across his group defending London and the south-east. Arthur Tedder, a senior British Air Force commander in 1940 and Marshal of the RAF (the highest rank in the service) said after the war of Park, 'If ever any one man won the Battle of Britain, he did.'

132. Hugh Dowding, Fighter Command's C-in-C, looks on as Alan Deere (New Zealand) of 54 Squadron receives his Distinguished Flying Cross (DFC) from King George VI at RAF Hornchurch, 27 June 1940. Adolph 'Sailor' Malan (South Africa), John Allen and Robert Stanford Tuck received their DFCs at the same ceremony. It was not uncommon for the king to present medals on site; good for morale of the whole airfield and less time away from the fight for such precious airmen. Dowding's own son, Derek, was a Spitfire pilot with 74 Squadron in summer 1940.

133. Hurricane pilot decamps after returning from a scramble. The erks (ground staff) immediately begin refuelling.

134. 601 Squadron Hurricanes being rearmed at RAF Tangmere, July 1940. Note the cluster of four machine guns next to one another on each wing; this gave a more concentrated hail of fire than the Spitfire, which had its machine guns spaced out along its wings. Each set of four machine guns on each wing were grouped in a single bay, which enabled the cleaning out and rearming to be faster on Hurricanes.

135. Spitfire IA, P9386 'QV-K', of 19 Squadron being rearmed between sorties in 1940 at RAF Fowlmere, Cambridgeshire. P9368 was often flown by Squadron Leader Brian 'Sandy' Lane (see chapters 7, 43 and 55).

Above: 136. Ground staff overhauling the Rolls-Royce Merlin engine of a Hurricane.

Right: 137. RAF Tangmere, July 1940. Armourers of 601 Squadron rearm a Hurricane's .303 Browning machine guns while an erk refuels the fighter. This process was honed by ground staff (like a pit stop at a Grand Prix race) so that a fighter could be turned around and put in the air again within minutes.

Below: 138. Hurricanes of 601 Squadron being refuelled on their return to base at RAF Tangmere in July 1940. By the wing of the Hurricane on the left is (with his back to camera) Squadron Leader John 'Max' Aitken (4 kills in 1940). In white overalls next to the aircraft on the right is William Rhodes-Moorhouse (7 kills and 3 shared kills in 1940, KIA 6 September 1940).

139, 140, 141. *UNUSAL KILLS.* Some of the rarer German aircraft engaged in the Battle and shot down by Fighter Command included the Arado Ar 196 (145 Squadron Hurricanes shot one down on 12 October); Henschel Hs 126 (one was found near Hastings on reconnaissance, its gunner shooting down the Hurricane of Ian Kestin and killing the pilot before being shot down by Ernest Wakeham of 145 Squadron); Heinkel 115 (Alastair Jeffrey of 64 Squadron shot one down while it was laying mines in the Thames Estuary on 19 July).

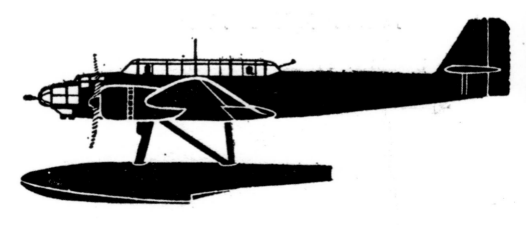

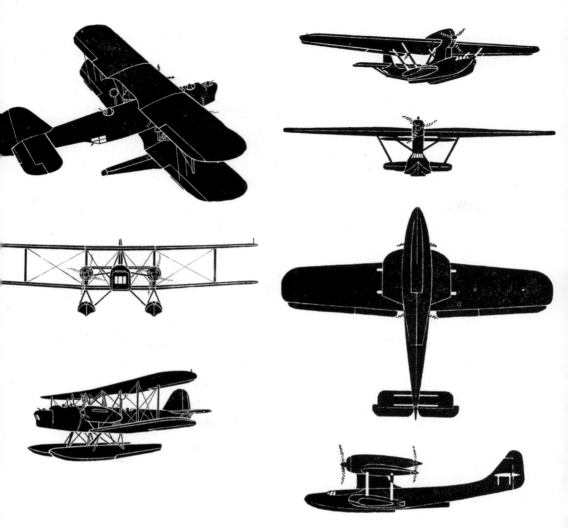

142, 143. The German air-sea rescue operated He 59 and Do 18 flying boats which were often armed (with some of the sharpest shots in the Luftwaffe as gunners) and flying Red Cross markings. The Luftwaffe were far more advanced in their air-sea rescue service of downed aircrew. Many an RAF airman drowned or died of exposure after baling out over the Channel, though the lifeboat service rescued many who came down close to the coast. The RAF soon worked out that the Luftwaffe flying boats were also acting as military reconnaissance, flying close to convoys, and Air Ministry Order No. 1254 of 29 July 1940 sanctioned fighter pilots to take them down. An He 59 was caught near a convoy 20 July by Hurricanes of 43 Squadron but escaped into cloud after shooting down Joseph Haworth, who baled out but drowned. The floatplane was later tracked down by 601 Squadron and dispatched; all crew were lost. A Do 18 seaplane was shot down by the Blenheim of Graham Russell of 236 Squadron on 25 September.

Above: 147. A trapped young victim of an October 1940 daylight raid on London being rescued.

Left: 144, 145, 146. *BLITZ.* Civilians and the Battle of Britain in Kent. A large bomb crater in Ashford, 26 September 1940. Children in Bearsted play around a bomb crater. A photograph taken in Maidstone just after bombs had fallen on the town on 2 September; bloody and tearful, these civilians have clearly had a lucky escape.

Left: 148. John Simpson (see chapters 8 and 48) and his fellow pilots were very conscious of the human cost of the Blitz. Simpson, on attacking a fully laden He 111 bomber: 'I saw a comforting red glow in his belly. Below the glow was hanging an immense object. I could see the silhouette of it. I suppose it must have been a very heavy bomb or a mine and I think I must have hit it. I was still firing when the Heinkel blew up, with a terrific explosion which blew me upwards and sideways. I found out afterwards that bits of metal from the Hun had hit my left wing and had made a tear in the fuselage by the tail plane. When I righted myself, I was delighted to see showers of flaming pieces, like confetti on fire. I was able to enjoy the satisfaction of knowing that I had brought the bastard down before he had dropped his bombs on Belfast.' *Right:* 149. London Blitz, 29 December 1940, Ave Maria Lane.

Left: 150. 11 November 1940, Elephant and Castle tube platform. Londoners used to sleep on the platforms of the London Underground during the Blitz. *Right:* 151. A London street, 1940. Householders return after a night's blitz to their shattered home.

152. Not only did the civilian population have to contend with being bombed, but also the bombers themselves crashing onto their homes. The remains of an He 111 shot down and crashed at Hornchurch, Essex, on 1 November 1940. The pilot and observer survived, and gave themselves up the following day. The other two crewmen were found in the wreckage.

Above: 153. War didn't bring out just the good in British people; poster attached to bomb-damaged commercial premises warning that looting was punishable by death. *Left:* 154. Shattered London homes, occupants rescuing scant possessions, 1940. Bill Rolls (see chapter 37) received a warm welcome when he went to collect a fellow pilot who had crash-landed in London and been 'entertained' by locals of an East End pub. The two pilots arrived back at their squadron and discovered pound and ten-shilling notes had been surreptitiously stuffed in their pockets!

movie *The Battle of Britain*. Deere died in 1995 and his medals and a large archive of documents and photographs (including the notes and original manuscript of *Nine Lives*) were sold in 2003 to RAF Museum Hendon for £138,000.

1941 broadcast Next morning I was just taking off, doing about 100 mph over the ground, when bombs whistled down on the aerodrome. The Hun was dive-bombing us. One bomb landed just in front of me, blew the engine clean out and sent me and my Spitfire hurtling upside down along the ground for 150 yards. My leather helmet was torn where it had caught the ground, but beyond slight concussion and bruises I was all right. I was helped out of the plane by a colleague who had been blown out of his aircraft. He revived me and we ran for shelter, as bombs were dropping thick and heavy. A couple of Jerries tried to machine-gun us as we ran, but they didn't get us. I was put to bed and I was still in bed the next day when another raid started. I felt I would rather be in the air than on the ground so I hopped out of bed, slipped on some clothes, went up in my Spitfire and brought down a Dornier.

54 Squadron ORB The squadron was ordered to off just as the first bombs were beginning to fall. Eight of our machines safely cleared the ground; the remaining section, however, just became airborne as the bombs exploded. All three aircraft were wholly wrecked in the air, and the survival of the pilots is a complete miracle. Sergeant [Jack] Davis, taking off towards the hangers, was thrown back across the River Ingrebourne two fields away, scrambling out of his machine unharmed. Flight Lieutenant [Alan] Deere had one wing and his prop torn off; climbing to about 100 feet he turned over and, coming down, slid along the aerodrome for 100 yards upside down. He was rescued from his unenviable position by Pilot Officer [Eric] Edsall, the third member of the section, who had suffered a smilar fate except that he landed the right way up. Dashing across the aerodrome with bombs still dropping, he extricated Flight Lieutenant Deere from his machine. 'The first and last time I hope' was the verdict of these truly amazing pilots, all of whom were ready for battle again by the next morning.

33 Richard Hillary Part 1, Spitfire Pilot, Flying Officer, Australian, 603 Squadron

First of two extracts from Hillary's bestselling wartime memoir, *The Last Enemy*. The first covers around 26 August to 7 September 1940. Hillary joined 603 Squadron in late June 1940, then based in Scotland at RAF Montrose (13 Group). The squadron moved into the thick of things in the south-east on 27 August 1940 (to RAF Hornchurch, Essex, in 11 Group) and within a week Hillary had shot down five Me 109s, becoming an 'ace'. However, on his last sortie he was shot down over Dungeness; the cockpit of his Spitfire became engulfed in flames and Hillary was grievously burned before he managed to bale out.

He was rescued by the Margate lifeboat and would become the most famous patient of pioneering plastic surgeon Archibald McIndoe. He endured months of painful surgery in an attempt to repair the injuries to his hands and face in order to return to active duty. He was treated at the Royal Masonic Hospital at Ravenscourt Park, London, and then Queen Victoria Hospital in East Grinstead. *The Last Enemy* was published in June 1942 and had been written during his long stay in various hospitals while being treated.

I've taken some liberties with the original text to be able to present his story in chronological order and added some dates in italics. The latter is important as Hillary plays a little fast and loose with the dates; for instance, he didn't move to Hornchurch on 10 August but on 27 August. Other explanatory comments, including surnames of fellow pilots where only a first name or nickname was originally used, I have put in square brackets. Due to confines of space I have edited out certain sections, denoted by '....'.

It was cold in Edinburgh and the damp mist lay heavy on the streets. We drove straight out to the aerodrome at Turnhouse and reported to our CO, Squadron Leader [George] Denholm (known by the squadron as Uncle George). From him we learned that the squadron was operating further north, A flight from Dyce and B flight from Montrose. There was one Spitfire replacement to be flown up to Dyce; Colin [Pinckney] got the job and so it came about that Peter [Pease] and I drove up together to join B flight at Montrose.

The aerodrome lay just beyond the town and stretched parallel to the sea, one edge of the landing field merging into the dunes. For a few miles around the country was flat, but mountain peaks reared abruptly into the sky, forming a purple backdrop for the aerodrome.

The first person to greet us in the mess was Michael Judd, whom neither of us had seen since our initial training. He was an instructor. He took us down to the dispersal point to introduce us to the squadron. Montrose was primarily an FTS where future pilots crowded the air in Miles Masters. As the only possible enemy raids must come from Norway, half a squadron was considered sufficient for its protection.

At our dispersal point at the north-west corner of the aerodrome there were three wooden huts. One of these was the flight commander's office; another was reserved for the R/T equipment and technicians; the third, divided into two, was for the pilots and ground crew respectively. It was into this third hut that Michael led us.

From the ceiling hung several models of German aircraft, on the back wall by the stove were pasted seductive creatures by Petty, and on a table in the middle of the room a gramophone was playing, propped at a drunken angle on a pile of old books and magazines. In a corner there was another table on which there were a couple of telephones operated by a corporal. Two beds standing against the longer walls, and several old chairs, completed the furniture.

As we came in, half a dozen heads were turned towards the door and [Frederick] Rushmer, the flight commander, came forward to greet us. Like the others, he wore a Mae West and no tunic. Known by everyone as Rusty on account of his dull-red hair, he had a shy manner and a friendly smile. Peter, I could see, sensed a kindred spirit at once. Rusty never ordered things to be done; he merely suggested that it might be a good idea if they were done, and they always were. He had a bland manner and an ability tacitly to ignore anything which he did not wish to hear, which protected him alike from outside interference from his superiors and from too frequent suggestions from his junior officers on how to run the flight. Rusty had been with the squadron since before the war: he was a flight lieutenant, and in action always led the Red section. As 603 was an auxiliary squadron, all the older members were people with civilian occupations who before the war had flown for pleasure.

Blue section leader Larry Cunningham had also been with the squadron for some time. He was a Scotsman, tall and thin, without Rusty's charm, but with plenty of experience.

Then there was Brian Carbury, a New Zealander who had started in 41 Squadron. He was six-foot-four, with crinkly hair and a roving eye. He greeted us warmly and suggested an immediate adjournment to the mess for drinks. Before the war he had been a shoe salesman in New Zealand. Sick of the job, he had come to England and taken a short service commission. He was now a flying officer. There was little distinctive about him on the ground, but he was to prove the squadron's greatest asset in the air.

Another from overseas was Hugh [Gerald] Stapleton, a South African. He hoped to return after the war and run an orange farm. He too was over six feet tall, thickset, with a mass of blond hair which he never brushed. He was twenty and married, with a rough *savoir faire* beyond his years, acquired from an early unprotected acquaintance with life. He was always losing buttons off his uniform and had a pair of patched trousers which the rest of the squadron swore he slept in. He was completely slap-happy and known as 'Stapme' because of his predilection for Popeye in the *Daily Mirror*, his favourite literature.

Pilot Officer [Ronald] Berry, commonly known as Raspberry, came from Hull. He was short and stocky, with a ruddy complexion and a mouth that was always grinning or coming out with some broad Yorkshire witticism impossible to answer. Above that mouth, surprisingly, sprouted a heavy black moustache, which induced me to call him the organ-grinder. His reply to this was always unprintable but very much to the point. Even on the blackest days he radiated an infectious good-humour. His aggressive spirit chafed at the squadron's present inactivity and he was always the first to hear any rumour of our moving south.

'Bubble' [Robin] Waterston was twenty-four, but he looked eighteen, with his short-cropped hair and open face. He too had been with the squadron for some time before the war. He had been studying in Scotland for an engineering degree. He had great curiosity about anything mechanical, and was always tinkering with the engine of his car. His unquestioning acceptance of everyone and his unconscious charm made him the most popular member of the squadron.

Then there was [John] Boulter, with jutting ears framing the face of an intelligent ferret, always sleepy and in bed snoring when off duty; 'Broody' [Noel] Benson, nineteen years old, a fine pilot and possessed of only one idea, to shoot down Huns, more Huns, and then still more Huns; Don MacDonald who had been in the Cambridge squadron and had an elder brother in A flight at Dyce; and finally Pip Cardell, the most recent addition to the squadron before our arrival, still bewildered, excited, and a little lost.

...

c. *26 August–2 September 1940* We retired early to bed and slept until, at two o'clock in the morning, a gillie banged on the door. Colin got up, took from the gillie's hand a telegram opened it, and read it aloud. It said: 'Squadron moving south stop car will fetch you at eight o'clock Denholm.' For us, the war began that night.

At ten o'clock we were back at Turnhouse. The rest of the squadron were all set to leave; we were to move down to Hornchurch, an aerodrome twelve miles east of London on the Thames estuary. Four machines would not be serviceable until the evening, and Broody Benson, Pip Cardell, Colin, and I were to fly them down. We took off at four o'clock, some five hours after the others, Broody leading, Pip and I to each side, and Colin in the box, map-reading. Twenty-four of us flew south that tenth day of August 1940 [in fact 27 August]: of those twenty-four eight were to fly back.

We landed at Hornchurch at about seven o'clock to receive our first shock. Instead of one section there were four squadrons at readiness; 603 Squadron were already in action. They started coming in about half an hour after we landed, smoke stains along the leading edges of the wings showing that all the guns had been fired. They had acquitted themselves well although caught at a disadvantage of height.

'You don't have to look for them,' said Brian. 'You have to look for a way out.'

From this flight Don MacDonald did not return.

At this time the Germans were sending over comparatively few bombers. They were making a determined attempt to wipe out our entire fighter force, and from dawn till dusk the sky was filled with Me 109s and 110s.

Half a dozen of us always slept over at the dispersal hut to be ready for a surprise enemy attack at dawn. This entailed being up by four-thirty and by five o'clock having our machines warmed up and the oxygen, sights, and ammunition tested. The first Hun attack usually came over about breakfast time and from then until eight o'clock at night we were almost continuously in the air. We ate when we could, baked beans and bacon and eggs being sent over from the mess.

On the morning after our arrival I walked over with Peter Howes and Broody. Howes was at Hornchurch with another squadron [54 Squadron] and worried because he had as yet shot nothing down. Every evening when we came into the mess he would ask us how many we had got and then go over miserably to his room. His squadron had had a number of losses and was due for relief. If ever a man needed it, it was Howes. Broody, on the other hand, was in a high state of excitement, his sharp eager face grinning from ear to ear. We left Howes at his dispersal hut and walked over to where our machines were being warmed up. The voice of the controller came unhurried over the loudspeaker, telling us to take off, and in a few seconds we were running for our machines. I climbed into the cockpit of my plane and felt an empty sensation of suspense in the pit of my stomach. For one second time seemed to stand still and I stared blankly in front of me. I knew that that morning I was to kill for the first time. That I might be killed or in any way injured did not occur to me. Later, when we were losing pilots regularly, I did consider it in an abstract way when on the ground; but once in the air, never. I knew it could not happen to me. I suppose every pilot knows that, knows it cannot happen to him; even when he is taking off for the last time, when he will not return, he knows that he cannot be killed. I wondered idly what he was like, this man I would kill. Was he young, was he fat, would he die with the Führer's name on his lips, or would he die alone, in that last moment conscious of himself as a man? I would never know. Then I was being strapped in, my mind automatically checking the controls, and we were off.

We ran into them at 18,000 feet, twenty yellow-nosed Me 109s, about 500 feet above us. Our squadron strength was eight, and as they came down on us we went into line astern and turned head on to them. Brian Carbury, who was leading the section, dropped the nose of his machine, and I could almost feel the leading Nazi pilot push forward on his stick to bring his guns to bear. At the same moment Brian hauled hard back on his own control stick and led us over them in a steep climbing turn to the left. In two vital seconds they lost their advantage. I saw Brian let go a burst of fire at the leading plane, saw the pilot put his machine into a half roll, and knew that he was mine. Automatically, I kicked the rudder to the left to get him at right angles, turned the gun-button to 'Fire', and let go in a four-second burst with full deflection. He came right through my sights and I saw the tracer from all eight guns thud home. For a second he seemed to hang motionless; then a jet of red flame shot upwards and he spun out of sight.

For the next few minutes I was too busy looking after myself to think of anything, but when, after a short while, they turned and made off over the Channel, and we were ordered to our base, my mind began to work again.

It had happened.

My first emotion was one of satisfaction, satisfaction at a job adequately done, at the final logical conclusion of months of specialised training. And then I had a feeling of the essential rightness of it all. He was dead and I was alive; it could so easily have been the other way round; and that would somehow have been right too. I realised in that moment just how lucky a fighter pilot is. He has none of the personalised emotions of the soldier, handed a rifle and bayonet and told to charge. He does not even have to share the dangerous emotions of the bomber pilot who night after night must experience that childhood longing for smashing things. The fighter pilot's emotions are those of the duellist – cool, precise, impersonal. He is privileged to kill well. For if one must either kill or be killed, as now one must, it should, I feel, be done with dignity. Death should be given the setting it deserves; it should never be a pettiness; and for the fighter pilot it never can be.

From this flight Broody Benson did not return.

During that August-September period we were always so outnumbered that it was practically impossible, unless we were lucky enough to have the advantage of height, to deliver more than one squadron attack. After a few seconds we always broke up, and the sky was a smoke trail of individual dogfights. The result was that the squadron would come home individually, machines landing one after the other at intervals of about two minutes. After an hour, Uncle George would make a check-up on who was missing. Often there would be a telephone call from some pilot to say that he had made a forced landing at some other aerodrome, or in a field. But the telephone wasn't always so welcome. It would be a rescue squad announcing the number of a crashed machine; then Uncle George would check it, and cross another name off the list. At that time, the losing of pilots was somehow extremely impersonal; nobody, I think, felt any great emotion – there simply wasn't time for it.

After the hard lesson of the first two days, we became more canny and determined not to let ourselves be caught from above. We would fly on the reciprocal of the course given us by the controller until we got to 15,000 feet, and then fly back again, climbing all the time. By this means we usually saw the Huns coming in below us, and were in a perfect position to deliver a squadron attack. If caught at a disadvantage, they would never stay to fight, but always turned straight back for the Channel. We arranged a system whereby two pilots always flew together – thus if one should follow a plane down the other stayed 500 feet or so above, to protect him from attack in the rear.

Often machines would come back to their base just long enough for the ground staff, who worked with beautiful speed, to refuel them and put in a new oxygen bottle and more ammunition before taking off again. Uncle George was shot down several times but always turned up unhurt; once we thought Rusty was gone for good, but he was back leading his flight the next day; one sergeant pilot in A flight was shot down four times, but he seemed to bear a charmed life.

The sun and the great height at which we flew often made it extremely difficult to pick out the enemy machines, but it was here that Sheep's [George Gilroy] experience on the moors of Scotland proved invaluable. He always led the guard section and always saw the Huns long before anyone else. For me the sun presented a major problem. We had dark lenses on our glasses, but I, as I have mentioned before, never wore mine. They gave me a feeling of claustrophobia. With spots on the windscreen, spots before the eyes, and a couple of spots which might be Messerschmitts, blind spots on my goggles seemed too much of a good thing; I always slipped them up on to my forehead before going into action. For this and for not wearing gloves I paid a stiff price.

I remember once going practically to France before shooting down a 109. There were two of them, flying at sea-level and headed for the French coast. Raspberry was flying beside me and caught one halfway across. I got right up close behind the second one and gave it a series of short bursts. It darted about in front, like a startled rabbit, and finally plunged into the sea about three miles off the French coast.

On another occasion I was stupid enough actually to fly over France: the sky appeared to be perfectly clear but for one returning Messerschmitt, flying very high. I had been trying to catch him for about ten minutes and was determined that he should not get away. Eventually I caught him inland from Calais and was just about to open fire when I saw a squadron of twelve Messerschmitts coming in on my right. I was extremely frightened, but turned in towards them and opened fire at the leader. I could see his tracer going past underneath me, and then I saw his hood fly off, and the next moment they were past. I didn't wait to see any more, but made off for home, pursued for half the distance by eleven very determined Germans. I landed a good hour after everyone else to find Uncle George just finishing his check-up.

From this flight Larry Cunningham did not return.

After about a week of Hornchurch, I woke late one morning [31 August] to the noise of machines running up on the aerodrome. It irritated me: I had a headache.

Having been on every flight the previous day, the morning was mine to do with as I pleased. I got up slowly, gazed dispassionately at my tongue in the mirror, and wandered over to the mess for breakfast. It must have been getting on for twelve o'clock when I came out on to the aerodrome to find the usual August heat haze forming a dull pall over everything. I started to walk across the aerodrome to the dispersal point on the far side. There were only two machines on the ground so I concluded that the squadron was already up. Then I heard a shout, and our ground crew drew up in a lorry beside me. Sergeant Ross leaned out:

'Want a lift, sir? We're going round.'

'No, thanks, sergeant. I'm going to cut across.'

This was forbidden for obvious reasons, but I felt like that.

'OK, sir. See you round there.'

The lorry trundled off down the road in a cloud of dust. I walked on across the landing ground. At that moment I heard the emotionless voice of the controller.

'Large enemy bombing formation approaching Hornchurch. All personnel not engaged in active duty take cover immediately.'

I looked up. They were still not visible. At the dispersal point I saw Bubble and Pip Cardell make a dash for the shelter. Three Spitfires just landed, turned about and came past me with a roar to take off downwind. Our lorry was still trundling along the road, maybe halfway round, and seemed suddenly an awfully long way from the dispersal point. I looked up again, and this time I saw them – about a dozen slugs, shining in the bright sun and coming straight on. At the rising scream of the first bomb I instinctively shrugged up my shoulders and ducked my head. Out of the corner of my eye I saw the three Spitfires. One moment they were about twenty feet up in close formation; the next catapulted apart as though on elastic. The leader went over on his back and ploughed along the runway with a rending crash of tearing fabric; No. 2 put a wing in and spun round on his airscrew, while the plane on the left was blasted wingless into the next field. I remember thinking stupidly, 'That's the shortest flight he's ever taken,' and then my feet were nearly knocked from under me, my mouth was full of dirt, and Bubble, gesticulating like a madman from the shelter entrance, was yelling, 'Run, you bloody fool, run!' I ran. Suddenly awakened to the lunacy of my behaviour, I covered the distance to that shelter as if impelled by a rocket and shot through the entrance while once again the ground rose up and hit me, and my head smashed hard against one of the pillars. I subsided on a heap of rubble and massaged it.

'Who's here?' I asked, peering through the gloom.

'Cardell and I and three of our ground crew,' said Bubble, 'and, by the Grace of God, you!'

I could see by his mouth that he was still talking, but a sudden concentration of the scream and crump of falling bombs made it impossible to hear him.

The air was thick with dust and the shelter shook and heaved at each explosion, yet somehow held firm. For about three minutes the bedlam continued, and then suddenly ceased. In the utter silence which followed nobody moved. None of us wished to be the first to look on the devastation which we felt must be outside. Then Bubble spoke. 'Praise God!' he said, 'I'm not a civilian. Of all the bloody frightening things I've ever done, sitting in that shelter was the worst. Me for the air from now on!'

It broke the tension and we scrambled out of the entrance. The runways were certainly in something of a mess. Gaping holes and great gobbets of earth were everywhere. Right in front of us a bomb had landed by my Spitfire, covering it with a shower of grit and rubble.

I turned to the aircraftsman standing beside me.

'Will you get hold of Sergeant Ross and tell him to have a crew give her an inspection.'

He jerked his head towards one corner of the aerodrome: 'I think I'd better collect the crew myself, sir. Sergeant Ross won't be doing any more inspections.'

I followed his glance and saw the lorry, the roof about twenty yards away, lying grotesquely on its side. I climbed into the cockpit, and, feeling faintly sick, tested out the switches. Bubble poked his head over the side.

'Let's go over to the mess and see what's up: all our machines will be landing down at the reserve landing field, anyway.'

I climbed out and walked over to find that the three Spitfire pilots were quite unharmed but for a few superficial scratches, in spite of being machine-gunned by the bombers. 'Operations' was undamaged: no hangar had been touched and the officers' mess had two windows broken.

The station commander ordered every available man and woman on to the job of repairing the aerodrome surface and by four o'clock there was not a hole to be seen. Several unexploded bombs were marked off, and two lines of yellow flags were laid down to mark the runways. At five o'clock our squadron, taking off for a 'flap' from the reserve field, landed without incident on its home base. Thus, apart from four men killed in the lorry and a network of holes on the landing surface, there was nothing to show for ten minutes' really accurate bombing from 12,000 feet, in which several dozen sticks of bombs had been dropped. It was a striking proof of the inefficacy of their attempts to wipe out our advance fighter aerodromes.

Brian had a bullet through his foot, and as my machine was still out of commission, I took his place in readiness for the next show. I had had enough of the ground for one day.

Six o'clock came and went, and no call. We started to play poker and I was winning. It was agreed that we should stop at seven: should there be a 'flap' before then, the game was off. I gazed anxiously at the clock. I am always unlucky at cards, but when the hands pointed to 6.55 I really began to feel my luck was on the change. But sure enough at that moment came the voice of the controller: '603 Squadron take off and patrol base: further instructions in the air.'

We made a dash for our machines and within two minutes were off the ground. Twice we circled the aerodrome to allow all twelve planes to get in formation. We were flying in four sections of three: Red Section leading, Blue and Green to right and left, and the three remaining planes forming a guard section above and behind us.

I was flying No. 2 in the Blue Section.

Over the radio came the voice of the controller: 'Hello, Red Leader,' followed by instructions on course and height.

As always, for the first few minutes we flew on the reciprocal of the course given until we reached 15,000 feet. We then turned about and flew on 110° in an all-out climb, thus coming out of the sun and gaining height all the way.

During the climb Uncle George was in constant touch with the ground. We were to intercept about twenty enemy fighters at 25,000 feet. I glanced across at Stapme and saw his mouth moving. That meant he was singing again. He would sometimes do this with his radio set on 'send', with the result that, mingled with our instructions from the ground, we would hear a raucous rendering of 'Night and Day'. And then quite clearly over the radio I heard the Germans excitedly calling to each other. This was a not infrequent occurrence and it made one feel that they were right behind, although often they were some distance away. I switched my set to 'send' and called out *'Halts Maul!'* and as many other choice pieces of German invective as I could remember. To my delight I heard one of them answer: 'You feelthy Englishmen, we will teach you how to speak to a German.' I am aware that this sounds a tall story, but several others in the squadron were listening out and heard the whole thing.

I looked down. It was a completely cloudless sky and way below lay the English countryside, stretching lazily into the distance, a quite extraordinary picture of green and purple in the setting sun.

I took a glance at my altimeter. We were at 28,000 feet. At that moment Sheep yelled 'Tally-ho' and dropped down in front of Uncle George in a slow dive in the direction of the approaching planes [Sheep was a Scotsman and a farmer, with a port-wine complexion and features which gave rise to his name]. Uncle George saw them at once.

'OK. Line astern.'

I drew in behind Stapme and took a look at them. They were about 2,000 feet below us, which was a pleasant change, but they must have spotted us at the same moment, for they were forming a protective circle, one behind the other, which is a defence formation hard to break.

'Echelon starboard,' came Uncle George's voice.

We spread out fanwise to the right.

'Going down!'

One after the other we peeled off in a power dive. I picked out one machine and switched my gun-button to 'Fire'. At 300 yards I had him in my sights. At 200 I opened up in a long four-second burst and saw the tracer going into his nose. Then I was pulling out, so hard that I could feel my eyes dropping through my neck. Coming round in a slow climbing turn, I saw that we had broken them up. The sky was now a mass of individual dogfights. Several of them had already been knocked down. One I hoped was mine, but on pulling up I had not been able to see the result. To my left I saw Peter Pease make a head-on attack on a Messerschmitt. They were headed straight for each other and it looked as though the fire of both was striking home. Then at the last moment the Messerschmitt pulled up, taking Peter's fire full in the belly. It rolled on to its back, yellow flames pouring from the cockpit, and vanished.

The next few minutes were typical. First the sky a bedlam of machines; then suddenly silence and not a plane to be seen. I noticed then that I was very tired and very hot. The sweat was running down my face in rivulets. But this was no time for vague reflections. Flying around the sky on one's own at that time was not a healthy course of action.

I still had some ammunition left. Having no desire to return to the aerodrome until it had all been used to some good purpose, I took a look around the sky for some friendly fighters. About a mile away over Dungeness I saw a formation of about forty Hurricanes on patrol at 20,000 feet. Feeling that there was safety in numbers, I set off in their direction. When about 200 yards from the rear machine, I looked down and saw 5,000 feet below another formation of fifty machines flying in the same direction. Flying stepped up like this was an old trick of the Huns, and I was glad to see we were adopting the same tactics. But as though hit by a douche of cold water, I suddenly woke up. There were far more machines flying together than we could ever muster over one spot. I took another look at the rear machine in my formation, and sure enough, there was the swastika on its tail. Yet they all seemed quite oblivious of my presence. I had the sun behind me and a glorious opportunity. Closing in to 150 yards I let go a three-second burst into the rear machine. It flicked on to its back and spun out of sight. Feeling like an irresponsible schoolboy who has perpetrated some crime which must inevitably be found out, I glanced round me. Still nobody seemed disturbed. I suppose I could have repeated the performance on the next machine, but I felt that it was inadvisable to tempt providence too far. I did a quick half roll and made off home, where I found to my irritation that Raspberry, as usual, had three planes down to my one.

There was to be a concert on the station that night, but as I had to be up at five the next morning for dawn readiness, I had a quick dinner and two beers, and went to bed, feeling not unsatisfied with the day.

Perhaps the most amusing though painful experience which I had was when I was shot down acting as Arse-end Charlie to a squadron of Hurricanes. Arse-end Charlie is the man who weaves backwards and forwards above and behind the squadron to protect them from attack from the rear. There had been the usual dogfights over the South Coast, and the squadron had broken up. Having only fired one snap burst, I climbed up in search of friendly Spitfires, but found instead a squadron of Hurricanes flying round the sky at 18,000 feet in sections of stepped-up threes, but with no rear-guard. So I joined on. I learned within a few seconds the truth of the old warning, 'Beware of the Hun in the Sun'. I was making pleasant little sweeps from side to side, and peering earnestly into my mirror when, from out of the sun and dead astern, bullets started appearing along my port wing. There is an appalling tendency to sit and watch this happen without taking any action, as though mesmerised by a snake; but I managed to pull myself together and go into a spin, at the same time attempting to call up the Hurricanes and warn them, but I found that my radio had been shot away. At first there appeared to be little damage done and I started to climb up again, but black smoke began pouring out of the engine and there was an unpleasant smell of escaping glycol. I thought I had better get home while I could; but as the windscreen was soon covered with oil I realised that I couldn't make it and decided instead to put down at Lympne, where there was an aerodrome. Then I realised that I wasn't going to make Lympne either – I was going at full boost and only clocking 90 mph, so I decided that I had better put down in the nearest field before I stalled and spun in. I chose a cornfield and put the machine down on its belly. Fortunately nothing caught fire, and I had just climbed out and switched off the petrol, when to my amazement I saw an ambulance coming through the gate. This I thought was real service, until the corporal and two orderlies who climbed out started cantering away in the opposite direction, their necks craned up to the heavens. I looked up and saw about 50 yards away a parachute, and suspended on the end, his legs dangling vaguely, Colin. He was a little burned about his face and hands but quite cheerful.

We were at once surrounded by a bevy of officers and discovered that we had landed practically in the back garden of a brigade cocktail party. A salvage crew from Lympne took charge of my machine, a doctor took charge of Colin, and the rest took charge of me, handing me double whiskies for the nerves at a laudable rate. I was put up that night by the brigadier, who thought I was suffering from a rather severe shock, largely because by dinner time I was so pie-eyed that I didn't dare open my mouth but answered all his questions with a glassy stare. The next day I went up to London by train, a somewhat incongruous figure, carrying a helmet and parachute. The prospect of a long and tedious journey by tube to Hornchurch did not appeal to me, so I called up the Air Ministry and demanded a car and a WAAF. I was put on to the good lady in charge of transport, a sergeant, who protested apologetically that she must have the authorisation of a wing commander. I told her forcibly that at this moment I was considerably more important than any wing commander, painted a vivid picture of the complete disorganisation of Fighter Command in the event of my not being back at Hornchurch within an hour, and clinched the argument by telling her that my parachute was a military secret which must on no account be seen in a train. By the afternoon I was flying again.

That evening there was a terrific attack on Hornchurch and, for the first time since coming south, I saw some bombers. There were twelve Dornier 215s flying in close formation at about 12,000 feet, and headed back for France. I was on my way back to the aerodrome when I first sighted them about 5,000 feet below me. I dived straight down in a quarter head-on attack. It seemed quite impossible to miss, and I pressed the button. Nothing happened; I had already fired all my ammunition. I could not turn back, so I put both my arms over my head and went straight through the formation, never thinking I'd get out of it unscratched. I landed on the aerodrome with the machine, quite serviceable, but a little draughty.

From this flight Bubble Waterston did not return.

And so August drew to a close with no slackening of pressure in the enemy offensive. Yet the squadron showed no signs of strain, and I personally was content. This was what I had waited for, waited for nearly a year, and I was not disappointed. If I felt anything, it was a sensation of relief. We had little time to think, and each day brought new action. No one thought of the future: sufficient unto the day was the emotion thereof. At night one switched off one's mind like an electric light.

It was one week after Bubble went that I crashed into the North Sea.

...

3 September 1940 dawned dark and overcast, with a slight breeze ruffling the waters of the Estuary. Hornchurch aerodrome, twelve miles east of London, wore its usual morning pallor of yellow fog, lending an added air of grimness to the dimly silhouetted Spitfires around the boundary. From time to time a balloon would poke its head grotesquely through the mist as though looking for possible victims before falling back like some tired monster.

We came out on to the tarmac at about eight o'clock. During the night our machines had been moved from the dispersal point over to the hangars. All the machine tools, oil, and general equipment had been left on the far side of the aerodrome. I was worried. We had been bombed a short time before, and my plane had been fitted out with a new cockpit hood. This hood unfortunately would not slide open along its groove; and with a depleted ground staff and no tools, I began to fear it never would. Unless it did open, I shouldn't be able to bale out in a hurry if I had to. Miraculously, 'Uncle George' Denholm, our squadron leader, produced three men with a heavy file and lubricating oil, and the corporal fitter and I set upon the hood in a fury of haste. We took it turn by turn, filing and oiling, oiling and filing, until at last the hood began to move. But agonisingly slowly: by ten o'clock, when the mist had cleared and the sun was blazing out of a clear sky, the hood was still sticking firmly half-way along the groove; at ten-fifteen, what I had feared for the last hour happened. Down the loudspeaker came the emotionless voice of the controller: '603 Squadron take off and patrol base; you will receive further orders in the air: 603 Squadron take off as quickly as you can, please.' As I pressed the starter and the engine roared into life, the corporal stepped back and crossed his fingers significantly. I felt the usual sick feeling in the pit of the stomach, as though I were about to row a race, and then I was too busy getting into position to feel anything.

Uncle George and the leading section took off in a cloud of dust; Brian Carbury looked across and put up his thumbs. I nodded and opened up, to take off for the last time from Hornchurch. I was flying No. 3 in Brian's section, with Stapme Stapleton on the right: the third section consisted of only two machines, so that our squadron strength was eight. We headed south-east, climbing all out on a steady course. At about 12,000 feet we came up through the clouds: I looked down and saw them spread out below me like layers of whipped cream. The sun was brilliant and made it difficult to see even the next plane when turning. I was peering anxiously ahead, for the controller had given us warning of at least fifty enemy fighters approaching very high. When we did first sight them, nobody shouted, as I think we all saw them at the same moment. They must have been 500 to 1,000 feet above us and coming straight on like a swarm of locusts. I remember cursing and going automatically into line astern: the next moment we were in among them and it was each man for himself. As soon as they saw us they spread out and dived, and the next ten minutes was a blur of twisting machines and tracer bullets. One Messerschmitt went down in a sheet of flame on my right, and a Spitfire hurtled past in a half roll; I was weaving and turning in a desperate attempt to gain height, with the machine practically hanging on the airscrew. Then, just below me and to my left, I saw what I had been praying for – a Messerschmitt climbing and away from the sun. I closed in to 200 yards, and from slightly to one side gave him a two-second burst: fabric ripped off the wing and black smoke poured from the engine, but he did not go down. Like a fool, I did not break away, but put in another three-second burst. Red flames shot upwards and he spiralled out of sight. At that moment, I felt a terrific explosion which knocked the control stick from my hand, and the whole machine quivered like a stricken animal. In a second, the cockpit was a mass of flames: instinctively, I reached up to open the hood. It would not move. I tore off my straps and managed to force it back; but this took time, and when I dropped back into the seat and reached for the stick in an effort to turn the plane on its back, the heat was so intense that I could feel myself going. I remember a second of sharp agony, remember thinking 'So this is it!' and putting both hands to my eyes. Then I passed out.

When I regained consciousness I was free of the machine and falling rapidly. I pulled the ripcord of my parachute and checked my descent with a jerk. Looking down, I saw that my left trouser leg was burnt off, that I was going to fall into the sea, and that the English coast was deplorably far away. About twenty feet above the water, I attempted to undo my parachute, failed, and flopped into the sea with it billowing round me. I was told later that the machine went into a spin at about 25,000 feet and that at 10,000 feet I fell out – unconscious. This may well have been so, for I discovered later a large cut on the top of my head, presumably collected while bumping round inside.

The water was not unwarm and I was pleasantly surprised to find that my lifejacket kept me afloat. I looked at my watch: it was not there. Then, for the first time, I noticed how burnt my hands were: down to the wrist, the skin was dead white and hung in shreds: I felt faintly sick from the smell of burnt flesh. By closing one eye I could see my lips, jutting out like motor tyres. The side of my parachute harness was cutting into me particularly painfully, so that I guessed my right hip was burnt. I made a further attempt to undo the harness, but owing to the pain of my hands, soon desisted. Instead, I lay back and reviewed my position: I was a long way from land; my hands were burnt, and so, judging from the pain of the sun, was my face; it was unlikely that anyone on shore had seen me come down and even more unlikely that a ship would come by; I could float for possibly four hours in my Mae West. I began to feel that I had perhaps been premature in considering myself lucky to have escaped from the machine. After about half an hour my teeth started chattering, and to quiet them I kept up a regular tuneless chant, varying it from time to time with calls for help. There can be few more futile pastimes than yelling for help alone in the North Sea, with a solitary seagull for company, yet it gave me a certain melancholy satisfaction, for I had once written a short story in which the hero (falling from a liner) had done just this. It was rejected.

The water now seemed much colder and I noticed with surprise that the sun had gone in though my face was still burning. I looked down at my hands, and not seeing them, realised that I had gone blind. So I was going to die. It came to me like that – I was going to die, and I was not afraid. This realisation came as a surprise. The manner of my approaching death appalled and horrified me, but the actual vision of death left me unafraid: I felt only a profound curiosity and a sense of satisfaction that within a few minutes or a few hours I was to learn the great answer. I decided that it should be in a few minutes. I had no qualms about hastening my end and, reaching up, I managed to unscrew the valve of my Mae West. The air escaped in a rush and my head went under water. It is said by people who have all but died in the sea that drowning is a pleasant death. I did not find it so. I swallowed a large quantity of water before my head came up again, but derived little satisfaction from it. I tried again, to find that I could not get my face under. I was so enmeshed in my parachute that I could not move. For the next ten minutes, I tore my hands to ribbons on the spring-release catch. It was stuck fast. I lay back exhausted, and then I started to laugh. By this time I was probably not entirely normal and I doubt if my laughter was wholly sane, but there was something irresistibly comical in my grand gesture of suicide being so simply thwarted.

Goethe once wrote that no one, unless he had led the full life and realised himself completely, had the right to take his own life. Providence seemed determined that I should not incur the great man's displeasure.

It is often said that a dying man relives his whole life in one rapid kaleidoscope. I merely thought gloomily of the squadron returning, of my mother at home, and of the few people who would miss me. Outside my family, I could count them on the fingers of one hand. What did gratify me enormously was to find that I indulged in no frantic abasements or prayers to the Almighty. It is an old jibe of God-fearing people that the irreligious always change their tune when about to die: I was pleased to think that I was proving them wrong. Because I seemed to be in for an indeterminate period of waiting, I began to feel a terrible loneliness and sought for some means to take my mind off my plight. I took it for granted that I must soon become delirious, and I attempted to hasten the process: I encouraged my mind to wander vaguely and aimlessly, with the result that I did experience a certain peace. But when I forced myself to think of something concrete, I found that I was still only too lucid. I went on shuttling between the two with varying success until I was picked up. I remember as in a dream hearing somebody shout: it seemed so far away and quite unconnected with me …

Then willing arms were dragging me over the side; my parachute was taken off (and with such ease!); a brandy flask was pushed between my swollen lips; a voice said, 'OK, Joe, it's one of ours and still kicking'; and I was safe. I was neither relieved nor angry: I was past caring.

It was to the Margate lifeboat that I owed my rescue. Watchers on the coast had seen me come down, and for three hours they had been searching for me. Owing to wrong directions, they were just giving up and turning back for land when ironically enough one of them saw my parachute. They were then fifteen miles east of Margate.

While in the water I had been numb and had felt very little pain. Now that I began to thaw out, the agony was such that I could have cried out. The good fellows made me as comfortable as possible, put up some sort of awning to keep the sun from my face, and phoned through for a doctor. It seemed to me to take an eternity to reach shore. I was put into an ambulance and driven rapidly to hospital. Through all this I was quite conscious, though unable to see. At the hospital they cut off my uniform, I gave the requisite information to a nurse about my next of kin, and then, to my infinite relief, felt a hypodermic syringe pushed into my arm.

I can't help feeling that a good epitaph for me at that moment would have been four lines of Verlaine:

> *Quoique sans patrie et sans roi,*
> *Et très brave ne l'étant guère,*
> *J'ai voulu mourir à la guerre.*
> *La mort n'a pas voulu de moi.*

The foundations of an experience of which this crash was, if not the climax, at least the turning point were laid in Oxford before the war.

PM 3–7 September 1940 I was falling. Falling slowly through a dark pit. I was dead. My body, headless, circled in front of me. I saw it with my mind, my mind that was the redness in front of the eye, the dull scream in the ear, the grinning of the mouth, the skin crawling on the skull. It was death and resurrection. Terror, moving with me, touched my cheek with hers and I felt the flesh wince. Faster, faster … I was hot now, hot, again one with my body, on fire and screaming soundlessly. Dear God, no!

No! Not that, not again. The sickly smell of death was in my nostrils and a confused roar of sound. Then all was quiet. I was back.

Someone was holding my arms.

'Quiet now. There's a good boy. You're going to be all right. You've been very ill and you mustn't talk.'

I tried to reach up my hand but could not.

'Is that you, nurse? What have they done to me?'

'Well, they've put something on your face and hands to stop them hurting and you won't be able to see for a little while. But you mustn't talk: you're not strong enough yet.'

Gradually I realised what had happened. My face and hands had been scrubbed and then sprayed with tannic acid. The acid had formed into a hard black cement. My eyes alone had received different treatment: they were coated with a thick layer of gentian violet. My arms were propped up in front of me, the fingers extended like witches' claws, and my body was hung loosely on straps just clear of the bed.

I can recollect no moments of acute agony in the four days which I spent in that hospital; only a great sea of pain in which I floated almost with comfort. Every three hours I was injected with morphia, so while imagining myself quite coherent, I was for the most part in a semi-stupor. The memory of it has remained a confused blur.

Two days without eating, and then periodic doses of liquid food taken through a tube. An appalling thirst, and hundreds of bottles of ginger beer. Being blind, and not really feeling strong enough to care. Imagining myself back in my plane, unable to get out, and waking to find myself shouting and bathed in sweat. My parents coming down to see me and their wonderful self-control.

They arrived in the late afternoon of my second day in bed, having with admirable restraint done nothing the first day. On the morning of the crash my mother had been on her way to the Red Cross, when she felt a premonition that she must go home. She told the taxi-driver to turn about and arrived at the flat to hear the telephone ringing. It was our squadron adjutant, trying to reach my father. Embarrassed by finding himself talking to my mother, he started in on a glamorised history of my exploits in the air and was bewildered by my mother cutting him short to ask where I was. He managed somehow after about five minutes of incoherent stuttering to get over his news.

They arrived in the afternoon and were met by matron. Outside my ward a twittery nurse explained that they must not expect to find me looking quite normal, and they were ushered in. The room was in darkness; I just a dim shape in one corner. Then the blinds were shot up, all the lights switched on, and there I was. As my mother remarked later, the performance lacked only the rolling of drums and a spotlight. For the sake of decorum my face had been covered with white gauze, with a slit in the middle through which protruded my lips.

We spoke little, my only coherent remark being that I had no wish to go on living if I were to look like Alice. Alice was a large country girl who had once been our maid. As a child she had been burned and disfigured by a Primus stove. I was not aware that she had made any impression on me, but now I was unable to get her out of my mind. It was not so much her looks as her smell I had continually in my nostrils and which I couldn't dissociate from the disfigurement.

They sat quietly and listened to me rambling for an hour. Then it was time for my dressings and they took their leave.

The smell of ether. Matron once doing my dressing with three orderlies holding my arms; a nurse weeping quietly at the head of the bed, and no remembered sign of a doctor. A visit from the lifeboat crew that had picked me up, and a terrible longing to make sense when talking to them. Their inarticulate sympathy and assurance of quick recovery. Their discovery that an ancestor of mine had founded the lifeboats, and my pompous and unsolicited promise of a subscription. The expectation of an American ambulance to drive me up to the Masonic Hospital (for Margate was used only as a clearing station). Believing that I was already in it and on my way, and waking to the disappointment that I had not been moved. A dream that I was fighting to open my eyes and could not: waking in a sweat to realise it was a dream and then finding it to be true. A sensation of time slowing down, of words and actions, all in slow motion. Sweat, pain, smells, cheering messages from the squadron, and an overriding apathy.

8 September 1940 Finally I was moved. The ambulance appeared with a cargo of two somewhat nervous ATS women who were to drive me to London, and, with my nurse in attendance, and wrapped in an old grandmother's shawl, I was carried aboard and we were off. For the first few miles I felt quite well, dictated letters to my nurse, drank bottle after bottle of ginger beer, and gossiped with the drivers. They described the countryside for me, told me they were new to the job, expressed satisfaction at having me for a consignment, asked me if I felt fine. Yes, I said, I felt fine; asked my nurse if the drivers were pretty, heard her answer yes, heard them simpering, and we were all very matey. But after about half an hour my arms began to throb from the rhythmical jolting of the road. I stopped dictating, drank no more ginger beer, and didn't care whether they were pretty or not. Then they lost their way. Wasn't it awful and shouldn't they stop and ask? No, they certainly shouldn't: they could call out the names of the streets and I would tell them where to go. By the time we arrived at Ravenscourt Park I was pretty much all-in. I was carried into the hospital and once again felt the warm September sun burning my face. I was put in a private ward and had the impression of a hundred excited ants buzzing around me. My nurse said goodbye and started to sob. For no earthly reason I found myself in tears. It had been a lousy hospital, I had never seen the nurse anyway, and I was now in very good hands; but I suppose I was in a fairly exhausted state. So there we all were, snivelling about the place and getting nowhere. Then the charge nurse came up and took my arm and asked me what my name was.

'Dick,' I said.

'Ah,' she said brightly. 'We must call you Richard the Lion Heart.'

I made an attempt at a polite laugh but all that came out was a dismal groan and I fainted away. The house surgeon took the opportunity to give me an anaesthetic and removed all the tannic acid from my left hand.

At this time tannic acid was the recognised treatment for burns. The theory was that in forming a hard cement it protected the skin from the air, and encouraged it to heal up underneath. As the tannic started to crack, it was to be chipped off gradually with a scalpel, but after a few months of experience, it was discovered that nearly all pilots with third-degree burns so treated developed secondary infection and septicaemia. This caused its use to be discontinued and gave us the dubious satisfaction of knowing that we were suffering in the cause of science. Both my hands were suppurating, and the fingers were already contracting under the tannic and curling down into the palms. The risk of shock was considered too great for them to do both hands. I must have been under the anaesthetic for about fifteen minutes and in that time I saw Peter Pease killed.

He was after another machine, a tall figure leaning slightly forward with a smile at the corner of his mouth. Suddenly from nowhere a Messerschmitt was on his tail about 150 yards away. For two seconds nothing happened. I had a terrible feeling of futility. Then at the top of my voice I shouted, 'Peter, for God's sake look out behind!'

I saw the Messerschmitt open up and a burst of fire hit Peter's machine. His expression did not change, and for a moment his machine hung motionless. Then it turned slowly on its back and dived to the ground. I came-to, screaming his name, with two nurses and the doctor holding me down on the bed.

'All right now. Take it easy, you're not dead yet. That must have been a very bad dream.'

I said nothing. There wasn't anything to say. Two days later I had a letter from Colin. My nurse read it to me. It was very short, hoping that I was getting better and telling me that Peter was dead.

Slowly I came back to life. My morphia injections were less frequent and my mind began to clear. Though I began to feel and think again coherently I still could not see. Two VADs fainted while helping with my dressings, the first during the day and the other at night. The second time I could not sleep and was calling out for someone to stop the beetles running down my face, when I heard my nurse say fiercely, 'Get outside quick: don't make a fool of yourself here!' and the sound of footsteps moving towards the door. I remember cursing the unfortunate girl and telling her to put her head between her knees. I was told later that for my first three weeks I did little but curse and blaspheme, but I remember nothing of it. The nurses were wonderfully patient and never complained. Then one day I found that I could see. My nurse was bending over me doing my dressings, and she seemed to me very beautiful. She was. I watched her for a long time, grateful that my first glimpse of the world should be of anything so perfect. Finally I said:

'Sue, you never told me that your eyes were so blue.'

For a moment she stared at me. Then, 'Oh, Dick, how wonderful,' she said. 'I told you it wouldn't be long'; and she dashed out to bring in all the nurses on the block.

I felt absurdly elated and studied their faces eagerly, gradually connecting them with the voices that I knew.

'This is Anne,' said Sue. 'She is your special VAD and helps me with all your dressings. She was the only one of us you'd allow near you for about a week. You said you liked her voice.' Before me stood an attractive fair-haired girl of about twenty-three. She smiled and her teeth were as enchanting as her voice. I began to feel that hospital had its compensations. The nurses called me Dick and I knew them all by their Christian names. Quite how irregular this was I did not discover until I moved to another hospital where I was considerably less ill and not so outrageously spoiled. At first my dressings had to be changed every two hours in the daytime. As this took over an hour to do, it meant that Sue and Anne had practically no time off.

But they seemed not to care. It was largely due to them that both my hands were not amputated.

Sue, who had been nursing since seventeen, had been allocated as my special nurse because of her previous experience of burns, and because, as matron said, 'She's our best girl and very human.' Anne had been married to a naval officer killed in the *Courageous*, and had taken up nursing after his death.

At this time there was a very definite prejudice among the regular nurses against VADs. They were regarded as painted society girls, attracted to nursing by the prospect of sitting on the officers' beds and holding their hands. The VADs were rapidly disabused of this idea, and, if they were lucky, were finally graduated from washing bedpans to polishing bed-tables. I never heard that any of them grumbled, and they gradually won a reluctant recognition. This prejudice was considerably less noticeable in the Masonic than in most hospitals: Sue, certainly, looked on Anne as a companionable and very useful lieutenant to whom she could safely entrust my dressings and general upkeep in her absence. I think I was a little in love with both of them.

The Masonic is perhaps the best hospital in England, though at the time I was unaware how lucky I was. When war broke out the Masons handed over a part of it to the services; but owing to its vulnerable position very few action casualties were kept there long. Pilots were pretty quickly moved out to the main Air Force hospital, which I was not in the least eager to visit. Thanks to the kind-hearted duplicity of my house surgeon, I never had to; for every time they rang up and asked for me he would say that I was too ill to be moved. The Masonic's great charm lay in that it in no way resembled a hospital; if anything it was like the inside of a ship. The nursing staff were very carefully chosen, and during the regular blitzing of the district, which took place every night, they were magnificent.

The Germans were presumably attempting to hit Hammersmith bridge, but their efforts were somewhat erratic and we were treated night after night to an orchestra of the scream and crump of falling bombs. They always seemed to choose a moment when my eyes were being irrigated, when my poor nurse was poised above me with a glass undine in her hand. At night we were moved into the corridor, away from the outside wall, but such was the snoring of my fellow sufferers that I persuaded Bertha to allow me back in my own room after matron had made her rounds.

Bertha was my night nurse. I never discovered her real name, but to me she was Bertha from the instant that I saw her. She was large and gaunt with an Eton crop and a heart of gold. She was engaged to a merchant seaman who was on his way to Australia. She made it quite clear that she had no intention of letting me get round her as I did the day staff, and ended by spoiling me even more. At night when I couldn't sleep we would hold long and heated arguments on the subject of sex. She expressed horror at my ideas on love and on her preference for a cup of tea. I gave her a present of four pounds of it when I was discharged. One night the Germans were particularly persistent, and I had the unpleasant sensation of hearing a stick of bombs gradually approaching the hospital, the first some way off, the next closer, and the third shaking the building. Bertha threw herself across my bed; but the fourth bomb never fell. She got up quickly, looking embarrassed, and arranged her cap.

'Nice fool I'd look if you got hit in your own room when you're supposed to be out in the corridor,' she said, and stumped out of the room.

An RASC officer who had been admitted to the hospital with the painful but unromantic complaint of piles protested at the amount of favouritism shown to me merely because I was in the RAF. A patriotic captain who was in the same ward turned on him and said: 'At least he was shot down defending his country and didn't come in here with a pimple on his bottom. The Government will buy him a new Spitfire, but I'm damned if it will buy you a new arse.'

One day my doctor came in and said that I could get up. Soon after I was able to totter about the passages and could be given a proper bath. I was still unable to use my hands and everything had to be done for me. One evening during a blitz, my nurse, having led me along to the lavatory, placed a prodigiously long cigarette holder in my mouth and lighted the cigarette in the end of it. Then she went off to get some coffee. I was puffing away contentedly when the lighted cigarette fell into my pyjama trousers and started smouldering. There was little danger that I would go up in flames, but I thought it advisable to draw attention to the fact that all was not well. I therefore shouted 'Oi!' Nobody heard me. 'Help!' I shouted somewhat louder. Still nothing happened, so I delivered myself of my imitation of Tarzan's elephant call of which I was quite proud. It happened that in the ward opposite there was an old gentleman who had been operated on for a hernia. The combination of the scream of falling bombs and my animal cries could mean only one thing. Someone had been seriously injured, and he made haste to dive over the side of the bed. In doing so he caused himself considerable discomfort: convinced of the ruin of his operation and the imminence of his death, he added his cries to mine. His fears finally calmed, he could see nothing humorous in the matter and insisted on being moved to another ward. From then on I was literally never left alone for a minute.

34 Donald Stones Part 2, Hurricane Pilot, Pilot Officer, British, 79 Squadron

This second extract from Stones's memoir covers 27 August–7 September, when he was based in southern England flying from RAF Biggin Hill. By the end of 1940 his score was nine kills (plus several probables), five shot down over France and four during the Battle of Britain.

Donald would go on to fight in Malta and Burma and rise to become a squadron leader before he lost an eye in a flying accident in 1945. He joined the Colonial Service after the war and died in 2002. His two volumes of memoirs have recently been republished together as an ebook, *A Pilot's Passion: The Story of Dimsie*, and re-edited by Adrian Burt. Thanks to Adrian and Donald Stones's widow, Beryl Stones, for giving permission.

I got back to Acklington just in time to prepare for the squadrons return to Biggin, fully operational again. But I had missed the 'big day' in mid-August when the northern based squadrons, including 79, had totally defeated a massive German raid from Norway. Some of our new pilots had done well, so morale was high as we flew south to relieve 32 Squadron at Biggin, where we arrived on 27 August. 32 was more than ready for a rest and we were very impressed when we heard about their experiences during the much increased savagery of the fighting over southern England. Now began the phase of massive attacks on most of our sector's aerodromes. On 30 August, Biggin was bombed by an enemy formation which had evaded interception. John Parker and I were running across the aerodrome to get from the mess to our dispersal hut when the bombers dropped their load and we went flat on our faces. It was rather noisy, but when the dust cleared we ran on unhurt. Some of our Hurricanes were hit and, sadly, some ground crew were killed.

Now that we were seeing the enemy in large numbers streaming above the glorious countryside of Kent, I felt a sense of outrage. It was like the rape of a sleeping beauty. Their black Prussian crosses looked malevolent enough, but the crooked cross of the swastika on their tails now seemed idolatrous and obscene. How dare these descendants of Atilla the Hun's barbarians have the impertinence to violate the skies of our 'sceptred isle'? We pilots never discussed our innermost feelings about the enemy, preferring the simple maxim: 'It's him or me', but what we had regarded as merely enemy aircraft within the vaguely defined frontiers of France were now invaders as they crossed our sea marked coasts. We fell upon them with a new found righteous fury, determined to give no quarter. Teddy Morris exemplified this on 30 August when we attacked some Heinkel 111s and Dornier 17s near the Thames. He pressed home his head-on attack on one Heinkel and would not give way until the crew was dead. This resulted in collision and the total destruction of both the bomber and the Hurricane. Teddy found himself alone among small bits of debris but with his parachute undamaged. He calmly pulled the cord and landed with only a broken leg. I fired at two Dorniers, saw bits fly off one, then tracers from a 109 right behind me which missed, the 109 pulling up ahead and being seen off by a Spitfire, then another Do 17 on its own in front of me. I got in two good bursts on this one, more bits off him. He straightened out and went for the ground but my Hurricane was faster and another burst into that same port engine, now lots of black smoke as he went screaming across Kent to the South Coast. He was still flying though, now on one engine, as I put my last burst into his other engine, came in again and pressed my gun button – dead silence – out of ammunition. Still he flew on, now very slowly at about 300 feet. Surely he couldn't make France? As always in these shambles, at one moment the air is full of crazily wheeling aircraft, and the next it is empty except for yourself and this stricken pig-headed Do 17. I felt it only needed a spanner to throw at him and he would hit the deck. But eventually he did, in a field near Newchurch, north of Dungeness. He ploughed across the field, coming to rest near the hedge and was immediately surrounded by farm workers. I flew around him for a minute or so and saw some of the crew get out, then went in to Hawkinge to re-fuel and re-arm. At Hawkinge I was told to wait as Biggin was being bombed and the operations room was out of action. Eventually I was told to stay overnight at Hawkinge and while there, the recovery party which had gone out to the Dornier, brought in the survivors of its crew and gave me the pilot's goggles and Very pistol as souvenirs. Some idea of the effects of the Hurricane's eight machine guns at close range may be gained from the fact that one of the Do 17's gunners was lifted out of the wreck in two pieces.

Returning to Biggin next morning, I heard that David Haysom, our other South African, had a message from Teddy Morris in hospital. Teddy had missed France, as he was recovering from meningitis at the time, which had turned his hair white. So this had been his first combat and he was very cross with us as we had told him that the best way to split up a formation of enemy bombers was to attack them head-on, when they might break away. He complained that the Heinkel had not broken away but flew straight at him. David explained to Teddy that as he had obviously killed the Heinkel pilot with his accurate burst, the corpse could not turn at all, so it was up to the Hurricane to get out of the way.

While I was away at Hawkinge, the ops room at Biggin had been badly damaged and our mess had also been hit. Worse than all that, some of our WAAFs had been killed in a shelter, but there was little time to brood on these blows as we were immediately in action against 50 Do 17s escorted by Me 110s right above Biggin, but our ten Hurricanes could not stop them dropping their bomb load and causing a lot more damage, particularly to our hangers. Orders to scramble were now being sent from our almost useless ops room by despatch riders, because our telephone line to dispersal was also out of action. It seemed that the radar system was swamped by the incessant raids and we were being scrambled too late to get any height on them.

Some of us were now billeted out with local civilian families and I was very fortunate in my hostess, the dowager Lady Avebury in her beautiful house near Biggin, the ancestral home of the Lubbock family, which had had a close connection with Charles Darwin. I recall large glass cases displaying fossils and other evidence connected with *The Origin of the Species*. She was a fascinating and charming old lady, whose hospitality and kindness I shall never forget. She still employed a full staff and for the few nights I stayed there, I was waited upon hand and foot. She was very much aware of what was happening at Biggin, a mile or so away, and each night she would ask me for full details of the day's action. Quite fearless, she had no thoughts of moving to a safer place and was determined to maintain her peacetime standard of composure. No mere German armada was going to upset that great lady.

The summer days continued hot and mostly cloudless, as it had been almost without a break since May, and we were beginning to think that we would never get a typical English day with torrential rain so that the Luftwaffe would take a day off flying and give us a bit of a rest too. Harvey Heyworth singled me out for a public dressing down outside the dispersal hut where we were all sitting in deckchairs or lying on the grass, fully booted and wearing our Mae West life jackets, ready to scramble into our aircraft. 'Now look here, Dimsie, you went on that fighter navigation course in August didn't you? And part of it was meteorology, was it not? Presumably you studied weather patterns?' 'Yes, sir. Very interesting and technical it was too.' 'Well,' he continued, 'may I point out that since you came back, it hasn't bloody rained ONCE! Why is that? We might just as well not have sent you!' I muttered something about a large area of high pressure stationary over the Azores and stretching as far as the whole of northern Europe. 'That's not good enough,' he boomed. 'We want rain, fog, sleet, or snow for at least a week. What are you, the squadron met man, going to do about it?' I suggested prayer.

'Now there's a good idea,' said Harvey. 'Everyone down on his knees. O God of battles, steel my soldiers' hearts, but give us fog or snow or sleet or anything but sunshine. Amen.' He intoned. We said the FOG PRAYER every morning at dawn after that, but the sun kept shining. Harvey said that the Great Lord of the Weather must be on leave in the Azores as he certainly could not hear us.

The squadron was now restricted to aerodrome defence until our ops room could be fully repaired, but on 4 September we succumbed to temptation and went after 15 Me 110s which formed a defensive circle over Beachy Head. We attacked them, hoping to break up their circle, and got one of them in our first attack. I was so close to him before breaking away that I could see a red dragon painted on his nose. His wreckage was confirmed later in the day by the anti-aircraft gunners. Fortunately for me, John Parker shot another 110 off my tail while I was dealing with the red dragon, but we lost Sergeant [John] Wright. Back at Biggin we were bombed again that afternoon and the damage was getting rather serious we were now taking off in a series of zig-zags to avoid bomb craters, which the hardworking repair gangs tried to fill in at night.

The fighting became even more fast and furious, and during one typical mêlée, my engine stopped and I glided down to Biggin in tight turns to avoid being picked off by the keen-eyed 109s, but in so doing, with my canopy open, my lucky red scarf blew off my neck and was lost.

They say bad luck comes in packets of three. Coming into land after the next scrap, my starboard wheel stuck in its housing and refused to unlock whatever violent manoeuvres I tried, so I had to land wheels up on the grass, putting yet another precious Hurricane out of action. I wondered what number three gremlin was cooking up for me. Not long to wait, for on the following afternoon, 7 September, the Luftwaffe changed its tactics and thereby lost the battle, and perhaps the war. A huge radar plot of German bombers and fighters was building up over Cape Gris Nez on the French coast and we were told to patrol at 24,000 feet between Biggin and the Thames to await their arrival. We now know that this was not to be the coup de grâce for Biggin and neighbouring aerodromes, but an attack on London itself. The Germans, particularly Goering, thought these bases were now out of action and needed no further attention. We went off just before 3pm and clambered up to 24,000 feet, where we arrived, surprisingly for once, without being jumped, and awaited our customers. We patrolled north to south and back, across the afternoon sun. According to ground control, the radar plot showing a massive raid, was still building up. Fuel was getting low after about an hour, so Harvey, wisely I thought, sent the squadron down for urgent refuelling and return to patrol height. He told me to remain with him as his No. 2, so back and forth we flew, one of us going north along our patrol line and the other south, to keep a full view of our area. Before the squadron could rejoin us, our controller suddenly told us that the German armada was now coming in fast. I heard this message as I was on my northern course, with Harvey going south. Almost at once I heard his R/T saying: 'Tally ho! I'm going into this lot. Come on Red 2.' Whipping around I caught a glimpse of great fires already burning along the Thames, and Harvey, diving almost vertically into a mass of Dorniers heavily escorted by swarms of 110s and 109s above and around them. I turned to dive after him, but at once saw another gaggle nearer to me. The only way to attack such large formations on one's own is to fly straight at them in a frontal attack, in the hope that destroying or crippling one of the leaders will split them up or cause collisions amongst the densely packed horde. I went through my lot, trying to concentrate my fire on a particular Dornier 17, but the trouble with frontal attack was that the combined closing speeds of the attacking fighter and the targets was a good 500 mph, even in those days. I did not see any of my brief targets waiver, so pulled through them avoiding collision by what seemed to be a hair's breadth and turned to see if there was any damage or perhaps even a cripple to knock down. Completing my turn, I came out right on the tail of a fat Me 110 filling my sights and an absolute sitter. I was about to fire and finish him when my Hurricane was hit from tail to cockpit by a blast from the 110s little friend, a 109 I had been too busy to notice. Things happened rather quickly now. I reacted instinctively into a tight turn like a startled rabbit and went into a spiralling dive to get away from the 109, knowing there was damage but not how much. He didn't fire again as far as I know and I tried to regain full control but the Hurricane was hell-bent downwards and was not answering the controls properly. Everything was happening fast, but it can only have been for a couple of seconds that I struggled to open my cockpit canopy and prepared to bale out, finding the canopy jammed through damage.

I remember I prayed for a miracle, and it was answered as I felt the spin slowing and gradually we straightened out. I was now at about 2,000 feet and had time to look around. There was a large gap in the starboard side of the cockpit, near my leg which began to tingle as the adrenalin dried up and, looking aft in my mirror, I could see damage to my rudder and tail plane. There was a grass airstrip ahead of me. The wheels dropped down and locked, but the flap selector had been shot off. I taxied to a hanger and someone climbed on the wing to wrench open my bent canopy and help me out. The rear fuselage and tail of my sturdy Hurricane was tattered and torn. Once more I was grateful for the ruggedness of that machine. Soon an ambulance arrived and I was taken to hospital, where I was given a jab and bits of metal were taken out of my leg. I remember hoping, before I went into a drugged sleep, that someone should tell Lady Avebury that I wouldn't be in to dinner that night.

Awakened early in the morning by a very pretty young nurse, I was told that this was Preston Hall Hospital near Maidstone, Kent, and that the other five beds in this room were also occupied by wounded pilots. I looked around at the others, in various stages of minor disrepair. On the bed to my right, however, was a body completely swathed in white bandages. In spite of the usual hospital smell of antiseptics, there was a sickly sweetness in the air near this bed, and I realised that he was a badly burned case. The only hole in the bandages was for his mouth. I never discovered his identity as he was taken away later in the day, whether to a special burns unit or a grave, no one would say. According to the nurses, they had watched the fiery glow in the sky over London all night, easily seen as far away as Maidstone, and German night bombers had kept the fires stoked up. I made sure that the hospital had reported my whereabouts to Biggin Hill and began to take stock of the position. My leg seemed pretty good and, though sore, I could hobble with a stick to the lavatory when the nurses were not looking. The small amount of cash I had with me was enough for cigarettes, the food was good, and the staff superb. I spent a lot of time sleeping during the first two or three days and nights. The other chaps had arrived a few days before me and their stories were similar to mine, stupidly not seeing a 109 or getting too close to a good rear gunner. None was badly wounded and all were expecting to be released very soon, as Preston Hall was only an emergency post. It's major function was for tuberculosis patients, they said. For what? TB? I at once hobbled down to see the matron, told her that I was feeling perfectly fit and must get back to Biggin at once. She had a very strong personality and absolutely refused to discharge me. I saw the surgeon to no avail. He palmed me off by saying I must stay just 'another day or so'. The thought of TB made me nervous.

Meanwhile the battle raged above us. Some of us sat on the lawn in the hot sun and watched the endless fighting in frustration. From what we could gather, the whole attack had been switched from our aerodromes to London itself, and this we realised was good news for our squadrons. The Luftwaffe losses were announced every evening and as they mounted to cricket score levels, even 185 on 15 September, one of the chaps said disparagingly: 'We seem to have got some shit-hot pilots from somewhere. Must be the Poles.'

Whatever the real score on the 15th, it was too much for me. I had an idea. I asked the pretty nurse if she would take me for a walk, purely for exercise, when she was off duty that evening. To my delight she agreed, with the proviso that it would not be publicly known. I crept out at dusk and, holding her hand for quite unnecessary support, steered her determinedly into the local pub and kept her there until closing time. Making sure that she slipped into her quarters unseen while I waited in the darkness, I now banged on the main door and was let in by the porter. I bumped into the startled night sister, who was very cross and I was sent to bed. The next morning I was discharged with ignominy and on my way to Biggin by train. I could have kissed that little nurse. Well, I had anyway.

On my way back to Biggin, I began to wonder why I had had no message or a visit from my parents. Some of the other pilots had been visited by families and girlfriends, and most at least had telegrams or letters. Perhaps my people hadn't heard.

Arriving at Biggin, I went into the mess and there was no one I knew. My squadron had gone to Wales, replaced by Spitfires. Biggin had been declared a Spitfire only area, as Hurricanes could not climb as fast as was now imperative to meet the enemy before he got undeterred to London.

35 Josef Koukal, Hurricane Pilot, Sergeant Pilot, Czech, 310 Squadron

Contemporary newspaper article including an anonymous account by a Czech, 'Sergeant Josef K', reprinted in an anthology of first-hand accounts of Poland's fight against the Nazis and first published in early 1941.

This was by Josef Koukal, who was born in Czechoslovakia in 1912 and was serving in the Czech Air Force when the Nazis occupied his country on 15 March

1939 and disbanded the air force. He escaped to Poland despite his wife being four months pregnant, and flew against the Luftwaffe when Poland was invaded. When Poland fell in September 1939 Josef evaded capture and shipment to Siberia (by the invading Russians who had seized eastern Poland as part of the non-aggression pact signed with Hitler) and escaped once more, this time to France. One of his fellow airmen was killed during this escape, which took Josef via Romania and on board a ship to Turkey, Beirut and Syria. He arrived in France in January 1940 and joined the l'Armee de l'Air. When France capitulated he escaped a third time to England on the Polish ship *Robur III*, arriving in Falmouth on 21 June 1940. He joined 310 Squadron in July 1940 and shot down an Me 110 on 3 September.

The sortie he describes in harrowing detail took place on 7 September 1940, when 310 Squadron were flying from RAF Duxford, Cambridgeshire (12 Group). Before Koukal was shot down in flames, he had shot down an Me 109. Koukal was one of Dr Archie McIndoe's early burns patients and a member of the Guinea Pig Club (Richard Hillary met him in hospital, see chapter 50). Despite his serious injuries he returned to operational flying in 1942 with 312 Squadron.

Koukal survived the war and returned to Czechoslovakia in August 1945, meeting his six-year-old son for the first time. After the communist takeover of 1948 Koukal and his family were to suffer years of harassment by the state, who remained suspicious of those who had fought with the Allies during the war. When the crash site of his Hurricane at Capel Fleet, Harty Marshes in Kent was excavated in 1972 he returned to England and met the widow of the soldier who helped him following his baling out. The recovered items of the dig are now on display at Kent Battle of Britain Museum.

Josef died in 1980 and was posthumously 'rehabilitated' after the Velvet Revolution of 1989. After his death he was promoted to Colonel of the Czech Air Force, a plaque was erected on his house in his home town of Luze and the town square was named after him.

I lost control of the machine at once, as I think the explosion had wrecked the controls; she began to nose-dive at a rapidly increasing speed. The cockpit cover was open, as I had had it all through the fight, so I slipped off my safety belt and tried to scramble out of my burning machine, but the position of the aircraft and the air pressure of my speed held me into my seat as if I was anchored there. Flames from the burning petrol were roaring all round my head – I never heard such a row in all my life. It was just like being in Hell itself, and I gave up all hope; I know now something of what a chap can live through before dying. I thought of my wife and our boy, and of quite a lot of other people; then I summoned up courage to open my eyes in spite of the flames, and I could see my own flesh burning on my arms and legs. I was in the most awful pain, but still quite fully conscious.

The bust up had happened at about 20,000 feet, and just as I had given up all thought of saving my life Fate took a hand: the second petrol tank went up, and I was shot out of the aircraft into space. Then I realised just how I should have to pay for my foolishness in going into a fight with my cockpit open. The second explosion must have been at about 13,000 feet. The remains of my clothes with petrol, and, of course, I simply fell through the air like a flaming torch! I didn't dare release my parachute, as I thought it would simply catch fire at once, and leave me to drop headlong. At last, when my clothes had stopped burning, I pulled the release, about 2,000 feet from the ground. The parachute opened faultlessly, and in a short time I came down in the garden of a farm on the Isle of Sheppey. With my burnt hands I could not release the catch of my parachute, and it was only after a long struggle that I could get rid of it. Half naked, and in great pain, I managed to get to the main road, where I met, and was helped by, first a British soldier and then an ambulance car. They took me to hospital at Minster, and there I was visited a few days after by the farmer's wife into whose garden I had fallen. The burnt skin over three-quarters of my body was as hard as leather, and my hands and feet were beginning to curl up from the contraction of the scars.

36 Svatopluk Janouch Part 2, Hurricane Pilot, Pilot Officer, Czech, 310 Squadron

The second account from Svatopluk Janouch is a newspaper account quoting the words of 'Lieutenant J', republished in the anthology of first-hand accounts of Poland's fight against the Nazis and first published in early 1941. Lieutenant J is in fact Janouch, and the extract covers his first kill over Britain, an Me 110 on 7 September, when Janouch was flying from RAF Duxford, Cambridgeshire (12 Group). He would go on to share in the kill of a Dornier 17 on 18 September, bringing his 1940 total to four kills and one shared kill. Janouch survived the war and wrote a book about his wartime experiences which was published in Prague in 1947 as *Svetla a Stiny* (*Light and Shadow*). He died in New York in 1966.

Once the actual fight begins you don't see much except just the rings or cross that mark a friend or an enemy, white streaks flying round you which are probably tracers, and then a momentary glimpse of a machine going down in flames out of control, or occasionally of a parachute. But in the moments when you are not fighting, it's almost majestic. Great black bombers in close formation, but little disturbed by anti-aircraft fire, and above them, or along with them, formations of fighters. And all of them seem sliding so quietly and somehow calmly through the air – til the fight actually starts. Below, some thousands of feet down, you can see puffs of smoke and dust from bursting bombs, but the air round you seems marvellously clear and quiet.

You attack out of the sun, and, for the moment, you see nothing but the cross marking your enemy, and the little gleaming bead of your gunsight. Then one of my comrades suddenly is gone from my side, a Messerschmitt after him, and I go after him in turn, to help before it may be too late. And then, quite suddenly, I find myself alone, all my ammunition gone, with the Thames below me and London a little farther on, almost hidden in a light layer of smoke and mist.

Another time we were flying in three flights in step formation, a Canadian flight above us and an English flight below. The German bombers were escorted by a considerable number of fighters, and it was these we had been ordered to attack. We had a group of Messerschmitts in front of us, and I picked out one and got behind a 110 by manoeuvring. The German pilot nose-dived, but just too late; I pressed my trigger, and got at least 150 rounds into him, and saw smoke starting out of his engines. I didn't get time to see what happened after that, but a comrade flying behind me saw him go out of control and straight into the ground. I believe the pilot baled out by parachute.

37 William Rolls, Spitfire Pilot, Sergeant Pilot, British, 72 Squadron

Extract from his memoir, *Spitfire Attack*, first published in 1987 and covering 2–14 September. Born in Lower Edmonton, London, in August 1914, 'Bill' Rolls joined the RAF in March 1939 and 72 Squadron on 19 June 1940. His squadron moved from the comparative calm of RAF Acklington in Northumberland to RAF Biggin Hill, south-east London (11 Group), on 31 August just as the Battle was reaching its zenith (during this period he also flew from RAF Croydon, south London).

This is a brilliant account, not least because it comes from a sergeant pilot rather than an officer, but also because it covers the high point of the Battle from its epicentre in the south-east. Notably, unlike all his friends in the squadron, Bill was at the time both married (to Rene) and had a young baby girl (Carole). Carole tragically died of heart trouble in 1941. Later in the war he had a son, Derek, born in 1942. Note the interesting story of Bill collecting his friend Johnny White from an East End pub after crash-landing nearby.

Rolls would shoot down seven enemy aircraft by the end of the Battle and end the war with a total of seventeen kills and four probable kills. He died in 1988. Many thanks to his son, Derek Rolls, for permission to use this extract.

2 September 1940 At 7.30 a.m. the telephone rang and the flight sergeant answered it. He put the phone down and told us all to get airborne immediately. No one asked why. We simply ran to the nearest aircraft, yelling to the crews to start up the engines and in no time we were taxiing out to take off. The flight sergeant took the first four aircraft and I took the second four as Green 1. There were no officers with us as the squadron had not even been called to readiness from the thirty minutes; availability state. It was only because we were in the tents waiting for breakfast that we were able to take off. The combat report for this action is J/2/15 dated 2/9/40, and is reproduced below.

SECRET. FORM 'F' COMBAT REPORT.
Sector Serial No. (A) [blank]
Serial No. of Order detailing Flight or Squadron to Patrol (B) [blank]
Date (C) 2/9/40
Flight, Squadron (D) Flight: 'B' Sqdn: '72'
Number of Enemy Aircraft (E) 30 bombers + fighters
Type of Enemy Aircraft (F) Do 17, Me 110, Me 109

Time Attack was delivered (G) 0800

Place Attack was delivered (H) Approx Maidstone

Height of Enemy (J) 13–30,000

Enemy Casualties (K) Me 110, Do 17 destroyed

Our Casualties: Aircraft (L) nil / Personnel (M) nil

GENERAL REPORT (R) I took off from Croydon as Green 1 and followed Blue section in wide formation and was instructed to climb to 15,000 feet. We saw the enemy approaching from ESE and Blue section led the attack on the bombers while I followed above them. I saw Blue section break away and the enemy was then turning to south as I approached. I saw one Me 110 leave the formation and dive on to the tail of a Spitfire and as no other Spitfire was near enough, I dived after it and came in at the Me 110 from 15° above and astern from port. I aimed at the Me 110 port engine and put about 640 rounds into it. It caught fire and appeared to fall away with part of the wing and the machine went over on its back and then went down with flames from the port wing. I had opened fire at 200 yards but did not see any return fire. I dived down to the starboard side of it and saw 17 Do 17s below me at about 12,000 feet. I had one in my sights and I fired all my other rounds at it. The fuselage blew to pieces and then the engine (port) caught fire. I closed my fire at about 175 yards to 50 yards and then dived again to starboard and went into a spin to avoid the Me 109 behind. I found myself flying at 4,000 feet when I pulled out of the spin. Above me rather separated I saw 3 parachutes drifting down and to my starboard I saw the Do 17 coming down in flames and it crashed into the wood NE of Maidstone. I went up to investigate the parachute being as I could not see the enemy again. I saw that one was empty, another appeared to be a sergeant pilot with Mae West, and the other had no Mae West and I circled round him and he landed near a factory at Chatham. I climbed up again to 3,000 feet and made for base as we were ordered to return.

Sgt Rolls, B flight, Green section, 72 Squadron.

When we later landed back at Croydon we were faced with some very irate officers. The audacity of sergeant pilots taking off without their officers was something unheard of and they seemed at a loss to know what to do about it, until our flight commanders took over. They had been on the phone in one of the tents while we were landing and when we were all together they came into our tent to ask us how many enemy aircraft we had destroyed. Control had kept them informed as to what had happened. My own flight commander came over to me and said, 'Bloody good show, Rolls.' The other sergeants were likewise congratulated.

This time we had had no order to break and we were at the right height and distance when we made our attack, with maximum fire power. The enemy did not know what had hit them as they went down fast and furious. I had got two confirmed destroyed, Johnny White had a Dornier 17 destroyed and one damaged and also one Me 110 probable. Stickey [Sergeant Pilot Norman Glew] had one probable and Johnny Gilders one Do 17 destroyed. The flight sergeant had been successful also. I think each one of us had made contact, if only to damage the enemy aircraft.

When we were making out our combat reports I asked Johnny White what position he was flying in and he told me was Blue 3. He also told me that he had been hit by an Me 110 on his tail but someone took it off him. I had the pleasure of telling him that it was me and that it had crashed at the edge of Birling woods near Maidstone. We were very happy at the results we had achieved without any officer to lead us and this fact only went to prove the value of the training Flying Officer [Thomas 'Jimmy'] Elsdon had put us through. Some of the credit for these victories should go to him.

That afternoon six of our squadron were scrambled to go to forward base at Kenley. When I was airborne I noticed that after a few minutes when we started to climb I was losing power and the engine was not sounding so good. As the flight was not likely to be long I decided that I would continue and get it seen to at Kenley. It was forty minutes before we landed and by then the aircraft was losing pressure in the oil system and I was glad when I arrived at dispersal. I told the flight sergeant to see if he could see what was wrong with the engine and went into the flight room to wait as we were supposed to still be at readiness.

Within the next ten minutes we had been ordered to scramble and I ran to my aircraft and the flight sergeant told me it was u/s as the magneto was not working on either mag. I had to watch the others take off after having tested the mags to satisfy myself that they were too bad for an operational sortie.

I went back to dispersal and listened to the controller on the R/T set in the hut. Our flight of five aircraft was being vectored onto the target and I felt sick. Johnny White was up there and here I was on the ground without an aircraft. I could not listen any more so I went out onto the grass to lie and wait for their return.

About forty minutes later I saw two aircraft returning and watched them land. One had been hit and had made a bad landing, I thought immediately that the pilot must be injured. I then saw two others return and land and saw with relief that Johnny had landed and seemed to be all right. There was no sign of the fifth aircraft as I walked over to Johnny. I knew what had happened by the bullet holes in the aircraft which had landed.

As we were walking to dispersal I told Johnny what had happened to my aircraft. 'It's a good job it was u/s, Bill because we were jumped by Me 109s and did not have a chance. Blue leader was hit and he did not bale out. I got hit on the tail unit and only just managed to break away in time.' He paused for breath and then continued, 'You know, Bill, I was scared out of my life when I saw all those Me 109s coming down on us. We had no time for avoiding action before they hit us.'

'Perhaps if I had been there as well, it might have made a difference,' I said.

'Don't be a bloody fool. It would have given them a better chance to knock another one down. At least you are here to fight another day. Poor old Snowy [Douglas Winter] has had it'.

The flight commander agreed that it would have made no difference to what had happened even if there had been a dozen aircraft there at that particular moment. He asked about my own aircraft and I told him that they were changing the magneto, but that although it would be ready later in the day to fly back to Croydon, it would not be operational until a full inspection of the aircraft was done by our own ground staff. An inspection of the other aircraft showed that they could be flown back to Croydon to be serviced there. When this was reported to the controller he stood the flight down so that they could return to Croydon, having brought the flight that was still there to readiness again.

My aircraft was not ready until about an hour after the others had gone and although I still did not like the sound of the engine I took off and landed at Croydon in time to be stood down with the rest of the squadron.

That evening we went out to celebrate our day's victories and Johnny White was the first up to the bar and had whispered something to the barmaid and then turned to ask us what we wanted as there were six of us altogether and two were tee-total. Johnny gave the girl the order and then took from her a glass of whisky which he came up to me with; he put his arm round my shoulder and kissed me lightly on my cheek. I was flabbergasted and so were the others.

Stickey was the first to retort: 'Christ, I knew you two were bosom pals but I had no idea it had reached this stage.' The others were laughing but Johnny still had his hand on my shoulder, he said, 'Bill took a 110 off my tail this morning, otherwise I might not have been here tonight.'

'Cheers, Johnny, perhaps you'll do the same for me one day,' was my reply.

A gentleman who was standing near to us walked the couple of paces up to the middle of our group. 'Congratulations, lads, on today's effort. May I have the pleasure of asking you to join me in a drink?'

'It will be our pleasure, sir,' Stickey replied, and the gentleman told the barmaid to repeat the order for us. We duly toasted the gentleman's health and thanked him for his kind thoughts.

As more people came into the bar, we seemed to be the centre of interest. I don't think they had seen RAF sergeant pilots before, only officer pilots by the interest we seemed to be causing. After a short while the barmaid came up to us and pointed to the drinks on the bar; when asked where they had come from, she pointed to a man and presumably his wife. We all looked over to them and the man waved his hand to us and called, 'Cheers, lads.'

This was amazing, two free drinks in four minutes, it was just like being back at The Trap.

We had started on this second free drink when Johnny Gilders, pint in hand, walked over to the table where the man and wife who had bought us the drink were sitting. He spoke to them but not loud enough for us to hear what he was saying, but as the people on the other tables were all looking at him, we were beginning to wonder. He came back to us and we asked him what he had been telling them.

'I think their gesture was worthy of our personal thanks and so I thanked them for their round of drinks and told them that we would try and shoot down another half dozen bloody Jerries tomorrow.'

Needless to say, we did not have to buy any more drinks that night, and after a while had drunk as much as we could and still appear respectable. Good old Sergeant [Malcolm 'Mable'] Gray was still sober and so our ride back to the billets was uneventful. That night even our metal bedsteads seemed comfortable.

The next day was rather a quiet one for me and I only did one sortie, but had no action. The 4 September saw us taking off at 1250. I was Blue 3 in the leading section and we were told the enemy were a mixed bunch of aircraft, making for Ashford in Kent. We intercepted them near Tunbridge Wells and made our attack. The combat report for this action is reproduced below.

SECRET. FORM 'F' COMBAT REPORT.

Sector Serial No. (A) [blank]

Serial No. of Order detailing Flight or Squadron to Patrol (B) [blank]

Date (C) 4/9/40

Flight, Squadron (D) Flight: 'B' Sqdn: '72'

Number of Enemy Aircraft (E) 30

Type of Enemy Aircraft (F) Me 110, Ju 86

Time Attack was delivered (G) 1330

Place Attack was delivered (H) Ashford and Tunbridge Wells

Height of Enemy (J) 15,000

Enemy Casualties (K) Two Ju 86s

Our Casualties: Aircraft (L) nil / Personnel (M) nil

GENERAL REPORT (R) I took off from Croydon as Blue 3 in leading section at 12.50. We intercepted the enemy who were approaching us from the NE at right angles to our course. The leader gave the order line astern and turned to port to attack. His first burst hit the leading machine and the rest started to form a circle. I turned steeply to port and did a quarter attack on one of the end Ju 86s. The port engine started to fire and two of the crew baled out as I went beneath. I turned steeply again to port and came up from the quarter on another Ju 86 which was in a steep bank. I gave a ring and a half deflection shot and my bullets hit the fuselage at about 200 yards range, and I saw the port engine smoke and the machine fall in. I followed it down and it was burning before it hit a wood SE of Tunbridge Wells. As I was about to climb up I saw another one crash not far away and it was followed down by Sergeant Gray who joined up on me. We then went to investigate 3 parachutes and saw that 2 were German and one was an officer from our own squadron. I then flew back to base as I had run out of ammunition.

Rounds in First machine: about 800 to 1000

Rounds in Second machine: the remainder

Speed of Ju 86 about 160–180 mph

Firing cannon from back and what appeared to be cannon from the side window. Also tracer and incendiary bullets.

W. Rolls, Sergeant, Blue section 3, B flight, 72 Squadron

That evening we had another interception over the London Docks, but I did not destroy any enemy aircraft. The same evening we again went into Croydon. It had not taken us long to understand what the 79 Squadron sergeant had said about getting away from the camp at night and also that if you don't drink now, you will after a few days here. I am not trying to excuse our desire to go out on the binge. We had seen some of our officers killed and wounded and some who had baled out, all of this in a few days. It was no wonder that we thought our turn would soon come for the high jump, so why not enjoy ourselves while we could? That was the kind of mentality most of the fighter pilots had adopted for the first few days in action, but directly you realised you had survived some aerial battles and had got the better of the enemy, you tended to sober up and take it easier of a night. I even found time to write some letters home and this made my fight for survival necessary, even more than my mates who were all single, though they were of the same opinion as I was. We would have a drink at night when we were not on dawn readiness.

The next morning I was in a flight which was ordered to forward base at Hawkinge in Kent on the coast. We met some Me 109s and attacked them but it was impossible to get your sights on one of them long enough to get the right deflection. Unfortunately we lost one of our officers.

We returned to Croydon after lunch and the rest of the squadron were again scrambled later in the day but I did not go on that trip. One of our officers had to bale out and we lost one aircraft in sight of the aerodrome. He was right behind a Heinkel 111 and from the ground it seemed that the Heinkel was afire. At that moment a 109 dived down on the Spitfire and the Heinkel and the Spitfire fell to earth not very far from Croydon.

Those of us who were in the dispersal tent, waited anxiously for news as to who baled out and who was shot down. We knew that two of our aircraft had not yet returned but as other squadrons were involved we hoped the one we saw crash was not one of ours. The period of waiting was one of the worst I had encountered to date and it was a relief when the ops phone rang to give us the news. The flight commander told us that our Australian officer, one of the nicest officers in the squadron, had baled out and was wounded. He looked at the sergeants who were by the tent opening:

'Sorry, chaps, have some bad news for you. Sergeant Gray has been killed.'

Until now we had lost some of our officers and had some injured and others who had baled out, but this was the first sergeant we had that had been killed and the fact that it was our dear old mate, 'Mabel', to those that were his friends, made it very hard to take. We had got used to it when we heard that one of the officers had been killed, you kind of expected that as they were the leaders, for they were more vulnerable, but when it came to our mate, who had taken us out each night, it was now personal and a great shock to all, as he was such a likeable chap. He would drink only a shandy so that he would be able to drive us home safely.

When we had finished for the day, we decided that we would get off the airfield as quickly as possible. We would go into Croydon and have something to eat and then have a drink in our local pub. We had a duty to perform. Later that evening after having had a meal we went back to the pub we had been using since we arrived at Croydon.

It was quite full and as we got near the bar Stickey called out for the usual four beers and a shandy. People soon made way at the bar for us and the manager asked where the other chap, the quiet one was. I pointed my finger towards the ceiling and the people round us all stopped talking. It went right through the lounge and yet no word had been spoken. We picked up our four beers and just said quietly, 'Cheers, Mabel' and took a few mouthfuls. Stickey then picked up the glass of shandy and poured it into each of our glasses. People were still looking at each other and did not say a word. They all seemed to know what it was all about and as most of them had seen Mabel on the other occasions, I think they were as shocked as we were.

Within a couple of minutes we were talking to the manager and things started to get back to normal. In the conversation I managed to tell him that we had agreed a long time ago that if one of us were killed, the others would drink his health and share his drink among us. We had even suggested that it might even come to one of us having to get drunk in order to carry out this request. We did not stay until closing time, I think we had depressed the other customers for long enough and so we caught a cab back to our billets for a more miserable night's rest.

I did not fly at all on the next day as our flight was at 30 minutes' availability and was not called to readiness.

That night we did not go out at all and wrote letters home instead.

On 7 September at late afternoon, we were scrambled and met 50 plus Dornier 17s with fighter escort going for the London Docks. Johnny White and I were in the section led by Flying Officer Elsdon and it was just like the training flights we had been doing with Jimmy back at Acklington. As we approached the enemy aircraft, he ordered echelon to port and I went underneath to come up on John's port side. This way we went into the bombers. As we were almost head on there was little chance to get a single target in your sight so it left you to open fire at everything in front of you as you flew through the formation of enemy bombers. At the same time the gunners in the front and rear turrets of the bombers were firing at us.

I saw a hell of a lot of crosses, but did not see any going down and by the time I had got through the formation, I was on my own without ammunition and was diving as fast as I could away from a Me 109 that I saw in my mirror. There were dozens of Spitfires from other squadrons attacking the bombers and I could see the fires down by the docks.

I was now over the reservoir at Chingford and not far from my parents' home at Edmonton. I flew low over the house and waggled my wings, I knew that if my parents did not see me, one of the neighbours would and they would tell my mother. They had seen me do the same thing when I was at Hatfield.

I then flew back to Croydon and landed. Flying Officer Elsdon and Johnny White had not yet returned and I was getting worried as I had not seen either of them after the attack had started. On landing I learned that Flying Officer Elsdon had baled out and that Johnny White had crash-landed somewhere near the docks. They had been seen by one of the other officers. It was now getting dark and we were stood down from readiness and would soon be going for our dinner, I decided that I would wait a while to find out where Johnny had landed as I knew he would phone in as soon as he was able. It was not very long before the phone rang and we got the message that he was in a pub in Rotherhithe and the MT driver who knew the pub would soon be going to pick him and his gear up. I asked our CO if I could go with the car to pick Johnny up and he readily agreed.

He rang the MT section and ordered the car to come and pick me up; he asked me if I would like to go now or after dinner and I said 'He may be hurt and I don't want to wait if the driver is ready.' In minutes the driver had arrived to pick me up. I had not even had the time to have a wash, but that could wait.

As we were approaching the East End we could see the glow of the fires round the dock area; it looked as though London was going to be the target for the German bombers from now on. It was not long before we reached the pub, where the driver had been before. I expected that it would be busy, being a Saturday night, but as I pulled the blackout curtain aside, I was met with a solid wall of people and the noise was deafening. The people near the door saw us go in and immediately made way for us to get to John who was seated at the end of the room. He was surrounded by a bevy of ladies and had obviously had a couple of scotches by the looks of him.

On the floor by his side was his Mae West and parachute. His arms were round two ladies' waists.

As I got nearer to him, he saw me and jumped up and put his arms round me and lifted me off the floor.

'I knew you would come for me,' he told me, and with that he put me down and sat me in his chair and one of the ladies stood up to let him sit down next to me. I had hardly sat down when a large whisky was put in my hand and I was told to drink up. I stood up and called, 'Cheers, everyone, and thanks for looking after my pal.' Then I saw myself in the mirror behind the bar.

My hair was a mess and looked dirty, my face was spotted with oil blobs some of which had been rubbed and my white scarf about my neck was likewise spotted with oil. I put my drink down and took my scarf off and tried to wipe my face and as I was doing so, an elderly lady whom I presumed was the owner of the pub came over to me and wiped my face with a nice warm flannel and got the spots off. She then took a comb and combed my hair back. The noise had by now died down considerably and we were the centre of interest. When the lady had finished she took my face in her two hands and kissed me saying afterwards, 'Thanks, son, for what you have been doing for us.' The next few minutes I did not know where I was because the other ladies young and old were kissing John and me and at the same time their men folk were slapping our backs and saying, 'Good show, mate.' Eventually sanity returned and another drink was put in our hand. One of the men asked me how the one who had baled out was and I told them he was safe and unhurt. Someone asked me if I had been with John when he crash-landed and I told them I was the other one of the three they saw go head-on to attack.

I noticed that my scarf was missing and was looking for it when one of the ladies told me not to worry because the lady of the house was washing it to get the oil out before it dried in. I learned that her name was Edna and a few drinks later she came up to me and handed me the scarf which was still damp but clean. One of the ladies gave her a seat next to us and she asked why it was that all fighter pilots wore silk scarves round their neck, and nice black leather boots lined with lambs' wool. Johnny told her that the boots were for keeping one's tootsies warm and this caused some laughter. I told them that the scarf had two uses; one was for wiping any oil off your goggles or even your windscreen and in case you were wounded you might be able to use it as a tourniquet or bandage. I stopped here and one of the ladies asked, 'What is the other use then?'

I answered, 'Pure vanity. It looks good.'

This made them laugh even more and another drink was on its way down. I noticed at this point that our driver was not drinking at all but was enjoying himself talking to the women. It was now getting late and the driver asked if we were ready for the trip back and we said we were. There was a little bit of pushing from the back of the crowd and a large fat lady came and looked at us as though we were monkeys in a cage or something. She was obviously well known as it had gone quieter.

'Why, they are only a couple of ordinary blokes!' she exclaimed and with that she took a beautiful silk white scarf from around her neck and tied it round mine, then folded it into my tunic neck and patted my shoulder.

'Can't have you catching cold on the way back,' Emma said.

I did not know what to say to this very generous gesture so I bent down and lightly kissed her and said, 'Thanks, ma.' I was almost in tears and Johnny was the same. It was worth all the flying and danger to meet people like these, who really appreciated what we were doing.

After much kissing and back-slapping we crawled into the car and went back to our billet.

When we arrived back, Stickey and Johnny Gilders were waiting for us, they had not gone out on their own. We had hardly got in the room when Stickey came over and pulled something from John's side pocket, and then came over to me and did the same.

'Where have you two been to? We expected you back two hours ago. And what's this stuffed in your pockets?'

We both put our hands in our side pockets and pulled out what seemed to be a lot of old papers but instead turned out to be pound and ten shilling notes; they were in the side pockets, the top pockets and even in the trouser pocket although I can't remember any unfamiliar moves by any of the ladies we had been with earlier.

We then related as best we could what had gone on in that pub.

'Next time any of us comes down in London, I will come and get him,' said Stickey.

When I was on my own I had another look at the white silk scarf. It was about a yard square but very fine and warm. I knew that it was going to see a lot of service in the future and I would not forget her remark when she saw us, 'They are only a couple of ordinary blokes.' How right she was. We were all ordinary blokes fighting for ordinary people, like that lovely lady and all those lovely ordinary people in an ordinary pub and all of us in an extraordinary land of Great Britain and most of all the Eastenders of London.

The next morning I was on readiness again and we were scrambled to patrol near Maidstone at 25,000 feet. It was a very cold and cloudy day and involved a lot of cloud flying to get above them. It was while climbing that I got something in my eye as at the time I had my goggles above my eyes, which gave you a much better all round view. You would pull them down over your eyes when going into the attack. I tried wiping my eyes with my scarf but to no avail; it only made it worse. I decided that I would have to take my gloves off to be able to get a finger into the eye socket and pull the lid down over the other one. I removed my three pairs of gloves and felt the cold immediately and tried to clear my eye. My eyes were now watering so much I had a job keeping in formation as we were still climbing. I was attempting to pull the lid down when we went into a steep turn and I changed hands and just managed to keep the aircraft in formation, but in doing so my gloves fell from my knee into the bottom of the cockpit and I was unable to recover them.

My hands were getting colder and we were now at 25,000 feet and being vectored onto the enemy bombers and in desperation I again wiped my eyes with my scarf and this time I was successful although my eyes were still watering and I was not able to see very clearly. I knew we were now getting very near to the enemy. I went to put my firing button on to 'fire' but could not turn the switch, my fingers were numb. I could hardly hold the control column and I was getting out of formation. I only had seconds left to decide what I should do. I dare not use the R/T to tell the CO what had happened. Then it suddenly came to me. The silk scarf round my neck! I pulled it off and tied it round my hand onto the control column and decided that I would have to follow the rest of the squadron even if I did not fire my guns, it would help break them up. I went into the attack with the rest of the squadron and kept as close to my number one as I could. They made a few kills but I did not fire my guns and my hand was still freezing but the silk scarf was beginning to have its effect in warming the hand. At least it was keeping my hand tied to the control column. Without it I would have had difficulty in controlling the aircraft.

I returned to base a very unhappy man but grateful that the feeling was now back in my hands. I untied the scarf and put it back round my neck, I remembered thinking that if I had the cotton scarf on I could not have tied it round in the same way as I could this lovely silk scarf and it wouldn't have had the warmth of the silk one. I would liked to have thought that perhaps the lady who gave it to me had given with it a little bit of her own warmth. God bless you, Emma.

I had learned a very valuable lesson though, and that was, never take your gloves off at altitude on an operational patrol.

On 9 September we had one short trip only, as the weather was not very good. On 10 September we had a day off and I decided to go to London and see my parents and in-laws. John Gilders was also going to see his parents. Stickey and Johnny White had decided to go down to the coast for the day. The money we had been given was as good as a week's pay for each of the four of us and so we could afford a bit of luxury.

I decided that I would leave after having had some tea and catch a train to London and stay the night with my parents. As I was approaching Holborn viaduct I could see the fires still burning and I thought at first that it was the station which was burning but on arrival I saw that it was on the other side of the road and quite a lot of buildings were burning round the whole area of St Pauls. It was frightening and I wanted to walk to Holborn viaduct to catch a tube train. I had hardly got out of the station when I saw these firemen pulling away some wreckage of a building which had been on fire. I went nearer to them and started to help them when I soon felt someone taking my arm and pulling me away; I turned to see who it was and saw that it was a fireman.

'What's that for?' I asked him.

'You have done enough work for one day. You are more important up there than down here. I can't take the risk of your getting hurt by falling masonry. Besides it's an experienced job which my men can handle.' He then let go of my arm.

'Now, son, I suggest you go down the shelter until it's all over.'

I thanked him, but told him that I was going to Edmonton to see my parents to put them at ease a bit. I then shook hands with him and started to walk the short distance to Holborn tube station. I had only gone a few paces when a young lad about twelve years of age came up beside me and took hold of my right hand and held it tight. I looked down at him and asked him what he was doing out of an air raid shelter and where were his parents?

'Don't worry about me, Guv. I'm used to the raids. You told the firemen you are going to Holborn tube station. Can I walk with you to keep you company?'

I did not want to upset the lad so I said it was all right by me.

'Are you a fighter or bomber pilot?' he enquired after a few moments of looking me over.

'A fighter pilot,' I replied.

'Well, why haven't you got your bleeding top button undone?'

'Because I am not on duty at the moment and I would be improperly dressed if I did not have my buttons done up.'

'Do you mean to tell me that someone is going to put you on a charge for one bleeding button, in the middle of a bleeding war?'

I admit that this conversation was taking my mind off what was going on around me, but there were too many bleedings in the conversation and from such a young lad I did not like it so I asked him why he had to swear. I also mentioned casually 'anyway it's not a bleeding button, it's a brass button, young man.'

At this remark he roared out laughing, 'You must be a stranger to London, if you don't know that that word ain't a swear word. Everybody says it where I live.'

By now we had reached the entrance to the tube and there were a lot of people about and some of them were looking at us as the boy was still holding my hand. I was anxious to get to my parents and as much as I liked this youngster I did not want to delay any longer but so many people were looking at us I was figuring how to say goodbye to him without people wondering what he was doing with me and holding my hand.

I saw a space on a seat near the ticket office and I walked over to it and put my arms under the lad's and lifted him on the seat, in a standing position. I quickly put my arms round him and kissed him on the cheek and said loudly so that the people would hear me.

'Cheerio, little brother. Don't forget to look after your mum while I'm away.'

I put a ten shilling note in his top pocket and walked quickly to the top of the escalator and as I reached it I felt a tug on my arm. It was him again. He handed me the folded ten shilling note and said, 'Thanks, brother, I did not help you for the sake of money'. He was crying as he ran away.

I was standing waiting for the train and a man and woman came up to me. The woman said, 'Your little brother was upset at you leaving him, it's a shame you have to go back to your squadron.'

I only nodded in reply. I could not talk, I was too choked up myself and all the way to Edmonton I thought of this young lad. I had become a brother to a complete stranger, if only for a little while. I also thought of the moaning we had been doing over our billets etc and when I saw in the past two days what the people of London had to contend with, sleeping in shelters and tube stations, I vowed I would never again complain of what was happening to me.

When I reached my parents' home I found my mother and sisters in the Anderson shelter at the bottom of the garden. My father was with the air raid warden just along the road. No need to enlarge on the greetings from my family. They had seen me fly over two days earlier and were surprised to see me because I had not let them know that I was going to visit them because of the short notice I had received of my day off.

The air raid was still on and as my mother was not very well she had a bed in the shelter. I was appalled at her having to live under these conditions but as she pointed out to me there were a lot worse than she was. It was at that moment that I realised the full horror of what this war was like to the civilian population who could do nothing but wait and take it. I was more than grateful that my own wife and baby and younger sister were away in Gloucestershire, so far out of the way of the bombings.

I wanted to get outside the shelter to see my father but my mother said that he would be back soon and did not want me to leave her. That night was a night I would not forget in a hurry. I realised how ill my mother was and the claustrophobic effect the shelter was having on me made it unbearable, but for my mother's sake I had to put up with it. I spent the next day visiting some aunts and my in-laws, but I was thankful when it was time to go back to my squadron and once again help to stop the bombers from reaching London.

The next morning I was at readiness and we talked about our respective days off and in the afternoon we were scrambled at 1500 hours to intercept 100 plus Dornier 17s escorted by Me 110s and Me 109s. We met them east of Maidstone, the combat report for this action is reproduced below.

SECRET. FORM 'F' COMBAT REPORT.
Sector Serial No. (A) [blank]
Serial No. of Order detailing Flight or Squadron to Patrol (B) [blank]
Date (C) 11/9/40
Flight, Squadron (D) Flight: 'B' Sqdn: '72'
Number of Enemy Aircraft (E) 100+
Type of Enemy Aircraft (F) Do 17, Me 110 and 109
Time Attack was delivered (G) 1550
Place Attack was delivered (H) East of Maidstone
Height of Enemy (J) 20,000
Enemy Casualties (K) One Do 17 and 1 Do 17 probable
Our Casualties: Aircraft (L) nil / Personnel (M) nil
Searchlights: (Did they illuminate enemy if not, were they in front or behind) (N.1) [blank]
A.A. Guns: (Did shell bursts assist pilot intercepting enemy?) (N.2) [blank]
Range at which fire was opened in each attack delivered, together with estimate length of bursts: (P) 200 yards closed one No. 1 at 25 to 30 yards 6 sec burst on No. 1
Total No. of Rounds fired: 2600
Name of Pilot (Block Letters): ROLLS, W.T. Sgt.
GENERAL REPORT (R) See Below
I took off from Croydon as No. 3 in Yellow section and we met the enemy at Ashford region where they were flying on a NW course. We attacked them from the beam and by the time our section had got into position we were attacking dead astern of the Do 17. We dived down from 25,000 to 20,000 and made our attack. I saw return fire from the Do 17 and immediately I opened fire it stopped and I saw pieces flying away from the machine and smoke start coming from the engine. I closed range at about 25 to 30 yards as it hauled over to starboard and went on its back as I did a steep turn to watch it go down. It continued to spin with smoke and flame coming from it and I saw it crash over a wood and lake at an estimated position Cranbook. I started to climb up again

and I saw the other enemy machines above me. I continued to climb up below them from astern and saw the Me 109s above me but they did not attack then. I was about 300 yards below them and I aimed full deflection on the leading machine and directly I fired I saw pieces flying off the underneath of it. I pulled the stick back gradually and finally saw the machine slip in but no smoke or fire came from it. By this time I had stalled and found myself in a spin. When I had pulled out I saw 3 Me 109s coming down towards me and I had to get them off my tail. They opened fire and I got hit on the tail plane and I kept doing steep turns and finally got rid of them at 3–5,000 feet and then I dived down to about 800 feet and came back home to Croydon. I had 13 rounds left in each gun approx. Before I fired my guns I saw Yellow 1 hit a Do 17, which went down between the hills near my own Do 17.

Sgt Rolls, 72 Squadron, B flight.

Johnny White destroyed a Do 17 and a probable Do 17. Johnny Gilders got a Me 109. There were other claims for destroyed and damaged and we all returned safely to base. We had helped pay back the Germans for what they had done to the people of London the night before, but better still was that there would be a few aircraft less for them to use another night.

That evening one of my old pals from the other squadron which had arrived at Biggin Hill came to visit us in his car and took us to a pub way out in the country. We had a wonderful evening away from it all and even the regulars let us enjoy our evening together to talk of old times at Cambridge.

On the morning of 12 September we took off to intercept a 100 plus raid and once again it was a question of breaking up the formation for other squadrons to get at more easily and although I fired all my ammo I did not wait to see any results and hoped the camera gun would show something. I was about to pull up and turn after diving on the formation with the rest of our squadron when I felt my aircraft judder and felt something hit my throttle which stunned my hand. I felt a terrific draught coming into the cockpit and I knew that I had been hit somewhere although I could not see any aircraft near enough to me that could have fired at me.

When I landed back at Croydon, and having taxied over to our dispersal point I saw the holes in the cockpit; one of the instruments had been smashed too. Then I saw holes on the other side of the cockpit and wondered how I had got hit both sides at the same time. I soon found out because before I could get out of the cockpit, I saw a metal rod coming through one of the holes and an airman on my wing put his hand on the rod and pushed it through the other side of the cockpit. The rod was now four inches from my Mae West at chest height.

The airman then said, 'Sergeant, do you realise that one ten-thousandth of a second later that bullet would have gone right through your heart.'

I looked at him and thought he had gone mad. I climbed out of the aircraft and told him not to do a stupid thing like that again. As an afterthought I asked him how he had worked that out so quickly. He showed me a chart he had made out showing various speeds of the aircraft and how far the aircraft would travel in one second, he had reduced this to inches and was thus able to calculate immediately how long it would take for the aircraft to travel the number of inches the bullet was away from you. This is why they used the cleaning rod of the Browning guns on the aircraft as it was the right size to penetrate the bullet holes on either side of your cockpit.

We had not been refuelled very long and I had only just put my parachute into another serviceable machine, when we were again ordered to scramble. This time the instructions from the controller were music to our ears. We were told to return to Biggin Hill for future operations.

Although we had some very good memories of some very nice people at Croydon, nothing could compensate for going back to a sergeants' mess where the other squadron pilots were. We had missed the atmosphere of good-hearted rivalry and especially the food and beds. During the afternoon we were again scrambled but did not intercept as the enemy formation had turned back at the coast. The four of us were told that we would be off the next afternoon.

That evening in the comfort of my room I was able to write to my wife and tell her of my visit to my parents and her parents and sister. I also told her about the Anderson air raid shelter and said it was a good job we never had to use the one we had before moving to Watermoor at South Cerney. I did not tell her about how many aircraft I had shot down or even about my own near misses, as long as I was well, that's all she need to know. I told her about Johnny and me in the pub in the East End and as she knew Johnny she was amused by it.

That evening we had a booze up with the sergeants from the other squadron at Biggin and also discussed a visit we were going to make to Bromley to buy an old car as we would certainly need one to get about in. There was an ample supply of cars among our rivals so we had to get something in order not to be outdone by them as far as the drinking stakes and even the girlie stakes were concerned. We decided that we would go to the pub first and that we would spend up to twenty pounds for the car; that was about as much as we could afford, nearly one week's pay each.

The next afternoon we got a lift into Bromley and were just in time to get into the pub and order a beer each. It turned out to be a most profitable pint because we found out that the barman was a friend of the garage where we were going for the car. He told us to ask the garage owner to let us have a Humber Essex 19HP car, which was in the garage and as it was heavy on petrol and insurance we would get it for a song.

We finished our drink and went to the garage to look at the cars on the forecourt and soon a man came up and asked us if we had seen anything of interest. We told him we had except that the price was too high.

'How much do you want to spend then?' he enquired.

'Nothing above twenty pounds,' said Stickey.

'You are sure you are looking for a car which goes under its own steam?'

It was a beautiful car, in almost perfect condition. The upholstery inside was luxurious. He started the engine and it went first time and purred like a kitten. I was almost wishing that he had not showed it to us as it was obviously worth a lot of money, more than we could afford.

He asked us how we liked it. There was no need, for our faces gave us away. We would have to have it and mortgage our pay for the next six months by the looks of it. He handed us the log book and a big volume instruction manual, and told us that it had been owned by an American lady and had been chauffeur driven. I would well believe it because of its condition. We were waiting for him to tell us the price.

'Well, let me have the twenty pounds then,' he said.

Stickey had been holding the money and took it out of his wallet. He kept it in his hand and said to the man, 'On one condition.' 'Oh, Stickey, for heaven's sake don't cock it up,' I was saying under my breath.

The man looked at Stickey somewhat puzzled as were we, 'And what might that be?' he asked.

'That you fill it up with petrol.'

'Do you realise that the petrol tank holds twenty gallons and even the autovac takes half a gallon before you can start it?' He then roared out laughing. 'I thought I was doing you the favours, lads, but I will put three gallons in for free.'

'Done,' we all cried, and with that Stickey paid over the cash and was about to count out the last pound in change and the man said, 'Forget the other pound. Let's make it a pound a horsepower. Will that satisfy you?'

Thanks to a grand gentleman we had a car of our own. How we were going to tax and insure it none of us knew or cared and it was with great pride that Stickey drove the car back to the aerodrome. To our amazement the guard on the gate never said a word to us and let us proceed to the mess. We were now the proud possessors of a prestige limousine; no more would we have to rely on MT for trips from the mess to dispersal. The world of Kent was now our oyster, except for that one little item, petrol and insurance. We solved that the next day quite simply; we considered that as we were going to use it officially on the camp, then the RAF should pay for it, so we painted RAF roundels on each wing and RAF on the windscreen and filled up with petrol from the bowser. 100 octane petrol worked fine on that car.

On the morning of 14 September we were airborne and met the Me 109s and bombers going back across the Channel but I had no claim.

In the late afternoon we were again intercepting 50 plus Me 109s west of Canterbury. The combat report for this action is reproduced below.

SECRET. FORM 'F' COMBAT REPORT.

Sector Serial No. (A) [blank]

Serial No. of Order detailing Flight or Squadron to Patrol (B) [blank]

Date (C) 14/9/40

Flight, Squadron (D) Flight: 'B' Sqdn: '72'

Number of Enemy Aircraft (E) 50+ Me 109s

Type of Enemy Aircraft (F) Me 109

Time Attack was delivered (G) 1825 approx.

Place Attack was delivered (H) West of Canterbury

Height of Enemy (J) 20,000

Enemy Casualties (K) Me 109 damaged (confirmed crashed)

Our Casualties: Aircraft (L) nil / Personnel (M) nil

Search Lights was enemy illuminated. If not they were in front or behind target (N) [blank]

GENERAL REPORT (R)

I took off from Biggin Hill at 1800 as Blue 3 and we were told to patrol Canterbury at 20,000 feet. We met the enemy west of Canterbury and as we were about to get in line astern to attack an Me 109 dived down from behind and started to do a quarter attack on Blue 2 as he was going underneath Blue 1. He had fired a few rounds at Blue 2 and then I was in a position to do a quarter attack on the Me 109. I was at 150 yards range approx where I opened fire. I gave about 4 sec burst with full deflection and saw my bullets and tracer sweep down the side of the Me 109. It suddenly pulled back as though to do a loop and then spun down with what appeared to be glycol fumes coming from it. I watched it spin for about 6,000 feet then suddenly another Spitfire flew up to it so I left it to him in case it wanted finishing, while I went back to try and make contact again. The Me 109 eventually crashed in flames near Betherston after the other pilot had put another burst into it. Rounds Used 1,000 about.

Sgt W. Rolls 72 Squadron B flight Blue section.

The other pilot who I had thought put a burst of fire into this aircraft as it was going down did not do so, and it was later confirmed that I had shot it down.

We soon found out the real value of having our own car. It saved the officers from having to deviate their car to pick us up and we were able to get to dispersal much quicker. It was even better when we stood down for the day because we could get away without having to wait for the officers. For the cost of the petrol the RAF were getting an extra transport vehicle and it was a good booster for our morale.

We went in to Bromley that evening and found a nice club called the Country Club. Here we found some of the 92 Squadron sergeants who had found it days before and they were not too pleased that opposition had arrived, especially with those nice young ladies who used to dance there.

38 Douglas Bader, Hurricane Pilot, Acting Wing Commander, British, 242 Squadron

Copy of a personal combat report by an anonymous RAF fighter pilot included in the Air Ministry & Ministry of Information propaganda booklet about the Battle of Britain first published in 1941. The narrative below would have been preceded by a 'tick box' list of questions, date and time of combat, type and number of aircraft and any official claim of a 'kill'.

The pilot is probably the best-known fighter pilot of all from the Battle of Britain, Douglas Bader. He joined the RAF in 1928. This remarkable man successfully fought tooth and nail to rejoin the RAF as a fighter pilot in 1939 after being medically retired against his will after he lost both legs in a flying accident in 1931. Flying with two artificial legs, he would shoot down twenty enemy aircraft by the end of the war, one during Dunkirk and seven during the actual Battle of Britain. He wasn't perfect, his 1940 theories of the 'Big Wing' (the idea of forming massed squadrons before attacking Luftwaffe raids) stirring up opposition to the two desk-bound heroes of the Battle of Britain, Air Chief Marshal Hugh Dowding, commander of Fighter Command, and New Zealander Air Vice-Marshal Keith Park, commander of 11 Group. Both Dowding and Park were 'moved' from their respective positions after securing victory in the Battle of Britain, suffering a fate similar to that of Winston Churchill after the end of the Second World War. Several other pilots in this book reflect upon the idea of the 'Big Wing'; I suggest you draw your own conclusions.

Bader survived the war and his biography by Paul Brickhill, *Reach for the Sky*, was published in 1954. It was a publishing sensation and a similarly successful film of the same name followed in 1956. This cemented Bader in the British consciousness as a true hero and, thanks to Kenneth More's genial portrayal of him in the film, one with not a single flaw. Truth be told he was a blunt and opinionated man who held some unpopular views which made him a rather easy target for his detractors. At the same time he courted publicity and no doubt was imperfect in his dealings with some people. This editor's favourite anecdote of Bader is how, during a visit to a party of ex-Luftwaffe pilots (invited by Adolf Galland, a great friend and his nearest equivalent in Germany), he walked in and exclaimed, 'My God, I had no idea we left so many of you bastards alive.'

Bader went on to work tirelessly for the rights of disabled people and was knighted for this work in 1976. He died in 1982. A bronze statue of Bader was unveiled by his widow, Joan, at Goodwood, formerly RAF Westhampnett, West Sussex, on the sixtieth anniversary of his last combat mission. His work in support of disabled people is carried on through the Douglas Bader Foundation, created by his friends, family and fellow pilots following his death.

The combat report dates from an action at 11.22 a.m. on Sunday 15 September 1940, on what became 'Battle of Britain Day', when the largest bomber formation to date arrived over London but was broken up by more than 300 fighters of Fighter Command, a resounding defeat for the Luftwaffe. Brian Lane (see chapter 43) was part of the same patrol with Bader that day. I have restored the actual names of Bader's fellow pilots in square brackets stripped by the wartime censor from the 1941 propaganda booklet. Norman Campbell was KIA on 17 October 1940 with one kill and two shared kills in the Battle; Richard Cork was an ace by the end of the Battle but was killed in a flying accident in 1944.

Patrolled south of Thames (approximately Gravesend area) at 25,000 feet. Saw two squadrons pass underneath us in formation travelling north west in purposeful manner. Then saw AA bursts, so turned wing and saw enemy aircraft 3,000 feet below to the north west. Managed perfect approach with two other squadrons between our Hurricanes and sun and enemy aircraft below and down sun. Arrived over enemy aircraft formation of twenty to forty Do 17s: noticed Me 109 dive out of sun and warned our Spitfires to look out, Me 109 broke away and climbed south east. Was about to attack enemy aircraft which were turning left-handed, ie, to west and south, when I noticed Spitfires and Hurricanes engaging them. Was compelled to wait for risk of collisions. However, warned wing to watch other friendly fighters and dived down with leading section in formation on to last section of five enemy aircraft. Pilot Officer [Norman Campbell] took left-hand Do 17, I took middle one and Flight Lieutenant [Richard Cork] took the right-hand one which had lost ground on outside of turn. Opened fire at 100 yards in steep dive and saw a large flash behind starboard motor of Dornier as wing caught fire: must have hit petrol pipe or tank; overshot and pulled up steeply. Then carried on and attacked another Do 17, but had to break away to avoid Spitfire. The sky was then full of Spitfires and Hurricanes queueing up and pushing each other out of the way to get at Dorniers, which for once were out-numbered. I squirted at odd Dorniers at close range as they came into my sights, but could not hold them in my sights for fear of collision with other Spitfires and Hurricanes. Saw collision between Spitfire and Do 17 which wrecked both aeroplanes. Finally ran out of ammunition chasing crippled and smoking Do 17 into cloud. It was the finest shambles I've been in, since for once we had position, height and numbers. Enemy aircraft were a dirty looking collection.

39 Eugene 'Red' Tobin, Spitfire Pilot, Pilot Officer, American, 609 Squadron

Air Ministry- and Ministry of Information-endorsed BBC radio broadcast by an anonymous RAF fighter pilot in October 1940. The pilot is Eugene 'Red' Tobin (American), 609 Squadron, and the combat took place on 15 September 1940 with 609 Squadron flying from RAF Middle Wallop, Hampshire (10 Group).

Tobin, from Los Angeles, and two other Americans, Andrew Mamedoff and Vernon Keough, had originally intended travelling to Finland to help fight the Russians. When Finland surrendered, they headed instead to France and then endured a long and tortuous escape to England to continue the fight, arriving in June 1940. In a London pub they chanced across an air commodore and explained how they were having difficulty joining the RAF and were told to contact him the next day. By noon the following day they were accepted into the RAF, Tobin joining 609 Squadron on 8 August. When a 'scramble' was called Red would yell to his ground crew, 'Saddle her up boys, I'm ridin'!' David Crook flew with him and his two American friends in 609 Squadron (see chapters 13, 24, 45 and 49).

Tobin achieved two shared kills in the Battle but was KIA in September 1941, shot down over France by an Me 109. He was twenty-four. He is buried in Boulogne Eastern Cemetery, France.

I expect it must seem a long hop from guiding visitors round the movie studios in Culver City to fighting in an eight-gun Spitfire over London. But that's just how it happened to me, and all within a little more than a year, with some exciting adventures in between.

It was only my second air fight when I helped rout Goering's mass attack on 15 September. And I had the good luck to shoot down my first raider.

During the battle, the air over Surrey, Kent and Sussex, was full of bombers and fighters. At 20,000 feet I met a formation of Me 110s. I gave one a burst and saw him giving out smoke. But I lost him in the cloud before I could press home my attack.

Then below me I saw a big Dornier 215 bomber trying to seek the safety of some clouds. I followed it down and gave it a long squirt. Its left motor stopped and its right aileron came to bits. Smoke was pouring from it as the bomber disappeared in cloud. I followed. Suddenly the clouds broke and on the ground I saw a number of crashed aircraft. It was an amazing sight. They had all crashed within a radius of about twenty miles from our fighter station. My Dornier was there too. I was quite sure I could see it. A little later I learned that the intelligence officer's report on the damage to the crashed Dornier agreed with my own, so I knew I had claimed my first definite German victim.

That was a great day for England. I thought this little island was going to sink under the weight of crashed enemy planes on that day. And was I proud to be in the battle! It was the fulfilment of a year's ambition.

But let me go back and tell you the story of this momentous year.

My home is in Hollywood. It was in the wonderful Californian climate that I was born, educated and learnt to fly. I don't suppose there are more than seven days in a year when you can't take the air in California. I learnt to fly at the Mine Fields, Los Angeles. I was always pretty keen on flying and whenever there were no classes at school I hurried out to the airfield to put in all the time I could learning about aircraft and their vices. My instructors were mostly Army people. I went through the various graduations and by July last year I was a fully qualified charter pilot.

For nearly two months last year I flew parties up to the High Fierres in California on hunting and fishing expeditions. It was pretty tricky flying, because you get some fierce down draughts and you can't be too careful.

I had a civilian job of course in the MGM studios at Culver City; I finally acted as guide for visitors to the studios. I used to meet all the film stars and found them nice ordinary folk. But my studio jobs didn't keep me from flying and in the winter of 1939 I took a course in aerodynamics at evening school.

Then a number of us met Colonel Sweeney, whose name you will know from his association with the Escadrille Lafayette in the last war. With him we decided it would be a grand idea to form a flight and go out and fly for Finland. But, I guess, that war was over before we could get going.

In May of this year we decided to form a squadron of all American flyers, another Escadrille Lafayette. The adventure was off.

Several of us went by train from Los Angeles, through the States to Canada. Finally we finished up at Halifax, Nova Scotia, where we got split up. I joined a large French motor vessel, which was part of a big convoy sailing for France. My boat could do about sixteen knots but she had to travel at only six. In front of us was a boat with 400 mules on board. The stench from the mules was something awful and so was the weather. We had pursuit planes, bombers, and munitions of all sorts on board, cargo worth in all about seven and a half million dollars. We rolled and pitched all the way across the Atlantic and were mighty thankful after seventeen days to tie up at St Nazaire.

All our plans went haywire at St Nazaire. I had no passport and had lost my birth certificate. Naturally the French treated me with suspicion.

Incidentally, there's a story about that birth certificate. In all my journeys up and down France, I stuck to an old shirt just in case I wanted a spare one any time. Only last week I took out that shirt and from it dropped my birth certificate.

The next thing was to get to Paris and meet the rest of the boys. I took three and a half days to reach the capital and there I met my friends who had disembarked at Bordeaux. Just outside Paris while in the train I had my first experience of being bombed. The scream of the bombs dropping on the suburban houses from about 20,000 feet was awful.

We made our way to the French Air Ministry, saw high officials there, and were given our physical examination. The French didn't hurry, and we were in and out of the ministry for three days. They kept telling us that all would be well and that we would be flying any day soon. Actually we spent a whole month in Paris, doing nothing, for nothing could be done for us.

Then suddenly one day we realised that Paris was going to be evacuated. As the Air Ministry had gone, we made up our minds to get going as well – to Tours. A pall of smoke – which might have been a smoke screen – covered the city and you couldn't see more than a block away. There must have been 10,000 people at one station, all patiently waiting for trains to take them to safety – staunch solemn queues all round the station, men, women and children.

It took us a day and a half to reach Tours and it was an awful journey. Sometimes we had to ride between the cars to get a breath of fresh air. But there was no panic among the refugees, just fear and depression. We didn't lose a bit of luggage on this journey. We spent a week at Tours and were bombed by Heinkels and Dorniers every day. There was a pretty big party of us by now, most of them belonging to the French Air Force. We left Tours by bus for Chinon about an hour's ride away. We got away just in time, for the Nazis bombed and machine-gunned the main bridge out of Tours just as it was packed with refugees. The bridge was completely destroyed and very many refugees were killed.

Things weren't looking at all good. We were tired and food was getting scarce. We set out for Arcay about four hundred of us of all ranks, and from there walked another fifteen miles to Air Vault. Our boots were completely worn out, and we had no food and no water. Dog-tired, we lay down in some fields at Air Vault, but not for long. At nearly midnight we were ordered by an elderly French officer to get going once again, this time to Bordeaux. It took us three and a half days in a packed train to reach Bordeaux, and when we got there we found that the French Air Ministry could do nothing for us. We Americans were pretty sore by this time and thought that the best thing we could do would be to take some aircraft and fly to England. But that little plan didn't come off and we began our travels again determined to get out of the country.

Our little bunch went by bus to Bayonne. The British consul had left. We had no money and were starving. Eventually we made our way to St Jean-de-Luz and were lucky enough to get the American consul. He was a fine guy and treated us pretty handsomely. But he told us the situation was pretty bad and advised us to quit. There was a crowd pouring into St Jean-de-Luz and the quay side was crowded with refugees. They came any old way they could, in cars, on motorcycles and cycles. The cycles they did not bother to park but simply threw them in the water.

We boarded a British ship, *Boron-Nairn*, a little old-timer of seven knots. We were a mixed crowd on board. Our number included seven hundred Polish refugees. A tragedy occurred as we were going on board. We had only one suitcase between our little bunch. The handle came off and into the water she went with all our belongings. All the extras I had then was a pair of shorts and a couple of shirts. We sailed across the Bay of Biscay. It was a three day journey and all we had to eat was a dog-biscuit – even the one dog on board wouldn't eat them. The boat had no cargo and rolled pretty badly. But the crew were rather kind and did all they could for us.

Eventually we made Plymouth, although I thought at one time we were bound for South Africa judging by the ship's course.

I guess we weren't too popular at Plymouth. We had no papers and we were evacuated straight away to London. We were put in an ice skating rink and had to stay there for three days. We weren't allowed out at all. We rang up the Air Ministry, who sent round an officer to see us. He was very kind but didn't hold out much hope that the Air Force could use us at the moment.

We talked it over between us and made up our minds to return to America. We rang the embassy who sent round a representative to see us. He got our particulars, checked them over with Washington, fixed us up with passages to America and lent us £15 for food and clothing. It looked as if the adventure was over.

Then, I forget how, we met a very fine English lady, who after hearing our story told us she was sure that a friend of hers, a well-known member of Parliament, could do something for us. We met him next day in the Houses of Parliament and he sent us to the Air Ministry. We were given our physical examination at once. All passed, and so we were in the Volunteer Reserve of the Royal Air Force for the duration of the war.

We felt pretty good when we went to the American embassy. The officials there were mad with us at first for upsetting all the arrangements, but we soon smoothed that out. Things moved rapidly. Three of us, all in RAF uniforms, were sent north to an Officers' Training Unit. I had not flown for two months, but after twenty minutes in an advanced trainer I was put into a Spitfire.

After twenty hours' flying in Spitfires I was attached to a station in the south, just in time for the opening of the big Blitz. But I had several weeks' training before I became operational, that is, fit to fight. And I guess my first fight was lucky.

I was patrolling high over an English port on the South Coast when I saw some Me 110s. I went into them and hit the first guy with my first burst. He was quickly lost in cloud. Then another Me 110 shot ahead of me. I gave him a long burst and saw my stuff entering his fuselage. He climbed steeply then, and then as steeply dived in a sort of spin. I couldn't turn on oxygen and suddenly had what they call over here a blackout. I went into a sort of dream from which I awakened when I was only 1,000 feet from the ground. I think I heard myself say 'you'd better come to, you're in trouble.' Anyway, I landed safely with two probables in my 'bag'.

And now, we Americans are a separate squadron. We wear RAF uniforms with the American eagle on the shoulder. It's a grand idea this Eagle squadron of all American flyers. We must try and make a name for ourselves, just like the famous Escadrille Lafayette. After all, we're all on the same side and all fighting in the same cause. The fellows in the squadron come from various parts of America – New York, Idaho, Minnesota, Oklahoma, Illinois and California, we're all flyers and very keen. We have got a lot to learn yet, of course, and that is why I'm so glad to have been with an English fighter squadron, first. These English pilots certainly know their fighting tactics. My old squadron has brought down at least one hundred German aircraft. The German airmen may be pretty good formation flyers, but the British pilot has got the initiative in battle. He thinks quickly and gets results. He knows how to look after himself.

And are we lucky with our fighter planes? I guess the Spitfire is the finest fighter aircraft in the world. It's rugged and has no vices. I'd certainly rather fight with one than against one.

We like England and its people who are cheerful and very easy to get on with. I miss the Californian weather, of course, and if I could only have the English people and the Californian weather combined, everything would be grand. Everyone in the Royal Air Force is most kind to us all. They somehow seem to understand us and go out of their way to be helpful.

It's grand to say hello to everyone on behalf of the Eagle squadron. You can be sure we will do our very best, because we're in this business to try and do a little job of work for England.

40 Tom Neil, Hurricane Pilot, Pilot Officer, British, 249 Squadron & Eric 'Sawn Off' Lock, Spitfire Pilot, Pilot Officer, British, 41 Squadron

Air Ministry- and Ministry of Information-endorsed BBC radio broadcast by two anonymous RAF fighter pilots broadcast on 21 October 1940. The two pilots are Tom Neil of 249 Squadron and Eric 'Sawn Off' Lock of 41 Squadron, and the sortie described took place on 15 September 1940.

Tom Neil was born in Liverpool in 1920, began work in a Manchester bank in 1938 and at the same time joined the RAF reserve (Royal Air Force Volunteer Reserve, RAFVR). He was posted to his first operational squadron, 249, in May 1940 and remained in the relative calm of northern England until his squadron was moved south to RAF North Weald on the front line of the Battle of Britain at the beginning of September. He recorded in his logbook his reaction to his first real dogfight: '3 Sept 1940 first fight, nearly died of shock.' The nineteen-year-old, known as 'Ginger' by his fellow pilots, was six foot four and cut quite a dash. He was photographed several times during that summer by press photographers and notably by Cecil Beaton.

Eric Lock, known as 'Sawn Off' due to his short stature, was born near Shrewsbury in 1919 and would become the top-scoring Allied ace of the Battle of Britain with twenty-one kills (mostly Me 109s). He completed his training in May 1940 and was posted to 41 Squadron, then based in the comparatively quiet north of England. He had little contact with the enemy until his squadron was sent south in early September, and he shot down fifteen enemy aircraft in four weeks.

Neil recalled in his Battle of Britain memoir *Gun Button To Fire* (first published 1987, reissued by myself at Amberley Publishing in 2010) how the script for the broadcast was first put together at the officers' mess at RAF Hornchurch by himself, Eric Lock and two intelligence officers over 'innumerable whiskies and ginger-ales'. He also describes their actual performance in the live broadcast on Monday 21 October 1940. 'Sawn Off' was a bag of nerves at the prospect of speaking to an audience of 40 million listeners, and Neil admits to feeling 'a bit queasy in the stomach' too! *Gun Button* was based on the extensive collection of over 600 letters he had sent to his parents during the war from May 1940 to 1945.

The broadcast is reproduced below together with Tom Neil's combat report of the day. Neil's report only details one and a half kills (Dornier 215s), his memoir explains how two further Me 109s were not confirmed until four days after he'd submitted his report, after Eric Lock had told his side of the story and the intelligence officers came to visit Neil's squadron to confirm it and capitalise on a good news story.

Tom Neil's score for 1940 was thirteen kills, and after the Battle of Britain he was sent to fight again over the skies of Malta where he shot down another. He famously featured along with fellow 249 Squadron pilots in an iconic photograph taken on 21 September 1940 at RAF North Weald and used extensively in the press and in the *Battle of Britain* booklet published by the Ministry of Information in 1941 that sold six million copies. Later in the war he was an RAF liaison officer with the USAAF. Neil survived the war and, aged ninety-five, is chairman of the Battle of Britain Fighter Association and one of a mere twenty-five surviving Battle of Britain veterans at the time of writing.

Eric Lock disappeared on a combat mission over occupied France on 3 August 1941. He was last seen strafing German troops on a road at Hardelot, on the northern tip of France, but failed to return and is likely to have been shot down by ground fire. Neither his body nor the aircraft were ever found, despite a detailed post-war search by both the RAF and the Commonwealth War Graves Commission.

Both pilots were married during the war, Lock to Margaret Meyers in July 1940 and Neil to Eileen Hampton, an RAF plotter whom he married in 1945 and remained with for the next seventy years. Many thanks to Tom Neil for permission to use this broadcast.

Tom Neil (Hurricane): I'd like to go through that day again. When I first saw you come alongside in your Spitfire I thought you were a Messerschmitt. Then, you remember, I pointed at the Dornier about a mile in front, and saw you go away from me, because a Spitfire certainly has the legs of a Hurricane at that height. When you'd made your first attack, I caught up with him and we took our time finishing him off. As a matter of fact, I ran out of ammunition towards the end, when he was down to fifty feet. I made several dummy attacks on him before I saw you send him into the sea.

Eric Lock (Spitfire): And I thought you were playing the little gentleman. It just seemed that you were saying: 'Look, you have this one, it's your turn.'

Announcer: Now you are getting on too fast. Let's start again with the Spitfire.

Eric Lock (Spitfire): What happened to me was this: Our Spitfire squadron was over London when the battle began and pretty soon we were all split up into a series of dogfights. When you are tearing about the sky you don't see much, and you sometimes find yourself alone when you do get a chance to look round. That was what happened to me. I could see no sign of my squadron or of the enemy formation. There were plenty of clouds about, remember. I looked around and saw, about 2,000 feet above me and away to the north east of London, three Dorniers and three Messerschmitts being dogged by a Hurricane.

I decided to go up and give whatever help I could, but before I could get up there the Hurricane was milling around with the Messerschmitts and two of them were walloping down through the clouds absolutely done for, in my opinion. When I got up there I shot down the odd Messerschmitt. Then I saw you blaze away at a Dornier. He did a somersault – a couple of somersaults. As he whirled over, bits of his wings fell off, and he went crashing down through the clouds.

After that I drew alongside your Hurricane and you pointed forward. I looked where you were pointing, and saw a Dornier about a mile ahead, heading off for the sea. I opened up and drew away from you, made an attack and the Dornier went down through the clouds. We both followed him through, and took it in turns to attack him. By the time he had reached the coast he was at 1,000 feet, still going down steadily. He was only at fifty feet when we passed down the middle of a convoy. We were below the tops of the masts all the way between the ships. Then, about forty miles off Clacton-on-Sea, I gave the Dornier a final burst and in he went.

He alighted on the water tail first, quite comfortably, you might say. Then a wing cracked off, his back broke, and down he sank.

Announcer: What does the Hurricane say to that?

Tom Neil (Hurricane): I really didn't notice your Spitfire until you flew alongside when the chase of the final Dornier began. I remember cracking one Dornier down, and attacking another, and then being set on by three Messerschmitt 109s. And after the milling around with the Messerschmitts I started after the Dornier. I know I hit at least two of the 109s, but I didn't see them go down. I was too busy. I remember, though, attacking a Dornier earlier on. Maybe two. It's hard to say.

Eric Lock (Spitfire): I saw you do it. The first one was lovely. And the other went straight down through the clouds in a vertical dive.

Tom Neil (Hurricane): The main thing is that we beat them up, isn't it? What I liked was when you shot off in front of me chasing that last Dornier. When you caught him up and started squirting at him I was about half a mile behind you. He dived through the clouds, so I dived through after him. I came out below the clouds and the Dornier came out a short distance away. I think he was a bit of a nit-wit, don't you? If he had stayed in those clouds he might have been safe.

Eric Lock (Spitfire): You're right. But, mind you, he had a lot of my bullets inside him even then, and maybe he wanted to stay in the clouds and couldn't. It was easy after that, wasn't it? Those quarter attacks we made on him, in turn. First you from the right, swinging across his tail, then me going at him from the left. We just criss-crossed as he flew on a straight course, though losing height all the time. I should say he was about 1,000 feet when we reached the coast, and he got down to fifty feet before we finished him off.

Tom Neil (Hurricane): Before YOU finished him off, you mean. I liked the way we both flew back to the coast, grinning at each other. I thought once of coming along with you to your aerodrome so that we could discuss the battle together. Then I thought I'd better get back. I only had a few gallons of petrol left when I landed.

Eric Lock (Spitfire): So had I.

Announcer: Well, your story certainly shows that it doesn't really matter – to the Germans, I mean – whether a Spitfire or a Hurricane attacks them.

Tom Neil (Hurricane): There's no doubt about that at all. Nevertheless, I'm used to the Hurricane, so give me a Hurricane every time.

Eric Lock (Spitfire): And give me a Spitfire. By the way, a Spitfire is a lot easier to handle than some of the trainer aircraft I learned in. I do hope that my old instructor is listening in to this, for he always said I was the world's worst pupil in any kind of aircraft.

Tom Neil (Hurricane): That's funny. That's what my old instructor used to tell me.

Announcer: Perhaps that's part of the instruction.

Tom Neil's Combat Report, 15 September 1940:

SECRET. FORM 'F' COMBAT REPORT.

Sector Serial No. (A) [blank]

Serial No. of Order detailing Flight or Squadron to Patrol (B) [blank]

Date (C) 15 Sept 1940

Flight, Squadron (D) Flight: A Sqdn: 249

Number of Enemy Aircraft (E) 15–20 bombers 50 plus fighters

Type of Enemy Aircraft (F) Dornier 215 Me 109

Time Attack was delivered (G) 1450 approx

Place Attack was delivered (H) S.E. London

Height of Enemy (J) 15,000

Enemy Casualties (K) 2 destroyed Do 215

Our Casualties: Aircraft (L) nil / Personnel (M) [blank]

GENERAL REPORT (R)

P/O T. F. NEIL CLAIM 2 DORNIER 215 DESTROYED.

At approximately 1450 249 Sqn intercepted a formation of about 15 Dornier 215s. I was Yellow 2. Over S.E. London at 15,000 the squadron did a quarter attack. I eventually found myself behind a Dornier. I gave a one second burst to the port engine. Large pieces of cowling and engine flew apart. The crew immediately baled out whilst the aircraft went vertically into the clouds.

Later I saw another Dornier flying about 16,000. I climbed, chasing him. I finally caught a little north of the estuary and fired several 2 and 3 sec bursts. Faint smoke was seen to come from the port engine.

The bomber flew out to sea. Gradually losing height it passed over a convoy sailing south about 10 miles out to sea.

I fired all my ammunition at close range the E.A. gradually lost height and crashed into sea about 30 miles off English coast. No evasive action was engaged by the bomber.

Shared with Spitfire EBE. ['EBE' was Eric Lock's Spitfire, the squadron code 'EB' for 41 Squadron and the 'E' the individual aircraft call sign. The RAF roundel would be painted between these sets of letters on the fuselage.]

41 John Sample, Hurricane Pilot, Squadron Leader, British, 504 Squadron

Air Ministry- and Ministry of Information-endorsed BBC radio broadcast by an anonymous RAF fighter pilot in September 1940. The pilot is John Sample of 504 Squadron as the facts fit the introduction given to a transcript of the broadcast published in 1941. This provided details that the pilot was previously an estate agent from Northumberland and had joined an auxiliary squadron in 1934. The day described is 15 September 1940, when 504 Squadron was flying from RAF Hendon, north London (11 Group).

John Sample was called up on 24 August 1939 to 607 Squadron, and shot down a German Do 18 flying boat on 17 October 1939 in an antiquated Gloster Gladiator biplane fighter. His squadron moved to France as part of the Air Component of the RAF Component of the British Expeditionary Force (the other part was the AASF, Advanced Air Striking Force, which included Hurricane fighter squadrons 1, 73 & 501) in November, where he shot down two enemy aircraft before the squadron was withdrawn on 21 May 1940. He was made squadron leader of 504 Squadron at the end of May.

He died in a flying accident in October 1941 with three kills under his belt and two shared kills. He is buried in St Andrew's churchyard, Bothal, Northumberland.

At lunchtime on Sunday, my squadron was somewhere south of the Thames estuary behind several other squadrons of Hurricanes and Spitfires. The German bombers were three or four miles away when we first spotted them. We were at 17,000 feet and they were at about 19,000 feet. Their fighter escort was scattered around. The bombers were coming in towards London from the south-east, and at first we could not tell how many there were. We opened our throttles and started to climb up towards them, aiming for a point well ahead, where we expected to contact them at their own height.

As we converged on them I saw there were about twenty of them, and it looked as though it were going to be a nice party, for the other squadrons of Hurricanes and Spitfires also turned to join in. By the time we reached a position near the bombers we were over London – central London, I should say. We had gained a little height on them, too, so when I gave the order to attack we were able to dive on them from their right.

Each of us selected his own target. Our first attack broke them up pretty nicely. The Dornier I attacked with a burst lasting several seconds began to turn to the left away from his friends. I gave him five seconds and he went away with white smoke streaming behind him.

As I broke away and started to make a steep climbing turn I looked over the side. I recognised the river immediately below me through a hole in the clouds. I saw the bends in the river, and the bridges and idly wondered where I was. I didn't recognise it immediately, and then I saw Kennington Oval. I saw the covered stands round the Oval, and I thought to myself: 'That is where they play cricket.' It's queer how, in the middle of a battle, one can see something on the ground and think of something entirely different from the immediate job in hand. I remember I had a flashing thought – a sort of mental picture – of a big man with a beard, but at that moment I did not think of the name of W. G. Grace. It was just a swift, passing thought as I climbed back to the fight.

I found myself very soon below another Dornier which had white smoke coming from it. It was being attacked by two Hurricanes and a Spitfire, and it was still travelling north and turning slightly to the right. As I could not see anything else to attack at that moment, I went to join in. I climbed up above him and did a diving attack on him. Coming in to attack I noticed what appeared to be a red light shining in the rear gunner's cockpit, but when I got closer I realised I was looking right through the gunner's cockpit into the pilot and observer's cockpit beyond. The red light was fire.

I gave it a quick burst and as I passed him on the right I looked in through the big glass nose of the Dornier. It was like a furnace inside. He began to go down, and we watched. In a few seconds the tail came off, and the bomber did a forward somersault and then went into a spin. After he had done two turns in his spin his wings broke off outboard of the engines, so that all that was left as the blazing aircraft fell was half a fuselage and the wing roots with the engines on the end of them. This dived straight down, just past the edge of a cloud, and then the cloud got in the way and I could see no more of him.

The battle was over by then. I couldn't see anything else to shoot at, so I flew home. Our squadron's score was five certainties – including one by a sergeant pilot, who landed by parachute in a Chelsea garden.

An hour later we were in the air again, meeting more bombers and fighters coming in. We got three more – our squadron, I mean. I started to chase one Dornier which was flying through the tops of the clouds. Did you ever see that film *Hell's Angels*? You remember how the Zeppelin came so slowly out of the cloud. Well, this Dornier reminded me of that.

I attacked him four times altogether. When he first appeared through the cloud – you know how clouds go up and down like foam on water – I fired at him from the left, swung over to the right, turned in towards another hollow in the cloud, where I expected him to reappear, and fired at him again. After my fourth attack he dived down headlong into a clump of trees in front of a house, and I saw one or two cars parked in the gravel drive in front. I wondered whether there was anyone in the doorway watching the bomber crash.

Then I climbed up again to look for some more trouble and found it in the shape of a Heinkel 111 which was being attacked by three Hurricanes and a couple of Spitfires. I had a few cracks at the thing before it made a perfect landing on an RAF aerodrome. The Heinkel's undercarriage collapsed and the pilot pulled up, after skidding fifty yards in a cloud of dust. I saw a tall man get out of the right-hand side of the aircraft, and when I turned back he was helping a small man across the aerodrome towards a hangar.

42 Eric 'Boy' Marrs Part 3, Spitfire Pilot, Pilot Officer, British, 152 Squadron

This third set of letters from Eric to his father covers 3 September – 1 October 1940. The 152 Squadron pilot lost on 4 September was John Barker (two kills in the Battle); his body eventually washed up on the French coast. It is interesting to note Marrs's unbending confidence in Britain's ability to repel any invasion and his informed view of the strength of the Luftwaffe, made without the benefit of hindsight.

I have added in some dates and pilots' names in square brackets. The pilot shot down and killed on Monday 30 September and mentioned in the last paragraph was Lesley Reddington. Reddington's wife was pregnant at the time and this, his second daughter, was born in February 1941 and named Lesley after her father.

3 September 1940 We have been having a very slack time here since I last wrote. The Hun has been concentrating entirely on the south east and the London area and doesn't seem to be bothering about Southampton and Portsmouth any more.

I have christened my aeroplane 'Old Faithful' as it is about the oldest aeroplane in the squadron and has now done nearly 300 flying hours. Looking through my log book I find I have now done over 130 hours on Spitfires, fourteen hours of which are night flying. I have also flown ten different types of aeroplanes at various periods of my career. My total flying hours add up to over 300.

You were asking my score. It is two and a half confirmed and one unconfirmed; the half being one I shared with another chap and the unconfirmed one being the Heinkel which I left with both engines giving off a lot of black smoke and which poured a lot of oil over my aeroplane. The two and a half consist of one Ju 87, one Me 110 and a half Dornier 17. I have shot down all these in my own aeroplane, which is another reason for my calling it 'Old Faithful'.

5 September 1940 We unfortunately lost another pilot yesterday. He was chasing a Dornier out to sea when his glycol cooling system was punctured. He lost all his coolant and had to come down in the sea about 30 miles out. We sent out aeroplanes to search for him, but he was not to be found. There is a good chance that he may have been picked up by one of those German seaplanes which always search the seas after any battle.

The weather continues to be stifling hot and very clear down here, for which we are not at all thankful. A long period of rain would be most welcome.

10 September 1940 How are things going with you with all this bombing of London? Poor old London! It has received a terrible hammering and so long as this moon lasts is bound to receive worse. The casualties are colossal. This is the sort of thing I have been expecting for a long time and it is what everybody thought would come at the beginning of the war.

We are still doing nothing down here. The Hun has been concentrating entirely on London just lately and it seems to go to show that Germany has not the colossal bomber force she claims to have, otherwise she would be able to concentrate on a greater number of places at the same time.

I am glad we did not waste time and bombs on large scale reprisals against Berlin. If the invasion is going to come before next spring, I feel it must come during this moon and concentrations of shipping at Channel ports, etc seem to show that they may be going to have a crack at it soon and that we should waste bombs on Berlin is probably just what Hitler would like.

The more I think about it, the more confident I feel that we shall be able to stop any invasion attempts. One has only to put oneself in Hitler's shoes and try to work out a plan of invasion to realize how difficult it is for him.

What is the general feeling in London about this bombing? Are the people terrified of it or are they taking it calmly? I think a great deal depends upon how the public can take such treatment. I have never been bombed myself and so don't know what it is like, but I can't think of anything worse unless it is being shelled, which I am told is much the same.

Our squadron is now up to strength again and we have managed to train quite a number of new pilots during the lull in operations down this way.

22 September 1940 I have just received your letters dated the 17th. They take a shocking long time to come now, but considering the amount of bombing London has received I don't think the Post Office has been doing too badly.

London certainly has received a pasting, but the Germans have paid heavily for it and don't seem to have achieved much damage of military importance. This indiscriminate bombing seems to me to be a somewhat pointless affair. They haven't been able to demolish completely any large area as they did at Rotterdam and Arras. At those places they were unhampered by any opposition and they caused tremendous havoc and killed all the civilians in the areas they laid waste.

The weather has broken at last, for which I am most thankful, and I expect many others are too. The moon is also going and there is now not much more than a half left. This, of course, hampers our bombers as much as his and may in a way be a bad thing because I think we have been wreaking havoc amongst his barges just lately with our night bombing. The sea was beautifully rough during that gale but is now unfortunately calm again. Still, his invasion is by no means made easy by that fact. The weather is still bad and so he loses all backing by his bombers.

We have had some more excitements during this last week. Last Sunday, the famous day of the 185 [15 September 1940 when the RAF claimed to have shot down 185 enemy aircraft], we had 30 Heinkel 111 bombers over Portland. There was only one flight up at the time and I was leading it. A flight is six aircraft. I had been patrolling the aerodrome for some time already with one other chap, when the other four were sent off to join me. Before we had joined up we were sent off to intercept this raid coming in from the SW of Portland Bill.

I was over Weymouth when I first saw them. They were coming at Portland from the west. I climbed up to come in behind them from the sun, but they were going faster than I thought. They were in tight formation and they dropped their bombs on Portland Bill from 16,000 feet, doing pattern bombing. We then came in on their tails and they turned out to sea. We chased them for about 10 miles, nibbling at the rear end of their formation, and we knocked down two of them. I myself did not get one, though I must have damaged two of them. If we had had the whole squadron up we could have broken up their formation and knocked down quite a number. The extraordinary part about this raid was that there was no fighter escort. I was keeping a very good lookout though in case such a thing should suddenly appear from out of the sun. On Tuesday [17 September] I was leading a section of three and we were ordered on to a Junkers Ju 88 bomber up near Bath. I attacked first and hit the radiator of his starboard engine with my first burst. His glycol poured out in white streams and his starboard motor finally packed up. The other two then attacked in order and then we each nibbled around attacking when we could.

He then managed to reach the clouds, which were thick, puffy cumulus. I followed him into one and lost him. The other two went around and were able to find him again. When I'd lost him I circled round looking for him and then noticed a strange smell. I looked down and saw slight fumes arising from under the dashboard. During the scrap I had noticed an aerodrome with big runways standing out and showing up well. I made for it, and as I was still at about 12,000 feet I was able to make it easily. My engine began to shudder very violently, making the whole aeroplane shake. It then seized up solid. I then noticed that my aerodrome was covered with small, square concrete blocks to prevent German transport aeroplanes landing. I had to come down and was able to pick a spot more or less free from blocks, where I landed without damage to the aeroplane. The aerodrome was one just being built and that was the reason for the concrete blocks.

I inspected my aeroplane and found one bullet through my oil cooler. I had lost my oil and my engine had seized up.

When I got back here I found that the 88 had come down at Imber, a little village about three miles from Dauntseys. The next day the three of us who had shot it down motored up to inspect it. We did not get away from here until 3pm and arrived at 5pm. It was in very good condition and we were extremely interested. Of the crew of four, two were killed and one seriously wounded, only the pilot getting away scot-free. There were four bullet marks on the back of his armour-plated seat. We arrived to find quite a crowd all round the machine, though kept at a distance by a rope. We were able to climb all over it and see where our bullets had gone and I was able to see where I had hit his radiator. We stayed two hours and then pushed on to Salisbury.

The unfortunate part about that engagement was that I lost 'Old Faithful'. It will go to a maintenance unit to be repaired and then because of its age will probably go to a training unit. Poor 'Old Faithful'. I had become very attached to it.

On Thursday, that is the day after we went up to see the 88, I was leading a section of two when we happened upon another 88 just off Lulworth Cove. He dived to sea level and headed at top speed for France. We chased him over the wave tops for 10 miles out to sea until he disappeared into a bank of fog. I think I put his rear gunner out of action because he fired at me to begin with and then ceased. I had a new sergeant pilot with me and he was able to have his first crack.

On returning I beat up the dispersal hut as I was in high spirits, but it is strictly 'verboten', and I was seen. I was therefore given four days duty pilot to cool me off and here I languish having completed one and a half days of my sentence. Still, it is a good opportunity to read and to write some very necessary letters...

1 October 1940 On Wednesday morning [25 September] a flight was sent off to patrol. Soon afterwards the rest of the squadron was told to get into the air as quickly as possible. The result was we all went off in bits and pieces. I went off with one other chap, and as a pair we went looking for the trouble. We climbed up to 16,000 feet and saw a tremendous cloud of aircraft just round Yeovil way going north. There were two large groups of bombers consisting of about 40 bombers each. Milling around and above and behind them were numerous Me 110s acting as guard.

Well the two of us proceeded north, passed the enemy and came round in front of them. We waited just south of Bristol for them. Then we attacked. We went head-on straight for the middle of the foremost group of bombers. Firing as we went, we cut through the heart of them like a knife through cheese; but they wouldn't break. They were good, those Jerry bombers – they stuck like glue.

On coming through the first group I ran into some Me 110s. I milled around with those for a bit trying to get on the tail of one of them, but there was always another to get on to my tail. Things became a bit hot, and seeing a 110 very close to getting a lovely shot in on me, I pulled the stick back hard and pushed on full left rudder. I did three smart flick rolls and span. I came out of the spin below everything. I climbed up to sunwards of everything to have another crack at the bombers, climbed to the same height and slightly in front of them on their starboard side. I saw a Heinkel lagging behind the formation and dived to attack it from the starboard quarter. I put a long burst into it and it also streamed glycol from its starboard engine. My attention was then occupied by a Me 110 which came to the help of the Heinkel. A steep turn was enough to get behind it as it did not seem very anxious to stay and fight. I came in from the starboard quarter again and kept my finger on the firing button, turning in behind it. Its starboard engine (becoming a habit now) streamed glycol. Suddenly there was an almighty bang and I broke away quickly. I looked around glanced at my engine and oil tanks and positioned myself for another attack, this time going for the port engine. I just began to fire when my ammunition petered out. I broke away and dived below cloud, throttled back, heaved a deep sigh and looked around to see where I was. I steered south, came to the aerodrome and landed. I had a look at my machine and counted 11 bullet holes in it. The one that made a bang in my cockpit had come along from the rear, nipped in the right-hand side of the fuselage and smashed the socket into which the R/T is plugged.

We lost one pilot that morning and knocked down about five Huns. I also forgot to mention that two days previously one of our best pilots just disappeared over the sea. He went up to chase a lone Hun that was making a condensation trail along the coast. The last that was heard of him was an R/T message to say that he was on fire.

Well, to continue the story, that afternoon A flight (I'm in B flight) went up to patrol Portland. Suddenly the flight commander looked round and saw a Me 109 formating on his last man and pumping lead into him. He nipped round and shot down the 109, but not before the 109 had got his man. This man [William Silver] was killed in the air and dived vertically into the sea. It shows how careful one must be to watch one's tail.

That finished Wednesday's operations. On Thursday [26 September] we had a bad time. We were sent off to a raid on Southampton, but we were off late and only arrived when their bombers were crossing the south coast of the Isle of Wight on their way home. We were just about to attack when some Me 109s came down on our tails. I did not see them at first, but the chap I was flying alongside saw one coming up under my tail. He whipped around and shot at it and probably saved me.

I was not able to get a shot in at anything, and for me and for most of the squadron the show was a failure. Some of our chaps managed to get to the bombers and I believe shot down three, but against that we had two pilots shot down in the sea. One was picked up with a bullet through the thigh [Edward Deanesley] and the other was killed [John Christie].

Friday [27 September] was a good day. I set the ball rolling by finding a lone Ju 88 at 23,000 feet. I had a long running fight during which we came down to 50 feet and skimmed the hills of Devon. I did continuous quarter attacks aiming at his engines and was able to hit both of them. Glycol streamed forth and I hovered around waiting. As I expected, both engines soon stopped. He made for the south coast of the Bristol Channel and landed about 20 yards from the beach in the water, running his machine up on to the beach. I circled around and watched the crew get out. They waved to me and I waved back and then hordes of civilians came rushing up. I watched the crew taken prisoner, beat up the beach and then climbed away. The place he came down at was Porlock and no doubt you heard that little engagement mentioned over the wireless on the news that night. Well, his rear gunner had landed a few bullets in my machine. One had penetrated the leading edge of my machine, going through the well into which the wheel was retracted and puncturing the tyre. One other had landed in the fuselage about 6 inches from my left knee. When I landed at the aerodrome I could, feel the aeroplane slewing and swinging and tending to tip forward on its nose, but was able to pull off the landing ok in spite of a bust tyre.

The pilot of the German Ju 88 shot down this morning sent a message of congratulation on a very fine fight. He would like to meet me. This German pilot was also a pilot in civilian life.

There was a big show later on in the morning, but my machine was still unserviceable and I had to sit on the ground. This was a successful show and the squadron knocked down another four and a half, the half being shared with another squadron. This was without loss to us. On Saturday [28 September] we had nothing till the afternoon, when we were caught napping again by another of these offensive patrols which the Hun keeps sending over. One of our chaps was shot down but he made a forced landing. He is now in hospital with some chunks of cannon shell in his arm. We did not shoot down any Jerries. They mill around at about 30,000 feet and when they see us stooging underneath they send down two or three of their men to attack the last two of ours. They just nip down and nip up again before we can catch them, having a pot shot on the way.

On Sunday [29 September] we had a quiet day. On Monday [30 September] things began again. In the morning some of us (not me luckily) became mixed up with another of their offensive patrols which consisted of about 80 Me 109s and Me 110 fighters. We did not lose anybody, nor did we shoot down anything.

In the afternoon we were sent off to patrol Portland. Soon we saw a large formation of enemy bombers arriving with a large number of Me 110s as guard.

We were just going in to attack when somebody yelled 'Messerschmitts' over the R/T and the whole squadron split up. Actually it was a false alarm. Anyway, being on my own I debated what to do. The bombers were my object, so I snooped in under the 110s and attacked the bombers (about 40–50 Heinkel He 111s) from the starboard beam.

I got in a burst of about three seconds when – crash! And the whole world seemed to be tumbling in on me. I pushed the stick forward hard, went into vertical dive and held it until I was below cloud. I had a look round. The chief trouble was that petrol was gushing into the cockpit at the rate of gallons all over my feet, and there was a sort of lake of petrol in the bottom of my cockpit. My knee and leg were tingling all over as if I had pushed them into a bed of nettles. There was a bullet hole in my windscreen where a bullet had come in and entered the dashboard, kocking away the starter button. Another bullet, I think an explosive one, had knocked away one of my petrol taps in front of the joystick, spattering my leg with little splinters and sending a chunk of something through the backside of my petrol tank near the bottom. I had obviously run into some pretty good crossfire from the Heinkels. I made for home at top speed to get there before my petrol ran out. I was about 15 miles from the aerodrome and it was a heart-rending business with all that petrol gushing over my legs and the constant danger of fire. About 5 miles from the 'drome smoke began to come from under the dashboard. I thought the whole thing might blow up at any minute, so I switched off my engine. The smoke stopped. I glided towards the 'drome and tried putting my wheels down. One came down and the other remained stuck up. I tried to get the one that was down up again. It was stuck down. There was nothing for it but to make a one-wheel landing. I switched on my engine again to make the aerodrome. It took me some way and then began to smoke again, so I hastily switched off. I was now near enough and made a normal approach and held off. I made a good landing, touching down lightly. The unsupported wing slowly began to drop. I was able to hold it up for some time and then down came the wing tip on the ground. I began to slew round and concentrated as much as possible with the brake on the wheel which was down. I ended up going sideways on one wheel, a tail wheel and a wing tip. Luckily the good tyre held out and the only damage to the aeroplane, apart from that done by the bullets, is a wing tip which is easily replaceable.

I hopped out and went off to the MO to get a lot of metal splinters picked out of my leg and wrist. I felt jolly glad to be down on the ground without having caught fire.

That was yesterday. Today, Tuesday [1 October], we have not up to now been engaged. We went up this morning, but the raid turned out to be a very large number of fighters on an offensive patrol. We steered clear of them as they were not bombing and we would do no good by attacking them. There were about 50 of them.

I forgot to mention yesterday's scores. We lost another man and shot down two and a half of the Hun. We did, however, stop the bombing raid from reaching its objective – Yeovil. They dropped all their bombs on Sherborne. I am just wondering what is going to happen this afternoon and whether the weather is ever going to break properly.

43 Brian Lane Part 2, Spitfire Pilot, Squadron Leader, British, 19 Squadron

The second of three extracts from his 1942 memoir, covering 11–30 September, when 19 Squadron (based in 12 Group and flying from RAF Fowlmere, Cambridgeshire) formed part of Douglas Bader's 'Big Wing', the famous pilot's idea to mass several squadrons together to meet the enemy's own mass formations on an almost equal basis. This was a more aggressive strategy. However, during the Battle it proved rather ineffective as it took too long to form up so many aircraft, which often led to the 'Big Wing' failing to intercept the enemy in time. It also rather missed the point of Dowding's strategy for Fighter Command, which was to carefully marshal his limited resources of men and machines to prevent the Luftwaffe achieving air superiority. Central to this was not being tempted into unnecessary combat, which in the summer of 1940 would have led to unrecoverable losses of pilots in particular. Hit-and-run attacks on the Luftwaffe bomber formations to disrupt and minimise bombing damage was the order of the day.

Lane took command of 19 Squadron when Squadron Leader Philip Pinkham was shot down and killed on 5 September 1940.

11 September, and we took off and joined up with two other Spitfire squadrons to make up the wing. Again we were to act as a covering patrol over the London area.

Thirty-six Spitfires climbed towards the afternoon sun. I was leading the show and it felt like old times looking back at the formations behind me.

At 22,000 feet I turned east and flew along the Thames watching to the south for any trade which might be about. I had been told over the R/T that a raid was coming in towards the capital.

As I looked a cluster of black mushrooms of smoke appeared at about 20,000 feet two or three miles away. It was the South London guns opening up. I called up the ground station and the rest of the formation as I sighted a swarm of aircraft in the middle of the Ack-Ack and turned to meet them. It was the sort of interception a pilot dreams of. We were going for them head on from slightly above. Behind the bombers I could see the fighter escort stepped up in layers above their charges; and they couldn't touch us until after we had carried out the first attack on the bombers!

I called up again on the R/T, and then we dived on the 12 leading Heinkels. I took the right hand Hun, the rest of the flight each picking out a target so as to cover the whole front of the formation. Down we went, rushing to meet them at something like 500 mph, with the combined closing speed. A fleeting burst of fire and we were into them.

I think it must have shaken those Huns a lot. It must have been rather frightening to see the Spitfires rushing to meet them apparently in a head-on collision, forty-eight guns of the leading flight spanning the space between with white pencils of tracer.

I held on to the last minute and then ducked to one side as a huge dark green monster flashed past. I caught an impression of the whirling airscrews, a black cross outlined in white, a gun in the rear cockpit swinging after me, a pink blur of the gunner's face showing behind it. Then they were gone.

I turned hard round to the left to come back. To my utter astonishment almost every aircraft had disappeared. Above me the flash of the sun on wings told of a dogfight going on. No doubt the fighter escort and the rest of the Spitfires, but of what must have been over 50 bombers not one could I see! Nor could I see the rest of the flight, much less the squadron!

Then towards the river I saw seven Heinkels turning for home, dropping their bombs as they turned: the leading bombers which we had attacked. There didn't seem to be much to stop them going on to the centre of London if they wanted to – only me! But no – they looked to have had enough and were going home. Well, we seemed to have got five of them down in that first attack – probably the leader had gone down and these other lads were lost and didn't know quite what to bomb. Anyway, they were on the run.

I turned after them, scanning the sky all the time for signs of fighters. Two Me 110s swam into view and joined up one each side of the bombers. They made no attempt to interfere with me, one of them merely dropping back behind the Heinkels. I closed in and fired at him from dead astern. I hit him with the first burst, a shower of pieces flying off from his starboard engine as the airscrew stopped. He made no attempt to avoid my fire, he just flew straight on. Puzzled, I broke away as I overshot him and turned to come back in again. Taking a sight on the port engine I opened fire again. At the second burst a huge cloud of smoke and flame belched out and the aircraft slowly went down in a dive. Breaking away I glanced down but he was lost from view. Looking back at the other aircraft I was amazed to see the remaining Me 110 diving away as hard as he could for home!

I obviously couldn't catch him, and anyway the bombers were more important to knock down. The Heinkels had tightened up their formation and were steaming along as fast as they could. I picked out the rearmost aircraft and then frowned. There were only six! I counted them again. Definitely six. I looked round but there was not another aircraft to be seen in the sky. Where the other Heinkel had gone I don't know to this day. When I broke away from the 110 I temporarily lost sight of the bombers, and it must have been then that he broke away or was possibly shot down by Ack-Ack.

I closed in behind the last Hun and eased the sights on to one of the engines and fired. I stopped for a moment to steady my kite in the slipstream and then fired again. Nothing happened.

Breaking away I climbed up to one side of the formation and came down in a beam attack on the leader. Still nothing happened. No return fire came from the Huns at all. Their crews might have been dead for all the response I got to my attacks. Turning round again I closed in behind No. 6 and opened fire at his starboard engine. After a short burst a cloud of white vapour streamed out from below the engine. Ah! I'd got his radiator! I fired again but my guns stopped after a second – out of ammunition – but not before I saw flames and black smoke come licking out around the engine cowling.

I broke away above him and looking back saw there were only five Heinkels now.

I could account for that – a thin streak of black smoke showed where No. 6 had gone plunging down.

Feeling rather exhilarated on getting two down, I dived back across the Thames and headed for home and a glass of beer – it was too late for tea!

Chapter 12 Der Tag! 14–15 September 1940 14 September saw the wing on two patrols, but no E/A were seen. Perhaps the Hun was saving himself for the morrow. I think this was actually the case for the next day saw the record bag of 185 Huns shot down – these only the certainties, the real total therefore probably even higher.

We carried out two patrols, the first, at 1130 hours I very nearly missed as my aircraft refused to start. After about ten minutes my fitter managed to get it going and as two other aircraft had just been made serviceable I took off with a section consisting of the Admiral and Jock.

We climbed away south as hard as we could without much hope of catching up with the wing. At 20,000 feet just over the outskirts of London I sighted some Ack-Ack fire ahead. We were luckier than I had even hoped, for as we drew nearer I saw a loose formation of about 15 Dorniers with several 109s above them. They were flying west and it looked as if the wing had already been at them, as in fact they had.

Keeping an eye on the 109s, which apparently hadn't seen us, I turned in from ahead of the formation and dived at the leader, the Admiral and Jock picking a target each side of me.

We weren't quite dead ahead of the E/A and coming in at a slight angle I misjudged the deflection when I opened fire, the bullets going behind the Dornier. I flashed through the formation and pulled up in a climbing turn as a 109 came down on me. He came at me from the side and dived straight on underneath me and disappeared. Where he went to I don't know – he may have been out of ammunition and going home.

The sky was clear above, the sun shining down from the blue of the heavens on to the dazzling layer of cloud 10,000 feet below us, the Dorniers standing out starkly black against the snowy whiteness. As I came round behind the formation again I saw the Admiral's aircraft behind one of the E/A and marked the white streaks from the wings as he opened fire – then I was closing behind my own target.

I came in rather fast and fired a short burst as the aircraft bumped in the bomber's slipstream, breaking away hard down below the twin rudders as they seemed to rush almost into the cockpit. Pulling out of the half loop I began to turn again towards the enemy formation when I saw a Dornier diving past me going east. Reversing the turn I followed, firing from the quarter at the starboard engine. As I slipped in astern of the Hun a Hurricane swam up beside me firing also. I turned away to one side and saw two more Hurricanes behind him. Dammit! Who saw this Hun first?

Then I realised that the Hurricanes had probably been chasing this Dornier when I had come in and attacked. Perhaps after all I was horning in on them! I looked back to see if there was anything else about. No – the sky was empty save for the Hun, the Hurricanes, and me.

Taking my place in the queue I waited my turn to fire! The German pilot seemed to be taking no evasive action at all, the Dornier just diving slightly towards the clouds. Getting impatient I pulled out to one side and began a quarter attack aiming at the starboard engine again. This time I think I hit him, but it may have been one of the Hurricane pilots who was firing at the same time, as the E/A began to dive more steeply and as it went through a hole in the clouds, two white mushrooms blossomed forth as the wretched Huns baled out. The pilot was probably dead, as only two parachutes were floating down. Throttling back I dropped one wing to get a better view of the black-crossed aircraft. Behind, rushing over trees and hedges, fields and roads to meet the stricken machine, I saw its shadow. As the two came nearer and nearer a house loomed up, apparently in the path of the raider. With a sigh of relief I watched it miss the obstacle and then shadow and master met with a huge gush of flame as the aircraft hit the ground and the petrol tanks exploded. I circled, watching the pillar of black smoke rising up towards the clear blue sky above to mark the grave of another of Goering's pride. Turning back I saw the two white shapes of the parachutes as the rest of the crew floated down. One landed in a field and then I was on top of the other. I saw the black figure at the end of the shroud lines gesticulating violently and felt tempted to give him the burst he was so obviously expecting. Anger surged up inside me as I remembered the unbroken layer of cloud over London through which these 'brave' Huns had been shovelling their bombs! Looking back I saw the parachute swinging violently in my slipstream only a few feet from the top of a wood and laughed –

I hope that breaks your neck, you bloody little swine!

The morning's party was only a very small foretaste of what was in store after lunch. The sun was only just past the zenith when we were in the air again, forming up in the usual wing formation. As we climbed away towards London, Squadron Leader B [Douglas Bader], Woody and I exchanged wisecracks as we usually did on the way to our patrol line, in between more serious messages.

The weather was fine, the golden blaze of the sun high in the blue picking out the fleecy layer of clouds far below us. At 20,000 feet a message came crackling through in my 'phones – Woody's calm familiar voice saying, 'There's some trade heading NW to the south of you.'

'Lovely,' came from B in reply and then ahead some black puffs of smoke showed up a myriad black specks. Huns and plenty of them!

The old feeling fluttered again at my stomach as I settled myself more comfortably in my seat, tested the reflector sight, which I knew perfectly well was working ok, and glanced round at the rest of the squadron.

Looking back again at the rapidly growing black specks I saw above them a tangle of white condensation trails – the whole sky ahead seemed filled with aircraft. As we got closer I recognised the bombers as Dorniers, about 30 in each formation stretching away towards the coast to the south. Above the bombers weaved Me 109s and 110s, the escort. Never before, or since, have I seen so many enemy aircraft in the sky at one time. There were literally hundreds of them! It was an amazing sight and one which I shall remember all my life – it made the mass fly past at the Hendon Display seem small by comparison. It must have been about the maximum effort of the Luftwaffe.

As we climbed as hard as we could towards the Huns, the leading Dorniers crossed our bows and headed away to our right with their attendant escort.

I kept glancing up at those white trails just above, a gleaming speck at the head of each showing the fighters themselves. As we headed across the stream of aircraft I heard B call up but I didn't catch what he said, then I saw him turn away into the nearest formation of bombers with the rest of the Hurricanes, whilst I continued up into the escort with the Spitfires to try and hold them off while the bombers were being attacked. Glancing at No. 2 of my section, I noticed that he was just beginning to make a trail and looking up again as a 109 passed over the top of me I judged we were about 1,000 feet below them. I have never felt so uncomfortable in all my life; we were a perfect target and could do nothing save continue climbing into the fighters, waiting all the while to be attacked from the ideal position – above and behind. I didn't feel scared now, there was too much to occupy my attention, but my 'sit-me-down' was twitching as if I was expecting someone to kick me there and all the time I was squinting up into the glare above trying to keep an eye on all those damned Huns.

Suddenly I caught sight of a flash in my mirror, and turned as a couple of 109s came down on the rear section of the squadron. We opened out and after a few seconds split up as we swam up into the middle of a whole horde of 109s and 110s.

Why they hadn't attacked before I cannot think, but probably their idea was to draw us up into them to distract our attention from the stream of unescorted bombers which I later found were following at intervals behind the leading mass of aircraft. It almost seemed as if they hadn't sufficient fighters to escort all the bombers they sent over.

Ahead of me was a squadron of Me 110s and after a quick look round to see that no other Huns were immediately concentrating on me I climbed up after the rearmost 110. Unfortunately, before I could get close enough to fire they saw me and paid me the compliment of all forming a defensive circle! Remembering the pilot who managed to get inside one of these circles going round in the opposite direction and keeping the firing button pressed as the string of targets passed through his sights, I decided now was the time to do likewise. But for the fact that I was now below the Messerschmitts I think I might have succeeded, but as it was I couldn't get into the middle of them quickly enough and was forced to break away as the leader came round behind me. As I straightened out again and began to climb up, a pair of 109s descended on me, but I managed to sidestep, so to speak, and they passed harmlessly to one side and pulled up in a climb ahead of me. As I opened the throttle wide and climbed after them they did a very foolish thing. The leader turned left and No. 2, instead of following him, turned away in the opposite direction, right across my nose.

He saw me as I turned after him and putting on full inside rudder as he turned, skidded underneath me. Pulling round half stalled, I tore after him and got in a short burst as I closed up on him again before he was out of my sights again. That German pilot certainly knew how to handle a 109 – I have never seen one thrown about as that one was, and I felt certain that his wings would come off at any moment. However, they stayed on, and he continued to lead me a hell of a dance as I strove to get my sights on him again. Twice I managed to get in a short burst but I don't think I hit him, then he managed to get round towards my tail. Pulling hard round I started to gain on him and began to come round towards his tail. He was obviously turning as tightly as his kite could and I could see that his slots were open, showing that he was nearly stalled. His ailerons were obviously snatching too, as first one wing and then the other would dip violently.

Giving the Spitfire best, he suddenly flung out of the turn and rolled right over on his back passing across in front of me inverted. I couldn't quite see the point of this manoeuvre unless he hoped I would roll after him, when, knowing no doubt that my engine would cut whereas his was still going owing to his petrol injection system, he would draw away from me. Either that or he blacked out and didn't realise what was happening for a moment, for he flew on inverted for several seconds, giving me the chance to get in a good burst from the quarter. Half righting himself for a moment, he slowly dived down and disappeared into the clouds still upside down, looking very much out of control.

The sweat was pouring down my face and my oxygen mask was wet and sticky about my nose and mouth. I felt quite exhausted after the effort and my right arm ached from throwing the stick round the cockpit. At speed it needs quite a bit of exertion to move the stick quickly and coarsely in violent manoeuvres.

Looking round, the sky seemed empty and I dived down to follow the 109 and see if he had crashed or whether I could find him and finish him off if not. As I reached the top of a cloud layer I noticed away to the west a formation of about 20 aircraft flying south east.

Climbing up again as hard as I could I got up into the sun above them and waited until they approached beneath me. They were Dorniers again, with no escort. Before I came down on them I had a good look round but could see nothing else in the sky at all.

I don't think they saw me until I was on top of them and what tracer did come from the rear guns was not very close to me. I fired at the leader in a quarter attack but with the speed of the dive I couldn't get in a very long burst and had to break away quickly underneath the formation, rolling over and pulling out in the opposite direction to that in which they were flying. As I pulled out, there in front of me was another formation of about the same number of Dorniers.

I was in a fairly good position for a head-on attack and since this seemed to be about the only way I could break up a formation of this size by myself, I sailed in at them. As I fired at the leader I saw the aircraft on his right wobble a bit and wondered whether my bullets weren't going quite where I thought they were, or whether the pilot just didn't like the look of a Spitfire coming at him head on.

The Huns rushed to meet me, and I remember involuntarily ducking my head as the leader's port wing flashed over the cockpit, then I was through the formation and turning back after them again.

Far from breaking up the formation, my efforts seemed to have had the opposite effect as the Dorniers had closed up until they were flying with their wings almost overlapping. Those Huns certainly could fly in formation, and since there wasn't enough room to get through them again from the front, I pulled up to one side, got slightly ahead of the leader and then came down in a beam attack. I was certain from the sight and the tracer that my burst hit at least one other aircraft, if not the leader, but there was no visible effect, they just sailed on towards the coast.

Breaking away behind them I noticed that the last man on the starboard flank of the formation was straggling a little. A steep left hand turn and I came in behind him firing at one engine. I heard a sharp metallic bang and then my guns stopped. I broke away as obviously I was out of ammunition, and that bang I had heard was obviously a bullet from the German rear gunner. I quickly glanced over all the engine instruments but all was well – he hadn't hit the engine.

A last regretful glance after the Dorniers and I turned for home, feeling rather annoyed at not getting any of those bombers. I was sure I had been shooting straight – they must be carrying a lot of armour on them these days – Blast them!

Ah well – 'Home James,' and find out how the others fared.

Back on the deck once more everyone was busy over their combat reports, Cras fussing round getting the score as he collected the completed forms, and a good score it was too. Twelve certain and five probables. Sergeant R had got a bullet in his engine and had forced-landed, and Sergeant P was missing – these were our only casualties. Young Leonard had excelled himself and got three certain, two 109s and a 110, and Grumpy had got three as well, all 109s. Grumpy with some 109s always reminded me of a terrier amongst rats! Of the others, Sergeant Chad got a 109, Flight Sergeant S a Dornier certain and a 109 probable, and Wilf a 110 and a Dornier both certainties, and Jock and the Admiral each a 109.

Of the rest of the wing, Squadron Leader B hadn't been quite so lucky, as his squadron and the Czechs close behind had been jumped on before we could get into the escort and hold them off, but for all that they had done well, the Czechs also having a good bag. The total for the day for the wing amounted to 52, our own casualties being covered on the fingers of one hand. That night the sun was blood red as it sank beyond the western horizon.

Chapter 13 Out of Control: 16–27 September 1940 The blitz was not yet over, but 15 September saw the climax of it. Activity continued, however, on a fairly heavy scale for several days, and the wing carried out at least one patrol almost every day. On the 18th of the month we went off three times, and the first two patrols yielding nothing, I decided I might go over to my office to get on with a bit of work.

I was there when shortly after four o'clock the wing was ordered off again. Jumping into my car which I always had with me for these occasions, I tore round to dispersal point just in time to see 12 Spitfires taxiing away down the aerodrome. Some cad had taken my aircraft! It didn't matter from the operational point of view, as Wilf used to lead when I was away at any time, but I was furious at getting left behind. At the same time I couldn't help smiling and remembering another instance when a flight commander found his aircraft unserviceable and ordered another pilot over the R/T to give up his kite, whereat the latter developed mysterious R/T failure until he was in the air! It showed a grand spirit, and I could hardly imagine such a thing happening in a German squadron.

Alternately swearing and smiling to myself I repaired to the operations room, there to watch the progress of the wing. Woody, as usual, had come from his office to take over and very unsympathetically roared with laughter when I told him why I was there.

As luck would have it this third patrol which I had missed was the one in which the wing got into a party, a large formation of Heinkels, Junkers 88s and Mes being sighted east of London.

I made my way back to dispersal point as the aircraft returned and waited with

Cras for the pilots to taxi in. From their faces it was quite obvious that they had had some fun. Out of the total for the wing of 28, the squadron had accounted for six plus one probable. Wilf had got a Ju 88, Leonard shared a Ju 88 and a probable 109; Dolly and Sergeant P, our Czech pilots, each a He 111, and Grumpy (as usual) had added to his score with a Me 110. Flight Sergeant S had also got a Heinkel and shared a Ju 88 with Leonard, and F and his section had polished off another Ju 88 between them. Unfortunately F had had to force-land at E aerodrome with a bullet in his coolant tank. News came through that he was quite ok, however, to our relief. Two days later came the news that Grumpy had got the DFM. We were all very pleased about it.

22 September was a dirty day, low rain clouds obscuring the sun. Taking advantage of this, a Dornier paid us a visit, dropping a stick of bombs along B flight's dispersal point. They were only small bombs and apart from blowing one of the aircraft up on its nose and filling the cockpit with earth, no damage was done. F had taken off with his section just before this to try and intercept the raider and caught him over the aerodrome, getting in a burst before the Hun got back into the clouds again.

Five days later the wing was on patrol south of London and intercepted a formation of Me 109s. The Hun by now had almost completely given up large-scale bombing raids, contenting himself instead with sending over 109s on offensive sweeps, some of these fighters carrying bombs in order to increase their nuisance value more than anything else, I think, judging by the results they obtained.

We were flying south east at the time and some bursts of AA fire ahead showed us a formation of about twenty or thirty 109s flying north in loose formation. As they saw us they turned to meet us and Squadron Leader B waded into them, the rest of us following. As the squadron broke up, I noticed two yellow-nosed Huns creeping round underneath us to try and attack from below and behind.

Half rolling I dived down on them, getting in a short burst at each of them as they passed through my sights. I was coming down rather fast in the dive and felt the aircraft skidding slightly. My left hand felt for the rudder bias control and wound the wheel back. Still the aircraft continued to skid and trying to pull out of the dive I found that I couldn't. I was doing a fair rate of knots and the controls had stiffened up a great deal accordingly, but a backward movement of the stick did not have the customary effect! Pressing as hard as I could on the left rudder pedal had little or no effect either, as it was almost impossible to move it at this speed.

A glance at the airspeed indicator showed me I was doing well over 400 mph and the altimeter was giving a good imitation of one of those indicators you see in lifts. To say that I was a trifle worried about all this would be a slight understatement. I had started this blasted dive at 25,000 feet and the altimeter now showed 10,000. I was just beginning to think about stepping out, and then began wondering whether I could at this speed. I decided to have one last attempt at getting control.

Bracing myself against the back of the seat I put both feet on the left pedal and pressed as hard as I could, pulling back on the stick at the same time. Relieved was hardly the word, as I felt the aircraft straighten up and saw the nose rising to meet the horizon. Determined to make no mistake about pulling out of the dive completely, I kept the stick back and not unnaturally blacked out completely as the controls regained their full effect.

Easing the stick forward again I came to and was confronted with the sight of a parachute upside down and apparently ascending instead of descending. Further examination of this phenomenon drew my attention to the fact that the sun was below me! I had completed a half loop while I was blacked out without knowing it.

I rolled out right way up and circled round the white mushroom of silk, trying to recognise the pilot at the end of the shroud lines. High above me one or two aircraft were still circling round but the dogfight seemed to be over. Circling round I waited until the pilot came to rest in the top of a tree and then diving down (slowly this time!), caught a glimpse of him climbing down to the ground. He was obviously ok and I couldn't help laughing at his predicament. As he reached the ground he waved, and I turned for home.

Back on the aerodrome I found out that it was Gordon who had taken to the silk. His machine had been set on fire and he had had to get out in a hurry. He had left us a couple of months ago to take over a flight in the Czech squadron.

Our score for the day was good. Seven 109s down plus one probable. F, P, S, Grumpy and our Czech Sergeant P, had each got one, the Admiral had got two and Sergeant J had a probable – and I had had a fright! The trouble was later traced to a 'bowed' rudder, and the rudder bias out of adjustment. This had prevented me from being able to trim the aircraft straight in the dive, the ensuing skid causing the rudder to blank off one side of the elevators, thus causing the effectiveness of this control to be greatly decreased. Later I went up to test the aircraft again and all was well, the faults having been remedied.

The same day we learned that Jock and Leonard had both got the DFC, and we had a celebration that night in the mess to mark the occasion.

44 Anthony Bartley, Spitfire Pilot, Pilot Officer, British, 92 Squadron

Known to everyone as Tony, Anthony Bartley was born in India in 1919 into an Irish family. He joined the RAF in May 1939 and 92 Squadron in November. This extract is from his memoir, *Smoke Trails in the Sky*, and covers 12–27 September 1940, when 92 Squadron was based at the quintessential Battle of Britain base, Biggin Hill, south-east London (11 Group). The book was published in 1984 and was based on the author's collection of contemporaneous diaries, letters sent to his parents and logbook entries.

92 Squadron was a rather interesting outfit; it had more than its fair share of famous ace pilots who would publish memoirs or have biographies written about them. As a result we probably know more about their antics on the ground and in the air than we do about any other squadron. All the following feature in 3's memoir (though not all in this extract): Geoff Wellum (whose memoir *First Light* was published in 2002), Robert Stanford Tuck (*Fly for Your Life*, 1956), Brian Kingcome (*A Willingness to Die*, 1999) and Johnny Kent (*One of the Few*, 1971).

Kingcome on Bartley: 'Our archetypical playboy ... he was so good looking it was almost in poor taste. He was also a brilliant, successful pilot.' Fellow 92 Squadron pilot Allan Wright, also mentioned, is one of the few Battle of Britain pilots still alive today. 72 Squadron were also based at Biggin Hill during September, so Bartley, without knowing it, probably flew sorties with Bill Rolls (see his account of 2–14 September in chapter 37). By the end of 1940 he had destroyed eight enemy aircraft and damaged many more.

Bartley survived the war and worked as a test pilot and sales executive for Vickers Armstrong. He married his first wife, actress Deborah Kerr (whom he had met in Brussels in March 1945), and moved to Hollywood to start a career in television. He died in 2001. I am very grateful to Victoria Bartley, Anthony's widow, for permission to use the extract.

12 September 1940 As my Anson transport plane made a quick circuit of Biggin, I had looked at the scene below. The whole environment was a mess of bomb-scarred earth and bombed-out buildings. The hangars were in ruins, the entire airfield pock marked with bomb holes ringed with obstruction warning flags. There were newly laid patches on the runways where craters had been filled in and tarmacked.

The Anson picked its way cautiously between the obstacles, and taxied up to the nearest dispersal point.

A squadron of Spitfires were dispersed in their pens with starter trolleys and ground crews at readiness. With a surge of excitement I saw the 92 Squadron markings on their fuselages.

The boys, in their flying boots, fur coats and Mae Wests were either standing by their aircraft talking to their ground crews, or lounging in chairs outside the wooden pilots' dispersal hut. Brian's (Kingcome) bulldog was sprawled at his master's feet.

The ferry pilot wasn't going to switch off, and gestured me to get moving. He'd seen all he wanted to of Biggin Hill, for sure. No sooner had I humped my baggage out the back of the Anson than it swung around, and took off cross-wind.

The boys helped me stow my gear in the aircrew station wagon while I shot questions at them on the form.

'We shoot at Huns all day, dear boy, and get bestially drunk at night,' Brian answered. 'Station stores has been blitzed, so you can help yourself to anything in the line of flying clothing. I got two of everything for a rainy day.'

As he spoke, the ack-ack guns started barking at a Ju 88 which had emerged momentarily from cloud cover over the airfield heading south, having, evidently, dropped his bombs, as he ignored us.

'What does one do on these occasions?' I asked, a little nervously.

'Just put on a tin hat, and strike a hostile attitude,' Brian said.

Suddenly the Tannoy loud hailer crackled to life: '92 Squadron at 30 minutes available', and the fighter pilots made a concerted dash for the station wagon, which took off packed, with others hanging on to the outside wherever there was a foothold.

'Where's my V8?' I shouted at Brian above the roar of the unsilenced exhaust.

'Sorry about that, chum. Norman (Hargreaves) drove it into a bus and wrote it off when you were on leave. Had up for drunk driving, but fortunately, the local beak had a son in Fighter Command and let him off with a pound fine.'

'I'll fix him, for this,' I yelled.

'Been fixed already, poor chap, on the dawn patrol, yesterday,' Brian sighed. Tuck's taken over 257 Squadron at Martlesham. Hurricanes, poor sod. Al's got his flight.'

'Guess I'd better check in with the CO,' I said.

'He's out of action. Set himself on fire with his cigarette lighter. Seems someone had cleaned his uniform with a hundred octane,' Brian replied laconically.

Over a NAAFI lunch in the crew room, I asked John Bryson what the action was after dark, and he just winked 'plenty'.

The guns started roaring again, and a stick of bombs crashed across the airfield. Most of us had dived under cover when we had heard the dive-bomber coming, except Brian who had remained seated. 'This gives me the most terrible indigestion,' was all he said.

Climbing, self-consciously, back on to my chair, I assumed that this was something that I would have to acclimatize myself to.

The regular officers' mess had been bombed and evacuated, as far sleeping accommodation was concerned, so we were billeted in an old army establishment, adjacent to which were a number of wooden huts which had been divided into rows of small bedrooms. Having stowed my kit, and met up with my batman, I found station stores, and helped myself to two of everything, as Brian had advised. I drew another parachute from the section, chatted up a WAAF packer, and made sure that she knew, and had done a good job. By that time, it was almost dark, and the squadron had been released.

As we dined in the old army mess the night bombers started pouring over the airfield in a steady stream, heading for their target, London. Biggin was in their flight path. Their high-pitched, desynchronized engines droned above the yapping of the anti-aircraft guns.

After one large explosion had rocked the building, Johnnie Bryson suggested, 'Let's all get out of here, and watch the bombing from the White Hart at Brasted. Far more fun.'

Wimpey Wade wouldn't be hurried over his dessert, and Allan Wright declined. He was more interested in processing the war photographs he took, and reading, we figured. He took the war quietly, in his stride, unworried. We couldn't level with him. He liked a party, but only one a week. The rest of us liked one every night. Having taken over Bob Tuck's flight, Al had a lot of responsibility. We secretly admired him because we knew that we needed the alcoholic tranquillizer and stimulant in order to keep going, all the time, while he relied on his sober self-control, and a philosophy all of his own.

The station wagon set off at demoniacal speed, with John Bryson at the wheel.

'Ninety-two fighter squadron,' everybody yelled in unison, as response to the sentry's challenge, and we swept through the guard room gates on our way to Brasted.

The White Hart was a typical country pub, with low beamed oak ceilings. The appendages of hunting horns and horse brasses were now interspersed with squadron crests and war souvenirs. Two very tall and identical twins were talking to a short little man with a goatee beard. They greeted the boys effusively, and Brian introduced me to the MacNeal sisters. Drinks started coming up from all directions, with someone or other's compliments.

'Who's paying for all this?' I asked.

'Don't know, who cares, as long as I'm not. The natives are very friendly,' Brian said.

'What's the scene upstairs?' I asked.

'Plenty to shoot at. They come in their hundreds.'

'Time, gentlemen, please,' yelled the barman.

'Who's for the Red House?' said one of the twins. I couldn't tell the difference. There was a unanimous howl of approval.

And then, I saw her coming down the stairs.

She had honey blond hair down to her shoulders and the bluest of eyes. Her figure was like what most men dreamed about. She seemed preoccupied and unhappy. Her escort was an over-fed army major.

'Who the hell is that one?' I whispered to Brian.

'Not for you, Tony boy. She's army property. A London model. Bombed out of her flat. She's staying down here.'

She passed quite close to me and I could smell her perfume.

'Paula, meet Tony,' one of the twins said. I could only say:

'Hello, Paula.'

'Come on, chaps, let's get up to the Red House,' pleaded someone.

I didn't want to leave her, but I guessed there was no alternative. I hated the army major.

We piled into the station wagon like sardines again, and after a short drive, arrived in front of a fine old red brick manor house. The twins had gone ahead, and were waiting for us at the door. I was shown into the drawing room, and a very large whisky thrust into my hand. Someone put on the radiogram and John Bryson grabbed one of the twins and started to dance her around the floor. He was the only one taller than they were.

Several hours, and three bottles of Scotch later, I suggested that we should be getting back to the airfield. Geoff Wellum had been sick in the garden. Brian said that he was staying on for a while, but I couldn't figure which twin was the attraction. I wondered how we were going to make dawn readiness, but I wondered more about Paula.

13 September My batman called me at 4.30 a.m. with a cup of tea. I struggled into my clothes and bumped into Wimpy Wade in the corridor. He had thrown on his uniform over his pyjamas. It was cold and dark outside. The boys converged from various rooms of our barrack block, dressed in polo-necked sweaters, corduroy trousers and flamboyant scarves.

We clambered aboard the station wagon, and started for the dispersal area. No one spoke, and only the shattered exhaust pipe broke the silence.

Our Spitfires stood silhouetted against the backdrop of the dawn sky. In the middle of our dispersal hut stood a pot-bellied stove which had already been lit by the duty ops telephone operator. Around the walls, the pilots' cots were distributed, head to toe. I strapped on my Mae West and walked out to my aircraft. My fitter Wallace was sitting in the cockpit making his final check.

'Everything under control?' I asked.

'Yes, sir. Running like a bird. Wouldn't let anyone else fly her. Kept her unserviceable 'til you got back.'

'Good work, Wallace,' I said.

As I strolled back to the dispersal hut, I wondered how much we owed our lives to the devotion of people like Wallace. Our fitters, riggers and armourers.

When I re-entered the crew room, I watched the boys lying on their iron cots in Mae Wests and flying jackets, some tossing in uneasy sleep. Others played nervously with flying helmets and oxygen tubes, or studied enemy aircraft identification charts, and the sector maps pinned to the wooden plank walls. Someone had stuck up a warning poster with black crosses painted on it, and underneath written '*Remember the Hun in the Sun*'.

The duty ops airman was sitting at his corner desk with his hand ready to pick up the direct line to the controller. Suddenly, the silence was shattered by the roar of an engine starting up the other side of the airfield.

'God how I hate this waiting. Why don't the buggers come?' someone said. As if in answer, the ops phone bell broke the silence, and as one man, the pilots were on their feet.

Brian grabbed the instrument and held it to his ear. 'Ok, chaps, it's scramble Angels 20, rendezvous with 72 (72 Squadron stationed at Biggin Hill when we arrived) over base.' It was a rush for the door, and a race for our Spitfires, as the Tannoy loud hailer howled the alarm.

Twelve pilots leapt into their cockpits and strapped on their parachutes. Twelve Merlin engines of one thousand horsepower coughed and roared into life.

I pushed my throttle open in pursuit of Brian, and the squadron gathered momentum, then launched itself into the air, in close formation. Climbing slowly, in a left hand circuit, we joined up with 72, then reached for the sky, and operational altitude.

I looked down at the earth below. Under my port wing, I could see the River Thames winding through the city of London, the early morning mist enveloping it in a semi-transparent shroud. The rising sun glinted on the myriads of barrage balloons that looked like grotesque fungi sprouting from the ground. I could see no other fighters in the sky, and I thought, there we were, twenty-four Spitfires barring the way to the destruction of the capital city of the British Commonwealth of Nations, by a ruthless enemy. Obviously, the after effects of the previous night's drinking were still with me.

'Keep up, Red 2,' someone barked on the R/T, and I suddenly realized the remark was addressed to me. I had been day-dreaming, and slipped well behind my leader.

Then, 'Hello, Gannic, leader! Gannic leader! Carfax calling! 200 plus coming in over Red Queen. Vector 120. Angels 22.'

'Hello, Carfax. Gannic leader. Message received. Over.' Brian's voice.

'Hello, Gannic. Gannic leader. Carfax calling. Watch out for snappers above. Many snappers above. Hear me?'

'Loud and clear, Carfax. Over and out.'

I looked over my starboard wing, and in the distance, could make out hundreds of little black puffs of cotton wool in the sky. They were approaching fast, and travelling in the wake of an armada of dark bombers flying in V formations.

The 'snappers' were made visible by smoke trails in the sky. *Jeesus*, I thought. Where the hell do we start on this lot? I saw six squadrons of Hurricanes tearing up on our port side and I felt less lonely.

'Tally ho, right. Here they come, chaps,' somebody yelled on the R/T, and the squadron swung towards the approaching enemy which were making straight for London.

'Ok, boys, let's go.' Brian half rolled, and tore into the leading formation from the quarter. I lowered my seat, crouched over my gun sight, and followed him.

As we closed in on them, I pushed my face close to the armour plated glass, and tried to make myself as small as possible. This was like the Dunkirk days. The thrill of the chase. The scent of the kill.

I watched as Brian opened fire. Flames spurting from his eight machine gun ports. I filled my gun sight with a fat Dornier, and pressed the trigger. My guns started their staccato chatter, and lead crashed into its fuselage with flashing De Wilde. He jettisoned his bombs, and started to burn. I transferred my aim to another, and his engine cowling flew off before I was caught in his slip stream and tossed to one side as my ammunition ran out.

Simultaneously, my ailerons gave a jolt as one of them was hit, and I saw two 109s flash by.

I yelled, 'snappers', on the R/T, half rolled, and dived for the deck. Aircraft were falling, in every direction, out of the sky which was now full of smoke trails and parachutes.

I made a dicey landing due to my crippled aileron, taxied up to my dispersal point where my apprehensive crew helped me out of my cockpit.

I hurriedly lit a cigarette, before I said anything.

'You all right, sir?' Wallace asked me anxiously.

'Bit of 109 trouble, that's all. Got my aileron.'

I walked over to the dispersal hut, and slumped down in a chair. Some of the boys had preceded me, and Tom Weiss, our Norwegian intelligence officer was trying to get their combat reports. I asked him if all the boys had got back, and he told me that Gus Edwards and Sergeant Eyles hadn't checked in yet. Geoff Wellum said that a Spitfire had spun down quite close to him, in flames, but too fast to get its squadron markings.

Within a couple of hours, my mechanics had fixed my damaged aileron, and shortly after, the Tannoy loud hailer cried out its fateful air raid warning:

'92 Squadron scramble. Angels 20.'

High over the cliffs of Dover, we saw them coming in their hundreds. Look left, look right, behind into the sun where the Me 109s always lurked.

'Keep up, Blue 2. Snappers above.'

Back wet with sweat. Breathing faster. The waiting and the watching that is fear. They are near now. Legs strong on rudder pedals, safety catch off, hands firm. Then, 'Tally ho' from Brian, and the wing over and dive into attack, after one look behind.

Within range, a thumb depresses the trigger button as the enemy fills the gun sight. A backlash of eight machine guns, a reek of cordite in the cockpit, a stream of tracer pouring forward.

A cry over the R/T: 'Watch out. Snappers coming down.' Then, the sky full of planes. Twisting. Sniping. A hailstorm of lead. Blinding centrifugal forces. Ammunition gone. Alone and unarmed in a hostile sky. A dive for the deck, and a heading for home. Unsteady landing, and switch off at dispersal point. A welcoming hoist out of the cockpit by mechanics who secretly thought they might not have seen you again. Intelligence reports gabbled to the IO. A count up of score. Five confirmed, and three probables.

'Good show,' from the station commander – Group Captain Grice.

'Who's for the White Hart?' somebody shouts, and a spontaneous show of hands, all except Allan Wright's. 'In twenty minutes, then.'

'Time, ladies and gentlemen, please,' called the barman, and a sad silence descended upon the civilian customers as we left the White Hart Inn.

'Get one for me,' said a man with one arm.

'Who's for the Hilden Manor?' Bob Holland shouted. A howl of 'ayes' greeted his suggestion, then a scramble for the station wagon, a roar of its motor and a screech of tyres.

John Bryson drove the station wagon up to the front door of the road-house, and struck a major whom he had failed to see, in the buttocks.

'Why the bloody hell don't you look where you're going?' the soldier shouted.

'Why the hell didn't you get your fat ass out the way?' John shouted back.

'Get out of there, and come inside,' barked the infuriated major.

'He wants to play,' John grinned, as he heaved his six foot four of carcass from under the wheel.

The victim took one look at John, and stalked through the door into the road-house. John followed him up to the bar, and bought him a double whisky. The boys were greeted effusively by some quite pretty hostesses, and the head waiter who asked what our day's score had been while leading us to a prominent table. When we told him, he bowed and said that the drinks would be on the house.

A combo was playing *Tuxedo Junction*, and couples moving lethargically on the dance floor, as the first bottle of whisky appeared. John had brought the prettiest hostess with him, and after we had helped ourselves liberally to the gratuitous liquor, Bob swallowed a couple of Benzedrine tablets, got up and walked over to the band who had just finished their number.

'Going to play for us tonight, Bob?' asked the pianist, vacating his stool in anticipation.

Bob needed no encouragement. After flying, piano playing was his life. He started with something slow and nostalgic which reminded him of times before the war. Full whisky glasses appeared one by one on the top of the piano, and Bob helped himself with one hand while keeping on playing with the other.

Then, as the Benzedrine started to take effect, his tempo quickened. Sweat had started to pour down his face, and he closed his eyes as he rocked his head from side to side in ecstasy at his music making. Some of the guests stopped dancing, or left their tables to gather around this impromptu performer who helped himself to booze and Benzedrine in turn, and played piano like the greatest. All of a sudden he stopped, grabbed one of the hostesses, and walked her out of the room, through the black-out curtained French window, into the garden and into the swimming pool. The band resumed their playing, the customers their dancing, and the fighter boys their drinking on the house, until it closed.

The first opportunity I had, I located and bought, with parental financial support, a twelve cylinder Lincoln Zephyr coupe. It went for £100, as no civilian could get enough petrol to sustain its voracious consumption.

Bob Holland had a supercharged Bentley, Kingcome had been lent the SS100 racer which belonged to one of the MacNeal twins, and Wimpy Wade, a Packard convertible. None was licensed or insured, and the local constabulary were fully aware of this omission, and once in a while, a police sergeant would come up to the airfield to remonstrate to our adjutant who would take him to the bar in the officers' mess to which we were summoned.

After copious drinks and choruses of 'good old serg' the reprimand would turn into a warning, not of prosecution, but of the date of the next police road check-up of all unlicensed vehicles.

We filled our cars with 100-octane fuel from the aircraft petrol bowsers, without conscience, and everyone turned a blind eye.

18 September I was firing at Dornier 17 and so pre-occupied with my target that I forgot the cardinal rule of air fighting. *Remember the Hun in the Sun.* I heard a cannon shell explode behind my armour-plated seat back, a bullet whizzed through my helmet, grazing the top of my head and shattering my gun sight, while others punctured my oil and glycol tanks. A 109 flashed by.

Fumes then started to fill my cockpit, and I knew without doubt that I had had it, so I threw open my hood, undid my straps and started to climb over the side. As I braced myself to bale out I saw my enemy preparing for another attack, and knew it meant suicide to jump with him around. Escaping airmen over their own territory were fair game in some combatants' log book, and a friend of mine had been shot down in his parachute. So, I decided to bluff it out, climbed back into my aircraft, and turned on my attacker.

My ruse worked; he didn't know how hard he'd hit me, but he did know that a Spitfire could turn inside a Messerschmitt, and I fired a random burst to remind him, whereupon he fled for home. By this time I was too low to jump, so I headed for a field and prayed.

At a hundred feet, my engine blew up, and I was blinded by oil. I hit the ground, was catapulted out, and landed in a haystack unharmed. I hit the buckle of my parachute to release it, and as it fell to the ground, the pack burst open spewing forth the silk which had been shredded by splinters of cannon shell. I said a hasty prayer before the first of the rescue party could reach me.

I was soon surrounded by a crowd of farmers, and inmates from a public house nearby. I asked them where I was, and they told me Appledore, before sitting me on a stool at the bar counter with a first pint of beer. Five pints later, an army officer turned up in a jeep with a couple of military policemen. He drove me to his command post, where I was given a large whisky. The commander told me that the Dornier had crashed with no survivors.

From there, I was taken to the office of the Chief Constable of Kent who opened a bottle of sherry which we drank before he gave me lunch. I slept the entire journey back to Biggin where I was driven by a very large police officer in a very fast squad car. He delivered me to the officers' mess with the remains of my parachute and demanded a receipt for me from the adjutant.

The boys then broke the news that Roy Mottram had been killed and Bob

Holland wounded. We drowned our sorrows, and John Bryson and Kingcome carried me to bed.

19 September, letter to my mother, RAF Biggin Hill As you will have guessed we have been desperately busy since we have been here – taking a leading part in nearly all the fighting. Of course, we have had our casualties which are only to be expected. Gus Edwards and Norman Hargreaves are still missing and several of the boys are in hospital with wounds.

I got three more bombers, but yesterday I was shot down by a Me 109 which crept up behind me while I was blowing up a Do 17. I crashed near Dungeness, but thank God I was unhurt, and am ready for anything again now.

The German Air Force are doing their utmost to smash us. We certainly know that we are up against it, but the morale of the fighter boys is terrific – we will crack the German Air Force, at all costs. This is our greatest and diciest hour, but we are proud to have the chance to deal with it.

Please on no account worry about me – I am safe until my predestined time runs out. I am happy, and almost enjoying myself. In these times of danger one gets drawn much closer to one's friends, and a great spiritual feeling of comradeship and love envelops every one. I can't explain, but everyone seems a much better man, somehow.

I met Chris (my doctor brother, now senior physician at St Thomas's Hospital) in London and we spent the night at the Regent Palace Hotel. The bombing proved only a distraction and we found a bottle of gin far more fortifying than an air-raid shelter. The Londoners, although deadly tired, are standing up to it well, and are full of determination to see things through. Tony

21 September Although I had made very strong resolutions not to get in front of an Me 109 again, I was shot up by one a couple of days later. We were mixing it with a bunch of them, when a salvo of lead crashed into my fuselage behind my armour-plating. I didn't even see my opponent who must have been a pretty good sportsman, as I was doing aerobatics when he hit me. I may even have flown through a stream of bullets that had been aimed at somebody else.

However, when my control column wouldn't respond how I wanted it to, I rolled out of the conflict, found a friendly layer of cloud and set a compass course vaguely in the direction of where I thought Biggin Hill was, scarcely daring to sneeze in case I broke the last of the tail plane cables which I knew had been hit.

When I broke cloud at 800 feet, I had made up my mind to jump, as my engine was beginning to lose power, but I found myself right over Sevenoaks where I dared not jettison my Spitfire for fear of the destruction it might cause in the built-up area. By the time I had passed it, I was too low to bale out, so it was Biggin or bust.

When I made my landing approach, I found this could only be achieved by winding the tail trimming tab fully forward to depress the nose, and control this tendency by easing back on the 'stick', which had lost its forward effect.

I motored in slowly, sweating profusely, and made a pretty commendable landing.

As I turned at the end of the runway and headed towards my dispersal point, I yanked back on the control column, and the last cable broke.

A somewhat bizarre arrangement had been made with the factory where our Spitfires were built. When a pilot assessed that his aircraft was shot up badly enough to necessitate a crash landing, he was encouraged to crash on the factory airfield instead of his own, and pick up a new aircraft from the production line. Another unorthodox arrangement had been established with the Luftwaffe. We had mutually organized a radio communications system whereby we could each report to one another the position of our respective pilots shot down in the Channel. It was the responsibility of whichever air sea rescue boat was closest, to pick up the airmen before they drowned. No one shot at air sea rescue boats – an unwritten law which I experienced three miles off Calais when I took part in a successful air sea rescue operation of one of my pilots.

I wondered what the others felt when they saw the tracer and the black crosses. We never discussed it. John Bryson, whose main thoughts seemed focussed on having a good time with girls. The huge, wise-cracking ex-Canadian Mountie who had become my best friend. His dismissal from his previous service, according to his account, was due to progress in the shape of helicopters. Lonesome, stationed in some north Canadian outpost, he had moved in a couple of Eskimo babes, and was teaching them to play ice hockey when the commandant literally descended upon them.

Brian was a bit of an enigma. He loved his dog and one of the twins which took up all his spare time.

Bob Holland had his piano and his Benzedrine. Al Wright, his letter writing and photos. He and Pat Learmond had shared their love for the same girl. Now Pat was dead, leaving Al a clear field.

Wimpy was an atheist who loved flying and himself, but nice with all. Geoff Wellum, we nicknamed 'the boy'. A youngster who fought and drank as hard as any of us.

From an hour before dawn until dusk we lived at our dispersal point on the airfield, and fought until we ran out of ammunition. At night we drank and played and made love like there was no hereafter. I can't remember all the pilots who flew with us. Some came in the morning and were dead by nightfall. The Biggin Hill chapel keeps the record. I swore never to hate anyone again after I'd seen one of our team I loathed blow up beside me when caught by a 109. First, Norman Hargreaves had gone, then Sergeant Eyles. Gus Edwards was found dead a week after he went missing, in the middle of a forest. Similarly, Howard Hill, after three weeks, lodged in the top of a tall tree, decomposing in his cockpit, his hands on the controls and the top of his head blown off by a cannon shell. Pat Patterson, though badly burned in a previous escape, refused to be grounded. I saw him spin down quite close to me, having been hit and struggling to get out of his blazing cockpit. A burned offering to the god of war.

After Judy's accident followed two replacement COs with no previous combat experience who flew number two to Brian in consequence: Lister had won a DFC on the North West Frontier; McLoughlan, from Training Command. Neither lasted much more than a week being shot down in quick succession. This was no game for inexperience, and Brian continued to lead the squadron with no promotion.

Brian was the only one of us who seemed unaffected by the war. We would have happily accepted a rest if it had been offered us. Maybe it was, and he never told us. His private life revolved around the White Hart Inn and the Red House of the twins.

The war in the air seemed just an incidental interruption which kept him occupied during the day. He appeared unmoved by our casualties. He seemed to take it for granted. A complete enigma to us who loved and followed him, with complete faith in his leadership. When we had lost one of our sergeant pilots, and one of us asked what became of him, Brian answered, 'Lee's a cinder' which I remember to this day.

On his way to Chequers, Churchill would pay us a visit from time to time. He would burst into our crew room, unheralded, and sit and chat with us while he puffed on a huge cigar. He was an honorary air commodore of an Auxiliary squadron, an inspiration, and we were proud to think of him as a friend as well as our leader.

On 24 September John Bryson was shot up in a dogfight, but managed, how I'll never know, to land on North Weald airfield. When the ground crew lifted him out of his cockpit, they found him dead. One leg had been blown off just below the knee.

I didn't remember much of John's funeral. I got so drunk that I wouldn't. But I do remember one of the pilot boys, drunker than I was, giving his farewell salute beside the grave, then falling into it.

26–27 September Just as our destroyed Spitfires were replaced with others, so were dead men's shoes refilled with raw young recruits. If they lasted, they gradually got incorporated in our team. Many of them only lasted a few days before they died. Some never returned from their very first sortie. We never even remembered their names.

Quite a number were sergeant pilots of every nationality. They fought with our team by day, but were segregated by rank from us when off duty. An anachronism of our service. We were all one breed of fighting men.

Don Kingaby was one of these whose companionship I would have cultivated, had I the chance, amongst others, but there was little opportunity, the way we were forced to live. He joined Brian Kingcome's flight of which I was a member.

Sergeant Pilot Don Kingaby got off the London train at Bromley South and boarded a bus on the last leg of his journey to Biggin where he'd been posted to join 92 Squadron. At Leaves Green, a village at the bottom of the hill, the conductress chirped out a cheery 'All change', and in answer to his query, pointed the way up the road leading towards the airfield. The buses had given up driving past the camp since the recent bombings, and this one was no exception. It turned around and hastily departed in the direction from which it had come. Don hoisted his kitbag and set off towards his destination.

Upon reaching it Don found a scene of complete desolation, and one weary-looking aircraftman who directed him to a shattered building bearing the sign 'sergeants' mess' beyond the wreckage of a hanger. As he approached it, he heard overhead the sound of unfamiliar aero engines, and looking up, spotted a Ju 88.

Don jumped into a convenient ditch and watched the aircraft makes its run over the airfield, then turn and head south. Obviously on a photograph reconnaissance job, he reckoned. Then, he emerged from his cover and continued his hike. On entering the mess, he found it deserted, but located a telephone, called 92 Squadron orderly room and reported his arrival. A voice told him to check in next morning.

It was getting dark when pilots started to arrive from the squadron dispersal points, and a flight sergeant greeted him, and showed him to a room which he was to share with two other pilots. After further introductions, a couple of beers and a hasty supper, most of the pilots took off for their local pub, but weary after his journey, Don decided to turn in early.

At what hour he knew not, he was rudely awoken by an ear-shattering bang, quickly followed by two others, jumped out of bed and started reaching for his clothes. Desynchronized motors droned overhead. 'Only ack-ack' came a drowsy voice from the bed next to him. 'Go back to sleep. You're going to need it.'

The gun battery kept up its infernal racket all night long. The building shook, and the windows rattled. Every now and again came the whistling of descending bombs followed by their bursts to add to the cacophony of noise. Not another wink of sleep did he get that night as he listened, and wondered at the composed slumber of his room mates who appeared to accept the holocaust as par for the course.

At dawn, Don reported at the squadron dispersal with two other pilots who had just arrived. They had already collected parachutes. One of the flight commanders interviewed them in the pilots' crew room.

'Have you ever seen a Hun?' he asked.

'No,' replied a sandy-haired lad beside Don.

'Yes,' Don and the third of the trio said simultaneously. His name was Bowen-Morris.

'Have you ever fired at a Hun?' the flight commander added.

'Only once,' Don and Bowen-Morris replied, again in unison.

'Ye gods,' exclaimed the flight commander to the pilots lounging at readiness. 'They've sent us a couple of veterans,' and thus was their introduction to Brian Kingcome.

Don Kingaby had noticed another flight lieutenant in the crew room with the most terrible blood-shot eyes and a crimson face. 'Jesus,' he thought, 'there's a real booze hound, if ever I saw one. Hope I'm not in his flight.' He wasn't, and learned later that the pilot was New Zealander Pat Patterson who had been shot down in flames a few days previously, but refused to take a rest because of the shortage of pilots.

Don put on his overalls and Mae West, sorted out helmet and gloves and picked up his parachute. Brian Kingcome led him out to the Spitfire he was to fly and showed him how to stow his gear, arrange his straps for a quick getaway and introduced him to his ground crew upon whom his life would partly depend. Returning to the crew room he was introduced to his section leader who told him he'd fly his number three, to stick with him, and always remember the 'Hun in the Sun'.

The rest of the fighter pilots were lounging in chairs or trying to catch up on lost sleep on iron beds scattered around the floor. The ops telephone rang from time to time as the sector controller checked on the aircraft and pilot readiness state, and each time the boys would open a sleepy eye, and cock an ear to the ops clerk, Aircraftman Webber, who would sooner or later order a 'scramble'. When the phone was returned to its cradle, silence would return, only interrupted by the stertorous breathing of Brian's massive bulldog as he dreamed of despatch riders, his bêtes noirs and as soon as they delivered at the dispersal point, they would beat a hasty retreat before Zeke could get his teeth into a leg. Until, one time, he fastened on to a hot exhaust pipe which discouraged further attacks.

The ops phone rang once more, but this time Webber shouted, 'Scramble Maidstone, angels fifteen.'

The pilots hurled themselves from bed and chair, with a mad rush for the open door. Some, whose aircraft were dispersed nearby made them running. Others, parked at some distance, hopped aboard the squadron truck which whisked them to their destination. The Tannoy blared out the 'scramble' alarm. Tongues of flame and belches of blue smoke burst from the Spitfire's exhausts.

Tense and apprehensive, Don clambered up the wing root and into the cockpit. By the time he was strapped in, some of the others were taxiing out, and he panicked in fear of missing his section leader's aircraft, before he spotted him waiting for him, and took up his position. The squadron lined up across the airfield in battle formation, then opened up, and started to roll forwards together; then they were airborne, clearing Biggin's last remaining hangar with a few feet to spare.

Ninety-two were still using the standard vic formation which Douglas Bader and Sailor Malan had discarded in favour of the 'four finger' concept. Don had been delegated as one of the two 'weavers' to protect the squadron's rear. 'Arse-end Charlies', they were dubbed, and the most precarious position in the squadron. The squadron climbed over Maidstone to fifteen thousand feet; then we were ordered to twenty-five where we reached vapour trail height.

'Smoke trails, Gannic leader', a voice came over the R/T and Brian, who was leading, eased down out of the treacherous zone which would betray our position to the enemy.

'Hello, Gannic leader.' The voice of the controller came over the R/T. 'I have some trade for you. Twenty plus bandits with many snappers heading for Red King, angels twenty. Over.'

'Roger,' Brian answered, and turned south east. Then suddenly: 'Gannic leader. Bandits now over Red King. Watch out for many snappers above.'

'Gannic leader, I see them. Tally ho, and over.'

Don saw the black puffs of flak reaching for the sky over Dover, then their target, small compact dots constituting the bomber formation. His weaving became more violent as he set himself to guard, not only the tail of the squadron, but his own. The gap between pursuers and pursued was quickly closing, and then Brian's section, wide opening their taps, dived into their attack on the dark grey fat bombers, followed by Pat Pattersons.

Don saw their 109 escort coming down, and shouting a warning. Then all was a maelstrom of fighting aeroplanes. He saw a spurt of flame emerge from Patterson's fuselage in front of his cockpit, and then it blossom into an all consuming fire ball as the aircraft fell away. Then his number two followed, streaming thick black smoke. Don attacked one of a vic of three Dorniers. He saw his de Wilde bullets flickering on wings and body as he glued his finger to the trigger button. Then he saw the tracer bullets zipping past his starboard wing as the 109s came down on their prey, and swung into a tight turn which temporarily blacked him out. When his sight returned he found himself on the tail of one of four, closed the gap and finished his ammunition on it, again seeing the de Wilde bullets as they peppered his enemy's wings and fuselage, which started to smoke. Then he flick-rolled and dived out of the combat arena, towards mother earth.

On his landing back at Biggin, Don's ground crew greeted him with eager questions on seeing that the canvas patches over his gun ports had been shot away.

'Did you get one, serg? How many? What were they?'

Don answered that he could possibly claim a 109, and they started to regale him with the news from the other pilots who had landed.

'Mister Kingcome got another one, and Mister Bartley a Ju 88.'

The squadron claims were an assorted bag of six, and another four were claimed by 72. Pat Patterson had been reported killed, and two 92 Spitfires missing. One of them was Wimpy Wade's who turned up by car later. He had taken on a formation of Dorniers, and after hitting one, had been caught in their rear gunner's cross-fire and forced landed on Lewis race track with a punctured radiator.

Sergeant Pilot 'Tich' Havercroft, even smaller than Don, seated himself at the battered crew room piano, and started to play 'boogi' to relieve the tension everyone was feeling. He wasn't very adept and the boys shouted at him to make room for Bob Holland who took over with his magic touch.

Mid-afternoon the ops telephone again gave the alarm, but Brian had stood Don down. Newcomers were treated leniently. Don watched the squadron scramble, then the sirens started their wailing, and the Ack-Ack cracking. He would have gone to earth but for the casual conduct of Flight Sergeant Stewart and Sergeant 'Tubby' Back, armourer and mechanic, who stood their ground, looking skywards for the approaching enemy.

Don watched, fascinated, a formation of Ju 88s with their fighter escort approach remorselessly overhead, then 92 and 66 (our sister squadron) tear into them. The formation started to break up and scatter all over the sky. A lone 88 passed low overhead with a Spitfire close on its tail, firing a continuous burst from its eight machine-guns. From its letter on the fuselage, he knew it was Tommy Lund's. The bomber started to shed bits and pieces, then dive towards the ground beyond the airfield perimeter.

The long waiting at 'readiness' in our crew room was full of tension which we tried to relieve with cat-napping, play and shop talk, and interminable squadron tactics. In respect of the latter, two things had been worrying us. The first was the vulnerability of our weavers, and Don Kingaby who was in Brian's and my flight seemed invariably to get this precarious job, shared with Tich Havercroft, and in an unexpected manoeuvre both were liable to become separated from the squadron and priority targets for the 109s.

Don suggested that, instead, they should weave in front where they could do their job just as well, and stick with the group, which was agreed. It worked well, and was, thereafter, adopted as a standard operational procedure.

A further consideration was the practicality of flying with the cockpit hood open, two arguments being advanced in favour of this. One, that the reflections from the perspex were distracting, and the other that speck of dirt on it could be mistaken for an enemy fighter and give a false alarm. But an even more compelling reason was that we had found it exceedingly difficult to open the hood at high speed, and there was no jettison mechanism on it, causing a predominant feeling that one could become trapped in a burning cockpit, the fighter pilot's greatest fear. This sticking hood problem exercised the inventive talents of Sergeant Ronnie Fokes, and together with the squadron engineer officer and a senior flight mechanic, the first hood jettisoning mechanism was developed and incorporated in all our aircraft, without reference to the designers or the bureaucrats at the Air Ministry.

45 David Crook Part 3, Spitfire Pilot, Pilot Officer, British, 609 Squadron

Third extract from Crook's 1942 memoir based on his diaries, covering 7–30 September, when he was flying from RAF Middle Wallop, Hampshire (10 Group).
September opened quietly as far as we were concerned, and though we did a number of patrols, nothing much happened. The days were now getting noticeably shorter and we benefited accordingly, as we could now be released at dusk, between 7 p.m. and 8 p.m., and get out more in the evenings.

This was a great contrast with the state of affairs in July, when for several days on end we were on duty (and doing a lot of flying) from 3.30 a.m. till 10.45 p.m.

We were able to do quite a lot of practice flying and I had a lot of dogfights with Geoff. There was a tremendous rivalry between us, and altogether they proved to be most energetic affairs – turning, diving, and climbing all over the sky at anything between 300 mph and 400 mph in a desperate attempt to get on each other's tails. But dogfighting in a Spitfire is a very tiring business owing to the high speeds and heavy strains involved, and after about ten minutes we had generally had enough.

So we flew home with honours generally about even, and the loser stood a pint of beer.

At the beginning of the month, the London night bombing started to get rapidly worse, and so rather reluctantly we decided that Dorothy would have to go north to Huddersfield. This was the only thing to do, but it meant the end of our pleasant evenings every week in town. From now onwards we could see each other only on the comparatively rare occasions that I could get up home.

However, on 7 September John and I got the Magister and flew up to Yeadon for twenty-four hours' leave. It seemed very odd to be piloting a little aeroplane at 100 mph again. I found it more difficult to fly than a Spitfire, so accustomed had I become to the latter.

We did a very neat bit of navigation between us (fighter pilots are not generally renowned for their navigational skill) and dived over John's house at Cawthome, and flew over Glenwood, where I could see the family waving hard from the lawn.

We found everybody in very cheery form when we got back. The first big daylight raid on London had taken place the previous day and 609 had their first fight for about a fortnight, during which time we had become very bored with inactivity. We got about six Huns confirmed, and everybody got back safely (except Noel who had a bullet in his engine and forced-landed). The whole squadron then adjourned to Gordon Harker's cocktail party in aid of the Spitfire Fund.

They all thought this most appropriate! So altogether we had missed quite a lot of fun!

In the next week or two we flew up to London almost everyday, sometimes twice a day, in order to give the overworked London squadrons a helping hand. They certainly needed it; the weight and intensity of these raids exceeded anything ever seen before.

Day after day great masses of German bombers with enormous fighter escorts tried to battle their way through to the capital.

Sometimes they were beaten back, sometimes a number of the bombers got through, always they suffered terrible losses.

Day after day, battles of incredible ferocity were taking place, often at a height of five or six miles, and the great conflict raged and thundered through the summer skies of southern England.

Many hundreds of German bombers and fighters littered the fields and countryside, and yet each morning brought a fresh wave of enemy aircraft, manned by crews who generally showed a fine determination and doggedness in the face of such murderous losses.

The strain on everybody in Fighter Command was very heavy indeed during this period. There were so many attacks to meet and so few pilots to do it – only a few hundred of us in all, and on many occasions only about half that number were actually engaged. A number of these pilots had only just arrived in squadrons to replace the losses of the previous months. At the end of Dunkirk in June one quarter of the pilots in Fighter Command had been killed, and now, halfway through September, there were not many left of those who had started the summer's fighting. I think the death of one experienced pilot was a bigger loss to a squadron in those days than ten Spitfires or Hurricanes, because however many fighters we lost or damaged, replacements always turned up immediately. This must have demanded the most terrific efforts from both the factories and the ground crews, and though we couldn't see the efforts we did appreciate the results. But experienced pilots could never be replaced. You could only train the new ones as best you could, keep them out of trouble as much as possible in the air, and hope they would live long enough to gain some experience. Sometimes they did.

The Germans were now making some very heavy attacks on our fighter stations, and many aerodromes were bombed till hardly a building of any importance was left standing, yet they continued to function at full operational efficiency. One or two squadrons lost almost all their pilots in a matter of a few days and had to be withdrawn in order to be rested and reformed. To many pilots in the London squadrons, the strain at times must have seemed almost unbearable, and yet everybody held out, badly outnumbered though they were, and at the end of a few weeks it was the Luftwaffe and not the RAF who had to cry halt.

'Hard pounding, gentlemen,' said the Duke of Wellington at Waterloo, 'let us see who pounds the longest.'

In this prolonged and bitter encounter, it was certainly the RAF who pounded the longest – and the hardest.

We did not get our full share of these battles, however, and though we always went towards London and generally patrolled Guildford or Brooklands, we were often sent off with orders to patrol at a low altitude, about 10,000 feet, in order to deal with any dive-bombing or low level attacks.

This was quite sensible, as we had a long way to go and might not have had sufficient time to get up to very big altitudes before the Germans arrived. The London squadrons on the other hand, had ample time in which to get up to 25,000 feet or more, and therefore got a lot more fighting than we did, as the enemy bombers used to take full advantage of the cloudless skies and do their bombing from about 18,000 feet, while their escorting fighters circled above them at anything up to 30,000 feet.

It was always a rather tricky and unpleasant business attacking the bombers while their fighter escort were still in position above. Often it was almost impossible to see them because of the blinding sun, but you always knew that they were there, and as soon as they saw a favourable opportunity, they would dive down and attack. Generally, therefore, we had to try to get in one very quick attack on the bombers and then turn round before the fighters arrived on the scene.

Some squadrons used to do head-on attacks at the bombers, approaching them from the opposite direction, firing at them hard in the split seconds as they drew nearer (their aggregate rate of closing being about 550 mph), and then pull up quickly at the last moment in order to avoid collision. These tactics, carried out with the utmost recklessness and abandon, were generally very successful in destroying some bombers and, more important still, splitting up the formation so that the machines separated, and were then shot down far more easily. Moreover, they rather shook the morale of a number of enemy pilots, and many prisoners, when questioned after capture, said how terrifying they found these attacks.

Certainly, after the offensive had been in progress for a few weeks, enemy bombers showed a much greater tendency to jettison their bombs and turn back when attacked, and this was a great contrast to their earlier showing, when attacks were usually pressed home with the utmost determination.

We were patrolling over south western London one afternoon in early September, during a big raid, and were watching the sky intently, waiting for the Hun to appear. Suddenly somebody said, 'Enemy formation above us on the right'.

I looked up and a moment later saw the biggest German bomber formation that I have ever seen. Like a great wedge in the sky, it moved steadily on, black, menacing, apparently irresistible. Above it, a terrific fight was going on between the German fighters and our own squadrons, but nobody apparently had been able to get near the bombers yet. The whole formation had already passed over London from the east, dropped its bombs, and was now running for the coast as hard as it could, being harassed and worried the whole way by our Hurricanes and Spitfires.

We were too low to attack it and started to climb, and a terrific chase took place all the way down to Brighton. But we had too much leeway to be made up over such a short distance, and they crossed the coast before we managed to get into range, though a number were shot down by other squadrons.

I saw one Hurricane pilot, whose machine had been hit, jump out and open his parachute. Immediately four other Hurricanes made straight for him and circled round and round till he reached the ground, watching carefully to see that no enemy fighter shot him in mid-air.

On 13 September I got four days' leave, and accordingly packed my things and prepared to get away at midday. Geoff and Michael had just come back from twenty-four hours in London and I had a chat with them both before leaving. Geoff and I made the usual arrangement that we always made when either of us got leave, that the one who went away would ring the other one's people when he got home and tell them that everything was ok.

F and I got into the Magister and started it up, and Geoff having bade me give his love to Dorothy, waved goodbye and wandered down to his Spitfire with Michael to check it over.

My last glimpse of him was very typical: in high spirits after an amusing day with Michael, full of zest and appreciation of life, and looking as fit and pink and massive as he always did.

Together we had had a grand few weeks of flying and fighting, sleeping in deck chairs in the sun, playing our rough game of cricket, and spending the usual amusing evenings at the Square Club. Geoff had entered into all this with his usual infectious enthusiasm, and I have never seen him so happy or in such excellent form. Certainly, he never had any premonition of death, and up to the very last moments of his life I believe he was as happy, as carefree, and as gay as he always had been.

And thus, with a few casual remarks and jokes, I said goodbye to the person who had been one of my closest friends for the whole of my life.

F and I took off in the Magister and flew to Peterborough, where I made a somewhat exciting landing in a very high wind and nearly tipped the poor little Magister up on its nose.

F then continued on his way to London, and I walked to the station, caught a train north, and arrived home a few hours later.

Sunday morning, 15 September, dawned very bright and clear, and I remember thinking when I got up that if the weather in the south was as good as this, then the squadron would probably have a fairly busy day. My guess seemed to have been justified when we heard on the 9 p.m. news that there had been a terrific blitz on London, and 185 Huns had been shot down. I wondered how many the squadron had bagged.

The following morning I came into the house just before lunch, and Mother told me that Mrs Gaunt had just rung up to say that Geoff was reported missing. I immediately wired to Michael asking for information, and he replied saying that Geoff had not come back after a fight over London.

I think that the Gaunts and our family also were still pinning a few last hopes on the word 'missing', but I knew perfectly well from previous experience that this merely meant that the body and aircraft had not yet been found or at any rate identified.

I left home the following day and went up to London on my way back to the squadron. I had not been in London since the real 'Blitz' started, and found everything changed very much.

By 8 p.m. very few people were to be seen in the West End, and the bars and restaurants were doing about one tenth of their normal trade. However, I met a very amusing Canadian and we had a few beers together.

I said goodbye to my Canadian friend at about 11 p.m., and walked back to the hotel through practically deserted streets. I could hear one or two German machines quite plainly and the guns were firing at them rather spasmodically, but the whole business was not nearly as spectacular or as noisy as I had been led to believe. I went to bed and slept soundly all night, despite the fact that John Lewis's and various other stores in Oxford Street were hit that night.

Next morning, after a good night's sleep, bath and shave, I bounced down to breakfast in grand form to find everybody coming up from the shelters looking blear-eyed and dishevelled after a sleepless night. I felt rather guilty!

And so back to the squadron to hear all the known details of Geoff's death.

On 15 September, the day of his death, there had occurred the biggest enemy raids yet experienced, and in terrific battles over London and the south east, 185 raiders had been definitely destroyed, besides many more probables and damaged. The RAF losses were about twenty-eight fighters, but only twelve pilots, and Geoff had been one of these.

The squadron took off about 11.30 a.m. and flew up to west London. They were then ordered south east, and at 12.15 they met a very big bomber formation at nearly 20,000 feet over Kenley (just south of Croydon). 609 attacked immediately.

Geoff was one of a section of four machines led by Michael, with Geoff No. 2 and two others behind him.

Michael led the section in against the bombers, but could give only a short burst of fire because a lot of Messerschmitts were coming up from the rear to protect the bombers. So Michael broke away very quickly and the last two pilots in the section, Johnny and Shorty (the American) did not even have time to fire but dived away immediately.

They last saw Geoff following Michael into the attack, and after that he was never seen alive again. He had either been hit by one of the rear gunners in the bombers (Michael came under very heavy fire from them), or more probably, in his intense desire to destroy a bomber, he stayed too long firing at them and was destroyed by the Me 110s from behind.

Apart from this accident, 609 had quite a good day and destroyed several enemy aircraft. 'Ogle', a Canadian, chased a Dornier across London and shot it down near Victoria Station. Incidentally, the Queen of Holland saw this action from her bedroom window and sent a letter of congratulations through her ADC to Ogle.

The squadron were in action again in the afternoon and over the Channel they caught two Dorniers that had dropped behind the rest of the enemy formation. Michael was leading Green section and he decided to do a really pansy attack in the approved style, so he gave the order 'Green section, number one attack, number one attack, go.' He then discovered that there was nobody behind him – they had all dived away and attacked without waiting for orders. So instead of leading a superb charge, he arrived last of all!

The two wretched Dorniers were overwhelmed by the twelve Spitfires and were literally shot to pieces in mid-air. Everybody in B flight was absolutely determined to have a squirt at the Hun, and as a result there was a mad scramble in which people cut across in front of each other and fired wildly in the direction of the Dorniers, regardless of the fact that the air was full of Spitfires. Fortunately, nobody collected any of the bullets that were flying about, and their energy was duly rewarded as each pilot was able to claim one sixth of one Dornier very definitely destroyed!

For four days after Geoff's death we heard absolutely no details of the crash or anything. However, on the Thursday, the RAF at Kenley wired to say that the body and Spitfire had been found near there. The crash had been seen by a number of people, but the machine, having fallen for about 20,000 feet, was absolutely smashed and impossible to identify by any number or letter. Geoff's body was identified only by the name in his collar band. He had made no attempt to escape from the machine, though in such a long dive he would have had ample time, had he been alive.

The funeral took place at Huddersfield on 26 September, and I flew up home in order to be present and also to represent the squadron. Unfortunately, however, the Magister had something wrong with one wheel and though one or two men worked nobly to get it right in time, I was rather late in starting. I landed at Yeadon and raced over to Huddersfield by car, and arrived at the church about fifteen minutes after the service had finished. Everybody had gone.

The grave was still open and I walked over to it and stood there for a moment, looking at the inscription on the coffin of this very gallant and delightful friend.

We had known each other all our lives and been at school together for about twelve years, and after that we were in the same squadron. He possessed a most attractive and vital personality, and entered into everything with the utmost keenness and zest; I don't think I have ever known anybody who appeared generally to derive as much enjoyment from life. And what grand times we have had together – the amusing evenings we used to enjoy before the war, those glorious summer days we spent rock climbing on Scafell and Doe Crag, or sailing unskilfully but with endless amusement in the dinghy on Windermere.

And then, during this last summer, the good days we spent fighting together, having our practice dogfights, playing tip and run, and going out every evening with the rest of the squadron. The memories which I shall always have of Geoff will be those of happiness and laughter and gaiety.

Only a week or two before his death I said to him one evening that if anything were to happen to him, I should feel rather responsible because he was an only son, and I had persuaded him to join the RAF with me. He replied that he would always be grateful to me for my persuasion, because the year that he had spent in the RAF since the beginning of the war had been the best year of his life and he wouldn't have gone into the Army for anything and missed all this glorious fun.

Looking back, I don't think that his death was altogether a surprise to me, because for some time past I had the feeling that he would not survive this war. I had the same feeling about some other friends, notably Basil and Gordon, and two months before Gordon's death I told Dorothy that I was sure he would be killed. She reminded me of this remark soon after she heard of his death.

On the other hand, I am firmly convinced that some other people, Michael for instance, will not be killed. I cannot explain this feeling; it is not based on their qualities as pilots, because they were all good pilots and Geoff particularly so, even though he hadn't much experience of air fighting. But none of us had to start with.

The other fact that impressed me about Geoff's death (and one or two other deaths that occurred soon after) was that they seemed to have no effect on the squadron's spirit. This was a great contrast to the feeling after the casualties at Dunkirk and Weymouth a month or two before. Everybody was naturally very shocked, because Geoff had been so popular, but we were now so consistently successful and strong in our confidence that we had the enemy 'just where we wanted him' that nobody was shaken in the least.

But for me it was the biggest loss that I had ever experienced. I could not believe that such a vital spark was now extinguished for ever, and that I would not see him again. I still can't believe it now, sometimes.

I left the churchyard and went down to see the Gaunts.

They were being very brave about it all, but it was an absolutely overwhelming blow to them because he was their only son. It reminded me only too well of Gordon's death – another only son.

Geoff, Gordon, and I were always very pleased to reflect that three Old Leysians should be together in the same squadron. But I was the only one left now.

I had a pleasant journey down next day and flew through Gloucestershire and over the village where our old FTS was. It was all looking as peaceful and sleepy as ever, and I could see the New Inn where we had spent the whole winter, and the village street and Hartwell's garage, and the stream flowing gently through it all. I could even see the orange curtains in our bedroom.

How much had happened since we were all there together! It was only just over four months since we left, and yet it seemed like an age, because so much had happened in that time.

I got back to the squadron to find that I had missed a lot of excitement the previous day. A very big daylight raid had penetrated to Bristol and 609 had been heavily engaged and got quite a good score, about six confirmed with no losses.

A running fight had been taking place from Weymouth, where they crossed the coast, all up through Somerset to Bristol and then back again. A number of our squadrons were engaged and the Germans suffered fairly heavy losses, though I think on the whole they could claim it as a moderately satisfactory raid.

Shortly after my return, a raid approached Southampton and we took off to intercept it. As we were climbing over the Isle of Wight at about 25,000 feet we sighted the German bombers some distance away to the south, a great mass of machines coming steadily on in very good formation. Above them, ranging up to about 35,000 feet, the Me 109s were circling round and round so that every now and then I could see a quick flash as their wings caught the sun. They were watching us like cats, just waiting for us to attack the bombers, and then the fun would start and it would be the usual hair raising competition to see if we could get to the bombers before the 109s got to us.

The CO swung B flight into echelon starboard and prepared to do a beam attack. God, I thought, now for it. In that instant somebody shouted 'Look out, 109s', and I whipped round just as a whole pack of Messerschmitts tore over our heads not more than thirty feet above us. They came down at terrific speed out of the sun and we never saw them at all till they were on us. We split up in all directions, diving and turning to avoid them. I went down about two thousand feet, and then looked round and saw a few Spitfires forming up again and chasing some Dorniers out over the Isle of Wight. I went after them as hard as I could, but was about half a mile behind, and as we were all going flat out I didn't seem to get much nearer.

One Dornier was rather behind the rest of the Hun formation, and two black streaks of smoke from his engines showed that he realized his danger and was doing everything he could to catch up. A moment later the leading Spitfire (I learned later that it was Sergeant F) opened fire on the Dornier and gave him a long burst. The bomber flew steadily on for a moment and then he turned slowly over on his back and started to spin down. We all watched him; it was rather a shaking sight. Down he went, spinning faster and faster at an incredible rate for such a big machine, and then suddenly a wing was wrenched off. The Dornier gave a lurch and continued to dive, but now turning crazily over and over. The crew must have been all dead inside the cabin, for nobody got out. I saw the other wing and the tail break away, and the fuselage then went straight down like a stone and disappeared from sight. A moment later, looking down, I saw a patch of foam appear on the sea over 20,000 feet below, showing where he had dropped.

We turned back for the English coast, as the other Huns were too far away to catch. It had not been a very satisfactory action for us; as a result of the attack by the Me 109s we were so split up that several people like myself never found a target. However, we got five confirmed destroyed, and very fortunately suffered no casualties. Why those Me 109s didn't kill half of us in that attack God only knows. They can't have been very good; had the position been reversed and we had dived on them like that, not many of them would have seen the Fatherland again.

Unfortunately, the following day Mac had to go to hospital with ear trouble, and the doctors told him that he would not have to go above 5,000 feet in future. This meant, of course, that he could not remain in a fighter squadron, and poor Mac was very sad about it.

So were we all – he had been a grand chap and an excellent flight commander, besides being very successful individually. I am glad to say that he got the DFC a few days later, which bucked him up a lot.

He was the third case of ear trouble that we had in two months. High altitude flying and fighting imposes a very great strain on the ears owing to the rapid changes of pressure when diving from big heights. One day in a fight at nearly 25,000 feet he failed to turn on sufficient oxygen and he lost consciousness almost immediately and woke up again to find he was doing a screaming dive at well over 400 mph and very near to the ground. He managed to pull out just in time, but he had dived nearly five miles in a few seconds and it was this incident which ruined his ears.

On Friday, 27 September, another big raid tried to get through to Bristol and we took off to intercept. When we sighted the bombers we were too far behind to be able to catch them, but they were very well taken care of by other squadrons.

Also the CO had a bad cold and the height caused him such agony in his ears that he had to drop out. He was off flying for over a week as a result of this effort.

Anyway, we continued our patrol, and soon after we saw a squadron of Me 110s circling over Swanage at 25,000 feet, waiting to protect their bombers on their return. We immediately turned towards the enemy fighters and started to climb above them.

They had formed one of their defensive circles, going round and round on each other's tails – altogether quite a tough nut to crack.

Incidentally this was the first time in this war that we had met the enemy on even terms. Generally we were outnumbered by anything from three to one up to ten to one. But on this glorious occasion there were fifteen of them and twelve of us, and we made the most of it.

We were very close to them now and we started to dive. I think that these moments just before the clash are the most gloriously exciting moments of life. You sit there behind a great engine that seems as vibrant and alive as you are yourself, your thumb waits expectantly on the trigger, and your eyes watch the gun sights through which in a few seconds an enemy will be flying in a veritable hail of fire.

And all round you, in front and behind, there are your friends too, all eager and excited, all thundering down together into the attack! The memory of such moments is burnt into my mind for ever.

I was flying just behind Mick and he turned slightly left to attack an Me 110 which was coming towards him. But the German was as determined as Mick, and refused to give way or alter course to avoid this head-on attack. Their aggregate speed of closing was at least 600 mph and an instant later they collided.

There was a terrific explosion and a sheet of flame and black smoke seemed to hang in the air like a great ball of fire. Many little shattered fragments fluttered down, and that was all.

Mick was killed instantly and so were his two German opponents, and hardly any trace of them was ever found.

Poor old Mick! I had known him for a year, as he was at FTS with me. His brother, also in the RAF, was killed only two months before in a raid on Germany.

All this happened in an instant, and I turned right in order to get on to the tail of a Hun. My Spitfire immediately went into a very vicious right hand spin – the atmosphere at these great altitudes is so rarefied that machines are very much more difficult to manoeuvre – and when I recovered I had lost my German.

The whole enemy circle had been broken up by our attack, and various Messerschmitts were streaming out to sea with our people chasing after them.

I saw an Me 110 about half a mile ahead and went after him on full throttle. He also was going flat out and diving to get extra speed, but my beloved Spitfire rose nobly to the occasion and worked up to over 400 mph, and I caught him fairly easily, though we were about twenty miles out to sea by this time.

The enemy rear gunner, who obviously had wind up, opened fire at me at rather long range, though I could see his tracer bullets flicking past me. It is an odd thing when you are being fired at by a rear gunner that the stream of bullets seems to leave the machine very slowly and in a great outward curve. You chuckle to yourself, 'Ha, the fool's missing me by miles!' Then, suddenly, the bullets accelerate madly and curl in towards you again and flick just past your head. You thereupon bend your head a little lower, mutter 'My God,' or some other suitable expression and try to kill the rear gunner before he makes any more nuisance of himself.

I dived slightly to get underneath his tail, as he could not fire at me in that position, and when in range I opened fire. I must have killed the gunner, because he never fired again, though I must have been visible to him at times and at very close range. I put all my ammunition into the fuselage and port engine and the latter started to smoke furiously. To my intense disgust my ammunition ran out before he went down and I thought that I might have to let him go after all, badly damaged though he was.

I should have been able to shoot him down easily, but on thinking it over afterwards I decided that I must have opened fire too soon – always a temptation during a hard chase – and thus I wasted the first part of my ammunition at too great a range.

But at this moment a voice said on the R/T 'Ok, ok, help coming,' and Bishop gradually overtook us and finished off the Messerschmitt, which fell into the sea. Bishop and I were credited with one half each in this affair.

Apart from Mick's death, the whole fight had been a great success and six Huns were destroyed and one or two more probables. I bet that German squadron don't look forward to their next trip over England. I know what we should feel like if we were attacked by an equal number of Messerschmitts and half our squadron was destroyed in four minutes.

From *The Times*, 28 September 1940: 'At one time bombers with escorting fighters crossed the Dorset coast in two waves each of at least fifty machines. They were hotly attacked by AA fire and RAF fighters and six were seen to fall in flames. One had a direct hit from an AA shell and exploded in the air. Three crashed west of Poole and another fell into the sea. The funerals of four German airmen who were killed in an air battle two days ago were taking place during yesterday's air battle.' (This statement is not quite correct. The enemy aircraft seen to explode in the air was actually the collision between Mick and the Me 110, but as it happened at about 27,000 feet the onlookers on the ground naturally could not see exactly what occurred.)

It's a very good thing to instil into the Hun a healthy respect for the RAF!

I remember walking into the mess for lunch and sitting down and suddenly recollecting that at breakfast, only a few hours before, I had sat next to Mick at this very table and we had chatted together. And now, here we were at the next meal, everything quite normal, and he was dead.

That was the one thing I could never get accustomed to; seeing one's friends gay and full of life as they always were, and then, a few hours later, seeing the batman start packing their kit, their shaving brush still damp from being used that morning, while the owner was lying dead in a shattered aeroplane 'somewhere in England'.

The following day was rather cloudy and nothing very much happened except that we were bombed by a single Ju 88 which came over under cover of cloud. Some Hurricanes were up after him and one of them sighted him when about five miles south of the aerodrome. A terrific chase ensued with the Hun dodging in and out of cloud and the Hurricane firing madly at him whenever he could see him. They passed right over our heads at about 1,000 feet; I had never heard a fighter's eight machine-guns firing before except when in the cockpit myself, when the noise is very muffled, and I was amazed! It's the most terrific, tearing, ripping sound, just like hundreds of girls ripping sheets of calico. I must say this Hun pilot was very cool, because, despite the Hurricane on his tail, he still did his run-up towards his target and let go four big bombs. They fell just beyond our mess, made four huge craters in a field, shook everybody in the mess, but did no damage whatsoever. A very lucky escape.

Novi got so excited when the Hurricane started firing that he jumped up on to some sandbags and shouted at the top of his voice to the Hurricane, 'Shoot, shoot!' The Junkers got back into cloud again before the Hurricane could shoot him down, but he had to land about twenty miles away as one of the Hurricane's bullets had hit an oil pipe. So we got him after all.

Just about this time Michael made a joke which I think is worth recording. We pilot officers are not exactly over paid for our services, and Michael suggested the following variation of Mr Churchill's now famous phrase – 'Never in the history of human conflict has so much been owed by so many to so few – for so little.'

Monday, 30 September, was a very eventful day for me and easily the most successful that I had experienced. The weather was brilliantly clear, and when we got up we shook our heads dismally, as we knew there would be a lot of trouble. As Mac used to remark, 'We should have quite a job to keep the Grim Reaper at bay.'

We arrived down at our aircraft about 7.30 a.m., and I walked over to my Spitfire, as I always did first thing every morning, and checked over everything in the cockpit with the utmost care, because if later we got any orders to 'scramble' we always had to get off the ground in such a hurry that we had no time to look at anything.

So I checked over the whole machine carefully, looked at the petrol gauges and turned on the petrol, checked that the mixture control was in 'rich' and the airscrew in fine pitch, set the elevator trim, opened the radiator, turned on the oxygen, and checked it, switched on the reflector sights, checked the air pressure for the gun system, and switched on the camera gun. Everything was perfect, as indeed it always was. I walked back to the hut, put on my Mae West, and started to write up this diary, my daily occupation.

All the rest of the squadron who happened to be on duty were down there too, twelve of us in all, some writing or reading, some asleep, and the rest playing cards. Thus we spent the war.

Soon after 10.30 a.m. we heard the telephone bell ring in the next room, and the telephone orderly ran to our door and yelled in his usual stentorian voice, 'Squadron take off, patrol 25,000 feet'.

I threw this diary into a chair, the card players dropped their hands, and everybody sprinted out of the door towards their machines. All the airmen were running hard too, and by the time I got to my Spitfire two men were already there to help me on with my parachute and then fasten my harness when I was in the cockpit. I put on the starter and ignition switches, turned on the R/T, gave the priming pump a couple of strokes, and pressed the starter button. The engine started immediately, and I put on my helmet and oxygen mask, and within ninety seconds of the alarm coming through we were all taxiing out on the aerodrome. I was leading Green section with Novi and Johnny behind me, and we got out to our taking-off point and turned into wind. I looked round at Novi and he gave me 'thumbs up', meaning all ok, and Johnny did likewise. I dropped my hand, opened the throttle and we all accelerated rapidly over the aerodrome and took off. The rest of the squadron were either taking off or already in the air, and we all joined up and started to climb towards Swanage, nearly fifty miles away.

I used to love flying with the squadron like this. It was always a grand sight to see twelve Spitfires sweeping along together in formation – twelve pilots, fifteen thousand horsepower, and ninety six machine-guns with a total fire power of 120,000 rounds a minute. Altogether quite a formidable proposition!

A few minutes later the controller in the operations room called us up on the R/T 'Hallo, Blue leader, more than 100 enemy aircraft now approaching Swanage, height 20,000 feet.' The CO replied immediately, 'Blue leader answering, your message received and understood.'

We continued to climb – 10,000 feet, 15,000, 20,000, 25,000 feet, and as we got higher, I kept turning on more oxygen for myself and every few moments looking at the dashboard to check the oil pressure, and temperature, radiator temperature, boost pressure, and oxygen delivery. Everything was running like clockwork, always very reassuring when you know that a big fight is imminent.

We were now high over Dorset, nearly 27,000 feet, and rapidly approaching Swanage, when somebody called up on the R/T, 'Enemy ahead on the left'. I looked round and saw a long way in the distance a big formation of enemy fighters circling over the coast. I don't think there were any bombers on this occasion; it was just a very strong fighter patrol sent over to annoy us and destroy as many of our fighters as possible.

Frank (who was leading us that day, as the CO was ill) altered direction slightly and we flew right out into Weymouth Bay and then turned in towards land again, so as to approach the enemy from the sun. This was a clever move, as it turned out.

It was now obviously a matter of moments only before we were in the thick of it. I turned my trigger on to 'Fire', increased the engine revs, to 3,000 rpm by slipping the constant speed control fully forward, and 'pulled the plug', ie pushed the small handle on the throttle quadrant that cuts out the automatic boost control thus allowing one to use emergency full power.

A few seconds later, about six Me 109s flew across right in front of us. I don't think they saw us till too late as we were coming out of the sun. Michael was leading Blue section and I was leading Green, and immediately we swung our sections round and turned on to the tails of the enemy. They then saw us – too late – and tried to escape by diving.

We all went down after them in one glorious rush and I saw Michael, who was about a hundred yards ahead of me, open fire at the last Messerschmitt in the enemy line. A few seconds later, this machine more or less fell to pieces in mid-air – some very nice shooting on Michael's part. I distinctly remember him saying on the R/T, 'That's got you, you bastard,' though he never recollects it!

The victim that I had selected for myself was about 500 yards ahead of me, and still diving hard at very high speed. God, what a dive that was! I came down on full throttle from 27,000 feet to 1,000 feet in a matter of a few seconds, and the speed rose with incredible swiftness – 400 mph, 500, 550, 600 mph. I never reached this speed before and probably never shall again. I have a sort of dim recollection of the sea coming up towards me at an incredible rate and also feeling an awful pain in my ears, though I was not really conscious of this in the heat of the moment. I pulled out of the dive as gently as I could, but the strain was terrific and there was a sort of black mist in front of my eyes, though I did not quite 'black out'.

The Messerschmitt was now just ahead of me. I came up behind him, and gave him a terrific burst of fire at very close range. The effect of a Spitfire's eight guns has to be seen to be believed. Hundreds of bullets poured into him and he rocked violently, then turned over on his back, burst into flames and dived straight down into the sea a few miles off Swanage. The pilot made no attempt to get out and was obviously dead.

I watched him hit the water in a great cloud of white foam, and then turned round to see what was going on.

A few of our Spitfires were chasing Messerschmitts all over the place and obviously a very nice little massacre was in progress, as a few seconds later I saw another Hun go into the sea. I then saw another Me 109 going back to France as hard as he could and I chased after him, caught him fairly easily, and put a good burst into him. He swerved slightly, his cockpit covering broke off the machine and flew just past my head and he then dived steeply.

I waited to see him hit the water, but he was only shamming, as he flattened out again just above the sea, and continued full speed for home, though his machine was now smoking and obviously badly hit.

For the first time in this war, I felt a certain pity for this German pilot and was rather reluctant to finish him off. From the moment I saw him, he really had no chance of escape as my Spitfire was so much faster than his Messerschmitt, and the last few moments must have been absolute hell for him. I could almost feel his desperation as he made this last attempt to get away.

But if I let him go, he would come back to England another day and possibly shoot down some of our pilots. In the few seconds during which all this was happening, I did not consciously make these reflections; my blood was up anyway and I was very excited, but I distinctly remember feeling rather reluctant.

However, I caught him up again and made no mistake this time. I fired almost all my remaining ammunition at very close range, and he crashed into the sea, going at terrific speed, and disappeared immediately. I circled round the spot, but there was no trace of anything.

I now looked round and discovered that I could see the French coast clearly ahead and that I was only about fifteen miles from Cherbourg. England was nowhere to be seen.

In the excitement of the chase I had not realized how far we were going, and I turned round very hastily and started on my sixty mile trip back to the English coast. It seemed to take a long time, and I was very relieved when, still a long way out to sea, I saw the white cliffs begin to appear ahead. One never knows what an engine may do after running it so long on absolutely full throttle and the idea of drowning out in mid-Channel never did appeal to me.

I was now feeling very happy and pleased with myself – I had always wanted to get two Huns in one fight. I approached the cliffs in Weymouth Bay, flying only a few feet over the water at nearly 300 mph, and when I was almost hitting the cliff I pulled the stick back and rocketed over the top to the very considerable amazement of some soldiers who were on the other side. And so back home, flying very low the whole way, generally playing the fool and feeling gloriously happy and elated!

Everybody was safely back and we had destroyed five Messerschmitts – quite a nice morning's work.

In the afternoon there was another alarm at about 3.30 p.m., and again we took off and made for the coast at Swanage, climbing all the time. We passed over Weymouth, and then turned round and approached Swanage down from the sun.

A few moments later we saw a few machines down on our left, which I thought were Hurricanes. However, Frank, who was leading the squadron, told me to take Green section down to investigate, so three of us, Novi, Johnny, and I, broke away from the squadron, and dived down to the left. Unfortunately Johnny's engine was giving trouble, and he could not keep up with Novi and me, and got left a long way behind.

I was still under the impression that these machines were Hurricanes, but as we got nearer I recognized them as Me 109s and shouted to Novi accordingly.

We both attacked together and he opened fire on the last one on the line and shot it down almost immediately. I don't think they ever saw us till we opened fire as we dived on them out of the sun.

They split up quickly and I went after one and gave him a quick deflection burst, which I don't think hit him, but certainly startled him, as he promptly proceeded to take the most violent evasive tactics. For nearly two minutes we dived and zoomed and turned madly all over the sky in a desperate effort to get on each other's tails. It was just like the practice dogfights that Geoff and I used to have together, except that in this case the slightest mistake would probably cost the loser his life, instead of a pint of beer.

But the Spitfire is more manoeuvrable than the Messerschmitt, and I had no difficulty in keeping on his tail more or less, though he was sufficiently quick in his turns to prevent me getting my sights on him for more than a fraction of a second.

Finally, after a dive even faster than before, he zoomed up almost vertically for two thousand feet, going straight into the sun in an effort to shake me off that way. Almost completely dazzled, I managed nevertheless to follow him up and when he did a stall turn at the top I got another quick burst at him without apparent effect.

At the top of the zoom I rolled over on to my back, but the recoil of the guns practically stalled me and I hung there for a second upside down and then fell away in a very drunken dive after the 109. He streaked away in front of me, going hard for a layer of cloud. I went down vertically after him, gathering speed like a bullet and doing a quick aileron turn to get into line again. Outside the cockpit I could see the earth and the clouds and the sky all apparently revolving crazily round my head, but they did so in a curiously detached way because I was conscious only of the small racing object in front.

He managed to reach the cloud below and I chased after him, missed him with another burst, and then hunted him through this cloud for some miles, dodging in and out, and seeing him for a fleeting instant every now and then.

He wasn't very clever about this, and he never changed course in the cloud, and thus, if I lost him, I had only to keep straight on and I would pick him up again.

We tore over Weymouth, going very fast indeed, and passed out to sea. This was his undoing, as he probably thought he had shaken me off and he made the bad mistake of climbing out of the cloud. I climbed up behind, came into very close range, and then absolutely blasted him. He turned over, and spun down into the cloud, streaming glycol smoke, which meant that his radiator had been hit. I dived below cloud but could see no trace of him at all, and I think there can be very little doubt that he crashed into the sea, as he was badly hit and certainly could not have reached France with a radiator leaking like that. But I had not seen him actually crash, and therefore could only claim him as a 'probable'.

My camera gun film showed later that I had him for several seconds in the middle of my sights at very close range, so I don't think he could possibly have survived.

I hung round for a few minutes but saw no other Huns and returned home. The rest of the squadron had not been in action, and so Novi and I were the only lucky ones. He had shot down two of the Me 109s, and the pilot got out of the second machine and tried to open his parachute. One of the rigging lines fouled it however, and it only opened slightly, and the unfortunate German therefore continued his drop with scarcely any reduction in speed, and was killed.

Novi, bloodthirsty as ever where Germans are concerned, recounted this story to us with great relish and a wealth of very descriptive gestures.

This had been a good day for B flight, and we all felt in very good form that evening. Michael, Noel, Johnny and I went over to Winchester and had dinner with the Berrys. We had a very amusing evening together; Major Berry stood us all some champagne and we returned home taking a distinctly rosy view of life. It was one of the best days I ever had in the squadron.

And thus ended that eventful month, September 1940.

46 Roger Hall, Spitfire Pilot, Pilot Officer, British, 152 Squadron

Extract from Roger Hall's memoir, first published 'quietly' in 1975 as *Clouds of Fear*. According to the introduction in the book, the unnamed 'editor' bemoans having to cut two-thirds of the original manuscript, including great swathes of 'vivid combat narrative', material now presumably lost forever. It was reissued (by myself at Amberley Publishing) in 2013, and stands out for its incredibly dramatic and detailed descriptions of aerial combat.

The extract starts with the tail end of a long evening sortie on Tuesday 24 September 1940, and goes on to describe the following day, which is also recounted by fellow 152 Squadron pilot Eric Marrs (see chapter 42) in his letter to his father (dated 1 October). Hall's memoir is graphic and highly personal – he is not afraid of relating to the reader his blind panic and stifling fear. He refers to his fellow pilots only by nickname, so below is a list of who is who. Ferdie, Frederick Holmes; Brains, 152 Squadron's intelligence officer; Watty, Arthur Watson; Bottle, Derek Boitel-Gill; Chumley, Richard Inness; Cocky, Graham Cox; Dimmy, Ian Bayles; Sgt Woolton, Ralph Woolton; Dudley, William Dudley Williams; Boy Mars, Eric Marrs.

Post-war, Roger served for many years with the Air Training Corps (ATC), Kent Wing, helping hundreds of teenage cadets in the area get a taste of Air Force life, including experience of flying gliders and trainer aircraft. Roger Hall was also a long-time supporter of the Battle of Britain Memorial Trust and their National Monument to the Few at Capel-le-Ferne atop the famous White Cliffs of Dover. He was a regular visitor to this site and contributor to events. Towards the end of his life Hall lived alone in poor health and members of the trust were very supportive. When he died in 2002 his nephew Nicholas Hall recounted how at his funeral 'it seemed that the whole of Dover turned out – uniformed cadets, other

RAF associates, neighbours and many civilians from the town which, it seems, had taken him to its heart'.

I could see a single Spitfire in front of me and a little lower. It must be Ferdie, I thought at once, and chased after it to catch it up. It would be nice to go back to base together. When I got closer to it I noticed a white stream of Glycol coming away from underneath. There wasn't very much but it was enough to tell me that the machine had been hit in its radiator. It seemed to be going down on a straight course in a shallow dive. I got to within about three hundred yards of it and called up Ferdie to ask his position, feeling that he would be sure to tell me if he had been hit in the radiator, although he might not have wanted me to know in the first instance. I got no reply and for a second I became convinced that he had been attacked since I had last spoken to him. I opened up my throttle, although I ought to have been conserving my fuel. From the direct rear all Spitfires look exactly the same and I had to get up close to it to read the lettering. I came up on its port side and at a distance of about twenty yards. It wasn't Ferdie. I felt relief. It didn't belong to Maida Squadron at all. It was 'G' for George and belonged to some totally different squadron. I made a mental note of the lettering for 'Brain's' benefit. I closed in a bit to see what it was all about. The Glycol leak wasn't severe. I couldn't think what to make of it at all. Perhaps the pilot wasn't aware of the leak. Perhaps he had baled out already and the machine, as they have been known to, was carrying on alone, like the *Marie Celeste*. Perhaps it was my imagination, an hallucination after the excitement and strain of the past hour. I came in very close to it as though I were in squadron formation and it no longer presented a mystery to me. The pilot was there, his head resting motionless against the side of the perspex hood. Where it was resting, and behind where it was resting, the perspex was coloured crimson. Now and then as the aircraft encountered a disturbance and bumped a little, the pilot's head moved forward and back again. The hood was slightly open at the front which gave me the impression that he had made an instinctive last minute bid to get out before he had died. The wind had blown into the cockpit and had blown the blood which must have gushed from his head, back along the entire length of the cockpit like scarlet rain. I became suddenly and painfully aware that I was being foolhardy to stay so close as this for a sudden reflex from the pilot, dead though he was, a sudden thrust of the rudder bar or a movement from the stick could hurl the aircraft at me. I swung out and left it. I didn't look back any more. Before I left it, it had started to dive more steeply, and the Glycol flowed more freely as the nose dipped and the speed increased.

I thanked God for many things as I flew back away from the din and noise of the battle through the cool and the peace of the evening across the New Forest and above Netley to base. I landed my machine at six-thirty, stepped out and went to the hut.

Brains was very much in evidence and busy collecting reports from different people. Most of the pilots had landed and Ferdie, I was glad to see, was among them. I gave my report to Brains and Ferdie checked it. I was granted two damaged aircraft and Ferdie got one confirmed and two damaged. There were still three of our pilots unaccounted for. P/O Watty was not down and Red two and Blue two were overdue. We were allowed up to the mess in parties of six at a time, for we were still on readiness until nine o'clock. Ferdie and I went together and discussed the events of the last hour or so. We had some supper and then went down to dispersal again to relieve the others. It was unlikely, I was told, that we should be scrambled again in any strength for it was getting late now and the Germans would hardly be likely to mount another large offensive as late as this.

Brains was still down in the hut and was spending most of his time at the telephone answering calls from Group Intelligence and making enquiries from other stations as to the possible fate of our own missing pilots. Eventually news came through that Watty was safe but had been shot down near Southampton on his way back to base. He had been attacked by two Me 109s in this area and his machine had been hit in the Glycol tank but he had managed to force land. He was taken to the hospital there because the medical officer had found a rip in his tunic which, upon further investigation, had revealed that he had got some shrapnel of some sort into his arm. We heard later that Red two and Blue two had both been shot down and both of them had been killed. Blue two had gone down in flames in front of a Me 110 and Red two had pressed his attack too closely to a Heinkel 111 and had gone into it. Both of these were sergeant pilots.

The squadron, according to Brains' assessment, had accounted for eight confirmed aircraft, three probables and seven damaged. There was no further flying that day and we were released at nine o'clock. We went up to the mess as usual and after some drinks we got into our cars and left the camp. We were to rendezvous at the Sunray.

We got to the Sunray after five minutes or so. It wasn't far from the aerodrome and was tucked away at the end of a lane leading from the main Weymouth-Wareham road.

The Sunray was blacked out and it was pitch dark outside when we switched off our lights. We groped our way to the door which Chumley seemed able to find in some instinctive manner. He opened the front door calling to me 'Switch your radar on Roger' and pulled aside a blanket which had been rigged up to act as a further precaution to prevent the light from escaping as the main door was opened. We got inside to find the others already drinking. Cocky seemed to be in the chair as Chumley and I came in and he called out 'Lost again White Section – biggies coming up for both of you.'

The Sunray was an old pub and full of atmosphere. The ceilings were low and oak beams ran the entire length of them. In between the beams, the ceiling itself was made of wood of the same colour. It seemed dark at first but there was a liberal amount of lamps, not on the ceiling itself but on the walls, and these gave a soft light that was distinctly cosy. There were tables of heavy oak around which were chairs made out of barrels, highly polished and each containing soft plushy cushions. Around the walls ran an almost continuous cushion-covered bench, and the windows, from what I could see of them, for they were heavily curtained, were made of bottle-glass and were only translucent. The serving bar in the middle of the room was round and from it hung a varied assortment of brilliantly polished copper and brass ornaments. There were roses in copper vases standing on some of the tables and a bowl or two on the bar itself. There were sandwiches beneath glass cases and sausage-rolls as well. The visible atmosphere in the room was cloudy with tobacco smoke which seemed to reach its optimum height a foot or so from the ceiling where it appeared to flatten out and drift in horizontal layers until someone passed through it and then it appeared to follow whoever did so for a moment. There was a wireless somewhere in the room, for I could hear music coming from near where I was standing.

I was by the bar with the others and I had finished my third pint of bitter and was talking to Cocky. The night was quite early yet and Bottle was standing up at the bar with Dimmy, Chumley and Pete; they were all laughing at the top of their voices and a bit further along was Ferdie listening to what might, I think, have been a rather long-drawn-out story from one of the sergeant pilots, while two others seemed impatiently trying to get him to the point. Ferdie seemed to be quite amused at the process. There were two of our Polish pilots here too, both non-commissioned and their names were so difficult to pronounce that we simply called them 'Zig' and 'Zag'. They didn't seem to take any offence at this abbreviation. They were excellent pilots, both of them.

The wireless now started to play the theme of Tchaikovsky's 'Swan Lake' ballet and when I'd got my sixth pint I mentally detached myself from the rest for a moment.

'Wotcher Roger, mine's a pint of black and tan – have one yourself.' I was jolted back to reality by this, accompanied by a hearty slap on the back from Ferdie, who had wormed his way across to me.

I had my seventh pint with Ferdie and we both edged up closer to the bar where the main body of the squadron seemed to have congregated. It was Cocky who, high spirited and irrepressible as ever, said 'Come on boys, we've had this – next stop the Crown.' We picked up our caps and made for the door. 'Mind the light,' someone shouted as the protective blanket was thrust aside for a moment. The air outside was cold and it hit me like a cold shower for a brief second while I gathered my wits. Chumley piled into the passenger seat. I was feeling perhaps a little too self-confident after the drinks but I felt sure I would make it somehow.

We got on to the main road again and Chumley directed us to the Crown in Weymouth. The road was fairly free of traffic and I gave the little car full rein for a while. It was dark and just in front of me there seemed to be an even darker but obscure sort of shape which I found difficulty in identifying for a moment. 'For Christ's sake, man' Chumley shouted. Cocky's large Humber had pulled up on the verge and its occupants were busy relieving themselves by the roadside, but one of them was standing in front of the rear light and obscuring it. We were travelling at not much less than seventy-five mph when Chumley shouted at me and the Humber was only about thirty yards from us when I recognised it. My slow-wittedness only now became evident but I felt quite confident and in complete control of my faculties as I faced the emergency. I pulled the wheel over to the right, not abruptly but absolutely surely and with a calculated pressure to allow me only inches, inches enough to guide the left mud-guard past the Humber's off rear bumper. At the time I was in full control and thinking how fine and assured were my reactions, how much finer they were now than they ever were when I had had no drink. The sense of complete infallibility and the consequent denial of any risk had overtaken me and the feeling, if anything, became accentuated when the little car had passed Cocky's large Humber, which it did by the barest fraction of an inch, to an accompanying shout of 'Look out, 109s behind' from those who were standing by the verge and otherwise engaged. 'No road sense, those boys,' Chumley remarked.

The Crown was quite a different sort of place from the Sunray. From the outside it was distinctly unpretentious in appearance, just a flat-sided building flanking the back street down by the harbour. It had four windows, two top and bottom and a door in the middle. We went in, and as I had rather expected, it was an ordinary working-man's pub. There were no furnishings to speak of, the floor was just plain wooden boards and the few tables were round with marble tops and the conventional china ash-trays advertising some type of lager or whisky. The bar occupied the whole of one side of the room and the barman greeted us warmly as we arrived. Chumley ordered two pints of bitter. Apparently the squadron were well known and held in high esteem.

The others arrived soon after we got there and the drinks were on me this time. There was a dartboard in the corner of the room and, not surprisingly, we threw badly. What did it matter how we played I thought, as long as we let off some steam.

When we left the Crown at closing time I was drunk, but we didn't return to the aerodrome. Bottle had some friends in Bournemouth and it was to Bournemouth that he'd decided to go. I was too drunk to drive and so was Chumley, who had left the Crown before closing time and taken up his position in the passenger seat of my car where he was now fast asleep. Dimmy and I lifted him out, still asleep, into the back of Cocky's Humber. Dimmy, who, so he claimed, was more sober than I, said he would drive my car. I made no protest. I relapsed into the passenger seat and fell asleep as the car gathered speed towards Bournemouth. I woke up as soon as the car came to a standstill, feeling a lot more sober. It was about half-past eleven when we went through the door of this quite large private house. Bottle's and Cocky's car had already arrived and the occupants had apparently gone inside. The door opened and a girl greeted us. 'I'm Pam, come on in the others are here,' she said. Everyone was seated in or on some sort of chair or stool and all had a glass of some sort in their hand. There were two other girls there besides Pam.

I was beginning to feel rather tired about this time and I would have been glad to get back to camp, especially as I had to be on dawn readiness again. The atmosphere here didn't seem conducive to any sort of rowdery like the Crown or the Compass and the girls didn't somehow seem to fit into the picture. They weren't on the same wavelength. It was about two-thirty in the morning when we finally left.

We arrived back at the mess just after four o'clock, having stopped at an all-night cafe for eggs and bacon and coffee. I had to be on readiness at five-thirty and it seemed hardly worthwhile going to bed, so I decided to go straight down to dispersal, to find I was the only one there. I had just an hour and a half's sleep before I was due to take off on dawn patrol.

Chapter 5: Angels Two-Zero: 25 September 1940 We took off at six o'clock. We were Red Section, and as soon as we were in the air, Bottle called up control to say that Maida Red Section were now airborne. I was flying in port vic of Bottle and was in quite loose formation. I felt much better now that I was in my machine once more. The heavy cloud that had obscured the sunlight an hour ago had now almost disappeared and as we continued climbing in an easterly direction we could see the remains of what must have been a gorgeous sunrise. The horizon itself was purple and the sky above the horizon was the same colour. Above this there were a few wisps of cirrus, brushed delicately with a vivid crimson, and above these were pieces of open sky, pure gold in colour. It was really beautiful. The gold gave way to yellow as it got higher and this in turn to pale green and finally to blue. Among the blue, much higher than we could ever go, was more cirrus, exquisite to gaze upon, golden cirrus, icily remote in the uppermost realm of the atmosphere.

The air was calm and quiet as it so often is at this time of day and our two Spitfires hummed easily along the air paths, not bumping or jolting at all but keeping station one with the other with no effort at all. The world of last night seemed a long way off, and I wondered how, by contrast to this ecstatic feeling I had now, I could ever have descended to the general debauchery which characterised last night's behaviour. I wondered what the alternatives were. Were we to sit in our rooms and read a book, or sit in the mess and do the crossword puzzle or read all about the war, or write letters to our loved ones in case we got no further opportunity, or should we go to the cinema? I didn't think any of these activities would really be adequate as a sequence to the events of the day.

It would be physically possible to sit down by oneself in one's room and read a book after fighting Germans at a great height and at great speed at intervals during the day – but it would be unnatural. I concluded, by a process of eliminating the alternatives, that I should either have to become unnatural and estrange myself from the squadron, or become a drunk by night. It was no longer a mystery to me why fighter pilots had earned such a reputation for being somewhat eccentric when they were on the ground. I knew why it was, and I knew that if I were alive this evening I should get drunk with the others and go wherever they went.

We were now over Portland harbour at twenty thousand feet and orbiting this position. Control had not called us during our ascent, which had taken us a little less than a quarter of an hour.

We continued to orbit in a wide circle the diameter of which, when related to the ground, stretched from Dorchester through Weymouth to some five or six miles south of the Portland peninsular. I was still in 'V' formation with Bottle for there seemed to be no immediate cause for me to get into line astern and start weaving. If I had said this to anyone at the time I should have immediately evoked from them the comment 'famous last words', which was intended to prevent a state of over-confidence.

'Hallo Maida Red one – Mandrake calling – are you receiving me?' 'Hallo Mandrake – Red one answering – receiving you loud and clear – over.' 'Hallo Maida Red one – Mandrake answering – receiving you loud and clear also – I may have some information for you shortly – continue to orbit your position – Mandrake to Maida leader over.' 'Hallo Mandrake, Red leader answering – your message received and understood – continuing to orbit – listening out.' I don't suppose we had been in the air for more than half an hour when this message came through and I can't say that it meant very much to me when it did. I expect it meant something to Bottle. He would probably connect it with events which had followed messages of a similar nature before, but he showed no sign of alarm. Bottle from this distance, about fifty yards I should think, might have been anyone sitting there in his cockpit. His helmet gave him a certain anonymity. He seemed to be doing nothing in particular, but just sitting there in the cockpit of his 'A' for Arthur. If it had been possible to smoke, I'm sure that Bottle would have been puffing away contentedly, elegantly tapping the ash from a cigarette held in its holder into some convenient receptacle, probably the map-case. Such was his composure that I don't suppose he would have bothered to remove the cigarette from his mouth even during a dogfight with half a dozen 109s. Of course this is only conjecture, for one cannot smoke in a single engined aircraft with any degree of safety. The petrol tank and the fumes from it are just in front of you and fumes are highly volatile. Apart from this, one has one's oxygen mask continually on one's face and even if the aircraft is not high enough to warrant having to use oxygen it is necessary to wear it, for the radio-transmitter is incorporated in it. If these limitations did not exist I'm quite certain that Bottle would smoke and I'm dead certain I would all the time.

'Hallo Maida Red leader – Mandrake calling, Vector 090 – Vector 090 degrees – over.' 'Hallo Mandrake, Red leader answering – your message received and understood – 090 degrees it is – listening out.' We set off due east, still maintaining our height of angels twenty. Due east would take us south of Swanage, across Poole Harbour, and up the Solent if we kept on this course. I thought immediately of Southampton. Most of the scrambles for the squadron had been to the Southampton area except those for the London battles.

'Hallo Maida Red leader – Mandrake calling – increase your angels to two-five – there is one bandit approaching 'Bandstand' at angels two-zero from the south – Mandrake to Red leader, over.' 'Hallo Mandrake, Red leader answering – understand angels two-five, your message received listening out.'

Looking at my code card for the day I saw that 'Bandstand' was Southampton, which was rather what I had expected. One bandit at this time of day, so the others had told me, was most certainly a reconnaissance plane either photographing the previous night's raid damage or assessing the suitability of the weather conditions for a raid today or possibly both.

Bottle pulled the nose of his machine up in what I thought was a particularly perilous angle but who was I to say? My airspeed dropped to 120 mph or less and my climb indicator passed the three thousand feet a minute mark. Apart from Bottle's machine on my left, I saw only the sky and wisps of cirrus, now turned silver, high above us. Despite all our vaunted technical mastery we were no match for the cirrus nor would we be for some years to come. We were but insects which had just learnt to leave the ground, angrily scratching about on the earth's boundary layer. We took just over five minutes to get up to our new altitude, and flattened out immediately we got there.

'Hallo Mandrake, Maida leader calling – we are now at angels two-five have you any further information for us? over.' 'Hallo Maida leader – Mandrake answering – your message received – no further information – continue on your present course – over.'

Looking down for a minute I could see the white pointed tops of the needles as they rose out of a layer of mist covering the sea. The Isle of Wight was only partly visible beyond them. The horizon was indistinct and it was difficult to distinguish the sea from the sky, for the whole of the distant background was a sort of slate grey with no apparent depth or perspective to it. Vertically beneath us however, visibility was good. We were now over the Solent and Bottle called up control once more to ask for further instructions. Control told us to orbit our position. We did so.

It was wonderful up there and flying conditions were perfect. We were in a different world, a new world. I felt as though the world of last night had been just make-believe, a two-dimensional world, where little people think that they are bigger than they are, and in so doing become smaller. I wondered if it were possible to feel depressed in this new world and I thought that psychiatrists and mental quacks might be well advised to inaugurate a course of flying therapy to add to their many other therapies.

'Hallo Maida leader – Mandrake calling, bandit is now just south of Battleship – angels two-zero – you should see it very soon – Mandrake to Maida leader, over.' 'Battleship', according to the code card, was the Isle of Wight, I looked in its direction but could see nothing.

'Hallo Mandrake, Maida leader answering – your message received and understood – can't see it yet – will keep you informed – listening out,' Bottle replied. 'Better get into line astern Red two' he continued, speaking to me. I acknowledged his order and slid my machine into position behind him, keeping some distance away. I searched feverishly for any sign of the bandit. I suppose I had instinctively conjured up in my mind the shape of the bandit, I thought it would be a Junkers 88, the others had said that the 'Recce' planes were usually these. Suddenly I did see it, almost exactly as I had expected. It was a Junkers 88 and it was flying almost due north and seemed to be going very fast. At once I called to Bottle 'Hallo, Red leader – Red two calling – there it is – below at three o'clock – over.' 'OK, Roger, I see it, thanks,' came his reply. Bottle called up control and Tally ho'd. Control seemed satisfied with what they considered was their interception and bid us *bon voyage*.

Bottle waited until the German machine had gone past us underneath before going down on it. When it had crossed the Hampshire coast just west of Calshot he said 'All set, Roger? keep well out behind me.' I just replied 'OK Red one.' Bottle turned his machine over on to its back and I followed in the same style. My sights were on and so was my firing button. When I was upside-down I saw Bottle's 'A' for Arthur through the top of my hood going down vertically towards the Hampshire panorama, but for the moment I had lost sight of the Junkers 88.

I wasn't concerned with it, but only with sticking close to 'A' for Arthur. I pulled the stick hard back into my stomach to get my machine into a vertical attitude as quickly as possible. The engine spluttered and threatened to stop but soon caught itself again and I was now following 'A' for Arthur and travelling at over four hundred mph. My controls stiffened up and my ear drums became painful for a minute until I could swallow. I could see the bandit now and it had apparently become aware of our presence too, for it had turned in a wide arc to port and was obviously shedding quite a bit of its altitude at the same time, for it was going at an enormous speed. The Junkers 88 was now going almost due west towards Poole but we were coming down on it rapidly. I was thrilled. The excitement of the chase consumed me and something of the great speed of the moment seemed to infuse itself into my thinking and feeling. I was no longer an ordinary mortal, I was a god. I had the fire power of an infantry battalion at my fingertips and the speed of thirteen hundred horses in my gloved left hand. Nothing could stop the leaden wall that I was soon to unleash and nothing could stem it or stand in one piece before it. What rubbish I was thinking, but that's how it was.

Bottle's 'A' for Arthur started to flatten out below me and I accordingly heaved back on my own stick and disappeared into the night of a sustained blackout and could see nothing. I kept it like this until I felt I was level and then eased the stick forward a little. The black veil dropped from beneath my eyes to reveal 'A' for Arthur just about twenty yards in front of me and not more than two hundred yards behind the Junkers 88. Bottle must be firing I thought, he was well within range. Yes, he was. I could see the tell-tale spirals of cordite and tracer leaving his machine and going straight into the target. The Junkers 88's port engine was on fire already and was leaving behind a plume of black smoke which was now describing a shallow 'U' shape as the machine itself turned to port. We too turned to port and as we did so I could see tracers coming away from its rear-gun but they were quite innocuous for they were going yards to our starboard. The Junkers 88 now turned into a steep tight turn to port and the rear-gunner stopped firing. I supposed that he had blacked out for a minute. We followed and Bottle opened fire again on the turn, giving, I suspect, a lot of deflection to his aim. I hadn't fired yet but was becoming impatient to do so. We were turning inside the German machine's arc and it must have realised that it couldn't out-turn us.

The black smoke from its engine was starting to get in our way as we had to turn through it. We were very close to it and I could at times smell its pungent vapour. It smelled foreign. We continued to turn until at length the Junkers 88 turned completely over on its back and after describing a hundred and eighty degrees on its longitudinal axis now faced the opposite way. It started to pull away to starboard in a contrary steep turn but Bottle had whipped 'A' for Arthur on to its starboard wingtip with the rapidity of a striking cobra and his tracers were now pouring into the German aircraft's starboard engine nacelle. I was still behind Bottle and utterly fascinated by his demonstration. Flames, with a little accompanying smoke burst from the starboard engine and the machine levelled out of its turn as if to say that it had had enough. There certainly didn't seem much else it could do under these circumstances.

We had lost a lot of height since this somewhat uneven dogfight had begun but I hadn't noticed it while it was happening. We were down now to about eleven thousand feet and were somewhere over the Isle of Wight. The Junkers 88 had started to go into a slow spin and was going down vertically towards the sea. 'That seems to have done it,' I heard Bottle say, 'I think we will follow it down to make sure,' he added. We spiralled slowly down after the bandit, keeping a respectful distance from it in case the rear-gunner in a final act of defiance should feel inclined to hit back at us before he snuffed it.

'Why the hell don't you get out, you clots,' I thought aloud, 'you can't all be dead.' Someone ought to have baled out by now, surely. I kept my eyes on the machine the whole time, expecting to see black figures trailing white canopies jump away from it. The machine was still spinning and the spin seemed to become more vicious and faster the lower it came. I wondered how long a comparatively large aircraft could stand this before something snapped. I thought perhaps the crew, if there were any alive, were being prevented from getting out by the centrifugal force that must be exerting itself on them. I could imagine the panic that must have prevailed among them if this was so as the altitude ran out on them. I felt sorry for them. At five thousand feet the aircraft's port wing came off and hovered for a moment almost stationary in the airflow of the bomber and then started to fall like a leaf. 'It won't get home like that, I don't think,' I heard Bottle say in a rather laconic tone. If it had not been so entirely tragic and had no lives been involved, the whole episode might have been almost amusing, especially when Bottle enlivened the drama with a little wit.

As soon as the wing had fallen off the remainder of the aircraft stopped spinning and almost immediately two figures became separated from it, their parachutes as yet unopened, trailing behind them. They hadn't got much further to fall, but I thought they would be all right if their parachutes were good ones. The body of the aircraft hit the water with an enormous splash and at once a white spume of spray rose out of it, hung for a second and cascaded back on to it, settling itself into a white circle about the remains of the Junkers 88, which still floated on the surface. One of the parachutes had billowed out and the little figure on the ends of the shroud lines started to oscillate from side to side, his legs kicking the air as if to stop this. The other man was not so fortunate; he was still falling fast towards the sea, and still trailing behind him was the white unopened canopy. The air seemed to refuse to unfold the pleats. Maybe the body, for body it would soon be, was twisting to such an extent that the canopy was becoming twisted too so that the air could not get into it. The body and the canopy hit the sea together, and again a small spume of water rose to mark the spot and again it fell and covered both. The sea had exacted its toll. We circled over the spot only feet above the water and there was blood on it and among the blood – German blood, but even so human blood – there were bits of a German flying suit.

Bottle called me up to say 'One confirmed, I think, Roger,' and I agreed, but could not feel quite so light-hearted about it as he was. Bottle was used to this sort of thing by now, and I wondered if I should ever get used to it. We started to climb up and when we had got to two thousand feet called up Mandrake to tell them what had happened and also to say that one German aircrew was floating in the Solent at a certain spot and that it would probably be appreciated by the airman in question if some form of rescue were sent. We needn't have worried, for rescue boats were already racing towards the position. The whole of our battle had been witnessed from the coast.

Control seemed pleased with Maida Red Section and congratulated us as we flew to base. We landed at seven fifteen. When we got back inside the hut Brains, inevitably, was there waiting for us. He was looking a bit dishevelled, and had obviously been summoned from his bed at an unaccustomed hour, for he had a roll-top pullover on instead of a collar and tie, the pilot's privilege, and he had certainly not shaved. 'Wotcher Brains … One Junkers 88 confirmed … positions somewhere in the Solent, time … five past seven … number of bursts, three, range … two hundred yards shortening to fifty … two occupants baled out … one dead … the other now in the process of being rescued … anything else you want to know, Brains?' queried Bottle after giving this highly colourful account of our combat to the all-inquiring Intelligence. Brains was not impressed by this version and demanded it all over again. Bottle was always baiting Brains. He took his 'Mae-West' off, took out his cigarette case, put a cigarette into its holder, lit it, got on to his bed, inhaled deeply and said 'Come and sit on the bed and I'll tell you all about it, Brains.' Bottle was as cool as ever; his hands were not shaking as he fingered the long cigarette holder, I noticed. Mine always seemed to shake a bit after flying, whether we had been in action or not. I had not yet acquired that composure essential to an airman. Sooner or later I should just have to if I were to go on flying, or I should quickly become a nervous wreck.

At eight o'clock the whole of 'B' Flight came to readiness and Bottle and I were released to the mess for breakfast. The dawn readiness section normally didn't have to come back to dispersal until after lunch unless there was a major flap on, and so I was able to look forward to a comparatively civilised sort of morning.

I sat in the mess all the morning and read the papers and felt quite relieved to be able to do so. At half-past twelve I had lunch and went down to dispersal to relieve two of the others at one o'clock.

When I got down there 'B' Flight were getting ready to come up to lunch and the remainder of 'A' Flight were coming to readiness. There were Cocky, Ferdie, Sgt Woolton, myself, Dudley and Boy Mars to comprise the 'A' Flight readiness sections. At a quarter past one Red Section were scrambled to angels twenty over Portland. Dudley was leading and Boy Mars was his number two. This was the first scramble of the morning. There had been no flying at all, though the weather had been lovely.

The sun was hot outside and the remainder of the flight were enjoying its heat sitting in deckchairs up against the side of the hut. I was dozing and both Ferdie and Sgt Woolton were reading. Cocky was giving his dog Pooch a hip bath in an enamel basin. I was trying to sleep but I could do no more than doze. Perhaps I should have had a dog to whom I could periodically give a hip-bath in an enamel basin if only to take my mind off other things. Perhaps I should have had a girl whom I could go to visit instead of drinking after we were released at night. Perhaps I would go to see Anne again. I hadn't seen her now for almost a year and we hadn't written to each other for some time. I decided that it would be quite a good idea to get in touch and resolved to ring her up that evening and find out what she felt about it. I must confess that I had given little thought to her or for that matter any other girl since I had started flying. Flying had so totally absorbed me that I felt quite adequate without the opposite sex. In a purely selfish sort of way I had come to regard her now as unnecessary. I was still in love with her but I didn't think anything could possibly come of our association for her mother was quite adamant upon the subject of our ever getting married. I think Anne herself also wanted things to be that way, although she had said when we last met, that she was not certain. She never seemed to be certain. I would ring her up tonight, anyhow.

At about half-past two, over an hour after Blue Section had been scrambled, Cocky broke the silence by shouting 'For Christ's sake, off the deck 'A' Flight.' I was hurled out of my uneasy stupor back into reality. I had no need to ask the reason why 'A' Flight should be off the deck, for a little way off was a formation of almost a hundred German bombers about fifteen thousand feet up, headed in the direction of the aerodrome. The four of us rushed to our aircraft. I rushed to mine with precious little heroism, I'm afraid. I didn't see myself as a St George about to take off to slay the dragon but merely as someone who considered that there would be less danger in the air than on the ground when the bombs started to fall. Why had we not been scrambled ages ago, I wondered as I got into my aircraft, and what the hell had Red Section got up to. Perhaps they had been shot down. But this was no time for conjecture. We must get off the ground as quickly as possible. Cocky and Sgt Woolton as Yellow Section took off first as soon as they had taxied into position and I was frantically awaiting Ferdie's arrival as my leader, White one. Ferdie's machine seemed difficult to start, from what I could see. It would happen now of all times. His propeller was turning but the engine refused to fire. I started to feel panic as the bomber formation drew closer to the aerodrome and I tried to calculate the position from which they would release their bombs in order to hit it. It must be soon now. I tried to repress the impulse to take off without him and orbit the aerodrome to wait for him, and just managed to do so, but I resolved to take off whatever happened if I saw the bombs leave the bomb-bays of the enemy machines, feeling that I should just be able to get airborne before they reached the ground. The bombers were overhead now and still their bombs hadn't been released. If they were going to bomb the aerodrome it was too late now, they would have to make another turn over it. It was evident that they were not going to, for they were well past it now and going northwards. I suppose it was just a coincidence that they had been right over us at all. The oil temperature of my machine was getting dangerously high, as it always did when the engine idles on the ground. I opened up the engine to get some wind into the oil cooler if possible, but it seemed to get even hotter. At last Ferdie started his engine and without further ado was coming hell for leather towards me. I hoped his brakes would work.

As soon as he had turned into the wind he opened up, giving me a cursory wave as he did so. I followed in starboard 'V' formation. We got off the ground in no time at all and as soon as our wheels were retracted Ferdie turned his machine sharply to port in a climbing turn towards the north. 'Hallo Maida Yellow one … where the hell are you … White one calling,' I heard Ferdie calling. 'Hallo, Ferdie … Yellow one answering … due north of base … angels four climbing like a flipping thunderbolt … pull your finger out, White Section' Cocky replied. It struck me at the time that thunderbolts fell to earth, but I let it pass. We were traveling at full throttle and climbing at nearly three thousand feet a minute in the general direction of the enemy formation, which was just visible high up above and in front of us. I could see Yellow Section in front and above us also, going at full boost. Black streams of petrol vapour were coming away from both their engines. 'Better use your energy boost, Roger,' Ferdie called out to me, as he started to increase speed himself.

The makers stipulated that the emergency boost must not be used for more than five consecutive minutes, but now the occasion seemed to warrant the risk. I throttled back, pushed the red half-lever fully forward and then opened up the main throttle again. Immediately the aircraft seemed to leap forward with a jolt, hitting me in the back as it did so, and the engine started to vibrate – black smoke pouring out of each exhaust port. The engine vibration transmitted itself to the entire aircraft and I began to appreciate the maker's instructions. The strain on the engine must have been phenomenal. I opened my radiator to its fullest extent to try to cool it a bit, for the Glycol temperature was rising rapidly and threatening to pass the danger mark. We were gaining on Yellow Section, who, in turn, were getting up to the level of the bombers. Control, for the first time since we had taken off, came up on the air and made some quite unnecessary remark to which Cocky replied pretty curtly.

'Pull your fingers out, Mandrake. What the bloody hell are you playing at? Get off the air, I can see them, you boys should learn to keep awake, stupid clots.' Control had certainly slipped up badly here. We should have been scrambled long before the bombers had got anywhere near the English coast. However, there was nothing to be gained by acrimony now. It was quite clear what we had to do and we were trying desperately to do it. We reached the level of the bomber formation after about twenty minutes and levelled out at sixteen thousand feet behind and to their starboard. There were about eighty bombers dispersed in ten rows of eight machines each and stepped up from front to rear. At about five thousand feet above the formation there were another twenty Me 109s as escort, flying in two lines of ten, line astern of each other. They were making vapour trails. The enemy formation was about halfway between the English and Bristol Channels when we gained their altitude. Yellow and White Sections had now formed up in line astern and we were starting to overhaul the German formation when Cocky called up and said 'OK, chums, prepare for head-on attack.' I wondered how Cocky was going to lead us into this lot for it would have been suicide to have attacked them from the rear in the face of a coordinated battery of rear-guns. I put my goggles on and opened my sliding hood. I hadn't bothered to do this before when going into action although it was advised at OTU, mainly to facilitate the baling-out process and as a precaution against splinters from the windscreen or hood. I did it this time for I had no illusions about my chances of survival against this lot. There were only four of us and I began to feel respect for the law of averages.

Despite this I was still optimistic. I was a bit vague about the break-away procedure following a head-on attack, in fact I had never discussed the subject with anyone, feeling that when it came to the point, it would work itself out. I was at the rear of our formation and black smoke continued to pour out of my engine and I could smell it as it swept past my open cockpit. I had been using my emergency boost for twice the permitted length of time now but I wasn't caring much about the possible effects of this any more.

We were about three miles in front of the bombers when Cocky led us into them with a steep turn to port. I prayed very earnestly as we turned, and placed my right thumb on the firing button. I remember thinking my goggles seemed a bit misty as I slid out to echelon starboard of Ferdie as we completed our turn and were now heading straight for the enemy formation. I opened fire immediately, not aiming at any machine in particular, but at the whole target. It was a compact target, a great juggernaut of metal flying extremely close together and it was difficult to see daylight between the individual machines. The fighter escort above were still in station and had not molested us yet. The four of us were in a shallow echelon to starboard and in good relative formation, being fairly steady and all firing together. Thirty-two machine guns firing at the rate of thirteen hundred rounds a minute for each gun were hitting something, somewhere about that target. We had only seconds in which to fire for we were approaching each other at a speed of not much less than six hundred mph. I was watching for the results of our fire during those brief seconds but could see none. From the corner of my eye I saw Cocky turn his machine on to its port wing and go down beneath the leading rank of the bombers, followed immediately by Yellow two, and then Ferdie started the turn, but being at the rear of the echelon I hadn't done so yet. I thought there was a little more time in which to hit the bombers. I was wrong for I pushed up my goggles from my eyes for a second and saw the sort of thing that one sees only in nightmares or aerial fighting. I was about to collide with the leading bomber of the front row. All I was conscious of was the perspex nose section of a Heinkel III coming straight at me. It seemed as though a single frame of a cinema film had stopped dead as they do when the projector breaks down.

I was in total darkness at once and my body seemed to contract into itself like a concertina. I was certain that I wasn't going to get away with this. If I wasn't going to hit an enemy machine, then the wings of my aircraft were going to come off with the force of the 'G' I was exerting on them. I felt a jolt round about my tail section and I thought that I must have hit it against some part of the bomber and I awaited the consequences. There didn't seem to be any. I still couldn't see anything and my hands were like ton weights on the controls. My aircraft shuddered for a moment. It was a stall shudder. Then the machine whipped round into a spin and I could see again. I could see the ground turning round beneath the nose of my aircraft. The English countryside was going round and with it some barrage balloons above a town. I didn't mind this happening. Nothing seemed to register with me and the aircraft just continued to spin and I made no effort to stop it. My thumb was still pressed on the trigger on the control column and intermittently bursts of fire came from my gun ports, the bullets presumably burying themselves somewhere in the English fields below. I looked at my altimeter and it registered only eight thousand feet. I had lost quite a lot of height during this semi-coma of mine. I felt distinctly shaken and started to take corrective action to recover from the spin which I was still in. I was spinning to port and so I pushed forward the starboard rudder pedal and the spin slowed up until it stopped, but I didn't remove the pressure on the pedal when it stopped and the machine whipped into another but contrary spin to starboard. This spin was faster and more vicious than the first and I applied the opposite rudder to stop it. The machine began to spin more slowly, until it stopped, but my reactions were too slow and again I didn't release the pressure of my foot on the rudder pedal in time, so the machine again whipped over into another spin to port. It spun faster than the last time and even more viciously. What was the matter with me? Had I forgotten how to fly? I thought the tail unit had been damaged possibly. Perhaps I had touched one of the bombers after all. I looked round at it to see if it was all in one piece, and it appeared to be. The ground was getting nearer. It was now three thousand feet off and I made a supreme effort to pull myself together. I must be suffering from some sort of psychological shock, and my reactions had become clumsy. There was nothing wrong with the machine, I had assured myself of that. It was human frailty that was at fault. I pulled myself together, got the aircraft out of its spin and let it continue its dive for a bit to rid itself of any further tendency to stall. When it had recovered flying speed, I pulled the machine up into its level position and found my altimeter reading two thousand feet.

I felt horribly shaken and I just flew around aimlessly for a while to try to regain some sort of self-confidence. I thanked God for many things. I looked about the sky for the others and for the battle but both of these seemed to have passed over and gone. No one else seemed to be in the sky. I realised at once what I must do. If I didn't conquer myself now while I was in a state not far removed from cowardice, then I never would. I should eke out the remainder of my life in a state of nervous apprehension in some sort of institution, and the horror of the leading Heinkel would remain indelibly imprinted upon my mind for ever. I must get back to the battle wherever it was and suffer other experiences which would serve to expunge from my mind the one through which I had just passed.

I started to climb towards the north and immediately began to feel very alone and vulnerable. I also felt very foolhardy. There was no cover, there were no clouds of any sort and the glare from the sun was intense. A few moments before there had been a lot of enemy fighters about me and I could see no reason why there should not be now. A climbing machine labouring slowly up a steep incline is an easy target and an almost impotent opponent. It cannot turn suddenly without stalling, it cannot even manoeuvre without losing precious altitude, and of course the sun is a menace. Unless its camouflage is perfect, and that depended on what the ground beneath it was like, it was an easy-eye-catcher for a lookout flying above.

I was alone in the battle area for the first time. It was entirely up to me what I did now. I could fly straight back to base if I liked. It was so easy to turn back under such conditions. No one could see, no one could gainsay what I would say by way of explanation; technical failure, lack of ammunition, oxygen failure, wireless indistinct, engine overheating. One could invent a host of lies to save oneself from further immediate danger. Why bother to be brave, why stick one's neck out further than was necessary.

Suddenly I was aware and enormously conscious of the real significance of God in my life, and I was alone no longer.

My immediate goal was to regain my altitude. I did this and flattened out, increasing speed as I did so. Self-confidence seemed to flow back into me as I threw my aircraft about the open spaces of the sky, challenging it to do its worst. I could see no sign of the others or for that matter anyone else, German or British. The sky seemed empty, and after some minutes I called up to say that I was returning to base.

I landed to find the other three of our two sections already down and they were amazed to see me when I came into the hut. Cocky said by way of greeting 'Well, if it's not Roger the rammer himself, I thought you were after getting yourself a posthumous VC or something. Why didn't you break below with Ferdie?' he asked. I felt like crying with joy for a moment, then I did my best to explain what had happened, assuring him that my apparent bravado was entirely involuntary and at best could only be described as the result of being a clumsy clot. Cocky had shot a Heinkel III down in flames over Bristol, which the formation had bombed, and Ferdie and Sgt Woolton had both claimed a Junkers 88 each as destroyed. 'B' Flight had taken off about ten minutes after we had and the CO had got one enemy machine but had been hit in his petrol tank by something and had crash-landed near Yeovil. In all, the squadron had been credited with five confirmed and three probables. We had lost two pilots, one sergeant pilot and one flying officer from 'B' Flight – both killed.

47 Witold Urbanowicz, Hurricane Pilot, Pilot Officer, Polish, 303 Squadron

Account contributed by an anonymous Polish RAF fighter pilot to an anthology of first-hand accounts of Poland's fight against the Nazis and first published in early 1941.

Like other allied airmen from occupied Europe, Polish Air Force pilots had a difficult time reaching England after their country had been overrun in late 1939. The Polish pilots were experienced and well trained and performed exceptionally well during the Battle. Despite only becoming operational in late August, 303 Squadron, the first all-Polish squadron, was one of the highest-scoring in the Battle of Britain. Fighter Command was initially dubious of the usefulness of Allied airmen who couldn't speak English and didn't know the 'ways' and systems of the RAF. Non-Poles were put in charge of the Polish squadron. They would soon be proved wrong. The Polish pilots stood out in fact, firstly in their level of experience (most had been in the Polish Air Force before the war) and secondly in their aggressive tactics and hatred of the enemy. The latter was understandable as these pilots had witnessed first-hand the brutal treatment of their fellow countrymen and families at the hands of the Nazis during the blitzkrieg unleashed on their homeland.

The pilot is Pilot Officer Witold Urbanowicz as the byline of the piece is 'Pilot Officer W. U. of Fighter Squadron No. 303'. Urbanowicz was the top-scoring Polish pilot in the Battle of Britain with fifteen kills. 'Flying Officer Pashko' is Flying Officer Ludwik Paszkiewicz, who was also a member of 303 Squadron and flew a Hurricane with 'M' as its call sign (which formed the suffix or prefix to the squadron code on the two sides of the fuselage of the aircraft). The sortie took place on 27 September 1940, and 303 Squadron were flying from RAF Northolt, west London (11 Group). This is the day the official records note Ludwik Paszkiewicz as having been shot down and killed. There are some discrepancies between this account and Battle of Britain reference books but this should be viewed in the context of these reference books (which decant combat reports and squadron operations record books into a chronological record of the Battle) also contradicting one another in turn. Record-keeping during wartime was imperfect. Witold Urbanowicz settled in America and died there in 1987.

The fighter pilots were standing by, fully dressed for battle, and ready to take off at a moment's notice. The day was warm and sunny, and the crews and ground staffs of the squadron were lounging in front of the hut; some resting in deck chairs, others stretched out on the grass.

We were all in high spirits. Only Flying Officer 'Pashko' seemed to be out of sorts, perhaps because during his previous flight there had been 'nothing doing'.

We were chatting about air attacks, about single fighters and mass attacks, and exchanging experiences, when someone casually observed that it would be interesting to know the individual preferences of each of us. I turned to 'Pashko' and asked him what was his greatest desire.

'All I want is that my last shot should not be wasted. Apart from that ...'

The telephone bell cut him short. The operator on duty lifted the headphones and shouted the order 'Take off!'

In two minutes the squadron was up in formation, one flight behind the other, heading for the south east of London. 'Pashko's' flight followed flight No. 1. The squadron climbed to 25,000 feet before reaching the Thames estuary. Visibility was good; only tiny white cloudlets were brushing past our wing-tips. Presently we could see the shining surface of the Channel, and beyond it the shadowy blue outline of the French coast.

On our left we had as neighbours two British fighter squadrons, which climbed as fast as we did. From the moment of taking-off we were directed by wireless, but soon our radio began to register the sharp, rapid sound of Morse signals which often warned us that the enemy was near.

Our squadron received the order: 'Course 110 degrees!' but soon afterwards we heard: 'Change course to 120 degrees: Enemy bombers approaching you from south east. Height, 25,000 feet.'

The squadron gently wheeled to the right, and immediately in front of us we saw a group of enemy bombers flying in the direction of London. At a glance I estimated their number at about sixty. Above them glittered the yellow-nosed Messerschmitt 109 chasers, of which there were a great many. They certainly outnumbered us.

The squadron hovered lightly, while our formation loosened into flights of threes, and changing into battle order turned in the direction of the barrage thrown out by our anti-aircraft batteries. I released the catch of my machine guns.

The enemy's bombers were flying in flights of threes in a tight formation, which is difficult to disperse, and the protecting Messerschmitts that were circling above the bombers were grouped in twos or fours.

Our squadron gained the necessary superiority in height to give it a convenient position for attack, which is most effectively launched frontally from above at an angle of about 120 degrees.

The first machine of our squadron rolled over on its right wing, followed by the second and third machine, and then by the second flight, and the third, making straight for the German bombers. Our machine guns, housed in the wings, belched forth streams of bullets. Our squadron cut through the enemy formation, followed by the two British squadrons. The German formation was broken. I could see several of the Heinkels dropping out, leaving a trail of heavy black smoke. Single enemy bombers attacked by individual fighters attempted to escape by zigzagging sharply: but they were too clumsy for our agile fighters. We just sat on their tails until a burst or two sent them down.

Some of the German machines attempted to break off and turn back, but they could not escape. In the general mêlée of dog-fights the sparkling tracks of the machine gun bullets cut across the white smoke streaks issuing from the exhausts, and soon one more enemy bombing expedition against London was broken up.

At this very moment, however, the yellow-nosed Messerschmitts poured down and attacked us. The air became one great quivering confusion of planes, flying in threes or singly: Hurricanes, Messerschmitts, Spitfires, and Heinkels. The black crosses flashed menacingly before my eyes, followed by the red and white circles, the markings of our own Kosciuszkos and of the British fighters. Three or four burning machines left a parabolic trail of black smoke in the sky as they tumbled helplessly to earth. I could see a number of poor devils who had baled out. The white cupolas of the parachutes were clearly visible against the green background of the earth.

One flight of three German bombers, taking advantage of the general confusion, turned sideways, and I could see them making in the direction of a chimney stack close to the river. I was going all out, and decided to cross their path. I was getting my sights on them, when suddenly, like a flash, one of our Kosciuszkos, with the letter M painted on its frame, overtook me, diving from above and going straight into the three bombers.

I could not observe the exact sequence of the events which followed. At one moment I noticed a torn mass of the frame and a few yards away a fragment of the wing of a Heinkel III, but the next moment I could see a Hurricane spinning down and leaving a dense streak of smoke behind it. It was the Kosciuszko Hurricane bearing the letter M.

By this time the other two German bombers were already far away, making for home. It was time to return. Our machines were flying singly at different levels, but in a northerly direction. I received by wireless the order: 'Return. Land.'

All my ammunition was spent by then, and automatically I secured the catch of the guns. One more wide circle, and I was off for home.

On landing I learnt that Hurricane M was 'Pashko's'. Though he was killed not on the Vistula but on the Thames, he knew that his last shot was not wasted.

Part 4
The End of the Battle
October – December 1940

48 John Simpson Part 2, Hurricane Pilot, Flight Lieutenant, British, 43 Squadron

Simpson's final series of letters covers 14 September to late November and begins with a letter to Hector Bolitho while on leave convalescing from wounds received when he was shot down on 19 July.

'Killy' is Flying Officer John Kilmartin (Irish, twelve kills in 1940), and the two Czech pilots are Jaroslav Sika and Josef Pipa, both of whom survived the war. The letters are very personal and dwell on the loss of his friends and colleagues in his squadron and elsewhere in Fighter Command. His attitude towards Germans hardens noticeably over the course of the Battle of Britain. He became an ace during the Battle of Britain and survived the war with ten confirmed kills. He died in 1949.

14 September 1940 On leave recovering from wounds, Cornwall For two days I have been thinking of Caesar [Hull, KIA 8 September]. I loved him as I would a brother. He was more than a rare person in the RAF, and there can never be anyone to replace him in character, charm and kindliness. We came to 43 together and grew up in it together. We knew each other from A to Z and it was a privilege no one else could share.

This hell cannot go on for ever. And reassure yourself with the feeling and knowledge that we do the same to them. I was glad I was here, in a quiet, calm place when the news came. I swim and fish with the wonderful old fishermen, and I walk miles into the woods every day. They are full of giant hydrangeas and wild orchids.

I had a wonderful letter from Mummy. My God, her courage is astounding.

I go down to the Sloop at St Ives for my glass of beer. The fishermen are there and some of them saw me in my uniform on the day I arrived. They are so grateful to the RAF it is frightening. Their stories of the sea and of their own courage, which they tell without realising what they are saying, put any bravery I thought I had in the shade. They make me feel very humble.

I have received my golden caterpillar for the parachute jump.

It is very pretty and it has two rubies for eyes. I am looking forward to wearing my uniform again so that I can show it off.

Your letter about Caesar. I don't know what to say. I thought I was quite used by now to people dying. Do you realise that there are only three of us who were with the squadron when the war began ... still alive and serving with the squadron? But Caesar was like a brother. I went for a long walk in the woods when the news came and I cried for the first time since I was little.

Poor 43. But we can take it. We will have to begin all over again. New CO new pilots. But the squadron spirit is safe. Dear old Caesar. He commanded the squadron he began in as a pilot officer. I would have loved to fly with him as my CO.

It seems funny to think that I shall never see him shaking that left foot of his as he used to do when he was excited. And how he used to rub his nose between his thumb and forefinger when he was nervous. And that laugh!

He had a good life and I think that he loved every minute of it. I never heard anybody say an unkind thing about Caesar and I never heard him say an unkind thing about anybody else. One can't say more than that, can one?

c. *30 September 1940, John visiting Hector Bolitho in Essex before his return to 43 Squadron.*

Hector: Soon after breakfast eight Hurricane fighters rose from the aerodrome, five odd miles away. For me the war had been limited to raids on London and I did not realise the full horror of what was to come. But John knew. He could hear the drone of the German bombers and their escorts coming from the east. We went back to the garden and lay on the grass, with our hands beneath our heads, looking up. John suddenly pointed and said, 'Look!'

A German bomber was hurtling down from the sky, with a scarf of smoke at its tail. It dived into a distant field. We heard the explosion as it hit the ground. Then we looked up. High in the sky, four parachutes were floating down... lovely, flower-like parachutes, with men swinging to and fro beneath them.

The sound of machine-gun bullets guided our eyes. Over our heads were two formations of bombers surrounded by fighters ... the fighters darting backwards and forwards so that it was not easy to know if they were ours or theirs. The bombers moved towards the aerodrome and then we heard the thud of the bombs. Debden was getting it.

Then another bomber was flung out of the pattern above us ... flung so that it crashed into a thousand pieces. Then a third fell and the flaming pieces of fuselage made a dangerous rain over the garden. All six of the enemy came down ... before they could recross the coast. Two of ours limped out of the battle and crashed among the distant trees.

We went into the fields to watch the parachutes slowly descending. Then we jumped into the car and sped down the narrow Essex lanes. The hedges bristled with guns. It was strange how the whole countryside had suddenly awakened ... the sleepy acres of farmland became belligerent. We left the car and ran through clover with the old farmers, to wait for the Germans to land. In one hollow we came upon a burning Messerschmitt. I shall never forget the fierce core of the flame. There was no vestige of the crew.

John and I followed an old farmer we knew. He had seen a German land ... the fluttering parachute settling slowly into the stubble. He was a few yards ahead of us, so we left him to his victory.

He peeped through the hedge, to be certain first that his prisoner was not holding a grenade. Centuries of peace had not dulled the edge of his valour or his caution. He was a fine old man, with a beard and quick eyes. He climbed through the hedge and captured his man.

John and I drove back to the house. When we went down to the pub in the evening, John was no longer the only hero in the village. The old farmer was there and he was stealing John's thunder. We gathered about him as he said, 'That German! He was no more than eighteen years old. A boy, you might say. Trembling all over. I was working in the field when they came. And he landed in the next field. I heard tell what they did with they hand grenades so I looked through the hedge first and I saw him walking away, you see, so I ran after him, you see, and I called after him. I said, "Hey!" and he stopped and put his hands up and young George took his revolver and we took him over to the cottage.'

I asked him then, 'Did you feel angry? Did you feel that you would like to shoot him?' He answered, 'No, oh, no. He was a trembling sort of boy. So I just took him back to my cottage until the military came for him. He could not speak English, but he understood when I said, "Cocoa." So my missus made him a cup of cocoa.'

As we drank our beer, the old farmer added a footnote to the story. 'You know, women are queer creatures. All my wife said to me was, "You should have brought home the parachute as well. They're made of fine silk and it would have given me blouses to last me to Doomsday."'

On the way back to the house, John was critical.

'Those cups of cocoa must be stopped,' he said. 'It bolsters up their arrogance.' And then he told me a story. 'Only last week some friends of mine took a German prisoner into the mess and gave him drinks and were kind to him. After he had gone they found out that just before he forced landed, he had flown around one of our pilots while he was descending by parachute and shot him down. These farmers have got to be taught that it isn't all just friendly fun. I have no qualms now in killing Germans. I have seen so many of my own friends shot down that I can't be sentimental any longer.

c. *October 1940* I am as tired as I was two months ago. None of the pilots here are operational. Czechs and Poles for the most part, who cannot speak English and who understand very little.

c. *October 1940* I was wrong about the Czechs and Poles. I suppose I was a bit depressed, finding so many new people. It did not seem like the old 43. I miss Caesar and the others terribly. Thank God for Killy. He is like Laurie in many ways. Nice, unreasonable Irish. He knows all the old jokes and slang and the songs we used to sing. So we are like a couple of old veterans, sighing for the old days and snorting at the young. But I took your lecture to heart. It is very good for all of us having to work and fly with the Czechs and Poles. Their flying is wizard and they are grand.

Killy has three Poles in A Flight and I have two Czechs in mine. They are Sergeants Sika and Pipa. Nice names, don't you think! Sika and Pipa. They are grand pilots and very keen to go south and have a smack at the Hun.

You were right. The Poles are the most amazing people. They hate so passionately. One of them has a very sad face. Sometimes I see him sitting in the mess, and he runs his hands over his face, and sighs.

And what my two Czechs have been through! I'd like to feel that every Englishman would face the same for his country. These boys went through all that happened in Czechoslovakia, then to fight in France, and then escaped and made their way to this country. It shakes one to the core ... seeing patriotism like that. They both wear the Czech war cross and the French Croix de Guerre. Sika, who flies with me as my No. 2, is a charmer, but very naughty. Now that we can talk easily I find their sense of humour not so very different from ours. We laugh at the same things. I am teaching him to sing some of the Air Force songs. You should see his face when he tries to sing: *We are the fighting 43, Up from Sussex by the sea ...*

His English is now quite good. The Czechs seem to pick it up very quickly. I am going to the sergeant's mess to drink with them tonight. I'm told that they drink spirits neat.

It has been interesting to see the way everybody now likes them. I suppose we are a lot of stodgy Englishmen, imagining that foreigners are difficult. Now everybody likes the Czechs and the Poles and the ground crew are wonderful with them. All out to help. It is good to see the fitters leap to it and treat Sika and Pipa with just a little more kindness because they are strangers. As Killy says, 'It's a good thing.'

The Poles are very intelligent. Tom Morgan, Killy and I took them to the local last night, and by the end of the evening they had taken possession of the pub. We were given bacon and eggs and beer with the owner and his wife. And they were both so charming to the Poles. They were very touched and the quiet one, who sits in the mess alone, was obviously moved. They kept saying, 'Sank you' and one of them bowed over the pub lady's hand when he said, 'Goodnight.'

Now that we are all settling down, the spirit of the squadron is incredible. After all those knocks! Killy and I feel very pleased about it. The 43 spirit can never die, however much it is mauled.

30 November 1940 Our work here is local defence and the defence of the coastal areas where occasional Huns might snoop about, hoping to tell their headquarters the position of our convoys. By catching them in time, before they can transmit the good news, we may ward off a big attack. Sometimes in bad weather, a sneak raider will come in under cover of the cloud and drop a stick of bombs on a shipyard. We are here for all these things, and to rest while we are pulling ourselves together again.

Now I'll tell you what happened. I was at readiness with my flight in the early afternoon. The weather was lousy, low cloud at 200 feet and visibility the width of the aerodrome. It did not seem likely that anything would happen so we were not at instant readiness. We were sitting in the dispersal hut, rather cold, browned off and hating life. I was asked for on the telephone. There was a report of one aircraft off the coast near Newcastle. I was asked if I could send off two aircraft to have a look for it. I did not like the look of the weather so I decided to go alone. The little Czech Sergeant, Sika, was very fussed. He is my No. 2, and I find that now we are getting over the language difficulty I understand him much better. He is very keen and his eyes sparkled and then went sad when I said he could not come with me.

I took off through the mist and cloud. It was filthy. I flew out to sea and at about five thousand feet, I emerged into bright sunlight, above the clouds. The surface of the clouds below me was perfectly level. I am told that this has something to do with atmospheric conditions near big industrial areas, but that is all too clever for me. Well, I did not know where I was. I was told over the R/T where to go and after about fifteen minutes I saw an aircraft. It was also flying over the top of the clouds, going east. I felt that it must be a Hun. As I closed on him I recognised it as a Ju 88. I was about a quarter of a mile away and above him. Apparently he had not seen me. I closed in, fired and hit his starboard motor. He dived for the clouds, but I fired again from closer quarters. This stopped his starboard engine and pieces fell from his port wing root. He waffled in the air banked over and dived steeply into the clouds. It was too risky in that weather to follow him. So I fixed my position over the R/T and returned with some difficulty. I could only claim a 'probable' but I hoped that that dive was his last. Fortunately for me, the Hun had crashed through the cloud into the sea, near to a trawler. The captain reported that a Ju 88 had crashed near by and as the time was the same my 'probable' became a 'destroyed.'

49 David Crook Part 4, Spitfire Pilot, Pilot Officer, British, 609 Squadron

Final extract from Crook's memoir, covering most of October when 609 Squadron were operating from RAF Warmwell, Dorset (10 Group). Crook was KIA on 18 December 1944. His Spitfire was seen to crash into the sea off Aberdeen, and his body was never recovered. He had ended the war with four kills and two shared kills, all during the Battle of Britain.

In the first few days of October, to our very real regret, the news came through that the CO was leaving us. He had been promoted wing commander and was going to command another station.

We were all delighted to hear, just before he left, that he had been awarded the DSO.

We expected that Frank, A flight commander, would take command of the squadron, and certainly it would have been a very good thing, because in the CO's absence he always led us so well that everybody had complete confidence in him.

However, the powers that be decreed otherwise, and we got Squadron Leader R, who proved to be a very good CO and an excellent leader. He was a pilot who, about two months before, shot down two Me 109s, and having finished his ammunition, saw a third 109 and chased it for forty miles, and finally so frightened the German pilot by making dummy attacks at him, that he landed in a field and was captured. The CO then threw him a packet of Players, waved, and the German waved back, and then he flew off. A very cool bit of work!

We had a terrific farewell party the night before the CO left. Pamela and Maurice came over for the early part of the evening, and we adjourned to the Square Club. We then came back for dinner in the mess and went down to the CO's house, where a large barrel of beer had been installed for the occasion, and a very good and rather rowdy time was had by all.

The next morning the CO came down and bade us all goodbye and good luck, and said how proud he had been to command such a grand squadron. He stood there, looking exactly like a rather sheepish schoolboy, while we all sang 'For he's a jolly good fellow' at the top of our voices, and then he drove off.

That afternoon we took off to do some practice flying, when we came in to land again and put our undercarriages down, only one of Novi's wheels would come down and the other remained locked obstinately in the raised position. Try as he would he was unable to move it. This meant that it was very dangerous to land, as one wheel would hit the ground and the Spitfire – still doing about 75 mph – would then somersault towards the missing wheel. I called him up on the R/T and told him that he must not land but instead climb up and bale out.

I was flying very close to him and we climbed up to 5,000 feet over Salisbury Plain, and then Novi opened his sliding hood, took off his helmet, undid his harness and prepared to abandon ship. However, he seemed to experience some difficulty in getting out of the cockpit into the slipstream, and finally he turned the machine over on to its back and dropped neatly out of his seat. The Spitfire promptly dived into the corner of a small wood and burst into flames. Novi, after fumbling for his release cord, opened his parachute, and a few minutes later he dropped into the middle of a hen run, to the consternation of the poultry.

People seemed to spring up from all over the place and rush towards him, and so I circled the spot for a few minutes, as I thought that, with his rather broken English, he might be mistaken for a German parachutist. But everything was ok. We sent out a car to collect him, and half an hour later he was in the mess again, none the worse for his experience except for a bruised arm. The machine that he had been flying was not a very good one – it was rather old and slower than the new ones – so we were all very grateful to him for writing it off!

The following day, 6 October, was misty and rainy and we sat in the mess, read the papers, and had a beer before lunch. The weather seemed so thick that obviously no Hun would get over – or so we thought.

However, at about 12.30 p.m. the loudspeakers announced that an enemy aircraft was approaching us in the clouds. We could do nothing about it, as we could not possibly intercept him in such weather, so we ordered another beer apiece and were rather amused by the whole business.

A few seconds later we all heard a very sharp whistle, and everybody in the mess – about thirty people in all, lounging in armchairs and reading the papers – suddenly threw themselves with astonishing agility on to the floor. I remember that Michael and I met with a crash under the table and spilt all the beer, while our intelligence officer, McK, who is too fat to get underneath anything, merely lay hopefully on his back.

There were two big flashes outside the window, and two terrific explosions that seemed to rock the whole building to its foundations. We cowered and waited expectantly for the next, but nothing happened and we rose cautiously to our feet.

No windows were broken (except one in the billiard room, where Johnny was just playing a shot as the bomb dropped, and he was so surprised that he slung his cue through the window).

The bombs had fallen in a field just in front of the mess. We walked over to inspect the craters, picked up a few splinters and wandered back and ordered more beer before lunch, to replace that spilt in the rapid dive on to the floor.

The following day, Monday, 7 October, dawned very bright and clear, and we expected trouble from the moment we got up.

But nothing happened till about 3.30 p.m., when we were ordered off to patrol Weymouth at a height of 25,000 feet. We took off and climbed up steadily in a south westerly direction, trying to get as much height as possible before reaching the coast.

I don't think I have ever seen such a clear day in my life. From 15,000 feet I could see Plymouth and far beyond into Cornwall; up in the north the whole coast of South Wales was clearly visible, from the Severn at Gloucester and away beyond Swansea in the west, while on our left, to the south, the Channel glistened and sparkled in the sun, and the French coast and the Channel Islands, although seventy-five miles away, seemed to lie just under my wing tip.

But I can't say that I appreciated this superb view very much under the circumstances, because I was busily engaged behind the squadron, anxiously scanning the sky for the Messerschmitts which we knew would soon be arriving.

The sun was so brilliant and dazzling that it was very difficult to see anything clearly in the glare, and yet this made it even more important to maintain the utmost vigilance, as the Me 109s are very good at jumping on one out of the sun.

When we were almost at Weymouth, at about 20,000 feet, we saw an enemy bomber formation some miles out to sea, and at the same moment, various people saw a lot of Me 109s above us, apparently about to dive down and attack us. About four people at once started to shout warnings on the R/T and there was a perfect babel of excited voices, which rather added to the confusion.

B flight was rather behind A flight, and we started to break up, as it is quite hopeless to watch enemy aircraft above and behind, and at the same time keep in formation with the rest of the squadron.

I hardly saw anybody again for the rest of the action, and most of us never engaged at all. Several of us continued to patrol for about half an hour, by which time the whole affair was obviously over and operations room told us to land. When we got back we found that A flight had been rather more successful. Being in front of us and therefore to some extent guarded by us, they managed to keep together, and they attacked a formation of Me 110s and destroyed five or six of them. We now had a very anxious half hour, as four pilots were still missing. However, some news soon started to come through – John's machine had been hit by a cannon shell from an Me 110 which came up behind him as he was engaged in shooting down an Me 109. The shell burst in the wing, and put a lot of little splinters into his side, but he wasn't badly hurt and landed safely and returned to us the next day. Mike got a bullet in his leg, and baled out and landed near Blandford, where they took him to hospital, and he was ok, though with a rather big hole in his leg.

Frank shot down an Me 110 in flames, but the rear gunner managed to hit Frank's engine and he had to land in a field.

Within two minutes a crowd of people had sprung up from an apparently deserted countryside, and offered him cups of tea and coffee. The police and soldiers then arrived on the scene, and had a great argument as to who should give him a party that night. The police won, and bore Frank off in triumph to the local pub, where the police and the inhabitants plied him (and themselves) with pints of beer for four solid hours and then drove him back and delivered him into the mess in a distinctly intoxicated condition.

Well, that was three out of the four safe, but Sergeant F was still missing. We waited for some hours, hoping to hear that he had landed somewhere, but later that evening somebody rang up to say that his body had been found. He was last seen by us when attacking the Me 110s, and his machine must have been hit, because a number of men saw his Spitfire spinning down from a great height.

He recovered from the spin, got into another one, recovered again, spun again and then apparently decided to get out. But he had left it too late, because his parachute did not have time to open properly and he was killed by the fall. He had not been hit at all and if only he hadn't stayed so long in the damaged machine he would almost certainly have got away with it.

A great pity, as he was a very good and resolute pilot, and had been all through the summer's fighting.

Weymouth certainly seemed to be an unlucky spot for 609. Apart from the Dunkirk casualties, we lost eight pilots during the summer, and seven of these – Peter, Pip, Gordon, Buck, G, Mick, and Sergeant F were all killed in the south west.

Only Geoff was killed near London, and when one considers how much fighting we did both in the London and Southampton areas, it does seem curious that all our losses should occur in one place.

[By a very tragic coincidence, on the afternoon that this paragraph was written, 28 November, both John and B were killed over the Isle of Wight during a raid into Southampton. The last heard of John was when he called up on the R/T and said that he had shot down an Me 109. He never came back and a few days later the German official communiqué said that one of their most successful fighter pilots, Major Wieck, had been shot down by an English fighter near the Isle of Wight, and that the English machine itself was immediately shot down by another member of the German formation. As no English pilots claimed any victims in this fight, Major Wieck must have been the Messerschmitt pilot that John spoke about on the R/T, and this has since been confirmed by the Air Ministry.

B also just disappeared, and two months later, in January, Berlin sent a telegram to the Air Ministry via Geneva, saying that his body had been washed ashore at Boulogne and buried there.

John was the most successful pilot in the squadron and an exceptionally good fighter pilot. He was given a bar to his DFC shortly after his death, and I don't think an award was ever better deserved. He possessed also a brilliant intellect and was a well known journalist on the *Yorkshire Post*.

I did not know B so well, as he had not been in the squadron for long, but I liked him and the loss of these two was a big shock to everybody.]

A few days later I got five days' leave and again flew to Peterborough and caught the train north from there. Dorothy and I spent a very happy few days at home. As usual, I caught the afternoon train from Wakefield and arrived in London nearly two hours late, as there was a big raid in progress. It was almost impossible to get a taxi at King's Cross, but finally about six of us crowded into one, and drove through the dark and deserted streets to Piccadilly. There was a lot of gunfire, and every now and then the deep 'whoom' of a bursting bomb could be heard.

I walked round to the Trocadero and had some dinner and then met an amusing Canadian soldier (I always seemed to meet Canadians on my evenings in town). We had a few beers together, and then decided that we could do with some bacon and eggs. It was just about midnight and we walked round to Lyons' Corner House in Coventry Street, and ordered our food. We had just started our meal when there was a terrible crash outside – all the glass in the windows fell in and the whole building seemed to rock to its foundations.

I was amazed by the complete lack of any panic or confusion; most people just looked up for a moment and then resumed their conversation again.

A few minutes later we went outside and found that the bomb had fallen just on the other side of the road next to the Prince of Wales Theatre. Very little structural damage had been done as it exploded in a small open space, but there was hardly a window left in the whole of Coventry Street.

The pavements were almost ankle deep in broken glass, and a large squad of men were just assembling to start the job of clearing it all up.

A few moments later I bade my Canadian friend goodnight, and went back to bed at the hotel. There was no further excitement that night.

When I got back to the squadron I found that very little had happened in my absence, and for the next few days life continued to be very quiet. However, the weather improved slowly, and a few days later we were sitting down near the aircraft when the order came through to take off. We all got off the ground and started to climb towards the coast. At about 10,000 feet there was some cloud, and as soon as we got above this I looked round and above, and saw many thousands of feet above us at least thirty Messerschmitt 110s, accompanied by a lot of Me 109s. At first I thought they were our own fighters and called up to the CO and suggested that they were some Hurricanes. The CO took one look and replied, 'No, they must be Huns'. And so they were, as I recognized a moment later.

We were in a hopeless position, a long way below them and outlined against the white cloud underneath us. However, we continued to climb, in the hope of somehow managing to get in one attack, and all the time we watched the Messerschmitts like cats, as sooner or later they would obviously drop down on us. Altogether rather an unpleasant few minutes.

It was very difficult watching them, as they were almost in the sun, and the glare was awful.

Suddenly I saw two Me 109s just behind John's Spitfire. How they got there I don't know – I never saw them come down and nobody else did either. They must have dived very fast indeed, and they had just opened fire when I saw them. I remember distinctly their yellow noses and the white streaks caused by their cannon shells.

I immediately shouted on the R/T, 'Look out, Messerschmitts, they're coming down'. I have never seen the squadron break up so quickly. The machines turned sharply away in all directions and dived hard for the cloud. I went down with everybody else, pulled out after a few thousand feet and looked round. Apart from a few Spitfires dashing around, there was nothing to be seen. We all waited a little longer, but met no more enemy, and soon afterwards we were ordered to land. And so a lot of very angry pilots returned home.

Nobody was missing and John was quite ok, though there were one or two bullet holes in his wings. Those Me 109 pilots must have been bad shots; if any of us had fired at them in similar circumstances they wouldn't have got away.

And there was more good news. We had shot down a couple of Me 109s, though it seemed incredible when we were at such a disadvantage. When the squadron broke up and dived away, both Noel and Novi stayed up there with the Me 109s – a very cool and risky thing to do, since they were in such a hopeless position. However, like some other audacious schemes, it worked.

Noel was just turning round when a bullet crashed through his cockpit roof three inches above his head, and several more hit his machine. He whipped round and saw two 109s calmly flying away and not paying the slightest attention to him – perhaps they thought they had shot him down. So he caught them up and shot down the rear one.

Novi was also attacked, but managed to shoot down another 109, which crashed near Bournemouth. When the machine was near the ground, the pilot got out and just managed to open his parachute in time, but landed very heavily and lay on the ground, probably winded by the fall. Novi circled round and said afterwards, in his rather broken English, 'I circle round, bloody German lies down, he is dead, ok. But I look again, he is now sitting up, no bloody good.' He was very disappointed; in his opinion the only good Germans are dead Germans.

After this little affair the bad weather set in again and we did very little for the next few weeks. After the long strain of the summer and autumn, when we hardly ever got out in the evening, as we were on duty till dark, the reaction now began to set in, and we seemed to go out on parties nearly every night.

On Thursday, 17 October, after an uneventful and rainy day, we came into the mess for tea and I got a plate and settled down in a chair to read the paper. A few minutes later the CO came up to me and put something on the paper with the remark, 'Look what the post has just brought for you'.

It was the DFC ribbon!

I was so surprised that I just stared at it for a moment without grasping what it meant. I remember getting to my feet, still rather dazed and being congratulated by various people.

Johnny had got one also, and he soon produced a needle and thread and sewed his on. I took mine to my batman to fix it on my tunic, and then walked downstairs again feeling better than I'd ever felt before.

We had the most terrific party that night and, I should imagine, consumed most of the mess stock of Pimms. Altogether a riotous evening!

In the action on 7 October, in which Sergeant F was killed and Mike wounded, we had brought our score of Huns definitely destroyed to ninety-nine, and as we seemed to get some fight every few days it looked as though we should complete our century very quickly. But, unfortunately, the German air force did not seem very keen to offer themselves up for the slaughter, and so we waited impatiently for over a fortnight, hoping every day that our luck would change. No batsman, hovering on the edge of his century, was ever more keen than we were to see the 100 up. But after the murderous losses inflicted on them in the previous two months, the Germans had reduced their daylight bombing activity practically to nil, and nothing seemed to come our way.

However, on Monday, 21 October, our chance arrived. The day was cloudy – ideal conditions for single bombers to carry out hit-and-run raids, and about 12.30 p.m. a Junkers 88 appeared out of the clouds and bombed a place in the Midlands. He then turned south again towards the coast at Bournemouth, on his way home, flying very low the whole way so as to escape detection by any of our fighters who might be above.

Two of our people, Frank and Sidney, were up after him and were waiting near the coast to try to intercept him on his way out. A few moments later operations room called them up on the R/T and said, 'He should be near you now, flying very low'.

A second later they saw him practically underneath – a very nice bit of work on the part of Ops.

They both dived down to attack and Frank went in first, opened fire at very close range, and damaged an engine badly. It must have been an exciting chase, as the Ju 88 was going down below the level of the trees in his desperate efforts to escape.

Frank then broke away, and Sidney opened fire, and almost immediately the Hun dived into a field. There was a terrific explosion and the wreckage was scattered over four fields. All the crew were killed instantly.

And that was that. There was great rejoicing at the aerodrome when the news came through a few minutes later, and a considerable party was organized for that night.

About 6.30 p.m. we trooped into the writing room and there found a couple of waiters behind the bar and almost hidden by the large stock of champagne and brandy that had been installed for the occasion. A satisfactory if somewhat boozy party ensued; everybody was in top form and we all felt distinctly pleased with ourselves and life generally. We drank to the CO, we drank to the Poles, we drank to the squadron, and in fact we toasted practically everything we could think of, in round after round of champagne cocktails.

It was a very good party.

50 Richard Hillary Part 2, Spitfire Pilot, Flying Officer, Australian, 603 Squadron

The final extract from Hillary's bestselling wartime memoir, covering October 1940 to about February 1941, which charts his treatment by pioneering burns specialist Archibald McIndoe. Here he meets fellow burns victims Tom Gleave (see chapter 31), Eric Lock (see chapter 40) and Josef Koukal (see chapter 35). Hillary twisted many arms to get posted back to operational duty and returned to service with 54 Operational Training Unit at RAF Charterhall in Scotland, but was killed on a night-flying training flight in January 1943.

For the first few weeks, only my parents were allowed to visit me and they came every day. My mother would sit and read to me by the hour. Quite how much she suffered I could only guess, for she gave no sign. One remark of hers I shall never forget. She said, 'You should be glad this has to happen to you. Too many people told you how attractive you were and you believed them. You were well on the way to becoming something of a cad. Now you'll find out who your real friends are.' I did.

When I was allowed to see people, one of my first visitors was Michael Cary (who had been at Trinity with me and had a First in Greats). He was then private secretary to the Chief of Air Staff. He was allowed to stay only a short time before being shoo'd away by my nurses, but I think it may have been time enough to shake him. A short while afterwards he joined the Navy as an AB. I hope it was not as a result of seeing me, for he had too good a brain to waste polishing brass. Colin came down whenever he had leave from Hornchurch and brought me news of the squadron.

Ken MacDonald, Don's brother who had been with 'A' flight at Dyce, had been killed [on 28 September 1940]. He had been seen about to bale out of his blazing machine at 1,000 feet; but as he was over a thickly populated area he had climbed in again and crashed the machine in the Thames.

Pip Cardell had been killed [on 27 September 1940]. Returning from a chase over the Channel with Dexter, one of the new members of the squadron, he appeared to be in trouble just before reaching the English coast. He jumped; but his parachute failed to open and he came down in the sea. Dexter flew low and saw him move. He was still alive, so Dexter flew right along the shore and out to sea, waggling his wings to draw attention and calling up the base on the R/T. No boat put out from the shore, and Dexter made a crash landing on the beach, drawing up ten yards from a nest of buried mines. But when they got up to Pip he was dead.

Howes had been killed, even as he had said. His squadron had been moved from Hornchurch to a quieter area, a few days after I was shot down. But he had been transferred to our squadron, still deeply worried because as yet he had failed to bring anything down. The inevitable happened; and from his second flight with us he failed to return.

Rusty was missing, but a clairvoyant had written to Uncle George swearing that he was neither dead nor captured. Rusty, he said (whom he had never seen), had crashed in France, badly burned, and was being looked after by a French peasant.

As a counter to this depressing news Colin told me that Brian, Raspberry and Sheep all had the DFC, and Brian was shortly to get a bar to his. The squadron's confirmed score was nearing the hundred mark. We had also had the pleasure of dealing with the Italians. They had come over before breakfast, and together with 41 Squadron we were looking for them. Suddenly Uncle George called out, 'Wops ahead.'

'Where are they?' asked 41 Squadron.

'Shan't tell you,' came back the answer. 'We're only outnumbered three to one.'

Colin told me that it was the most unsporting thing he had ever had to do, rather like shooting sitting birds, as he so typically put it. We got down eight of them without loss to ourselves and much to the annoyance of 41 Squadron.

Then one day I had an unexpected visitor. Matron opened the door and said 'Someone to see you,' and Denise [Peter Pease's fiancée] walked in. I knew at once who she was. It was unnecessary for her to speak. Her slight figure was in mourning and she wore no make-up. She was the most beautiful person I have ever seen.

Much has been written on beauty. Poets have excelled themselves in similes for a woman's eyes, mouth, hair; novelists have devoted pages to a geometrically accurate description of their heroines' features. I can write no such description of Denise. I did not see her like that. For me she had an inner beauty, a serenity which no listing of features can convey. She had a perfection of carriage and a grace of movement that were strikingly reminiscent of Peter Pease, and when she spoke it might have been Peter speaking.

'I hope you'll excuse me coming to see you like this,' she said; 'but I was going to be married to Peter. He often spoke of you and wanted so much to see you. So I hope you won't mind me coming instead.'

There was so much I wanted to say, so many things for us to talk over, but the room seemed of a sudden unbearably full of hurrying jolly nurses who would not go away. The bustle and excitement did little to put her at her ease, and her shyness was painful to me. Time came for her to leave, and I had said nothing I wanted to say. As soon as she was gone I dictated a note, begging her to come again and to give me a little warning. She did. From then until I was able to get out, her visits did more to help my recovery than all the expert nursing and medical attention. For she was the very spirit of courage. It was useless for me to say to her any of the usual words of comfort for the loss of a fiancé, and I did not try. She and Peter were two halves of the same person. They even wrote alike. I could only pray that time would cure that awful numbness and bring her back to the fullness of life. Not that she was broken. She seemed somehow to have gathered his strength, to feel him always near her, and was determined to go on to the end in the cause for which he had given his life, hoping that she too might be allowed to die, but feeling guilty at the selfishness of the thought.

She believed passionately in freedom, in freedom from fear and oppression and tyranny, not only for herself but for the whole world.

'For the whole world.' Did I believe that? I still wasn't sure. There was a time – only the other day – when it hadn't mattered to me if it was true or not that a man could want freedom for others than himself. She made me feel that this might be no mere catchphrase of politicians, since it was something to which the two finest people I had ever known had willingly dedicated themselves. I was impressed. I saw there a spirit far purer than mine. But was it for me? I didn't know. I just didn't know.

I lay in that hospital and watched summer turn to winter. Through my window I watched the leaves of my solitary tree gradually turn brown, and then, shaken by an ever-freshening wind, fall one by one. I watched the sun change from a great ball of fire to a watery glimmer, watched the rain beating on the glass and the small broken clouds drifting a few hundred feet above, and in that time I had ample opportunity for thinking.

...

The day came when I was allowed out of the hospital for a few hours. Sue got me dressed, and with a pair of dark glasses, cotton wool under my eyes, and my right arm in a sling, I looked fairly presentable. I walked out through the swing-doors and took a deep breath.

London in the morning was still the best place in the world. The smell of wet streets, of sawdust in the butchers' shops, of tar melted on the blocks, was exhilarating. Peter had been right: I loved the capital. The wind on the heath might call for a time, but the facile glitter of the city was the stronger. Self-esteem, I suppose, is one cause; for in the city, work of man, one is somebody, feet on the pavement, suit on the body, anybody's equal and nobody's fool; but in the country, work of God, one is nothing, less than the earth, the birds, and the trees; one is discordant – a blot.

I walked slowly through Ravenscourt Park and looked into many faces. Life was good, but if I hoped to find some reflection of my feeling I was disappointed. One or two looked at me with pity, and for a moment I was angry; but when I gazed again at their faces, closed in as on some dread secret, their owners hurrying along, unseeing, unfeeling, eager to get to their jobs, unaware of the life within them, I was sorry for them. I felt a desire to stop and shake them and say: 'You fools, it's you who should be pitied and not I; for this day I am alive while you are dead.'

And yet there were some who pleased me, some in whom all youth had not died. I passed one girl, and gazing into her face became aware of her as a woman: her lips were soft, her breasts firm, her legs long and graceful. It was many a month since any woman had stirred me, and I was pleased. I smiled at her and she smiled at me. I did not speak to her for fear of breaking the spell, but walked back to lunch on air. After this I was allowed out every day, and usually managed to stay out until nine o'clock, when I drove back through the blitz and the blackout.

'London can take it' was already becoming a truism; but I had been put out of action before the real fury of the night attacks had been let loose, and I had seen nothing of the damage. In the hospital, from the newspapers, and from people who came to see me, I gained a somewhat hazy idea of what was going on. On the one hand I saw London as a city hysterically gay, a city doomed, with nerves so strained that a life of synthetic gaiety alone prevented them from snapping. My other picture was of a London bloody but unbowed, of a people grimly determined to see this thing through, with manpower mobilised; a city unable, through a combined lack of inclination, facility, and time, to fritter away the war in the night haunts of the capital. I set out to see for myself.

London nightlife did exist. Though the sirens might scream and the bombs fall, restaurants and cocktail bars remained open and full every night of the week. I say restaurants and cocktail bars, for the bottle parties and striptease cabarets which had a mushroom growth at the beginning of the war had long been closed. Nor was prostitution abroad. Ladies of leisure whose business hours were from eleven till three were perhaps the only citizens to find themselves completely baffled by the blackout. London was not promiscuous: the diners-out in a West End restaurant were no longer the clientèle of café society, for café society no longer existed in London. The majority of the so-called smart set felt at last with the outbreak of war a real vocation, felt finally a chance to realise themselves and to orientate themselves to a life of reality. They might be seen in a smart restaurant; but they were there in another guise – as soldiers, sailors, and airmen on forty-eight hours' leave; as members of one of the women's services seeking a few hours' relaxation before again applying themselves wholeheartedly to their jobs; or as civil servants and government workers who, after a hard day's work, preferred to relax and enjoy the bombing in congenial company rather than return to a solitary dinner in their own flats.

While the bombs were dropping on London (and they were dropping every night in my time in the hospital), and while half London was enjoying itself, the other half was not asleep. It was striving to make London as normal a city by night as it had become by day. Anti-aircraft crews, studded around fields, parks, and streets, were momentarily silhouetted against the sky by the sudden flash of their guns. The Auxiliary Fire Service, spread out in a network of squads through the capital, was standing by, ready at a moment's notice to deal with the inevitable fires; air-raid wardens, tireless in their care of shelters and work of rescue, patrolled their areas watchfully. One heavy night I poked my nose out of the Dorchester, which was rocking gently, to find a cab calmly coasting down Park Lane. I hailed it and was driven back to the hospital. The driver turned to me: 'Thank God, sir,' he said, 'Jerry's wasting 'is time trying to break our morale, when 'e might be doing real damage on some small town.'

With the break of day London shook herself and went back to work. Women with husbands in government jobs were no longer to be seen at noon draped along the bars of the West End as their first appointment of the day. They were up and at work with determined efficiency in administrative posts of the Red Cross, the women's voluntary services, and the prisoners of war organisations. The Home Guards and air-raid wardens of the previous night would return home, take a bath, and go off to their respective offices. The soldier was back with his regiment, the airman with his squadron; the charming frivolous creatures with whom they had dined were themselves in uniform, effective in their jobs of driving, typing, or nursing.

That, I discovered, was a little of what London was doing. But what was London feeling? Perhaps a not irrelevant example was an experience of Sheep Gilroy's when flying with the squadron. He was sitting in his bath when a 'flap' was announced. Pulling on a few clothes and not bothering to put on his tunic, he dashed out to his plane and took off. A few minutes later he was hit by an incendiary bullet and the machine caught fire. He baled out, quite badly burned, and landed by a parachute in one of the poorer districts of London. With no identifying tunic, he was at once set upon by 200 silent and coldly angry women, armed with knives and rolling-pins. For him no doubt it was a harrowing experience, until he finally established his nationality by producing all the most lurid words in his vocabulary; but as an omen for the day when the cream of Hitler's Aryan youth should attempt to land in Britain it was most interesting.

All this went on at a time when night after night the East End was taking a terrible beating, and it was rumoured that the people were ominously quiet. Could their morale be cracking? The answer was provided in a story that was going the rounds. A young man went down to see a chaplain whom he knew in the East End. He noticed not only that the damage was considerable but that the people were saying practically nothing at all. 'How are they taking it?' he asked nervously. The chaplain shook his head. 'I'm afraid,' he said, 'that my people have fallen from grace: they are beginning to feel a little bitter towards the Germans.'

The understatement in that remark was impressive because it was typical. The war was practically never discussed except as a joke. The casual observer might easily have drawn one of two conclusions: either that London was spent of all feeling, or that it was a city waiting like a blind man, unseeing, uncaring, for the end. Either conclusion would have been wide of the mark. Londoners are slow to anger. They had shown for long enough that they could take it; now they were waiting on the time when it would be their turn to dish it out, when their cold rage would need more than a Panzer division to stamp it out.

...

c. 3 November 1940 I had now been in hospital something over two months and it was thought that I was sufficiently recovered for operation.

Shortly after my arrival at the Masonic the Air Force plastic surgeon, A. H. McIndoe, had come up to see me, but as I had been blind at the time I could recollect his visit but vaguely, remembering only that he had ordered the gentian violet to be removed from my eyes and saline compresses to be applied instead, with the result that shortly afterwards I had been able to see.

He was expected this time at about eleven o'clock, but I was ready a good hour before, bathed and shaved and dressings elaborately correct. The charge nurse ushered him in fussily. Of medium height, he was thickset and the line of his jaw was square. Behind his horn-rimmed spectacles a pair of tired friendly eyes regarded me speculatively.

'Well,' he said, 'you certainly made a thorough job of it, didn't you?'

He started to undo the dressings on my hands and I noticed his fingers – blunt, capable, incisive. By now all the tannic had been removed from my face and hands. He took a scalpel and tapped lightly on something white showing through the red granulating knuckle of my right forefinger.

'Bone,' he remarked laconically.

He looked at the badly contracted eyelids and the rapidly forming keloids, and pursed his lips.

'Four new eyelids, I'm afraid, but you're not ready for them yet. I want all this skin to soften up a lot first. How would you like to go to the south coast for a bit?'

He mentioned the official RAF convalescent hospital on the south coast, generously supplied with golf courses, tennis and squash courts. But as I could not use my hands, and abhorred seaside resorts in winter, I wasn't very enthusiastic. I asked instead whether I could go down to a convalescent home a couple of miles from his hospital. He raised no objection and said that he would fix it with the commandant.

'And I'll be able to keep an eye on you there,' he added. He had got up to go when I asked him how long it would be before I should fly again. I had asked the same question on his previous visit, and when he had said 'Six months' I had been desperately depressed for days. Now when he said, 'Next war for you: those hands are going to be something of a problem,' I wasn't even surprised. I suppose I had known it for some time. I felt no emotion at all.

He took his leave and I went off to have lunch with my mother.

Two days later, after the disentangling of a few cross wires in official circles, Air Ministry permission came through and I was driven down to Sussex.

The house was rambling and attractive, and ideal for a convalescent home. I was greeted at the door by matron and led in to tea. There were about twenty other inmates drinking tea, mostly Army men, not particularly exciting and with not particularly exciting complaints. About them hung the listless air and furtive manner of undertakers, born no doubt of their prolonged inactivity combined with the dreary nature of their intestinal afflictions. By dinner-time I was preparing to resign myself to a comfortable if not stimulating period of relaxation, when a couple of genial souls came rolling in very late and I met Colin Hodgkinson and Tony Tollemache.

Hodgkinson was twenty and in the Fleet Air Arm: it was not until he got up after dinner that I noticed his two artificial legs. While training in an Albacore he had come into collision with a Hurricane. His two companions and the Hurricane pilot were killed instantly and Colin was found in a field six hours later.

Tony Tollemache had crashed in March, night flying. Coming in to land, his Blenheim had turned over and caught fire, throwing him free. His passenger was also thrown free and killed; but under the impression that he was still inside, Tony had climbed in again and wandered up and down the flaming machine, looking for him. He had been badly burned on his face, hands, and, above all, legs. For this action he got the Empire Gallantry Medal and nearly a year in hospital. He had already had several operations, and he was due at the hospital in another two days for a graft on his left hand.

We sat long by the glow of the open fire talking of many things and it was late when we finally climbed the stairs to bed. As I turned on my side and closed my eyes I was content. Tomorrow I should have my breakfast in bed, be given a bath, and come down only for lunch: I was the autocrat of the bolster, the aristocrat of fine linen: there were many worse ways of spending the war.

The following afternoon an eye specialist took a look at me: the pupil of my left eye, dilated by regular treatment with belladonna, interested him particularly.

'Can't close your eyes at all, can you?' he asked.

'No, sir,' I said.

'Well, we'll have to get some covering over that left eye or you'll never use it again.'

He went into the commandant's office where there was a telephone, and returned a few minutes later.

'McIndoe is going to give you a new pair of top lids,' he said. 'I know your eyes are still infected but we'll have to take that chance. You're to go in with Tollemache tomorrow.'

At the Masonic I had been the only action casualty. I had been very ill and in a private ward; subsequently I had been outrageously spoiled. Having little previous experience of hospitals, I had taken it all as a matter of course. At the convalescent home the food was exceptional and the living conditions bordering on the luxurious: as a result the new hospital was something of a shock. It was one of several hundred Emergency Medical Service hospitals. Taken over by the Ministry of Health at the beginning of the war, these were nearly all small country-town hospitals in safe areas. Erected by subscription for the welfare of the district and run by committees of local publicity-loving figures in the community, they had been perfectly adequate for that purpose. They were not, however, geared for a wartime emergency; they were too small. To overcome this difficulty the Ministry of Health had supplied them with 'blisters' to accommodate the anticipated flow of troops. I had heard of these 'blisters' and was vaguely aware that they were huts, but this hospital provided my first introduction to them.

It was of fairly recent construction and of only one storey. There were two main wards: one reserved for women and filled with residents of the district; the other for men, one half for local civilians and the other (eight beds) for action casualties. Then there were the 'blisters'; a dental hut, and two others set at an angle to the main building.

Ward Three, housing some of the worst cases, stood about fifty yards away from the hospital. It was a long, low hut, with a door at one end and twenty beds down each side. The beds were separated from each other only by lockers, and it was possible without much exertion to reach out and touch the man in the next bed. Towards the far end the lockers degenerated into soap-boxes. They constituted the patients' furniture. Windows were let into the walls at regular intervals on each side: they were never open. Down the middle there was a table with a wireless on it, a stove, and a piano. On either side of the entrance passage were four lavatories and two bathrooms. Immediately on the left of the entrance passage was the saline bath, a complicated arrangement of pipes that maintained a constant flow of saline around the bathed patient at a regulated temperature. McIndoe had been using it with great success for the rapid healing of extensive burns. Next to this, in a curtained-off bed, was a little girl of fifteen, by name Joan, terribly burnt by boiling sugar her first day in a factory. Joan was in this ward because there was no other saline bath in the hospital (there were only three in England), and she could not be moved any distance. She screamed fairly regularly, and always before being lifted into the bath; her voice was thin and like that of a child of seven. As the time for her bath approached there was a certain tension throughout the hut; and then everyone would start talking rather loudly, and the wireless was turned up.

For the rest, there was a blind man at the far end learning Braille with the assistance of his wife, a squadron leader, several pilot officers, a Czech, and sundry troops, unlikely to forget Dunkirk as quickly as most.

But my first taste of Ward Three was not yet. It was to the main building that I went for my new eyelids, and with little graciousness. Tony and I came in late, a fair measure of whisky inside us, and started noisily to get undressed. Our beds were next to each other: opposite us were two Hurricane pilots, one with his legs badly burned and the other with a six-weeks growth of beard and a thick surgical bandage over his eyes. He was being fed by a nurse.

'Is he blind?' I whispered to Tony.

'Blind?' he roared. 'Not half as blind as we are, I'll bet. No, me boy. That's what you're going to look like tomorrow when McIndoe's through with you.'

'Are you daft, Mr Tollemache, coming in here late and making all that noise? If it's trouble you want you'll get it when Sister Hall sees you. And tell your fine friend to take his shoes off the bed.'

This was my first introduction to the ward charge nurse. She rose from feeding the man with the bandaged eyes and stood feet apart and hands on hips, her cap awry, one tooth nibbling her lower lip as though it was lettuce.

Tony turned to me.

'Begad,' he said, 'I forgot to warn you, it's back in hell's kitchen we are. The ward is lousy with Irish and 'tis better to lie and rot than let them lay a finger on your dressings. They'll give you a dig for De Valera as soon as look at you.'

'Ach! you needn't show off now, Mr Tollemache. That's not funny and I'm not laughing.'

She drew herself up to her full five feet and stalked majestically from the ward, somewhat spoiling the effect by a shrill cackle of laughter when she caught sight of the pair of red pyjamas that I was unpacking.

'It's the wrong address you're at with those passion pants,' she said. 'This is a hospital, not an English country house weekend.'

'Be off with you, woman,' I said, and putting on the offending garments I climbed into bed and settled down to read.

Shortly afterwards Sister Hall came into the ward, her dark-blue uniform proclaiming her rank.

'More Ireland,' whispered Tony as she approached.

She stopped at the foot of my bed and I noticed that she was short, that her hair was grey, and that a permanent struggle between a tight-lipped mouth and smiling eyes was at the moment being very definitely won by the mouth.

'Good evening, Mr Tollemache,' she said.

'Good evening, Sister Hall,' said Tony in his blandest manner.

She turned to me.

'Mr Hillary, both you and Mr Tollemache are to be operated on tomorrow morning. As you know, you should have been in earlier for preparation; now it will have to be done in the morning. I hope you will settle in here quickly; but I want it understood that in my ward I will tolerate no bad language and no rudeness to the nurses.'

'My dear Sister,' I replied, 'I've no doubt that you will find me the mildest and most soft-spoken of men,' and sitting up in bed I bowed gravely from the waist. She gave me a hard look and walked through the ward.

Tony waited until she was out of earshot. Then: 'A tough nut, but the best nurse in the hospital,' he said. 'I don't advise you to get on the wrong side of her.'

Shortly before the lights were put out McIndoe made a round of the ward followed by half a dozen assistants, mostly service doctors who were training under him. 'You're first on the list, Tony,' he said, 'and you're second. By the looks of you both we'll need to use a stomach pump before we can give you any anaesthetic.'

He took a look at my eyes. 'They're still pretty mucky,' he said, 'but I think you'll find it a relief to have some eyelids on them.' He passed on through the ward and we settled down to sleep.

In the morning we were wakened early and 'prepped' by Taffy, the Welsh orderly. 'Prepping' consists of sterilising the area of skin to be used for the graft and shaving completely any surrounding hair. My eyelids were to be a 'Thiersch' graft (a layer of skin thin as cigarette paper) taken from the inside of my left arm, so Taffy shaved the arm and armpit, then sterilised the arm and bound it up in a loose bandage. He did the same thing to Tony's leg, from where the skin was to be taken for his hand, and we were both ready to go. The charge nurse then trundled in a stretcher on wheels, parked it beside Tony's bed, pushed his feet into an enormous pair of bed socks, and whipped out a hypodermic needle. This contained an injection to make one drowsy half an hour before being wheeled into the operating theatre.

'Bet you she's blunted the needle,' said Tony; 'and look at her hand; it's shaking like an aspen leaf.'

'Be quiet, Mr Tollemache, let's have less of your sauce now.'

After much protesting she finally caught his arm and stuck him with the needle. He then climbed on to the trolley, which was screened off, and after about half an hour he was wheeled away.

I hoped that the operation would not be a lengthy affair, for I was hungry and could have no food until after I had been sliced up. Finally Tony was wheeled back, very white on the unburned patches of his face and breathing ether all over the room. It was my turn for the trolley. The injection did not make me particularly drowsy, and feeling bored I asked for a cigarette from one of the others and puffed away contentedly behind the screen. But I had not counted on the sharp eyes of Sister Hall. For a second she stared unbelievingly at the thin spiral of smoke; then she was inside the screen, the confiscated cigarette glowing accusingly in her hand and herself looking down on me with silent disapproval. I gazed back innocently; but pulling the screen to with a jerk, she walked on, her measured tread the silent voice of outraged authority.

It was time for me to go. Two nurses appeared at either end of the trolley and I was off, Tony's stertorous breathing and the coarse cries of the others following me down the ward. I was welcomed by the anaesthetist, vast and genial, with his apparatus that resembled a petrol station on wheels. As he was tying up my arm with a piece of rubber tubing, McIndoe came in sharpening his knife and wearing a skull cap and multi-coloured gown, for all the world like some Bedouin chieftain. The anaesthetist took my arm and pushed the needle in gently. 'Well, goodbye,' he said. A green film rose swiftly up my throat and I lost consciousness.

When I came round I was not uncomfortable, and unlike Tony I was not sick. I could not see; but apart from a slight pricking of the eyes I had no pain, and but for the boring prospect of five days without reading I was content. Those of us with eyelid grafts had of course to be fed and given bed baths, but we could (thank God) get up and walk to the lavatory, escorted by a nurse. Were there no nurses about, the others would sing out instructions to the needy one until he arrived safely at his destination.

Being unable to see, had, I discovered, some distinct disadvantages. As I could not read, I talked; and as everyone knows, there are few more pleasant pastimes when one is indisposed than grousing and swearing. After a few unfortunate incidents I always asked Tony if any nurses were about before opening my mouth, but Tony was unreliable, getting a hideous pleasure out of watching the consequences. Then – I think it was on the third day of my incarceration – some nurse further down the ward dropped a bedpan with a crash that made me start up in bed.

'Jesus Christ,' I said, 'what a hospital! It stinks like a sewer, it's about as quiet as a zoo, and instead of nurses we've got a bunch of moronic Irish amazons.'

'Mister Hillary!' The voice was so close that I almost fell out of bed.

'That's done it,' I thought; and I was right.

'Not another dressing do you get until you apologise.' Sister Hall was standing at my elbow. Tony, of course, was delighted and I could hear him chuckling into the bedclothes. I opened my mouth to apologise but no words came. Instead, I realised with horror that I was laughing, laughing in a manner that could in no way be passed off as a mere nervous titter, that could be taken, indeed, for nothing but what it was – a rich fruity belly-laugh.

Nothing was said, but I had a sense of impending doom. A few minutes later my suspicions were confirmed: I felt my bed begin to move.

'What goes on?' I asked.

'Two orderlies are shipping you off next door,' said Tony. 'They're going to separate us.'

Now I had no wish to be separated from Tony. He was amusing to talk to, and especially at a time when I could not see, I felt the need of his presence. Further, there is nothing more depressing than being moved in hospital just after getting the feel of a ward. So I got out of bed. The orderlies were for a moment nonplussed; but, as Tony explained to them, their orders were to move the bed, not me. I could almost see their faces clear and I heard the bed being pushed through the door.

'Trouble ahead,' said Tony. 'Haven't enjoyed myself so much for ages.'

Sure enough, a few minutes later Sister Hall returned accompanied by one of the younger surgeons, unhappy and embarrassed by the whole thing.

'Now what's all this?' he asked nervously.

'Well, among other things,' I said, 'I have told Sister Hall that I object to being treated as though I were still in a kindergarten.'

'He said more than that, doctor,' said Sister Hall with some truth. 'He and Mr Tollemache together make it impossible to run the ward.

By this time the pettiness of it was boring me, and when the harassed doctor said that he could not interfere with Sister Hall's running of the ward I made no demur and allowed myself to be led off to the all-glass covered-in balcony extension of the ward to which my bed had been moved. I made some remark to Tony as I passed his bed but sister had the last word.

'And we'll have no bad language while I'm in charge here,' she said, and shut the door firmly behind me.

I found myself next to an Army doctor with smashed insides, sustained running into a stationary lorry in the blackout. He had difficulty in getting his breath and roared and whistled all night. I began to regret the haste of my outburst.

The hospital visiting hours were from two till four in the afternoon, a change from the Masonic and an arbitrary rule which in my present state of mind I considered nothing short of monstrous. Denise, who was now back in the ATS with an important job, could get off only at odd moments but wanted to come and see me. I asked the matron if she might be allowed to come in the morning if she could get down from London, and the matron very reasonably agreed. Denise duly arrived and called up from the station to ask when she might appear. Due to a misunderstanding, she was told that visiting hours were from two till four, and she had therefore to kick her heels for several hours in the town. By this time I was so enjoying my sense of persecution that, even if I had realised that it was a misunderstanding, I should doubtless have chosen to ignore the fact. When, therefore, on the stroke of four Sister Hall entered and said coldly, 'All visitors must leave now,' I would willingly have committed murder, but Denise laid a warning hand on mine and I held my peace.

The next day McIndoe took down the dressing from my eyes and I saw again.

'A couple of real horse blinkers you've got there,' he said; and indeed for a day or so that is what they felt like. In order to see in front of me I had to turn my face up to the ceiling. They moulded in very rapidly, and soon I could raise and lower them at will. It was a remarkable piece of surgery, and an operation in which McIndoe had yet to score a failure.

Shortly afterwards I was allowed to have a bath and soak the bandage off my arm from where the graft had been taken. This laborious and painful process had already taken me half an hour when Sister Hall came in. I was down to the last layer, which I was pulling at gingerly, hurting myself considerably in the process.

'Well, really, Mister Hillary!' she said; and taking hold of it she gave a quick pull and ripped the whole thing off cleanly and painlessly.

'Christ!' I started involuntarily, but stopped myself and glanced apprehensively at sister's face. She was smiling. Yes, there was no doubt about it, she was smiling. We said nothing, but from that moment we understood each other.

Tony's graft had been a success, and within a few days we were allowed out for a fortnight's convalescence before coming in again for further operations.

As I was getting ready to go, sister took me on one side and slipped a small package into my hand.

'You'll be wanting to look your best for the girls, Mr Hillary, and I've put in some brown make-up powder that should help you.'

I started to protest but she cut me short.

'You'll be in again in a couple of weeks,' she said. 'Time enough for us to start quarrelling then.'

We returned after a short but very pleasant convalescence – Tony for his last operation, one top lid, and I for two lower ones.

This time when the dressings were taken down I looked exactly like an orang-outang. McIndoe had pinched out two semicircular ledges of skin under my eyes to allow for contraction of the new lids. What was not absorbed was to be sliced off when I came in for my next operation, a new upper lip. The relief, however, was enormous, for now I could close my eyes almost completely and did not sleep with them rolled up and the whites showing like a frightened negro.

Once again we retired to our convalescent home, where our hostess did everything possible to relieve the monotony of our existence. She gave a large party on Christmas night, and every few weeks brought down stage or screen people to cheer up the patients.

There had been some changes among the other inmates since our last visit, and two of de Gaulle's Frenchmen had arrived from an Aldershot hospital. One of them, an Army officer, had been in plaster since Dunkirk, where he got an explosive bullet in the arm. The other had been in the French Air Force but had decidedly un-Gallic features. When I first saw him he was wearing a beard and looked like a Renaissance Christ. Later he shaved it off and was indistinguishable, from any chorus-boy in the second row.

When France fell he was completing his flying training in Morocco. He had taken off in an antiquated trainer and landed at Gibraltar. Eventually he managed to reach England and to continue his training on Magisters with French instructors whom he described as old, blind, and incompetent. Apparently he was sent up to practise spins without having been told how to come out of them. His command of English was picturesque and somewhat erratic, yet he managed to convey to me a vivid picture of his crash.

'I am diving at about 4,000 feet,' he said, 'when I start the spin. I am told only two turns, so after these I think I centralise the stick and rudder and come out. Nothing happens, so I cross the controls, open the gas and push the stick further forward. I do not wish to jump out, you understand, as I have done this before and do not like.

So I try an inverted loop but nothing happens. By this time I have done many turns and am feeling dizzy, so I say to myself, "I must now bale out," and I undo my straps and stand up. When I look over the side a haystack is spinning round the plane and I am stepping over the side, when crash! And we are no more.'

A most remarkable recital! His back and one foot were broken. His body and leg were swathed in plaster of Paris, and his fellow-countryman, who was an artist, had painted the picture of the crash across his chest.

On Tuesdays and Thursdays the inmates always drove into town in the station wagon to go to the pictures. This involved sitting in the local tea shop for an hour afterwards, eating sickening cakes and waiting for the car to drive them back. As tea shops have the most appalling effect on me, depression descending like a fog, I seldom went along.

...

But on our first Thursday out of the hospital our two Frenchmen asked Tony and me to accompany them, and we duly set off.

We were having tea when a pretty waitress came up and said to my bearded friend, '*Vous êtes Français?*'

'*Oui, et vous?*'

'*Canadienne-Française.*'

'*Dommage que je n'aille mieux. J'aimerais vous prouver que je vous trouve gentille.*'

'*Faudrait aussi que je le veuille!*'

'*N'importe. J'aimerais toujours tenter la chance.*'

The rest of us sat there like cold suet.

Tony and I went often to London, where we settled ourselves down in some restaurant, ordered a most excellent dinner, and surveyed the youth and beauty around us with a fatherly eye. For while we were now medically fit and perfectly content, yet we were still naturally enough drained of any exuberance of youthful vitality.

One night over a particularly good dinner I summed it up to Tony. 'Well,' I said, waving a vague hand at the crowded dance floor, 'we're a lucky pair. Here we are enjoying all the pleasures of old men of sixty. To us it has been granted to pass through all the ages of man in a moment of time, and now we know the joys of the twilight of man's existence. We have come upon that great truth, that the warmth in the belly brought on by brandy and cigars leaves a glow that is the supreme carnal pleasure. Not for us the exacerbation of youthful flesh-twitchings, not for us palpitations and agony of spirit at a pretty smile, a slender waist. We see these things with pleasure, but we see them after our own fashion – as beauty, yes, and as a joy for ever, but as beauty should be seen, from afar and with reverence and with no desire to touch. We are free of the lusts of youth. We can see a patch of virgin snow and we do not have to rush out and leave our footprint. We are as David in the Bible when "they brought unto him a virgin but he gat no heat".'

Tony nodded owlishly and lit a cigar. Then, jabbing it through the air to emphasise his words, he spoke. Slowly and deliberately and with great sorrow he spoke.

'Alas,' he said, 'it is but a dream, a beautiful, beautiful dream, but still a dream. Youth will catch us up again. Youth with all her temptations, trials, and worries. There is no escape.' He lowered his voice and glanced nervously over his shoulder.

'Why, even now I feel her wings fluttering behind me. I am nearly the man I was. For you there is still a little time, not much but a little. Let us then enjoy ourselves while yet we may. Waiter, more brandy!'

One night when we were in town we walked around to see Rosa Lewis at the Cavendish Hotel. Suddenly caught by a stroke, she had been rushed to the London Clinic, where she refused to allow any of the nurses to touch her. After a week she saw the bill and immediately got up and left.

When we arrived, there she was, seventy-six years old, shrieking with laughter and waving a glass of champagne, apparently none the worse. She grabbed me by the arm and peered into my face. 'God, aren't you dead yet either, young Hillary? Come here and I'll tell you something. Don't you ever die. In the last two weeks I've been right up to the gates of 'eaven and 'ell and they're both bloody!'

A few weeks later a heavy bomb landed right on the Cavendish, but Rosa emerged triumphant, pulling bits of glass out of her hair and trumpeting with rage. Whatever else may go in this war, we shall still have Rosa Lewis and the Albert Memorial at the end.

Thus did I while away the time between operations living from day to day, sometimes a little bored, a little depressed, aware of being restless but analysing this restlessness no further than as the inevitable result of months in bed.

It was already January of 1941 when I returned to the hospital for the removal of the ledges under my eyes and the grafting of my new upper lip.

I had lunch at home, saying goodbye to London with two dozen oysters and a bottle of Pol Roget, and just caught my train. On the way down I began to regret the richness of my lunch and I was in no way cheered by the discovery that the only available bed was in Ward Three. McIndoe came round on his tour of the ward, and I asked if I might be first on the list, feeling that the great man would be at his best in the early morning. It was true that he never seemed to tire. Indeed he had been known to operate all day, and finally at ten o'clock at night, stretch himself comfortably and say to an exhausted theatre staff, 'Now let's do something!'

I was wakened early to have my arm 'prepped' by one of the orderlies. I had decided on the arm, and not the leg, in order to be spared the bother of shaving my new upper lip. We chose a piece of skin bounded on one side by a vaccination mark and on the other by the faint scar of what are now my upper lids.

Sister gave me an injection at about nine o'clock, and an hour later, wearing my red pyjamas for luck, I climbed on to the trolley and was wheeled across the fifty yards of open space to the hospital. There was something a little lowering about this journey on a cold morning, but I reached the theatre feeling quite emotionless, rather like a business man arriving at his office. The anaesthetist gave me an injection and I lost consciousness.

On coming round, I realised that I was bandaged from forehead to lip and unable to breathe through my nose. At about three o'clock Tony Tollemache and his mother came to see me; I had by then developed a delicate froth on both lips and must have resembled a perhaps refined stallion. They were very kind, and talked to me quite normally. I'm afraid I replied little, as I needed my mouth to breathe with. They went at about four. After that the day was a blur: a thin wailing scream, the radio playing 'Each day is one day nearer', injections, a little singing, much laughter, and a voice saying, 'Naow, Charlie, *you* can't do it; naow, Charlie, you *can't* do it; naow, Charlie, you can't *do* it.' After this, oblivion, thank God.

The next morning I awoke in a cold sweat after a nightmare in which my eyelids were sewn together and I was leading the squadron in an Avro Tutor. In the evening one of the doctors took the bandages off my eyes. I was left with a thick dressing across my upper lip which pressed against my nose, and two sets of semicircular stitches under my eyes. Peering into a mirror, I noticed that my right eyebrow had been lifted up higher to pair it off with the left. This was also stitched. Later McIndoe made a round and peered anxiously at the scar under my right eye, which was blue and swollen. He moved on. There was comparatively little noise, but the ward smelt and I was depressed.

The next few days remain in my memory as a rather unpleasant dream. Rumour started that eight of us were to be isolated, owing to suspicion of a bug. It proved true. We climbed on to trolleys and were pushed across the yard to one of the main wards, from which a bunch of protesting old women had been evacuated. On the way over I passed a new victim of tannic acid being wheeled in to take my bed: all I could see was an ebony-coloured face enveloped in a white cowl. As we were pushed up the steps to our new quarters we were greeted by four nurses wearing masks, white aprons, and rubber gloves. Our luggage followed, and was tipped into the storeroom outside.

Opposite me was Squadron Leader Gleave with a flap graft on his nose and an exposed nerve on his forehead: in Ward Three he had been unable to sleep, nor could the night nurse drug him enough to stop the pain. Next to him was Eric Lock, a tough little Shropshireman who had been with me at Hornchurch and collected twenty-three planes, a DSO, a DFC and a bar: he had cannon-shell wounds in the arms and legs. On my left was Mark Mounsdon who trained with me in Scotland and was awaiting an operation on his eyelids. Beyond the partition was Joseph, the Czech sergeant pilot, also with a nose graft; Yorkey Law, a bombardier, blown up twice and burned at Dunkirk, with a complete new face taken in bacon strips from his legs, and no hands; and Neft, a clever young Jew (disliked for it by the others), with a broken leg from a motorcycle accident.

We were of course allowed no visitors and could write no letters.

On the second day Neft's face began to suppurate and a small colony of streptococci settled comfortably on the squadron leader's nose. The rest of us waited grimly. Neft showed a tendency to complain, which caused Eric Lock to point out that some of us had been fighting the war with real bullets and would be infinitely grateful for his silence.

On the third day in our new quarters the smell of the bandage under my nose became so powerful that I took to dosing it liberally with eau de cologne. I have since been unable to repress a feeling of nausea whenever at a party or in company I have caught a whiff of this scent.

Our heads were shorn and our scalps rubbed with special soap and anointed with M & B powder. We submitted to this with a varying amount of protestation: the squadron leader was too ill to complain, but Eric Lock was vociferous and the rest of us sullen. A somewhat grim sense of humour helped us to pass this day, punctuated by half-hours during which Neft was an object of rather cruel mockery. He had been a pork butcher before the war and of quite moderate means, but he made the mistake of mentioning this fact and adding that foul-mouthed talk amused him not at all. From that moment Yorkey Law, our bombardier, gave him no peace and plied him with anecdotes which even curled what was left of my hair. By the evening Neft had retired completely under the bed clothes, taking his suppurating face with him.

After the huts our new ward was luxurious: the beds were more comfortable, and above each a pair of earphones hung on the wall. A large plain window ran the whole length of one side and ensured an adequate ventilation: the ward was kept dusted and tidy.

The nurses were efficient and not unfriendly, though the enforced wearing of masks and rubber gloves made them a little impersonal. Our language was always rough and sometimes offensive; Eric, with an amiable grin on his face, would curse them roundly from dawn till dusk, but they seldom complained. They did their best to make up to us for our lack of visitors. Tony Tollemache came down once from the convalescent home and said goodbye through the window: he was returning to Hornchurch. Otherwise we saw nobody.

It was announced that our swabs had returned. We all clamoured to know who was, and who was not, infected. Apparently two were not, but which two the doctors would not say.

On 14 February I developed earache. Short of breath and completely blocked in the nose, I gave a snort and felt something crack in my right ear. Never having had earache before, I found the experience disagreeable to a degree: it was as though someone with a sharp needle was driving it at regular intervals into the side of my head.

An ear, nose, and throat man, on a course of plastic surgery under McIndoe, came along to see me. He regarded me dispassionately for a minute, and then withdrew with sister to the other end of the ward. That night I was put on to Prontosil and knew beyond any doubt that I had the streptococcus.

I slept fitfully, aided in my wakefulness by the pain in my ear, Eric's snores, and the groans of the squadron leader.

In the morning the pain in my ear was considerable and I felt sick from the Prontosil. But it was now eight days since my operation, and the dressing on my lip was due to be taken down. For this mercy I was grateful, as the smell under my nose was proving too strong for even the most frequent doses of eau de cologne. At lunchtime one of the doctors took off the bandages and removed the stitches, at the same time cutting the stitches from under my eyes to the accompaniment of appreciative purrs from his satellites. I asked for a mirror and gazed at the result. It was a blow to my vanity: the new lip was dead white, and thinner than its predecessor.

In point of fact it was a surgical masterpiece, but I was not in the mood to appreciate it. I fear I was not very gracious. The lip was duly painted with mercurochrome, and the doctors departed. The relief at having the bandages removed was enormous, but I still dared not blow my nose for fear that I should blow the graft away. I took a bath and soaked the bandage off the arm from which my lip had been taken. This was a painful process lasting three-quarters of an hour, at the end of which time was revealed a deep narrow scar, neatly stitched. Sister then removed the stitches. During this little operation an unfortunate incident occurred. As soon as the stitches were out, instead of behaving in an approved and conventional manner and remaining pressed together, the two lips of the wound opened out like a fan, exposing a raw surface the size of a half orange. Everyone clustered round to inspect this interesting phenomenon but were hastily ordered back to bed by a somewhat harassed sister. That night I slept not at all: the pain in my ear was a continuous throbbing and I felt violently sick from the Prontosil. At about two o'clock I got up and started pacing the ward. A night nurse ordered me back to bed. I invited her to go to hell with considerable vigour, but I felt no better. She called me a wicked ungrateful boy and I fear that I called her a cow. Finally I returned to bed and attempted to read until morning.

In the conversation of the next twenty-four hours I took little part but lay, propped up in bed, watching the squadron leader rubbing his eye with pieces of cotton wool. The hair from his scalp was making it acutely uncomfortable. This is not so odd as it sounds, for during a flap graft on the nose the scalp is brought down to the top of one's eyebrow where it is neatly rolled and feeds the new nose. It is of course shaved but the hair tends to grow again.

February 17 was a Friday, the day on which an ear, nose, and throat specialist was in the habit of visiting the hospital. It was arranged for me to see him, and putting on my dressing gown, I walked along to the out-patients' department. His manner was reassuring. He felt behind my ear and inquired if it pained me. I replied that it did.

That being so he regretted the necessity, but he must operate within half an hour for what appeared to be a most unpleasant mastoid. I asked if I might be moved to Sister Hall's ward, and after one look at my face the doctors very decently agreed.

I went back, changed into my red pyjamas and climbed once more on to the trolley. I was wheeled along to the 'horsebox', the title affectionately bestowed on the emergency theatre which was the converted end of the children's ward. McIndoe was already at work in the main theatre.

With the usual feeling of relief I felt the hypodermic needle pushed into my arm, and within five seconds I was unconscious.

For the next week I was very ill, though quite how seriously I could only judge by the alacrity with which all my requests were granted. I was again in the glass extension of Sister Hall's ward and she nursed me all day and most of the night. I had regular morphia injections and for long periods at a time I was delirious. The bug had got into my lip and was biting deep into the skin at three places. I remember being in worse pain than at any time since my crash. After the plastic operations I had felt no discomfort, but now with the continuous throbbing agony in my head I thought that I must soon go mad. I would listen with dread for the footsteps of the doctors, knowing that the time was come for my dressings, for the piercing of the hole behind my ear with a thin steel probe to keep it open for draining, a sensation that made me contract within myself at the mere touch of the probe on the skin.

It was during my second night in the glass extension that a 2,500 lb bomb landed a hundred yards away but did not explode. I heard it coming down with a curious whirring rustle, and as I heard it I prayed, prayed that it would be near and bring with it peace, that it would explode and take with it me, the extension, the ward, the huts, everything. For a moment I thought it had, so great was the force of impact, but as I realised slowly that it had not exploded I found that the tears were pouring down my face: I was sobbing with mingled pain, rage, and frustration. Sister immediately gave me another morphia injection.

It was decided that while the excavation squad was digging it out, everybody possible must be evacuated to the convalescent home. Those who were too ill to be moved would go to Ward Three on the far side of the hospital. I imagined that I would go along with the others, but after taking a look at me McIndoe decided that it would be too dangerous to move me. Sister Hall offered to send a special nurse with me, but they thought even so the risk was too great.

Sister looked at me: 'I'm afraid that means the huts,' she said. At that something exploded inside me. McIndoe's chief assistant came into the ward to arrange for me to be moved and I let fly. I had not spoken since my operation and I saw the surprise in his face as I hauled myself up in bed and opened my mouth. Wild horses, I said, would not drag me back to that garbage-can of human refuse. If anyone laid a finger on my bed I would get up and start to walk to London. I preferred to die in the open rather than return to that stinking kitchen of fried flesh. I had come into the hospital with two scars on my upper lip: now I had a lip that was pox-ridden and an ear with enough infection in it to kill a regiment. There was only one thing to be said for the British medical profession: it started where the Luftwaffe left off. An outburst to which I now confess with shame, but which at the time relieved my feelings considerably.

'You're not making this very easy,' he answered mildly.

'You're damn right, I'm not,' I said, and then felt very sick and lay down.

It was then that Sister Hall was magnificent.

'I think perhaps he should stay here in his present state, sir,' she said. 'I'll see if I can fix up something.'

The doctor, only too willing to have the problem off his hands, looked grateful, and left. I saw that she was smiling.

'Well, Mr Hillary,' she said, 'quite like old times,' and went off to see what she could arrange. Somehow she obtained permission to convert one of the consulting rooms further down the hospital into a ward, and my bed was pushed along.

That night McIndoe came in to see me. He was still wearing his operating robes and sat down on the end of the bed. He talked to me for some time – of the difficulties of running a unit such as this, of the inevitable trials and setbacks which must somehow be met. He knew, he said, that I had had a tough break, but I must try not to let it get me down. I noticed that he looked tired, dead tired, and remembered that he had been operating all day. I felt a little ashamed. The next day my mother and Denise motored down to see me. I was grey in the face from all the Prontosil that I was taking and they both thought that I was on the way out, though of this they gave no sign. Poor Mother. The crash, the sea, the hospital, the operations – she had weathered them all magnificently. But this last shock was almost too much. She did not look very well.

During the last five months I had gradually built up to my usual weight of twelve stone, but in the next week I sweated my temperature down to normal and my weight down to nine stone. I also began to feel more human, and as the bomb had been removed and the evacuated ones brought back, I returned to the main ward and the regular hospital routine.

If there is one thing I really loathe it is to be awakened an hour earlier than necessary with a cup of cold brown tea. Unfortunately I could not approach Tony's imperious sarcasm, which was proof against all nurses until nine o'clock, but I finally hit on an idea for stopping this persecution. Nurse Courtney promised that if I made no more remarks about Ireland, she would no longer wake me with tea. I agreed with alacrity, saying that I could easily dispense with both. She at once bristled but was calmed down by sister.

My God, I thought, who would be a nurse! They must suffer all the inconveniences of convent celibacy without the consolation of that inner glow which I take to be an integral part of the spiritual life.

It was shortly after this that Edmonds was readmitted to the hospital and placed in the bed next to mine. He was the worst-burned pilot in the Air Force to live. Taking off for his first solo in a Hampden at night, he had swung a little at the end of his run and put a wing in. The machine had immediately turned over and burst into flames. He had been trapped inside and fried for several minutes before they dragged him out. When he had first been brought to McIndoe he had been unrecognisable and had lain for months in a bath of his own suppuration. McIndoe performed two emergency operations and then left it to time and careful dressings to heal him enough for more.

Never once had Edmonds complained. After nine months McIndoe had sent him away to build up his strength. Now he was back. It would take years to build him a new face. He was completely cheerful, and such was his charm that after two minutes one never noticed his disfigurement.

He was first on the list for operation the day after his readmission. Both his top lids and his lower lip were done together and he was brought back to the ward, even-tempered as ever. The man on his other side diverted him for most of the day with endless funny stories of crashes. Sometimes I think it would be very pleasant to be invested with the powers of life and death.

Three days went by and I noticed an ominous dribble down Edmonds' right cheek from under the dressing across his eyes. That night McIndoe took the dressing down: the right eyelid graft had not taken. He took it off and threw it away: it was the streptococcus at work again, and bitterly ironical that McIndoe's first eyelid failure should be on Edmonds. He was immediately put on to Prontosil and by the next morning was a greeny blue, with his lower lip jutting out like an African tribeswoman's.

After lunch some idiotic woman came in and exclaimed at how marvellously well he looked. I held my breath but I need not have worried. Instead of turning his face to the wall or damning her soul, he managed to smile and said:

'Yes, and I'm feeling much better too.'

I could not but marvel at his self-control and unruffled good manners. I remembered a few of my own recent outbursts and felt rather small.

Here was a twenty-six-year-old South African with no ties in this country, no mere boy with his whole life to make, terribly injured without even the satisfaction of having been in action. Sometimes he behaved as though he had been almost guilty not to have been shot down, as though he were in the hospital under false pretences; but if ever a pilot deserved a medal it was he. He read little, was not musical, yet somehow he carried on. How? What was it that gave not only him but all these men the courage to go on and fight their way back to life? Was it in some way bound up with the consciousness of death? This was a subject which fascinated me and I had discussed it with McIndoe. Did people know when they were about to die? He maintained that they did not, having seen over two hundred go, none of them conscious that their last moment had come.

'How about Charles II's apology for being such an unconscionable time a-dying?'

He admitted that in some cases people might have a premonition of death, but in cases of terrible physical injury he would say never. Their physical and mental conditions were not on a different plane: the first weakened the second (if I report him accurately), and there was neither consciousness of great pain nor realisation of the finality of physical disintegration.

That, then, would account for my calmness when in the sea. I knew well enough, meanwhile, that sheer anger had pulled me through my mastoid complication. But what of the men who, after the first instinctive fight to live, after surviving the original physical shock, went on fighting to live, cheerfully aware that for them there was only a half-life? The blind and the utterly maimed – what of them? Their mental state could not remain in the same dazed condition after their bodies began to heal. Where did they get the courage to go on?

It worried me all day. Finally I decided that the will to live must be entirely instinctive and in no way related to courage. This nicely resolved any suspicion that I might recently have behaved rather worse than any of the others, might have caused unnecessary trouble and confusion. Delighted with my analysis of the problem, I settled myself to sleep.

51 Mark 'Hilly' Brown Part 3, Hurricane Pilot, Pilot Officer, Canadian, 1 Squadron

Resting north of the main action at RAF Wittering in Cambridgeshire, Hilly still managed to find the enemy. This series of letters and a combat report covers late September to 20 November 1940. 'Alex' Kent is the famous fellow Canadian ace Johnny Kent.

Brown was shot down by flak over Gela in Sicily on 12 November 1941 while leading 249 Squadron in Malta, and a few weeks later the Italians notified the British that he had been buried with military honour. He now lies in Catania War Cemetery, Sicily. By the end of 1940 he had sixteen confirmed victories and four shared kills, the majority shot down over France.

For more information on his time in France, read fellow 1 Squadron pilot Paul Richey's memoir *Fighter Pilot: A Personal Record of the Campaign in France – September 8th, 1939 to June 13th, 1940* (first published 1942), which refers to Hilly Brown frequently, and his sister Jean Brown Segall's biography of her brother, *Wings of the Morning* (first published 1945). Also see Gordon Olive's extract (see chapter 18); he met Brown in August 1940 after he was shot down in flames and injured.

26 September 1940, Wittering, Peterborough, letter home We came up here for a rest, and now it looks as if we shall stay here. There were a number of the boys in need of a good rest.

22 October 1940, Wittering, Peterborough, letter home The Huns keep cracking at London and the south, but we don't see any of the big stuff up here. The weather is very seldom favourable for large formations now anyway. I haven't been in London since the blitz on it started, the but the people are bearing up very well. I would rather be there than in Berlin or Hamburg.

25 October 1940, letter home I am still at the same job. Another chap and I shot down a Hun yesterday. We don't get a crack at much up here, so it is quite an event now.

I saw Alex Kent today. He has just been promoted to squadron leader and was on his way to his new squadron.

Don Miller was sent on an instructors course when he got out of hospital after he cracked up, and I believe is going to Moose Jaw now.

I would love to have about six months in Canada, myself, but expect that by that time I would be itching to be in it again. I have my heart set on getting home, but in any case I will be a squadron leader by spring if I stay here.

Form F, Combat Report 24 October 1940. Time attack delivered 12.05; Enemy casualties 1 Do 17 destroyed crashed nr St Neots; Place attack delivered East of Banbury; General report: Enemy sighted at 12.04 near Banbury by No. 2 who proceeded ahead. Height of E/A on sighting 10–12,000 feet. First attacked by No. 2 at about 6–7,000 feet. E/A half rolled and came back towards Red 1 & 3. I attacked from above as Red 2 broke away commencing with full deflection at 400 yards to 6 degrees deflection at 100 yards when he disappeared in cloud. Fired 1,448 rounds in one burst. Camouflage and markings normal. He did not use cloud cover as much as would be expected, and I am of the opinion he was not a very experienced pilot. I was then separated from Red 2 and 3 so asked for a separate pip squeak. I was vectored to St Neots where I was told to orbit. It was clear of cloud at this spot. I had orbited for several minutes watching for him to come out of the cloud when I was told he had crashed at St Neot. I did not know I was over the place mentioned. The E/A must have been below cloud before he came to the clear space.

20 November 1940, letter home Ernie is now wing commander, and is here studying operations. He wants to go back to Canada, but is having a bit of a struggle to fix it.

McGregor is now commanding the (all-Canadian) squadron.

The Spitfire is a very nice machine, and a better match for the Me 109 in speed, but just the same, nobody on Hurricanes wants to change. Our big advantages are a steadier gun platform, better manoeuvrability and easy servicing. Also we can operate under worse conditions re size and surface of landing fields.

When I came back from France I had 16 Huns to my credit, and have since accounted for one and a half and two damaged. I missed a lot of fights when I was U/S (unserviceable) with my burns.

The business of my last CO killing himself in a foolish crash, when he was the last person in the world I would have expected to do such a thing, was a very strange trick of fate. It seems so strange that one who was so much against dangerous flying should finish himself in such a way as to be an example for one of his strictest orders.

I had everything all set to get an instructors course and get back to Canada, but this happens; the station commander recommends that I become Squadron Leader M. H. Brown, DFC, OC No.1 Fighter Squadron RAF.

As far as I know, I am the only squadron leader to come right up from acting pilot officer to squadron leader remaining in the same unit. I was looking forward to seeing you so much, but now I must do another year or so of much harder work than I have done before, and then maybe I will get some reward. As a matter of fact, I couldn't have been better rewarded for staying when the old stalwarts came back (from France) than I have been. There are still a lot of chaps senior to me who have not been given a command.

We aren't seeing much action these days, but should do so once in a while this winter.

52 René Mouchotte Part 2, Hurricane Pilot, Flying Officer, French, 615 Squadrons

The final extract from the posthumous publication of Mouchotte's diaries covers 1 October to early November 1940, during which time he was finally posted to the centre of the Battle at RAF Northolt, west London (11 Group). The Polish squadron relieved by Mouchotte's squadron is the famous 303 Squadron.

Mouchotte would go on to command an RAF squadron, have tea with Churchill and be decorated by General de Gaulle. He did not write his diaries with any intention of publishing them, and was shot down and killed in combat over the French coast on 27 August 1943 while escorting American B-17 Flying Fortress bombers. But his story does not quite end there. The body of one 'René Martin' was washed up on a beach in Belgium on 3 September 1943 and duly buried with military honours by the Belgium authorities. This is relevant as 'René Martin' was Mouchotte's alias, a necessity to avoid reprisals against his family in occupied France if he ever fell over enemy soil. It was recorded on the death certificate that the name 'Adjt René Mouchotte' was written in ink on a tailors label on the inner pocket of his jacket. The grave was eventually correctly identified as René's through sterling work by an unnamed RAF liaison officer of the War Graves Commission, and his remains were brought back to France and reburied in the family vault in 1949. His mother and a family friend named André Dezarrois later edited the diaries into a book.

As for the fates of his two compatriots who escaped Algeria, Charles Guérin was KIA on May 1941, his body never recovered; Henry Lafont survived the war.

For permission to quote from the Diaries I would like to thank the Quentin-Mouchotte Family Archives and Hubert de Lisle. I'd also like to thank Jan Leeming for her help.

1 October 1940 Much excitement on waking up. Two of us are going to the outskirts of London. Alas! Ten times alas! I am staying... Another separation. Two Frenchmen here, in two different flights. The bitterness I feel is mixed with a trace of jealousy. Those who are leaving are going to the north east of London, on the Thames estuary, over which all the German squadrons coming to England have to pass. It is there that the Battle of London is being fought at this moment, upon which the fate of the world depends. Why have they been chosen rather than me? I make absurd suppositions which end in the conclusion that chance has decided it thus and that my turn will soon come. I am sorry to see the departure of two good friends with whom I had, in pure imagination, taken part in so many fierce battles. Must my dream of being the first Frenchman to shoot down a Boche be abandoned?

Two accidents in a few days, one fatal. The first was due to the pilot's inattention. He came down in the sea, near the shore, and was able to be picked up. The second is inexplicable. During a combat exercise, at 3,000 metres, the plane dived at full speed to the ground and crashed... The pilot had vertigo, probably, or a black-out. Combat at these speeds involves extremely steep turns and pretty fierce pulling out to shake off the enemy, which, on account of the centrifugal force, produces a rush of blood to the lower part of the body, causing blindness for a few seconds. With your eyes wide open, you see nothing but blackness. That is sometimes enough to make you lose control of the plane. They say a pilot cannot stand two minutes of black-out. During acrobatics and in combat in the Hurricane I am always having black-outs; it is rather unpleasant but I console myself by thinking that the man behind me, on my tail, certainly has a black-out too.

I have been here a fortnight, flying more than I ever did in France. I often go on missions, not very dangerous ones, for the Germans rarely show their noses here. Nearly all my French comrades are in the south and are certainly in combat every day...

8 October At last we are leaving for London with the whole squadron. Perhaps in a few days I shall have my duel. At last I shall be able to try and avenge my mother for all the misery she is suffering. Sometimes I have bloodthirsty impulses which astonish me. I should die content if I first slaked this thirst for revenge. Each time my thoughts fly to France (God knows how many times a day) I am haunted by these memories; each time, I feel a weight on my heart, like a physical pain. Shall I have made all these sacrifices uselessly? I do not think so; I have faith in my star. I am sure I shall see France again, return to all I love... But when?

10 October, RAF Prestwick, Scotland (13 Group) We took off southward, sixteen planes. Shocking weather, very low cloud, thick mist in places. But it was absolutely necessary to go. We are replacing a squadron of tired Poles who are taking our place at Prestwick. No trouble on the trip; marvellously fast.

Chapter 4: At Northolt with the Churchill Squadron, 10 October, RAF Northolt, West London (11 Group) We have arrived at Northolt, a modern aerodrome with runways, at the gateway to London, since the underground reaches it. It is much nearer the capital than Le Bourget is to Paris. We are at readiness from today. They do not lose time in England. For we are exclusively charged with the defence of the biggest city in the world. It was with some little pride that I learned I was to be one of the guardian angels of this very proud city.

'The job goes on all the time,' two Poles, who are leaving tomorrow for a rest, told me, 'you'll always be at readiness!' This Polish squadron has done a first class job; in a month they have shot down 115 planes. This promises to be enormously interesting for us, but alas, what casualties! Nearly 50 per cent of their comrades have not returned from the battle and some are wounded... These last details left us thoughtful.

11 October My first fighting mission: an event. Greatly excited. We took off, twenty-four of us, in three minutes: a record. There is always a layer of mist over London which nowadays almost completely hides the city and its suburbs. We soon went through this ceiling and at once found ourselves beneath an immensely blue sky. The radio was guiding us, probably to meet a German squadron making for England. In places we saw the ground, very small, for we were already at 22,000 feet. I was thinking hard. Memories, ideas rushed into my mind, while my hands were busy.

I saw France. Far, far, very far off, the coast stood out clearly. Without wanting to be emotional, I abandoned myself to a feeling of great sadness and pity...

Instinctively I scanned the sky from which, fiercely and treacherously, might rush the danger we were fighting. Fighter work is like a dagger in the back. Each opponent dodges, escapes, returns, seeks the advantage of altitude, a spot in the sun, the better to achieve surprise, and at the moment when he is least expected he drops on the other like a stone and kills him from behind. That is the law...

The light patrol therefore has a plane to make S's behind it to protect it from surprise. A few metres to starboard I saw my squadron leader, his head continually turning to all the visible points of the sky. Behind us followed three groups of four, slightly below us, in perfect formation. From time to time came radio instructions, followed at once by the leader's answer, and the whole formation turned on a new course. What wonderful discipline and what a terrible engine of war we are handling! Still nothing in the sky. I was intensely awaiting the moment of meeting the Germans... My heart beat faster, for far off, much higher than we were, I had just seen a cloud of furiously fast black specks. Would they be Messerschmitts? I pointed them out over the radio to my squadron leader, who signalled me the meteors' nationality: they were no other than Spitfires.

The time came to turn back; the order rang in my ears. I was not sorry; my hands were horribly cold. In the rush to get away I had forgotten my silk gloves. Also I am not yet accustomed to breathing oxygen for so long.

12 October Our squadron has just had the honour of a visit, between two spells in the air, from Air Vice-Marshal Park. He shook hands with all the pilots. When he came to me he asked me about my escape and, after wishing me luck, congratulated me on my English. He must be deaf.

An hour later, Eve Curie came. What sweetness and simplicity! After listening to us, she talked about her propaganda in America and her lectures on Free France. She told us of her faith in the future and in our early return to a liberated France. We French in Britain who go on fighting from here enable her to make her propaganda tours. She talked to us about her sister and brother-in-law, still in Paris. I am very proud; she has asked me to telephone her when next I go to London.

14 October Our flights over London go on almost without interruption. I am beginning to get used to high altitudes. This morning we put to flight a group of Messerschmitts much bigger than ours. They crossed the Channel again without our being able to get at them. I find the Hurricane is no longer fast enough for modern combat. The latest German bombers can almost keep up with it. In spite of these disadvantages in speed and manoeuvrability it has been noticed that the Germans generally refuse battle unless they have superiority in numbers and the advantage of altitude.

Every night, about seven o'clock, the sirens sound, and immediately afterwards the first bombs crash on London and the suburbs. We are not spared. All night, till dawn, the bombers keep coming over and dropping their load. Londoners have good nerves; during the day nothing of their nightly ordeal shows and work goes on everywhere.

17 October Yesterday I had my first engagement with Messerschmitts, for an instant. I confess I didn't see very much, the Germans being well above us. I saw a Spitfire dive earthwards at terrifying speed, trailing a cloud of black smoke after it. Poor lad! Another one. Up to us to carry on his work.

At this season of the year the sun is almost entirely lost in cloud, so that in the air the pilot is dazzled by the contrast between the white immensity stretching out beneath him and the limpidity of the sky. The Germans, who can go much higher than we can, therefore have the frightful advantage of seeing us coming far off and are consequently able to manoeuvre to approach unseen by us out of the sun; they have the advantage of height, speed, and often of numbers. Yesterday we flung our poor Hurricanes up desperately, throttles wide open. They wouldn't climb and we had the unpleasant impression of standing still. Appallingly unpleasant moments.

18 October The finest day I have had since coming to Great Britain. I long to shout my joy to the whole world. In London I met a woman who runs a club where Frenchmen often go. She herself is French, married to a Russian. She very kindly lent me her name to try and write to France. The letters apparently did not arrive so I sent a telegram to Cannes. My uncle has just replied, 'Family all well.' Now he will know I am here; I am happy.

19 October Two-hour patrol over London and Dover. Saw quite a few Germans, always, alas, perched five or six thousand feet above our heads. We leap, but by the time we arrive they have long ago decamped. We landed almost without petrol. I was at the head of the squadron, next to the squadron leader, when I noticed 50 feet from the ground that I only had one wheel down. I circled the aerodrome and tried the mechanism to lower the undercarriage several times. Nothing happened. I pressed the safety lever: no result. Looking at my fuel, I noticed that I had only four gallons in the reserve tank. I climbed to 3,000 feet, and made a dive followed by an abrupt pull-out, hoping thus to dislodge my recalcitrant wheel. Nothing doing... I asked for instructions on the radio, not wanting to land without permission. I saw the whole squadron, which had landed an instant ago, with faces uplifted to watch me turning desperately, like a one-legged man. I tried all the mechanisms once more. No. My petrol exhausted, I should have to make a belly landing. A pretty prospect. Well, that was the order on the radio. The ground came nearer and nearer. I had taken the precaution of retracting the other wheel. I was well strapped in. I made a very shallow glide. I kept the plane in the air as long as possible. Finally the tail touched down first. The plane bumped savagely on the ground. I felt myself flung forward. But I was well wedged in and went about 60 metres with the nose ploughing up the earth. I stopped without hurting myself. But up came the ambulance and the fire-tender at full speed.

'Not worth the trouble, gentlemen!'

I had been expecting everything except the congratulations, and they came from every side.

21 October I have not yet succeeded in seeing any good reason for the necessity of balloons of the sausage variety, ranged in their thousands over towns and country. I remember having seen our balloons at an altitude of about 6,000 metres in Paris. They therefore put up effective opposition to the German raids. Here the sausages rarely go as high as 2,000 metres, giving the enemy no trouble; far from it, indeed, for comically enough, when a raid is announced, they are lowered lest the Germans should shoot them down. On the other hand, the barrage balloons are extremely harmful to pilots here who have to return to their base deep in very thick mist (nine days out of ten at this season). An Englishman touched a cable last week and was killed. Five days ago, guided by radio, a patrol of three Poles crashed in the same way. Our landing ground is literally ringed with balloons, and yesterday in particular I only just had time to yell over the radio to the leader of my patrol, 'Balloons! Balloons!' There was a monster less than 50 metres ahead of us. We made steep turns, each to his own side, and I immediately lost him. I must confess I felt far from pleased with myself, with visibility nil in that field of balloons... In the end I managed, after much worry and perspiration, to find my way back to the landing ground. They were waiting anxiously for me.

24 October I returned to London this morning and my first visit was to 'René Ignatieff', my letterbox. One never knew... In fact my kind friend greeted me with a broad smile. 'Good news tonight, René; another telegram for you.' This one came from Dordogne. My uncle must have written to my sister and given her my address. So now I am in touch, but still without direct news of my mother.

Actually, a few days afterwards, a far from ordinary looking letter came by airmail for me, covered with crossings-out, and censored. I opened it. Oh, surprise! It was my mother's writing! I did not believe my eyes. In a few words she contrived to tell me that she approves of my conduct and is proud of it. Poor mother, you are paying dearly for that pride; what fearful anxiety you must feel on my account! Deep in action as I am, I have no more time for thought. I must not think. An excess of emotion can only spoil the top mental and physical form which is indispensable in the great fight we are carrying on. But you, over there, all on your own, are worn with anxiety. What sleepless nights you must pass! Leaning over the radio I imagine you feeling like the stab of a knife the lying news that a terrifying daily total of English fighters is shot down by the glorious Messerschmitts...

I wrote at once to thank the American lady who had agreed to forward this blessed letter to me.

25 October An engagement with three enemy planes this morning. This time again I did not see much. I could not take the initiative because I did not know where the danger was coming from; I followed the formation into a dive. I had a black-out. Then the shouting stopped, the squadron reformed and went up to the ceiling. Three

Messerschmitts, apparently, attacked us. They must have passed quite close to me for I was right in the rear of the formation, highest in the air. The cold is beginning to make itself seriously felt. At 9,000 metres thighs and hands feel the pin pricking of the temperature. Tomorrow I shall wear more clothes.

Evening 25 October I very nearly covered myself with glory; unfortunately Providence wouldn't permit it today. Patrolling above the squadron, like a dog with sheep, I suddenly saw a big twin-engined plane 10,000 feet below us just above the cloud. I went into a dizzy dive, passing just in front of another Hurricane to draw it after me. Unfortunately the other saw us soon enough to have time to plunge into the thick cloud and disappear without trace. This is not a very interesting tale to tell, but it was such a disappointment to see the prey before me that I make a point of recording it. These pages are meant only to be read by me in a few years' time.

28 October Today is mother's birthday. I should love to shut my eyes and be transported to her. We would go out gaily, arm in arm, for a walk, talking about nothing and everything. One day, perhaps?

30 October Attacked by Messerschmitts, higher up than we were; we did not see them, the sun is so dazzling. They dropped out of the sky like three stones and climbed back without giving us time to say 'Ouf!' In the scrap that followed I saw two of ours shot down. One of them was my only French comrade in the squadron. Luckily he was not hit and landed in a field. The enemy has a terrible advantage in superiority of altitude.

31 October It was our turn to attack this morning: an unhappy bomber, making off like the devil, turning starboard and port and diving desperately for France. Two comrades and I chased him three-quarters of the way across the Straits of Dover. He was hit and I think we damaged him; black smoke came out of his port engine for a moment. I threw my hand in; I have no desire to be brought down and shot in France.

That is what has just happened to three unhappy young men who bravely landed in Morocco with the intention of attracting other French pilots to England. Unfortunately they were caught and executed at once. I knew one of them very well. Shame on the men who order such crimes! An obscure death, but glorious and beautiful … Our task will not be done when we return.

2 November 615 has just had a visit from Mr Churchill. What a surprise! What an honour! We were all there, the twelve pilots at readiness, wearing our yellow pneumatic lifejackets in case of coming down in the sea. He came in a car and shook hands with everyone, saying a few words to each. He speaks French very well. He is most informal and extremely likeable. To think that the future of the world depends on this man's will… A square jaw; he certainly has the jaw of the English bulldog which grips but does not let go its prey. He talked to our squadron leader, smiling all the time and sucking the end of a match. He wanted to see our flying monsters. I learned that he is the godfather of 615. Churchill our godfather!

When he had gone I was told that he has promised us, soon, a transcendant new plane with speed, altitude and armament superior to the Germans. Figures were mentioned to me; I dare not believe them, these machines are so prodigious.

I have just been a spectator rather than a participant in a terrific air battle involving at least 100 enemy fighters. They were everywhere. As fast as we saw them overhead (as usual) we saw more of them coming. It was like an hallucination to have them moving so fast and always above us. We tried to get at them and were at our poor planes' ceiling when we were attacked by a squadron of Messerschmitts which calmly turned barely 100 metres above us and placed themselves in the sun to dazzle us the better. There was nothing we could do but clear out fast, which we did, I as fast as the rest, taking very little time to drop to 5,000 feet in zig-zags. At each turn I blacked out. We went at over 430 miles an hour...

TESTAMENT

If Fate allows me only a brief fighting career, I shall thank Heaven for having been able to give my life for the liberation of France. Let my mother be told that I have always been very happy and thankful that the opportunity has been given me to serve GOD, MY COUNTRY and THOSE I LOVE, and that, whatever happens, I shall always be near her.

René Mouchotte

53 Arthur 'Art' Donahue Part 3, Spitfire Pilot, Pilot Officer, American, 64 Squadron

Final extract from Art's 1941 memoir, covering the beginning of October to the end of November 1940. Art had been in hospital recovering from the wounds received when he was shot down on 13 August and then on a period of leave. He returned to his squadron, which was by then resting in Yorkshire at RAF Leconfield (13 Group), around 26 September.

Art is pretty sure he gets his first kill (an Me 109) on 11 November, but the records show he was only awarded a 'damaged'; my sense is of an overzealous intelligence officer and I think the kill was made. Art doesn't come across as a 'line shooter'. Donahue flew Hurricanes later in the war in Singapore against the Japanese, which he wrote about in his second book, *Last Flight From Singapore*, published posthumously in 1944. He went MIA in 1942 with two kills under his belt.

Chapter 8 Impatience: c. *2 October–7 November 1940 (based RAF Leconfield, Yorkshire in 13 Group to 13 October, then RAF Biggin Hill, Bromley, Greater London in 11 Group to 15 October, then RAF Coltishall, Norfolk in 12 Group)* The day we were waiting for, when we could go back to frontline fighting, was a long time coming. Occasionally an order would come through posting one of our new pilots to one of the squadrons that were in the blitz and replacing him with a new pilot for us to train up. Then there would be a lot of goodbyes and well-wishes to the boy who was off for the front, including the oft repeated counsel to 'watch your tail and keep your rear vision mirror polished.'

But though we grew more and more impatient to get back into the fray no orders came for the squadron to move. I was particularly anxious to get back and even things up for my own defeat. I had no confirmed victories before being shot down myself, and as I told my friends I hated to go about with a score of minus one to my credit.

The great squadron of all Polish pilots and ground personnel joined us, having been sent up here to rest also. They had gotten 126 confirmed victories in less than six weeks, which I believe is a record for any RAF squadron in that length of time. They fought savagely, for their pilots had nothing to lose. Most of them had seen so much of murder and terror and tragedy among their people before they escaped from Poland that they didn't care to live. One night I traded one of my uniform buttons with one of their ace pilots, for one of his, and I still wear it and am very proud of it.

Gilly [Ernest Gilbert] told me a great deal of how the squadron fared after I was shot down in August, for the rest of the time that they remained in the blitz. The day after I was downed had been pretty bad. He was leading the squadron's rearguard section on a patrol when they were sent to break up a raid that was forming up over Cape Gris Nez on the French coast. The squadron had sighted sixty Messerschmitts and turned to sail into them, and Gilly's section happened to be on the outside of the turn because of their rearguard maneuvers, with the result that they got left quite a way behind.

And then the three of them were attacked from behind by nearly fifty Messerschmitts. Gilly alone of the three in his section got back. He shot down one Messerschmitt off Bud's tail, but Bud was already going down in flames, and then his own machine was being riddled from behind, by another Messerschmitt. Steam blinded him so he couldn't see, and he had to open his hatch, unfasten his straps, and stand up to see out; and that way he flew all the way back across the Channel with this Messerschmitt following him and shooting at him, so that he had to keep twisting violently one way then the other, all the time.

Somehow his wrecked engine managed to keep going until just before he reached the coast, when it seized up, out of oil and with radiator dry of course, and he made a forced landing on the belly of his machine with the wheels retracted. The Messerschmitt pilot had exhausted his ammunition by the time Gilly's engine stopped, and he gave up the chase. Gilly's machine was riddled with bullets and completely ruined.

A day or two later [Jack] Mann got a bullet in his hip and his machine badly damaged, but he managed to fly back to the airdrome. He was still in the hospital and was expected to be laid up for several months. The CO had his machine shot down in flames on one of those days, and he baled out unhurt, although when he landed in his parachute in a small village he had a hard time convincing the residents that he wasn't a German spy who should be shot.

The climax of the week's events was the raid on the squadron's own airdrome. They were on patrol right over the airdrome, trying to intercept a German formation at twenty-five thousand feet, when another big formation of bombers attacked the airdrome from low altitude. The squadron dived straight down at more than six hundred miles per hour and sailed into the bombers. Altogether they shot down ten bombers with no casualties to themselves.

Gilly got one of them, a Heinkel. He got it away from its formation and the pilot must have been pretty good, for when Gilly attacked he did all sorts of acrobatics with the big machine to evade him. Gilly followed, shooting whenever he got a chance, and finally caught him in a stalled turn and gave him a good long burst that finished him, and the Heinkel turned over and dived straight down in from about five thousand feet, bursting into flames when it hit.

Other squadrons that joined the fight shot down eighteen German planes and the ground defenses got two, which with the ten our squadron got made a total of thirty machines and crews that the raid cost the Luftwaffe.

Considering that only a small amount of damage was done by the bombing it was quite a victory for the RAF. However, it very nearly finished the frazzled nerves of some of the boys of our squadron, and that night the grateful news came that they were to pack up and move to this place in the north next day.

Early in October we were ordered to move to a base farther south, which though not yet in the blitz area was nevertheless quite close to it, and there was a lot more activity by hit-and-run bombers. An outside factor unfortunately interfered just then and kept me out of the squadron and in idleness for the first two weeks, but I finally got back with them again and started doing my share of the work. The bombers were coming over individually and trying all sorts of tricks to get us side-tracked long enough to get through and bomb a city or harbour in our area. Often they came over very high, carrying only small bomb loads. The whole squadron was seldom sent up at once, but there were many patrols by sections of three.

Have you ever made clouds? I have. It was on these patrols that I first made them and became acquainted with the strangest, weirdest, and most beautiful phenomenon that I have encountered in flying. They are generally called 'vapor trails' by pilots, and the phenomenon usually occurs only in the thin cold air at high altitudes, although I have seen it as low as eight thousand feet in the winter. I had seen these trails a few times in the summer, when fighters were flying at thirty or thirty-five thousand feet overhead, appearing as thin white lines curving about the sky overhead. Now in the fall the air was cold enough for trails to be made sometimes as low as twenty thousand feet.

I understand that the wings and propeller of a high-speed airplane rushing through the air cause sudden changes in the air pressure in its path, so that moisture in the air condenses into cloud and the condensed droplets then freeze instantly, before they have time to evaporate again.

Whatever be the cause, the effect is the weirdest thing imaginable. As a formation of planes enters the altitude at which vaporization begins to take place, each pilot begins to notice what seem like wisps of white smoke streaming back from the tails of the other machines. When they have climbed a little bit higher these become good-sized clouds billowing back, about the size of the cloud of dust that a car rolls up when moving fast on a dusty road, though of course streaming back several times as fast. Indeed, the pilot's view in the rear vision mirror of his machine while he is 'vaporizing' is just like what you get looking in the rear vision mirror of your car when billowing clouds of dust behind you obscure everything else in your mirror.

As a rule these trails stay put for an hour or so, recording in the sky the tracks of the planes that have been there and gone, until they gradually widen out and diffuse themselves in the atmosphere. From the ground the machines, when they are vapourizing, look like invisible paint brushes drawing silvery white lines across the blue dome of the sky, slowly and majestically; for the planes are too high to be seen themselves usually, and because of the distance the movement seems to be very slow.

To sit on the ground watching the trails made by, say, a section of three planes of your own squadron on patrol, and try to realize that at the head of each silver line curving across the sky five or six miles overhead is a pal who was sitting beside you in the pilots' hut a half-hour before, is in my belief to stretch the imagination beyond its capacity. It's certainly beyond mine! And it's interesting too, to land after having flown high overhead, and to look up and see your own track inscribed up there in the sky.

One bright sunny morning three of us were up on patrol, trying to find a bandit which was reported approaching the coast at a point in our area, and we headed out over the sea. We were at about twenty thousand feet, which is not in the stratosphere, but is so high that the sky is a more intense blue and the sun brighter and everything more frigid and wintry-looking. I had been engrossed for a moment checking my instruments and closing my radiator shutter, because it was very cold up there and my engine was beginning to run too cold. Glancing up, I noticed, emblazoned in the sky far above and ahead of us, something that I could only imagine at first as being a comet. It was a little patch of brilliant silver against the blue, in the exact shape of a comet, awe-inspiring in the weird stratosphere, and it nearly scared me out of my wits.

Then reason came back, and after making a quick estimate of its height and position I called over the R/T to our formation leader, 'Bandit ahead and to starboard! He's about thirty thousand feet and making a very short vapour trail!'

We opened throttle and gave chase, but after a minute the trail disappeared, and as we were too far away to see the airplane itself we of course lost it. Its pilot had apparently observed that he was making this trail and had dived to a lower altitude where it quit forming. Apparently the atmospheric conditions at his altitude were such that the cloud formation made by his machine evaporated and became invisible again after a split second, so that his visible trail remained only a few hundred feet long and took on the appearance of a comet. That was the first short vapour trail I had seen, although I've seen many since.

While at this place we got a good demonstration of the intelligence and initiative of Nazi bombing pilots one morning. This was a big airdrome and should have been an ideal bombing target, for there were dozens of big military buildings built close together – enormous hangars, shops, office buildings, big permanent barracks and messes, and dozens of houses for 'married quarters.' On an airdrome of this kind nearly two thousand men are required. It wasn't much over a hundred miles from the nearest German air base in Holland, yet not a single building had been hit by bombing so far, though I understand that the Nazi news dispatches had had it completely wiped out twice and badly damaged several times in addition.

One morning three of us who were on 'dawn readiness' had just finished our early breakfast and were walking out of the officers' mess toward the car we would drive to the dispersal hut when we heard the droning of strange engines nearby that resembled the sound of Daimler-Benz engines too much for comfort. It was in the quarter-light before dawn, and the stars were beginning to disappear.

Out of the east and not over two thousand feet up we saw the majestic outlines of a big Heinkel bomber coming directly overhead. If the pilot had released his bombs just then he couldn't have helped scoring hits on our hangars or other buildings, or on us. We waited expectantly, ready to throw ourselves on the ground, but no bombs came, and we gazed almost thunderstruck as the big machine sailed serenely on over. The crew couldn't possibly have helped seeing the buildings of the airdrome as they passed over.

Cosmer, our flight commander, shouted: 'Come on! He's going to turn around and make his 'bombing run' coming back! Let's get down to our machines as quick as we can!'

Stan, who was driving, kept one hand on the horn button, and the guards threw aside barbed wire and other barricades in advance of us as we raced through the camp and out across the field. Cosmer was raging and calling the Hun names. The thought of having our airdrome bombed maddened all of us.

'The lousy ___!' he kept repeating. 'He's going to bomb us for sure! Oh, why weren't we up five minutes earlier and down by our machines now?' He was on his knees on the back seat of the careering car, looking out the back window.

All at once he shouted: 'Look! He's dropping 'em now!' Then, in a puzzled tone, 'I wonder where that is?'

Great terrifying yellow splashes of light were flickering against the dim blue sky just above the horizon, seemingly four or five miles west of us, several of them in succession; and after they ceased a lurid yellow glow remained.

'Oh, he's started a fire too!' Cosmer was almost crying with rage. 'Come on, let's get in our machines and get off as quick as we can!'

We were at the pilots' hut now, and we dashed in and grabbed our helmets and parachutes. There was no time to bother with flying suits. Mechanics seeing our car racing across the field had already started up three machines for us, and we were airborne in no time; but we found no trace of the Hun, who had apparently headed out to sea and homeward as soon as he dropped his load. Neither could we find the spot which he had bombed, though after we gave up the chase we circled the area where the flashes had seemed to come from. There wasn't any fire to be seen either. There was a little village, but we could see no signs of damage in it.

An hour later we learned that the bombs had been aimed at the little village, though for what possible reason the pilot preferred a harmless little country village to a big military airdrome I don't know. Fortunately his aim was terrible considering how low he was, and all the bombs landed in an open field nearby. The yellow glow we had seen after the bombs had finished exploding, and which we thought was a fire that had been started, was merely from a bunch of incendiary bombs he had dropped along with the big ones. They were burning away harmlessly in the field.

The only explanation that we could imagine for it all was that the pilot didn't notice our airdrome until he was too far over it to drop his bombs, and then he didn't have nerve enough to come back again and take a crack at us. So he just dumped his bombs in the direction of the village and beat it, probably returning home to tell his superiors about 'direct hits on hangars, fuel depots, and ammunition dumps.' That seems to be a popular rhyme in Nazi war communiques.

Just after we got back from that chase another section was sent off to hunt two bandits that were reported over the sea near the coast. One of the pilots of this section had trouble getting his machine started and didn't take off until the others were out of sight. He was a Free French pilot, whom we called 'Chifi' [Maurice Choran].

The other two machines returned after about half an hour, having had no luck; but there was no sign of Chifi. We began to worry. He hadn't joined up with the other two at all, and hadn't been heard from after he took off. Soon, however, we saw another Spitfire coming in and began to relax a little.

It was Chifi's machine all right, and when he landed he seemed to have some trouble taxiing. Then we saw that one of his tires was flat. When he got closer to us we could also see that his guns had been fired, because the fabric covers over the holes in the wings in front of the guns were shot away. He was grinning from ear to ear as he climbed out of his machine, and in his halting English told us the story of the squadron's first action in several weeks.

He had gone out to sea in the direction that the other two planes had taken, hoping to find them and join up with them. Instead, after searching around for about twenty minutes he found two twin-engined Heinkel 115 German seaplanes flying low over the water together. He attacked, and in the running fight which followed he shot one of them down and got a few bullets in his own machine, one of them puncturing his tire.

This sort of life was of course occasionally exciting, but it seemed dull to us, with our hearts set on getting back into the frontline fighting. We began to get quite well settled, learned our way to and from all the local pubs in the black-out, got acquainted with the local townspeople, and so on.

One day I received a registered letter in the mail, containing a little jewel case. In it was a little solid gold badge in the shape of a caterpillar about an inch long, with an inscription engraved in very tiny letters on the back – a souvenir of my 'party' on 12 August. It is the emblem of the Caterpillar Club, to which anyone is eligible who has saved his life by a parachute. The idea is that caterpillars make the silk from which the parachutes are made. It came from the Irving Company, makers of parachutes.

October ended and the great 'Battle for Britain' seemed to be abating considerably according to the news, and still we were not moved into the frontline fighting. And then one day early in November it came! Forty-eight hours' notice for the squadron to move to, a famous airdrome on the outskirts of London! Jubilantly always, if occasionally a bit grimly, we bade goodbye to our friends and to our comparatively secure life here, and prepared to move back to the battle zone!

Chapter 9 Back to the Front – Tally-Ho Again: 8 November – AM 10 November 1940 (based RAF Coltishall, Norfolk in 12 Group, thereafter RAF Hornchurch, Essex in 11 Group) The two days we were given were busy ones. It's always a big event when a squadron moves. While twelve pilots are all that fly in a squadron at one time, it also has its own personnel of mechanics and helpers who move with the squadron; its own office and staff, a hundred per cent reserve of pilots and a fifty per cent reserve of airplanes, as well as all sorts of equipment and spares. The total personnel is well over two hundred.

There was a lot of packing to do and there were lots of arrangements to make, particularly in regard to transportation. The order came on Friday. Saturday night some of us had a little farewell party with some friends in a nearby village, and Percy got tight for the first time in his life and was murmuring all the way home about wanting to get four Huns down before Christmas.

Next day we moved. That was 10 November. Three of our reserve airplanes were ready to go (there were six in reserve but the other three were undergoing maintenance) so we flew down as a squadron of fifteen instead of the regular twelve.

The station personnel at our new airdrome greeted us warmly. We were replacing a squadron which had been there through most of the blitz and were being moved up north to rest just as we had been in August.

With wisdom born of previous moves I made a beeline for the officers' mess as soon as I was free, and 'signed in.' The best rooms are first come first served, and I got a very nice double room for myself and Jonah, with whom I'd arranged to room. Jonah was going on leave shortly and was to get married, so he'd be living out most of the time; but he would want a place in the mess to keep his flying equipment and some of his clothes, and to sleep nights when he had to be on duty early in the morning.

I was particularly delighted because our room had a fireplace, for fireplaces are the English institution that I love most of all. (This was a very old station that had been established in the First World War, and in the entry to the mess there were on display pieces of Zeppelins that had been shot down by planes operating from here in 1915 and 1916.) There were also a couple of the most beautiful, colored photos of Spitfires in flight, framed and hanging on the wall.

A second Spitfire squadron was stationed at this airdrome, and I found that their CO [41 Squadron, Donald Finlay] had been a roommate of mine in the hospital in August. In peacetime he had been a world-famous athlete.

Our first shift at readiness was to be from dawn to one o'clock the next day, which was Armistice Day – of all days to be going back into action!

I went to bed that night with mingled feelings of tenseness and fear, of course, and a kind of a fierce joy. From now on it would be playing for keeps again. Instead of hunting in threes after timid bombers and reconnaissance machines without having to guard against being attacked ourselves, we should now fly nearly always as a full squadron, hunting an enemy far superior in numbers who would also be hunting us and watching for a chance to attack us by surprise under circumstances favorable to hit-and-run tactics.

Because the only type of attack which the Nazi fighter pilots ever carry out against British fighters is by surprise, we had to fly in a type of formation that could guard itself well from surprises and be effective for attacking also. We were shown the newest type of formation used by the frontline squadrons, which while not spectacular was simple and very flexible.

Getting my machine ready next morning, I practically made a ceremony of changing the setting of my gunsight – in my efforts to be nonchalant and unceremonious about it. These sights can be adjusted for the wing span of the type of plane you expect to be shooting at. As you move the adjustment, a gap in a line across the middle of the sight narrows or widens; and the wingspan of whatever machine it's set for will just fill the gap when you are at the proper distance behind it to open fire.

Up north, where the enemy's fighters never came, I'd had it set for machines of seventy-foot wing span, for that's about the average span of the Heinkel, Junkers, and Dornier bombers that we hunted. Now I changed it to thirty-two and one-half feet, which is the span of the Messerschmitt 109 fighters.

I also gave my rear vision mirror an extra going over with my handkerchief. The memory of the month I'd spent in hospitals for not watching my mirror was still quite fresh in my mind.

This airdrome was equipped with a loudspeaker system, with speakers on all the buildings; and about nine o'clock a voice boomed over them: 'Squadron take off. Patrol base at ten thousand feet!'

Three minutes later we were in the air and climbing in squadron formation to the altitude ordered. Further orders followed over the R/T; Control was trying to bring us into contact with some enemy planes that were approaching London. Finally in the distance south of and above us we saw, among some puffs of anti-aircraft smoke, several enemy fighters scurrying about, very tiny in the distance. We climbed after them and they turned back. We weren't able to catch them because they had the advantage in height and we lost speed in climbing; and after following them out to the east coast and part way across the Channel we were ordered back to land. It was a nice little exercise, giving the new members of the squadron a chance to see what the new area of operations looked like and giving the rest of us a chance to refresh our memories of it.

We had only been on the ground a short time when we were off again under orders to join another squadron and fly with them, the two squadrons together making a wing, with ourselves leading.

It sounded as if something big might be up. We picked up the other squadron at about ten thousand feet over the airdrome, and after they were in line behind us we started climbing. Then our controller's voice sounded in our headphones: 'Steer towards Ramsgate and climb to twenty-five thousand feet.'

Ramsgate is a town on the southeast coast, a few miles north east of Dover. We climbed steeply and nearly wide open. It was a dark morning, with the sky covered by a high overcast. We entered the overcast at about eighteen thousand feet, and it proved to be sort of heavy haze, from which we emerged at about twenty-three thousand. About that time Control's voice came again with another order.

'In a couple of minutes I will give you a new course to steer that will lead you toward an objective. There are Junkers 87 and Messerschmitt 109 aircraft approaching this objective.'

My heart began to pound as I switched on my gunsight, removed the cover from my firing button, and turned the safety ring on the button to the position which read 'FIRE.' The news that there were Junkers 87s involved filled me with anticipation. Those are the 'Stuka' dive-bombers that were so terrible in their attacks on the armies in France. They hold no terrors for British fighter pilots, for they are the most vulnerable of all the standard German machines. Pilots who have been fortunate enough to engage them usually report that a two- or three-second burst of fire is all that's necessary to bring them down, and they are so slow and big that they are easy to hit. I'd never engaged anything but enemy fighters before, and the prospect of finding something easy was inviting.

Putting two and two together I guessed that our 'objective' must be a ship convoy, and the Junkers 87s would be coming to dive-bomb it. The 87s got treated so badly whenever they came over England that the Nazis hardly ever used them now except against shipping. The Messerschmitts would be accompanying the Junkers 87s as an escort to protect them from our fighters.

A moment later we were ordered to steer a course of 45 degrees and lost height quickly to five thousand feet. We headed northeast and began diving at about a thirty-degree angle, back into the haze, and just then someone in the squadron called over the R/T, 'Bandits ahead and above us!'

Sure enough, the queer little figures of about twenty Messerschmitt 109s were streaking towards us from in front, passing right over us and so close that we could easily make out details of their markings. It was almost like seeing old friends again. They were painted very dark gray, with their black crosses outlined in white so they could be seen against the gray, and their noses, clear back to their cockpits, were a dull yellow. In the summer they had all been almost white, or light blue-gray.

'Keep formation! Keep formation!' Our CO's voice warned us. 'Stay in formation and let them alone!'

I caught on. This was a Hun trick to keep us diverted up here while the raid was going on down below. As these Huns were above us we should be at a disadvantage in attacking them anyway. We kept going downward, and they turned around after they were behind us and followed us down very half-heartedly, not getting close enough to attack.

We broke through the haze and saw we were out over the sea. Far below and ahead were the dim outlines of a long line of ships, and we began to dive very steeply. Our speed was terrific, and my controls were becoming rigid from it. Tiny gnat like figures were milling about over the sea near the distant convoy, and the air around there was peppered with black puffs of smoke from anti-aircraft guns. A good-sized battle must be in progress.

Our CO led us in a gentle diving turn at the last, curving around toward where most of the airplanes seemed to be. It was dull and murky out here, and hard to make out at any distance what kind of machines they were. There were no formations now, just dozens of airplanes scurrying about in ones, twos, and threes.

I strained my eyes to identify the nearest ones, and finally discerned the square-cut wing tips of Messerschmitts. Then we were closing down into a swarm of them and we could see they were all Messerschmitts, and our CO's voice seemed calm and almost nonchalant in all the confusion of speed and noise and emotions as we heard him call out the battle cry once more. 'TAL-L-LY—HO-O!'

We overshot the first enemy machines because we had too much speed left from our dives, and turned back toward them, breaking formation as we did so in order not to hamper one another. Trying to remember to be careful, I kept close watch on my tail as I swung around toward the Huns. In the distance I saw one coming straight toward me, head on. Under such circumstances it's best to keep heading directly at the approaching machine, not giving way until the last instant. If you turn ahead of time while the other is still heading toward you, he gets a good shot at your exposed flank while you cannot shoot at him at all because you've pointed your airplane away from him and your guns point with your airplane.

This Nazi must have panicked when he recognized my machine as an enemy, and that was probably fatal for him. For he started turning away from me when we were still about five hundred yards apart. I could hardly believe my eyes as I saw myself presented with the easiest shot I'd ever had – at his unprotected side. The pilot is protected from the front by his engine and from the rear by his armour; but there is no protection from bullets from the side.

When we were about four hundred yards apart and he had turned about fifteen degrees I opened up on him, allowing for his speed and aiming just ahead of his machine. Once more I was sensing the terrific thrill and sense of power that come from the sound and feel and smell of one's guns in combat.

He kept turning and exposing himself even more to me as we closed together, and at the last I was just firing point blank at him and had to jerk back on the stick to avoid ramming his machine, and passed over his tail. Just then I saw two other Huns on my right and went on the defensive again, trying to be careful. They turned away from me, and I swung back to see what became of my victim; I couldn't find him and as we were so low over the water I thought I knew where he had gone.

Then I turned back toward the other two, but they were heading homeward and were too far away for me to overtake. I climbed up a little and headed toward the convoy, hoping to find some more trouble. On the way I met three 109s in formation, heading homeward. They ignored me and I let them alone too, remembering that the last time I had attacked three enemy fighters singly I got shot down myself. Besides, I still had Junkers 87s in my head. That's why I was heading toward the convoy, as I thought they would be trying to bomb it.

I had been four or five miles from the convoy when I attacked the Messerschmitt. Going to the convoy and circling it, I investigated and was investigated by various aircraft that I saw; but they always turned out to be Spitfires or Hurricanes when we got close enough for identification. I just couldn't find any more Huns at all.

There's something amusing about the way fighter pilots investigate each other under such circumstances. It reminds me of the way two strange dogs approach each other – very much alert against any hostile moves, circling sideways around each other until they decide whether or not they're going to be friends. Two fighters will approach and start circling each other while they get closer, neither one giving the other any advantage and each ready to change the gentle turn he's making into a vicious pirouette to get on the other's tail if he proves hostile; until finally they are close enough to identify each other's machines. At times of poor visibility like this we are especially careful.

I flew up and down the length of the convoy for several minutes, hoping to find some more enemies, but all I found were other Spitfires and a few Hurricanes, all doing what I was. The enemy had apparently fled completely.

I watched the ships to see if any of them had been damaged in the raid, but could only see one that looked as if it had been hit; and it was sailing right along in its place.

Next day, incidentally, we were all edified to learn from the German High Command communique, relayed from New York, that eleven ships were sunk in the raid! I imagine Great Britain would be in a more favourable position in this war if she had ever had as many ships as Herr Goebbels has already sunk.

Finally, satisfied that there weren't any more enemies about, I headed homeward, joining on the way three or four other boys of the squadron who were drifting toward the airdrome too.

Taxiing my Spitfire to its position on the edge of the field I saw mechanics grinning as they observed the tattered bits of yellow cloth fluttering from the leading edges of my wings around the gun holes. This was all that remained of the cover patches over these holes, the rest having been shot away, as occurs each time the guns are fired. The mechanics always watch for this on each machine as it taxis in from a patrol, to see if these covers have been shot away indicating a fight. They are fully as interested as we are in the accomplishments of the squadron, in which they play such a highly important part. Armorers made haste to remove the plates above and below the guns, in my wings, as soon as I stopped taxiing, so that they could check the guns and install fresh ammunition belts. The kid who helped me out of the cockpit asked, 'Did you get anything, sir?'

'I think I got a 109, but I doubt if I'll get it confirmed.'

Excitement filled the air, as always after a fight. When pilots return from a 'show' they are in a hurry to get out of their machines and meet the other pilots and find out what each knows about what happened as a whole, and how each made out.

Each individual pilot usually knows little of the whole of what happened after the leader's cry of 'Tally-ho.' He careens about, cramped in his little tight cockpit with limited visibility, seeing little of what goes on except in his immediate vicinity, watching his tail against surprises, evading Huns that get behind him and attacking others when he is in a favourable position to do so (and other times too, if he chooses); but like one bee in the middle of a swarm he doesn't get much idea of what has happened as a whole. The fights usually spread out over too big an area. When he can't find any more enemies or runs out of ammunition or low on fuel, or when his machine is damaged, he returns home.

Naturally then he is anxious to find out as much as he can from the other boys. How many Huns were there? Why were they there, and what were they up to? Was there more than one formation? Could he have found more trouble in a different area or higher up or lower down? What other squadrons took part? How many did we get?

Most important question of all is, 'Is everybody allright?' – meaning the other pilots. Often that question can't be answered for a while. It is common after a good scrap for one or two or even more planes of a squadron not to show up at the airdrome; but there can be a number of reasons for that. The pilot of one may have had to land at another airdrome, having run short of fuel or lost his bearings in the fight. Maybe he had to make a forced landing somewhere, with his radiator punctured or his engine damaged by bullets or cannon shells. He may have had to 'bale out' with his machine on fire or out of control. In any of these cases the news is likely to be slow in coming through. And of course sometimes the heartbreaking word finally comes through that one of the familiar faces in the mess is now but a memory to us and his loved ones; in which case tonight when we have time one or two of us who knew him well can spend an hour or so going through his belongings and personal effects, packing them and sending them home.

That way his room will be empty for someone else to occupy without delay. We try to keep sentiment to a minimum; we're all in the same boat more or less, and he'll find plenty of friends where he's going, who got there ahead of him.

This time there were no casualties of any kind in our squadron, and everyone got back to the home airdrome without mishap. Jack and Chaddy had had some shots at a 109, and Jack was very proud of a bullet hole the mechanics found in his rudder. Our CO had damaged another 109, and one or two of the other boys had had shots. We hadn't accomplished much, all told, but several new pilots had been brought through their first fight safely, which was important. The whole story of the fight revealed that we were a little late in arriving, which explained why we didn't have more to do.

A large formation of these Junkers 87 'Stukas,' escorted by Messerschmitt 109 fighters, had approached the convoy, and two squadrons of British Hurricanes had intercepted them first before they got to the convoy. The Hurricanes shot down seven of the 87s and most of the rest fled. Only a few got through to drop their bombs. The Messerschmitts then staged a sort of hit-and-run attack on the Hurricanes, and we got there just when they were running.

The Hurricanes shot down three or four of the Messerschmitts too, but they lost two of their own machines and pilots in the last part of the scrap. Jonah saw one of them go down. He first saw it making for shore with steam and glycol streaming back from the radiator, but it appeared to be under good control and he thought the pilot was trying to make a forced landing on the beach. Then just as it reached shore and was about a hundred feet up it nosed straight down and dived into the ground and went up in flames.

That was the morning the Italians made their first and last raid on England. It was going on at the same time that our fight occurred but farther south. We had learned some time previously that Italian bomber and fighter squadrons were being based in northern France, but they hadn't made an appearance over the Channel or England.

On this morning, however, a good-sized formation of old Caproni bombers and Fiat biplane fighters were intercepted by a Hurricane squadron. After the Hurricane pilots recovered from the shock of seeing such ancient aircraft in modern war skies they waded in and shot down thirteen of them without getting a single bullet in any of their own machines. The Hurricane pilots who did it said it was like shooting tame ducks.

After that some of the Italian fighters used to fly out over mid-Channel once in a while, stooging around and trying to look fierce apparently, until one day near the end of the month the other squadron that was stationed at our airdrome found them and shot down another eight. That apparently was enough, and a few days later the remaining Italians moved back to Italy. They hadn't shot down a single British airplane in all the time they had been based across the Channel from us, 'daily ranging far and wide over England, side by side with the German Air Force, seeking out and destroying the remnants of the Royal Air Force,' or something like that, according to the silly Italian dictator.

It was cold-blooded murder to send their pilots up in their little slow, unarmoured biplanes with only two or four machine guns against our powerful eight-gun Spitfires and Hurricanes, and they must have been sent for political reasons, like some pilots that were killed in the United States in 1934. I hope the era of dictators is drawing to a close. Lust for power makes even good men turn to doing ruthless deeds.

Chapter 10 Hun-Chasing: PM, 11–30 November 1940 (based RAF Hornchurch, Essex in 11 Group) In the afternoon after our combat I saw a mechanic doping new fabric covers over the holes in the wings in front of the guns on my airplane, to replace those that were shot away. 'You're wasting your time doing that!' I told him cheerfully.

He replied, 'I hope you're right, sir.'

I expected to be using my guns often now, but in this I was mistaken. The Luftwaffe was in the process of abandoning the mass day raids, and what raiding they did now was cautious, and on a small scale. The great air offensive which they had boasted would destroy the Royal Air Force and pave the way for the scheduled German invasion of England was entering its final and ignominious stages.

I have often heard doubts expressed that the RAF's accounts of our own and enemy losses could be correct. The abandoning by the Nazis of these mass raids should be proof that RAF accounts of casualties, which showed that the Nazis lost at least four times as many airplanes as we did, could not have been exaggerations.

At the beginning of their air onslaught the Luftwaffe outnumbered us several times over. England admitted it, and Germany boasted of it. They deliberately announced their intention to wipe us out, as a first step to bombing freely and preparing for and supporting the invasion of England which they promised, and which is necessary for them ever to win this war.

The Royal Air Force had to maintain an overwhelming ratio of victories to losses in order to continue to exist! – and in order for England to continue to exist, too, for that matter. If the Huns could have destroyed even half as many British machines as they lost themselves, it would have paid them to continue the mass raids until the RAF was wiped out, for they (the Huns) would still have plenty of airplanes left. The fact that we still existed after the mass raids were abandoned proves that we must have maintained at least a four-to-one ratio of victories to losses; and the fact that the Nazis abandoned the mass raiding was an admission that, in spite of their tremendous numerical superiority, they were losing a bigger percentage of their air force than we were losing of ours. In other words, their big air force was being worn down faster than our little one!

They were starting now a new type of raiding which, while it didn't accomplish much, was far less costly to them. Because their big bombers, slow and unwieldy, were such cold meat for our fighters and were shot down in such a wholesale manner during the day raids, they fixed up some of their little Messerschmitt fighters to carry bombs. They of course couldn't aim the bombs; there was no room for an extra person or a bomb aimer in the machines, and they didn't even have a bomb sight in them.

But that was immaterial in their program of terrorizng the civilians of London, for London is so big and thickly populated that they didn't have to aim the bombs – if they just flew anywhere over the city and dropped them, there was a good chance of killing some people. Each plane so equipped usually carried a 550-pound bomb under its belly. The weight and wind resistance of the bomb of course impaired the performance of the Messerschmitts, but they were still much faster than any regular bombers, and being small they weren't as easy for us to spot when we were hunting for them. Also, once they had released their bombs, they had all their original performance back again and had just as much chance to race or fight their way home as any other fighter. They carried their regular machine guns and cannon just the same when they were carrying bombs as otherwise. In case they were intercepted before they reached their objective they jettisoned their bombs wherever they were, so that they'd have a better chance to get away without fighting, or could fight better if they had to fight.

So now we were often sent up to chase 'Messerschmitt 109 bombers.' Chasing them was easier than catching them, for they were very careful about it, coming over only when conditions were favorable for them to get through to London without having to fight. They flew at twenty-two or twenty-three thousand feet, usually,which seemed to be as high as they could get when carrying bombs; and they were often escorted by others without bombs, flying above them at any altitude up to thirty-five thousand feet.

Both the British and the Germans have listening devices on their respective sides of the Channel, by which each side can tell when an enemy formation is flying on the opposite side, if it's anywhere near the coast; and they can keep track of its position and height. As soon as a formation of Messerschmitts would take off on the other side (all the fighter airdromes are near the coast) one or more of our squadrons would be sent up on patrol to be ready to intercept them if they came across. The Nazis of course kept track of the positions of our squadrons; and if our machines seemed to be in a good position to intercept their planes the Nazi controllers would order their pilots (by radio) not to start across.

Then they'd just fly up and down the French coast, and we'd fly up and down the English coast, 'figuratively glaring at each other across the Channel,' as I said in one of my letters home at about that time. They'd be hoping that we'd get sidetracked long enough for them to make a dash across and get by us; and we would sit up there hoping they'd try it. They got to using all sorts of tricks, sending over several small formations at a time at different points to draw us off guard, playing hide and seek in the clouds, and leading us all sorts of merry chases.

For example, one afternoon we were scrambled and ordered to patrol over Canterbury at fifteen thousand feet. Canterbury is a fairly large place a few miles from the coast, and is a handy point to stay around because it is easy to see and keep track of when pilots are busier watching the sky above than the ground below. After we'd hung around over there a few minutes Control called and said, 'Steer a course of 150 degrees and climb to twenty-three thousand feet. There are several bandits approaching Dungeness from Boulogne at about that altitude.'

Our leader acknowledged the message and we went roaring out toward Dungeness, our gunsights switched on, firing buttons off safety, and blood in our eyes, I suppose.

We steamed out over Dungeness, our CO anxiously calling Control. 'Can you tell me where the bandits are now? We are circling Dungeness but can't see anything.'

Control's voice answered: 'Sorry, they must have smelled you. They've turned back again. Steer three six zero. There is another formation of about fifteen bandits now approaching Manston from Cape Gris Nez at about your altitude.'

We turned north ward as ordered, and as we approached Manston Control called out: 'Be careful. Keep a sharp lookout above! There may be more bandits very high above them!'

This was the warning for all of us to watch the sky above for vapour trails. We weren't 'vaporizing' at our present altitude, but airplanes very much above us probably would be.

A moment later one of our boys called out, 'Vapour trails above and starboard!'

I looked carefully, and then I saw them, about twenty eerie little silver lines crawling across the sky above from the south east, close together. They were undoubtedly the trails of Messerschmitts without bombs, flying at thirty or thirty-five thousand feet in the stratosphere, supposedly to protect those lower down which we were searching for and which would be carrying bombs.

We couldn't bother about those high ones now. If they wanted to come down to our level and fight, ok, but we weren't going to climb up after them when there were others at our own altitude. Our rear guard would keep close watch on them so they couldn't pull a surprise attack from above. We kept going straight and level towards Manston, and when we got there Control called and said: 'Sorry again! They are getting very careful. The bandits which were at your altitude have turned back. You may use your discretion about the ones above you.'

The vapour trails were almost directly over us now.

Our CO answered Control: 'Thank you. I think we'll climb up and try to have a go at them.'

And heading south west to get us out from under them he led us upward in a steep climb to try to reach their altitude. Soon it grew very cold in our cockpits, as our altimeter needles approached the thirty-thousand-foot mark on their dials. I could see the fluffy cloud trails streaming back from each of the other planes in the formation, for of course we were making vapour trails ourselves now. The Huns above, after making a big circle, had turned north now, and we did likewise, following them and climbing. They were still some distance above us. As we got farther up in the stratosphere the sky grew a more intense blue, and the sun was weirdly bright and wintry. We climbed on above thirty thousand.

The air at that altitude is so thin that even these high-powered machines lose most of their beautiful flying qualities. Controls work very easily and the airplane responds to them only sluggishly, as a car responds to the steering wheel on ice, instead of with the rigid alertness one gets accustomed to in these machines at normal altitudes. The powerful engine becomes lazy too. Somehow the air one is riding on feels terribly unsubstantial, and until one gets used to it he gets a feeling of insecurity, a feeling that he and his machine are on the verge of losing what little support the air gives up there, and just falling off into the eerie, seemingly limitless space below. The ground seems as far away as a distant continent, and he wonders if he will ever find his way back.

Visibility is unbelievable in the thin air up there. If there are no clouds below it isn't uncommon to see the whole of south east England, north east France, and Belgium, as well as the sea in between, just like looking at a map.

We could watch our enemies by their vapour trails, and they likewise could watch us; and as we drew near their altitude they turned south east and headed homeward.

We tried to head them off, but they had too much of a start. It is very hard to fight with an unwilling enemy.

These German attacks by bomb-carrying fighters began about mid-October, I believe, and were more or less abandoned by the first of December. They had become less and less successful and more and more expensive to themselves as our controllers and squadron leaders became experienced in combating them. Our squadron intercepted one of the last ones they attempted.

We were on patrol one morning at about twenty-two or twenty-three thousand feet, having chased around quite a bit after raids that started across the Channel and then turned back. We were right over Dungeness, heading about straight east, our only recent information being that 'there are several bandits somewhere in your vicinity.'

Suddenly one of our new pilots who hadn't had a fight yet called out on the R/T, in a very subdued voice that we all laughed about afterwards, 'Bandits coming up on the starboard!'

And there they were, little rat like 109s streaking across so that they passed just under us, going at right angles to our course. If they had been two hundred feet higher we'd have collided with them! They had simply blundered into us, and we into them.

Our CO shouted a quick 'Tally-ho!' and the squadron exploded in all directions. So did the Hun formation. I didn't get to see it, but the boys who were closest to the 109s saw them let their bombs go – a dozen or so big bombs jettisoned to fall harmlessly on the beaches of Dungeness.

The Messerschmitts were scattering and diving, and it was more or less of a hide-and-seek proposition to find them. I didn't get a single shot. After hunting around for two or three minutes I gave up trying to find any of them as they had quite obviously taken the shortest route home.

However, I could see three or four pairs of vapor trails scattered about the sky higher up, all coming in-land, and I decided to try to stalk one pair of them, climbing to a higher level and getting 'up sun' of them. I was getting along pretty well, when looking above me in the other direction I saw the vapor trails of two others that were stalking me, and were just getting to a good position to attack. I panicked a little then and dived away from them, making the excuse to myself that I couldn't do anything but get hurt if I stayed up there with these two getting ready to take a crack at me.

Returning to our base, I found that once again the squadron had had no casualties and a little had been accomplished. Our CO had shot one Messerschmitt down into the sea for his eleventh confirmed victory, and one other pilot had damaged another 109. Our CO had also gone back up, the same as I did, to stalk one of the pairs that came over higher, and he got 'jumped' by two Heinkel 113 fighters and had the sliding hatch over his cockpit shot away!

I took forty-eight hours' leave shortly after that, and spent it shopping in London. There was little bombing in London now, and the city had recovered quite well from the bombings it had undergone in the fall. I had a very pleasant and interesting time walking about and shopping and seeing the thousands of historical sights. I got some genuine English plum puddings, or Christmas puddings, and sent them to my folks for Christmas presents.

When I got back to the squadron I found that I had missed a spot of action with them, in which they hadn't fared so well. They had chased after some Messerschmitts among cloud and fog over the Channel and some of them got separated from the squadron. Chaddy found a 109 and damaged it and got shot up by another and had to make a forced landing with his engine wrecked by cannon shells.

'Hop' didn't come back. The last they saw of him he was diving in among some scattered clouds after some 109s that he had spotted, shouting 'Tally-ho' over his R/T. No one ever found out what became of him; but we felt pretty sure that, however they got him, they knew they had a job on their hands before he went down.

With the end of November I had had three more weeks of 'front-line' service since we moved to this airdrome, and as yet I had only used my guns the one time. I wasn't very proud of that record, but it was as much as most of the rest had done. Of course the weather interfered a lot, keeping both sides on the ground a good share of the time. But the Huns just weren't fighting anyway. They liked to come over our territory whenever they got a chance, but they avoided combat when they did so.

54 Eric Marrs Part 4, Spitfire Pilot, Pilot Officer, British, 152 Squadron

The final instalment of letters from Eric to his father, here covering 10 October to the end of November. I have inserted in square brackets some identifiable pilots and dates. Interestingly he reports how he is gradually improving his technique in shooting down enemy aircraft. By the end of 1940 he was an ace, with five confirmed victories (excluding 'probables' and 'shared' kills). He was killed by flak later in the war while flying over France and is buried in Kerfautras Cemetery, Brest, France.

Thursday 10 October 1940 We have had some more excitements down our way. We had a show on Monday [7 October] with a large number of Jerry bombers and fighters, and it was very lucky that we did not have it the day before (Sunday) as the Hun would have had a walk-over with regard to our squadron.

The squadron had decided to have a party in celebration of its 60th Hun and we had arranged to have it in Swanage, come what might. As it happened it was rather unfortunate because we had to drink on empty stomachs. We all missed our lunch and tea, due to having to go off on 'flaps' and we finally stopped flying at about seven. We then all went off to Swanage and began drinking cocktails and sherry. We began eating at about nine and had an excellent dinner with champagne and port, etc to accompany it. We then all moved off to another hotel, where we seemed to be able to drink without any limitation till any hour of the morning. It actually turned out that the proprietor of this hotel had been registered and was waiting to be called up. He was therefore selling off all his stock of which he had plenty. His licence had run out and he had not bothered to renew it and he was therefore not very careful as to what hours he kept. I finally arrived back at camp at about 5.30 a.m. to find

Dudley Williams 'out' on my bed. I woke him up and we picked up our blankets and staggered off to dispersal where we slept as we were 'on' at 6.30 a.m. in the morning. We both of us passed out pretty efficiently when we reached dispersal, and even a telephone ringing for half an hour failed to wake us up. Luckily for us the weather, for the whole of that day, was absolutely lousy and the whole squadron was able to sleep off the after-effects unhindered by the activities of the Hun.

Next day [Monday 7 October] the weather cleared up. We were now sufficiently recovered and were all ok for flying again. We had a quiet morning and people were beginning to think, somewhat prematurely, that we were going to be let off lightly that day. However, off we went in the afternoon to intercept a big raid.

This raid consisted of about 40–50 Junkers Ju 88s and about an equal number of Me 110s. Some people say that there were also Me 109s about, but I saw none. They crossed the coast and went north just to the east of Warmwell and then they turned north west and made for Yeovil. We attacked them just about as they turned north west. The bombers were in loose formation at about 16,000 feet with their guard of Me 110s behind and above them. We were at 20,000 feet and to one side of the bombers. We all dived down on the latter to try and split them up thoroughly. I was not able to get in a good shot at them and pulled away to the right and up again. I then took stock of the position. I was in a bad position to go for the bombers again, so I thought I would have a crack at the fighters. These I found were going about in strings of about 10 aircraft sneaking along behind the bombers. From time to time the leader of each string would come round behind the last man in the string to form a defensive circle. The leader would then break the circle again to catch up the bombers. After one or two attempts I found I was able to sneak up behind one of these 'strings' and attach myself to the end of it for a short spell, shooting at the end machine in the line. Every time the leader came round to form a defensive circle I had to break away and wait till the circle broke up again. I was, however, able to tack myself on again. In this way I was able to make the end of one of these lines stream glycol from one of its engines. I was not able to finish it off as the leader of this particular string was forming one of the defensive circles and was coming round behind me.

I then drew away for a bit to take stock of the position. The Huns were now making for the coast again, and I saw a straggler all by himself. I swooped up on him from the starboard rear quarter. He saw me coming and opened up, but I was able to catch him up quite easily. I opened fire and his starboard engine streamed glycol. I switched on to the fuselage and then over to the port engine. I was by now overtaking him somewhat fast, so I drew out to the left. Suddenly the back half of his cockpit flew off and out jumped two men. Their parachutes streamed and opened and they began drifting slowly earthwards. They took an awful long time to come down, as they baled out at about 15,000 feet. They came down on land and I watched the army rush up and capture them. I then returned to the aerodrome and landed to see what had happened to the rest of the squadron.

The squadron's score was three confirmed and one probable that day. We unfortunately had one chap shot down [Harold Akroyd]. He was very badly burnt and died of his burns next day. This was a most unfortunate case. The man was a sergeant pilot and he had just received his commission. He was due to go on leave that morning, but was not able to owing to the fact that there were no spare pilots in our flight. The flight commander had gone ill the day before and I, being the next senior officer in the flight, was acting flight commander.

23 October 1940 Very little has happened down here while I have been away, but one pilot [Edmund Shepperd] was killed in a crash. Two were sent off in some foul weather. One managed to get back all right, but the other flew into the ground and was killed outright. Luckily, the chief controller was down here at the time, and so found out all about it first-hand. He will see that somebody is well and truly 'administered unto' for that episode.

I have flown twice since I have been back, but I have seen nothing. There is a lull on down this way with regard to enemy activity on the large scale, though they still send over lone raiders. The weather today is wonderfully lousy and we haven't got anybody at 'readiness.' We are all 'available' in the mess.

19 November 1940 How goes things at home? I wonder whether you have had any Italians round your way. I wish they would come over here, but their last show over the Thames seems to have scared them pretty thoroughly.

We continue to get an occasional fighter sweep over the Isle of Wight or that district, but have not connected up with any of them. I have had some luck, though, in that I met up with a lone Junkers Ju 88 the other day [14 November]. I was leading a section of two when we saw a condensation trail moving across above us about 5,000 feet higher. We turned round and climbed flat out after it. It was going north and it took us some time to catch up, so when we did it was well inland. I was able to get within about 800 yards of it before it saw me, and when finally it did see me it began a gentle turn to the left. This was very nice for me and I was able to close in and give it a burst from the port rear quarter. I made three attacks from port and starboard quarters, but could see no visible result from my fire. I therefore thought to myself, 'Damn this,' and coming in from dead astern and slightly underneath I held my fire until within about 180 yards. I then gave it a good burst at point blank range and smoke began to come from the port engines. Unfortunately the rear gunner of the 88 landed one plumb on the middle of my windscreen splintering it in all directions and making it quite opaque, I drew away to the left and saw that I had started a fire under the port engine, an ominous red glow being clearly visible. I could not sight any more through my cracked windscreen, but my number two was going hard at it. All this time the enemy had been diving hard south. We had caught him up at 24,000 feet and had now got down to about 5,000 feet and were over Poole. My number two finished his ammunition and broke away. The Hun was now obviously in a bad condition and badly on fire. He began left hand turn which became steeper and steeper and ended in a vertical dive. He hit the ground over the vertical, on a street corner in Poole. There was a great mushroom of orange flame edged with oily black smoke, as all his bombs exploded with his petrol. I dived down to have a look and could see nothing left of the aeroplane except a large number of little pieces scattered over a wide area, and each burning fiercely. There were also three houses on fire and I was very sorry about that. It was a pity it could not have come down in a field. Luckily there were no civilian deaths, though I believe two people were injured. I had six bullets in my machine. Two through the prop, one on the windscreen, one in the wing and two others had penetrated the engine cooling,

one bouncing off the crankcase and the other half severing three plugleads and
finishing up in the fireproof bulkhead.

2 December 1940 More excitements to report. In my last letter I wrote saying that
we had not had any of those offensive patrols for a long time. Well, the day after I
wrote they came again and it was a very eventful day [28 November]. The first one
was at lunchtime and I had just had about one mouthful of soup when we were
called out. As usual they came over at about 35,000 feet and we were below them.

They began to come down on us, but we saw them coming and turned to meet
them. As soon as they saw that we had seen them they turned round and climbed
back out to sea. We were by now all split up and after patrolling for some time
looking for odd stray Huns I returned and landed. I found, on landing, that after we
had split up, one of the pilots [Norman Hancock] had found a lone Me 110 and shot
it down in the sea, after a longish chase to the south of the Isle of Wight.

We managed to stay on the ground till our tea arrived out at dispersal, but just as
I was taking my first bite of bread we were all sent off again. Once more we were
sent off late, and we were only at 23,000 feet over the Isle of Wight when we saw
the blighters coming in above us at about 30,000 feet to 35,000 feet. We were not
making condensation trails at 23,000 feet, but the Huns were, and when we saw
some of the trails stop we knew that they were coming down on us.

The next thing that happened was that, on looking over my right shoulder, I saw
one of those beastly yellow-nosed blighters about a hundred yards on my right. I had
obviously dived down and had a pot at somebody in our formation and I must have
first seen him just after he had finished shooting. My instinctive reaction was to pull
up sharply to the right to see if anything was coming down on my tail. As I did this,
the Me 109 slid across under me to my left and dived full speed for France. I flipped
over to the left and dived flat out after him. The 109 was very keen to get home,
and was a fool or over confident, for he never looked round once to see whether he
was being pursued or not. It took me some time to catch up, especially as I was not
such a fool and weaved slightly to keep a look out behind my tail. I was very angry
with him for having surprised us and I knew that one of us must have been shot up
by him. I distinctly remember muttering to myself as I flipped over and dived after
him, 'You dirty b...r! This is where you get yours!' I crept up on him slowly, keeping
beneath him in his blindest spot. Slowly he got bigger in my sights – then in was
in range, but I did not open fire, I was going to make absolutely sure of him, so I
waited till I was within about 100 yards. Then aiming carefully I fired – a one second
burst was enough. Black smoke belched forth, and oil spattered over my windscreen.
He half-rolled and dived away, I followed in a steep spiral to see what was going to
happen, but my speed became so great I pulled away and my wing hid him for a bit.
When I looked again there were a large number of flaming fragments waffling down
to the sea. One large black lump, which was not on fire, trailed a white plume which
snapped open and became a parachute. This was the pilot and he must have baled
out just before the petrol tank blew up. However, he landed in the sea and might
just as well have blown up, for he was never found. I went home in great spirits, but
this joy soon evaporated, for when I landed I heard of the death of the chap [Arthur
Watson] who had been flying just behind me. The 109 had shot at him, hitting his
glycol system. Streaming smoke, he made for land and then tried to bale out. He

bungled up his baling out and tore his parachute in doing so, with the result that his descent to earth was somewhat swift. His parachute streamed out behind him, but owing to the tears did not open. We lost one other pilot that day, one of the Polish sergeants [Zygmunt Klein]. He just disappeared and nobody saw what happened to him. He got separated and must have become involved with a large number of enemy fighters. So we lost two for two and that is not very satisfactory. I found that I had shot down my 109 with 440 rounds, that is 55 rounds from each gun. This is the easist victory I've had and fulfilled a long-felt ambition to shoot down one of these damned yellow-nosed blighters.

The next day we had another of these fighter sweeps over, but did not contact at all. A most extraordinary thing happened, however. I was leading the flight up to 30,000 feet as we had been ordered to patrol Swanage at this disgustingly great altitude. At about 26,000 feet my number two called up something on the R/T which I did not hear properly. I waited for him to repeat it. Then number three rang up to say that number two had broken away and gone down. I thought nothing more of it until we landed, when he found that this pilot was missing. Later we found that a Spitfire had dived vertically into the ground from some colossal height. Bits of the aeroplane and pilot were spread over a large area but were found found to belong to the poor chap who had been flying behind me. We can only surmise that he passed out due to lack of oxygen and had not come to before hitting the ground.

That was the third pilot in two days and all from B flight – the flight I'm in. Since that day we have been very quiet again; we will probably have a tremendous blitz tomorrow.

My total score now is six and a third confirmed, one unconfirmed and four damaged, and is made up as follow:-

Destroyed confirmed: A half Dornier 17, one Ju 87, one and a half and a third Ju 88, one Me 109, two Me 110s. Probably destroyed: One He 111. Damaged: Two He 111s, two Me 110s.

55 Brian Lane Part 3, Spitfire Pilot, Squadron Leader, British, 19 Squadron

The final extract from the fighter pilot's 1942 memoir covers his experiences in the days following the 'end' of the Battle, 5–15 November. Lane disappeared on 13 December 1942 after getting into combat with Focke Wulf 190s over the North Sea near Holland. By this time Lane had shot down six enemy aircraft plus one additional shared kill. His body was never recovered.

Lane's memoir, like many others featured in this book, has been long forgotten by its original publishers, who in this case brought out only a single hardback edition. Battle of Britain historian Dilip Sarkar brought the book back into print in 2009 with an introduction and substituted Lane's anonymous comrades' pseudonyms with their real identities. Sarkar was also involved with the unveiling in 2011, to a

Spitfire and Hurricane flypast, of a memorial plaque on the house in which Lane grew up in Pinner. Guests of honour included Lane's rigger from summer 1940, John Milne, who was responsible for refuelling and repairing the airframe on his Spitfire. *John died in his 90's. (Lived in Winston) WG*

Chapter 14 Quiet Days: 5–15 November 1940 (based at RAF Foulmere, Cambridgeshire in 12 Group to 1 November 1940 then RAF Coltishall, Norfolk also 12 Group) It was obvious now that the blitz was over and that at any rate for the time being the Luftwaffe had shot its bolt.

Enemy activity declined, offensive patrols by Me 109s, some carrying bombs to increase their nuisance value, took the place of the mass bombing raids. As a result of this there wasn't enough trade to go round! And although the wing continued patrols whenever any enemy activity occurred in the Channel, it became obvious that we should have to be very lucky to get any more action. As it happened we did have a bit of luck, but not until 5 November .

On this occasion I was unfortunate in missing the patrol, F leading the squadron. His R/T, however, became unserviceable shortly after taking off and Flight Sergeant S took over the lead. Over Canterbury a considerable amount of cloud was experienced, and the squadron became separated from the rest of the wing. Shortly afterwards a formation of 109s was sighted and attacked. The E/A dived into the clouds and disappeared, but not before F had fired at one from 150 yards range and seen the cockpit cover break off. He fired again, giving a five-second burst, and the 109 disappeared in a vertical dive into the clouds and apparently crashed into the sea 10 miles south of Dungeness.

Sergeant C claimed his first victim since joining the squadron. He climbed up after three E/A which were circling 500 feet above him and after four turns got on the tail of one, the other two breaking away and disappearing from sight. Opening fire at the remaining Hun from about 200 yards he fired six bursts closing to 50 yards before breaking away to see the 109 with smoke and flame pouring from the engine.

In the afternoon F again was lucky over the same area, running into another bunch of 109s and the new Heinkel 113s. This time he made certain of his opponent and had the satisfaction of seeing the E/A completely break up in the air after he had fired only about 20 rounds per gun. It was excellent shooting.

Grumpy also added another to his score, chasing a 113 across the Channel and catching it over the French coast. It was the first and only E/A of this type to be shot down by the squadron.

Unfortunately the squadron came back without H, one of our two Czech officers, and a report was later received that a Spitfire had been seen falling in flames over the Thames at the time of the fight. His body was never found and it obviously must have been poor H who had been seen.

The next ten days were quiet, and although we carried out several patrols nothing was seen.

Then, on the morning of the 15th, two squadrons, Squadron Leader B's and ourselves, were sent off to patrol a convoy off the estuary.

We climbed up towards the sun and set course over the banks of rolling mist covering the tree-tops. It was a glorious morning, the sun shining down from a cloudless blue sky on to the wisps of white vapour clothing the earth below.

Out to sea the mist had cleared a little and before long B picked up the convoy and began running up and down the line of ships.

Owing to the limited visibility he decided to patrol fairly low at about 7,000 feet, whilst I climbed up behind him to keep a lookout for any higher stuff that might come in.

Away to the south over the French coast a tangled mass of smoke plumes high up in the blue showed where some Huns were having a morning trip: It was not our job to chase them, however, so I sat back idly watching the white trails weaving a fantastic pattern against the heavens.

Glancing farther to the east towards Dunkirk I saw two more white plumes and watched to see which way the E/A were heading. They seemed to be coming our way.

Switching on my transmitter I called up B and told him I was going up higher in case the Huns should come within reach.

'Ok, pal,' came back in my 'phones as I turned towards the trails. Climbing south I edged round towards the sun to try and take the Huns by surprise. There was about 10 miles separating the two aircraft and I called up Wilf and told him to break away with B flight and take the rearmost one whilst I went after the other with A flight. Up and up we climbed, and after a few minutes Wilf called up and asked if I could head his chap off a bit as they weren't gaining on him very quickly.

Telling Grumpy with his section to break away and try to cut off the Hun in question, I climbed on after the other one; at about 22,000 feet he passed over the top of us heading up the estuary and I turned in behind getting between him and the sun.

At 25,000 feet I noticed that we were making condensation trails as well and began to wonder when our quarry would see us. We were still several miles behind him and at least 5,000 feet lower but I could now pick out the aircraft at the head of its white tail of smoke. I could see that it was a twin-engined kite but we weren't near enough yet to recognise the type.

The Ack-Ack batteries were firing at the E/A and I sat watching the white puffs of the exploding shells bursting below and behind him to come floating lazily back to meet us as we climbed on and on after him.

I began to think we were never going to catch up as we didn't seem to be gaining on the Hun to any great extent and it seemed as if our climbing speed was the same as his cruising speed. Accordingly I eased the stick forward a little until we were flying level and we began to catch up. As we got nearer, I began climbing slightly again trying to get the happy medium between maximum climb and forward speed.

We were now at almost 30,000 feet and over the outskirts of London. Apparently this was as far as the Hun wanted to go, for he turned slowly round the way he had come … and then he saw us and did a very foolish thing. He dived down as hard as he could back towards the sea.

As it was I turned and dived after him, Jock and Arthur following in line astern. Down, down we went, the needle of the airspeed indicator going farther and farther round the dial until it showed 400 mph. In reality, our speed must have been nearly 500 mph, as in the rarified air at these altitudes there is quite a large error of anything up to 100 mph in the instrument.

The controls were solid now with the force of the air flow over them, and it needed two hands and a lot of strength to move the stick even a little.

We were gaining on the Hun now and gaining fast, and at 10,000 feet I began to ease the sights on to the fuselage of the target. I say 'ease' but perhaps heave would be a better word. I was sweating with the strain of holding my aircraft steady in the bumps as I began to get the Hun's slipstream. My head felt thick and I was almost deaf from the sudden change from the rarified atmosphere above to the increased pressure lower down.

At last I was in range and squinting through the sight. I pressed the firing button.

The muffled 'Br-r-r-r-p' of the guns came to my ears as streams of tracer leaped from the wings and flashed towards the E/A in my sight. I fired three bursts steadying my aim between each and then pulling away to the left, a stream of black smoke coming from the port engine as I did so. Straightening up I watched Jock firing and then the starboard engine spluttered and a tongue of flame licked out around the cowling. Good show! Jock. We've got him.

I watched Arthur close in behind the 110 and as he broke away the E/A pulled up in a climbing turn and I closed in from the side and gave him another squirt. He turned over on his side and a parachute blossomed out behind as the burning aircraft dived through a patch of cloud and crashed in a huge fountain of white foam and steam into the blue waters of Father Thames.

We were now at 2,000 feet and watching until the German pilot had been picked up by a boat. I turned and called up the other two of the section, heading home over the carpet of mist still covering the land.

After a while I picked up a town through a gap in the mist and a few minutes later sighted a familiar landmark sticking up through the white vapour and came to the aerodrome.

Landing, I found that B flight had accounted for the other E/A, which had also turned out to be a Me 110. The two were obviously on reconnaissance flights and it was nice to think that the Huns had lost two aircraft and a lot of photographs which they probably thought they could get without trouble.

Wilf's scheme for getting the second 110 had worked admirably and Grumpy had headed him off just as B flight came up behind the quarry. Thus nine Spitfires had pounced on the wretched Hun at the same time and it was small wonder that he had not survived the encounter. He had dived headlong towards the sea in an effort to escape, the Spitfires streaming after him, and one wing had broken off before he hit the water. It was rather hard to say who had been most instrumental in getting him, as everyone except Wilf had fired.

Over a glass of beer before lunch I heard Wilf's account.

'The bastards just shouldered me out of the way,' he said indignantly. 'I couldn't get near enough to fire at all!' Roars of laughter greeted this remark. That the flight commander, who was supposed to be leading the attack should be pushed aside, so to speak, by the rest of his flight, all determined to get in a burst, struck everybody as being extremely funny.

56 Peter 'Cowboy' Blatchford, Hurricane Pilot, Flight Commander, Canadian, 257 Squadron

Air Ministry- and Ministry of Information-endorsed BBC radio broadcast by an anonymous RAF fighter pilot in November 1940. The pilot is Peter 'Cowboy' Blatchford (Canadian), 257 Squadron. This combat took place on 11 November 1940 with 257 Squadron flying from RAF Martlesham Heath, Suffolk (11 Group).

Hitler's Italian allies had very limited involvement in the Battle of Britain. Mussolini insisted that his air force (Corpo Aereo Italiano or Italian Air Corps) be permitted to help the Luftwaffe and dispatched an expeditionary force to fight in the last few months of 1940. Their aircraft were totally outclassed by Fighter Command's Spitfires and Hurricanes, and it was the latter from 46, 41 and 257 squadrons that shot down the Fiat CR42 biplane fighters and twin-engined Fiat BR20 bombers on 11 November. One of the CR42s on the raid suffered engine overheating just before the engagement, landed on the beach at Orfordness and was captured by the RAF. It was subsequently flown by 'No. 1426 Flight RAF', the unit that operated captured Axis aircraft (and nicknamed the 'Rafwaffe') and is today on display at RAF Museum, Hendon.

The fellow Canadian and friend referred to by Blatchford is Lionel Gaunce, squadron leader of 46 Squadron, whose kill on this day made him an ace. Shortly after returning to Martlesham, Blatchford visited one of the crashed CR20 bombers with his squadron leader, Robert Stanford Tuck, who had missed the sortie due to illness, and together they liberated two large hampers containing Italian cheeses, salami and Chianti!

Blatchford achieved ace status before he was shot down and ditched in the sea in May 1943. His body was never found.

Well, we started with the usual afternoon blitz, just like any other day during the past three months, and we were ordered up on patrol out to sea. Our job was to join up with another Hurricane squadron, as their bodyguard. When we were about 12,000 feet up, I saw nine planes of a type I had never seen before, coming along. They were in tight 'V' formation. I didn't like to rush in bald-headed, until I knew what they were, so the squadron went up above them to have a good look at them. Then I realised that at any rate they were not British, and that was good enough for me. So we went into attack starting with the rear starboard bomber and crossing over to attack the port wing of the formation.

I must say that the Italians as they turned out to be, stood up to it very well. They kept their tight formation and were making for the thick cloud cover at 20,000 feet, but our tactics were to break them up before they could do that and we succeeded. I singled out one of the enemy and gave him a burst. Immediately he went straight up into a loop. I thought he was foxing me as I had never seen a bomber do that sort of thing before. So I followed him when he suddenly went down in a vertical dive.

I still followed, waiting for him to pull out. Then I saw a black dot move away from him and a puff like a white mushroom – someone baling out. The next second the bomber seemed to start crumpling up and it suddenly burst into hundreds of small pieces. They fell down to the sea like a snowstorm. I must have killed the pilot. I think he fell back, pulling the stick with him – that's what caused the loop. Then he probably slumped forward, putting the plane into an uncontrollable dive. But what usually happens then is that the wing or the tail falls off, and it was a surprising sight to see the plane just burst into small pieces.

Then I started to climb again and I saw another two of the bombers in the sky. They were mixed up in a fight and were both streaming smoke. At that moment another one shot past me flaming like a torch, and plunged into the sea. After seeing that I thought the battle was over and I could go home, but just as I turned to do so I saw a dogfight going on up above with another type of aeroplane I had never seen before. They were Fiat fighter biplanes. There must have been about twenty of them milling round with the Hurricanes, I went up to join in the party, but the fighter I singled out saw me coming and went into a quick turn with me on his tail. His plane was very manoeuvrable, but so was the Hurricane and we stuck closely enough together while I got in two or three bursts. It was a long dogfight, as dogfights go. We did tight turns, climbing turns and half-rolls till it seemed we would never stop. Neither of us was getting anywhere until one of my bursts seemed to hit him and he started waffling. For a moment he looked completely out of control and then he came in at me and we started all this merry-go-round business over again. I got in two or three more bursts and then ran out of ammunition. That put me in a bit of a fix and I didn't know what to do next. I was afraid if I left his tail he would get on to mine. Then he straightened up – he was just thirty yards ahead and I was a few feet above. At that moment I decided that as I could not shoot him down I would try and knock him out of the sky with my aeroplane. I went kind of haywire. It suddenly occurred to me what a good idea it would be to scare the living daylight out of him. I aimed for the centre of his top main plane, did a quick dive and pulled out just before crashing into him. I felt a very slight bump, but I never saw him again and somehow I don't think he got back.

By now the scene had changed a bit. Another squadron of Hurricanes was chasing the Italians all over the sky. I did not know at the time, but I found when I got down that their squadron leader was a great friend of mine from my home town of Edmonton, Alberta.

He bagged a couple in that fight.

And now I thought it's home for me, but the day wasn't over yet. As I was flying back, keeping a good look-out behind, I saw a Hurricane below me, having the same kind of affair with a Fiat as I had just had. I went down and did a dummy head-on attack on the Italian. At 200 yards he turned away and headed out to sea. I thought: 'Good, I really can get home this time,' but just before I got to the coast, still keeping a good look-out behind, I saw another Hurricane, with three Fiats close together worrying him. So down I went again, feinting another head-on attack, and again when I was about 200 yards away the Italians broke off and headed for home. That really was the end of the battle.

I was a bit worried because my plane had started to vibrate badly, but I managed to land all right. Just as I had got out of my Hurricane and was walking away – my fitter and rigger ran after me saying that I had six inches missing from one of my propeller blades and nine inches from another. All the same, it certainly was a grand day for the squadron.

Appendix 1: List of RAF Squadrons Engaged in the Battle of Britain

A total of 71 Squadrons and other units from Fighter Command, Coastal Command and the Fleet Air Arm are listed as having taken part in the Battle. The first number in the list below is the squadron number (it didn't run in consecutive numbers), next is the squadron code made up of twin capital letters (randomly chosen) displayed prominently on the aircraft fuselage and finally the aircraft type flown by the squadron.

1 JX, Hurricane
1 (RCAF Canadian) YO, Hurricane [also known as 401 Squadron]
3 OQ, Hurricane
17 YB, Hurricane
19 QV, Spitfire
23 YP, Blenheim
25 ZK, Blenheim, Beaufighter
29 RO, Blenheim
32 GZ, Hurricane
41 EB, Spitfire
43 FT, Hurricane
46 PO, Hurricane
54, KL, Spitfire
56 US, Hurricane
64, SH, Spitfire
65 YT, Spitfire
66 LZ, Spitfire
72 RN, Spitfire
73 TP, Hurricane
74 ZP, Spitfire
79 NV, Hurricane
85 VY, Hurricane
87 LK, Hurricane
92 QJ, Spitfire
111 JU, Hurricane

141 TW, Defiant
145 SO, Hurricane
151 DZ, Hurricane
152 UM, Spitfire
213 AK, Hurricane
219 FK, Blenheim, Beaufighter
222 ZD, Spitfire
229 RE, Hurricane
232 EF, Hurricane
234 AZ, Spitfire
235 (Coastal Command), QY, Blenheim
236 (Coastal Command) FA, Blenheim
238 VK, Hurricane
242 (Canadian), LE, Hurricane
245 DX, Hurricane
247 HP, Gloster Gladiator
248 (Coastal Command), WR, Blenheim
249 GN, Hurricane
253 SW, Hurricane
257 DT, Hurricane
263 HE, Hurricane, Westland Whirlwind
264 PS, Defiant
266 UO, Spitfire
302 (Polish), WX, Hurricane
303 (Polish), RF, Hurricane
310 (Czechoslovak), NN, Hurricane
312 (Czechoslovak), DU, Hurricane
421 Flight, L–Z, Spitfire
422 Flight, not known, Hurricane
501 SD, Hurricane
504 TN, Hurricane
600 BQ, Blenheim, Beaufighter
601 UF, Hurricane
602 LO, Spitfire
603 XT, Spitfire
604 NG, Blenheim, Beaufighter
605 UP, Hurricane
607 AF, Hurricane
609 PR, Spitfire
610 DW, Spitfire
611 FY, Spitfire
615 KW, Hurricane
616 QJ, Spitfire
804 Fleet Air Arm, Gloster Gladiator, Grumman Martlet
808 Fleet Air Arm, Fairey Fulmer
FIU (Fighter Interception Unit), not known, Blenheim, Beaufighter

Appendix 2: List of Luftwaffe Units Engaged in the Battle of Britain

Each Luftwaffe *luftflotte* or air fleet was organised by a bewildering designation system. The next level down was the *geschwader* (75 aircraft in each) and the Luftwaffe further described these military units to reflect the role of the aircraft so that most of the aircraft that flew against Britain in 1940 were in one of the following: *jagdeschwader* (abbreviated to 'JG') were single-seat Me 109 fighters; *zerstorergeschwader* ('ZG') were 'destroyers', the heavy fighters, twin-engined Me 110s (and rarer Ju 88Cs where the glazed nose cone of the regular Ju 88 bomber was replaced with a solid one with canons mounted in it); *stukageschwader* ('StG') were dive-bombers; *kampfgeschwader* ('KG') were bombers; *lehrgeschwader* ('LG') were experimental wings designed to test new equipment under operational combat conditions and to evaluate new tactics, comprising a variety of aircraft types. Each *geschwader* was given Arabic numbers, for example, 'JG2' or '*Jagdeschwader* 2'. In addition other more specialist *geschwader* military units were also encountered: *Kustenfliegergruppe* (generally not abbreviated, though sometimes to 'Ku Fl Gr', usually just the unit number is used, e.g. '106'), whose main role was mine laying; *aufklarungsgruppe* (generally not abbreviated, though sometimes is to 'Aufkl Gr', usually just the unit number is used, e.g. '122') were reconnaissance aircraft. *Kampfgruppe* (generally not abbreviated, though sometimes is to 'KGr', usually just the unit number is used, e.g. '100') mostly pathfinder bombers; *Erprobungsgruppe* (abbreviated to 'Erpr Gr'), an experimental unit testing fighter bomber roles. *Wettererkundungsstaffeln* (abbreviated to Wekusta or Westa) were weather reconnaissance units.

Below is a list of the *geschwader* units that were involved in the Battle of Britain, together with the unit code of all but the single-seat Me 109 fighter units and the aircraft they flew. The system for identifying units of Me 109s was even more complex as well as being colour-coded, so using a 1940 black-and-white photograph to pinpoint the unit to which a particular aircraft belonged is beyond the remit of this book. These *geschwaders* were further broken down into *gruppens* and *staffels*. Individual *gruppens* and *staffels* from a single *geschwader* unit sometimes operated in different *luftflottes*. Each *gruppe* consisted of around thirty-five to forty aircraft. In most books on the Battle, when describing which of these Luftwaffe units were in a raid or who had been shot down these abbreviations would be used, for example, 'I/KG1' or 1 Gruppe of Kampfgeschwader 1, i.e. Roman numerals for a *gruppe*. For a *staffel* (a smaller unit size, similar to an RAF squadron) Arabic numbers are used, for example '4/JG2' for '4 Staffel of Jagdeschwader 2'.

Luftwaffe aircraft like those of the RAF had a series of code letters/numbers on the fuselage (along with the national insignia, the black-and-white cross) which identified the unit to which the aircraft belonged. However, the Luftwaffe designation system was far more complex than that of the RAF. Again it is possible to outline the basics of identifying all Luftwaffe aircraft bar the Me 109s in 1940 photographs. The explanation below is not the complete story but a simplified model which will aid identification of most Luftwaffe aircraft in 1940 photographs. The letter and number to the left of the cross is the *geschwader* unit code. The letter immediately to the right of the cross is the individual aircraft ID within its squadron or *staffel* and the letter to the right of that is the squadron or *staffel* letter. To make matters worse, in the field these practices were sometimes ignored and transferred aircraft, for instance, sometimes flew for weeks under their previous codes.

Aufkl Gr 11 (unit code: MJ & 6M, aircraft: Do 17 & Me 110)
Aufkl Gr 14 (unit code: 5F, aircraft: Do 17 & Me 110)
Aufkl Gr 22 (unit code: 4N, aircraft: Do 17)
Aufkl Gr 31 (unit code: 5D, aircraft: Do 17, Me 110 & Ju 88)
Aufkl Gr 120 (unit code: A6, aircraft: Ju 88 & He 111)
Aufkl Gr 121 (unit code: 7A, aircraft: Ju 88 & Do 17)
Aufkl Gr 122 (unit code: F6, aircraft Ju 88 & Me 110)
Aufkl Gr 123 (unit code: 4U, aircraft Do 17)
Aufkl Gr Ob d L (unit code: K9 & T5, aircraft Do 215, Do 217, He 111, Ju 86, Ju 88, B&V 142 & Me 110)
Erpr Gr 210 (unit code: S9, aircraft: Me 109 & Me 110)
JG2 (aircraft: Me 109)
JG3 (aircraft: Me 109)
JG26 (aircraft: Me 109)
JG27 (aircraft: Me 109)
JG51 (aircraft: Me 109)
JG52 (aircraft: Me 109)
JG53 (aircraft: Me 109)
JG54 (aircraft: Me 109)
JG77 (aircraft: Me 109)
KG1 (unit code: V4, aircraft He 111)
KG2 (unit code: U5, aircraft: Do 17)
KG3 (unit code: 5K, aircraft: Do 17)
KG4 (unit code: 5J, aircraft: He 111 & Ju 88)
KG26 (unit code: 1H, aircraft: He 111)
KG27 (unit code: 1G & 1K, aircraft: He 111)
KG30 (unit code: 4D & 4K, aircraft: Ju 88)

KG40 (unit code: F8, aircraft: Ju 88 & Fw 200)
KG51 (unit code: 9K, aircraft: Ju 88)
KG53 (unit code: A1, aircraft: He 111)
KG54 (unit code: B3, aircraft: Ju 88)
KG55 (unit code: G1, aircraft: He 111)
KG76 (unit code: F1, aircraft Do 17 & Ju 88)
Ku Fl Gr 100 (unit code: 6N, aircraft: He 111)
Ku Fl Gr 106 (unit code: M2, aircraft: He 115)
Ku Fl Gr 406 (unit code: K6, aircraft: Do 18)
Ku Fl Gr 506 (unit code: S4, aircraft: He 115)
Ku Fl Gr 606 (unit code: 7T, aircraft: Do 17)
Ku Fl Gr 706 (unit code: 6I, aircraft: Do 18)
Ku Fl Gr 806 (unit code: M7, aircraft: Ju 88)
LG1 (unit code: L1, aircraft: Ju 87, Ju 88 & Me 110)
LG2 (unit code: 3X & L2, aircraft: Me 109 & Me 110)
StG1 (unit code: A5 or 6G, aircraft: Ju 87)
StG2 (unit code: T6, aircraft: Ju 87)
StG3 (unit code: S7, aircraft: Ju 87)
StG77 (unit code: S2 & F1, aircraft: Ju 87 & Do 17)
ZG2 (unit code: 3M & A2, aircraft: Me 110)
ZG26 (unit code: U8, E8 & 3U, aircraft: Me 110)
ZG76 (unit code: M8 & 2N, aircraft: Me 110)
Westa 26 (unit code: C5, aircraft: He 111, Me 110, Do 17)
Wett 51 (unit code: T4, aircraft: He 111, Ju 88, Do 17)
Wett X Fl Korps (unit code: n/k, aircraft: He 111)
Wekusta Ob d L (unit code: n/k, aircraft: He 111 & Do 17)

Acknowledgements

Rather than a full bibliography, I am opting for a list of authors whose books on the Battle of Britain I have consulted: Max Arthur, Philip Birtles, Patrick Bishop, Stephen Bungay, Basil Collier, Brian Cull, Len Deighton, Jonathan Falconer, John Foreman, Norman Franks, James Holland, Richard Hough & Denis Richards, David Isby, Jeff Jefford, Francis Mason, Richard Overy, Alfred Price, Winston Ramsey (*Then & Now*), John Ray, Dilip Sarkar, John Willis Derek Wood and Kenneth Wynn.

For various permissions in addition to those cited in the pilots' introductions, I would like to thank Max Dean, David Fox, Simon Jarvis, Robert Cartier, Mary Little, Hurricane Books and Gervase Lowney, National Archives, Kew, London (1940 Combat Reports AIR 50). Also a thank you to Geoff Simpson.

List of Illustrations

Jonathan Reeve JR2444b112fp12 19391945. **84.** Three fighter pilots of 111 Squadron. Courtesy of Jonathan Reeve JR1235b71pic15 19391945. **85.** 501 Squadron. Courtesy of Jonathan Reeve JR2445b112fp28 19391945. **86.** German Luftwaffe Me 110 pilots relax in France. Courtesy of Jonathan Reeve b584fp225t. **87.** Glendon Booth. Courtesy of Jonathan Reeve b570fp30b. **87b.** An unnamed fighter pilot. Courtesy of Jonathan Reeve JRb579fp96b. **88.** Parachute placed on the Spitfire wingtip. Courtesy of Jonathan Reeve JR2809b135fp107 19391945. **89.** Pilots 'scramble' to their Spitfires. Courtesy of Jonathan Reeve b593p15. **90.** Pilots 'scramble' to their Hurricanes. Courtesy of Jonathan Reeve JRb595fp17. **91.** Two 501 Squadron Hurricanes take off. Courtesy of Jonathan Reeve b577p90. **92.** David Crook. Courtesy of Jonathan Reeve b574fp57t. **93.** Me 109s preparing to take off. Courtesy of Jonathan Reeve JRb541 22b. **94.** A Hurricane coming in to refuel. Courtesy of Jonathan Reeve JR1210b71pic12 19391945. **95.** Luftwaffe pilot. Courtesy of Jonathan Reeve JRb541 23t. **96.** The crew of a Heinkel 111. Courtesy of Jonathan Reeve b574fp88b. **97.** An Me 109 shoots-up Dover barrage balloons. Courtesy of Jonathan Reeve b577p36tr. **98.** British gun-camera images. Courtesy of Jonathan Reeve. **99.** Gun-camera still. Courtesy of Jonathan Reeve JR1452b79p32 19391945. **100.** A Spitfire shoots great lumps off a Heinkel 111. Courtesy of Jonathan Reeve JR2401b109pic5 19391945. **101.** Gun-camera film from David Crook's Spitfire. Courtesy of Jonathan Reeve b574fp57b. **102.** A Dornier Do 17. Courtesy of Jonathan Reeve JR2454b112fp104 19391945. **103.** Rear cockpit gunner of a Dornier 17. Courtesy of Jonathan Reeve b584fp80b. **104.** View from the rear gunner position of an Me 110. Courtesy of Jonathan Reeve b584fp80t. **105.** A Do 17 with its starboard engine a wing on fire. Courtesy of Jonathan Reeve JRb542p804r. **106.** 56 Squadron. Courtesy of Jonathan Reeve b577p142b. **107.** Hurricanes of Ian Gleed's 87 Squadron. Courtesy of Jonathan Reeve b565fp32. **108.** Vapour trails. Courtesy of Jonathan Reeve JR2480b113p150 19391945. **109.** Hurricanes of 87 Squadron. Courtesy of Jonathan Reeve b565fp17. **110.** Pencil sketch portrait by Richard Frost. Courtesy of Jonathan Reeve b565fp80. **111.** Hurricanes of 85 Squadron. Courtesy of Jonathan Reeve JR1554b79p25 19391945. **112.** The Me 109 of Luftwaffe ace Franz von Werra. Courtesy of Jonathan Reeve b570fp49t. **113.** The tailplane of von Werra's crashed 109. Courtesy of Jonathan Reeve b570fp49b. **114.** Me 109 pilot Werner Voigt. Courtesy of Jonathan Reeve JRb543p492b. **115.** A KG54 Ju 88 (B3+DC). Courtesy of Jonathan Reeve JR2509b114p1156T 19391945. **116.** 18 August 1940 the day the Stuka met its match. Courtesy of Jonathan Reeve JR2475b113p108T 19391945. **117.** The remains of an Me 110. Courtesy of Jonathan Reeve JRb543p243mbr. **118.** Stuka (T6+HL). Courtesy of Jonathan Reeve JRb543p243mbr. **119.** Bullet ridden Heinkel 111. Courtesy of Jonathan Reeve b581fp35. **120.** A bullet-ridden Dornier 17. Courtesy of Jonathan Reeve JR1450b79p35B 19391945. **121.** Captured pilot, Oberfeldwebel Lange. Courtesy of Jonathan Reeve b570fp22b. **122.** A bullet-ridden He 111 (G1+FR). Courtesy of Jonathan Reeve JRb543p239mtr. **123.** A crewman from a Dornier 17. Courtesy of Jonathan Reeve b577p108mr. **124.** The sturdiness of the Hurricane! Courtesy of Jonathan Reeve JRb543p624b. **125.** A badly shot up Hurricane. Courtesy of Jonathan Reeve JRb543p316r. **126.** Wreckage of a StG1 Dornier 17. Courtesy of Jonathan Reeve b576p211b. **127.** Men of the

Observer Corps. Courtesy of Jonathan Reeve JR2494b113p89T 19391945. **128.** A pilot and intelligence officer. Courtesy of Jonathan Reeve JR2510b114p1165 19391945. **129.** The operations room at Bentley Priory. Courtesy of Jonathan Reeve JRb595fp4. **130.** Archibald Sinclair. Courtesy of Jonathan Reeve b568fp77. **131.** Keith Park. Courtesy of Jonathan Reeve b591bkp. **132.** Hugh Dowding. Courtesy of Jonathan Reeve b586fp32. **133.** Hurricane pilot decamps. Courtesy of Jonathan Reeve JR2511b114p1165B 19391945. **134.** 601 Squadron Hurricanes being rearmed. Courtesy of Jonathan Reeve b576p121b. **135.** Spitfire IA, P9368 'QV-K'. Courtesy of Jonathan Reeve b592fp2t. **136.** Ground staff overhauling the Rolls Royce Merlin. Courtesy of Jonathan Reeve JR1233b71pic13 19391945. **137.** Armourers of 601 Squadron re-arm a Hurricane. Courtesy of Jonathan Reeve JR1237b71pic17 19391945. **138.** Hurricanes of 601 Squadron being refuelled. Courtesy of Jonathan Reeve JR1234b71pic14 19391945. **139, 140, 141.** Some of the rarer German aircraft engaged in the Battle. Courtesy of Jonathan Reeve JRb540 55, JRb541 105t and Jonathan Reeve JRb561p30. **142, 143.** He 59 and Do 18 flying boats. Courtesy of Jonathan Reeve JRb561p15 and JRb561p35. **144, 145, 146.** Civilians and the Battle of Britain in Kent. Courtesy of Jonathan Reeve b570fp62b, b570fp56t and b570fp34b. **147.** A trapped young victim of a daylight raid. Courtesy of Jonathan Reeve JRb596p47. **148.** The pilots were very conscious of the human cost of the blitz. Courtesy of Jonathan Reeve JR1627b82p102 19391945. **149.** London Blitz. Courtesy of Jonathan Reeve JRb596p28. **150.** Elephant and Castle tube platform. Courtesy of Jonathan Reeve JRb596p63. 151. London street, 1940. Courtesy of Jonathan Reeve JRb596p79. **152.** The remains of a He 111. Courtesy of Jonathan Reeve JRb543p598bl. **153.** Poster attached to bomb-damaged commercial premises. Courtesy of Jonathan Reeve b570fp90b. **154.** Shattered London homes. Courtesy of Jonathan Reeve JRb596p72.

Internal illustrations in prelims and part pages courtesy of Jonathan Reeve.

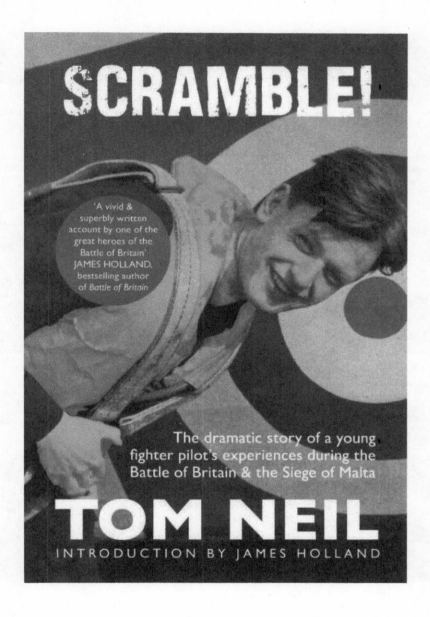

Battle of Britain Books From Amberley Publishing

GUN BUTTON TO FIRE Tom Neil
'A thrilling new book ... Tom Neil is one of the last surviving
heroes who fought the Luftwaffe' *THE DAILY EXPRESS*
£9.99   978-1-4456-0510-4   Paperback   120 illus

THE FEW Dilip Sarkar
'A captivating and frequently moving account ... anyone who wants to get
an insight into the human dimension of the battle will enjoy this book'
BBC WHO DO YOU THINK YOU ARE MAGAZINE
£9.99   978-1-4456-0701-6   Paperback

SPITFIRE MANUAL Dilip Sarkar
'A must' *INTERCOM: THE AIRCREW ASSOCIATION*
£9.99   978-1-84868-436-2   Paperback   40 illus

FIGHTER PILOT Helen Doe
'Among all the many stories of the Battle of Britain, Bob Doe's stands
out ... a sensitive & well researched biography' *RICHARD OVERY*
'Compelling and moving' *STEPHEN BUNGAY*
£25   978-1-4456-4611-4   Hardback

FIGHTER BOY
Barry Sutton
'A poignant & evocative
account of what it felt like to
be a young fighter pilot in the
Battle of Britain'
JULIA GREGSON
£10.99   978-1-4456-0627-9
Paperback   50 illus

SPITFIRE PILOT
Roger Hall, DFC
'An excellent memoir ... a lost
classic'
FLYPAST
£9.99   978-1-4456-1684-1
Paperback   66 illus

SPITFIRE
Brian Lane, DFC
'A very fine and vivid account'
MAX ARTHUR
£9.99   978-1-84868-354-9
Paperback   65 illus

FIGHTER ACE
Dilip Sarkar
'The definitive account'
*PROFESSOR PAUL
MACKENZIE*
£9.99   978-1-4456-3819-5
Paperback   60 illus

LAST OF THE FEW
Dilip Sarkar
'The Battle of Britain
rethought'
THE TIMES
£9.99   978-1-4456-0282-0
Paperback   57 illus

**ILLUSTRATED
INTRODUCTION
TO THE BATTLE OF
BRITAIN**
Henry Buckton
£9.99   978-1-4456-4202-4
Paperback   70 col illus

**BATTLE OF BRITAIN
VOICES**
Jonathan Reeve
£20   978-1-4456-4264-2
Hardback   150 illus, 50 col

**LIFE AS A BATTLE OF
BRITAIN SPITFIRE PILOT**
Arthur Donahue & Hannah
Holman
£6.99   978-1-4456-4468-4
Paperback   60 col illus

**HURRICANE
MANUAL**
Dilip Sarkar
£9.99   978-1-4456-2120-3
Paperback   65 illus

SPITFIRE ACE
Gordon Olive, DFC
£20   978-1-4456-4424-
Hardback   50 illus, 40 col

Also available as ebooks
Available from all good bookshops or to order direct
Please call **01453-847-800 www.amberley-books.com**